reference
NPS

rcsx

ANTIQUE MAPS
SEA CHARTS
CITY VIEWS
CELESTIAL CHARTS
&
BATTLE PLANS

PRICE GUIDE AND
COLLECTORS' HANDBOOK
FOR 1984

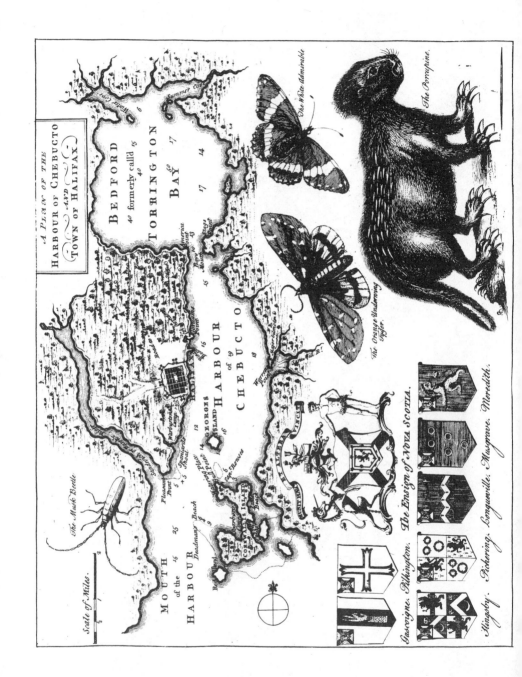

A PLAN OF THE
HARBOUR OF CHEBUCTO
AND
TOWN OF HALIFAX

Scale of Miles.

The Musk Beetle

MOUTH
of the
HARBOUR

Deadman's Beach

COLLYARD'S ISLAND

BEDFORD
4° formerly call'd
40

TORRINGTON
BAY

ISLAND HARBOUR
of
CHEBUCTO

The White Admirable.

The Orange Underwing
Tyger.

The Porcupine.

The Ensign of NOVA SCOTIA.

Gascoigne. Pilkington.

Kingsley. Pickering. Longueville. Musgrave. Meredith.

ANTIQUE MAPS
SEA CHARTS
CITY VIEWS
CELESTIAL CHARTS
&
BATTLE PLANS

PRICE GUIDE AND COLLECTORS' HANDBOOK FOR 1984

Compiled and edited by
David C. Jolly

Brookline, Massachusetts
David C. Jolly
1984

The typeface used for the text is Goudy Oldstyle, and the book is printed on 50-lb. Finch Opaque White paper. Text design and typography by Lee E. Fischer, Fine Print & Production, Inc., Cambridge, Massachusetts. Printing and binding by Halliday Lithograph, West Hanover, Massachusetts.

Requests for information on ordering this book or previous volumes, and all other correspondence, should be sent to:

David C.Jolly
Publishers
Post Office Box 931
Brookline, Massachusetts 02146

Frontispiece. One of the earliest depictions of Halifax, this map is a curious conglomeration of disparate elements. It appeared in the July 1750 issue of Gentleman's Magazine. Maps in later issues were much less flamboyant. Halifax was founded in 1749, and by 1752 had 4,000 inhabitants. The animals depicted are of some interest. The eastern porcupine, Erethizon dorsatum, is a clumsy, bark-eating rodent, vaguely resembling its depiction. The "White Admirable," now called the white admiral, Basilarchia arthemis, is an attractive blue-black butterfly. The "Orange Underwing Tyger" may be the Harris Checkerspot, Charidryas harrisii. (22.0 x 27.2 cm.)

CONTENTS

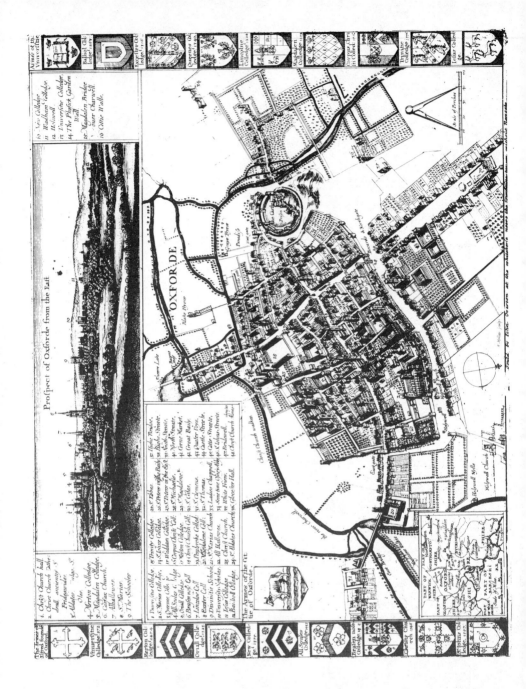

A view of Oxford by John Overton, circa 1670, engraved by the Bohemian Wenceslas Hollar. Just below the neat line at the bottom appears the legend, "Sould by Iohn Overton at the whitehorse neere the fountaine tavern without Newgate." The scale is given in perches, equal to 5½ yards or one rod. Although the engraving shows evidence of haste, the map is not only aesthetically pleasing and well composed, but is quite informative, showing details of every building. The modern observer can get an appreciation for life in Oxford 300 years ago by studying this map. (28.1 x 36.0 cm.)

PREFACE TO THE 1984 EDITION

Map collecting is a little-known but fascinating hobby. Unfortunately, potential collectors may become discouraged because useful advice on collecting is difficult to obtain. The market in old maps and charts is fragmented among specialists, rare book establishments, antique dealers, and print sellers. As a result, the beginner may become confused or intimidated. To help remedy this situation, this book provides practical advice for collectors, as well as serving as a price guide.

Information on old map and chart prices is not easily obtained without maintaining an extensive file of dealer catalogs. This is seldom practical for the beginning or casual collector, and even with such a file, locating the desired information can be tedious. Stamp and coin collectors have long enjoyed readily available price information, and people are able to take up stamp or coin collecting with confidence that they are paying fair prices. It is hoped that this work will similarly encourage persons to take up the fascinating hobby of map collecting.

Although primarily intended for map dealers and collectors, this book will also be useful to those who encounter maps occasionally: persons such as rare and used book dealers, antique dealers, print dealers, and appraisers. Libraries and historical museums will find this guide useful in making acquisitions, providing tax valuations for donors, evaluating holdings, and answering user inquiries. This work is a long-needed supplement to *American Book Prices Current* and *Bookman's Price Index* on the reference shelf. Finally, for the investment minded, statistical information on prices and rarity is provided.

Response to the 1983 edition has been enthusiastic, resulting in a decision to continue publication on a yearly basis. Minor changes have been made. An extensive directory of dealers has been added, along with a glossary of common Latin terms, and an index to the regional maps in Ptolemy's Geography. Some minor errors have been corrected. The price listings are, of course, entirely new. The statistical section compares some price levels with last year. The information on relative scarcity has been expanded and is now based on over 10,000 maps. A "News & Comments" section has been added to respond to readers' questions, mention new books, et cetera.

Thanks are extended to the many dealers whose cooperation in this venture is greatly appreciated. Thanks are also extended to all who wrote with helpful suggestions. Some of these are discussed in the "News & Comments" section. Suggestions are always welcome.

WARNING!

Users of this guide are warned that typographical errors may be present, and that prices for some items may not reflect the price that would be set by a majority of dealers. The publisher disclaims responsibility for any consequences of such errors and anomalies. Price information is given as an approximate guide to market values, and should be used with caution.

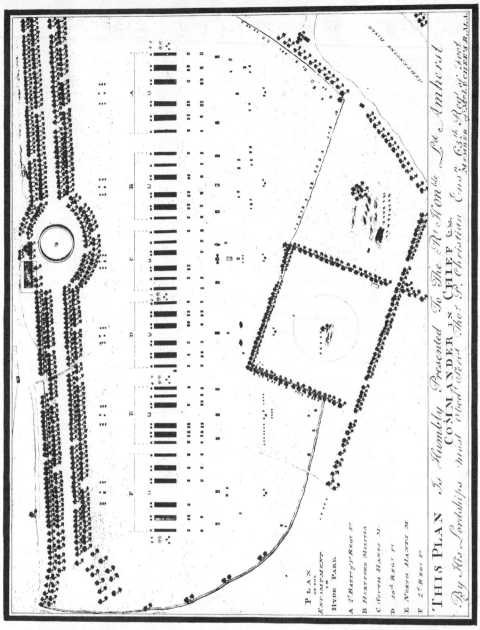

PLAN
OF THE
ENCAMPMENT
IN
HYDE PARK

A. 1st Battery 1st Regt Ft
B. Hertford Militia
C. South Hants M.
D. 18th Regt Ft
E. North Hants M.
F. 2d Regt Ft

THIS PLAN Is Humbly Presented To The Rt Honble La Amherst COMMANDER IN CHIEF &c &c By His Lordships most Obedt Servt Thos P. Christian Ensn 65th Regt of Foot MEMBER of Mr LIBGAIRE's R.M.A.

A manuscript plan of an encampment in Hyde Park, London, executed in india ink and watercolor with fanatical attention to detail. Although not visible on this reproduction, each tree trunk is shaded to indicate the direction of sunlight. Shown participating in the encampment were the Hertford, South Hants., and North Hants. militias, the 2nd and 18th Regiments of Foot, and the 2nd Battery of the 1st Regt. The map is dedicated to Lord Amherst, Commander in Chief, by Thomas P. Christian, Ensign, 65th Regt. of Foot. Amherst was a wily veteran of American campaigning in the French & Indian War. During that conflict, he had encouraged gifts of smallpox-contaminated blankets to unfriendly Indians. However, in 1775 he refused to fight against his many friends in America, and command was given to General Thomas Gage. Of average ability at best, Gage's previous American experience included such disasters as the repulse at Ticonderoga and Braddock's rout. Had the competent Amherst accepted command, the rebellion might have been crushed in short order. A punitive expedition here—a smallpox epidemic there—and soon the colonists would have been begging for peace. Fortunately, this was not to be. Manuscript maps are not included in the price guide, but collectors should always be on the alert for them, as they can be quite interesting. (22.5 x 28.6 cm.)

HOW TO USE THIS PRICE GUIDE

This book consists of several sections. The first portion contains helpful general information about maps and charts. Beginners should first skim these sections, reading any of special interest. Next is the price listing, followed in turn by the alphabetical title index. It is important that the price listing be used in the proper manner. If not, the desired information may not be found, or information that is found may be misinterpreted.

The prices represent retail prices taken from dealer catalogs. In most cases, all items in the catalogs used were abstracted. The exceptions are maps after 1899, manuscript maps, lots of more than one item, and incompletely described items. Where long runs of similar material occurred, only representative items were abstracted.

All entries in the price section are given in a standard format, reproduced here:

```
CLUVER
  SICILIAE ANTIQUAE DESCRIPTIO AUCTORE: PHILIP CLUVERIO [1729] 26x32cm.
     light staining in upper margin                           [99]    $60
```

The first part, underlined, is the mapmaker. There can be a good deal of uncertainty in assigning a map to a given name. For example, a map may be surveyed by Smith, drawn by Jones, engraved by Black, published by White in an atlas edited by Brown and later reprinted by Green. Thus, where one dealer might say the map is by White, another might say Brown or Black or Green. There is no consistent standard, and even if there were, catalogs usually do not give all names associated with the production of a map. The name assignments in this guide generally follow custom, but the same map might turn up under two makers. For this reason, it is vital to consult the title index. Where more than one map by the same maker is listed, the name of the maker is not repeated. Initials are not given. For example, maps by E. Bowen and T. Bowen are listed under "Bowen." Were this not done, three separate listings would be needed: "E. Bowen," "T. Bowen," and "Bowen." The same map might appear under "E. Bowen" and "Bowen," an unnecessary fragmentation.

Next is the title of the map. This ought to be straightforward, but it is not. Dealers may paraphrase or condense the title. "A New and Accurate Map by the Best Authorities" may be listed in a catalog as "America by the Best Authorities," or "A . . . Map of America . . . ," or "A New and Accurate Map of America etc." While this occurs in a minority of cases, it is wise to check some possible paraphrasings. Sometimes a map has two titles, and a catalog may list only one. For uniformity, "v" has been changed to "u" where appropriate, and the early form of s, resembling f, has been rendered "s." Diacritical marks such as the umlaut have been simply omitted. The ampersand "&" has been left unchanged, as has the English "ye." The slash "/" is used to separate titles of two or more maps appearing on one side of a sheet. A double slash "//" is used when two or more maps appear on opposite sides of a sheet. In rare cases, a map may have no title at all, in which case a descriptive title is supplied in parentheses. Usually, if an item is a view, this has been noted in parentheses after the title.

Next, in square brackets "[ ]" is the date. Some dealers give the actual date of the map, some give the date it first appeared, and others may give a range of dates.

1

The letter "C" is used to indicate explicitly that the date is approximate. However it is safest to regard all dates as approximate.

After the date are the dimensions, with height first and width second, both in centimeters. The precision of these measurements varies. Some dealers measure to the nearest millimeter. Others round off to the nearest centimeter or half-inch. Thus the dimensions are not necessarily exact. In most cases the dimensions are for the printed area and do not include the blank margins. On rare occasions, however, a dealer may list the paper size rather than the printed area. In some cases, the map is irregularly shaped, and the dimension might be the maximum extent in each direction. Sometimes dealers list a series of maps from the same atlas and give only one set of approximate dimensions for all. This can cause trouble when a few of the maps are in vertical format, and the dimensions imply a horizontal format. Because of this, and also because mistakes occur, the vertical and horizontal dimensions may occasionally be reversed. The letter "C" before the dimensions indicates that they are approximate.

Following the dimensions, in lower case, are comments on condition or other factors affecting the value of the map. These remarks are condensed from the catalog descriptions, and reference to the actual catalog is recommended if more detailed information is required. The comments are not always present. Their absence usually implies a sound copy. Laudatory remarks such as "a stunning example in mint condition" have been omitted. Some dealers give more detailed descriptions of condition than others. Thus, if two apparently similar maps are listed at different prices, it should not be concluded that one is overpriced or the other is underpriced. Differences might be apparent from the longer descriptions in the catalogs, and there is really no substitute for visual inspection. Coloring has not been noted.

Next, in square brackets, is a code number that designates the catalog from which the listing was taken. The corresponding catalog can be determined from the dealer listing.

Last is the price. Prices originally in foreign currency have been converted to American dollars using the values given in the foreign currency table. It should be borne in mind that the dollar during 1982 was historically very strong, and this depressed the converted value of foreign prices.

To look up a map, first check the alphabetical title index. Remember that the first article (i.e., a, an, the, etc.) has been included in alphabetizing. This makes the guide easier to use for those who may not know the Italian, Spanish, French, German, and Dutch articles. If the title cannot be found, and there is a name on the map, try the main price listing under that name. If still unsuccessful, check the title index for possible paraphrasings of the title. If the mapmaker is known, but that particular map is not listed, it should still be possible to estimate the value in comparison to the other maps listed under that maker. Refer to the section on what affects the value of a map.

WARNING!

Users of this guide are warned that typographical errors may be present, and that prices for some items may not reflect the price that would be set by a majority of dealers. The publisher disclaims responsibility for any consequences of such errors and anomalies. Price information is given as an approximate guide to market values, and should be used with caution.

NEWS & COMMENTS

Many thanks are extended to all who wrote with comments, questions, and suggestions. A few dealt with form, such as "add more pictures" or "make the title shorter," while others dealt with substance. Some are of sufficiently wide interest to merit answering in print:

Can a geographical index be added?
This is not easily done under the present system. The book is almost 300 pages long, and adding such an index would mean shortening the listings, adding pages, or using finer print. However, a geographical index is under consideration for the more distant future.

Could the listings be numbered for reference?
At the present time, the disadvantages of a more cluttered format and the space penalty outweigh any advantages. There seems to be little need to refer to specific items in the price guide. If necessary to refer to an item, the page should prove sufficient. Numbering may be adopted in the future if a geographical index is added.

Could the dimensions be given in inches?
The evil, dehumanizing effects of applying the metric system to everyday life are too well known to need comment. In fair competition in free societies, the English system invariably prevails. The metric system makes headway only where the reins of government have been seized by compulsive meddlers and self-important functionaries who bring the full weight of state power to bear on a helpless inch- and gallon-oriented citizenry. Nevertheless, the trend is toward the metric system for bibliographical usage. To facilitate comparison with reference books, the dimensions must be given in centimeters. It is not possible to give both because of space limitations. Try to remember that 30 cm. is about 12 inches.

Why are the titles not more uniform?
While obvious errors in catalog listings are corrected, the presumption must be that the catalog is correct. Changes cannot be made lightly because the dealer may be offering a little-known variant or the map may be obscure. Most problems occur when dealers paraphrase a title without any indication that this has been done. Dealers may leave out a portion of the title without so indicating by ellipses, or may add their own punctuation marks for clarity without using square brackets. Many actual titles end with "etc.," but some dealers occasionally use "etc." at the end of a partial title, and it is often impossible to know whether this has been done. Another frequent problem is the casual interchange of "&" and "and." Many dealers are sticklers for accuracy in their listings, and their efforts are greatly appreciated.

Could those maps which are illustrated in the catalogs be somehow designated?
Several people requested this. This is not being done since it is felt that most users do not have access to the original catalogs. Further, people interested in a particular map and possessing the catalog will very likely want to look up the original description whether illustrated or not.

Is the price guide advertising in disguise? Do dealers have to pay to have their catalogs included?

By the time the typical user obtains this guide, the listings are from two months to a year old. Although some items listed may still be on the market, the listings are not a substitute for the more extensive information appearing in the catalog listing, and are not really suitable for making purchases. Dealers do not pay anything for inclusion. On the contrary, dealers whose catalogs are used receive a free copy of the guide.

Do people ordering the guide get on all sorts of mailing lists?

No. The list of customers is confidential, and is not divulged to any third party. No unsolicited map catalogs will be received. At worst, buyers may receive brochures announcing future issues of the guide.

Two specialized books were received during the year which may be of interest:

Russell Morrison, Edward C. Papenfuse, Nancy M. Bramucci, and Robert J. H. Janson-La Palme, *On the Map, An Exhibit and Catalogue of Maps Relating to Maryland and the Chesapeake Bay Honoring George Washington at the beginning of the Third Century of Washington College at Chestertown, Maryland, February 21–March 6, 1983,* Chestertown, Maryland: Washington College (Map Exhibit, Clifton Miller Library, Washington College, Chestertown MD 21620, $10.63), 28 x 22 cm., viii, 102 pp. paper.

This is a finely produced, well-researched bargain for the Americana collector and dealer. A total of 58 maps, mostly antique, are reproduced and discussed authoritatively. The horizontal format makes the book a pleasure to read, since the book need not be rotated to view the figures right-side-up. The supply is said to be limited.

Christos G. Zacharakis, *A Catalog of Printed Maps of Greece 1477–1800.* Nicosia: A. G. Levantis Foundation (P.O. Box 1799, Nicosia, Cyprus, $65 pre-publication price), 1982. 21 x 29 cm., xv, 469 pp. paper.

This work is a valuable addition to any major dealer's reference collection and indispensable to the collector of Greek maps. Like all really good map reference books, it was many years in preparation. A total of 2173 maps of Greece and its regions are listed, and hundreds of these are illustrated. It is surprising that such an expensive book intended as a permanent reference was issued in paperback, but this may be due to a lack of production facilities in Greek-held Cyprus.

Collectors or dealers may wish to subscribe to *Mapline,* published by the Newberry Library. This is a quarterly newsletter with articles, news of the map world, and reviews of recently published books. The rate is $5.00 per year from Mapline, The Newberry Library, 60 West Walton Street, Chicago, IL 60610.

A notice was received announcing the formation of the Delaware Valley Map Society. For further details, write D.V.M.S., 33 Benezet St., Philadelphia, PA 19118, or phone 215-242-4750.

A preliminary profile of purchasers of the 1983 *Price Guide* showed that about 40 percent were dealers, 30 percent collectors, and 30 percent libraries. This suggests that most users are relatively sophisticated. However, information for beginners will continue to be provided.

GLOSSARY OF MAP-RELATED TERMS

AGE TONING.   A pleasant-sounding synonym for browning. See browning.

BACKED.   To protect a map, it is sometimes laid down, using paste, on cloth or paper. Properly done, this can make the map more resistant to damage from handling, improve its appearance, and prolong its life.

BLEACHING.   Sometimes done to a map to remove stains or to lighten browning. Bleaching should not be attempted without regard to modern conservation practices, or the map may be permanently damaged.

BORDER.   Usually refers to the printed area toward the edges of the map. The border may be a simple line or lines or may consist of scrollwork, costumed figures, or other decorative elements.

BROWNING.   As the organic material in paper ages, it undergoes a chemical transformation that causes the paper to darken. The earliest stages of browning often produce a pleasing tone. Extreme aging may cause the paper to become brittle. Maps should be protected from atmospheric pollutants, contact with cheap paper, and excessive ultraviolet exposure from sunlight and fluorescent lamps.

CARTOUCH, CARTOUCHE.   A bordered area enclosing information about the map, such as the title, author, or scale.

CENTERFOLD.   Many old maps have been removed from atlases. Often such maps have a vertical fold down the center. Opening and closing the atlas results in a weakening of the centerfold, frequently necessitating repair. Browning can occur at the centerfold because the paste used to hold the map in the atlas often attacks the paper.

CHAIN MARKS.   When handmade rag paper is held up to the light, a rectangular grid of lines can be seen. In one direction the spacing is close, about 1 mm., and in the other, about 2 or 3 cm. These marks are the impressions left by the wire screen on which the aqueous suspension of paper fibers was gathered to form sheets.

COLORING.   Color applied to the map, usually watercolor applied by brush. Not all maps were intended to be colored, but coloring can enhance the appearance of many of the more decorative maps.

COMPASS ROSE.   A small, starlike device from which rhumb lines usually radiate. North is indicated by a small pointer on the compass rose.

DECORATIVE.   A decorative map has definite aesthetic appeal. Decorative elements can include animals, sea serpents, mermaids, scrollwork, cherubs, costumes, etc. Many consider the 17th century to be the peak period of decorative mapmaking.

ENGRAVING.   An item printed from a metal plate on which a design has been scratched. When ink is applied to the plate and the plate wiped, ink adheres to the grooves in the plate. The plate is then pressed on a sheet of paper, transferring the design to the paper.

FOLIO.   A folio book is bound from sheets of paper folded one time. A map from such a book is sometimes said to be folio sized. Typically the vertical paper dimension of such a map is greater than about 11 inches or 24 cm. Large folio is about 17 to 22 inches (45 to 55 cm.) and imperial folio is greater than about 22 inches (55 cm.).

FOXING. Small dark spots on the paper surface caused by mold.

GORE. A printed sheet constituting a portion of a globe, often shaped like an American football. A complete set of gores can be pasted to a sphere of appropriate diameter to form a globe.

INSET MAP. A small map within the borders of a larger map.

LAID DOWN. See backed.

LINED. See backed.

LITHOGRAPHY. A form of printing first used for maps early in the 19th century. The image is printed from a stone on which ink adheres only to specially treated areas.

LOSS OF (PRINTED) SURFACE. Used in reference to a map that lacks a portion of the printed area. Sometimes such a map is restored by pasting similar paper over the hole and drawing the missing image with pen and ink.

MANUSCRIPT. Handwriting. A manuscript map is one drawn by hand.

MARGIN. The blank area outside the border of the map.

MOUNTED. See backed.

NEAT LINES. The straight, printed lines bounding the map.

OCTAVO. An octavo book is bound from sheets of paper folded in half three times. A map from such a book is sometimes said to be octavo sized. Typically the vertical dimension of such a map is about 8 to 9 inches, or about 20 to 23 cm. Abbreviated 8vo.

OFFSETTING. When the surface of a map contacts another surface, as in an atlas, there may be a transfer of color or ink, or a chemical reaction, which faintly reproduces a mirror image of the design. Offsetting can occur from a separate sheet, or, since maps are often folded on themselves, from one part of a map to another.

OUTLINE COLOR. Used in reference to maps with only the borders or coastlines colored.

PANELS. Areas around the border of a map with views or figures enclosed.

PLATE MARK. Impressions made from metal engraved plates often show an indentation of the paper just outside the printed area where the pressure of the plate compressed the paper.

PRINTER'S CREASE. When a map is printed, a wrinkle is occasionally compressed to form a permanent crease.

QUARTO. A quarto book is bound from sheets of paper folded in half twice. A map from such a book is sometimes said to be quarto sized. Typically the vertical paper dimension of such a map is about 9 to 11 inches or 23 to 28 cm. Abbreviated 4to.

6

RAG PAPER.   Paper made from cloth fibers.

RECTO.   The side of the paper on which the image of interest appears. See verso.

REMARGINED.   A remargined map has had paper added to the edges to extend them, protecting the original edges, and improving the appearance of the map.

REPRODUCTION.   A copy, usually photographically produced, of an original map. The reproduction may in some cases be difficult to distinguish from the original. See the section on detecting reproductions.

RHUMB LINES.   These are lines criss-crossing old charts at various angles, usually along the compass directions. They were used to facilitate plotting courses.

VERSO.   The reverse side to the side of the sheet on which the image of interest appears. See recto.

WATERMARK.   A design in the paper visible by transmitted light. For handmade paper, the watermark is made with bent wires placed on the rack on which the fibers are deposited to form the paper. Designs vary from simple initials to intricate coats of arms. Watermarks are often helpful in identifying the age of paper. See chain mark.

WOODCUT.   An image made by printing from a wooden block on which a mirror image of the design has been carved. Woodcut maps are most often associated with the earliest days of mapmaking, up to about 1600, but some were done later.

WORMING, WORM HOLES, WORM TRACKS.   Damage to paper by hungry insect larvae that eat the paper, leaving small holes or tracks.

FACTORS AFFECTING
THE VALUE OF MAPS

The value of a map is affected by supply and demand, and ultimately reduces to an agreement between buyer and seller. However, it is possible to make some generalizations helpful in estimating prices. Two broad groups of factors affect the value of a map, one dealing with the identity of the map, and the other with its condition. The factors related to the identity of the map will be discussed first:

THE AGE OF THE MAP. For similar maps, the older map is generally the more valuable. In fact, a table of the average price for various ages is given elsewhere in this guide. Using age as the sole basis for valuation is very dangerous, however. Maps from the 1500s can be had for under $100 while maps from the 1800s can be worth several thousand dollars (and vice-versa).

THE MAPMAKER. For similar maps, the maker can strongly influence the price. To take one example, Ortelius and de Jode both produced similar maps at about the same time. However, Ortelius produced far more editions of his atlas than de Jode, and de Jode maps are roughly triple the price of Ortelius maps, as indicated in the statistical section. A rough measure of rarity for each mapmaker listed in this guide can be obtained from the statistical tables. However, the sample size is small, and caution is urged.

AESTHETIC QUALITIES. Many persons buy maps intending to frame them and display them in their homes or offices. Such persons are more attracted to a map with scrollwork, fancy borders, sea monsters, fine coloring, etc., than to a plainer map of the same region and age. Some collectors also specialize in decorative maps. Naturally this increases the price of such maps.

REGION DEPICTED. Collectors in certain countries have developed a fondness for collecting maps of their own regions, which drives up prices for maps of those regions. The Germans, Dutch, English, Australians, Canadians, and Americans are some of the nationalities fond of maps of their countries. At the other extreme, the once dynamic and cultured people of eastern Europe have been reduced, through no fault of their own, to a state of penurious apathy. Thus maps of eastern Europe tend to be less expensive than those of the aforementioned regions. World maps are appreciated by collectors everywhere, and often the world map is the most expensive map in a given atlas. Maps of the continents, particularly America, are also in demand, as are maps of the Holy Land and Japan. Some idea of regional influence can be gained by inspecting listings for some of the more prolific cartographers such as Ortelius, Blaeu, Homann, Bowen, or Tallis.

SIZE. Most collectors prefer large maps. Such maps are usually more detailed and more decorative. Some idea of the influence of size can be obtained by comparing the large and small maps of Ortelius and Bellin in the price listings. Some collectors do prefer smaller maps since they are less expensive and easier to store.

Condition is another important factor in map pricing. It is difficult to be specific, since opinion among dealers varies. One dealer may regard one type of fault as very serious and may be complacent about another, while a second dealer might hold the opposite opinion. Ultimately the purchaser must make his or her own decision. If the map is being bought for decorative purposes, then flaws affecting the appearance should be closely evaluated. Sometimes discussion with the dealer may be useful. For example, the dealer may point out that a particular map is usually found with narrow margins or fold lines, and that such faults must be accepted. It would be helpful if some standard method of indicating condition were adopted, but this may be impractical, and dealers are too individualistic to use such a system. The factors below are generally taken into account in assessing the condition of a map:

STAINING.   Maps are subject to several different types of staining. Foreign matter such as ink can be spilled on a map. Water spills can leave visible traces. Browning can occur along the centerfold or at old repairs where the paste has caused chemical deterioration of the paper. The whole map sometimes browns. Mildew can result in spotting or foxing of the map. Offset staining also occurs (see glossary). The effect of staining on price depends on its visual impact and the type of map. The value of a decorative map is more affected by staining than is a rare map of scholarly interest. Stains located in the blank margins are much less serious than stains in the printed area.

RIPS.   Many maps become torn over the course of time. Sometimes this is the result of use, as in the case of maps that fold into a book. In such cases, tears or separations along the folds are relatively common. In general, tears are regarded as less serious if they are confined to the blank margin. Tears can be repaired by a skilled restorer. Such repairs are often almost invisible on the map side of the sheet. Tears should be repaired if the map is to be handled, since they tend to lengthen. Tears detract from the value of a map, but the effect on value is somewhat subjective. The collector should discuss such defects with the dealer.

BACKING.   Sometimes maps are found to be pasted or glued to something such as cardboard, pressboard, or brown paper. This can detract substantially from the value. In other cases, the map may have been backed by a conservator to protect it. Such conservation backing is usually done carefully with good materials, such as rice paper and acid-free paste, and helps protect the map from damage. This should be done only if necessary, since some collectors find it objectionable on an otherwise good map. Backing may obscure interesting text or figures on the back of the map. Some maps were published with backing. In that case, it obviously does not detract from the value.

COLORING.   Most people interested in decorative maps prefer them colored. This tends to give nicely colored maps a slight price premium. The magnitude of this premium is limited by the practice of coloring maps. The price differential settles at about the cost of coloring plus the perceived cost of the bother involved. The most desirable coloring is original color. Next would be recent color done in an authentic style. Least desirable is bad coloring, whether recent or original. Some maps were never issued colored, and knowledgeable collectors avoid colored examples. Some sophisticated collectors believe that coloring obscures the beauty of any engraved map. In the final analysis, it is a matter of taste.

MARGINS.   The blank margins on maps may have been trimmed at some time in the past. This reduces the value. Some maps, however, were issued with narrow margins. Because of this, there can be no general advice for the beginner, except to view narrow margins with a jaundiced eye. If part of the the border or some of the map itself is missing, the value can be reduced substantially.

CREASES.   This is perhaps the least serious fault. If a map has been folded, usually the resulting creases are almost invisible when unfolded properly. If a map was issued with fold lines, as in the case of maps folding into a book, its creases have no effect whatever on value. Many maps from atlases have vertical fold lines down the center. This is normal and does not affect the value.

HOW TO DETECT REPRODUCTIONS

An original generally means a copy printed more or less at the time the map first appeared. In some cases maps were printed for a century or more from the same plate or wood block, but they are still considered originals. Reproductions are copies, often photographically produced, which were printed after the production of originals ceased. Reproductions are not necessarily recent. A number of 19th-century reproductions exist, some of excellent quality. A few reproductions can be detected only by experts, but most can be discerned with a little experience. Some of the factors to be considered in distinguishing reproductions are listed below.

SIZE.   Reproductions not intended to deceive are often produced slightly larger or smaller than the original. Of course, the size of the original must be known. This price guide gives dimensions of all maps listed. Remember that since some dealers round off their dimensions, the dimensions in this guide are not necessarily exact.

COLORING.   Colored reproductions often employ halftone colors. These consist of patterns of small dots, geometrically arranged, which can be seen most easily using a magnifying glass. Some reproductions, however, are hand colored, just like the originals.

PRINTING QUALITY.   Sometimes reproductions have slightly blurred lines, or finely hatched areas may fuse together. It can be difficult to judge this, unfortunately, unless a known original is available for comparison.

PLATE MARK.   When an engraved map is printed, the impression of the metal plate crushes the paper, resulting in a depressed area extending to just outside the printed area. This usually can be felt or seen. Woodcut maps do not have such a plate mark, and sometimes it is not apparent on engraved maps. Occasionally a fake plate mark is added to reproductions to add "realism."

LEGENDS.   Many reproductions carry notations such as "Copyright 1968" or "From an original in the Library of Congress." Although this may appear obvious, personal experience indicates that people do not always notice such things. The notations are sometimes outside the border and can be trimmed off or erased.

PAPER.   On maps made before about 1800 look for chain marks (see glossary). Also look for any watermarks. Unfortunately, some reproductions are produced on paper designed to look old. This usually does not deceive an experienced collector or dealer, but the novice should beware. Originals also usually show some signs of age and use such as spotting, stains, browning, a limp quality, deterioration of the paper caused by the coloring, or offsetting of the color or printer's ink.

The above suggestions will decide the issue in most cases. However, before investing money, it is best to check with an experienced dealer or collector. Some dealers may charge a nominal fee for authenticating an old map. Local libraries or art galleries may also be willing to help you.

A *chart of Boston Harbor from* Atlas Maritimus & Commercialis; Or, A General View of the World . . . Together with a Large Account of the Commerce Carried on by Sea . . . to which are Added Sailing Directions . . . with a Sett of Sea-Charts . . . The Use of the Projection Justified by Dr. Halley . . . To which are Subjoin'd Two Large Hemispheres . . . containing all the Stars in the Britannic Catalogue: Of great Use to Sailors for finding the Latitude in the Night . . . *London* 1728. *The chart is terribly inaccurate, and any ship entering the harbor by this chart would be aground in a moment. The atlas is now somewhat scarce. Judging from the accuracy of this chart, some of the scarcity may be due to the large number of copies now reposing in the immense personal library of Davy Jones. This chart should be compared to the precise Admiralty survey of Boston Harbor done 20 years earlier and shown in the 1983 price guide. It is not terribly uncommon for an accurate map to be followed some years later by one much worse. The age of maps cannot always be judged by their accuracy. (27.2 x 24.6 cm.)*

HOW TO START A MAP COLLECTION

It is easy to start collecting. Look over the list of reference books elsewhere in this guide. These books and others are often available at the larger public libraries. Many dealers carry map books, both used and new, and will send you a price list upon request. You should read at least one or two books to gain familiarity with the history of cartography. You should obtain a few map catalogs as well. They can be quite educational. Often essays describe the importance of the maps listed. Write to a few of the dealers that are mentioned in the list of dealers, asking for catalogs or price lists. Some dealers charge a nominal fee for catalogs to defray the cost of their production. If you live near a dealer, you may wish to visit. Most dealers will be happy to discuss maps with you and to show you their stock. Some dealers require an appointment in advance. It is advisable to call first, in any event, since the dealer may not have the type of material you are interested in.

Most beginners have some sort of idea of what types of maps they wish to collect. In reading and looking through catalogs, your interests should become clearer. Some collectors choose to concentrate geographically, e.g., New England, Holy Land, Africa, Japan, Arctic, etc. Others collect only world maps or celestial charts. There are those who prefer decorative maps, while others like only maps before 1600 or miniature maps. Military history buffs collect battle plans. Students of exploration enjoy collecting early charts or the first maps to show certain features, e.g., Davis Strait or the Australian coast. City planners like to see the evolution of cities revealed by old city plans. Others prefer oddities, such as maps showing California as an island, or maps in the shape of animals or people. The possibilities are limited only by the imagination. When corresponding with dealers, it is best if you give them some idea of your interests. They may keep your name on file and quote prices to you on items that do not appear in their catalogs.

The beginner should avoid initial overenthusiasm. When buying a map, ask yourself if you really want to keep it for the next few decades. If the answer is yes, and the price reasonable, definitely buy it. Maps of interest have an uncanny habit of being sold quickly to someone else. If you are unsure about the map, it is better to think about it for a few days.

Some mention must be made of the investment aspects of map collecting. Acquiring an interesting collection need not require emptying the bank account, but anyone desiring to collect some of the more famous and rare maps must consider monetary aspects. It is a fact that many maps have appreciated rapidly in price over the last few decades. However, there is no guarantee that the trend will continue, although, of course, it may. It is dangerous to try to anticipate future demand. Buying maps of a particular type because they are sure to increase in value is risky. They may increase, but it is probably safer, and definitely more fun, to concentrate on maps of special interest to you. After all, if you like certain types of maps, others probably will also.

Maps can be bought by mail or in person. Buying maps in person is perhaps most satisfactory, since the map can be discussed with the dealer. A substantial portion of the antiquarian map trade is by mail, however. Usually new customers will be required to send payment with their order. Most dealers will let you return merchandise within a few days for a full refund. The return policy and shipping charges are given in their catalogs. Buying maps at auction is a possibility, but this is risky for the beginner. Auction catalogs often give very brief descriptions, and returns are more difficult. It is not sufficient to tell them that you changed your mind. Sometimes old maps are to be found in establishments that sell mainly other items, such as paintings or antique furniture. It is wise to avoid buying at these places until you have a good idea of market values.

If you plan to buy just a few maps, you may wish to frame them. This protects them and enhances their beauty. If you plan to assemble a larger collection, you should refrain from framing all your initial purchases. Victims of map collecting fever, a chronic and incurable malady, may wish to purchase a blueprint file. These can be ordered through office furniture establishments. Maps can be placed in pressboard folders and kept flat in the drawers. Maps can be stored rolled, but this may cause rips if they are inspected frequently.

USEFUL REFERENCE BOOKS

The following list of books has been kept brief. There are many other fine books, some dealing only with limited geographical regions. Most of the books listed are still in print or are available as used books from map dealers.

Leo Bagrow, *The History of Cartography*, Cambridge, Massachusetts: Harvard University Press, 1964. R. A. Skelton, editor.
This is perhaps the most sought after book on old maps. The text is definitive, and the numerous plates, some in color, are of the highest quality. It is difficult to obtain this book but worth the effort.

Roger Baynton-Williams, *Investing in Maps*, New York: C. N. Potter, Inc., 1969.
Despite the title, the major emphasis is on how maps were produced and who made them. There are many fine illustrations in this good book for beginners.

Lloyd A. Brown, *The Story of Maps*, Boston: Little, Brown and Company, 1949.
This is a scholarly, but readable, history of mapmaking.

Wilma George, *Animals and Maps*, Berkeley: University of California Press, 1969.
A zoologist finds that animals decorating old maps are not mythical beasts located at random. On the contrary, old maps turn out to be an interesting source of zoological data. This is not an essential book, but it is fun to read.

Raymond Lister, *Antique Maps & Their Cartographers*, London: G. Bell and Sons Ltd., 1970.
This is a very fine introductory book for beginners.

A. E. Nordenskiold, *Facsimile-Atlas to the Early History of Cartography*, Stockholm: 1889. Reprinted by Dover Publications, Inc., New York, 1973.
Although somewhat out of date, this is a useful reference work for those interested in maps of the 15th and 16th centuries. There are almost 200 illustrations of old maps.

R. A. Skelton, *Decorative Printed Maps of the 15th to 18th Centuries*, London: Spring Books, 1965.
This is a good reference for collectors of decorative maps. There are 84 plates, some in color.

R. V. Tooley, *Maps and Map-Makers*, New York: Bonanza Books, 1970.
This is perhaps the most useful general-purpose book for map collectors and should be obtained.

R. V. Tooley, *Tooley's Dictionary of Mapmakers*, Tring, England: Map Collector Publications Limited, 1979.
This book is expensive but gives information about almost any cartographer likely to be encountered.

R. V. Tooley, Charles Bricker, Gerald Roe Crone, *Landmarks of Mapmaking*, New York: Thomas Y. Crowell Company, 1976.
Numerous illustrations, including folding color plates and an informative text, make this an excellent book for the collector.

John Noble Wilford, *The Mapmakers*, New York: Alfred A. Knopf, 1981.
Very similar to Brown's book, this is essentially a history of cartography, and good background reading for the collector.

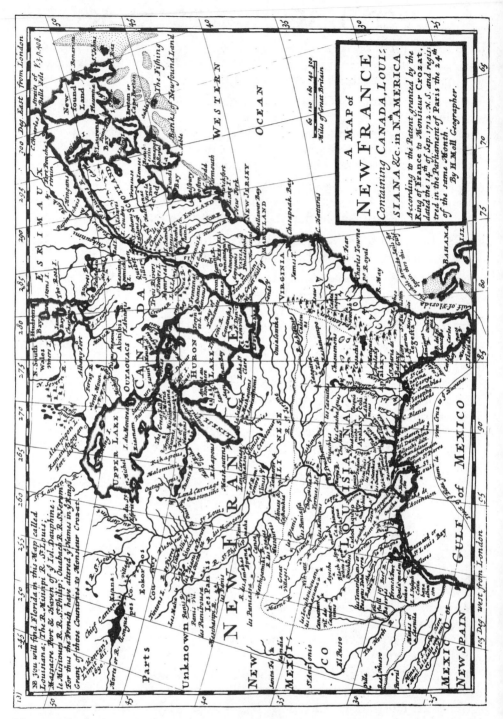

This map by Herman Moll, circa 1720, shows America in the days when France was an important country. Maps sometimes demonstrate better than any history book the ebb and flow of national power. The route of the treasure galleons is shown at the bottom. (18.3 x 25.8 cm.)

16

THE GEOGRAPHY
OF CLAUDIUS PTOLEMY

The maps of Claudius Ptolemy are among the earliest and most interesting that are available to the collector. Ptolemy, not to be confused with Egyptian kings of that name, lived from about 90–168 A.D., and probably worked in Alexandria, Egypt, where he produced a number of scholarly works on astronomy, astrology, music, optics, history, and geography. From the works of Marinus of Tyre and other geographers, and also from the accounts of travelers, Ptolemy compiled his *Geographia*, an atlas of the known world. Aside from the lost works of Marinus, it is the only ancient atlas that we know about. Fortunately, copies survived into the Middle Ages, perhaps in Constantinople, apparently passing into Europe around the year 1400 as the Eastern Roman Empire disintegrated. Handmade copies circulated until the advent of engraving and printing made mass production possible. The 27 maps are believed to date back to ancient times, providing a valuable record of early geography. The classical Ptolemaic maps usually consist of the world, 10 maps of Europe, 4 of Africa, and 12 of Asia. The maps for each continent are numbered, and maps from Ptolemy are usually recognizable by a legend such as "Tabula Europae VI," i.e., the sixth map of Europe.

The earliest printed editions of Ptolemy adhered closely to the original maps. As geographers became more confident, so-called "modern" maps were added. So great was respect for ancient wisdom that the first standard atlas to break with Ptolemy was not printed until 1570, although specially assembled sets of maps could be purchased before that date. The debt of cartography to Ptolemy is not widely realized. Features now taken for granted stem directly from his maps, including north being at the top of the map, a labeled grid of latitude and longitude lines, the conventions depicting land and sea areas, and the use of mathematical projections. Lest these seem obvious, one need only look at medieval European maps not in the Ptolemaic tradition. Even locating the continents on such maps often takes the beginner a few moments. Maps by non-European cultures, such as the Eskimos or the Marshall Islanders, do not even look like maps to nonspecialists. In contrast, maps printed over 500 years ago for the Florence edition of Ptolemy are quite recognizable to laymen.

During the 16th and 17th centuries, some of Ptolemy's practices were abandoned. Elaborate decorations were added to maps, and the top of the map was often east, west, or even south. Towns were depicted as little castles, rather than dots. Gradually cartographers returned to Ptolemy's way of doing things. It is a measure of his genius that with little apparent tradition behind him, his maps so closely resemble the form finally adopted by cartographers 1800 years later.

The collector will often encounter maps from the various editions of Ptolemy in catalogs or in showrooms. To help identify these maps, the early editions of Ptolemy and closely related works are listed below. The list is believed to be complete and accurate, but additions or corrections will be appreciated. Several of the more significant reference works are given after the list of the editions of Ptolemy.

LIST OF THE EDITIONS OF PTOLEMY

1475	Vicenza	Folio	No maps. Latin text.
1477?	Bologna	Folio	24 crudely executed copperplate maps, usually colored: 1 world, 10 Europe, 4 Africa, 11 Asia. Latin text. The colophon is misdated 1462.
1478	Rome	Folio	27 copperplate maps: 1 world, 10 Europe, 4 Africa, 12 Asia. Latin text. Later editions: 1490, 1507, 1508.
1482?	Florence	Folio	31 crude copperplate maps including 4 ''modern'' maps of Italy, Spain, France, and Palestine. Italian text. This is the only edition of Ptolemy to use the original equidistant projection. It could have been published as early as 1478.
1482	Ulm	Folio	32 colored woodcut maps: 1 world, 14 Europe, 4 Africa, 13 Asia. These include 5 modern maps. All maps are double page except for Taprobane. Latin text. Later edition: 1486.
1486	Ulm	Folio	32 woodcut maps, same as 1482 Ulm edition. Latin text.
1490	Rome	Folio	27 copperplate maps, from the same plates as 1478 Ed. Latin text.
1507	Rome	Folio	33 copperplate maps, 27 the same as 1478 Ed. with minor alterations plus modern maps of Northern Europe, Spain, France, Central Europe, Italy, and Judea. Latin text.
1508	Rome	Folio	34 copperplate maps, same as the 1507 Ed. plus the world map of Ruysch, the first map in an edition of Ptolemy to show the New World. Latin text.
1511	Venice	Folio	28 woodcut maps: 2 world, 10 Europe, 4 Africa, 12 Asia. The heart-shaped world map is the first in an edition of Ptolemy to show part of North America, called ''Regalis Domus.'' Latin text.
*1512	Cracow	4to	An introduction to Ptolemy's Geography edited by Stobnizca, with 2 rare woodcut maps, one of the old world, the other of E. Asia and America. Latin text. Later edition: 1519.
1513	Strassburg	Folio	47 woodcut maps, 27 Ptolemaic maps, 20 new maps. Includes one map devoted to the discoveries in the New World. Latin text. Later edition: 1520.
1514	Nuremberg	Folio	No maps. Latin text.
*1519	Cracow	4to	2nd Ed. of the 1512 version. Apparently no maps were included in this edition.
1520	Strassburg	Folio	47 woodcut maps, same as 1513 Ed. except for the map of Switzerland. Latin text.
1522	Strassburg	Folio	50 woodcut maps similar to the 1513 Ed. but reduced in size. Latin text. Later editions: 1525, 1535, 1541.
1525	Strassburg	Folio	50 woodcut maps, printed from same blocks as 1522 Ed., except for Asia V. Latin text.
*1532	Strassburg	Folio	8 double page woodcut maps. Latin text.
1533	Basle	4to	No maps. Greek text. Later edition: 1546.
1533	Ingolstadt	4to	No maps. Latin text.

---

* Not a formal edition of Ptolemy.

1535	Lyons	Folio	50 woodcut maps, from the same blocks as the 1525 Ed. Latin text.
1540	Basle	Folio	48 woodcut maps: 27 Ptolemaic, 21 new. Latin text. Edited by Sebastian Munster. Later editions: 1541, 1542, 1545, 1551, 1552.
1540	Cologne	Small 8vo	No maps. Latin text.
1541	Basle	Folio	48 woodcut maps, Latin text. Reissue of 1540 Ed.
1541	Vienne	Folio	50 woodcut maps, from the same blocks as the 1525 Ed. Latin text.
1542	Basle	Folio	48 woodcut maps, same as 1540 Ed. Latin text.
1545	Basle	Folio	54 woodcut maps: 42 from 1540 Ed. with 12 new maps. Latin text.
1546	Paris	4to	No maps. Greek text. A reissue of the 1533 Basle Ed.
1548	Venice	Small 8vo	60 copperplate maps by Gastaldi: 26 Ptolemaic and 34 new. Italian text.
1551	Basle	Folio	54 woodcut maps, same as 1545 Ed. Latin text.
1552	Basle	Folio	54 woodcut maps, same as 1545 Ed. except "Lacus Constan" is replaced with "Pomerania." Latin text.
1561	Venice	4to	64 copperplate maps: 27 Ptolemaic and 37 new, most enlarged from the 1548 Ed., with Toscany, northern regions, Brazil, and the Ptolemaic world added. Italian text. Later editions: 1562, 1564 (2), 1574, 1598, 1599.
1562	Venice	4to	64 copperplate maps, from the same plates as 1561 Ed. Latin text.
1564	Venice	4to	64 copperplate maps, from the same plates as 1561 Ed. Italian text.
1564	Venice	4to	64 copperplate maps, from the same plates as 1561 Ed. Latin text.
*1571	Basle	Folio	27 woodcut maps from Munster's Ptolemy including 3 duplicates. This is an edition of Strabo. Latin text.
1574	Venice	4to	65 copperplate maps, same as 1561 Ed. except for the Ptolemaic world that is re-engraved on a conic projection. A map of Rome is added. Italian text.
1578	Cologne	Folio	28 copperplate maps by Mercator, no text. Later editions: 1584, 1605 (2), 1618–19, 1624, 1695, 1698, 1704, 1730.
1584	Cologne	Folio	28 copperplate maps from same plates as 1578 Ed. Latin text.
1596	Venice	4to	64 copperplate maps, newly engraved by Porro. All maps but world are single page. Edited by Magini. Latin text. Later editions: 1597 (2), 1597–98, 1608, 1617, 1621.
1597	Cologne	4to	64 copperplate maps. Latin text. 2nd Ed. of 1596 Ed.
1597	Cologne/Arnhem	4to	64 copperplate maps. Latin text. Variant of above.
1597-8	Venice	Small Folio	64 copperplate maps, same as 1596 Ed. Italian text.
*1597	Louvain	4to	19 copperplate maps of America. Latin text. Wytfliet's supplement to Ptolemy. Later editions: 1598, 1603, 1605, 1607, 1611.

---

* Not a formal edition of Ptolemy.

*1598	Louvain	4to	19 copperplate maps. Latin text. Wytfliet's supplement.
1598	Venice	4to	69 copperplate maps, similar to 1561 Ed., but decorations added. Italian text.
1599	Venice	4to	69 copperplate maps, similar to 1561 Ed., but decorations added. Italian text.
*1603	Douay	4to	19 copperplate maps. Latin text. Wytfliet's supplement.
*1605	Douay	4to	19 copperplate maps. Latin text. Wytfliet's supplement.
1605	Amsterdam	Folio	28 copperplate maps by Mercator. Greek and Latin text.
1605	Frankfort	Folio	28 copperplate maps by Mercator. Greek and Latin text. Variant of above.
*1607	Douay	4to	23 copperplate maps. Latin text. Enlarged version of Wytfliet's supplement.
1608	Cologne	4to	64 copperplate maps. Latin text. Reissue of 1596 Ed. of Magini.
*1611	Douay	4to	23 copperplate maps as in 1607 Ed. Latin text. Wytfliet's supplement.
1617	Arnhem	4to	64 copperplate maps, same as 1596 Ed. of Magini. Latin text.
1618–19	Amsterdam	Folio	47 copperplate maps, including 28 by Mercator and 14 from Ortelius. Greek and Latin text.
1621	Padua	Folio	64 copperplate maps. Italian text. Reissue of 1596 Ed. of Magini.
1624	Frankfort	Folio	28 copperplate maps by Mercator. Greek and Latin text.
1695	Franeker/Utrecht	Folio	28 copperplate maps by Mercator with ornamentation added. No text.
1698	Franeker/Utrecht	Folio	28 copperplate maps by Mercator. Latin text. Reissue of 1695 Ed.
1704	Amsterdam/Utrecht	Folio	28 copperplate maps by Mercator. Latin text. Reissue of 1695 Ed.
1730	Amsterdam	Folio	28 copperplate maps by Mercator. Latin text. Index added.

* Not a formal edition of Ptolemy.

REFERENCES:

Nordenskiold, A. E., *Facsimile-Atlas to the Early History of Cartography*, Stockholm: 1889. Reprinted by Dover Publications, Inc., New York, 1973.

Ruland, Harold L., "A Survey of the Double-page Maps in Thirty-five Editions of the Cosmographia Universalis 1544–1628 of Sebastian Munster and in His Editions of Ptolemy's Geographia 1540–1552," *Imago Mundi* XVI (1962), pp. 84–97.

Stevens, Henry N., *Ptolemy's Geography, A Brief Account of All the Printed Editions down to 1730*, London: Henry Stevens, Son and Stiles, 1908.

Winsor, J., *A Bibliography of Ptolemy's Geography*, Cambridge, Massachusetts: University Press: Henry Wilson and Son, 1884.

INDEX TO THE REGIONAL MAPS
OF PTOLEMY

The 26 ancient Ptolemaic regional maps are usually designated by continent and number. For example, *Tabula Europae III* would indicate the third map of Europe. To assist in cases where the map is not further described, the area covered by each map is given below.

EUROPE

I   The British Isles—Scotland, Ireland, England & Wales
II   Spain & Portugal
III   France & the low countries
IV   Germany
V   The Dalmatian Coast (present-day Yugoslavia)
VI   Italy & Corsica
VII   Sardinia & Sicily
VIII Eastern Europe from the Vistula River to the Sea of Azov
IX   Ancient Dace & Thrace (present-day Balkans north of Greece)
X   Greece & Crete

AFRICA

I   Ancient Mauretania (present-day Morocco & Algeria)
II   Present-day Libya
III   Egypt
IV   All of Northern Africa

ASIA

I   Asia Minor (present-day Turkey)
II   Ancient Sarmatia (present-day Crimea, Sea of Azov, & the northern Caucasus)
III   Armenia
IV   Holy Land, Cyprus & Mesopotamia
V   Persia (Iran)
VI   Arabia
VII   Ancient Scythia (present-day Caspian Sea & the land to the north & east)
VIII Central Asia, Tartary
IX   Present-day Pakistan
X   Southern Asia including India
XI   Present-day Burma & Malaya
XII   Ceylon

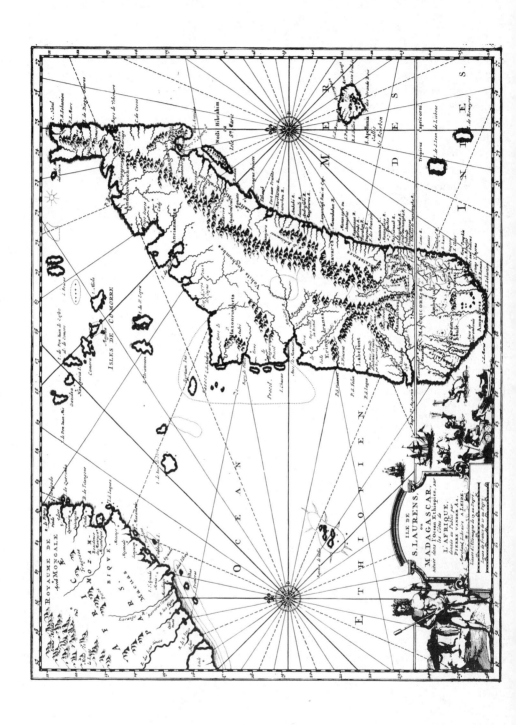

A decorative map of Madagascar by Pieter van der Aa, circa 1700. (18.0 x 36.7 cm.)

22

LATIN-ENGLISH LEXICON
OF MAP-RELATED WORDS

The following list of words may help beginners translate Latin titles and legends appearing on maps. The Renaissance Latin used on maps is very similar to classical Latin, although there are vocabulary differences.

One cannot teach Latin in a paragraph. However, as a reminder, Latin is an inflected language. Word endings change to reflect usage. Nouns are declined, and entries below give the nominative (subject) case, followed by the genitive (possessive) ending. Plurals and other cases exist, but are not given here. Adjective entries give the three endings for the masculine, feminine, and neuter nominative case. Verbs appear in the third person singular. The vocabulary below should be sufficient to extract the essence of simple phrases. Bear in mind that adjectives may appear before or after the nouns they modify. Also the letters *i* and *j* are often used interchangeably. In addition, words such as *sculpsit* and *scripsit* were often used loosely, and may merely indicate some unspecified connection between the person named and the map. Some actual examples may be helpful:

Henricus Hondius excudit. Literally, "Henry Hondius (he) engraved," or more loosely, "engraved by Henry Hondius."

Americae Nova Tabula. Here *America* has been inflected, and appears in the genitive (possessive) singular. Thus the title is "New Map of America."

Hispaniae Novae Descriptio. This is very similar to the above example, but now *Novae* agrees with, and thus modifies, *Hispaniae*. Therefore, the translation is "Map of New Spain," and not "New Map of Spain," which would have been written as *Hispaniae Nova Descriptio.*

a ab *prep* from, by

ac *conj* and, and also

accuratissimus -a -um *adj* most accurate

aliquot *indecl num* some, several

amplissimus -a -um *adj* most glorious, splendid, or esteemed

Amstelodamum -i *n* Amsterdam

Anglia -ae *n* England

annus -i *n* year

apud *prep* at the establishment of, near

aqua -ae *n* water

archducatus -us *n* archduchy

archiepiscopatus -us *n* archiepiscopate

atque *conj* and, and also

auctor -is *n* author, creator

australis -e *adj* southern

borealis -e *adj* northern

caelavit *v* he engraved or carved

Candia -ae *n* Crete

chalcographus -i *n* engraver

chersonesus -i *n* peninsula

chorographica -ae *n* geography

comitatus -us *n* county

comprehendens *adj* including

conatus -us *n* effort, endeavor; **ex conatibus** by the efforts of

confinis -e *adj* adjacent

confinis -is *n* neighboring region

continens -entis *adj* adjacent, neighboring

conventus -us *n* district assigned to a city, association

cum *prep* with

delineavit *v* he sketched or engraved

descriptio -ionis *n* map, representation, description

dicio (also **ditio**) **-ionis** *n* dominion, sovereignty

dioecesis -is *n* district, governor's jurisdiction, diocese

dominium -ii *n* ownership, property, rule

ducatus -us *n* duchy, dukedom

editus -a -um *adj* published, produced

emendatus -a -um *adj* corrected, improved, amended

episcopatus -us *n* episcopate, bishopric

et *conj* and

ex *prep* from, out of

exactissime *adv* most exactly

exactissimus -a -um *adj* most exact

excudebat excudit *v* he made, struck, or hammered out

exhibens *part adj* displaying

fecit *v* he made, produced, created, or prepared

florentissimus -a -um *adj* most flourishing, prosperous, or eminent

flumen -inis *n* river

fluvius -ii *n* river

fretum -i *n* strait, channel

Gallia -ae *n* France

Hibernia -ae *n* Ireland

hodie *adv* today, nowadays

hodiernus -a -um *adj* present, modern

imago -inis *n* image, likeness, copy

imperium -ii *n* empire, dominion

incola -ae *n* inhabitant

inferior -ius *adj* lower

insula -ae *n* island

integro -tegra -tegrum *adj* whole, entire

item *adv* likewise, also, in the same manner

iuxta (or **juxta**) *prep* near

lacus -us *n* lake

locus -i *n* place, district

marchionatus -us *n* marquisate

mare -is *n* sea, ocean

meridionalis -e *adj* southern

mundus -i *n* the world, the universe, the earth

nec (or **neqeu**) *conj* and besides, and also

nec non besides, and also

neotericus -a -um *adj* modern

novissimus -a -um *adj* newest, most recent

noviter *adv* newly

novus -a -um *adj* new

nunc *adv* now, nowadays

occidentalis -e *adj* western

officina -ae *n* workshop, factory

olim *adv* once, at that time, formerly

orbis -is *n* globe, circle, world, earth, orbit

orientalis -e *adj* eastern

pars partis *n* part, region

per *prep* through, by

pinxit *v* he drew, painted, or decorated

praecipuus -a -um *adj* excellent, extraordinary, special

proprius -a -um *adj* special, individual, particular

qui quae quod *rel pron* who, which, what, that

recens (or **recenter**) *adv* recently, newly

recens -entis *adj* recent

regio -ionis *v* line, boundary, region

regnum -i *n* kingdom, dominion

retectus -a -um *adj* discovered, opened, made accessible

Scotia -ae *n* Scotland

scripsit *v* he wrote or drew

sculpsit *v* he engraved or carved

secundum *prep* according to

septentrionalis -e *adj* northern

seu *conj* or

situs -a -um *adj* situated

situs -us *n* position, situation, site

sive *conj* or

subjacens -entis *adj* near

sumptus -us *n* cost; **sumptibus**, published at or by

superior -is *adj* upper, higher

tabula -ae *n* map

terra -ae *n* the earth, land

totus -a -um (*gen.* **totius**) *adj* all, entire, total

tractus -us *n* territory, district, region

typus -i *n* image, figure

urbs urbis *n* city

uterque utraque utrumque (*gen* **utriusque**) *adj or pron* each, both

vel *conj* or

verissimus -a -um *adj* truest

vernacule *adv* in the vernacular

vetus -eris *adj* old

vulgo *adv* commonly, generally, in the vernacular

DICTIONARY OF MAP AND VIEW MAKERS

The following list is intended for quick reference. For each entry, only the nationality and approximate date of publication are given. In some cases, the date may include a portion of an adjoining century. For example, "late 1600s" may include a little of the 1700s.

For more detailed information, the collector should refer to Tooley's *Dictionary of Mapmakers*, which lists maps or atlases associated with most mapmakers listed. A debt is owed to the *Dictionary of Mapmakers* for first names of some of the more obscure cartographers in this listing.

Name	Nationality	Period		Name	Nationality	Period
Albrizzi, Giambatista	Italian	Mid 1700s		Buchon, Jean Alexandre	French	Early 1800s
Allard (Family)	Dutch	Late 1600s		Bufford, J.H.	American	Mid 1800s
Allen, William and Co.	English	Mid 1800s		Bunting, Heinrich	German	Late 1500s
Andreas, Alfred	American	Late 1800s		Burgess, D.	American	Mid 1800s
Andrews & Dury	English	Late 1700s		Burney, J.	English	Early 1800s
Angelo, Theodore G.N.	Danish	Early 1800s		Burr, David H.	American	Early 1800s
Anson, George	English	Mid 1700s		Burriel	Spanish	Mid 1700s
Apianus, Peter	German	Early 1500s		Butler, Samuel	English	Early 1800s
Apianus, Philip	German	Mid 1500s		Cadell, Thomas	English	Late 1700s
Appleton, D. & Co.	American	Late 1800s		Camden, William	English	Late 1500s
Aquila, Prospero dell'	Italian	Late 1700s		Camocio, Giovanni Francesco	Italian	Mid 1500s
Arrowsmith, Aaron	English	Early 1800s		Carey & Lea	American	Early 1800s
Asher & Adams	American	Mid 1800s		Carey, Mathew	American	Early 1800s
Aspin, Jehoshaphat	English	Early 1800s		Carez, J.	French	Early 1800s
Atwood, J.M.	American	Late 1800s		Carleton, Osgood	American	Late 1800s
Baldwin & Cradock	English	Early 1800s		Carolus, Frans	Dutch	Early 1700s
Baldwin, Richard	English	Mid 1700s		Cary, John	English	Early 1800s
Barclay, James	English	Mid 1800s		Cassini, Giovanni Maria	Italian	Late 1800s
Barfield, J.	English	Early 1800s		Castilla, A. de	Spanish	Early 1800s
Barker, William	American	Late 1700s		Catlin, George	American	Early 1800s
Bartlett, W.H.	American	Mid 1800s		Chanlaire & Mentelle	French	Early 1800s
Baudin, Nicolas	French	Early 1800s		Chanlaire, Pierre Gregoire	French	Early 1800s
Beers (Family)	American	Late 1800s		Chapin, William	American	Mid 1800s
Beldin, H.	American	Late 1800s		Chapman & Hall	English	Mid 1800s
Bell, Peter	English	Late 1700s		Chapman, John	English	Late 1700s
Bellere, Jean	Dutch	Late 1500s		Charlevoix, P.F. Xavier de	French	Mid 1700s
Bellin, Jacques Nicolas	French	Mid 1700s		Chatelain, Henry Abraham	Dutch	Early 1700s
Benard, Jacques Francois	French	Early 1700s		Child, G.	English	Mid 1700s
Bernard, Jean Frederic	Dutch	Mid 1700s		Cluver, Philip	German	Early 1600s
Berry, William	English	Late 1600s		Collins, Greenville	English	Late 1600s
Bertius, Pieter	Dutch	Early 1600s		Colton, George Woolworth	American	Mid 1800s
Betts, John	English	Mid 1800s		Conder, Thomas	English	Late 1800s
Bien, Julius	American	Mid 1800s		Conservancy, Thomas	English	Late 1700s
Bion, Nicolas	French	Early 1700s		Cook, Capt. James	English	Late 1700s
Black, A. & C.	English	Mid 1800s		Coronelli, Vicenzo Maria	Italian	Late 1600s
Blackie & Son	Scottish	Late 1800s		Covens & Mortier	Dutch	Early 1700s
Blaeu (Family)	Dutch	Mid 1600s		Cowley, John	English	Mid 1700s
Blankaart, Nicolas	Dutch	Mid 1600s		Cowperthwait, H.	American	Mid 1800s
Blome, Richard	English	Late 1600s		Cram, George	American	Late 1800s
Blundell, J.	English	Early 1700s		Crawford, C.G.	American	Late 1800s
Bodenehr (Family)	German	Early 1700s		Crepy	French	Mid 1700s
Bohn, Carl Ernst	German	Late 1700s		Cruchley, George Frederick	English	Mid 1800s
Bolton, Solomon	English	Late 1700s		D'Anville, Jean B.B.	French	Mid 1700s
Bonne, Rigobert	French	Late 1700s		D'Apres de Mannevillette, J.B.	French	Late 1700s
Botero, Giovanni	Italian	Late 1500s		Dal Re, Marc Antonio	Italian	Early 1700s
Bouchette, Joseph	English	Early 1800s		Dalrymple, Alexander	English	Late 1700s
Bowen, Emanuel	English	Mid 1700s		Dampier, William	English	Early 1700s
Bowen, Thomas	English	Late 1700s		Danckerts (Family)	Dutch	Mid 1600s
Bowles, Carington	English	Late 1700s		Dapper, Olivier	Dutch	Late 1600s
Bowles, John	English	Mid 1700s		Darton, William	English	Early 1800s
Bowles, Thomas	English	Early 1700s		Davenport, S.	English	Mid 1800s
Bradford, Thomas Gamaliel	American	Early 1800s		Day & Son	English	Mid 1800s
Bradley, William	American	Late 1800s		De Belle Forest, Francois	French	Late 1500s
Braun & Hogenberg	Dutch	Late 1500s		De Berey, Nicolas	French	Mid 1600s
Brightly & Kinnersley	English	Early 1800s		De Bry, Theordore	German	Late 1500s
Brion de la Tour	French	Late 1700s		De Fer, Nicolas	French	Early 1700s
Brooke, W.H.	American	Mid 1800s		De Grado, Philip	Spanish	Early 1700s
Brue, Adrien Hubert	French	Early 1800s		De Hooghe, Romain	Dutch	Late 1600s
Bryant, A.	English	Early 1800s		De Jode (Family)	Dutch	Late 1500s
Buache, Phillipe	French	Mid 1700s		De L'Isle, Guillaume	French	Early 1700s

De La Potherie, B.	French	Early 1700s	Gold, Joyce	English	Early 1800s
De La Rue, Phillipe	French	Mid 1600s	Goodrich, Samuel Griswold	American	Mid 1800s
De Laet, Joannes	Dutch	Early 1600s	Goos (Family)	Dutch	Mid 1600s
De Lat, Jan	Dutch	Mid 1700s	Gordon, P.	Irish	Late 1700s
De Vaugondy, Didier Robert	French	Late 1700s	Gray, O.W.	American	Late 1800s
De Vaugondy, Gilles Robert	French	Mid 1700s	Greenleaf, Jeremiah	American	Mid 1800s
De Wit, Frederick	Dutch	Late 1600s	Greenleaf, Moses	American	Early 1800s
Dearborn, Benjamin	American	Early 1800s	Greenwood	English	Early 1800s
Delamarche, Charles Francois	French	Late 1700s	Gridley, R.	English	Mid 1700s
Den Schryver	Dutch	Early 1700s	Griswold	American	Mid 1800s
Denis, Louis	French	Late 1700s	Gussefeld, Franz Ludwig	German	Late 1700s
Denison, J.	American	Late 1700s	Guthrie, William	Scottish	Late 1700s
Des Barres, Joseph F.W.	English	Late 1800s	Hall, Sidney	English	Early 1800s
Desilver, C.	American	Mid 1800s	Halliburton, T.C.	Canadian	Early 1800s
Desnos, Louis Charles	French	Late 1700s	Harris, John	English	Early 1700s
Dezauche, J.A.	French	Early 1800s	Harrison, John E.	English	Late 1700s
Dicey, William & Cluer	English	Mid 1700s	Hayward, John	American	Mid 1800s
Dilly, Charles	English	Late 1700s	Hearne, Samuel	English	Late 1700s
Dixon, George	English	Late 1700s	Heather, William	English	Early 1800s
Dolendo, Bartholomew	Dutch	Early 1600s	Henriol, J.N.	French	Mid 1800s
Doncker, Hendrik	Dutch	Late 1600s	Herbert, William	English	Mid 1700s
Doppelmayr, Johann Gabriel	German	Early 1700s	Herisson, C.	French	Early 1800s
Dower, John	English	Mid 1800s	Herrera, Antonio de	Spanish	Early 1600s
Drayton, Michael	English	Early 1600s	Hill, J.W.	American	Mid 1800s
Drinkwater, John	English	Early 1800s	Hinshelwood, R.	American	Mid 1800s
Du Sauzet, Henri	Dutch	Early 1700s	Hinton, John	English	Mid 1700s
Du Val, Pierre	French	Mid 1600s	Hinton, Simpkin & Marshall	English	Early 1800s
Dudley, Robert	English	Mid 1600s	Hogenberg, Frans	Dutch	Late 1500s
Dufour, Adolphe Hippolyte	French	Mid 1800s	Hogg, Alexander	English	Late 1700s
Dunn, Samuel	English	Late 1700s	Hole, William	English	Early 1600s
Dwight, T.	English	Early 1800s	Hollar, Wenceslaus	Czech	Mid 1600s
Edwards, Bryan	English	Late 1700s	Holme, Thomas	American	Late 1600s
Ehrmann, Theodor Friedrich	German	Early 1800s	Homann, Johann Baptist	German	Early 1700s
Ellis, John	English	Late 1700s	Hondius (Family)	Dutch	Early 1600s
Ely, A.E.M.	American	Mid 1800s	Honter, Jan	German	Mid 1500s
Ertl, Anton Wilhelm	German	Early 1700s	Hornius, Georg	Dutch	Late 1600s
Euler, Leonhard	German	Mid 1700s	Houze, Antoine Philippe	French	Mid 1800s
Faden, William	English	Late 1700s	Hulsius, Levinus	German	Late 1500s
Fairburn, John	English	Late 1700s	Hume & Smollett	English	Mid 1800s
Farnham, Thomas	American	Mid 1800s	Huot, Jean Jacques Nicolas	French	Mid 1800s
Fenner, Sears & Co.	English	Early 1800s	Hutchins, Thomas	American	Late 1700s
Fielding, John	English	Late 1700s	Hutchinson, Thomas	English	Mid 1700s
Findlay, Alexander	English	Mid 1800s	Illman, T. & Sons	English	Mid 1800s
Finley, Anthony	American	Early 1800s	Imray, James	English	Mid 1800s
Fisher, H.	English	Early 1800s	Jacobz (Family)	Dutch	Mid 1600s
Fisk & Russell	American	Mid 1800s	Jaillot, Hubert	French	Late 1700s
Fisk & See	American	Late 1800s	Jansson, Jan	Dutch	Early 1600s
Franklin, John	English	Early 1800s	Janvier, Jean	French	Late 1700s
Fremin, A.R.	French	Mid 1800s	Jefferys, Thomas	English	Mid 1700s
Fullarton, Archibald	Scottish	Mid 1800s	Johnson & Browning	American	Mid 1800s
Fuller, Thomas	English	Mid 1600s	Johnson & Ward	American	Mid 1800s
Gall & Inglis	Scottish	Late 1800s	Johnson, A.J.	American	Mid 1800s
Galt & Hoy	American	Late 1800s	Johnston, W. & A.K.	Scottish	Mid 1800s
Gardner, James	English	Mid 1800s	Judd, James	English	Mid 1800s
Garnier, F.	French	Mid 1800s	Kaempfer, Engelbert		Early 1700s
Gaston, Samuel	American	Mid 1800s	Kelly, Thomas	English	Early 1800s
Gemma Frisius	Dutch	Early 1500s	Key, John R.	American	Mid 1800s
Gerritz, Hessel	Dutch	Early 1600s	Keyser, Jacob	Dutch	Early 1700s
Gibson, John	English	Mid 1700s	Kiepert, Heinrich	German	Mid 1800s
Goeree, Jan	Dutch	Early 1700s	Kilburn	American	Mid 1800s

King, Daniel	English	Mid 1600s	Miller, William	English	Early 1800s
Kip, William	English	Early 1600s	Mitchell, Samuel Augustus	American	Mid 1800s
Kircher, Athanasius	Dutch	Mid 1600s	Moll, Herman	English	Early 1700s
Kitchin, Thomas	English	Mid 1700s	Montanus, Arnoldus	Dutch	Late 1600s
Knight, Charles	English	Mid 1800s	Moon, F.G.	English	Mid 1800s
La Hontan, Baron Louis de	French	Early 1700s	Moore, J.H.	English	Late 1700s
La Perouse, Comte Jean de	French	Late 1700s	Morden, Robert	English	Late 1600s
Lacoste, Charles	French	Late 1800s	Morse & Breese	American	Mid 1800s
Lafreri, Antonio	Italian	Mid 1500s	Morse, Jedediah	American	Early 1800s
Lane, Michael	English	Late 1700s	Mortier, Pierre	Dutch	Late 1600s
Langley, Edward	English	Early 1800s	Mount & Page	English	Mid 1700s
Langsdorff, G.	German	Early 1800s	Moxon, Joseph	English	Late 1600s
Lapie, Alexandre Emile	French	Early 1800s	Mudie, Robert	English	Early 1800s
Lapointe, D.	French	Mid 1600s	Muller, Johann Ulrich	German	Late 1600s
Lauremberg, Johannes Wilhelm		Mid 1600s	Munster, Sebastian	Swiss	Mid 1500s
Laurie & Whittle	English	Late 1700s	Murray, John	English	Late 1700s
Laurie, Robert	English	Late 1700s	Neele (Family)	English	Early 1800s
Lavoisne, C.V.		Early 1800s	Nicholls, Sutton	English	Early 1700s
Le Page du Pratz	French	Mid 1700s	Nicol, G.	English	Late 1700s
Le Rouge, George Louis	French	Mid 1700s	Nicolosi, Giovanni Battista	Italian	Mid 1600s
Lea, Isaac	American	Early 1800s	Nolin, Jean Baptiste	French	Late 1600s
Lea, Philip	English	Late 1600s	Norrie, J.W.	English	Early 1800s
Lemercier	French	Mid 1800s	Nuttall, Fisher & Dixon	English	Early 1800s
Leval, P.	French	Early 1700s	Ogilby, John	English	Late 1600s
Levasseur, Victor	French	Mid 1800s	Olney, Jesse	American	Early 1800s
Lewis & Arrowsmith	English	Early 1800s	Ortelius, Abraham	Dutch	Mid 1500s
Lewis, Samuel	American	Late 1700s	Ottens (Family)	Dutch	Early 1700s
Liebaux, Jean Baptiste	French	Late 1600s	Overton, John	English	Late 1600s
Linschoten, Jan Huygen van	Dutch	Late 1500s	Padley, James	English	Mid 1800s
Lizars (Family)	Scottish	Early 1800s	Palfrey, John Gorham	American	Mid 1800s
Lloyd, H.H.	American	Mid 1800s	Paoli, Giovanni	Italian	Early 1700s
Lodge, John	English	Late 1700s	Papen, Augustus	German	Mid 1800s
Longman	English	Mid 1800s	Parr, Richard	English	Mid 1700s
Lopez de Vargas Machuca, Tomas	Spanish	Mid 1700s	Parry, William Edward	English	Early 1800s
Lotter (Family)	German	Late 1700s	Pease, R.H.	American	Mid 1800s
Lucas, Fielding	American	Early 1800s	Perthes, Justus	German	Mid 1800s
Luffman, John	English	Early 1800s	Petermann, Augustus Herman	English	Mid 1800s
Mackenzie, Murdoch	English	Late 1700s	Petri, Heinrich	Swiss	Mid 1500s
Magini, Giovanni Antonio	Italian	Late 1500s	Petrini, Paolo	Italian	Late 1600s
Mallet, Alain Manesson	French	Late 1600s	Petroschi, Giovanni	Italian	Early 1700s
Malte-Brun (Family)	French	Mid 1800s	Philip, George	English	Mid 1800s
Mante, J.	English	Late 1700s	Philippe de Pretot, E.A.	French	Late 1700s
Maspero, M.	Italian	Early 1800s	Phillips, Richard	English	Early 1800s
Maundressi, Henr.		Late 1600s	Pigafetta, Filippo	Italian	Late 1500s
Mayer, Johann Tobias	German	Mid 1700s	Pine, John	English	Early 1700s
McIntyre, A.	Scottish	Late 1700s	Pinkerton, John	Scottish	Early 1800s
McNally, F.	American	Mid 1800s	Pitt, Moses	English	Late 1600s
Mears, J.	English	Late 1700s	Plancius, Petrus	Dutch	Late 1500s
Meijer, Peter	Dutch	Mid 1700s	Playfair, James	Scottish	Early 1800s
Meisner, Daniel	German	Mid 1600s	Poirson, Jean Baptiste	French	Early 1800s
Meissas, Achille Pr. de	French	Mid 1800s	Pont, Timothy	English	Early 1600s
Melish, John	American	Early 1800s	Popple, Henry	English	Early 1700s
Mentelle, Edme	French	Early 1800s	Porcacchi, Tomaso	Italian	Late 1500s
Mercator, Gerhard	Dutch	Late 1500s	Porro, Girolamo	Italian	Late 1500s
Merian, Matthaus	German	Mid 1600s	Prevost D'exiles, A.	French	Mid 1700s
Metellus, Natalius Sequanus	German	Late 1500s	Probst, Johann Michael	German	Late 1700s
Meyer, H.	American	Mid 1800s	Purchas, Samuel	English	Early 1600s
Meyer, J.	German	Mid 1800s	Quad, Matthias	German	Late 1500s
Michault, R.	French	Late 1600s	Radefeld, Carl Christian Franz	German	Mid 1800s
Millar, Andrew	English	Mid 1700s	Ramsay, Andrew Crombie	English	Late 1800s

Name	Nationality	Period
Ramusio, Giovanni Battista	Italian	Mid 1500s
Rand, Avery & Co.	American	Late 1800s
Raspe, Gabriel Nikolaus	German	Late 1700s
Reed, John A.	American	Late 1700s
Reilly, F.J.J. von	Austrian	Late 1700s
Reland, Adrien	Dutch	Early 1700s
Renard, Louis	Dutch	Early 1700s
Renner	German	Mid 1800s
Robertson, George	English	Late 1700s
Robinson, G.G.	English	Late 1700s
Robson, T.	English	Early 1800s
Rocque, Jean	French	Mid 1700s
Rogers, Peet & Co.	American	Late 1800s
Rollos, G.	English	Late 1700s
Romans, Bernard	English	Late 1700s
Rossi, Luigi	Italian	Early 1800s
Rouargue, F.	French	Early 1800s
Roux, Joseph	French	Late 1700s
Ruscelli, Girolamo	Italian	Mid 1500s
Russell, John	English	Late 1700s
Sanson, Nicolas	French	Mid 1600s
Santini, P.	Italian	Late 1700s
Saxton, Christopher	English	Late 1500s
Sayer & Bennett	English	Late 1700s
Sayer, Robert	English	Late 1700s
Schedel	German	Late 1400s
Schenk (Family)	Dutch	Early 1700s
Scherer, Heinrich	German	Early 1700s
Schley, Jacob van der	German	Mid 1700s
Schmidt, M.F.	German	Early 1800s
Schouten, Willem Cornelisz	Dutch	Early 1600s
Scott, Joseph	American	Late 1700s
Seale, Richard William	English	Mid 1700s
Seile, Henry	English	Mid 1600s
Seller, John	English	Late 1600s
Senex, John	English	Early 1700s
Seutter (Family)	German	Mid 1700s
Smillie, J.D.	American	Late 1800s
Smith, Charles	English	Early 1800s
Soules, Francois	French	Late 1700s
Speed, John	English	Early 1600s
Stackhouse, Thomas	English	Late 1700s
Staehlin	German	Late 1700s
Stanford, Edward	English	Mid 1800s
Starling, Thomas	English	Early 1800s
Stedman, Charles	English	Late 1700s
Stockdale, John	English	Late 1700s
Stocklein, Joseph	German	Mid 1700s
Stoopendaal, Daniel	Dutch	Early 1700s
Stupnagel, F.	German	Mid 1800s
Swinston, W.	American	Late 1800s
Tallis, John	English	Mid 1800s
Tanner, Henry Schenck	American	Early 1800s
Tardieu (Family)	French	Early 1800s
Teesdale, Henry	English	Mid 1800s
Thevenot, Melchisedech	French	Late 1600s
Thierry	French	Early 1800s
Thomas, Cowperthwait & Co.	American	Mid 1800s
Thomson Bros. & Burr	American	Late 1800s
Thomson, John & Co.	Scottish	Early 1800s
Thornton, John	English	Late 1600s
Tindal, Nicolas	English	Mid 1700s
Tirion, Isaak	Dutch	Mid 1700s
Tombleson	English	Mid 1800s
Topham	English	Early 1800s
Torniello, Augustine		Late 1500s
Toudy, H.J.	American	Late 1800s
Trusler, John		Late 1700s
Valentyn, Francois	Dutch	Early 1700s
Valk & Schenk	Dutch	Early 1700s
Valk (Family)	Dutch	Early 1700s
Van Doetecum (Family)	Dutch	Late 1500s
Van Keulen (Family)	Dutch	Late 1600s
Van Lochom, Michael	French	Early 1600s
Van den Keere, Pieter	Dutch	Early 1600s
Van der Aa, Pieter	Dutch	Early 1700s
Vandermaelen, Philippe M.G.	British	Mid 1800s
Varte, P.C.	American	Late 1800s
Vascellini, G.	Italian	Late 1700s
Visscher (Family)	Dutch	Mid 1600s
Vivien, L.	French	Early 1800s
Vuillemin, Alexandre A.	French	Mid 1800s
Waghenaer, Lucas Janszoon	Dutch	Late 1500s
Wakefield, P.	English	Early 1800s
Walch, Johann	German	Early 1800s
Wales, William	English	Late 1700s
Walker, J. & C.	English	Mid 1800s
Wall, J. Sutton	American	Late 1800s
Walther, Johann Georg	German	Late 1600s
Walton, Robert	English	Mid 1600s
Ward, H.	English	Early 1800s
Ward, J.	English	Mid 1800s
Warden, D.	Scottish	Early 1800s
Weber, P.	German	Mid 1800s
Weigel, Christopher	German	Early 1700s
Weller, Edward	English	Late 1800s
Wells, Edward	English	Early 1700s
Wilkes, J.	English	Early 1800s
Wilkinson, Robert	English	Early 1800s
Willdey, George	English	Early 1700s
Willmann, Edward	German	Mid 1800s
Wilson, Charles	English	Mid 1800s
Winslow, E.N.	American	Late 1800s
Witsen, Nicolaas	Dutch	Early 1700s
Wright, Benjamin	English	Late 1500s
Wyld, James	English	Mid 1800s
Wytfliet, Cornelis	Dutch	Late 1500s
Zatta, Antonio	Italian	Late 1700s
Ziegler, Jacob	Austrian	Early 1500s

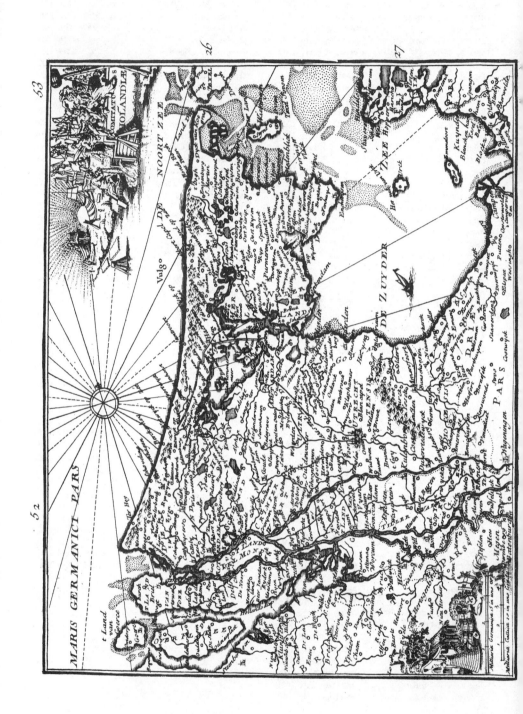

A miniature map of Holland by Jacobus Peeters, circa 1700. (14.5 x 18.3 cm.)

30

DIRECTORY OF DEALERS

The following list of dealers has been compiled from various sources. Questionnaires were sent to over 200 dealers, and the information received in reply has been incorporated below. It is believed that all the names and addresses are postally valid. However, some dealers may be retired or no longer active, while others may be book, print, or antique dealers who deal only occasionally in maps. One dealer in modern maps has been included so that collectors may obtain for reference and comparison modern maps of the regions they collect.

Because of the uniform format, when a dealer replied that he or she sometimes exhibited at fairs or occasionally issued catalogs, this appears as a definite affirmative in the list. Even though some entries do not indicate that an appointment is required, the information is not always complete, and even dealers with shop hours can be preoccupied with some activity such as preparation for a book fair. Therefore it is suggested that you write in advance, or at least telephone just before visiting. When writing to dealers for catalogs or quotes, please remember that it is far more productive to give a detailed description of the material you desire, and that some dealers charge a fee for sending catalogs.

The American list is in order of zip code to reflect regional proximity. The American and Canadian lists are believed to be reasonably complete. However, no questionnaires were sent outside North America, and the international list includes only addresses and telephone numbers.

Apologies are extended to any dealers inadvertently omitted or mistakenly included. Dealers omitted should request a questionnaire, and any errors should be called to the attention of the publisher so that corrections can be made in future editions.

Inclusion of a name should not be regarded as an endorsement by the publisher, nor should omission be regarded as a lack of such endorsement.

PAPERBOOK GALLERY, PALM PASSAGE, ST. THOMAS, VI 00801

JELTRUP'S BOOKS, THOMAS & DOROTHY JELTRUP, KING CROSS ST., CHRISTIANSTED, ST. CROIX, VI 00820

HISTORICAL TECHNOLOGY, 6 MUGFORD STREET, MARBLEHEAD, MA 01945   Phone 617-631-2275
   ANTIQUE INSTRUMENTS, CHARTS, BOOKS, GLOBES, ORRERYS by appointment, by mail, catalogs/lists

A.A. WILLS & SONS INC., PO BOX 148, MARSHFIELD HILLS, MA 02051

RUDISILL'S ALT PRINT HAUS, JOHN & BARBARA RUDISILL, 3 LAKEWOOD DRIVE, MEDFIELD, MA 02052

MICHAEL GINSBURG BOOKS, INC., PO BOX 402, SHARON, MA 02067

JOHN G. PANACY, 196 WALNUT STREET, STOUGHTON, MA 02072

GOODSPEED'S BOOK SHOP, DORIS B. ADAMS, 7 BEACON STREET, BOSTON, MA 02108   Phone 617-523-5970
   shop hours, by mail, book fairs/antique shows

EUGENE GALLERIES, 76 CHARLES STREET, BOSTON, MA 02114   Phone 617-227-3062
   shop hours

DAVID JOLLY ANTIQUE MAPS, PO BOX 1003, BROOKLINE, MA 02146   Phone 617-232-6222
   by appointment, by mail, catalogs/lists

YOLE G. ROSS, ANTIQUE MAPS & PRINTS, 84 SPOONER ROAD, CHESTNUT HILL, MA 02167   Phone 617-566-6747

K.C. OWINGS, JR., HISTORICAL AMERICANA, PO BOX 19, NORTH ABINGTON, MA 02351   Phone 617-587-6441
   by appointment, by mail, catalogs/lists

E.C. BREEDING, 27 NORTH LIBERTY STREET, NANTUCKET, MA 02554

EDWARD J. LEFKOWICZ, 43 FORT ST., PO BOX 630, FAIRHAVEN, MA 02719

THE CURRENT COMPANY, PO BOX 46, BRISTOL, RI 02809

THE MAP CENTER, 400 WICKENDEN STREET, PROVIDENCE, RI 02903   Phone 619-291-3830
   MODERN MAPS ONLY shop hours

THE ATLAS, 119 OLNEY AVE., PO BOX 3822, NORTH PROVIDENCE, RI 02911   Phone 401-353-1161
   by appointment, by mail

THE ANTIQUARIAN OLD BOOK STORE, 1070 LAFAYETTE ROAD, PORTSMOUTH, NH 03801

DOUGLAS N. HARDING, BOX 184, RT. 1, WEBHANNET FARM, WELLS, ME 04090   Phone 207-646-8785

R.T. LOMBARD, JR., CHARLES JORDAN ROAD, CAPE ELIZABETH, ME 04107

CHARLES ROBINSON RARE BOOKS, BOX 57, POND ROAD, MANCHESTER, ME 04351   Phone 207-622-1885
   by appointment, by mail, book fairs/antique shows, auction, catalogs/lists

VILLAGE BOOKSHIP, INC., RT. 130, BOX 169, NEW HARBOR, ME 04554

COUNTRY LANE BOOKS, PO BOX 47, COLLINSVILLE, CT 06022

CEDRIC L. ROBINSON, BOOKSELLER, 597 PALISADO AVE., WINDSOR, CT 06095   Phone 203-688-2582
   by appointment, by mail, catalogs/lists

TRADEWINDS GALLERY, 10 WATER STREET, MYSTIC, CT 06355   Phone 203-536-0119
   shop hours, by mail, book fairs/antique shows, catalogs/lists

CARTOGRAPHICS, PO BOX 67, NORTH STONINGTON, CT 06359   Phone 203-535-3152
   by appointment, by mail, book fairs/antique shows, catalogs/lists

BRANFORD RARE BOOK & ART GALLERY, 221 MONTOWESE STREET, BRANFORD, CT 06405   Phone 203-488-5882
   shop hours, by mail, book fairs/antique shows, auction, catalogs/lists

DONALD T. PITCHER, PO BOX 64, NORTH HAVEN, CT 06473

LUKE A. VAVRA, 1815 NOBLE AVENUE, BRIDGEPORT, CT 06610

ALFRED W. PAINE BOOKS, CAROLA PAINE WORMSER, WOLFPITS ROAD, BETHEL, CT 06801

AVIS & ROCKY GARDINER, 60 MILL ROAD, STAMFORD, CT 06903   Phone 203-322-1129

L.S. STRAIGHT, MAPS, 101 MAPLE STREET, WEEHAWKEN, NJ 07087   Phone 201-863-9115
   GENERAL, AMERICANA by mail, catalogs/lists

HOBBIT SHOP, 305 W. SOUTH AVE., WESTFIELD, NJ 07090

HAROLD NESTLER, INC., 13 PENNINGTON AVE., WALDRICK, NJ 07463   Phone 201-444-7413
   MAPS OCCASIONALLY OFFERED IN AMERICANA CATALOGS

MARTIN TORODASH BOOKS, 348 IVY LANE, ENGLEWOOD, NJ 07631

KEITH LIBRARY & GALLERY, 217 W. FRONT ST., RED BANK, NJ 07701

HEINOLDT BOOKS, T.H. HEINOLDT, CENTRAL & BUFFALO AVES., SOUTH EGG HARBOR, NJ 08215

ACADEMUS BOOK SHOP, HADDON HALL LOBBY, S. NORTH CAROLINA & BEACH, ATLANTIC CITY, NJ 08401

JOSEPH J. FELCONE INC., RARE BOOKS, PO BOX 366, PRINCETON, NJ 08540

PAGEANT BOOK & PRINT SHOP, 109 E. 9TH ST., NEW YORK, NY 10003   Phone 212-674-5296

SWANN GALLERIES, INC., 117 E. 24TH ST., NEW YORK, NY 10010

EL CASCAJERO, THE OLD SPANISH BOOK MINE, 506 WEST BROADWAY, NEW YORK, NY 10012   Phone 212-254-0905
   shop hours, by mail, book fairs/antique shows, catalogs/lists

ROSEJEANNE SLIFER, 30 PARK AVENUE, NEW YORK, NY 10016   Phone 212-685-2040
   AUTOGRAPHS, ATLASES, MAPS by appointment, by mail, catalogs/lists

THE OLD PRINT SHOP, 150 LEXINGTON AVE., NEW YORK, NY 10016   Phone 212-683-3950

H.P. KRAUS, 16 E. 46TH STREET, NEW YORK, NY 10017   Phone 212-687-4808

MAPS OF THE PROMISED LAND, HOWARD I. GOLDEN, 1450 BROADWAY, 40TH FLOOR, NEW YORK, NY 10018
  Phone 212-221-6050, 212-929-2052 EVES.
  HOLY LAND by appointment, by mail, book fairs/antique shows, catalogs/lists
J.N. BARTFIELD BOOKS INC., 45 WEST 57TH STREET, NEW YORK, NY 10019
NEW YORK BOUND BOOKSHOP, 43 W. 54TH ST., NEW YORK, NY 10019   Phone 212-245-8503
ANTIQUARIAN BOOKSELLERS' CENTER, 50 ROCKEFELLER PLAZA, NEW YORK, NY 10020
K. GREGORY, 222 EAST 71ST STREET, NEW YORK, NY 10021
LINLO HOUSE INC., 1019 LEXINGTON AVENUE, NEW YORK, NY 10021
SOTHEBY PARKE-BERNET, INC., 980 MADISON AVE., NEW YORK, NY 10021
W. GRAHAM ARADER III, 23 EAST 74TH STREET, SUITE 5A, NEW YORK, NY 10021   Phone 212-628-3668
  MAIN OFFICE IN KING OF PRUSSIA, PA
ARGOSY GALLERY, 116 E. 59TH STREET, NEW YORK, NY 10022   Phone 212-753-4455
PHYLLIS LUCAS GALLERY, 981 2ND AVE., NEW YORK, NY 10022
RICHARD B. ARKWAY, 538 MADISON AVENUE, NEW YORK, NY 10022   Phone 212-751-8135
  THIS ADDRESS EFFECTIVE OCTOBER 31, 1983 shop hours, by mail, book fairs/antique shows, catalogs/lists
B. ALTMANS, ANTIQUE MAP DEPT., 361 FIFTH AVE., NEW YORK, NY 10023
LUCIEN GOLDSCHMIDT, 1117 MADISON AVENUE, NEW YORK, NY 10023
THOMAS SUAREZ, RARE MAPS & PRINTS, 2142 BROADWAY, NEW YORK, NY 10023   Phone 212-877-7468
  EARLY WORLD, AMERICA, CURIOSA by appointment, by mail, book fairs/antique shows, catalogs/lists
XIMINES RARE BOOKS, INC., 120 EAST 85TH STREET, NEW YORK, NY 10028
N. & N. PAVLOV, 37 OAKDALE DR., DOBBS FERRY, NY 10522   Phone 914-693-1776
  by appointment, book fairs/antique shows
PARK AVENUE GALLERY, 15 ARMONK ROAD, MT. KISCO, NY 10549
JOYCE AMKRAUT, 35 WINDING WOOD ROAD NORTH, PORT CHESTER, NY 10573   Phone 914-939-1509
  by appointment, by mail, auction
BERNARD SUSSMAN, ANTIQUE MAPS, 19 DOUGLAS CIRCLE, RYE, NY 10580   Phone 914-698-4850
  by appointment, by mail, auction
HIGH RIDGE CORNER, PO BOX 286, RYE, NY 10580   Phone 914-967-3332
WALTER W. SMITH & SON INC., 51 PONDFIELD ROAD, PO BOX 66, BRONXVILLE, NY 10708
BERNARD BOOK COMPANY, BERNARD ZELANKA, PO BOX 272, RICHMOND HILL, NY 11418
CARAVAN-MARITIME BOOKS, 87-06 168TH PLACE, JAMAICA, NY 11432
WILLIAM ROBERTS CO., INC., PO BOX 543, MINEOLA, NY 11501   Phone 516-741-0781
  by appointment
WHITNEY ANTIQUES, B. STENARD, 60 FIRST STREET, GARDEN CITY, NY 11530
JO-ANN & RICHARD CASTEN, LTD., RR2 LITTLE BAY ROAD, WADING RIVER, NY 11792   Phone 516-929-6820
  WORLD, AMERICA, HOLY LAND, ASIA by appointment, by mail, book fairs/antique shows, catalogs/lists
WANTAGH RARE BOOK CO., PO BOX A73, WANTAGH, NY 11793
APOLLO, 391 SOUTH ROAD, POUGHKEEPSIE, NY 12601
MAPS UNLIMITED, MR. EDWIN ELLIS, LIMESTONE PLAZA, FAYETTEVILLE, NY 13066
ROGER BUTTERFIELD, INC., WHITE HOUSE, RTE. 205, HARTWICK, NY 13348
INTERELICO, INC., 4 CLINTON ROAD, BOX 189, NEW HARTFORD, NY 13413
THOMAS D. MAHONEY, 513 VIRGINIA STREET, BUFFALO, NY 14202
THE LAMP, WM. G. MAYER, JR., 204 AUBURN ST., PITTSBURGH, PA 15206   Phone 412-661-6600
  ATLASES & MAPS OF ALL U.S. STATES by appointment, by mail, book fairs/antique shows, auction, catalogs/lists
THE ERIE BOOK STORE, 717 FRENCH STREET, ERIE, PA 16501
GARY PLETCHER ANTIQUE ART, RD #8, BLOOMSBURG, PA 17815   Phone 717-784-7892
  by mail, book fairs/antique shows, auction
AMERICANA MAIL AUCTION, GEORGE M. RINSLAND, 4015 KILMER AVE., ALLENTOWN, PA 18104
GRAEDON BOOK SHOP, RD 1, NEW HOPE, PA 18938
EARL MOORE ASSOCIATES, INC., PO BOX 243, WYNNEWOOD, PA 19096   Phone 215-649-1549
BERNARD CONWELL CARLITZ, 1901 CHESTNUT ST., PHILADELPHIA, PA 19103   Phone 215-563-6608
  shop hours, auction
J.L. SMITH CO., 2104 WALNUT ST., PHILADELPHIA, PA 19103
SAMUEL T. FREEMAN & CO., 1808 CHESTNUT ST., PHILADELPHIA, PA 19103
CHARLES SESSLER, INC., 1308 WALNUT STREET, PHILADELPHIA, PA 19107   Phone 215-735-8811
  shop hours, by mail, catalogs/lists
GEORGE S. MACMANUS CO., 1317 IRVING ST., PHILADELPHIA, PA 19107
RICHARD PARRY, 8862 TOWANDA STREET, PHILADELPHIA, PA 19118   Phone 215-247-3925
  NORTH AMERICA by appointment, by mail
THE PHILADELPHIA PRINT SHOP, 8405 GERMANTOWN AVENUE, PHILADELPHIA, PA 19118   Phone 215-242-4750
  shop hours, by mail, book fairs/antique shows, catalogs/lists
CHAFEY'S BOOKS & PRINTS, 3511 SUNNYSIDE AVE., PHILADELPHIA, PA 19129

SWETS & ZEITLINGER, 19 WATERLOO AVE, BERWYN, PA 19312
W. GRAHAM ARADER III, 1000 BOXWOOD COURT, KING OF PRUSSIA, PA 19406   Phone 215-825-6570
  BRANCHES IN NEW YORK, ATLANTA & HOUSTON shop hours, by mail, book fairs/antique shows, catalogs/lists
GREENWOOD BOOK SHOP, 110 WEST NINTH STREET, WILMINGTON, DE 19801
BUXBAUM GEOGRAPHICS, PO BOX 465, WILMINGTON, DE 19899
BOOKED UP, 1214 31ST ST., NW, WASHINGTON, DC 20007
THE OLD PRINT GALLERY, 1220 31ST ST., N.W., WASHINGTON, DC 20007   Phone 202-965-1818
  shop hours, by mail, book fairs/antique shows, catalogs/lists
WILLIAM F. HALE BOOKS, 1222 31ST STREET N.W., WASHINGTON, DC 20007
THE HOLY LAND, 3041 NORMANSTONE TERRACE NW, WASHINGTON, DC 20008
ANTIQUE MAP MAIL AUCTION, TIM COSS, 5614 NORTHFIELD ROAD, BETHESDA, MD 20034
THE VEERHOFF GALLERIES, 1512 CONNECTICUT AVE, WASHINGTON, DC 20036
ANTIQUE SCIENTIFIC INSTRUMENTS, 4TH & SEVERN AVES., ANNAPOLIS, MD 21403
CAMELOT BOOKS, 7603 MULBERRY BOTTOM LANE, SPRINGFIELD, VA 22153   Phone 703-455-9540
  AMERICA by appointment, by mail, auction, catalogs/lists
JOBIN'S GALLERY, LOUIS L. JOBIN, 2315 SOUTHGATE DRIVE, ALEXANDRIA, VA 22306   Phone 703-430-5955
  by appointment, by mail, book fairs/antique shows
LIROS GALLERY, INC., 626 N. WASHINGTON ST., ALEXANDRIA, VA 22314   Phone 703-549-7881
  shop hours, by mail, catalogs/lists
SAMUEL YUDKIN & ASSOCIATES, 1125 KING STREET, ALEXANDRIA, VA 22314   Phone 703-549-9330
  MONTHLY AUCTION CATALOGS, NONE SOLELY CARTOGRAPHY shop hours, book fairs/antique shows, auction,
  catalogs/lists
PAUL VICTORIUS FRAMING SHOP, INC., 1413 UNIVERSITY AVE., CHARLOTTESVILLE, VA 22903
  Phone 804-296-3456, 804-293-3342
  shop hours
PAUL ROBERTS STONEY, PRINT & MAPSELLER, PO BOX F, WILLIAMSBURG, VA 23187   Phone 804-220-3346
  AMERICA, COLONIAL NORTH AMERICA by mail, book fairs/antique shows, catalogs/lists
THE BOOKPRESS, PO BOX KP, WILLIAMSBURG, VA 23187   Phone 804-229-1260
  LOCATED AT 420 PRINCE GEORGE ST. shop hours, by mail, book fairs/antique shows, catalogs/lists
BROADFOOT'S BOOKMARK, RT. 3, BOX 318, WENDELL, NC 27591   Phone 919-365-6963
  AMERICA IN GENERAL, THE CAROLINAS shop hours by appointment, by mail, book fairs/antique shows,
  catalogs/lists
NORTH CAROLINA BOOKS, DAVID STICK, KITTY HAWK, NC 27949
PAUL WHITFIELD, 503 COURT PLAZA BUILDING, 901 ELIZABETH AVENUE, CHARLOTTE, NC 28204
LITTLE HUNDRED GALLERY, 6028 BENTWAY DRIVE, CHARLOTTE, NC 28226   Phone 704-542-3184
  by mail, catalogs/lists
JEREMY NORTH, PO BOX 6, SHALLOTTE, NC 28459
ROBERT M. HICKLIN JR., INC., 509 EAST ST. JOHN STREET, SPARTANBURG, SC 29302   Phone 803-583-9847
  SOUTHEASTERN NORTH AMERICA shop hours, by mail, catalogs/lists
YESTERYEAR BOOK SHOP, 256 E. PACES FERRY RD., N.E., ATLANTA, GA 30305   Phone 404-237-0163
W. GRAHAM ARADER III, 1317 BERWICK AVE., ATLANTA, GA 30306
  MAIN OFFICE IN KING OF PRUSSIA, PA
HARVEY DAN ABRAMS, BOOKSELLER, PO BOX 13673, ATLANTA, GA 30324   Phone 404-233-6763
ROBERT J. MARTIN, JR., MAPS, PRINTS AND BOOKS, PO BOX 11510, ATLANTA, GA 30355   Phone 404-252-6496, 404-659-6700
  by appointment, by mail, catalogs/lists
THE NORTHERN MAP CO., STAR RT.1, BOX 15-2, DUNNELLON, FLORIDA 32630
MICKLER'S FLORIDIANA, PO BOX 38, CHULOTA, FL 32766   Phone 305-365-3636
  FLORIDA MATERIAL ONLY by appointment, by mail, book fairs/antique shows, catalogs/lists
ANTIQUE MAPS & PRINTS, 3583 COSMOS STREET, PALM BEACH, FL 33410
CAPT. KIT S. KAPP, ANTIQUARIAN MAPS, PO BOX 64, OSPREY, FL 33559   Phone 813-966-4181
  MAPS & PRINTS OF THE AMERICAS by appointment, by mail, book fairs/antique shows, catalogs/lists
WM. H. PETTIBON, 1911 OAK STREET, SARASOTA, FL 33577
DONALD & NANCY ORLANDO, 3135 MALONE DRIVE, MONTGOMERY, ALABAMA 36106
CHILTON'S INC., 940 CONTI STREET, MOBILE, AL 36604
TENNESSEE BOOKS & MAPS, ANN H. WELLS, PO BOX 50084, NASHVILLE, TN 37205
JOHN SHARP, ANTIQUARIAN GALLERY, 4004 HILLSBORO ROAD, NASHVILLE, TN 37215
MURRAY HUDSON, BOOKS & MAPS, RT. 1, BOX 362, DYERSBURG, TN 38024   Phone 901-285-0666
  BOOKS WITH MAPS, ATLASES, GEOGRAPHIES, S.E. & S.W. UNITED STATES by appointment, by mail, book fairs/antique shows,
  catalogs/lists
WILLIAM & PATRICIA HUTTER, ANTIQUARIAN BOOKS, RT. 3, BOX 123, OCEAN SPRINGS, MS 39564
W.C. GATES, 1279 BARDSTOWN ROAD, LOUISVILLE, KY 40204
ALZOFON BOOKS, 2662 GLENMAWR AVENUE, COLUMBUS, OHIO 43202

ROUSE'S BOOKHOUSE, RTE. 2, EATON RAPIDS, MI 48827
BONNS BOOKCENTER, 2009 1/2 SOUTH DIVISION AVE, GRAND RAPIDS, MI 49507
MCBLAIN BOOKS, BOX 971, DES MOINES, IOWA 50304
BOOK & RECORD LAND, 708 W. WISCONSIN AVE, MILWAUKEE, WI 53233
SADLON'S LTD., FINE PRINT GALLERY, 109 NORTH BROADWAY, DE PERE, WI 54115   Phone 414-336-6665
  shop hours, by mail, book fairs/antique shows, catalogs/lists
THE PRINT MINT GALLERY, BETTY D. SOBEL, 1147 GREENLEAF AVE., WILMETTE, IL 60091
GRATON AND GRATON, 1401 DAVIS STREET, EVANSTON, IL 60201
KENNETH NEBENZAHL, INC., 333 N. MICHIGAN AVE., CHICAGO, IL 60601   Phone 312-641-2711
  AMERICA, WORLD, GREAT LAKES, EARLY MAPS & PORTOLANS shop hours, by mail, book fairs/antique shows, catalogs/lists
RAND MCNALLY MAPSTORE, 23 EAST MADISON STREET, CHICAGO, IL 60602
HANZEL GALLERIES, 1120 S. MICHIGAN, CHICAGO, IL 60605
NEWBERRY LIBRARY BOOKSTORE, 60 WEST WALTON STREET, CHICAGO, IL 60610
HARRY L. STERN LTD., 620 N. MICHIGAN AVE., CHICAGO, IL 60611   Phone 312-787-4433
MARY BETH BEAL, 3919 NORTH CLAREMONT AVE., CHICAGO, IL 60618
MARSHALL FIELD CO., ANTIQUARIAN BOOK DEPT., 111 N. STATE ST., CHICAGO, IL 60690   Phone 312-781-3339
THE GLOBE, PO BOX A3398, CHICAGO, IL 60690   Phone 312-528-6228
  by appointment, by mail, book fairs/antique shows, catalogs/lists
ELIZABETH F. DUNLAP, BOOKS & MAPS, 6063 WESTMINSTER PL., ST. LOUIS, MO 63112   Phone 314-863-5068
  by appointment, by mail, catalogs/lists
BAYOU BOOKS, 1005 MONROE ST., GRETNA, LA 70053
LIBRAIRIE BOOK SHOP, 829 ROYAL ST., NEW ORLEANS, LA 70116
BARRISTER'S GALLERY AT NEARING'S ANTIQUES, 526 ROYAL, NEW ORLEANS, LA 70130   Phone 504-525-2767
  19TH CENTURY, SEARCH SERVICE FOR FINER ITEMS shop hours, by mail
TAYLOR CLARK'S INC., 2623 GOVERNMENT STREET, BATON ROUGE, LA 70806
ARK-LA-TEX BOOK COMPANY, L.S. HOOPER, PO BOX 564, SHREVEPORT, LA 71102
DAVID GROSSBLATT, BOOKSELLER, PO BOX 30001, DALLAS, TX 75230   Phone 214-373-0218, 214-271-6769
  by appointment, by mail, book fairs/antique shows, catalogs/lists
OLD MAPS & PRINTS, PRESTON FIGLEY, PO BOX 2234, FORT WORTH, TX 76113   Phone 817-923-4535
  AMERICA by appointment, by mail, catalogs/lists
ANTIQUE BROKERS, 1716 WESTHEIMER, HOUSTON, TX 77098
McCLENDON'S TRASH & TREASURE, 1714-16 WESTHEIMER RD., HOUSTON, TX 77098   Phone 713-522-7415
  shop hours
W. GRAHAM ARADER III, 2800 VIRGINIA STREET, HOUSTON, TX 77098   Phone 713-527-8055
  MAIN OFFICE IN KING OF PRUSSIA, PA
THE JENKINS COMPANY, PO BOX 2085, AUSTIN, TX 78768
THE ANTIQUARIAN SHOP, 4246 N. SCOTTSDALE ROAD, SCOTTSDALE, AZ 85251
TOMBSTONE AND WESTERN AMERICANA, TOMBSTONE, AZ 85638
RICHARD FITCH, OLD MAPS, PRINTS & BOOKS, 2324 CALLE HALCON, SANTE FE, NM 87501   Phone 505-982-2939
  NORTH AMERICA by appointment, by mail, book fairs/antique shows, catalogs/lists
GEORGE ROBINSON OLD PRINTS & MAPS, PO BOX 1239, TAOS, NM 87571   Phone 505-758-2278
  shop hours, by mail, catalogs/lists
MUSGRAVE'S ANTIQUE PRINTS & MAPS, MRS. HELEN MUSGRAVE, PO BOX 2224, CARSON CITY, NV 89702   Phone 702-882-2853
  by appointment, by mail, book fairs/antique shows
DAWSON'S BOOK SHOP, 535 N. LARCHMONT BLVD., LOS ANGELES, CA 90004
MANUEL URRIZOLA, 136 S. VIRGIL AVENUE, NO. 139, LOS ANGELES, CALIFORNIA 90004
WALTER NEUMAN, F.R.G.S., 10,500 WYTON DRIVE, WESTWOOD, CA 90024
BENNET & MARSHALL, 8214 MELROSE AVE., LOS ANGELES, CA 90028
KURT L. SCHWARZ, 738 S. BRISTOL AVE., LOS ANGELES, CA 90049
LEO MARTYN, PO BOX 49263, LOS ANGELES, CA 90049
THE HERITAGE BOOK SHOP, INC., 847 N. LA CIENEGA BLVD., LOS ANGELES, CA 90069
ZEITLIN & VER BRUGGE, BOOKSELLERS, 815 N. LA CIENEGA BLVD., LOS ANGELES, CA 90069
HARRY A. LEVINSON, RARE BOOKS, PO BOX 534, BEVERLY HILLS, CA 90213   Phone 213-276-9311
  by appointment, by mail, book fairs/antique shows, catalogs/lists
THE SCRIPTORIUM, 427 NORTH CANON DRIVE, BEVERLY HILLS, CA 90213
DAPHNE FROST, ANTIQUE MAPS, BOOKS & PRINTS, PO BOX 671, REDONDO BEACH, CA 90277   Phone 213-316-6990
  by appointment, book fairs/antique shows
F & I BOOKS, PO BOX 1900, SANTA MONICA, CA 90406
THE ARTHUR H. CLARKE CO., 1264 SOUTH WEST CENTRAL AVE., GLENDALE, CA 91204
MELVYN MASON, HISTORICAL MAPS, 4728 ROSITA PLACE, TARZANA, CA 91356
ROBERT ROSS & CO., OLD HISTORICAL MAPS, PRINTS & RELATED BOOKS, 6101 EL ESCORPION ROAD, WOODLAND HILLS, CA 91367
  Phone 818-346-6152
MAP CENTRE, 2611 UNIVERSITY AVE., SAN DIEGO, CA 92104

PENINSULA ANTIQUARIAN BOOKSELLERS, D. BEEK, 620 WEST OCEAN FRONT, BALBOA, CA 92661
MILTON HAMMER, BOOKS, SUITE 215 EL PASEO, SANTA BARBARA, CA 93101   Phone 805-965-8901
DREW'S BOOKSHOP, PO BOX 163, SANTA BARBARA, CA 93102   Phone 805-966-3311
  shop hours, by mail, catalogs/lists
VOLKOFF & VON HOHENLOHE, 1514 LA CORONILLA DR., SANTA BARBARA, CA 93109
CALIFORNIA BOOK AUCTION GALLERIES, 358 GOLDEN GATE AVE., SAN FRANCISCO, CA 94102   Phone 415-775-0424
  shop hours, auction, catalogs/lists
JEFFERY THOMAS, FINE & RARE BOOKS, 49 GEARY STREET, SUITE 215, SAN FRANCISCO, CA 94102   Phone 415-956-3272
  MAPS ONLY SOLD "PERIPHERALLY" shop hours, by mail, book fairs/antique shows, catalogs/lists
JEREMY NORMAN & CO. INC., 442 POST STREET, SAN FRANCISCO, CA 94102
JOHN HOWELL, BOOKS, 434 POST ST., SAN FRANCISCO, CA 94102   Phone 415-781-7795
  shop hours, by mail, book fairs/antique shows, catalogs/lists
SERGIO OLD PRINTS, 50 MAIDEN LANE, SAN FRANCISCO, CA 94108   Phone 415-434-3312
ARGONAUT BOOK SHOP, 792 SUTTER ST., SAN FRANCISCO, CA 94109   Phone 415-474-9067
KATHLEEN MANNING, 1255 POST STREET, SUITE 625, SAN FRANCISCO, CA 94109   Phone 415-621-3565
  by appointment
ARKADYAN BOOKS AND PRINTS, 926 IRVING, SAN FRANCISCO, CA 94122   Phone 415-664-6212
  CALIFORNIA AS AN ISLAND shop hours, by mail, book fairs/antique shows, catalogs/lists
WILLIAM P. WREDEN, 200 HAMILTON AVE., PALO ALTO, CA 94301
NEW ALBION ISLAND CLASSICS, SALLY A. LEWIS, PO BOX 390, DIABLO, CA 94528
THE HOLMES BOOK CO., 274 14TH ST., OAKLAND, CA 94612
NORMAN GREENE DESIGNS, PO BOX 8451, EMERYVILLE, CA 94662   Phone 415-652-7464
  ANTIQUE INSTRUMENTS, QUADRANTS, SUNDIALS, ARMILLARY SPHERES, ASTROLABES by appointment, by mail,
  book fairs/antique shows, catalogs/lists
JOHN P. COLL, 2944 PINE AVENUE, BERKELEY, CA 94705
ROY V. BOSWELL, PO BOX 278, GILROY, CA 95020
THE PRINTSELLER, 22A MT. HERMAN ROAD, SCOTTS VALLEY, CA 95066
RICHARD HANSEN, 11245 DRY CREEK ROAD, AUBURN, CA 95603   Phone 916-885-4878
  TRANS-MISSISSIPPI WEST by appointment, by mail, book fairs/antique shows, catalogs/lists
WENDELL P. HAMMON, 1115 FRONT, SACRAMENTO, CA 95814
LAHAINA PRINTSELLERS LTD., 991 LIMAHANA PLACE, LAHAINA, MAUI, HI 96761
ROBERT ELLIS RUDOLPH CORP., 1119 S.W. PARK AVE., PORTLAND, OR 97205
THE CLIPPER, PO BOX 803, BELLEVUE, WA 98009   Phone 206-453-8109
  GENERAL, UNITED STATES 1820-1880, LOCATED AT 525 121 PL. NE #6 by mail, book fairs/antique shows,
  auction, catalogs/lists
THE SHOREY BOOKSTORE, 110 UNION ST., SEATTLE, WA 98101
CAROLYN STALEY, FINE PRINTS, 313 FIRST AVE. S., SEATTLE, WA 98104   Phone 206-621-1888
  shop hours, by mail, book fairs/antique shows, catalogs/lists
FLEETSTREET RARE MAPS, BOOKS & ENGRAVINGS, PO BOX 4203, SEATTLE, WA 98104
BOB FINCH BOOKS, PO BOX 11254, BAINBRIDGE ISLAND, WA 98110   Phone 206-842-0202
  VOYAGES & MARITIME BOOKS, SELDOM INDIVIDUAL MAPS
COMSTOCK'S BINDERY & BOOKSHOP, DAVID G. COMSTOCK, 7903 RAINER AVENUE SOUTH, SEATTLE, WA 98118
GEORGE H. TWENEY, ANTIQUARIAN BOOKSELLER, 16660 MARINE VIEW DRIVE S.W., SEATTLE, WA 98166   Phone 206-243-8243
  by appointment, by mail, book fairs/antique shows, catalogs/lists
DONALD M. BARTON, 2336 MAGNOLIA BVLD WEST, SEATTLE, WA 98199   Phone 206-285-4500
  GENERAL, NORTH PACIFIC & NORTHWEST AMERICA by appointment, by mail, auction, catalogs/lists
DARVILLS RARE PRINT SHOP, PO BOX 47, EASTSOUND, WA 98245
METSKER MAPS, 111 S. 10TH ST., TACOMA, WA 98402
L.O. GANNON & SON, PO BOX 335, MABTON, WA 98935
ALASKANA BOOK SHOP, 4617 ARCTIC BLVD., ANCHORAGE, AK 99503   Phone 907-561-1340
  ALASKA, MOUNTAIN CLIMBING, HUNTING, U.S.G.S. shop hours, by mail
WILDWOOD BOOKS & PRINTS, 1972 WILDWOOD LANE, ANCHORAGE, AK 99503

CANADA

CANADIANA HOUSE, LTD., 509 2ND ST. SW, CALGARY ALBERTA T2P 1N8, CANADA   Phone 403-266-3714
  CANADIAN MAPS, PRE-CONFEDERATION shop hours, by mail
NORTH BY WEST, BOX 11538, EDMONTON MAIN P.O. ALBERTA T5J 3K7, CANADA   Phone 403-429-2226
  N. AMERICA, CANADA, ARCTIC, BOOKS ON EXPLORATION, TRAVEL, GEOGRAPHY by appointment, by mail, book fairs/antique shows,
  catalogs/lists
VANHALL ANTIQUES LTD., 1023 FORT STREET, VICTORIA BRITISH COLUMBIA, CANADA
THE ASTROLABE, JOHN W. COLES, THE ROYAL BANK BLDG., 90 SPARKS ST., OTTAWA ONTARIO K1P 5B4   Phone 613-234-2348
  shop hours, book fairs/antique shows, catalogs/lists
LEE PRITZKER, BOX 293, OAKVILLE ONTARIO L6J 5A2, CANADA
THE MAPPERY, PO BOX 113, ANCASTER ONTARIO L9G 3L3, CANADA
RUSSBOROUGH, PO BOX 422, STATION R, TORONTO, ONTARIO M4G 4C3 ONTARIO M4G 4C3, CANADA   Phone 416-425-2457
  EMPHASIS ON N. AMERICA, CANADA, ARCTIC, BRITISH ISLES by appointment, by mail, book fairs/antique shows,
  catalogs/lists
THE MAP ROOM, 18 BIRCH AVENUE, TORONTO ONTARIO M4V 1C8, CANADA
D. & E. LAKE LTD., 106 BERKELEY STREET, TORONTO ONTARIO M5A 2W7, CANADA   Phone 416-863-9930
  shop hours, by mail, book fairs/antique shows, catalogs/lists
CANADA BOOK AUCTIONS, REARDMORE BUILDING, 35 FRONT STREET EAST, TORONTO ONTARIO M5E 1B3, CANADA
HUGH ANSON-CARTWRIGHT BOOKS, 229 COLLEGE STREET, TORONTO ONTARIO M5T 1R4, CANADA
SPECIALTY BOOK CONCERN, PO BOX 293, OAKVILLE ONTARIO, CANADA
HELEN R. KAHN, ANTIQUARIAN BOOKS, PO BOX 323, VICTORIA STATION, MONTREAL QUEBEC H3Z 2V8   Phone 514-844-5344
  by appointment, by mail, book fairs/antique shows, auction, catalogs/lists
WILLIAM P. WOLFE INC., PO BOX 1190, POINTE CLAIRE QUEBEC H9S 5K7, CANADA
HUDSON ANTIQUES, BOX 438, HUDSON HEIGHTS QUEBEC, CANADA
OSIRIS, A.R. VAN PETEGHAM, 2065 CRESCENT, SUITE 3, MONTREAL H3G 2C1 QUEBEC, CANADA

INTERNATIONAL

ANTIQUARIAN MAPS & PRINTS PTY LTD, 247 VICTORIA STREET, DARLINGHURST, SYDNEY, NSW 10 AUSTRALIA   Phone 331 2745
SPENCER SCOTT SANDILANDS, 546 HIGH STREET;, EAST PRAHRAN 3181, VICTORIA AUSTRALIA   Phone (03) 51 5709
ROSENKILDE OG BAGGER A/S, KRON-PRINSENS-GADE 3-5, POSTBOKS 2184, DK 1017 COPENHAGEN K DENMARK   Phone 01-15 70 44
LEYCESTER MAP GALLERIES LIMITED, WELL HOUSE, ARNESBY, LEICESTER LE8 3WJ ENGLAND   Phone 053 758 462
WATERLOO FINE ARTS LTD, THE PENTHOUSE, CALCOT GRANGE, MILL LANE, CALCOT, READING ENGLAND   Phone 0734-411706
CHARLES WOOD, 9 RUTHERFORD ROAD, CAMBRIDGE ENGLAND   Phone 0223 840346
J. ALAN HULME, 54 LOWER BRIDGE ST., CHESTER ENGLAND   Phone 0244-44006
W.J. FAUPEL, 3 HALSFORD LANE, EAST GRINSTEAD, SUSSEX RH19 1NY ENGLAND
HENRY STEVENS, SON & STILES, 4 UPPER CHURCH LANE, FARNHAM, SURREY GU9 7PW ENGLAND   Phone (0252) 715416
JULIA HOLMES, ANTIQUE MAPS & PRINTS, MUIRFIELD PLACE, BUNCH LANE, HASLEMERE, SURREY GU27 1AE ENGLAND   Phone 2153
THE LYVER GALLERY, PAUL BREEN (FINE ART) LTD., 8 HACKINS HEY, LIVERPOOL, MERSEYSIDE L2 2AW ENGLAND   Phone 051-236 7524
EDNA WHITESON LTD, 343 BOWES ROAD, LONDON N11 ENGLAND   Phone 01-361 1105
SARUM, ERICSSON & CHRISTOPH, 10 CHAPEL STREET, BELGRAVE SQUARE, LONDON SW1 ENGLAND   Phone 01-235 6744
NICOLA THOMSON, PO BOX 122, LONDON SW16 1QX ENGLAND   Phone 01-677-1028
THOMAS E. SCHUSTER, 9 GILLINGHAM STREET, LONDON SW1V 1HN ENGLAND   Phone 01-828 7963
STEPHANIE HOPPEN LIMITED, 17 WALTON STREET, LONDON SW3 ENGLAND   Phone (01) 589 3678
THE MAPHOUSE OF LONDON, 54, BEAUCHAMP PLACE, KNIGHTSBRIDGE, LONDON SW3 1NY ENGLAND   Phone 01-589 4325
EIDDON MORGAN, 177 GRAYS ANTIQUE MARKET, 58 DAVIES STREET, LONDON W.1 ENGLAND   Phone 01-493-1578
AVRIL NOBLE, 177/8 AT GRAYS, 58 DAVIES STREET, MAYFAIR, LONDON W1 ENGLAND   Phone 01-493-1578
H.G. GIROU, 92 STERNDALE ROAD, LONDON W14 ENGLAND   Phone 01-602-4169
TOOLEY ADAMS & CO. LTD., 83 MARYLEBONE HIGH STREET, LONDON W1M 4AL ENGLAND   Phone 01-486 9052
JONATHAN POTTER LTD., NO. 1, GRAFTON STREET, LONDON W1X 3LB ENGLAND   Phone 01-491 3520
CHAS. J. SAWYER, BOOKSELLER, NO. 1, GRAFTON STREET, LONDON W1X 3LB ENGLAND   Phone 01-493-3810
ROBERT DOUWMA, 93 GREAT RUSSELL STREET, LONDON WC1B 3QL ENGLAND   Phone 01-636 4895
CARTOGRAPHIA LTD., COVENT GARDEN, 37 SOUTHAMPTON STREET, LONDON WC2E 7HE ENGLAND   Phone 01-240 5687
J.A.L. FRANKS, LTD., 7 NEW OXFORD STREET, LONSON WX1A 1BA ENGLAND   Phone 01-405-0274
L. WALTON, 41 WOODLAND ROAD, LEVENSHULME, MANCHESTER M19 2GW ENGLAND   Phone 061-224-6630
MAGNA GALLERY, 41, HIGH STREET, OXFORD ENGLAND   Phone (0865) 45805
CLIVE A. BURDEN LTD., 36 HIGH STREET, RICKMANSWORTH, HERTS. WD3 1ER ENGLAND   Phone 78097
NORTHWOOD MAPS LTD., 71 NIGHTINGALE ROAD, RICKMANSWORTH, HERTS. WD3 2BU ENGLAND   Phone 772258
BEACHES OF SALISBURY, 52 HIGH STREET, SALISBURY, WILTS. SP1 2PG ENGLAND   Phone 0722 3801
P.J. RADFORD, SHEFFIELD PARK NR. UCKFIELD, SUSSEX ENGLAND   Phone (0825) 790531
SUSANNA FISHER, SPENCER, UPHAM, SOUTHHAMPTON SO3 1JD ENGLAND   Phone (048 96) 291

IVAN R. DEVERALL, DUVAL HOUSE, THE GLEN, CAMBRIDGE WAY, UCKFIELD, SUSSEX TN22 2AA ENGLAND   Phone (0825) 2474
PAUL EISLER, 54 BRYANTS ACRE, WENDOVER, BUCKINGHAMSHIRE ENGLAND   Phone 0296 623709
COLLECTORS TREASURES LIMITED, HOGARTH HOUSE, HIGH STREET, WENDOVER, BUCKS HP22 6DU ENGLAND   Phone 624402
ANTIQUARIAT STENDERHOFF, ALTER FISCHMARKT 21, 4400 MUNSTER GERMANY   Phone (0251) 44749
A. SAPUNARU, OTTOSTR. 6, 8000 MUNCHEN 2 GERMANY   Phone 089/8112250
MONIKA SCHMIDT, TURKENSTRASSE 48, D-8000 MUNCHEN 40 GERMANY   Phone 089/284223
REISS & AUVERMANN, BUCH- UND KUNSTANTIQUARIAT, ZUM TALBLICK 2, 6246 GLASHUTTEN IM TAUNUS GERMANY
    Phone (0 61 74) 69 47
H. TH. WENNER GMBH & CO., HEGER STR. 2-3, POSTFACH 4307, D-4500 OSNABRUCK GERMANY   Phone 0541-25516
C. BROEKEMA, LEIDSEKADE 68, 1016 DA, AMSTERDAM HOLLAND   Phone (020) 22 21 26
SPECULUM ORBIS TERRARUM, PO BOX 380, 1000 AJ, AMSTERDAM HOLLAND   Phone (020) 26 78 74
NICO ISRAEL, 526 KEIZERSGRACHT, 1017EK, AMSTERDAM HOLLAND   Phone 020-22 22 55
GARISENDA LIBRI E STAMPE, STRADA MAGGIORE, 14A, 40125 BOLOGNA ITALY   Phone 23-18-93
NEIL McKINNON LIMITED, PO BOX 847, TIMARU NEW ZEALAND   Phone 81-931
DAMMS ANTIKVARIAT A/S, BOKHUSET, ECKERSBERGSGATEN 14, OSLO 2 NORWAY   Phone 56 45 33
LOUIS LOEB-LAROCQUE, 36, RUE LE PELETIER, 75009 PARIS   Phone 878.11.18
FINDEN S.A., VIA VOLTA 1, CHIASSO 6830 SWITZERLAND   Phone 091 445687

SUGGESTIONS FOR DEALERS PREPARING CATALOGS

Most dealer catalogs are prepared in an accurate, professional manner and are informative and interesting to read. However, in the course of summarizing thousands of listings from numerous catalogs, I have noticed a few features of listings that can occasionally be bothersome. A few of the more vexing are discussed here.

Most problems occur with the title of the map. For purposes of the alphabetical title index in this price guide, it is necessary that the title include the first words as well as the main portion of the title. To give an example, suppose the correct title is:

A NEW & ACCURATE CHART OF THE WORLD. DRAWN FROM AUTHENTIC SURVEYS, ASSISTED BY THE MOST APPROVED MODERN MAPS & CHARTS & REGULATED BY ASTRONL. OBSERVATIONS

The full title is to be preferred in a catalog listing, although sometimes the title is excessively long. Shortening is certainly permissible if done properly. A just barely acceptable abbreviation of the above title would be:

A NEW & ACCURATE CHART OF THE WORLD . . .

Some confusing abbreviations would be:

(a) **A NEW AND ACCURATE CHART OF THE WORLD . . .**

(b) **A NEW & ACCURATE CHART OF THE WORLD ETC.**

(c) **CHART OF THE WORLD**

(d) **. . . CHART OF THE WORLD . . .**

(e) **THE WORLD**

In (a) "&" has unnecessarily been replaced by "AND" and the title will not alphabetize properly. In (b) "ETC." has been used in place of ellipses, and it is not clear if "ETC." is part of the original title. In (c) and (d) the initial words have been omitted, and proper alphabetization is impossible. In addition, ellipses were omitted in (c). The paraphrase in (e) is virtually worthless for identification. If important data appear, such as cartographer or date, they should be included.

Sometimes dealers insert punctuation for clarity. For example, commas may be inserted to set off items in a long list of place names. They may be inserted to indicate the start of a new line in the title. Occasionally a terminal period is added. Additional information on the map is often strung after the title with no indication that it is not part of the title. For example, "E. Bowen Sc." appearing below the bottom neat line may be added to the end of the title. Such additions were almost impossible to detect and remove when compiling this guide. My recommendation is that the real title, if present, should be used. It should be clearly set off from other information by the use of quotes, boldface type, italics, or some other means. When the map is untitled, a descriptive title can be supplied, but it should be clearly indicated that this has been done.

The dates given for a map may be confusing. To take an example, suppose we are dealing with a map that first appeared in the 1570 edition of Ortelius, last appeared in 1612, and was actually taken from the 1587 edition. One dealer may date the item "1570," perhaps because the actual date cannot be ascertained. Another dealer may give "1570–1612," or "1570–87," while another may give "1587." Still another may give "1570-[1587]-1612." A more uniform notation should be adopted to convey more precisely what is meant. Perhaps "circa" should be used more liberally when information is uncertain.

A few minor problems occur with the dimensions. Most dealers measure the printed area. This is quite proper, since the paper size may vary. The majority of dealers and reference works put height first and width second, as in "24 by 32 cm." It would be sensible if this convention were universally adopted. Inches, centimeters, or millimeters are all quite acceptable as units. However, it would be helpful if metric measurements were done to a precision of one millimeter, and English measurements to the nearest one-eighth inch. This seems to be a modest request and would help in comparing map sizes with dimensions in this guide.

In describing condition, margin and border are sometimes used interchangeably. Margin should refer to the blank area outside the map, and border to the printed region enclosing the map. "Mounted" is also ambiguous. It usually implies pasting down, as in "mounted on linen," but sometimes implies that the map is matted. A better choice might be "backed."

The above are only a few random observations and do not constitute a requirement for listing in this guide. Comments are welcome.

Lloyd Brown's *Notes on the Care & Cataloguing of Old Maps* is a good source of information for catalog preparers.

STATISTICAL INFORMATION

The statistical information on the following pages is compiled from the data in this guide. Readers are warned that in some cases small numbers are involved, and the statistics can therefore be unreliable. Nevertheless, users are invited to peruse the data and ponder its significance, if any.

The information on prices for selected major mapmakers on this page provides information which may be useful in tracking price levels. Similar data will be compiled in future guides. For those untutored in statistics, the median price is the middle price if the prices are ranked in order. Thus the median of 11, 23, 25, 30, and 32 would be 25. For even numbers, the middle two values are averaged. The median may be more reliable than the average, which can be influenced by extreme values. Users should note that maps of each mapmaker have a wide price range. The average prices thus should not be used as a pricing aid. In compiling the statistics on this page, maps smaller than 20 cm. in either dimension were not counted. This eliminates the miniature Ortelius maps, most of the small Bellin and Moll maps, as well as map fragments and miscellaneous smaller maps.

AVERAGE PRICES
FOR MAJOR MAPMAKERS

MAPMAKER	NUMBER	MINIMUM PRICE $	MAXIMUM PRICE $	MEDIAN PRICE $	AVERAGE PRICE $
16th century					
Braun & Hogenberg	61	70	1600	210	265
De Jode	13	280	6500	2350	2770
Munster	16	214	2000	675	849
Ortelius	99	99	3200	439	781
17th century					
Blaeu	104	88	4800	351	601
Coronelli	37	15	3500	367	797
Ogilby	21	55	600	114	161
Sanson	23	70	2900	225	464
Speed	129	229	3750	550	760
Visscher	38	35	1600	289	460
18th century					
Bellin	65	35	1400	130	259
De l'Isle	14	105	2200	317	588
Homann	31	88	1050	425	478
Moll	21	42	1450	175	327
Mount & Page	16	88	1450	252	401
Seutter	15	275	1500	950	947
19th century					
Arrowsmith	32	35	1500	97	166
Fullarton	26	25	175	62	71
Mitchell	89	15	350	50	65
S.D.U.K.	25	24	195	53	73
Tallis	155	12	150	48	52
Thomson	28	7	325	125	135

PRICE CHANGES SINCE LAST YEAR

An attempt has been made to estimate the change in map prices from the previous year. This is a risky undertaking because of the limited amount of data. Everything said here should be taken with a grain of salt.

For both years, information was compiled on the average and median prices of some major mapmakers. From this data, it is possible to derive a statistical index reflecting price changes, just as security or commodity prices are reduced to a statistical index. To start with, the 1983 prices for each mapmaker are normalized to unity, and prices in succeeding years are expressed as a ratio relative to 1983. Thus if mapmaker Smith had an average price in 1983 of $200, and in 1984 of $250, the 1983 price would be reduced to 1.00, and the 1984 price would become 1.25. One could take these values for individual mapmakers as an index. However, at least for the first few years, the prices for individual mapmakers are too scattered to yield useful data.

To get around this problem, the average prices for the various mapmakers have been combined, much like a stock market index. The main question is what weighting function should be used to compute the index. One could use equal weighting, but then the few de Jode maps would have as much effect as the many Ortelius maps. If one went by number of maps, Tallis maps might have an inordinately large effect. It was decided to use total value as the weighting function. Thus, for equal numbers of maps, the inexpensive 19th century mapmaker would influence the average less than a more expensive 16th century mapmaker. In computing the weighting coefficients, data from 1983 and 1984 were combined. These same coefficients will be used in succeeding years. The table below shows the results of this procedure:

Category	1983	1984
16th century	1.00	1.04
17th century	1.00	1.20
18th century	1.00	1.40
19th century	1.00	1.21
Combined	1.00	1.18

Separate sets of weighting coefficients were derived for each of the five categories above, and the combined index is not necessarily the average of the four others. The procedure is not very sensitive to the weighting procedure. Weighting equally gives a combined 1984 index of 1.18, weighting by the number of maps gives 1.19, weighting by the square root of the number of maps gives 1.19, compared with the value-weighted 1.18 above. An index based on median values instead of the mean was tried, but it seemed more sensitive to the weighting scheme and less reliable. Future years will employ the same weighting coefficients used here.

Not too much significance should be given to these numbers yet, although the overall 18% price increase seems reasonable. The population is highly heterogeneous, as mathematicians say. However, the little-known and difficult-to-prove fundamental theorem of map-price averaging states that any mean of this type taken over a finite population will approach arbitrarily close to the mean taken over the entire population as the number of items averaged increases. In practical terms, what this boils down to is that perhaps five years will be needed before anything definite can be said about price trends. It is even possible that the index will go up one year and down the next. The trend over several years is what matters. Nevertheless, the raw data and the price indices are given for whatever edification and diversion they may provide.

HOW AGE AFFECTS PRICE

The table below shows how price varies as a function of the age of the map. This data should not be used for pricing since there is a wide range of prices for each decade.

DECADE	NUMBER	MINIMUM PRICE $	MAXIMUM PRICE $	AVERAGE PRICE $
1470–79	0	—	—	—
1480–89	4	2000	6800	4325
1490–99	3	246	3800	2344
1500–09	0	—	—	—
1510–19	20	175	4450	1099
1520–29	8	1275	3200	1853
1530–39	4	307	1450	1048
1540–49	46	90	10000	702
1550–59	24	38	2100	825
1560–69	34	37	2000	400
1570–79	136	23	3000	336
1580–89	62	70	3200	838
1590–99	105	23	6500	805
1600–09	109	35	2500	352
1610–19	63	35	1800	398
1620–29	127	31	3700	260
1630–39	141	50	4800	611
1640–49	104	35	3200	384
1650–59	50	31	2900	587
1660–69	67	80	4200	638
1670–79	192	40	4390	584
1680–89	142	15	3500	331
1690–99	222	15	3500	329
1700–09	227	45	3700	370
1710–19	84	41	3900	418
1720–29	134	12	2500	241
1730–39	69	25	5200	456
1740–49	144	20	3833	266
1750–59	192	4	1400	230
1760–69	168	15	900	134
1770–79	200	23	5750	422
1780–89	212	12	5200	223
1790–99	163	28	950	158
1800–09	93	15	1500	133
1810–19	161	20	1200	133
1820–29	244	6	1500	104
1830–39	243	7	3000	92
1840–49	208	14	2250	103
1850–59	443	12	3850	70
1860–69	190	8	1500	75
1870–79	118	7	850	74
1880–89	85	4	385	49
1890–99	54	4	1250	79

THE 100 MOST
FREQUENT MAPMAKERS

CUMULATIVE NUMBER OF ENTRIES IS 10432
TOTAL NUMBER OF DIFFERENT CARTOGRAPHERS IS 822

NAME	NUMBER	PERCENT	NAME	NUMBER	PERCENT
ORTELIUS	334	3.20	JOHNSON & WARD	54	.52
BELLIN	325	3.12	SCHENK	54	.52
JANSSON	287	2.75	QUAD	54	.52
BLAEU	275	2.64	PTOLEMY (1561-99 VENICE)	52	.50
SPEED	272	2.61	JAILLOT	50	.48
MERIAN	268	2.57	SEUTTER	50	.48
HOMANN	247	2.37	BERTIUS	47	.45
TALLIS	202	1.94	VAN DEN KEERE	47	.45
BOWEN	166	1.59	DE L'ISLE	45	.43
MOLL	166	1.59	MOUNT & PAGE	44	.42
MITCHELL	156	1.50	CAREY & LEA	39	.37
MERCATOR	145	1.39	LAURIE & WHITTLE	39	.37
BRAUN & HOGENBERG	138	1.32	LE ROUGE	37	.35
ANONYMOUS	136	1.30	DE FER	37	.35
HONDIUS	123	1.18	ROBINSON	37	.35
DE VAUGONDY	121	1.16	JOHNSON	37	.35
MORTIER	121	1.16	TANNER	36	.35
MUNSTER	111	1.06	GAZZETTIERE AMERICANO	36	.35
U.S.	106	1.02	POLITICAL MAGAZINE	36	.35
VISSCHER	99	.95	VON REILLY	35	.34
SANSON	95	.91	DES BARRES	35	.34
BONNE	92	.88	TIRION	34	.33
BRADFORD	90	.86	ALBRIZZI	34	.33
THOMSON	86	.82	BLACK	33	.32
JEFFERYS	85	.81	SANTINI	33	.32
ARROWSMITH	81	.78	WYLD	33	.32
FULLARTON	81	.78	LONDON MAGAZINE	31	.30
COLTON	78	.75	CRAM	31	.30
KITCHIN	76	.73	COVENS & MORTIER	31	.30
CARY	72	.69	LOTTER	30	.29
SDUK	70	.67	VAN DER AA	30	.29
CORONELLI	68	.65	SCHERER	29	.28
CAREY	67	.64	BOWLES	29	.28
PTOLEMY (1596-1621 MAGINI)	67	.64	MEISNER	29	.28
DE BRY	66	.63	DRAYTON	29	.28
SELLER	64	.61	DESILVER	29	.28
FADEN	63	.60	PTOLEMY (1548 VENICE)	29	.28
ZATTA	62	.59	WAGHENAER	28	.27
MORSE	61	.58	CAMOCIO	28	.27
THOMAS, COWPERTHWAIT & CO.	61	.58	COLLINS	28	.27
DE WIT	60	.58	D'ANVILLE	28	.27
MALLET	59	.57	CHATELAIN	27	.26
MORDEN	59	.57	DE JODE	27	.26
JOHNSTON	58	.56	KIP	27	.26
OGILBY	58	.56	PTOLEMY (1522-41 STRASSBURG)	27	.26
DE BRUYN	58	.56	FINLEY	26	.25
DEPOT DE LA MARINE	57	.55	BODENEHR	26	.25
U.S. COAST SURVEY	56	.54	D'APRES DE MANNEVILLETTE	26	.25
LUCAS	56	.54	WELLS	26	.25
GENTLEMAN'S MAGAZINE	55	.53	SMITH	25	.24

FREQUENCIES OF ALL MAPMAKERS LISTED: 1983-1984

Name	Freq	Name	Freq	Name	Freq
ABERT	1	BION	1	CARVER	2
ACKERMANN	1	BLACK	33	CARY	72
ADMIRALTY	24	BLACKIE & SON	13	CASE	1
ALBRIZZI	34	BLAEU	275	CASSINI	4
ALLARD	5	BLANCHARD	1	CASTILLA	2
ALLEN & CO	1	BLANKAART	3	CATESBY	1
ALMON	1	BLOME	20	CATLIN	3
ALTING	1	BLONDEAU	1	CELLARIUS	14
AMERICAN LITHO. CO.	1	BLUHME	1	CHABERT	3
AMERICAN PUBLISHING CO.	1	BLUNDELL	3	CHAMBERS	2
ANBUREY	1	BLUNT	13	CHAMOUIN	1
ANDREAS	4	BODENEHR	26	CHANLAIRE	3
ANDREWS	5	BOHN	1	CHANLAIRE & MENTELLE	2
ANDREWS & DURY	1	BOLTON	1	CHAPIN	1
ANDRIVEAU-GOUJON	4	BONNE	92	CHAPMAN	2
ANGELO	1	BONNEVILLE	1	CHAPMAN & HALL	6
ANONYMOUS	136	BORDIGA	1	CHARLEVOIX	7
ANSON	7	BORTHWICK	1	CHASTENET-PUISEGUR	1
ANTOINE	2	BOTERO	1	CHATELAIN	27
APIANUS	6	BOUCHETTE	5	CHILD	5
APPLETON	14	BOWEN	166	CHIQUET	11
AQUILA	1	BOWLES	29	CITTI	1
ARCHER	5	BOYNTON	4	CLAESZ	1
ARROWSMITH	81	BRADFORD	90	CLARK	1
ASHBY	1	BRADLEY	21	CLOUET	3
ASHER & ADAMS	13	BRAUN & HOGENBERG	138	CLUNY	1
ASPIN	2	BRIGHTLY	1	CLUVER	20
ATWATER	1	BRIGHTLY & KINNERSLEY	2	COCHIN	6
ATWOOD	3	BRION DE LA TOUR	7	COLBURN	4
BACHIENE	2	BROOKE	1	COLDEN	1
BAEDEKER	14	BROWN	1	COLLINS	28
BAILEY & HAZEN	1	BROWNE	1	COLNETT	1
BALDWIN	7	BRUE	12	COLTON	78
BALDWIN & CRADOCK	10	BRYANT	4	CONANT	1
BANKES	2	BUACHE	9	CONDER	8
BARCLAY	2	BUCHON	18	CONSERVANCY	1
BARFIELD	1	BUFFORD	2	COOK	12
BARKER	1	BUISSON	1	CORNELIS	1
BARNES & BURR	8	BUNTING	2	CORONELLI	68
BARROW	2	BURGESS	9	COTOVICUS	5
BARTHOLOMEW	8	BURNEY	1	COUNT & HAMMOND	1
BARTLETT	4	BURR	17	COUSEN	1
BASIRE	2	BURRIEL	1	COVENS & MORTIER	31
BAUDARTIUS	12	BUTLER	1	COWLEY	9
BAUDIN	1	CADELL	2	COWPERTHWAIT	2
BAUMGARTEN	5	CADELL & DAVIES	2	COX	2
BEAUTEMPS-BEAUPRE	1	CALLOT	2	COXE	1
BEERS	1	CALVERT	1	CRAM	31
BELDIN	3	CAMDEN	18	CRANTZ	4
BELL	12	CAMOCIO	28	CRAWFORD	3
BELLERE	1	CAMPANIUS HOLM	4	CREPY	1
BELLIN	325	CANADA	7	CREVECOEUR	1
BENARD	13	CANTELLI DA VIGNOLA	1	CROSS	1
BERNARD	2	CAPPER	10	CRUCHLEY	8
BERRY	3	CAREY	67	CUMMINGS	1
BERTELLI	2	CAREY & LEA	39	CUTLER	1
BERTIUS	47	CAREY & WARNER	2	D'ANVILLE	28
BETTS	1	CAREZ	1	D'APRES DE MANNEVILLETTE	26
BICKHAM	2	CARLETON	1	DAL RE	1
BIEN	2	CAROLUS	1	DALRYMPLE	4

Name		Name		Name	
DAMPIER	4	DU VIVIER	1	GERSTMAYR	2
DANCKERTS	23	DUDLEY	11	GIBSON	11
DANET	2	DUFOUR	7	GILLIAM	1
DAPPER	21	DUNCAN	1	GILMAN	1
DARTON	5	DUNN	1	GILPIN	1
DAVENPORT	3	DUPUIS	1	GIUSTINIANO	3
DAVIES	1	DURY	2	GLAZIER	1
DAWSON BROS.	1	DWIGHT	1	GLEASON'S PICTORIAL	1
DAY & SON	1	EDWARDS	14	GOEREE	3
DE BAR	1	EHRMANN	1	GOERING	3
DE BEAURAIN	1	ELLIOTT PUBLISHING CO.	1	GOLD	9
DE BELLE FOREST	8	ELLIS	13	GOODRICH	6
DE BEREY	1	ELWE	3	GOOS	19
DE BOUGE	1	ELY	1	GORDON	4
DE BRUYN	58	EMORY	1	GRATTON & GILBERT	1
DE BRY	66	ENTICK	4	GRAVIUS	3
DE FER	37	ERTL	24	GRAY	13
DE GRADO	1	ESQUEMELING	3	GREAT BRITAIN	1
DE HOOGHE	1	ETTLING	4	GREENLEAF	5
DE JODE	27	EULER	1	GREENWOOD	25
DE L'ISLE	45	EVANS	2	GRIDLEY	2
DE LA POTHERIE	4	EVERY SATURDAY	1	GRIERSON	3
DE LA RUE	1	EXSHAW	1	GRISWOLD	6
DE LAET	19	FADEN	63	GUICHARDIN	1
DE LAT	2	FAIRBURN	1	GUILQUIN & DUPAIN	1
DE LETH	2	FARNHAM	1	GUSSEFELD	5
DE RIENZI	1	FASSMANN	1	GUTHRIE	5
DE VAUGONDY	121	FAURE	1	HABERMANN	3
DE WIT	60	FENNER, SEARS & CO.	6	HACHETTE	1
DEAN & MUNDAY	1	FIDALGO	7	HADFIELD	1
DEARBORN	2	FIELDING	5	HALL	25
DELAMARCHE	7	FINDLAY	5	HALLIBURTON	3
DEN SCHRYVER	1	FINLEY	26	HALMA	1
DENIS	1	FISHER	1	HARDESTY	4
DENISON	1	FISK & RUSSELL	1	HARPER	1
DEPOSITO HIDROGRAFICO	1	FISK & SEE	1	HARPER & BROS.	1
DEPOT DE LA MARINE	57	FLEURIEU	1	HARPER'S WEEKLY	5
DES BARRES	35	FOOT	1	HARREWYN	1
DESILVER	29	FORSTER	1	HARRIS	8
DESNOS	3	FOSTER	1	HARRISON	9
DEZAUCHE	5	FRANK LESLIE'S ILLUSTRATED NEWSP	1	HAYDEN	1
DEZOTEUX	2	FRANKLIN	10	HAYWARD	2
DICEY	1	FREMIN	1	HEARNE	5
DIDOT	1	FREZIER	4	HEATHER	1
DILLY	1	FRICX	1	HENNEPIN	3
DIRECCION HIDROGRAFICA	3	FRIED	1	HENRIOL	1
DIXON	7	FULLARTON	81	HERBERSTEIN	1
DOLENDO	1	FULLER	20	HERBERT	1
DONALDSON	1	GALL & INGLIS	3	HERISSON	3
DONCKER	1	GALLE	3	HERRERA	8
DOPPELMAYR	3	GALT & HOY	1	HEYLIN	1
DORR, HOWLAND & CO.	1	GARDNER	6	HILDBURG INSTITUT	4
DOU	1	GARNIER	1	HILDEBRANDT	1
DOWER	14	GASKELL	1	HILL	1
DRAYTON	29	GASTALDI	1	HILL & CO.	1
DRINKWATER	1	GASTON	6	HINSHELWOOD	1
DRIPPS	1	GAZZETTIERE AMERICANO	36	HINTON	8
DU BOSC	1	GEDDES	2	HINTON & SIMPKIN	1
DU SAUZET	4	GENTLEMAN'S MAGAZINE	55	HINTON, SIMPKIN & MARSHALL	7
DU VAL	13	GERRITZ	1	HODGES	1

Name		Name		Name	
HOGENBERG	3	KRUIKIUS	1	MACPHERSON	1
HOGG	18	LA FEUILLE	2	MAFFEIUS	1
HOLE	19	LA HONTAN	9	MAGGI	1
HOLLAR	3	LA PEROUSE	15	MAGNUS	1
HOMANN	247	LABAT	1	MALLET	59
HONDIUS	123	LACOSTE	1	MALTE-BRUN	11
HONTER	3	LADIES REPOSITORY	6	MANTE	2
HORATIUS	1	LAFRERI SCHOOL	4	MARCY	2
HORNIUS	2	LAMBERT	1	MARIETTE	1
HOUZE	3	LANE	2	MARSHALL	2
HOWEN	1	LANGENES	1	MARTIN	1
HUBERTI	4	LANGLEY	12	MARZOLLA	1
HUGHES	1	LANGLOIS	1	MASPERO	1
HULSIUS	8	LANGSDORFF	1	MAST, CROWELL & KIRKPATRICK	2
HUMBOLDT	3	LAPIE	9	MATHER	1
HUME & SMOLLETT	1	LAPOINTE	1	MATTHEWS, NORTHRAP CO.	3
HUNTINGTON	2	LASOR A VAREA	4	MAUNDRESSI	1
HUOT	1	LATTRE	2	MANMAN	3
HURD	1	LAUREMBERG	7	MAYER	1
HUTCHINS	2	LAURENT	1	MCGREGOR	16
HUTCHINSON	1	LAURIE	2	MCINTYRE	3
ILLMAN	4	LAURIE & WHITTLE	39	MCNALLY	10
ILLUSTRATED LONDON NEWS	3	LAVOISNE	2	MEARS	11
ILLUSTRATED NEWS	1	LAW	1	MEGAREY	1
IMBERT	1	LAWSON	1	MEIJER	1
IMRAY	5	LE BEAU	1	MEISNER	29
IVISON & BLAKEMAN	2	LE BRUYN	15	MEISSAS	1
JACKSON	1	LE CLERC	9	MELISH	16
JACOBSZ	7	LE PAGE DU PRATZ	1	MERCATOR	145
JAILLOT	50	LE ROUGE	37	MERIAN	268
JAMES	1	LEA	2	METELLUS	2
JANSSON	287	LEIGH	10	MEYER	13
JANVIER	8	LEMERCIER	1	MICHAULT	2
JEFFERYS	85	LEVAL	1	MIDDLETON	1
JOHNSON	37	LEVANTO	2	MIGEON	1
JOHNSON & BROWNING	6	LEVASSEUR	13	MILLAR	3
JOHNSON & WARD	54	LEWIS	12	MILLER	1
JOHNSTON	58	LEWIS & ARROWSMITH	6	MILTON & CHEADLE	1
JUDD	1	LIEBAUX	1	MITCHELL	156
KAEMPFER	1	LIEFRINCK	1	MITCHELL, JOHN	1
KANE	1	LINSCHOTEN	11	MOFFAT	3
KELLER	1	LIZARS	8	MOLL	166
KELLY	6	LLOYD	1	MOLLHAUSEN	1
KEPOHONI	1	LODGE	7	MONIN & FREMIN	3
KEY	1	LONDON GAZETTE	2	MONK	2
KEYSER	3	LONDON MAGAZINE	31	MONTANUS	7
KEYSTONE PUBLISHING CO.	1	LONDON NEWS	9	MONTHLY CHRONOLOGER	1
KIEPERT	2	LONGMAN	6	MOON	1
KILBOURN	1	LOPEZ	2	MOORE	2
KILBURN	1	LOTTER	30	MORDEN	59
KING	1	LOWIZIO	1	MORDEN & BERRY	1
KINGMAN BROS.	6	LUCAS	56	MORGAN	1
KINGSBURY	1	LUFFMAN	4	MORRISON & WEST	2
KINO	1	LUFT	1	MORSE	61
KIP	27	LUTHER	1	MORSE & BREESE	16
KIRCHER	10	LYELL	1	MORTIER	121
KITCHIN	76	MACGREGOR	1	MOULE	5
KNIGHT	3	MACKENZIE	9	MOUNT & PAGE	44
KRAYENHOFF	2	MACKINLAY	1	MOXON	2
KREFFELDT	1	MACLURE & MACDONALD	1	MUDIE	1

MULLER	16	POLITICAL MAGAZINE	36	SAYER & BENNETT	21
MUNSTER	111	PONT	1	SCHEDEL	9
MURPHY & CO.	1	POPPLE	9	SCHENK	54
MURRAY	7	PORCACCHI	23	SCHERER	29
MUTLOW	1	PORRO	1	SCHLEY	6
MYERS	1	PORTLOCK	2	SCHMIDT	2
NATIONAL GEOGRAPHIC SOCIETY	1	PREVOST D'EXILES	7	SCHOMBURGK	2
NEELE	6	PRICE	1	SCHONBERG	1
NEW YORK MANUAL	1	PROBST	1	SCHOOLCRAFT	1
NEWBERY	1	PROUD	1	SCHOUTEN	3
NICHOLLS	1	PTOLEMY (1482 FLORENCE)	3	SCHRADER	1
NICOL	3	PTOLEMY (1482-86 ULM)	6	SCHRAEMBL	1
NICOLOSI	5	PTOLEMY (1511 VENICE)	1	SCHREIBER	1
NOLIN	8	PTOLEMY (1513-20 STRASSBURG)	21	SCOT'S MAGAZINE	4
NORDEN	1	PTOLEMY (1522-41 STRASSBURG)	27	SCOTT	15
NORRIE	2	PTOLEMY (1548 VENICE)	29	SDUK	70
NORWOOD	1	PTOLEMY (1561-99 VENICE)	52	SEALE	11
NUTTALL, FISHER & DIXON	2	PTOLEMY (1578-1730 MERCATOR)	2	SEILE	2
NUTZHORN	1	PTOLEMY (1596-1621 MAGINI)	67	SELIGMANN	1
OGILBY	58	PURCHAS	5	SELLER	64
OLNEY	3	QUAD	54	SENEX	17
ORTELIUS	334	RADEFELD	7	SERRES	1
OTTENS	22	RAIGNAULD	2	SEUTTER	50
OVERTON	1	RAILWAY NEWS	1	SILVER	1
OWEN	2	RAMSAY	3	SILVESTRE	1
OWEN & BOWEN	9	RAMUSIO	20	SIMONS	1
PADLEY	1	RAND MCNALLY	22	SLATTER	1
PALFREY	1	RAND, AVERY & CO.	1	SMILLIE	1
PAOLI	1	RASPE	1	SMITH	25
PAPEN	2	RATELBAND	1	SMOLLETT	1
PARKE	1	RAU	1	SMYTH	3
PARKER	2	RAWLINGS	1	SOLINUS	2
PARR	1	REED	1	SOULES	1
PARRY	9	REICHARD	3	SPEED	272
PAYNE	2	RELAND	1	SPEER	1
PEABODY & CO.	1	RENARD	7	SPILBERGEN	1
PEASE	1	RENNER	9	STACKHOUSE	4
PELHAM	1	RIEDEL	1	STAEHLIN	1
PENDLETON	1	ROBERTS	2	STANFORD	7
PENNSYLVANIA MAGAZINE	1	ROBERTSON	1	STARLING	3
PERELLE	2	ROBINSON	37	STAVELEY & WOOD	1
PERKINS	1	ROBSON	1	STEDMAN	15
PERTHES	3	ROCQUE	8	STEUDNER	1
PETERMANN	1	ROGERS	1	STEVENS	3
PETRI	1	ROGERS, PEET & CO.	1	STOCKDALE	16
PETRINI	1	ROLLINSON	1	STOCKLEIN	1
PHILIP	7	ROLLOS	8	STOOPENDAAL	3
PHILIPPE	1	ROMANS	1	STOPIUS	1
PHILLIPS	16	ROSS	1	STROBRIDGE & CO.	1
PICQUET	2	ROSSI	7	STUART	1
PIGAFETTA	1	ROUARGUE	1	STUPNAGEL	1
PIGOT & CO.	1	ROUX	2	SUDLOW	2
PINE	2	ROYAL GEOGRAPHICAL SOCIETY	2	SUHR	1
PINGELING	1	RUDOLPHI	5	SWINSTON	21
PINKERTON	16	RUSSEL	1	TALLIS	202
PITT	4	RUSSELL	19	TANNER	36
PLANCIUS	4	SANSON	95	TARDIEU	11
PLAYFAIR	1	SANTINI	33	TARLETON	1
PLUCHE	1	SAXTON	9	TASSIN	1
POIRSON	6	SAYER	12	TAVERNIER	2

TEESDALE	23	WALKER	12
TEGG	5	WALL	1
THEVENOT	1	WALLING & GRAY	1
THIERRY	1	WALLING, TACKABURY & CO.	1
THOMAS, COMPERTHWAIT & CO.	61	WALLIS & REID	17
THOMPSON BROS. & BURR	1	WALTHER	1
THOMSON	86	WARBURTON	1
THORNTON	4	WARD	3
TINDAL	23	WARDEN	1
TIRION	34	WATSON	1
TOMBLESON	1	WEBER	1
TOMS	1	WEIGEL	8
TOPHAM	1	WEIMAR GEOGRAPHISCHES INSTITUT	5
TORBETT	2	WELD	1
TORNIELLO	2	WELLER	18
TORRENTE	1	WELLS	26
TOUDY	1	WERNER	2
TRAMEZINI	2	WEST SHORE	1
TREMAINE	1	WHYMPER	2
TRUSLER	1	WILCOCKE	1
TRUTCH	1	WILD	1
TUNISON	1	WILKES	9
TURNER	1	WILKINSON	7
TYSON	1	WILLDEY	5
U.S.	106	WILLIAMS	2
U.S. COAST SURVEY	56	WILLIAMSON	2
U.S. EXPLORING EXPEDITION	1	WILLIS	1
UNIVERSAL MAGAZINE	19	WILLMANN	1
VALDOR	1	WILSON	2
VALENTINE'S MANUAL	2	WINKELMANNS CHRONIK	1
VALENTYN	3	WINSLOW	1
VALK	16	WITSEN	1
VALK & SCHENK	19	WOLFF	1
VAN ADRICHEM	1	WOODBRIDGE	5
VAN DEN HOEYE	1	WRIGHT	1
VAN DEN KEERE	47	WYATT	1
VAN DER AA	30	WYLD	33
VAN DER HAGEN	1	WYTFLIET	7
VAN DOETECUM	2	YOUNG	2
VAN KEULEN	22	ZAHN	1
VAN LOCHOM	4	ZATTA	62
VAN LOON	3	ZIEGLER	3
VANCOUVER	3		
VANDERMAELEN	18		
VARELA Y ULLOA	1		
VARLE	1		
VARTE	1		
VASCELLINI	1		
VERBIEST	1		
VIRTUE	4		
VISSCHER	99		
VIVIEN	2		
VON REILLY	35		
VRIENTS	3		
VUILLEMIN	1		
WAGHENAER	28		
WAGNER & MCGUIGAN	1		
WAKEFIELD	1		
WALCH	2		
WALES	1		

50

CURRENCY CONVERSION TABLE

The following exchange rates were in effect at mid-1983. Although fluctuations occurred throughout the year, these values provide a good approximation for converting the dollar values given in this price guide to other currencies.

COUNTRY	UNIT	VALUE IN U.S. DOLLARS	NUMBER PER DOLLAR
Argentina	Peso	0.1132	8.834
Australia	Dollar	0.8763	1.141
Austria	Schilling	0.0558	17.92
Belgium	Franc	0.0196	51.02
Brazil	Cruziero	0.00189	529.
Canada	Dollar	0.8133	1.230
Denmark	Krone	0.1096	9.124
Finland	Mark	0.1807	5.534
France	Franc	0.1310	7.634
Germany	Mark	0.3937	2.54
Great Britain	Pound	1.533	0.6522
Greece	Drachma	0.0119	84.
Hong Kong	Dollar	0.140	7.14
Ireland	Pound	1.238	0.808
Israel	Shekel	0.0212	47.2
Italy	Lira	0.000664	1506.
Japan	Yen	0.004184	239.
Mexico	Peso	0.0068	147.
Netherlands	Guilder	0.3512	2.847
New Zealand	Dollar	0.6545	1.528
Norway	Krone	0.1374	7.278
Portugal	Escudo	0.0085	118.
Saudi Arabia	Riyal	0.2899	3.45
Singapore	Dollar	0.4717	2.120
South Africa	Rand	0.9132	1.095
Spain	Peseta	0.00683	146.
Sweden	Krona	0.1313	7.616
Switzerland	Franc	0.4752	2.104
Turkey	Lira	0.00455	220.
Venezuela	Bolivar	0.0893	11.2

CATALOG CODES

Broadfoot's Bookmark
Rt. 3, Box 318
Wendell, NC 27591
[1] "Catalog #3"

C. Broekema
Leidsekade 68
1016 DA
Amsterdam, Holland
[2] "Catalogue 67"

Capt. Kit S. Kapp,
    Antiquarian Maps
PO Box 64
Osprey, FL 33559
[3] "Catalog XX"

Cartographia Ltd.
Covent Garden
37 Southampton Street
London WC2E 7HE
England
[4] "Catalogue 25"
[5] "Catalogue 26"

Charles Sessler, Rare Maps,
    Books and Prints
1308 Walnut Street
Philadelphia, PA 19107
[6] "Catalogue #11"

D. & E. Lake Ltd.
106 Berkeley Street
Toronto
Ontario M5A 2W7, Canada
[7] "Cartography No. 4"

Elizabeth F. Dunlap,
    Books & Maps
6063 Westminster Pl.
St. Louis, MO 63112
[8] "List 36-M, Americana in
    Maps"

George Robinson Old Prints &
    Maps
PO Box 1239
Taos, NM 87571
[9] "Catalog 15, Winter, 1982–3"
[10] "Catalog 16, Spring, 1983"
[11] "Catalog 17, Summer, 1983"

Ivan R. Deverall
Duval House, The Glen
Cambridge Way, Uckfield
Sussex TN22 2AA
England
[12] "Spring 1983"
[13] "Summer 1983"
[14] "Autumn 1983"

Jo-Ann & Richard Casten, Ltd.
RR2 Little Bay Road
Wading River, NY 11792
[15] "Catalog VII, 1983"

Jonathan Potter Ltd.
No. 1, Grafton Street
London W1X 3LB
England
[16] "Autumn 1983"

Kenneth Nebenzahl, Inc.
333 N. Michigan Ave.
Chicago, IL 60601
[17] "The Compass for Map
    Collectors, No. 45, 1983"

Louis Loeb-Larocque
36, Rue Le Peletier
75009
Paris, France
[18] "Le Benelux, Cartographie
    et Topographie Anciennes,
    1983"

Murray Hudson, Books & Maps
Rt. 1, Box 362
Dyersburg, TN 38024
[19] "Catalog One, Texas in Maps:
1721–1914"
[20] "Texas in Maps: an Addenda,
1747–1889"

North by West
Box 11538
Edmonton Main P.O.
Alberta T5J 3K7, Canada
[21] "Catalogue Number Two"

Old Maps and Prints
Preston Figley
PO Box 2234
Fort Worth, TX 76113
[22] "Catalog 4, Fall/Winter 1982–
83"
[23] "Catalog 5, Fall/Winter 1983–
84"

P. J. Radford
Sheffield Park. Nr. Uckfield
Sussex, England
[24] "Catalogue No. 39"
[25] "Americana No. 32"

Richard B. Arkway
131 Fifth Avenue
Suite 401
New York, NY 10003
[26] "Catalogue XXIII, Summer,
1983"

Richard Fitch
Old Maps, Prints & Books
2324 Calle Halcon
Santa Fe, NM 87501
[27] "Catalogue No. 39"

Robert Douwma
93 Great Russell Street
London WC1B 3QL
England
[28] "New in stock list 8, January
1983"
[29] "New in stock list 9, June 1983"

Russborough
PO Box 422, Station R
Toronto, Ontario M4G 4SL
Canada
[30] "A Collocation of Maps for a
Parsimonious Economy"

Stephanie Hoppen Limited
17 Walton Street
London SW3
England
[31] "Islands on Paper"

The Globe
PO Box A3398
Chicago, IL 60690
[32] "Catalog 6"

The Old Print Gallery
1220 31st St., N.W.,
Washington, DC 20007
[33] "Showcase, Vol. X, No. 1,
February 1983"
[34] "Showcase, Vol. X, No. 2,
May 1983"
[35] "Showcase, Vol. X, No. 3,
July 1983"
[36] "Showcase, Vol. X, No. 4,
October 1983"

Thomas Suarez,
Rare Maps & Prints
2142 Broadway
New York, NY 10023
[37] "Catalog 3, Codex Diversus"

W. Graham Arader III
1000 Boxwood Court
King of Prussia, PA 19406
[38] "Catalogue 39, April 1983"

W. J. Faupel
3 Halsford Lane
East Grinstead
Sussex RH19 1NY
England
[39] "Catalogue 83"

PRICE LISTING

ABERT
SKETCH OF A PART OF THE MARCH & WAGON ROAD OF LT. COLONEL COOKE FROM SANTE
   FE TO THE PACIFIC OCEAN [1848] 29.2x56.5cm.   [32] $85
ACKERMANN
FORT UTAH, VALLEY OF THE GREAT SALT LAKE (VIEW) [1852] 12.7x19.1cm.
   Ackermann Lith. N.Y.   [3] $30
ADMIRALTY
AMERICA, N.W. COAST: STRAIT OF JUAN DE FUCA [1864] 95.7x63cm.   [39] $175
CARTAGENA HARBOUR SURVEYED BY H.M.S. SCORPION [1856-85] 63.5x95.3cm. [3] $85
COAST OF NEW GRANADA CABO LA VELA TO CAYOS RATONES CHIEFLY FROM SPANISH
   DOCUMENTS [1837-73] 47.6x61cm.   [3] $75
NEW GRANADA, SAVANILLA HARBOUR & RIO MAGDALENA TO BARRANQUILLA [1886]
   45.7x61cm.   [3] $55
NORTH AMERICA, WEST COAST: HARO AND ROSARIO STRAITS [1864] 95.4x63.2cm.
                                      [39] $175
NORTH POLAR CHART...HYDROGRAPHIC OFFICE, LONDON 1881 [1891] 64.1x92.7cm.
   trimmed to border, minor splits and tears repaired, light browning in blank
   area, manuscript markings   [25] $68
WALES, NORTH COAST SHEET VII, POINT LYNUS TO ABERGELE... [1835-72] 47x62.9cm.
                                      [24] $107
ALBRIZZI
CARTA GEOGRAFICA DELLA AMERICA MERIDIONALE [C1750] 35.6x45.1cm.
   minor spotting, short tear at centerfold   [7] $110
CARTA NUOVA DELL' ARABIA [C1740] 28.5x35cm.   [4] $114
INGHILTERRA [C1740] 36.8x34.3cm.   [12] $88
IRLANDA [C1740] 38.1x32.4cm.   [12] $68
NUOVA CARTA DEL POLO ARTICO [1740] 27.9x33cm.   [3] $135
NUOVA CARTA DEL POLO ARTICO SECONDO L'ULTIME OSSERVATIONI. A AMSTERDAM DA ISAC
   TIRION [C1769] 29.8x35.6cm.   [7] $250
NUOVA CARTA DELL'ISOLE BRITANNICHE DIVISE NEI TRE REGNI D'INGHILTERRA, DI
   SCOZIA, E D'IRLANDA [C1740] 26.7x34.3cm.   [12] $91
NUOVA ET ACCURATA CARTA DELL' ISOLE FILIPPINES, LADRONES, ET MOLUCCUS O ISOLE
   DELLE SPEZIANIA COMO ANCO CELEBES & C [C1740] 28x35cm.
   light centerfold browning   [31] $61
SCOZIA [C1740] 38.1x31.8cm.   [12] $64
ALLARD
RECENTISSIMA NOVI ORBIS AMERICAE SEPTENTRIONALIS ET MERIDIONALIS TABULA
   [C1700] 50.2x59.1cm.   [23] $1400
ALMON
MAP OF THE ENVIRONS OF BOSTON DRAWN AT BOSTON IN JUNE 1775 [1775] 20.3x25.4cm.
                                      [3] $135
AMERICAN PUBLISHING CO.
PERSPECTIVE MAP OF THE CITY OF HELENA, MONT. CAPITAL OF STATE, COUNTY SEAT OF
   LEWIS & CLARKE CO. 1890 [1890] 66.7x99.7cm. 12 cm. tear at left repaired,
   backed with rice paper, attributed to Henry Wellge, published by his firm,
   The American Publishing Co., Milwaukee   [35] $1250
ANBUREY
VIEW OF THE WEST BANK OF THE HUDSON RIVER 3 MILES ABOVE STILL WATER, UPON WHICH
   THE ARMY UNDER THE COMMAND OF LT. GEN. BURGOYNE, TOOK POST ON THE 20TH SEPT.
   1777 [1789] 19.7x40.4cm. folds reinforced   [39] $95
ANDREAS
CITY OF DES MOINES FROM SOUTH PARK HILL [1875] 32.1x40.6cm. from A.T.
   Andreas, "Illustrated Historical Atlas of the State of Iowa," lithographed by
   Charles Shober & Co.   [35] $385
DAVENPORT, IOWA, AS SEEN FROM SOUTH WEST (VIEW) [1875] 33.3x41.3cm. from A.T.
   Andreas, "Illustrated Historical Atlas of the State of Iowa," lithographed by
   Charles Shober & Co., repairs in margins   [35] $350
ANDREWS
A MAP OF THE RAILROADS IN THE UNITED STATES... [1853] 99.1x106.7cm.
   a folding map restored & encapsulated   [20] $350

ANDREWS (continued)

A PLAN OF THE CITY OF LIMA [1772] 16.5x24.1cm.   [3] $55
MAP OF THE BASIN OF THE ST. LAWRENCE SHOWING ALSO THE NATURAL AND ARTIFICIAL
    ROUTES BETWEEN THE ATLANTIC OCEAN AND THE INTERIOR OF NORTH AMERICA...
    [1853] 88x190cm. on 6 sheets, joined, folded   [39] $350
MAP OF THE EASTERN PORTION OF BRITISH NORTH AMERICA INCLUDING GULF OF ST.
    LAWRENCE, AND PART OF NEW ENGLAND STATES COMPILED FROM THE LATEST SURVEYS AND
    CHARTS BY HENRY F. PERLEY... [1853] 66x117cm. on 2 sheets, joined   [39] $120
MAP OF THE RAILROADS IN THE UNITED STATES IN OPERATION AND PROGRESS... [1853]
    100x106cm. on 4 sheets, joined, folds reinforced   [39] $95

ANDRIVEAU-GOUJON

CARTE DE L'AMERIQUE DU NORD [1837] 49.5x38.1cm.   [27] $175
PAVILLONS ET COCARDES DES PRINCIPALES PUISSANCES DU GLOBE [1853] 45.7x57.8cm.
    a chart of 113 flags from around the world, hand colored   [24] $191

ANONYMOUS

A CARICATURE OF ENGLAND AND WALES [1808] 13x9.5cm.   [31] $191
A CARICATURE OF IRELAND [1808] 13x9.5cm.   [31] $191
A CHART OF DELAWARE BAY AND RIVER FROM THE ORIGINAL BY MR. FISHER OF
    PHILADELPHIA, 1776 [1776] 18.4x23.5cm.   [32] $85
A CHART OF HUDSON'S STRAITS AND BAY ACCORDING TO THE DISCOVERIES MADE IN THE
    YEARS 1746 & 1747 [C1760] 34.2x29.3cm. split repaired   [39] $175
A MAP OF MARCO POLO'S VOYAGES & TRAVELS IN THE 13TH CENTURY THROUGH A GREAT
    PART OF ASIA, ALL TARTARY, THE EAST INDIA ISLANDS & PART OF AFRICA [1744]
    20.3x30.5cm.   [10] $70
A NEW MAP OF NOVA SCOTIA [1823] 17.8x26.7cm.   [30] $73
AFBELDINGE VAN'T ZEER VERMAARDE EILAND GEKS-KOP [C1720] 28.6x22.9cm. a
    curiosity with several inset scenes surrounding a map in the shape of a
    fools-cap, with text below satirizing the Mississippi Bubble scheme, probably
    from Vol. 2 of "Het Groote Taferell der Dwaasheid," centerfold repaired
                                                                               [33] $285
AMERIQUE SEPTENTRIONALE [1823] 18.4x21.6cm.   [20] $40
ANCIENT FORTIFICATION ON THE MISSOURI/GREAT FALLS OF COLUMBIA RIVER [1814]
    10.1x17.4cm. 2 maps on one plate, dimensions are for each   [39] $40
BIRD'S-EYE VIEW OF NEW ORLEANS [C1860] 13.3x18.8cm.   [39] $25
BREDA OBESSSA... (sic) [C1625] 41x52cm. trimmed to border   [18] $175
CARTE DU WAEIGATZ OU DETROIT DE NASSAU [C1720] 15.2x29.2cm.
    folding, everything but title is in Dutch   [23] $40
CHARTE VON DEN VEREINIGTEN STAATEN VON NORD-AMERICA MIT LOUISIANA [1818]
    30.2x41.6cm. from "Neueste Lander und Boltersunde," Prague   [35] $185
CHARTE VON NORD-AMERICA [1818] 41.3x29.8cm.
    from "Neueste Lander und Boltersunde," Prague   [35] $165
CINCINNATI [C1833] 8.7x15.7cm.   [39] $25
EIGENTLICHE UND WOLFORMIERTE CARTE DARINNEN ZUFINDEN EIN THEIL DES
    GELLER-LANDS, BOMMELERWEERDT...AM 11 TAG MAY, ANNO 1600... [1600] 20x45cm.
                                                                               [18] $175
ENVIRONS OF ST. LOUIS/LEAD REGION/ENVIRONS OF LEXINGTON/ENVIRONS OF NASHVILLE
    [C1833] 15.2x13.4cm.   [39] $20
GALLAPAGOS ISLANDS, DESCRIBED BY AMBROSE COWLEY IN 1684/THE ISLAND SANTA MARIA
    DEL L'AGUADA... [C1800] 13.6x12.2cm.   [39] $35
GEORGIA AND ALABAMA [1833] 12.8x16.3cm.   [39] $20
GREAT FALLS OF MISSOURI [1814] 17.7x10cm.   [39] $25
HAVRE DE GRACE [C1760] 17.8x23.5cm. plan of Le Havre   [30] $40
ILLINOIS AND MISSOURI [C1833] 15.6x12.6cm.   [39] $20
INFERIORIS GERMANIAE PROVINCIARUM NOVA DESCRIPTIO [C1604] 41x53.5cm.
    perhaps by Willem Janszoon Blaeu   [18] $878
KENTUCKY AND TENNESSEE [C1833] 12.6x16.1cm.   [39] $20
KOPPENHAVEN (VIEW) [C1760] 19.1x26.7cm.   [10] $40
LA VERA DESCRITTIONE DELLA GALLIA BELGICA [1565] 39x30cm.
    published in Venice   [18] $1404
LOUISIANA AND MISSISSIPPI [1833] 15.6x12.5cm.   [39] $20

ANONYMOUS (continued)
LUIGIANA [C1740] 43.8x28.6cm. depicts the region of the future Louisiana
    Purchase, rivers & Indian tribes named, inset map of Pacific Northwest
                                                                        [23] $150
MAESTRICHT (VIEW) [1579] 27x40cm. cut to border, small tear repaired [18] $263
MAP AND ELEVATION OF THE SHUBENACADIE NAVIGATION FROM HALIFAX HARBOUR TO THE
    BASIN OF MINES [C1830] 11.4x31cm.   [39] $80
MAP OF PART OF THE PROVINCES OF RIO DE JANEIRO AND THE MINAS GERAES WITH THE
    AUTHOR'S ROUTE [C1820] 36.5x48.2cm.   [39] $50
MAP OF SCANDINAVIA [1899] 41.9x33cm.
    to accompany P.B. DuChaillu, "The Land of the Midnight Sun"   [30] $4
MAP OF THE COUNTRY DRAINED BY THE MISSISSIPPI [1823] 37.2x50.6cm.
    short tear repaired   [39] $95
MICHIGAN [C1833] 13.5x16.9cm. inset "Environs of Detroit"   [39] $25
NIEUWE KAART, VAN T'LAND DONAWERT, EN HOCHSTETT &C ALWAAR DE ROEMWAARDIGE
    BATTAILLE [C1740] 29.2x40.6cm.   [30] $130
NOORD-POOL [C1780] 17.8x23.5cm.
    shows routes of C. Duin in 1768 and Fredrik Pietersee in 1769   [23] $50
NOVA ZEMBLA EN'T WAYGAT [C1780] 17.8x22.9cm.   [23] $40
OHIO AND INDIANA [C1833] 12.5x15.5cm.   [39] $20
PENNSYLVANIA AND NEW JERSEY [1833] 12.2x15.3cm.   [39] $20
PLAN D'YORK EN VIRGINIE [1787] 29.8x38.1cm. the siege of Yorktown   [30] $134
PLAN DE LA BAYE DE MANILLE [C1780] 20x25cm.   [31] $61
PLAN OF THE PORT OF VERA CRUZ [1810] 20x25.2cm.   [39] $30
PLAN OF THE POST ROAD BETWEEN BUENOS AYRES AND SANTIAGO DE CHILE [C1850]
    14.8x37.4cm.   [39] $40
PROVINCES UNIES DES PAYS BAS [C1640] 41x44cm. left margin extended   [18] $105
RIO JANEIRO (VIEW) [C1850] 10.9x16.6cm.
    view from offshore with ships in foreground   [39] $20
RIVER ODER GEGENT VON MIT DER EROBERUNG DER INSUL SCHEPENSAMBT WEG NEHMUNG AND
    VER BRENUNG DER ENGLISCHEN SCHIFFEN AUFF DER RIVIER VON ROCHESTER, 1667
    [C1667] 21.6x34.3cm.   [24]
SIEGE D'OSTENDE EN 1601 [C1601] 31x44cm.   [18] $351
SKETCH OF NIAGARA RIVER BETWEEN QUEENSTON & CHIPPEWA [C1820] 18x22cm.
                                                                        [39] $40
SKETCH OF NOOTKA SOUND... [C1780] 26.2x20.3cm.   [39] $40
ST. SALVADOR (VIEW) [C1850] 11.1x16.7cm.   [39] $20
TEXAS [C1890] 40.6x55.9cm.   [19] $65
THE CITY OF BABYLON (VIEW) [1740] 33x47cm.   [10] $60
THE ISLES OF MONTREAL AS THEY HAVE BEEN SURVEY'D BY THE FRENCH ENGINEERS
    [C1770] 25.4x33cm. backed with archivists' tissue   [16] $150
THE UNITED STATES OF AMERICA AS SETTLED BY THE PEACE OF 1783 [1785] 21x25.4cm.
    narrow margins, from Andrews, "History of the War"   [30] $60
THE WORLD [C1850] 47x64.8cm. narrow margins, fold lines visible, backed with
    archivist's tissue, a double-hemisphere world showing "Principal Varieties of
    the Human Race" and "Female Costumes of Different Parts of the World,"
    separately published   [16] $250
VIEW OF THE ENGAGEMENT BETWEEN THE CAPES LA HOGUE & BARFLEUR [C1760]
    17.1x31.8cm.   [30] $24
VIEW OF THE ENGAGEMENT OFF THE ISLE OF MAN [1760] 18.4x27.3cm.   [30] $24
VIRGINIA, MARYLAND AND DELAWARE [1833] 12.4x15.5cm.   [39] $20
WEST INDIES [C1762] 17.8x29.2cm. shows the entire Caribbean, the cartouch
    shows the preparation of a ship's manifest on the dock   [23] $60
ANSON
A CHART OF THE PACIFIC OCEAN FROM THE EQUINOCTIAL TO THE LATITUDE OF 39 1/2 D
    NO. [1761] 27.3x88cm. 2 sheets joined, small repaired tear in margin
                                                                        [39] $155
A VIEW OF CUMBERLAND BAY AT THE ISLAND JUAN FERNANDES [1748] 20.3x34.3cm.
                                                                         [3] $30
A VIEW OF THE S.W. SIDE OF TENIAN [1748] 20.3x50.2cm.   [3] $40

ANSON (continued)
CAPE VIRGIN MARY AT THE NORTH ENTRANCE OF MAGELLAN'S STREIGHTS (VIEW) [1748]
   20.3x38.1cm.   [3] $30
ANTOINE
ETATS-UNIS ET N. BRETAGNE [C1848] 21.6x28.6cm.   [19] $75
MEXIQUE [C1848] 21.6x28.6cm.   [19] $70
APIANUS
(AMERICA ON A HEMISPHERE) [C1554] 12.4x10.9cm.
   a page from "Cosmographia..."   [39] $90
CHARTA COSMOGRAPHICA CUM VENTORUM PROPRIA NATURA ET OPERATIONE [1544-53]
   21.6x29.2cm.   [15] $1550
APPLETON
A MAP OF EGYPT AND SINAI [1890] 41.9x26cm. lithographed color   [30] $9
A MAP OF PALESTINE [1890] 41.9x26cm. lithographed color   [30] $9
CITY OF LOUISVILLE (VIEW) [1872] 15.2x22.9cm.
   from "Pictursque America"   [27] $25
CITY OF LOUISVILLE. A.C. WARREN. E.P. BRANDARD. ENTERED ACCORDING TO ACT OF
   CONGRESS...NEW YORK D. APPLETON & CO. 1872 (VIEW) [1872] 13.3x22.9cm.
      [25] $21
CITY OF PROVIDENCE. FROM PROSPECT HILL. A.C. WARREN, R. HINSHELWOOD...NEW YORK
   D. APPLETON & CO. (VIEW) [1872] 22.9x13.3cm.   [25] $24
SOUTHERN STATES [1881] 21x26cm.   [19] $20
ARCHER
BRITISH AND RUSSIAN AMERICA [1843] 22x27cm.
   from Gilbert, "Modern Atlas of the Earth"   [21] $36
CANADA, NEW BRUNSWICK, NOVA SCOTIA, ETC. [1843] 22x27cm.
   from Gilbert, "Modern Atlas of the Earth"   [21] $32
MEXICO & TEXAS [C1840] 22.9x28.6cm.   [20] $140
NORTH AMERICA [C1840] 28.6x24.8cm.   [20] $80
NORTH AMERICA [C1835] 15x21cm. margins badly scuffed   [21] $28
ARROWSMITH
A CHART OF THE GALAPAGOS SURVEYED IN THE MERCHANT SHIP RATTLER, AND DRAWN BY
   CAPT: JAMES COLNETT, OF THE ROYAL NAVY IN 1793 1794 [1798] 76x57cm.
      [39] $250
A MAP OF THE UNITED STATES OF NORTH AMERICA [1802-08] 121.9x141cm. on 4
   sheets joined to form 2, dimensions are overall, minor offsetting, minor wear
   at folds, the 3rd issue of the 1802 (2nd) edition, published in 1808 at 10
   Soho Square to which address Arrowsmith moved in that year   [16] $1500
AMERICA [1834] 61x47.6cm. 2nd edition   [3] $110
AMERICA. LONDON, PUBD. 15 FEBY. 1840 BY J. ARROWSMITH, 10 SOHO SQUARE [1840]
   63.5x53.3cm.   [7] $225
BRITISH POSSESSIONS IN AMERICA [1816] 20x25cm.   [21] $36
CANADA [1817] 19x24cm.   [21] $36
CANADA [1823] 20.5x25cm.   [21] $48
DARIEN [1825] 22.9x30.5cm.   [3] $45
DISCOVERIES IN WESTERN AUSTRALIA FROM DOCUMENTS FURNISHED TO THE COLONIAL
   OFFICE BY J.S. ROE [1838] 49x60cm.
   as published in "State Papers Western Australia 1837"   [14] $291
EMPIRE OF JAPAN [1820] 22.9x40.6cm.   [3] $45
LOWER CANADA, NEW BRUNSWICK, NOVA SCOTIA, PRINCE EDWARD IS... [1842]
   61x48.3cm. inset of Newfoundland   [3] $135
LOWER CANADA, NEW BRUNSWICK, NOVA SCOTIA, PRINCE EDWARDS ID. NEWFOUNDLAND, AND
   A LARGE PORTION OF THE UNITED STATES. LONDON, PUBD. 15 FEBY. 1842 BY J.
   ARROWSMITH, 10 SOHO SQUARE [1842] 62.9x53.3cm.   [7] $225
MAP OF PORTION OF THE ARCTIC SHORES OF AMERICA TO ACCOMPANY CAPTN.
   MC.CLINTOCK'S NARRATIVE. COMPILED BY JOHN ARROWSMITH. 1859 [1860] 34x50.2cm.
   light browning along one fold   [21] $117
MAP OF THE SOUTHERN COAST OF AUSTRALIA, FROM ENCOUNTER BAY TO KING GEORGE'S
   SOUND, SHEWING MR. EYRE'S TRACK IN THE YEARS 1839, 1840 & 41 IN HIS ATTEMPT
   TO PENETRATE INTO THE INTERIOR [1841] 32x77cm.   [14] $191

ARROWSMITH (continued)
```
  MARITIMES [1846-50] 60.3x47.6cm.                                   [30]   $142
  MEXICO [1817]  C22.9x24.8cm.                                       [20]   $150
  MEXICO [1832] 48.3x60.3cm.                                         [22]   $350
  NORTH AMERICA [1823] 25.5x20.5cm. from Arrowsmith, "New General Atlas"
                                                                     [21]    $48
  PERU AND BOLIVIA [1834] 48.5x60cm.                                  [4]    $76
  PLAN OF THE ANCHORING PLACE AT THE ISLAND QUIBO BY CAPT. JAMES COLNETT, ROYAL
     NAVY [1798] 37.5x52.1cm. top margin restored, minor repairs      [3]    $85
  SKETCH OF PART OF THE HUDSONS BAY COMPANY'S TERRITORY [1817] 28.6x32.4cm.
     one margin narrow, folds                                        [39]    $40
  SOUTH AMERICA [1840] 30.5x22.9cm.                                   [3]    $35
  THE COASTS OF GUATEMALA AND MEXICO FROM PANAMA TO CAPE MENDOCINO, WITH THE
     PRINCIPAL HARBOURS OF CALIFORNIA [1839] 36.8x50.8cm. usually bound into
     Alexander Forbes, "California," this copy was apparently sold separately,
     lacking the fold wear usually found on this map                 [16]   $250
  THE PROVINCES OF LA PLATA, THE BANDA ORIENTAL DEL URUGUAY & CHILE... [1842]
     63.5x52.1cm.                                                     [3]    $65
  THE WORLD DRAWN BY A. ARROWSMITH HYDROGRAPHER TO PRINCE REGENT... [1817]
     20.3x25.4cm.                                                     [3]    $40
  THE WORLD FROM THE DISCOVERIES & OBSERVATIONS MADE IN THE LATEST VOYAGES &
     TRAVELS [C1800] 30x45cm.                                        [13]    $68
  THE WORLD ON MERCATOR'S PROJECTION [1840] 49.5x59.7cm. light browning
                                                                      [3]    $80
  UNITED STATES [1828] 24.1x30.5cm. backed                            [3]    $45
  UPPER CANADA &C [1838] 61x50.8cm.                                   [3]   $120
  UPPER CANADA &C. LONDON, PUBD 15 FEBY 1842, BY J. ARROWSMITH, 10 SOHO SQUARE
     [1842] 63.5x53.3cm.                                              [7]   $225
  UPPER CANADA &C., LOWER CANADA, NEW BRUNSWICK, NOVA SCOTIA, PRINCE EDWARDS ID.,
     NEWFOUNDLAND, AND A LARGE PORTION OF THE UNITED STATES [1838] 61x95cm.
     folding map of 36 panels, on cloth                              [39]    $75
  W. INDIES [1840] 24.1x30.5cm.                                       [3]    $35
  WESTERN AUSTRALIA, FROM THE GOVERNMENT SURVEYS [1842] 24x32cm.
     from "Papers Relating to the Aborigines of the Australian Colonies"[14]  $160
```
ASHBY
```
  PRINCE EDWARD ISLAND [1798] 18.4x34.9cm.                           [30]   $243
```
ASHER & ADAMS
```
  (COLORADO) [1873-74] 40.6x57.2cm. dated 1873, published 1874       [27]    $75
  (IDAHO MONTANA, WESTERN PORTION) [1874] 57.2x40.6cm.               [27]    $65
  (UTAH) [1873-74] 40.6x57.2cm. dated 1873, published 1874           [27]    $60
  (WYOMING) [1874] 40.6x57.2cm. light browning at centerfold         [27]    $85
  ASHER & ADAMS' PART OF QUEBEC [1873] 56.5x40.5cm.                  [21]    $56
  GEOLOGICAL MAP OF THE U.S. & TERRITORIES [1872] 40.6x58.4cm.       [19]    $75
  MICHIGAN [1873] 58.4x40.6cm.                                        [3]    $60
  NEBRASKA [1873] 39.4x58.4cm.                                        [3]    $65
  ONTARIO [1871] 40.6x58.4cm.                                         [3]    $45
  OREGON [1872] 40.6x55.9cm.                                          [3]    $50
  TEXAS [1872] 57.2x40cm. 1st ed.                                    [19]   $120
```
ATLANTIC NEPTUNE
```
  See DES BARRES
```
ATWATER
```
  MAP OF THE STATE OF OHIO DRAWN BY A. BOURNE... [1820] 48.3x41.3cm. repairs to
     margins, 2 short tears into image, from Caleb Atwater, "Description of the
     Antiquities Discovered in the State of Ohio and Other Western States"
                                                                     [34]   $350
```
ATWOOD
```
  MASSACHUSETTS, RHODE ISLAND & CONNECTICUT [1873] 21.6x27.9cm.       [3]    $18
```
BACHIENE
```
  KAART VAN PERU MET EEN GEDEELTE... [1785] 33x21cm.                  [3]    $45
  NIEUWE EN ALGEMEENE VAN AMERICA [1783] 34.3x41.9cm. engraved by van Tagen,
     published by W.A. Bachiene in "Kuilenberg Atlas"                [16]   $200
```

BAEDEKER

ADIRONDACK MOUNTAINS [1893] 14.6x20cm.	[39]	$10
BOSTON [1893] 20x14.7cm.	[39]	$20
HALIFAX [1893] 20.1x14.7cm.	[39]	$30
MAP OF NEW BRUNSWICK, P.E.I. AND NOVA SCOTIA [1893] 14.6x27.2cm.	[39]	$20
MAP OF THE DOMINION OF CANADA BETWEEN THE BEAUFORT SEA AND THE SOUTHERN BORDER		
[1893] 14.7x29.7cm.	[39]	$25
MONTREAL [1893] 20x17.5cm.	[39]	$30
NEW ORLEANS [1893] 18.3x20.2cm.	[39]	$20
OTTAWA [1893] 14.7x20.2cm.	[39]	$30
PLAN OF MANHATTEN ISLAND (N.Y.) [1893] 14.7x49.4cm.	[39]	$40
QUEBEC [1893] 14.7x20.1cm.	[39]	$30
SAN FRANCISCO [1893] 19.5x24.5cm.	[39]	$30
ST. JOHN [1893] 9.8x14.7cm.	[39]	$25
TORONTO [1893] 14.7x20.2cm.	[39]	$30
WASHINGTON [1893] 23.5x27.4cm. Washington, D.C.	[39]	$25

BAILEY & HAZEN

BIRD'S EYE VIEW OF HOLYOKE, MASS. 1816 [1876] 61x86.4cm. 3 short tears
repaired, drawn & published by H.H. Bailey and J.C. Hazen, N.Y., lithographed
by G.H. Vogt, Milwaukee & printed by J. Knauber & Co. [36] $550

BALDWIN

A MAP OF THE WESTERN PARTS OF THE COLONY OF VIRGINIA [1754] 19.7x12.1cm.
map accompanied extracts from Geo. Washington's journal, minor repairs
[3] $185
A PLAN OF THE FORT AND BAY OF FRONTENAC WITH THE ADJACENT COUNTRY [1758]
10.8x17.8cm. [3] $85
PLAN OF A SURVEY FOR A RAIL-ROAD...NO.2 FROM SPRINGFIELD TO ALBANY; 1827 &
1828 [C1828] 19.7x74.9cm. thin paper, two sheets joined [22] $85
PLAN OF THE FORTS ONTARIO AND OSWEGO, WITH PART OF THE RIVER & LAKE ONTARIO
[1757] 19.1x10.2cm. a key at right [3] $60
PLAN OF THE TOWN AND FORTIFICATIONS OF MONTREAL OR VILLE MARIE IN CANADA
[1870] 17.8x24.8cm. [3] $125

BALDWIN & CRADOCK

EMPIRE OF JAPAN [1835] 39.4x31.8cm. backed [3] $75
MAP OF A PORTION OF CHILE WITH THE INTERMEDIATE MOUNTAIN RANGES AND PASSES OVER
THE CORDILLERA BETWEEN VALPARAISO & MENDOSA [1826] 25.4x43.2cm.
minor repairs [3] $55
NORTH AMERICA, THE NORTHWEST AND MICHIGAN TERRITORIES [1833] 32.4x38.7cm.
backed [3] $45
NORTH AMERICA. NEW YORK, VERMONT, MAINE... [1832] 35.6x30.5cm. 1st ed.
[3] $25
PARTS OF MISSOURI, ILLINOIS & INDIANA [1833] 32.4x36.8cm. [3] $30
PARTS OF MISSOURI...TENNESSEE, ALABAMA, MISSISSIPPI & ARKANSAS [1833]
33x39.4cm. backed [3] $30
PENNSYLVANIA, NEW JERSEY, MARYLAND, DELAWARE... [1833] 38.1x30.5cm. [3] $30

BANKES

NORTH AMERICA [C1785] 26x43.5cm. [4] $114
THE WEST INDIES... [C1787] 19.1x27.9cm.
notes for each island "according to the Treaty of Peace 1783" [23] $60

BARCLAY

BELIZE VIEW TAKEN FROM THE HARBOUR [1880] 14x19.1cm. [3] $20

BARNES & BURR

CHART OF THE HIGHLANDS & LOWLANDS OF THE WORLD/PRINCIPAL VOLCALOES & ISOTHERMAL
LINES [1854] 21.6x27.9cm. [3] $20
GEORGIA, FLORIDA & ALABAMA [1854] 27.3x21.6cm. [3] $20
MAINE, NEW HAMPSHIRE, VERMONT [1854] 22.9x27.9cm. [3] $18
MASSACHUSETTS, CONNECTUCUT & RHODE ISLAND [1854] 21.6x27.9cm.
inset of Boston [3] $18
MISSISSIPPI LOUISIANA & ARKANSAS [1854] 27.3x21cm. [3] $20
NEW YORK [1854] 20.3x27.9cm. [3] $18
SOUTH AMERICA [1854] 27.9x21cm. [3] $20

BARNES & BURR (continued)
WESTERN HEMISPHERE/EASTERN HEMISPHERE [1854] 27.9x45.1cm. on 2 sheets
                                                                    [3] $25
BARROW
A SKETCH BY COMPASS OF THE COAST OF THE PROMONTORY OF SHAN-TUNG WITH THE TRACK
   OF THE SHIPS... [1793] 68.6x49.5cm.   [3] $55
GENERAL CHART...TO SHEW THE TRACK...TO THE GULPH OF PEKIN IN CHINA 1796 [1797]
   55.9x92.7cm.   [30] $223
BARTHOLOMEW
ARCTIC REGIONS AND BRITISH AMERICA CONTAINING ALL DISCOVERIES IN ARCTIC SEAS UP
   TO 1853 [1853] 41.9x55.9cm.   [3] $65
CANADA, NEW BRUNSWICK, NOVA SCOTIA, CAPE BRETON ISLAND, PRINCE EDWARD ISLAND &
   NEWFOUNDLAND [1864] 62.2x53.3cm.   [3] $35
CANADA-WEST SHEET [1864] 62.2x53.3cm.   [3] $35
DOMINION OF CANADA [C1870] 23x30cm.   [21] $7
DOMINION OF CANADA//DOMINION OF CANADA (EASTERN PROVINCES) & NEWFOUNDLAND
   [C1877] 20x28cm.   [21] $7
NORTH & SOUTH WALES [1853] 58.4x41.9cm.   [11] $30
THE CONFEDERATE STATES... [1864] 50.8x61cm.   [20] $250
THE PACIFIC STATES, THE TERRITORIES... [1864] 50.8x61cm.   [20] $100
BARTLETT
HARPERS FERRY FROM THE BLUE RIDGE (VIEW) [1839] 16.5x18.4cm.   [3] $25
WILKESBARRE, VALE OF WYOMING (VIEW) [1838] 16.5x17.8cm.   [3] $20
BASIRE
PLAN OF THE TOWN AND FORTIFICATIONS OF GIBRALTER, EXACTLY TAKEN ON THE SPOT IN
   THE YEAR 1738... [1744-47] 36.8x58.4cm.   [24] $91
BAUMGARTEN
AMERICA DAS MITTERNACHTIGE [C1750] 32.4x41.9cm.   [19] $275
AMERICA DAS MITTERNACHTIGE NACH DER ZEICHNUNG DES HERRN WILHELM DELISLE IN
   VERLAG JOH. JUSTIN GEBANUS [C1753] 31.8x41.3cm. 4 folds   [8] $250
DIE INSEL HISPANIOLA, ODER SAN DOMINGO [1753] 21.6x29.2cm.
   based on a 1731 d'Anville map   [23] $50
DIE INSEL HISPANIOLA, VON DEN INDIANERN GENANT HAYTI [1753] 19.7x29.2cm.
   based on a 1731 d'Anville map   [23] $50
GEGEND UM DIE MEXICANISCHE SEE/DIE PROVINZEN MEXICO, PANUCO, UND TLASCALA
   [1753] 24.1x36.2cm. thin spot   [22] $75
BEAUTEMPS-BEAUPRE
CARTE GENERALE DE LA NOUVELLE HOLLANDE ET DES ARCHIPELS DE GRAND OCEAN [1807]
   49.5x75.5cm.   [4] $490
BELDIN
DOMINION OF CANADA. DISTRICTS OF ALGOMA, PARRY SOUND, ALSO PART NIPISSING
   DISTRICT AND RENFREW CO. [C1874] 40.6x61cm. by H. Beldin or H. Belden
                                                                    [3] $45
MAP OF PART OF THE NORTH WEST TERRITORY INCLUDING THE PROVINCE OF MANITOBA
   SHOWING ROUTE OF CANADA PACIFIC RAILWAY [C1874] 40.6x63.5cm.   [3] $65
BELL
See also SCOT'S MAGAZINE
CAMBRIDGESHIRE [1833-36] C24.1x19.1cm. from James Bell, "A New and
   Comprehensive Gazetteer of England and Wales;" many maps from this atlas have
   small decorative vignettes   [13] $24
DERBYSHIRE [1833-36] C24.1x19.1cm.   [13] $22
ESSEX [1833-36] C24.1x19.1cm.   [13] $22
HERTFORDSHIRE [1833-36] C24.1x19.1cm.   [13] $27
LEICESTERSHIRE [1833-36] C24.1x19.1cm.   [13] $22
NORFOLK [1833-36] C24.1x19.1cm.   [13] $27
OXFORDSHIRE [1833-36] C24.1x19.1cm.   [13] $24
SUFFOLK [1833-36] C24.1x19.1cm.   [13] $24
SUSSEX [1833-36] C24.1x19.1cm.   [13] $27
UNITED STATES OF AMERICA [1814] 23.5x18.4cm.   [3] $35
WORCESTERSHIRE [1833-36] C24.1x19.1cm.   [13] $24

BELLIN

See also DEPOT DE LA MARINE

AMERIQUE SEPTENTRIONALE [C1745] 22.2x29.2cm.	[23]	$85
CAPE BRETON [1744] 21x26.7cm. from Charlevoix's History	[30]	$81
CARTA DEL GOLFO DI S. LORENZO [1763-91] 22.2x35.6cm. from the Spanish ed.	[30]	$121
CARTE D'UNE PARTIE DE L'AMERIQUE SEPTENTRIONALE [1755-57] 34.6x45.4cm. tears in margins repaired, right margin narrow	[23]	$150
CARTE DE COURS DE RIVIERE DE SAGUEWAY [1744] 19.7x28.6cm.	[30]	$40
CARTE DE L'ACADIE ISLE ROYALE [1757-80] 21.6x33cm.	[30]	$130
CARTE DE L'AMERIQUE ET DES MERS VOISINES 1763 [1764] 45.7x30.5cm. one margin restored	[3]	$160
CARTE DE L'AMERIQUE SEPTENTRIONALE... [1743-44] 27.9x35.6cm. folding map, dated 1743 but published in 1744 in Pierre Charlevoix, "Histoire et Description Generale de la Nouvelle France..." 12mo. edition	[27]	$275
CARTE DE L'ENTREE DE LA RIVIERE DE CANTON [1757] 22.5x21cm.	[31]	$61
CARTE DE L'ENTREE DE LA RIVIERE DE KOUROU [1762] 21.6x16.5cm.	[3]	$30
CARTE DE L'ENTREE DU GOLPHE DU CHILOS ET DU PORT DE CACHAO AU CHILI [1764] 21.6x16.5cm.	[3]	$30
CARTE DE L'ISLE DE JAMAIQUE...1758 [1758] 21x31.5cm.	[31]	$84
CARTE DE L'ISLE DE LA BARBADE [C1758] 55x40cm.	[12]	$145
CARTE DE L'ISLE DE LA BARBADE [1764] 20.3x15.2cm.	[3]	$75
CARTE DE L'ISLE DE LA BARBADE POUR SERVIR A L'HISTOIRE GENERAL DES VOYAGES [1754] 20.3x15.2cm.	[3]	$65
CARTE DE L'ISLE DE SAINTE CROIX AU SUD DES ISLES VIERGES/CARTE DE L'ISLE DE SAINT JEAN DE PORTORICO [1764] 22.2x17.1cm.	[3]	$85
CARTE DE L'ISLE DE SAINTE LUCIE. DRESSEE AU DEPOST DES CARTES ET PLANS DE LA MARINE POUR LE SERVICE DES VASSEAUX DE ROY...PAR LE SR. BELLIN INGENIEUR DE LA MARINE 1763. P.A. RAMEAU, FECIT 1763 [1763] 87.6x55.9cm. tear at lower center repaired	[25]	$229
CARTE DE L'ISLE DE TERRE-NEUVE [1744] 28.6x36.2cm.	[30]	$130
CARTE DE L'ISLE ST. PIERRE [1764] 21.6x15.9cm.	[3]	$45
CARTE DE L'ISLE ST. THOMAS E UNE DES VIERGES [1764] 22.9x35.6cm.	[3]	$145
CARTE DE L'ISTHME DE PANAMA ET DES PROVINCES DE VERAGUA, TERRE FERME ET DARIEN [1754] 20.3x29.2cm.	[3]	$65
CARTE DE LA BAYE DE HUDSON [1757] 22.5x30.5cm.	[4]	$61
CARTE DE LA BAYE DE HUDSON PAR N. BELLIN... [1774] 21.6x29.2cm.	[3]	$125
CARTE DE LA BAYE DE PANAMA DANS L'AMERIQUE MERIDIONALE [1764] 21.6x17.1cm.	[3]	$65
CARTE DE LA CAROLINE ET GEORGIE [1746-61] 18.7x28.6cm. from "Histoire Generale des Voiages," 1757	[1]	$150
CARTE DE LA FLORIDE DE LA LOUISIANE [1757] 22.2x30.5cm.	[32]	$125
CARTE DE LA FLORIDE, DE LA LOUISIANE ET PAYS VOISINS. POUR SERVIR A L'HISTOIRE GENERALE DES VOYAGES. PAR M.B. ING. DE LA MARINE 1757 [1757] 22.2x30.5cm.	[25]	$130
CARTE DE LA FLORIDE, DE LA LOUISIANE, ET PAYS VOISINS POUR SERVIR A L'HISTOIRE GENERALE DES VOYAGES [1757] 22.9x30.5cm.	[3]	$125
CARTE DE LA FLORIDE, DE LA LOUISIANE... [1757] 21.6x30.5cm.	[19]	$225
CARTE DE LA GUYANE FRANCOISE ET L'ISLE DE CAYENNE FRANCOISE ET L'ISLE DE CAYENNE...PAR LE S. BELLIN...1763 [1763] 58.1x40.6cm.	[25]	$61
CARTE DE LA PARTIE ORIENTALE DE LA NOUVELLE FRANCE OU DU CANADA DEDIEE A MONSEIGNEUR LE COMTE DE MAREPAS MINISTRE ET SECRETAIRE D'ETAT, COMMANDEUR DES ORDES DU ROY. PAR N. BELLIN INGENIEUR DE LA MARINE 1744 [1744] 40x55.9cm. tear to fold repaired, margins narrow	[7]	$560
CARTE DE LA RIVIERE DE RICHELIEU ET DU LAC CHAMPLAIN [1744] 30.5x13.7cm. minor offsetting	[23]	$50
CARTE DE LA VIRGINIE, DE LA BAYE CHESAPEACK, ET PAYS VOISINS [C1765] 19.1x29.2cm.	[16]	$110
CARTE DES BAYES RADES ET PORTE DE PLAISANCE [1744] 19.7x28.6cm.	[30]	$60
CARTE DES COSTES DE LA FLORIDE FRANCOISE [1744] 20.3x14cm. 2 narrow margins	[23]	$75

CARTE DES COSTES DE LA FLORIDE FRANCOISE [1754] 20.6x14.4cm.
  narrow margins   [39] $45
CARTE DES ENVIRONS DE LA VILLE DE MEXIQUE POUR L'HISTOIRE GENERALE DES VOYAGES
  1754 [1754] 20.3x15.9cm. 1st ed.   [3] $60
CARTE DES ISLES BERMUDES OU DE SOMMER TIRE DE L'ANGLOIS [1763] 20.3x33cm.
                                                        [17] $300
CARTE DES ISLES CANARIES [1746-73] 21x27.9cm.
  additional title in Dutch   [24] $42
CARTE DES ISLES DE JAVA, SUMATRA, BORNEO &C [C1750] 25.5x29cm.   [4] $76
CARTE DES ISLES DE SAINT PIERRE ET MIQUELON LEVEE PAR ORDRE DE M. LE DUC DE
  CHOISEUL...1763...PAR LE SR. BELLIN... [1763] 58.4x88.9cm. minor
  offsetting, with Depot de la Marine insignia, priced at 30 sols, plate no.
  61   [7] $400
CARTE DES ISLES DU JAPON [C1760] 21.5x29cm.   [4] $114
CARTE DES LACS DU CANADA [C1757] 19.7x29.2cm.   [32] $185
CARTE DES PROVINCES DE TABASCO, CHIAPA, VERAPAZ, GUATIMALA...ET YUCATAN [1764]
  21x34.3cm.   [3] $60
CARTE DU COMTE DE KENT ET DU PAS DE CALAIS... [1759] 57.2x85.1cm. later issue
  with Depot de la Marine stamp with "R.F" on both sides of anchor, vertical
  fold   [24] $183
CARTE DU COURS DU FLEUVE DE SAINT LAURENT DEPUIS LA MER JUSQU'A QUEBEC EN DEUX
  FEUILLES DRESSEE AU DEPOST DES CARTES ET PLANS DE LA MARINE...PAR ORDRE DE M.
  BERRYER...1761 [1761] 60.3x86.4cm. covers the gulf and Anticosti Island,
  plate number 64, Depot de la Marine insignia, priced at 30 sols, with 4 inset
  maps   [7] $425
CARTE DU COURS DU FLEUVE DE SAINT LAURENT DEPUIS QUEBEC JUSQU A LA MER EN DEUX
  FEUILLES DRESSEE AU DEPOT DES CARTES ET PLANS...PAR LE S. BELLIN...1ST
  FEUILLE DEPUIS QUEBEC JUSQU'A MATANE ET RIVIERE DES OUTARDES 1761 [1761]
  60.3x89.5cm.
  plate number 63, Depot de la Marine insignia, and priced at 30 sols[7] $425
CARTE DU COURS DU FLEUVE ST. LAURENT [1757] 19.1x29.8cm.   [32] $85
CARTE DU FONDS DE LA BAYE DE HUDSON QUE LES ANGLOIS APPELLENT BAYE JAMES
  [1744] 20.3x14cm.   [3] $85
CARTE DU GOLPHE DE ST LAURENT [1748] 14x22cm.   [31] $76
CARTE DU GOLPHE DU MEXIQUE ET DES ISLES DE L'AMERIQUE [1754] 27.9x37.5cm.
                                                      [3] $95
CARTE DU KATAY OU EMPIRE DE KIN, POUR SERVIR A L'HISTOIRE DE JENGHIZ KHAN...
  [1749] 20.3x31.8cm.   [3] $55
CARTE HYDROGRAPHIQUE DE LA BAYE DE LA HAVANE AVEC LE PLAN DE LA VILLE ET DE SES
  FORTS POUR JOINDRE A LA CARTE DE L'ISLE DE CUBE. 1762. PAR LE S. BELLIN...
  [1762] 56.5x40cm.   [25] $99
CARTE REDUITE DE GRAND BANC ET D'UNE PARTIE DE L'ISLE DE TERRE NEUVE DRESSEE AU
  DEPOT DES CARTES PLANS ET JOURNAUX DE LA MARINE...PAR ORDRE DE M. LE DUC DE
  CHOISEUL...PAR LE S. BELLIN...M.DCCLXIV [1764] 56.5x81.9cm.
  plate no. 60, without insignia of Depot de la Marine or price   [7] $350
CARTE REDUITE DE L'ISLE DE SAINT DOMINGUE... [1754] 55.7x89cm.   [39] $190
CARTE REDUITE DE L'OCEAN SEPTENTRIONALE COMPRIS ENTRE L'ASIE ET L'AMERIQUE
  [1766] 55.9x85.7cm. margins somewhat ragged   [23] $750
CARTE REDUITE DE LA PARTIE LA PLUS MERIDIONALE D'AMERIQUE [1764] 21.6x16.5cm.
                                                  [3] $55
CARTE REDUITE DE LA PARTIE SEPTENTRIONAL DE L'ISLE DE TERRE NEUVE DRESSE AU
  DEPOST DES CARTES ET PLANS DE LA MARINE PAR ORDER DE M LE DUC DE
  CHOISEUL...PAR LE S. BELLIN INGENIEUR DE LA MARINE M.DCC.LXIV [1767]
  61.6x80cm. crease at lower edge, plate 59, "Corrigee en 1767, sur les Rems.
  des Navig."   [7] $425
CARTE REDUITE DES COSTES DE LA LOUISIANE, ET DE LA FLORIDE [C1764-95]
  56.5x85.1cm.   [32] $900
CARTE REDUITE DES COSTES ORIENTALES DE L'AMERIQUE SEPTENTRIONALE [1757]
  54.5x87.5cm.   [4] $643
CARTE REDUITE DES DESTROITS DE MALACCA, SINCAPOUR... [1764] 55x90cm. [31] $436

BELLIN (continued)

CARTE REDUITE DES ISLES ANTILLES...POUR SERVICE DES VAISSEAUX DU ROI [1758]
  87.6x56.5cm. minor repairs, inset of Virgin Islands   [3] $245
CARTE REDUITE DES ISLES BRITANNIQUES EN CINQ FEUILLES...PREMIERE FEUILLE
  [C1757-90] 55.9x61.6cm.   [13] $206
CARTE REDUITE DU GLOBE TERRESTRE [1764] 22.2x34.3cm.   [3] $95
CARTE REDUITE DU GOLPHE DU MEXIQUE ET DES ISLES DE L'AMERIQUE [1774]
  52.1x78.7cm. 2 vertical folds   [22] $700
CARTES DES ISLES PHILIPPINES CELEBRES ET MOLUQUES [1748] 15x23cm.   [31] $45
COURS DU FLEUVE SAINT LOUIS DEPUIS SES EMBOUCHURES JUSQUA LA RIVIERE
  D'IBERVILLE ET COSTES VOISINES [1764] 21.6x35.6cm.   [22] $150
FERNERE LAUF DES FLUSSES ST. LAURENTZ VON QUEBEC BIS AN SEE ONTRAIO [1757]
  18.4x28.6cm.   [3] $110
GRANDE OCEANO OUVERO QUINTA PARTE DE MONDE [1780] 20x25cm.   [31] $45
GRUNDRISS VON DER STADT BOSTON [1757] 16.5x16.5cm.
  also includes a key to features   [32] $125
GUYANE PORTUGAISE ET PARTIE DU COURS DE LA RIVIERE DES AMAZONES [1764]
  21.6x45.7cm.   [3] $40
INDIE OCCIDENTALI [1780] 18x30.5cm. the Italian ed.   [31] $27
INS KLEINE GEBRACHTE KARTE VON DEM MITTNAEGTIGHEN MEERE [1753] 20.2x35.5cm.
  from the German edition of Bellin, 1747-68, shows the Pacific   [13] $137
KARTE VON DEM LAUFE DES FLUSSES ST. LAURENS... [1757] 19.1x30.5cm.   [3] $95
KARTE VON DEN KUSTEN DES FRANZOSISCHEN FLORIDA [1744-56] 20.3x14cm.   [22] $85
KARTE VON DEN SEEN IN CANADA [C1757] 19.1x28.6cm.   [32] $175
KARTE VON DER INSEL BARBADE ZUR ALLGEMEINEN GESCHICHTE DER REISEN [C1758-74]
  14.6x19.7cm.   [25] $76
KARTE VON DER INSEL MONTREAL UND DEN GEGENDEN UMBER...1760 [1776] 22.9x27.9cm.
  fold repaired, inset of walled city of Montreal   [3] $145
KARTE VON NEU ENGLAND [1757] 20.3x29.2cm.   [32] $115
LE PORT AU PRINCE DANS L'ISLE DE ST. DOMINGUE [1764] 22.2x17.1cm.   [3] $55
LES PETITES ANTILLES OU LES ISLES DU VENT [1764] 23.5x16.5cm.   [3] $65
MERS DU NORD [1758] 33x44.5cm. folding, left margin narrow, repaired [23] $60
PARTIE DES ISLES ANTILLES, I PARTIE [1764] 22.9x15.9cm.   [3] $60
PARTIE DU FLEUVE ST. LAURENT AVEC LE PASSAGE DE LA TRAVERSE ET LES ISLE
  VOISINES [1764] 24.1x30.5cm.   [3] $85
PARTIE OCCIDENTALE DE LA NOUVELLE FRANCE [1755] 42.5x54cm.   [32] $1150
PARTIE OCCIDENTALE DE LA NOUVELLE FRANCE OU CANADA [1755] 47x61cm. major
  differences from his 1745 map of the same title, Fts. Detroit & Chartres
  added & geographical changes made   [16] $820
PARTIE OCCIDENTALE DE LA NOUVELLE FRANCE OU CANADA [1755] 47x60.3cm. [15] $1400
PARTIE ORIENTALE DE LA NOUVELLE FRANCE OU DU CANADA [1745] 47x62.2cm.
    [15] $800
PARTIE ORIENTALE DE LA NOUVELLE FRANCE OU DU CANADA. PAR. MR. BELLIN INGENIEUR
  DU ROY ET DE LA MARINE 1755 [1755] 49.5x60.3cm. one crease   [7] $875
PINCO OU PORT DE LA CONCEPTION AU CHILI [1764] 21.6x17.8cm.   [3] $35
PLAN DE L'ISLE VACHE A LA COSTE DU SUD DE S. DOMINGUE [1764] 21.6x16.5cm.
    [3] $35
PLAN DE LA RADE ET VILLE DU PETIT GOUAVE [1764] 22.9x30.5cm.   [3] $35
PLAN DE LA VILLE DE CAYENNE [1764] 22.2x15.9cm.   [3] $30
PLAN DE LA VILLE DE PARAMARIBO SUIVANT LES PLANS HOLLANDOIS [1764]
  22.2x15.2cm.   [3] $35
PLAN DE LA VILLE ET DU PORT DE MACAO [1757] 22.5x18cm.   [31] $53
PLAN DU PORT DAUPHIN [1744] 20.3x28.6cm.   [30] $60
PLAN DU PORT DE LA HAIVE [1744] 20.3x28.6cm. on the Nova Scotia coast
    [30] $60
PLAN DU PORT ET VILLE DE LOUISBOURG [1744] 20.3x27.9cm.   [30] $81
PLAN DU PORT ROYAL [1744] 22.9x27.9cm.   [30] $60
PLAN...DE LA HAVRE DE MILFORT [1744] 20.3x27.9cm.   [30] $60
SUITE DES ISLES ANTILLAS 2 PARTIE [1764] 22.2x17.1cm.   [3] $55
SUITE DU COURS DU FLEUVE DE ST. LAURENT [1757] 19.1x27.9cm.   [32] $95
SUITE DU COURS DU FLEUVE DE ST. LAURENT [1757] 19x28.5cm.   [5] $80

BELLIN (continued)
SUITE DU COURS DU FLEUVE ST. LOUIS DEPUIS LA RIVIERE D'IBERVILLE... [1764]
   21.6x34.3cm.   [22] $160
VILLE DE BUENOS AYRES [1764] 20.3x16.5cm.   [3] $45
BERNARD
L'ILE DE TERRE NEUVE ET LE GOLFE DE SAINT LAURENT SELON LES MEILLEURS MEMOIRES
   [1715] 21x31.8cm.   [3] $185
BERRY
A MAPP OF ALL THE WORLD [1680] 57.2x87.6cm.
   minor rubbing, lower centerfold   [15] $1875
NORTH AMERICA DIVIDED INTO ITS PRINCIPAL PARTS... [1680] 57.2x87.6cm.
                                              [15] $2800
BERTELLI
GALLIAE BELGICHAE ROMAE MDLXIIIII FERANDO BERTELI EXCUDEBAT [1565]
   34.9x47.4cm.   [18] $1404
TOTIUS GRAECIA DESCRIPTIO [1564] 18x51cm.   [31] $1494
BERTIUS
ARACHAN & PEGU [1616] 8.9x12.5cm.   [11] $35
CONGO, REGNUM CHRISTIAN IN AFRICA [1618] 10.2x12.7cm.   [10] $40
FRANCIAE COMITATUS [1616] 10.2x13.3cm.   [9] $40
GROENLAND [1626] 9.5x13cm.   [31] $73
ISLANDIA [1626] 9x13cm. small holes   [31] $61
NOVA GUINEA ET INS SALOMONIS [1626] 9x13cm.   [31] $61
PERU [1616] 8.9x12.7cm.   [9] $45
TRANSSILVANIA [1618] 8.9x13.3cm.   [9] $40
TYPUS ORBIS TERRARUM [1620] 9.5x13.3cm.   [22] $250
BICKHAM
A CHART OF THE SEA COAST [1748] 22.2x14cm.
   from "The British Monarchy..."   [12] $130
IRELAND, DIVIDED INTO THE PROVINCES AND COUNTIES [1748] 24.1x14cm.
   from "The British Monarchy..."   [12] $42
BIEN
TERRITORY OF NEW MEXICO [1879] 74.3x61.6cm.
   black & orange, mounted on cloth   [23] $180
BLACK
ARCTIC REGIONS AND BRITISH AMERICA. CONTAINING ALL THE DISCOVERIES IN THE
   ARCTIC SEAS UP TO 1853 [1856] 42x56cm.   [21] $56
CANADA, NEW BRUNSWICK ETC. [1844] 26x37cm.   [21] $32
CANADA, NEW BRUNSWICK, ETC. [C1849-55] 25.2x37.5cm.   [21] $20
EASTERN UNITED STATES [C1860] C26x37cm.   [21] $9
MEXICO, CALIFORNIA & TEXAS [1854] 25.4x36.8cm.
   yellow color denotes gold region in California   [27] $85
MEXICO, CALIFORNIA & TEXAS [C1860] 26x37cm. light staining along fold
                                              [21] $9
MOUNTAINS & RIVERS [C1853] 26x37cm.   [21] $13
POLAR REGIONS [C1859] 20x20cm.
   light foxing, 2 hemispheres, dimensions are for each   [21] $16
TEXAS, PART OF NEW MEXICO &C. [1856] 27.9x36.8cm.   [27] $85
TEXAS, PART OF NEW MEXICO &C. [1876] 27.9x36.8cm. plate numbered "44F"
                                            [27] $75
TEXAS, PART OF NEW MEXICO &C. [1873] 27.9x36.8cm.   [27] $75
UNITED STATES, SOUTHERN PART. [C1860] C26x37cm.   [21] $9
WEST INDIES [C1860] C26x37cm.   [21] $8
WEST INDIES. ENGRAVED BY S. HALL, BURY STRT. BLOOMSBURY. EDINBURGH PUBLISHED BY
   A. & C. BLACK [1854] 38.1x26cm. inset map of Jamaica   [25] $38
BLACKIE & SON
CANADA WEST, AND PART OF CANADA EAST [C1860] 35x50cm.   [21] $36
NEW BRUNSWICK, NOVA SCOTIA, PRINCE EDWARD ISLAND, AND PART OF CANADA EAST
   [C1860] 35x50cm.   [21] $40
THE UNITED STATES OF NORTH AMERICA [C1856] 34.3x50.2cm.   [22] $100

BLAEU

(FINLAND) [1662] 43.2x52.7cm. full title not given   [17] $650

AETHIOPIA INFERIOR... [1635] 38.1x49.5cm.   [17] $500

AETHIOPIA SUPERIOR VEL INTERIOR; VULGO ABISSINORUM SIVE PRESBITERI IOANNIS
    IMPERIUM [1638] 38.7x50.8cm. short tear in lower margin   [7] $425

AMERICAE NOVA TABULA [1650] 40.6x55.9cm. somewhat browned   [16] $1500

AMERICAE NOVA TABULA [1630] 40.6x55.2cm.   [17] $3600

AMERICAE NOVA TABULA [C1630] 40.6x54.6cm.   [15] $2700

AMERICAE NOVA TABULA [1640] 41x55.6cm. centerfold repaired in margin [35] $3200

AMERICAE NOVA TABULA [1630] 41.5x56cm.
    some staining, mostly in lower margin   [2] $1492

AMERICAE NOVA TABULA AUCT. GUILJELMO BLAEUW [1640] 41.3x55.9cm.
    centerfold tear repaired   [7] $2600

ASIA NOVITER DELINEATA [1630] 40.6x55.9cm.   [17] $2000

BERGARUM AD ZONAM [1649] C40x50cm.   [18] $140

BRABANTIA DUCATUS [1649] C40x50cm.   [18] $210

BRASILIA GENERIS NOBILITATE ARMORUM ET LITTERARUM SCIENTIA... [C1642]
    38.1x49.5cm.   [3] $400

BRITANNIA...ANGLO-SAXONIUM...HEPTARCHIA [1645] 42x53cm.
    light browning, backed with thin paper   [2] $779

BRUXELLA [C1640] 46x57cm.   [18] $351

BURGUNDIA... [1662] 43.2x57.2cm.   [17] $450

CANIBALES INSULAE [1662] 41.5x53.1cm.   [39] $275

CASTELLI AT SANTFLITAM [1649] C40x50cm.   [18] $175

CHAMPAGNE LATINE CAMPANIA, COMITATUS [C1650] 38.1x50.2cm.   [24] $88

CHINA VETERIBUS SINARUM REGIO NUNC INCOLIS TAME DICTA [1635] 40.6x49.5cm.
        [17] $650

COMITATUM HANNONIAE ET NAMURCI DESCRIPTIO [C1640] 38x50cm.   [18] $140

COMITATUS DORCESTRIA, SIVE DORSETTIA; VULGO ANGLICE DORSET SHIRE [1645-90]
    38.1x50.2cm. narrow margins, J. Overton issue of c1690   [24] $360

DELFLANDIA-SCHIELANDIA [1649] C40x50cm.   [18] $263

DRENTIA [1649] C40x50cm.   [18] $263

DUCATUS EBORACENSIS PARS ORIENTALIS; THE EASTRIDING OF YORKESHIRE [1645]
    38.1x48.3cm.   [13] $291

DUCATUS UPLANDIA [1638] 37.5x49.5cm.   [17] $650

EXTREMA AMERICAE VERSUS BOREAM, UBI TERRA NOVA NOVA FRANCIA, ADJACENTIAQ.
    [1662] 44.7x56.6cm.   [39] $875

FEZZAE ET MAROCCHI REGNA AFRICAE CELEBERRIMA, DESCRIBEBAT ABRAH. ORTELIUS
    [1638] 38.7x50.2cm.   [7] $400

FLANDRIA ET ZEELANDIA COMITATUS [C1640] 41.5x53cm.   [18] $175

FLANDRIAE PARTES DUAE [C1640] 41.5x52cm.   [18] $175

FLANDRIAE TEUTONICAE PARS ORIENTALIOR [C1640] 38x50cm.   [18] $140

FRISIA OCCIENTALIS [1649] C40x50cm.   [18] $351

GALLOFLANDRIA...AUCTORE MARTINO DOUE GALLO-FLANDRO [C1650] 38x50.5cm.
        [18] $263

GELDRIA ET ZUTPHANIA [1649] C40x50cm.   [18] $263

GERMANIA VULGO TEUTSCHLANDT [C1660] 49x56.5cm.   [4] $337

GRAECIA [1640-62] 40.6x52.1cm.   [24] $268

GROLLA OBSESSA ET EXPUGNATA... [C1640] 38x50cm.   [18] $263

GRONINGA DOMINIUM [1649] C40x50cm.   [18] $351

GUIANA SIVE AMAZONUM REGIO [1635-47] 37.5x49.5cm. repaired in margin [5] $200

GUILELMI ET JOANNIS BLAEU THEATRUM ORBIS TERRARUM SIVE ATLAS NOVUS PARS
    SECUNDUS (TITLE PAGE) [1640] 38.1x24.1cm.   [3] $95

GUINEA [1635] 38.1x50.8cm.   [17] $550

HIBERNIA REGNUM VULGO IRELAND [1635] 38.1x50.2cm.   [17] $550

HIBERNIA REGNUM VULGO IRELAND [C1660] 38.5x50cm. several minor stains
        [4] $337

HOLLANDIA COMITATUS [1649] C40x50cm.   [18] $351

HOLLANDIAE PART SEPTENTRIONALE [C1631] 38.1x49.5cm.
    deacidified, worm holes repaired   [30] $264

INSULA GADITANA... [1662] 38.1x50.2cm.   [17] $450

66

BLAEU (continued)

INSULAE ALBION ET HIBERNIA [C1654] 38x45cm.	[4]	$214
INSULAE AMERICANAE [C1660] 38x52.5cm.	[4]	$643
INSULAE AMERICANAE IN OCEANO SEPTENTRIONALI... [C1635] 38.1x52.7cm.	[22]	$750
INSULAE CANARIAE ALIAS FORTUNATAE DICTAE [1662] 38.5x50cm.	[2]	$298
JAPONIA REGNUM [1655] 41.9x57.2cm.	[15]	$885
KREMLENAGRAD... [1662] 37.5x48.9cm.	[17]	$850
LA PRINCIPAUTE D'ORANGE ET COMTAT DE VENAISSIN, PAR IAQUES DE CHIEZE ORANGEOIS.		
1627. EXCUDIT GUILJELMUS IANSSONIUS COESIUS [C1638-40] 38.1x50.2cm.		
tear in margin at centerfold repaired	[7]	$175
LACUS LEMANNI... [1635] 40.6x52.1cm. shows Lake Geneva	[17]	$850
LE GOUVERNEMENT DE L'ISLE DE FRANCE [1635] 40.6x52.1cm.	[17]	$350
LEODIENSIS DIOECESIS [C1640] 38x50cm.	[18]	$175
LIMBURGUM [1649] C40x50cm.	[18]	$210
LUTZENBURG DUCATUS [1640] 38x50cm. minor staining in margin, some wear		
	[2]	$263
LUTZENBURGUM [1649] 38.8x50cm.	[18]	$614
MAGNAE BRITANNIAE ET HIBERNIAE TABULA [1632] 38x50cm.	[31]	$536
MAGNAE BRITANNIAE ET HIBERNIAE TABULA [1648] 38.7x50.2cm.	[14]	$298
MAGNI DUCATUS LITHUANIAE...EXACTA DESCRIPTIO [1613] 75x73cm. worn, repairs at		
folds, first published by Hessel Gerritsz, and used by Blaeu in his		
"Appendix" of 1630	[2]	$245
MAPPA AESTIVARIUM INSULARUM, ALIAS BARMUDAS DICTARUM...ACCURATE DISCRIPTA.		
AMSTELODAMI GUILJELM BLAEUW, EXCUDIT [1630-63] 40.6x53.3cm.	[25]	$758
MAPPA AESTIVARUM INSULARUM ALIAS BARMUDAS... [1642] 40x53cm.	[31]	$574
MECHLINIA DOMINIUM, ET AERSCHOT DUCATUS [C1640] 41x52cm.	[18]	$140
MIDDLE-SEXIA [C1650] 39x41cm.	[4]	$398
MOMONIA, HIBERNICE MOUN ET WOUN; ANGLIC MOUNSTER [1654] 41.3x52.1cm.	[24]	$245
NAMURCUM COMITATUS, AUCTORE IOHANN SURHONIO [C1640] 41x51cm.	[18]	$140
NORVEGIA REGNUM VULGO NOR-RYKE [1662] 41.3x50.2cm.	[17]	$750
NOVA BELGICA ET ANGLIA NOVA [1635] 38.1x50.8cm.	[23]	$1100
NOVA BELGICA ET ANGLIA NOVA [C1650] 39.4x50.8cm.		
minor spotting, faint impression in places, some show-through of text		
	[16]	$1000
NOVA BELGICA ET ANGLIA NOVA [C1640] 38.7x50.2cm.	[32]	$1350
NOVA HISPANIA, ET NOVA GALICIA. GUILJELMUS BLAEUW EXCUDIT [C1635-40]		
38.4x50.2cm.	[25]	$398
NOVA TOTIUS TERRARUM ORBIS GEOGRAPHIA AC HYDROGRAPHICA TABULA [1630-35]		
40.6x54.6cm.	[15]	$4800
NOVA VIRGINIAE TABULA [1630-58] 37.5x47.9cm.	[33]	$1250
NOVA VIRGINIAE TABULA [1642] 37.5x48.3cm. one minor crease	[32]	$650
NOVUS XVII INFERIORIS GERMANIAE PROVINCIARUM TYPUS [C1640] 40x50.5cm.		
	[18]	$351
OVER-YSSEL [1649] C40x50cm.	[18]	$263
PALATIUM MANSFELDICUM, PROPE LUTZENBURGUM [1649] 42x52cm.	[18]	$526
PARS FLANDRIAE TEUTONICAE OCCIDENTALIOR [C1640] 39x50cm.	[18]	$140
PERU [C1660] 38x49cm.	[4]	$214
PLAN ET SIEGE DAMVILLERS, 1637 [C1640] 41.5x52cm.	[18]	$105
PRIMA PARS BRABANTIAE CUIUS CAPUT LOVANIUM AUCTORE MICHAELE FLORENTIO A		
LANGREN [C1640] 41x52cm.	[18]	$140
REGIONES SUB POLO ARCTICO [C1640] 41x53cm.	[5]	$600
REGIONES SUB POLO ARCTICO AUCTORE GUILJELMO BLAEU [C1663-67] 40.6x52.1cm.		
French text on verso	[7]	$950
RHENOLANDIAE ET AMSTELLANDIAE [1649] C40x50cm.	[18]	$263
SECUNDA PARS BRABANTIAE CUIUS URBS PRIMARIA BRUXELLAE [C1640] 41.5x52.5cm.		
	[18]	$175
SIEGE ET PRISE DE THIONVILLE, 1643 [C1645] 44x54cm.	[18]	$210
SYLVADUCUS [1649] C40x50cm.	[18]	$526
TABULA MAGELLANICA QUA TIERRA DEL FUEGO [1660] 41.3x53.3cm.		
left margin restored	[3]	$225
TERTIA PARS BRABANTIAE...MARCHIONATUS S.R.I. ANTVERPIA [C1640] 42x52.5cm.		
	[18]	$175

BLAEU (continued)

TRACTUS RHENI ET MOSAE [1649] C40x50cm.   [18] $263
ULTRAIECTUM DOMIN. [1649] C40x50cm.   [18] $263
VENEZUELA CUM PARTE AUSTRALI NOVAE ANDALUSIAE [1638] 37.5x48.3cm.   [3] $425
VENEZUELA CUM PARTE AUSTRALI NOVAE ANDALUSIAE [C1640] 48.3x37.5cm.   [25] $306
VIRGINIA PARTIS AUSTRALIS, ET FLORIDAE PARTIS ORIENTALIS... [C1640]
    38.1x50.8cm. light crease   [22] $700
VIRGINIA PARTIS AUSTRALIS, ET FLORIDAE PARTIS ORIENTALIS...NOVA DESCRIPTIO
    [1650] 38.7x50.2cm.   [3] $575
VIRGINIAE PARTIS AUSTRALIS, ET FLORIDAE PARTIS ORIENTALIS... [1650]
    38.1x50.8cm.   [16] $650
VIRGINIAE PARTIS AUSTRALIS, ET FLORIDAE... [1640] 40x38.4cm.   [26] $700
WALLIA PRINCIPATUS VULGO WALES [1645-62] 38.1x49.5cm.   [14] $298
WESTVRIESLAND [1649] C40x50cm.   [18] $351
YUCATAN... [1662] 41.9x52.7cm.   [17] $750
ZEELANDIA [1649] C40x50cm.   [18] $351
ZUYDHOLLANDIA [1649] C40x50cm.   [18] $263

BLANCHARD

CHICAGO IN 1812 [1850] 10.8x18.4cm. in Rufus Blanchard, "The discovery and
    conquest of the northwest," Chicago 1850   [3] $35

BLOME

A GENERALL MAPP OF THE COUNTY OF HEREFORD WITH ITS HUNDREDS... [1673]
    30.5x27.9cm.   [24] $76
A MAPP OF HANTSHIRE [1673] 30.5x25.4cm.   [24] $110
A MAPP OF HUNTINGDON SHIRE WITH ITS HUNDREDS... [1673] 31.8x25.4cm.   [24] $79
A MAPP OF ITALY... [1669-70] 29.8x39.4cm. plate signed by W. Hollar   [24] $122
A MAPP OF STAFFORD SHIRE WITH ITS HUNDREDS... [1673] 33x23.5cm.   [24] $79
A MAPP OF THE COUNTIES OF LEICESTER AND RUTLAND... [1756] 53.3x68.6cm.
                                                                            [24] $183
A MAPP OF THE COUNTY OF DARBYE WITH ITS HUNDREDS... [1673] 31.8x25.4cm.
                                                                            [24] $110
A MAPP OF THE COUNTY OF RUTLAND WITH ITS HUNDREDS [1673] 21.6x27.9cm.
                                                                            [24] $68
A MAPP OF WORCESTER SHIRE WITH ITS HUNDREDS... [1673] 26.7x32.4cm.   [24] $95
A MAPP OF YE COUNTY OF LINCOLNE, WTH ITS DIVISIONS & HUNDREDS: OR
    WAPONTACKS... [1673] 33x26.7cm. wormhole repaired   [24] $99
A NEW MAP OF AMERICA SEPTENTRIONALE... [C1673] 38.1x54.6cm. narrow margins,
    margins extended, arms of Jeffery Jefferys pasted over those of the Earl of
    Shaftesbury   [16] $1200

BLONDEAU

BASSE-LOUISIANE ET FLORIDE OCCIDENTALE... [1803] 19.1x40.6cm. cut in right
    margin, 2 repairs in margins, offsetting in margins, from "Vue de la Colonie
    Espagnole du Mississipi ou des Provinces de Louisiane et Floride," B.
    Duvallon ed.   [23] $125

BLUHME

AGGER CHANNEL-DENMARK [1838] 19.7x19.1cm.   [30] $6

BLUNT

ANNIS SQUAM [1806] C10.2x17.8cm.   [23] $35
BOSTON [1806] C10.2x17.8cm. light browning   [23] $35
CAPE POGE [1806] C10.2x17.8cm.   [23] $35
CHARLESTON HARBOUR [1806] 18.4x10.2cm.   [23] $40
CHART OF LONG ISLAND SOUND [1806] 17.8x43.2cm. folding   [23] $75
ISLE OF SABLE [1806] C10.2x17.8cm.   [23] $35
NEW YORK [1806] C10.2x17.8cm.   [23] $35
NEWBURYPORT [1806] C10.2x17.8cm.   [23] $35
NEWPORT [1806] C10.2x17.8cm.   [23] $35
PORTLAND [1806] C10.2x17.8cm.   [23] $35
PORTSMOUTH [1806] C10.2x17.8cm.   [23] $35
THE BAY AND RIVER OF DELAWARE [1806] 18.4x21.6cm.   [23] $65
THE BAY OF CHESAPEAKE, FROM ITS ENTRANCE TO BALTIMORE [1806] 17.8x17.8cm.
    folding   [23] $80

BONNE

```
AMERIQUE SEPTENTRIONALE [C1780] 21.2x31.8cm.                           [39]    $75
AMERIQUE SEPTENTRIONALE [1780] 21.6x31.8cm.                           [27]    $85
AMERIQUE SEPTENTRIONALE [C1780] 21.6x31.8cm.                          [19]   $125
CANADA IIE FEUILLE [C1770] 29.2x43.2cm.                               [23]   $140
CARTE DE L'ARABIE DU GOLFE PERSIQUE, ET DE LA MER ROUGH AVEC L'EGYPTE, LA NUBIE
   ET L'ABISSINIE [1780] 21.6x31.8cm.                                 [10]    $45
CARTE DE L'EMPIRE DE LA CHINE, DE LA TARTARIE...AVEC LES ISLES DU JAPON
   [C1780] 31.8x21cm.                                                  [3]    $40
CARTE DE L'EMPIRE DE PERSE... [1771-88] 31.8x42.5cm.                  [24]    $61
CARTE DE L'ISLE DE LA JAMAIQUE [1780] 21.6x31.8cm.                     [3]    $30
CARTE DE L'ISLE DE ST. DOMINGUE [1780] 21.6x30.5cm.                    [3]    $40
CARTE DE L'ISLE DE ST. DOMINGUE UNE DES GRANDES ANTILLES, COLONIE FRANCOISE ET
   ESPAGNOLE. PAR M. BONNE, INGENIEUR-HYDROGRAPHE DE LA MARINE [1780]
   32.1x21cm.                                                         [25]    $49
CARTE DE LA LOUISIANE ET DE LA FLORIDE PAR M. BONNE INGENIEUR [1780]
   33x21.6cm.                                                          [3]    $85
CARTE DE LA LOUISIANE, ET DE LA FLORIDE [C1780] 32x21.1cm.            [39]    $85
CARTE DE LA LOUISIANE, ET DE LA FLORIDE [1780] 31.8x20.3cm.           [10]   $120
CARTE DE LA NOUVELLE ZEELANDE [1788] 48x38cm.                         [13]    $99
CARTE DE LA NOUVELLE ZEELANDE PAR M. BONNE... [1778] 34.5x23cm.       [31]   $114
CARTE DE LA PARTIE MERIDIONALE DU BRESIL... [1780] 21.6x31.8cm.        [3]    $30
CARTE DE LA PARTIE NORD, DES ETATS-UNIS DE L'AMERIQUE SEPTENTRIONALE [1780]
   21.6x31.1cm.                                                        [3]    $60
CARTE DE LA PARTIE SUD DES ETATS UNIS DE L'AMERIQUE SEPTENTRIONALE [1778]
   21.6x31.8cm.                                                        [3]    $50
CARTE DE LA PARTIE SUD DES ETATS UNIS... [C1787] 21.6x31.8cm.         [23]    $70
CARTE DE LA TERRE VAN-DIEMAN [1782] 23.5x34.5cm.                      [13]   $130
CARTE DES ISLES ANTILLES OU DU VENT AVEC LA PARTIE ORIENTALES DES ISLES SOU LE
   VENT [C1780] 31.8x20.3cm.                                          [23]    $55
CARTE DU CHILI DEPUIS LE SUD PEROU JUSQU'AU CAP HORN, AVEC PARTIE DES REGIONS
   QUI EN SONT A L'EST... [1780] 34.3x21cm.                           [11]    $40
CARTE DU MEXIQUE DE LA NLLE. ESPAGNE [1771] 29.2x40.6cm.              [23]   $185
CARTE DU PEROU AVEC UNE PARTIE DES PAYS QUI EN SONT A L'EST... [1780]
   31.8x21cm.                                                         [11]    $45
CARTE DU PEROU OU SE TROUVENT LES AUDIENCES DE QUITO, LIMA ET LA PLATA...
   [1770] 43.2x31.1cm. minor repairs                                   [3]    $70
CARTE GEOGRAPHIQUE DE L'AMERIQUE MERIDIONALE [C1775] 59.2x42.3cm.     [39]    $55
L'ANCIEN ET LE NOUVEAU MEXIQUE [1787-88] 34.3x23.5cm.                 [30]    $89
L'ANCIEN MONDE ET LE NOUVEAU [C1780] 21.6x40.6cm.
   the world in hemispheres                                           [23]    $80
L'ANCIEN MONDE ET LE NOUVEAUX EN DEUX HEMISPHERES [1780] 21x40.6cm.
   3 folds, top margin reinforced                                      [8]   $125
L'ISLE DE TERRE NEUVE L'ACADIE OU LA NOUVELLE ECOSSE [1780] 21x31.8cm.
                                                                      [30]   $121
L'ISLE DE TERRE-NEUVE L'ACADIE, OU LA NOUVELLE ECOSSE, L'ISLE ST. JEAN ET LA
   PARTIE ORIENTALE DU CANADA. PAR M. BONNE [1780] 21.6x32.4cm.
   from Raynal, "Histoire Philosophique et Politique," Geneva 1780     [8]    $75
L'ISLE DE TERRE-NEUVE, L'ACADIE, OU LA NOUVELLE ECOSSE, L'ISLE ST JEAN ET LA
   PARTIE ORIENTALE DU CANADA [1780] 21.5x31.5cm.
   from Raynal's "Histoire Philosophique et Politique"                [21]    $60
LA GUYANE FRANCOISE, AVEC PARTIE DE LA GUYANE HOLLANDOISE; SUIVANT LES
   OPERATIONS ET LES CARTES RECENTES DES INGENIEURS-GEOGRAPHES FRANCOIS. PAR M.
   BONNE... [1780] 21.3x31.4cm.                                       [25]    $30
LE NOUVEAU MEXIQUE [C1770] 21x31.4cm.                                 [19]   $145
LE NOUVEAU MEXIQUE AVEC LA PARTIE SEPTENTRIONALE DE L'ANCIEN, OU DE LA NOUVELLE
   ESPAGNE [1780] 21x31.8cm.                                          [10]   $125
LE NOUVEAU MEXIQUE AVEC...NOUVELLE ESPAGNE [1770] 21.6x31.8cm.        [20]   $200
LES ETATE UNIS DE L'AMERIQUE SEPTENTRIONALE... [1781] 31.8x21.6cm.    [22]   $100
NLLE. GALLES MERIDLE. OU COTE ORIENTALE DE LA NOUVELLE HOLLANDE [1788]
   34.5x23.5cm. from "Atlas encyclopedique"                           [13]   $130
```

BONNE (continued)
NLLE. GALLES MERIDLE. OU COTE ORIENTALE DE LA NOUVELLE HOLLANDE [1774-89]
  36.5x79.5cm.   [13] $160
PARTIE DE L'AMERIQUE SEPTENTRIONALE [1776] 57.5x43.5cm.
  some foxing, mostly in margins   [5] $320
PARTIE DE L'AMERIQUE SEPTENTRIONALE, QUI COMPREND LE CANADA, LA LOUISIANE LE
  LABRADOR, LA GROENLAND, LES ETATS-UNIS ET LA FLORIDE...PAR MR. BONNE. A
  PARIS, CHEZ LATTRE, RUE ST. JACQUES E LA VILLE DE BORDEAUX...REVUE ET
  CORRIGEE 1783 [1783] 33x47cm. margins soiled   [7] $300
PARTIE DE L'AMERIQUE SEPTENTRIONALE. QUI COMPREND LE CANADA, LE LABRADOR, LE
  GROENLAND, LA NOUVELLE ANGLETERRE FLORIDA ETC [1776] 43.5x57.5cm.   [31] $275
PARTIE OCCIDENTALE DE CANADA, CONTENANT LES CINQ GRAND LACS... [C1780]
  21.1x31.8cm.   [39] $95
PARTIE OCCIDENTALE DU CANADA, CONTENANT LES CINQ GRANDS LACS AVEC PAYS
  CIRCONVOISINS [1780] 21x31.1cm.   [10] $125
PLANISPHERE GENERAL, POUR SERVIR A L'INTELLIGENCE DE LA NAVIGATION ET DU
  COMMERCE DES EUROPEENS... [1780] 20.3x31.8cm.   [10] $100
PLANISPHERE SUIVANT LA PROJECTION DE MERCATOR [1778] 22.2x32.4cm.   [3] $55
PLANSIPHERE SUIVANT LA PROJECTION DE MECATOR [C1780] 21.6x35.6cm.
  the world on Mercator's projection   [23] $75
SUPLEMENT POUR LES ISLES ANTILLES [C1780] 31.8x21cm.
  ten island maps on one sheet   [23] $55
BONNEVILLE
A MAP OF THE SOURCES OF THE COLORADO & BIG SALT LAKE, PLATTE, YELLOW-STONE,
  MUSCLE-SHELL, MISSOURI; & SALMON & SNAKE RIVERS, BRANCHES OF THE COLUMBIA
  RIVER [1837] 41.9x39.4cm. lower right margin trimmed, several minor flaws,
  map by Capt. B.L.E. Bonneville from 1st ed. of Washington Irving, "The Rocky
  Mountains: or, Scenes, Incidents, and Adventures in the Far West" [27] $200
BORDIGA
GIAPPONE [C1805] 20.3x21.6cm.   [3] $45
BORTHWICK
THE CALIFORNIA GOLD DISTRICT-KANAHA BAR WHERE GOLD WAS FIRST FOUND (VIEW)
  [1852] 24.1x35.6cm.   [3] $30
BOUCHETTE
PLAN OF OSWEGO HARBOUR [1815] 21.6x12.1cm.   [30] $48
BOWEN
See also GENTLEMAN'S MAGAZINE
(BEDFORDSHIRE) [1760] C17.1x19.1cm. "Engraved for the General Magazine of
  Arts and Sciences for W. Owen at Temple Bar"   [24] $42
(BEDFORDSHIRE) [1720] C11.4x11.4cm. large cartouch above map   [24] $18
(BERKSHIRE) [1758] C17.1x19.1cm. "Engraved for the General Magazine of Arts
  and Sciences for W. Owen at Temple Bar"   [24] $42
(BRECKNOCKSHIRE) [1720] C11.4x11.4cm. large cartouch above map   [24] $22
(BUCKINGHAMSHIRE) [1720] C11.4x11.4cm. large cartouch above map   [24] $38
(CAMBRIDGESHIRE) [1720] C11.4x11.4cm. large cartouch above map   [24] $41
(CUMBERLAND) [1762] C17.1x19.1cm. "Engraved for the General Magazine of Arts
  and Sciences for W. Owen at Temple Bar"   [24] $45
(FLINTSHIRE) [1720] C11.4x11.4cm. large cartouch above map   [24] $22
(GLOUCESTERSHIRE) [1720] C11.4x11.4cm. large cartouch above map   [24] $27
(HEREFORDSHIRE) [1760] C17.1x19.1cm. "Engraved for the General Magazine of
  Arts and Sciences for W. Owen at Temple Bar"   [24] $42
(KENT) [1720] C11.4x11.4cm. large cartouch above map   [24] $61
(LEICESTERSHIRE & RUTLAND) [1761] C17.1x19.1cm. "Engraved for the General
  Magazine of Arts and Sciences for W. Owen at Temple Bar"   [24] $42
(MONTGOMERYSHIRE) [1720] C11.4x11.4cm. large cartouch above map   [24] $22
(NOTTINGHAMSHIRE) [1761] C17.1x19.1cm. "Engraved for the General Magazine of
  Arts and Sciences for W. Owen at Temple Bar"   [24] $45
(NOTTINGHAMSHIRE) [1720] C11.4x11.4cm. large cartouch above map   [24] $41
(OXFORDSHIRE) [1720] C11.4x11.4cm. large cartouch above map   [24] $45
(SOMERSETSHIRE) [C1760] C17.1x19.1cm. "Engraved for the General Magazine of
  Arts and Sciences for W. Owen at Temple Bar"   [24] $45

BOWEN (continued)

(STAFFORDSHIRE) [1720] C11.4x11.4cm. large cartouch above map   [24] $38
(WILTSHIRE) [1720] C11.4x11.4cm. large cartouch above map   [24] $45
A CORRECT MAP OF THE UNITED STATES... [C1784] 31.1x44.5cm.
   tipped onto board   [20] $175
A CORRECT MAP OF THE UNITED STATES...AGREEABLE TO THE TREATY OF 1784 [C1785]
   32x45cm.   [4] $137
A MAP OF THE BRITISH AND FRENCH SETTLEMENTS IN NORTH AMERICA: (PART THE SECOND)
   CONTAINING PART OF NEW YORK, PENSILVANIA, NEW JERSEY, MARY LAND, VIRGINIA,
   NORTH & SOUTH CAROLINA, GEORGIA, LOUISIANA AND ALL THE COUNTRIES WESTWARD...
   [1755] 19.1x48.6cm.   [39] $150
A MAP OF THE BRITISH PLANTATIONS CANADA FLORIDA [1742] 10.8x13.3cm.
   from Cowley's Geography   [30] $203
A MAP OF THE DISCOVERIES MADE BY CAPT. WM. DAMPIER IN THE ROEBUCK IN 1699
   [1764] 20x32cm.   [2] $87
A MAP OF THE ISLAND OF TOBAGO DRAWN FROM AN ACTUAL SURVEY [1779] 19.1x24.1cm.
                                                                      [3] $100
A MAP OF THE SOUTH POLE WITH TRACK OF HIS MAJESTY'S SLOOP RESOLUTION IN SEARCH
   OF A SOUTHERN CONTINENT [1776] 22.9x21.6cm.   [3] $45
A MERCATOR CHART OF THE WORLD [1778] 33x44cm. fold lines   [21] $73
A NEW & ACCURATE CHART OF THE WESTERN OR ATLANTIC OCEAN DRAWN FROM THE MOST
   APPROVED MODERN MAPS...1778 [1778] 21.6x26.7cm.   [3] $50
A NEW & ACCURATE MAP OF ASIA. DRAWN FROM ACTUAL SURVEYS...BY EMMAN. BOWEN
   [C1747] 35.6x42.5cm.   [7] $150
A NEW & ACCURATE MAP OF CHINA. DRAWN FROM SURVEYS MADE BY THE JESUIT
   MISSIONARIES... [1747] 34.3x41.9cm.   [24] $73
A NEW & ACCURATE MAP OF LOUISIANA... [1747] 34.3x41.9cm.   [19] $350
A NEW & ACCURATE MAP OF SPAIN AND PORTUGAL [1747] 35.6x43.2cm.   [24] $53
A NEW & ACCURATE MAP OF THE ISLANDS OF HISPANIOLA AND PORTO RICO... [1747]
   17.1x41.9cm.   [3] $95
A NEW & ACCURATE MAP OF THE PROVINCES OF NORTH & SOUTH CAROLINA, GEORGIA &C...
   [1747] 34.9x43.2cm. 1st issue without Darien or Fork's River   [3] $220
A NEW & ACCURATE MAP OF TURKEY IN ASIA. ARABIA, &C. DRAWN FROM THE BEST
   AUTHORITIES... [1747] 34.9x42.5cm.   [24] $252
A NEW AND ACCURATE CHART OF THE WEST INDIES WITH THE ADJACENT COASTS OF NORTH
   AND SOUTH AMERICA [1744] 36.5x44cm.   [31] $206
A NEW AND ACCURATE CHART OF THE WESTERN OR ATLANTIC OCEAN DRAWN FROM THE MOST
   APPROVED MODERN MAPS ETC BY THOS. BOWEN 1778 [1778] 21.5x26.5cm.
   from Middleton's "New and Complete System of Geography"   [21] $48
A NEW AND ACCURATE MAP OF ALL THE KNOWN WORLD [C1747] 31.5x53.5cm.   [4] $367
A NEW AND ACCURATE MAP OF ALL THE KNOWN WORLD [C1750] 31x53cm.
   in 2 hemispheres   [2] $263
A NEW AND ACCURATE MAP OF AMERICA [1744] 34.3x44.5cm.
   repaired tear, offsetting, light centerfold stain   [32] $150
A NEW AND ACCURATE MAP OF SCOTLAND COMPILED FROM SURVEYS, AND THE MOST APPROVED
   MAPS AND CHARTS [1748] 31.8x22.2cm.   [24] $73
A NEW AND ACCURATE MAP OF THE ISLAND OF JAMAICA [1747] 34x42.5cm.   [2] $122
A NEW AND CORRECT MAP OF NORTH AMERICA WITH THE WEST INDIA ISLANDS, DIVIDED
   ACCORDING TO THE LAST TREATY OF PEACE, CONCLUDED AT PARIS 10TH. FEBY.
   1763...CORRECTED FROM THE ORIGINAL MATERIALS, OF GOVERR. POWNALL, MEMBR. OF
   PARLIAMT. 1777 [1755-77] 101.6x114.3cm. several tears, one affecting
   engraved surface, backed with cloth, on 4 sheets joined, 2nd issue of the
   1777 Pownall edition with eastern boundary of New York moved to the
   Connecticut River and "North Carolina" inserted on 2 lines   [7] $875
A NEW MAP OF GEORGIA WITH PART OF CAROLINA, FLORIDA AND LOUISIANA [1748]
   35.6x47cm. top margin ragged   [32] $375
A NEW MAP OR CHART OF THE WESTERN OR ATLANTIC OCEAN...SHEWING THE COURSE OF THE
   GALLEONS, FLOTA &C. TO THE WEST INDIES [1740] 35.6x29.8cm.   [3] $110

A NEW PROJECTION OF THE WESTERN HEMISPHERE OF THE EARTH ON A PLANE (SHOWING THE
   PORPORTIONS OF ITS SEVERAL PARTS NEARLY AS ON A GLOBE) BY J. HARDY (TEACHER
   OF MATHEMATICS & WRITING MASTER) AT EATON COLLEGE [1776] 24x22.5cm.
   margins damaged, fold lines visible   [21] $60
A NEW...MAP OF PERSIA, WITH THE ADJACENT COUNTRIES... [1747] 34.3x41.9cm.
                                                                [24] $52
A...CHART OF THE WORLD... [1787] 33x45.7cm.
   Mercator projection by T. Bowen   [30] $150
AN ACCURATE MAP OF CAMBRIDGESHIRE DIVIDED INTO ITS HUNDREDS [1753]
   72.4x52.1cm. long tear repaired, 1st issue, issued separately   [24] $199
AN ACCURATE MAP OF NORTH AMERICA... [1747] 15.2x20.3cm. folding   [20] $100
AN ACCURATE MAP OF THE COUNTY OF LANCASTER DIVIDED INTO ITS HUNDREDS... [1753]
   67.9x52.1cm. minor centerfold repairs, 1st issue   [24] $268
AN ACCURATE MAP OF THE COUNTY OF SUFFOLK DIVIDED INTO ITS HUNDREDS [C1753-60]
   52.1x69.9cm. the Bowles issue of this map from Bowen & Kitchin, "The Large
   English Atlas"   [14] $145
AN ACCURATE MAP OF THE COUNTY PALATINE OF CHESTER DIVIDED INTO ITS HUNDREDS
   [C1760] 53.3x69.2cm.   [13] $206
AN ACCURATE MAP OF THE ISLAND OF BARBADOES [C1747] 35x42.5cm.   [4] $214
AN ACCURATE MAP OF THE ISLAND OF BARBADOS DRAWN FROM ACTUAL SURVEY... [1747]
   42.5x34.9cm.   [3] $95
AN ACCURATE MAP OF THE WEST INDIES DRAWN FROM THE LATEST AUTHORITIES [C1747]
   34.3x41.9cm. minor split at fold   [8] $160
AN ACCURATE MAP OF THE WORLD LAID DOWN FROM THE MOST APPROVED MAPS AND CHARTS,
   REGULATED BY ASTRONOM. OBSERVATIONS [1747] 15.2x26cm.   [3] $70
AN EXACT CHART OF ALL THE COUNTRIES THROUGH WHICH CAPT. BEHRING TRAVELLED FROM
   TOBOLSKI CAPITAL OF SIBERIA, TO THE COUNTRY OF KAMTSCHATKA [C1747]
   17.8x32.4cm.   [23] $50
ATLANTIC OCEAN [1740] 36.2x43.8cm.   [32] $125
HUNTINGDON SHIRE, DIVIDED INTO ITS HUNDREDS [1767] 34.3x24.1cm. [24] $49
MEXICO OR NEW SPAIN [1758] 9.5x6.4cm.   [9] $30
NORTH AMERICA-SOUTH AMERICA [1773] 25.4x21.6cm.   [3] $45
NORTH EAST GERMANY [1751] 34.3x41.9cm.   [30] $182
NORTHAMPTON DIVIDED INTO HUNDREDS... [1767] 32.4x22.9cm.   [24] $45
PARTICULAR DRAUGHTS AND PLANS OF SOME OF THE PRINCIPAL TOWNS AND HARBOURS
   BELONGING TO THE ENGLISH, FRENCH, AND SPANIARDS, IN AMERICA AND WEST INDIES.
   COLLECTED FROM THE BEST AUTHORITIES. BY EMAN. BOWEN [1747] 43.8x35.6cm. 13
   maps on one sheet: Boston, Placentia, Louisbourg, New York, Annapolis, St.
   Augustine, Providence, Havana, St. Jago (Cuba), Charleston, Fort Royal
   (Martinique), Cartagena, and Porto Bello   [25] $183
PARTICULAR DRAUGHTS OF SOME OF THE CHIEF AFRICAN ISLANDS IN THE MEDITERRANEAN,
   AS ALSO IN THE ATLANTIC AND ETHIOPIC OCEANS [1744] 34.5x43cm.
   7 maps on one sheet   [31] $84
WEST INDIES [1744] 36.8x44.5cm.   [32] $160
WORCESTER SHIRE DIVIDED INTO HUNDREDS... [1767] 22.9x32.4cm.   [24] $58
BOWLES
A MAP OF THE MOST INHABITED PART OF NEW ENGLAND CONTAINING THE PROVINCES OF
   MASSACHUSETTS BAY AND NEW HAMPSHIRE WITH THE COLONIES OF CONECTICUT AND RHODE
   ISLAND... [1771] 63.5x52cm. left margin extended   [5] $1500
A MAP OF THE WHOLE CONTINENT OF AMERICA. PARTICULARLY SHEWING THE BRITISH
   EMPIRE IN THE NORTHERN PART OF AMERICA, WITH THE NEW GOVERNMENTS SINCE THE
   ACCESSION OF CANADA AND FLORIDA...FOR JOHN BOWLES...& CARRINGTON BOWLES...
   [C1765] 49.8x54.3cm.   [25] $551
A NEW AND CORRECT MAP OF THE COAST OF AFRICA...WITH EXPLANATORY NOTES OF ALL
   THE FORTS AND SETTLEMENTS BELONGING TO THE SEVERAL EUROPEAN POWERS. LONDON.
   PRINTED FOR JOHN BOWLES...AND CARRINGTON BOWLES... [C1775] 48.3x57.2cm.
   small tears in margin repaired   [24] $73
A NEW MAP OF THE KINGDOM OF HUNGARY AND OF THE COUNTRIES, PROVINCES &C.
   BORDERING THEREUPON... [1754-63] 64.8x100.3cm. folds reinforced   [24] $107

(continued)
BOWLES'S NEW ONE-SHEET MAP OF THE INDEPENDENT STATES OF VIRGINIA, MARYLAND,
   DELAWARE, PENSYLVANIA, NEW JERSEY, NEW YORK, CONNECTICUT, RHODE ISLAND
   &C...ALSO THE HABITATIONS AND HUNTING COUNTRIES OF THE CONFEDERATE INDIANS.
   BY LEWIS EVANS [1801] 48.3x63.5cm. two tears in margin repaired, dated by
   the Whatman watermark, similar to the Laurie & Whittle version of this map,
   but with additional notes & geographical changes   [16] $600
BOWLES'S NEW POCKET DRAUGHT OF FALKLAND ISLANDS...PUBLISH'D AS THE ACT DIRECTS
   1ST JAN. 1779. PRINTED FOR CARRINGTON BOWLES...LONDON [1779] 46.4x70.5cm.
   short tear repaired, creased   [7] $125
BOWLES'S NEW POCKET MAP OF THE DISCOVERIES MADE BY THE RUSSIANS ON THE NORTH
   WEST COAST OF AMERICA. PUBLISHED BY THE ROYAL ACADEMY OF SCIENCES AT
   PETERSBURG. PRINTED FOR THE PROPRIETOR CARINGTON BOWLES...LONDON [1780]
   46.4x62.2cm. tear in lower margin at centerfold   [7] $700
BOWLES'S NEW POCKET MAP OF THE DISCOVERIES MADE BY THE RUSSIANS ON THE NORTH
   WEST COAST OF AMERICA. PUBLISHED BY THE ROYAL ACADEMY OF SCIENCES AT
   PETERSBURG. PRINTED FOR THE PROPRIETOR...LONDON... [C1780] 45.1x61.3cm.
   centerfold separated in lower margin   [26] $650
BOWLES'S NEW POCKET MAP OF THE DISCOVERIES MADE BY THE RUSSIANS ON THE NORTH
   WEST COAST OF AMERICA...LONDON [1780] 45.1x61.3cm.   [36] $385
BOWLES'S NEW POCKET MAP OF THE EAST PART OF THE RUSSIAN EMPIRE IN ASIA, FROM
   THE SR. D'ANVILLE OF THE ACADEMY OF SCIENCES AT PETERSBURG. PRINTED FOR THE
   PROPRIETOR CARINGTON BOWLES...LONDON [C1755] 49.5x55.9cm.
   short tear in lower margin at centerfold repaired   [7] $110
BOWLES'S NEW POCKET MAP OF THE FOLLOWING INDEPENDENT STATES OF NORTH AMERICA,
   VIZ. VIRGINIA, MARYLAND, DELAWARE, PENNSYLVANIA, NEW JERSAEY, NEW YORK,
   CONNECTICUT & RHODE ISLAND...CARINGTON BOWLES, N. 69 IN S. PAULS CHURCH YARD,
   LONDON [C1784-93] 49.5x64.8cm.   [26] $875
BOWLES'S NEW POCKET MAP OF THE UNITED STATES OF AMERICA; THE BRITISH
   POSSESSIONS OF CANADA, NOVA SCOTIA, AND NEWFOUNDLAND WITH THE FRENCH AND
   SPANISH TERRITORIES OF LOUISIANA AND FLORIDA...SIGNED AT VERSAILLES THE 20TH
   OF JANY, 1783 [1784] 47x50.8cm. dated April 12, 1784   [27] $450
BOWLES'S NEW...MAP OF THE LAND OF CANAAN... [1792] 47x57.8cm.   [17] $375
NEW MAP OF KENT [1773] 41.5x53.5cm. margins extended, Thomas Bowles version
   of the Lea map c1693, inset of Canterbury and 8 coats of arms   [4] $728
NEW POCKET MAP OF PORTUGAL [1778] 64.5x48cm.   [2] $70
BOYNTON
MEXICO, GUATIMALA... [C1850] 8.3x15.2cm.   [19] $15
MEXICO, TEXAS, GUATIMALA... [C1847] 11.4x15.2cm.   [19] $25
SOUTHERN & WESTERN STATES [C1850] 8.3x15.2cm.   [19] $15
UNITED STATES [C1850] 21.6x36.8cm. minor creasing & foxing   [19] $65
BRADFORD
ALABAMA [1838] 35.6x28.6cm.   [26] $50
ALABAMA [1842] C35.6x29.2cm.   [36] $85
ARKANSAS [1842] C35.6x29.2cm.   [36] $90
ARKANSAS [1838] 35.6x27.9cm.   [26] $50
BALTIMORE [1838] 28.6x35.6cm.   [26] $50
BALTIMORE [1842] C35.6x29.2cm.   [36] $75
BRITISH AMERICA [1835] 19.7x24.8cm.   [8] $35
CONNECTICUT [1842] C35.6x29.2cm.   [36] $65
CONNECTICUT/RHODE ISLAND [1835] 19.7x25.4cm.   [26] $50
DELAWARE [1842] C35.6x29.2cm.   [36] $75
DISTRICT OF COLUMBIA [1836] 25.4x19.1cm.   [27] $50
EASTERN HEMISPHERE [1842] C35.6x29.2cm.   [36] $75
FLORIDA [1842] C35.6x29.2cm.   [36] $90
GEORGIA [1842] C35.6x29.2cm.   [36] $90
ILLINOIS [1842] C35.6x29.2cm.   [36] $85
ILLINOIS [1838] 36.2x28.9cm.   [8] $75
INDIANA [1842] C35.6x29.2cm.   [36] $75
INDIANA [1838] 35.6x28.6cm.   [26] $40
IOWA AND WISCONSIN [1838] 35.6x28.6cm. light foxing   [26] $50

KENTUCKY [1842] C35.6x29.2cm. small brown spot	[36]	$60
LOUISIANA [1842] C35.6x29.2cm.	[36]	$85
LOWER CANADA [1842] C35.6x29.2cm.	[36]	$65
MAINE [1842] C35.6x29.2cm.	[36]	$75
MAINE [1838] 35.6x29.2cm. minor foxing	[27]	$60
MARYLAND [1838] 28.9x36.2cm. small brown spot	[8]	$70
MARYLAND [1842] C35.6x29.2cm.	[36]	$85
MASSACHUSETTS [1842] C35.6x29.2cm.	[36]	$65
MEXICO, GUATEMALA & WEST INDIES [1835] 20.3x25.4cm.	[19]	$95
MICHIGAN [1842] C35.6x29.2cm.	[36]	$90
MISSISSIPPI [1842] C35.6x29.2cm.	[36]	$75
MISSISSIPPI [1838] 35.6x28.6cm.	[26]	$50
MISSOURI [C1838-42] 29.2x35.6cm.	[27]	$90
MISSOURI [1842] C35.6x29.2cm.	[36]	$125
NEW HAMPSHIRE [1842] C35.6x29.2cm.	[36]	$75
NEW JERSEY [1838] 35.6x28.6cm.	[26]	$60
NEW JERSEY [1842] C35.6x29.2cm. 5 cm. stain, lower right	[36]	$50
NEW YORK [1842] C35.6x29.2cm.	[36]	$75
NEW YORK CITY [1842] C35.6x29.2cm.	[36]	$65
NORTH AMERICA [1835] 25.4x19.7cm.	[19]	$65
NORTH AMERICA [1838] 35.6x29.8cm.	[19]	$100
NORTH AMERICA [1842] C35.6x29.2cm.	[36]	$225
NORTH CAROLINA [1842] C35.6x29.2cm.	[36]	$75
NORTH CAROLINA [1838] 29.2x36.8cm.	[27]	$80
NORTH CAROLINA [C1835-42] 20.3x25.4cm. light discoloration, from "A Comprehensive Atlas," Wilkins & Carter, Boston 1835(42?)	[1]	$45
OHIO [1838] 35.6x28.6cm.	[26]	$50
OHIO [1842] C35.6x29.2cm.	[36]	$65
OHIO [1838] 35.6x28.6cm.	[34]	$65
PENNSYLVANIA [1842] C35.6x29.2cm.	[36]	$75
PHILADELPHIA [1838] 48.3x39.4cm.	[27]	$100
PHILADELPHIA [1838] 36.2x29.2cm. minor repairs	[3]	$50
PHILADELPHIA [1842] C35.6x29.2cm. minor foxing	[36]	$75
RHODE ISLAND [1838-46] 36.8x27.9cm. "Corrected to 1846" in lower margin	[27]	$75
RHODE ISLAND [1842] C35.6x29.2cm.	[36]	$65
SOUTH CAROLINA [1842] C35.6x29.2cm.	[36]	$75
TENNESSEE [1842] C35.6x29.2cm.	[36]	$75
TEXAS [1838] 35.9x28.6cm.	[19]	$500
TEXAS [1835] 19.7x26.4cm. foxed	[19]	$300
TEXAS [1835] 19.7x26.4cm.	[19]	$300
TEXAS [1835-36] 20.3x26.7cm.	[22]	$400
TEXAS [1842] C35.6x29.2cm.	[36]	$350
UNITED STATES [1842] 35.9x57.8cm. light offsetting	[36]	$145
UNITED STATES [1838] 35.6x57.8cm. fold repaired	[19]	$175
UPPER AND LOWER CANADA [1835] 19.1x24.1cm. some browning, with page of text	[8]	$25
UPPER CANADA [1842] C35.6x29.2cm.	[36]	$65
VERMONT [1842] C35.6x29.2cm.	[36]	$75
VIRGINIA [1842] C35.6x29.2cm.	[36]	$85
WASHINGTON, NEW ORLEANS, LOUISVILLE AND CINCINNATI [1842] C35.6x29.2cm.	[36]	$65
WEST INDIES [C1818] 24.8x40cm. foxed	[19]	$85
WEST INDIES [1842] C35.6x29.2cm.	[36]	$75
WESTERN HEMISPHERE [1842] C35.6x29.2cm.	[36]	$85
WISCONSIN AND IOWA [1842] C35.6x29.2cm.	[36]	$90

BRADLEY

ARIZONA AND NEW MEXICO [1887] 36.8x55.9cm. dated 1886, published 1887	[27]	$55
IOWA [1887] 40.6x55.9cm.	[27]	$40

BRADLEY (continued)
```
 MISSOURI [1887] 43.2x53.3cm.                                             [27]    $45
 NEBRASKA [1884-87] 41.9x55.9cm. dated 1884, published 1887              [27]    $50
 NEBRASKA [1884-89] 41.9x55.9cm. dated 1884, published 1889, differs from 1887
    ed. in that blank area south of Cherry County has been divided into Arthur,
    Grant, Thomas, and McPherson Counties                                [27]    $50
 RAILROAD MAP OF THE UNITED STATES TOGETHER WITH VARIOUS STEAMSHIP LINES ALONG
    THE SEABOARD [1884] 36.8x58.4cm.                                      [11]    $25
 TEXAS [1887] 41.9x57.2cm.                                                [27]    $75
```
BRAUN & HOGENBERG
```
 (ALOST, PLAN) [1575] C30x45cm.                                          [18]    $70
 (AMERSFOORT, PLAN & VIEW) [1575] C30x45cm.                              [18]   $263
 (AMSTERDAM, PLAN) [1575] C30x45cm.                                      [18]   $351
 (ANVERS, PLAN) [1575] C30x45cm.                                         [18]   $175
 (ARNHEM/VENLO/GELDERN/RUREMONDE, PLAN) [1575] C30x45cm.                 [18]   $245
 (BERGEN OP ZOOM, PLAN) [1575] C30x45cm.                                 [18]   $210
 (BOLSWARD/STAVEREN/HARLINGEN/HINGE/DELOPEN, PLANS) [1575] C30x45cm. [18]   $175
 (BRIELLE, VIEW) [1575] C30x45cm.                                        [18]   $175
 (BRUGES, PLAN) [1575] C30x45cm.                                         [18]   $140
 (BRUXELLES, PLAN) [1575] C30x45cm. fold reinforced                      [18]   $175
 (CHARLEMONT/AVESNES/LANDRECY/BEAUMONT, PLANS) [1575] C30x45cm.          [18]    $70
 (DELFT, PLAN) [1575] C30x45cm.                                          [18]   $210
 (DEVENTER, PLAN) [1575] C30x45cm.                                       [18]   $210
 (DORDRECHT, BIRD'S EYE VIEW) [1575] C30x45cm.                           [18]   $263
 (DORDRECHT, PANORAMIC VIEW) [1575] C30x45cm.                            [18]   $421
 (ENKHUIZEN, BIRD'S EYE VIEW) [1575] C30x45cm.                           [18]   $175
 (GAND, PLAN) [1575] C30x45cm.                                           [18]   $140
 (GOUDA, BIRD'S EYE VIEW) [1575] C30x45cm.                               [18]   $263
 (GOUDA, VIEW) [1575] 18x48cm.                                           [18]   $263
 (GRONINGEN, BIRD'S EYE VIEW) [1575] C30x45cm.                           [18]   $263
 (GRONINGEN/BROUWERSHAVEN/GORCUM, VIEWS) [1575] C30x45cm.                [18]   $245
 (HAARLEM, BIRD'S EYE VIEW) [1575] C30x45cm.                             [18]   $210
 (HAINAUT, ARMORIAL) [1575] C30x45cm.                                    [18]    $70
 (HUY, VIEW) [1575] C30x45cm.                                            [18]   $210
 (JERUSALEM) [1588] 74.9x48.3cm.                                         [15] $1600
 (KAMPEN, BIRD'S EYE VIEW) [1575] C30x45cm.                              [18]   $175
 (KAMPEN, PANORAMIC VIEW) [1575] C30x45cm.
    light stains, small repaired tear                                    [18]   $421
 (LEEUWARDEN/FRANEKER, PLANS) [1575] C30x45cm.                           [18]   $140
 (LEYDEN, PLAN) [1575] C30x45cm.                                         [18]   $140
 (LIEGE, VIEW) [1575] C30x45cm.                                          [18]   $263
 (LIER, PLAN) [1575] C30x45cm.                                           [18]    $87
 (LIMBURG, VIEW) [1575] C30x45cm.                                        [18]   $105
 (LOUVAIN, PLAN) [1575] C30x45cm.                                        [18]   $140
 (LOUVAIN, VIEW) [1575] 13x47cm.                                         [18]    $70
 (MAASTRICHT, PANORAMIC VIEW) [1575] C30x45cm.                           [18]   $526
 (MAASTRICHT, PLAN) [1575] C30x45cm.                                     [18]   $245
 (MALINES, PLAN) [1575] C30x45cm.                                        [18]   $105
 (MALINES, VIEW) [1575] 13x47cm.                                         [18]    $70
 (MIDDELBURG, BIRD'S EYE VIEW) [1575] C30x45cm.                          [18]   $263
 (MONS, PLAN) [1575] C30x45cm.                                           [18]   $122
 (MONS, VIEW) [1575] 15x48cm.                                            [18]    $87
 (NAMUR, PLAN) [1575] C30x45cm.                                          [18]   $105
 (NAMUR, VIEW) [1575] C30x45cm.                                          [18]   $245
 (NIJMEGEN, PANORAMIC VIEW) [1575] C30x45cm.                             [18]   $526
 (NIJMEGEN, PLAN) [1575] C30x45cm.                                       [18]   $263
 (PHILIPPEVILLE/MARIEBOURG/CHIMAY/WALCOURT, PLANS) [1575] C30x45cm.      [18]    $70
 (ROTTERDAM, BIRD'S EYE VIEW) [1575] C30x45cm.                           [18]   $351
 (ROTTERDAM, VIEW) [1575] 19x48cm.                                       [18]   $351
 (S'HERTOGENBOSCH, BIRD'S EYE VIEW) [1575] C30x45cm.                     [18]   $263
 (S'HERTOGENBOSCH, VIEW) [1575] 11x49cm.                                 [18]   $175
```

BRAUN & HOGENBERG (continued)
(SLUYS, PLAN) [1575] C30x45cm.   [18] $140
(SNEECK/DOCCUM/SLOTEN/ILSTEN) [1575] C30x45cm.   [18] $140
(TIRLEMONT, PLAN) [1575] C30x45cm.   [18] $122
(TOURNAY, PLAN) [1575] C30x45cm.   [18] $122
(UTRECHT, PLAN) [1575] C30x45cm.   [18] $175
(YPRES, PLAN) [1575] C30x45cm.   [18] $87
(ZUTPHEN, PLAN) [1575] C30x45cm.   [18] $175
(ZWOLLE, BIRD'S EYE VIEW) [1575] C30x45cm.   [18] $263
ANTVERPIA (PLAN) [1618] 46x78cm. folds reinforced   [18] $526
EDENBURGUM SCOTIAE METROPOLIS (VIEW) [1581] 34.3x45.7cm.   [24] $306
FAMAGUSTA [1572] 15x23cm.   [31] $76
HEIRSOLYMA CLARISSIMA TOTIUS ORIENTIS CIVITAS INDAEQUE METROPOLIS (VIEW)
   [1588] 34x49cm.   [2] $333
HIERSOLYMA URBS SANCTA (VIEW) [1575] 33x42cm. light browning at fold [2] $368
LUCENBURGUM URBS... (VIEW) [C1598] 36x47cm. minor repairs   [18] $526
LUXEMBOURG LUTZENBURGUM [1581] 35x41cm.   [18] $280
MEXICO/CUSCO [1572] 26.7x47.6cm.   [23] $700
MOSCAUW [1574] 34.9x49.5cm.   [17] $750
RHODUS [1572] 15x23cm.   [31] $76
SEVILLA/CADIZ/MALAGA (VIEWS) [C1580] 34x47.5cm.   [2] $280
BRIGHTLY
NORTH AMERICA FROM THE BEST AUTHORITIES [1801] 19.1x21.6cm.   [3] $35
BRION DE LA TOUR
(ENGLISH COLONIES) [1778] 51.4x75.6cm.   [17] $850
L'AMERIQUE DRESSEE POUR L'ETUDE DE LA GEOGRAPHIE... [1764] 28x31.3cm.
   surrounded by a decorative border   [39] $85
L'AMERIQUE... [1764] 25.4x26.7cm. with descriptive panels laid down at sides,
   published in a school atlas by Desnos   [16] $100
MAPPEMONDE PHILOSOPHIQUE ET POLITIQUE [1799] 52.1x76.2cm. minor creasing at
   centerfold, double-hemisphere world with colored key, separately published
                                                                  [16] $400
BROWNE
PARAQUARIA VULGO PARAGUAY CUM ADJACENTIBUS. [C1690] 54.6x44.8cm. "Gerard
   Coeck, sculpsit. Sold by Christopher Browne at ye Globe at the west end of
   Saint Paul's Church;" this Blaeu plate of 1662 came into Browne's possession,
   no text on verso, some reinforcement on verso   [25] $145
BRUE
CARTE ENCYPROTYPE DE L'AMERIQUE SEPTENTRIONALE... [1815] 52.7x69.9cm.
                                                                  [36] $425
CARTE GENERALE DES ETATS-UNIS DES HAUT ET BAS-CANADA... [1835-39] 36.8x50.8cm.
                                                                  [22] $140
CARTE GENERALE DES ETATS-UNIS, DU CANADA ET D'UNE PARTIE DES PAYS ADJACENTS
   [1825] 37.5x51.4cm. backed   [3] $165
CARTE GENERALE DU PEROU DE LA BOLIVIE, DU CHILI ET LA PLATA... [1848]
   50.8x36.8cm.   [3] $30
MAPPE MONDE PHYSIQUE SUR LA PROJECTION REDUITE DE MERCATOR... [1821]
   36.8x50.8cm.   [3] $50
BRYANT
MAP OF THE COUNTY OF OXFORD FROM ACTUAL SURVEY BY A. BRYANT IN THE YEAR 1823
   DESCRIBED BY PERMISSION OF THE EARL OF MACCLESFIELD LORD LIEUTENANT...LONDON
   BY A. BRYANT 27 GRT. ORMOND STREET MAY, 1ST, 1824 [1824] 189.2x148cm. in 2
   portions, sectioned & mounted on cloth, dimensions are total, minor spotting
   & stains, with worn calf slipcase, both sheets marked as proof copies, inset
   of Christ Church   [7] $225
BUACHE
CARTE D'AMERIQUE DRESSEE POUR L'USAGE DU ROY...PAR GUILLAUME DE L'ISLE 1722...
   [1722-45] 48.3x59.7cm. backed   [3] $465
CARTE D'UNE PARTIE DE L'AMERIQUE POUR LA NAVIGATIONS [1740] 49.5x92.7cm.
                                                                  [15] $350

BUACHE (continued)
CARTE DE L'ISLE DE LA JAMAIQUE AUX ANGLOIS AVEC LES PASSAGES ENTRE CETTE ISLE
    ET CELLES DE ST. DOMINGUE [1740] 24.1x31.8cm.   [3] $125
CARTE DE LA LOUSIANE [C1745] 48.3x64.8cm. a reissue of de l'Isle's map
                                                                    [16] $820
CARTE DE LA PARTIE DE L'OCEAN VERS L'EQUATEUR ENTRE LES COTES D'AFRIQUE ET
    D'AMERIQUE... [1737] 48.3x64.8cm.   [3] $185
CARTE DES NOUVELLES DECOUVERTES AU NORD DE LA MER DU SUD, TANT A L'EST DE LA
    SIBERIE ET DU KAMTCHATKA, QU A L'OUEST DE LA NOUVELLE FRANCE. DRESSEE SUR LES
    MEMOIRES DE MR. DEL'ISLE PROFESSEUR ROYAL ET DE L'ACADEMIE DES SCIENCES
    [1752] 47x66.7cm. 1st state, "Philippe Buache de la meme Academie Et
    Presentee a l'Academie, dan son Assemblee publique du 8. Avril 1750. Par Mr.
    De l'Isle...sous le Privilege de l'Academie des Sciences...Guill. Delisle et
    Phil. Buache," minor faults   [7] $1225
CARTE DU CANADA OU DE LA NOUVELLE FRANCE ET DES DECOUVERTES...PAR GUILLAUME
    DEL'ISLE DE L'ACADEMIE ROYALE DES SCIENCES ET PREMIER GEOGRAPHE DU ROY. A
    PARIS CHEZ L'AUTEUR...AVEC PRIVILEGE...POUR 20. ANS 1703. PH. BUACHE...AVEC
    PRIVILEGE DU 30 AV. 1745 [1745] 50.8x66cm. 1st state, 6th issue [7] $775
CARTE DU COMTE DE FLANDRE. PARIS, CHEZ L'AUTEUR, SUR LE QUAI DE L'HORLOGE,
    1704. PH. BUACHE, 1745 [1745] 60x65cm.   [18] $105
BUCHON
CARTE GEOGRAPHIQUE STATISTIQUE ET HISTORIQUE DE L'AMERIQUE [1825] 48.3x64.1cm.
    dimensions include text   [3] $60
CARTE GEOGRAPHIQUE STATISTIQUE ET HISTORIQUE DE LA CAROLINA DU NORD [1825]
    44.5x60.3cm. dimensions include text, light foxing, similar to Carey & Lea
    map of 1823   [1] $110
CARTE GEOGRAPHIQUE, STATISTIQUE ET HISTORIQUE DE GEORGIE [1825] 45.7x61cm.
    includes text   [3] $90
CARTE GEOGRAPHIQUE, STATISTIQUE, ET HISTORIQUE DU TERRITOIRE D'ARKANSAS [1827]
    35.6x35.6cm. dimensions for map only, on a sheet of text   [22] $190
ETATS-UNIS D'AMERIQUE [1825] 41.9x52.7cm.   [32] $125
BUFFORD
LOVELL'S GROVE. NO. WEYMOUTH, MASS. (VIEW) [C1880] 45.4x63.8cm. lith. by J.H.
    Bufford's Sons, Boston, chromolithograph by S.S. Frizzell   [33] $385
BURGESS
(ARKANSAS, LOUISIANA, MISSISSIPPI, INDIAN TY. & EAST TEXAS) [1853-54]
    26.7x21.6cm.   [19] $35
GEORGIA AND ALABAMA [1845] 15.9x21cm.   [3] $25
MAP OF NORTH AMERICA [1853-54] 26.7x22.9cm.   [19] $45
MAP OF THE UNITED STATES & CANADA [1853-54] 26.7x44.5cm.
    foxing, fold reinforced   [19] $80
MAP OF THE UNITED STATES AND TEXAS [1839] 26.7x44.5cm. margins worn, some
    foxing, centerfold repaired, inset map shows Mexico and Guatemala [19] $110
MAP OF THE UNITED STATES AND TEXAS [1839-47] 26.7x44.5cm.
    fold repaired, offsetting, stain   [19] $90
TEXAS [1853-54] 26x22.2cm. foxing in margins   [19] $80
BURR
DELAWARE AND MARY-LAND [1836] 27.9x31.8cm. "Wm. Hall & Co."   [27] $85
LOUISIANA [C1834-35] 27.3x33cm.   [1] $85
MAINE [1836] 33x26.7cm. no date on map, from "New Universal Atlas" [27] $65
MAP OF THE CITY AND COUNTY OF NEW YORK, WITH ADJACENT COUNTRY [1839]
    125.7x49.5cm. on 2 sheets, joined, browning along joint, accompanied with a
    page of descriptive text, from the 3rd ed. of "Atlas of New York State"-3
    vertical folds as issued   [27] $350
MAP OF THE COUNTY OF SUFFOLK [1839] 45.7x83.8cm. minor staining in upper
    margin and centerfold, printer's creases, accompanied by a page of
    descriptive text, from 3rd ed. of "Atlas of New York State"   [27] $175
MAP OF THE STATE OF ALABAMA [C1834-35] 32.4x26.7cm.
    from "A New Universal Atlas"   [1] $85

BURR (continued)
MAP OF THE WORLD ON MERCATOR'S PROJECTION...SHOWING THE CENTRAL POSITION OF THE
  UNITED STATES, WITH EUROPE ON ONE SIDE, CONTAINING A POPULATION OF
  250,000,000, AND ASIA ON THE OTHER, WITH A POPULATION OF ABOUT
  700,000,000... [1850] 53.3x58.4cm. unfolded map by David Burr, issued
  separately, "Published by J. Haven, 86 State St., Boston, 1850"   [27] $160
MICHIGAN [1836] 30.5x26.7cm.   [27] $160
MISSOURI [1834] 29.5x32.7cm. light foxing   [1] $90
NEW YORK [1832-36] 25.4x31.8cm.   [27] $90
NORTH AND SOUTH CAROLINA [1834-35] 32.4x26.7cm.   [1] $80
OHIO [1831-36] 26.7x30.5cm. dated 1831, published 1836   [27] $110
BUSSEMACHER
 See QUAD
CADELL
PLAN OF THE SIEGE OF CHARLESTOWN IN SOUTH CAROLINA [1787] 25.4x29.2cm. top
  margin restored, map by Col. B. Tarleton, published by T. Cadell, London
                                                                    [3] $125
CALLOT
DISCRETIONE VERA DE L'ANTICA CITA DI GIERUSALEM (VIEW) [1620] 22.9x27.9cm.
                                                                    [15] $600
LA VERA CITA DI GIERUSALEM COME SI TROVA OGNI (VIEW) [1620] 22.9x27.9cm.
                                                                    [15] $950
CAMDEN
 (CHESHIRE) [1607-10] C28x38cm.   [4] $137
 (DERBYSHIRE) [1607-10] C28x38cm.   [4] $122
 (DEVONSHIRE) [1607-10] C28x38cm.   [4] $137
 (ESSEX) [1607-10] C28x38cm.   [4] $137
 (GLAMORGANSHIRE) [1607-10] C28x38cm.   [4] $137
 (HAMPSHIRE) [1607-10] C28x38cm.   [4] $153
 (HERTFORDSHIRE) [1607-10] C28x38cm.   [4] $168
 (MIDDLESEX) [1607-10] C28x38cm.   [4] $199
 (NORTHUMBERLAND) [1607-10] C28x38cm.   [4] $122
 (NOTTINGHAMSHIRE) [1607-10] C28x38cm.   [4] $107
 (OXFORDSHIRE) [1607-10] C28x38cm.   [4] $153
 (STAFFORDSHIRE) [1607-10] C28x38cm.   [4] $122
 (WARWICKSHIRE) [1607-10] C28x38cm.   [4] $137
 (WORCESTERSHIRE) [1607-10] C28x38cm.   [4] $137
 (YORKSHIRE E. RIDING) [1607-10] C28x38cm.   [4] $122
 (YORKSHIRE W. RIDING) [1607-10] C28x38cm.   [4] $137
CAMOCIO
DE ISLANDIA INSULA... [C1570] 26.5x19cm.   [31] $1034
INGILTERRA ET SCOTIA [C1574] 21.6x17.8cm.
  in "Isole famose, porti, fortezze...," Venice   [16] $1170
MOREA [1574] 21x15cm. dark impression   [31] $153
VENICE [C1562] 48x35cm. slight waterstaining, from "Isole Famose..." [31] $689
CAMPANIUS HOLM
 (NORTHWEST AMERICA) [1702] 9.6x14.8cm.
  shows "Terre de Iesso" between "Iapon" and "California"   [39] $85
CHRISTINAE SKANTZ OCH STATEN CHRISTINAE HAMNS BELAGRING AF HOLLANDERNE 1655
  [1702] 12.8x13cm.   [39] $650
EREFALL-DIGHEETZ FORTE [1702] 12.8x12.5cm.   [39] $225
CANADA
GEOLOGICAL MAP OF THE PROVINCE OF NOVA SCOTIA AND PART OF NEW BRUNSWICK [1886]
  32.4x45.7cm. published by the Geological and Natural History Survey of
  Canada to illustrate reports by Barlow, McOuat and Ells   [30] $6
MAP SHEWING DOMINION LANDS SURVEYED OR EXPLORED IN THE PROVINCE OF MANITOBA AND
  NORTH WEST TERRITORY. ALSO LANDS THAT IT IS DESIRABLE TO SURVEY IN THE SEASON
  OF 1873 [1892] 31x47cm. backed with linen, small tears repaired [21] $77
MAP SHEWING THE TOWNSHIPS SURVEYED IN THE PROVINCE OF MANITOBA AND NORTH-WEST
  TERRITORY IN THE DOMINION OF CANADA [1878] 65.5x96.5cm.
  backed with linen, litho by J. Bien, New York   [21] $89

CANADA (continued)

NORTH-WEST TERRITORY. MAP SHEWING DOMINION LAND SURVEYS BETWEEN WEST BOUNDARY
   OF MANITOBA AND THIRD PRINCIPAL MERIDIAN. FROM A MAP COMPILED BY E.
   DEVILLE...PUBLISHED BY AUTHORITY OF...SIR JOHN A. MACDONALD... [1881]
   77x88cm. some fraying at edges, upper right corner mission, breaks along
   folds, Burland Lith. Co., Montreal   [21] $60

CANTELLI DA VIGNOLA

ISOLE DELL'INDIA... [1688] 45x60cm.
   from "Mercurio Geografico" by Giacomo Cantelli da Vignola   [12] $536

CAPPER

CAMBRIDGE [1808] C10.2x17.8cm. engraved by Robert Cooper for Benjamin Pitts
   Capper, "A Topographical Dictionary of the United Kingdom"   [13] $21
CUMBERLAND [1808] C10.2x17.8cm.   [13] $18
DURHAM [1808] C10.2x17.8cm.   [13] $18
HERTFORDSHIRE [1808] C10.2x17.8cm.   [13] $21
LANCASHIRE [1808] C10.2x17.8cm.   [13] $21
NORFOLK [1808] C10.2x17.8cm.   [13] $21
OXFORDSHIRE [1808] C10.2x17.8cm.   [13] $18
SOMERSETSHIRE [1808] C10.2x17.8cm.   [13] $21
SUSSEX [1808] C10.2x17.8cm.   [13] $24
WORCESTERSHIRE [1808] C10.2x17.8cm.   [13] $18

CAREY

See also LEWIS
A CHART OF THE WEST INDIES FROM THE LATEST MARINE JOURNALS AND SURVEYS [1814]
   29.2x42.5cm. from "A General Atlas...," 3rd ed.   [6] $150
A CHART OF THE WORLD ACCORDING TO MERCATOR'S PROJECTON SHOWING THE LATEST
   DISCOVERIES OF CAPT. COOK [1814] 36.2x46.4cm.   [3] $95
A MAP OF BRAZIL NOW CALLED NEW PORTUGAL [1814] 46.7x37.5cm.
   from "A General Atlas...," 3rd ed.   [6] $150
A MAP OF CARACAS [1814] 33.7x52.7cm.
   from "A General Atlas...," 3rd ed.   [6] $75
A MAP OF IRELAND ACCORDING TO THE BEST AUTHORITIES [1814] 38.1x34.3cm.
   from "A General Atlas...," 3rd ed.   [6] $150
A MAP OF THE CARACAS [1814] 31.8x51.4cm. backed   [3] $95
A MAP OF THE COUNTRIES SITUATE ABOUT THE NORTH POLE AS FAR AS THE 50TH DEGREE
   OF NORTH LATITUDE [1814] 26x25.4cm. from "A General Atlas...," 3rd ed.
                                                                        [6] $125
A MAP OF THE DISCOVERIES MADE BY CAPTS. COOK & CLERKE IN THE YEARS 1778 & 1779
   BETWEEN THE EASTERN COAST OF ASIA AND THE WESTERN COAST OF NORTH
   AMERICA...ALSO MR. HEARN'S DISCOVERIES TO THE NORTH WESTWARD OF HUDSON'S BAY,
   IN 1772 [1814] 19.1x27.9cm.   [27] $100
A MAP OF THE DISCOVERIES MADE BY CAPTS. COOKE & CLERKE IN THE YEARS 1778 & 1779
   BETWEEN THE EASTERN COAST OF ASIA AND THE WESTERN COAST OF NORTH AMERICA,
   WHEN THEY ATTEMPTED TO NAVIGATE THE NORTH SEA. ALSO MR. HEARN'S
   DISCOVERIES... [1814] 20.3x29.8cm. from "A General Atlas...," 3rd ed.
                                                                        [6] $125
A MAP OF THE FRENCH PART OF ST. DOMINGO [1814] 39.4x49.5cm.
   from "A General Atlas...," 3rd ed.   [6] $50
A NEW AND ACCURATE MAP OF NEW SOUTH WALES, WITH NORFOLK AND LORD HOWE'S ISLANDS
   PORT JACKSON &C. FROM ACTUAL SURVEYS [1814] 29.2x24.1cm.
   from "A General Atlas...," 3rd ed.   [6] $250
A NEW MAP OF SOUTH AMERICA FROM THE LATEST AUTHORITIES [1814] 53.3x42.5cm.
   from "A General Atlas...," 3rd ed.   [6] $75
AN ACCURATE MAP OF ENGLAND & WALES WITH THE PRINCIPAL ROADS FROM THE BEST
   AUTHORITIES [1814] 36.8x33cm. from "A General Atlas...," 3rd ed.   [6] $150
AN ACCURATE MAP OF HINDOSTAN OR INDIA FROM THE BEST AUTHORITIES [1814]
   40x40.6cm. from "A General Atlas...," 3rd ed., light discoloration along
   centerfold   [6] $125
CHILE AND PART OF THE VICEROYALTY OF LA PLATA [1814] 41.3x25.4cm.
   from "A General Atlas...," 3rd ed.   [6] $50

CAREY (continued)
CHINA DIVIDED INTO ITS GREAT PROVINCES ACCORDING TO THE BEST AUTHORITIES
   [1814] 35.2x35.9cm. from "A General Atlas...," 3rd ed., light discoloration
     along centerfold   [6] $125
DELAWARE, FROM THE BEST AUTHORITIES [1795] 40.8x22.8cm.
   1st state, without reference numbers   [39] $135
EUROPE [1814] 40.6x48.3cm. from "A General Atlas...," 3rd ed.   [6] $125
FRANCE, DIVIDED INTO CIRCLES AND DEPARTMENTS [1814] 33.3x37.5cm.
   from "A General Atlas...," 3rd ed.   [6] $75
HOLLAND OR THE SEVEN UNITED PROVINCES, AND THE NETHERLANDS [1814] 44.5x37.5cm.
   from "A General Atlas...," 3rd ed.   [6] $85
ITALY AND SARDINIA FROM THE BEST AUTHORITIES [1814] 36.5x38.1cm. from "A
   General Atlas...," 3rd ed., light discoloration along centerfold   [6] $75
KENTUCKY [1814] 27.9x48.3cm.
   from "A General Atlas...," 3rd ed., small hole in margin repaired [6] $350
KENTUCKY [1814] 26x47cm. centerfold reinforced, minor staining   [26] $125
LOUISIANA [1814] 41.3x46cm. from "A General Atlas...," 3rd ed.   [6] $350
MAP OF THE UNITED STATES OF AMERICA [1814] 37.5x47cm.
   from "A General Atlas...," 3rd ed.   [6] $175
MARYLAND [1814] 31.8x45.1cm. from "A General Atlas...," 3rd ed.   [6] $350
MEXICO OR NEW SPAIN [1814] 45.4x41.3cm.
   from "A General Atlas...," 3rd ed.   [6] $1200
MEXICO OR NEW SPAIN [1814] 43.8x38.7cm. 1st ed.   [3] $185
MISSISSIPPI TERRITORY [1814] 31.1x35.6cm. some ink stains   [26] $150
MISSOURI TERRITORY FORMERLY LOUISIANA [1814] 30.5x35.6cm. backed   [3] $250
NORTH CAROLINA [1814] 29.5x48.3cm.
   from "A General Atlas...," 3rd ed., minor discoloration of centerfold
                                          [6]
                                          $275
PENNSYLVANIA [1814] 33x48.3cm. from "A General Atlas...," 3rd ed. [6] $250
PERU [1814] 41.9x30.5cm. from "A General Atlas...," 3rd ed.   [6] $50
PLAT OF THE SEVEN RANGES OF TOWNSHIPS BEING PART OF THE TERRITORY OF THE UNITED
   STATES NORTHWEST OF THE RIVER OHIO WHICH BY A LATE ACT OF CONGRESS ARE
   DIRECTED TO BE SOLD [1814] 61.6x34.9cm.
   from "A General Atlas...," 3rd ed.   [6] $350
PLAT OF THE SEVEN RANGES OF TOWNSHIPS...(OHIO) [1814] 60.6x33.3cm.
   light browning, some offsetting   [26] $150
SCOTLAND WITH THE PRINCIPAL ROADS FROM THE BEST AUTHORITIES [1814] 33x36.8cm.
   from "A General Atlas...," 3rd ed.   [6] $85
SPAIN AND PORTUGAL [1814] 36.5x44.1cm.
   from "A General Atlas...," 3rd ed.   [6] $75
SWEDEN, DENMARK, AND NORWAY FROM THE BEST AUTHORITIES [1814] 33x36.8cm.
   from "A General Atlas...," 3rd ed.   [6] $85
SWITZERLAND ACCORDING TO THE BEST AUTHORITIES [1814] 22.2x29.2cm.
   from "A General Atlas...," 3rd ed.   [6] $225
THE DISTRICT OF MAINE [1814] 40.6x31.8cm.
   from "A General Atlas...," 3rd ed.   [6] $275
THE ISLANDS OF THE EAST INDIES WITH THE CHANNELS BETWEEN INDIA, CHINA AND NEW
   HOLLAND [1814] 22.9x29.8cm. from "A General Atlas...," 3rd ed.   [6] $50
THE STATE OF MASSACHUSETTS [1814] 34.3x48.3cm.
   from "A General Atlas...," 3rd ed.   [6] $225
THE STATE OF NEW YORK [1814] 43.2x53.3cm.
   from "A General Atlas...," 3rd ed.   [6] $325
THE STATE OF OHIO WITH PART OF OHIO UPPER CANADA ETC. [1814] 40x36.8cm.
   from "A General Atlas...," 3rd ed.   [6] $475
THE STATE OF PENNSYLVANIA... [1796] 29.2x45.7cm.
   small tear in left fold, framed   [6] $375
THE STATE OF SOUTH CAROLINA FROM THE BEST AUTHORITIES BY SAMUEL LEWIS [1814]
   40x45.7cm. from "A General Atlas...," 3rd ed.   [6] $475
THE STATE OF TENNESSEE [1814] 26.7x54.6cm.
   from "A General Atlas...," 3rd ed.   [6] $350
THE UPPER TERRITORIES OF THE UNITED STATES [1814] 43.8x33.3cm.
   from "A General Atlas...," 3rd ed.   [6] $475

CAREY (continued)
TURKEY, IN EUROPE AND HUNGARY; FROM THE BEST AUTHORITIES [1814] 34.3x37.5cm.
   from "A General Atlas...," 3rd ed.   [6] $50
VERMONT [1814] 38.1x29.8cm. small ink stain   [26] $150

CAREY & LEA

GEOGRAPHICAL, HISTORICAL, AND STATISTICAL MAP OF CONNECTICUT [1822]
   24.1x29.2cm. on a sheet with text, dimensions are for map only   [27] $135
GEOGRAPHICAL, STATISTICAL & HISTORICAL MAP OF HISPANIOLA OR ST. DOMINGO [1822]
   43.2x53.3cm. text below map   [3] $65
GEOGRAPHICAL, STATISTICAL, AND HISTORICAL MAP OF ALABAMA [1827] 30.5x22.9cm.
   text on 3 sides, dimensions for map only, from 3rd edition of 1827 [27] $175
GEOGRAPHICAL, STATISTICAL, AND HISTORICAL MAP OF ALABAMA [1822] 30.5x22.9cm.
   text on 3 sides, dimensions for map only, from 1st edition of 1822 [27] $175
GEOGRAPHICAL, STATISTICAL, AND HISTORICAL MAP OF FLORIDA [1822] 29.2x24.1cm.
   on a sheet with text, dimensions are for map only   [27] $200
GEOGRAPHICAL, STATISTICAL, AND HISTORICAL MAP OF FLORIDA [1827] 30.5x24.1cm.
   on a sheet with text, dimensions are for map only   [27] $200
GEOGRAPHICAL, STATISTICAL, AND HISTORICAL MAP OF GEORGIA [1822] 29.2x22.9cm.
   on a sheet with text, dimensions are for map only   [27] $175
GEOGRAPHICAL, STATISTICAL, AND HISTORICAL MAP OF ILLINOIS [1827] 30.5x21.6cm.
   on a sheet with text, dimensions are for map only   [27] $200
GEOGRAPHICAL, STATISTICAL, AND HISTORICAL MAP OF INDIANA [1822] 27.9x21.6cm.
                                     [27] $175
GEOGRAPHICAL, STATISTICAL, AND HISTORICAL MAP OF KENTUCKY [1823] 28.6x45.7cm.
   light stain at fold, surrounded by text, dimensions are for map only
                                     [1] $85
GEOGRAPHICAL, STATISTICAL, AND HISTORICAL MAP OF LOUISIANA [1822-23]
   29.2x33.7cm. surrounded by text, dimensions are for map only, stain along
   centerfold   [1] $85
GEOGRAPHICAL, STATISTICAL, AND HISTORICAL MAP OF LOUISIANA [1827] 29.2x33cm.
   on a sheet with text, dimensions are for map only   [27] $200
GEOGRAPHICAL, STATISTICAL, AND HISTORICAL MAP OF MEXICO [1827] 38.1x36.8cm.
   one small spot stain, on a sheet with text, dimensions are for map [27] $275
GEOGRAPHICAL, STATISTICAL, AND HISTORICAL MAP OF MICHIGAN TERRITORY [1827]
   36.8x26.7cm.
   on a sheet with text, dimensions are for map only, from 3rd edition[27] $275
GEOGRAPHICAL, STATISTICAL, AND HISTORICAL MAP OF NEW HAMPSHIRE [1827]
   30.5x22.9cm. on a sheet with text, dimensions are for map only [27] $110
GEOGRAPHICAL, STATISTICAL, AND HISTORICAL MAP OF NEW HAMPSHIRE [1822]
   30.5x22.9cm. on a sheet with text, dimensions are for map only [27] $125
GEOGRAPHICAL, STATISTICAL, AND HISTORICAL MAP OF NEW YORK [1822] 30.5x45.7cm.
   centerfold split repaired, minor foxing, on a sheet with text, dimensions
   are for map only   [27] $125
GEOGRAPHICAL, STATISTICAL, AND HISTORICAL MAP OF NORTH CAROLINA [1827]
   27.9x48.3cm. surrounded by text, dimensions are for map only, small stain in
   text portion, small tear in left margin   [1] $135
GEOGRAPHICAL, STATISTICAL, AND HISTORICAL MAP OF NORTH CAROLINA [1822]
   27.9x47cm. on a sheet with text, dimensions are for map, accompanied by a
   page of text   [27] $175
GEOGRAPHICAL, STATISTICAL, AND HISTORICAL MAP OF PENNSYLVANIA [1822]
   29.2x44.5cm. on a sheet with text, dimensions are for map, accompanied by a
   sheet of text   [27] $125
GEOGRAPHICAL, STATISTICAL, AND HISTORICAL MAP OF TENNESSEE [1827] 29.2x47cm.
   on a sheet with text, dimensions are for map, accompanied by another sheet of
   text   [27] $200
GEOGRAPHICAL, STATISTICAL, AND HISTORICAL MAP OF VERMONT [1822] 30.5x24.1cm.
   on a sheet with text, dimensions are for map   [27] $125
GEOGRAPHICAL, STATISTICAL, AND HISTORICAL MAP OF VIRGINIA [1822] 41.9x52.1cm.
   on a sheet with text, dimensions are for map, accompanied by a sheet of
   text   [27] $175
MASSACHUSETTS [1822] 29.8x45.7cm. no text   [3] $50

CAREY & LEA (continued)
   PORTO RICO AND VIRGIN ISLANDS [1822] 41.9x52.7cm. text below map   [3] $95
   UNITED STATES OF AMERICA [1822] 43.2x53.3cm. 1st edition with note in Gulf of
      Mexico crediting Lewis & Clark, Pike & Long with western details   [27] $275
CAREY & WARNER
   EASTERN STATES WITH PART OF CANADA [1816] 19.4x24.1cm. light browning
                                                                          [8] $20
   NEW HAMPSHIRE BY SAM'L LEWIS. ENGRAVED FOR M. CAREY, SEXMEAR, SCUPT. [1816]
      19.1x14.3cm.   [8] $30
CARVER
   A PLAN OF CAPTAIN CARVERS TRAVELS IN THE INTERIOR PARTS OF NORTH AMERICA IN
      1766 AND 1767 [1778] 26.7x34.3cm. small tear into neat line repaired
                                                                          [22] $350
   CARTE DES VOYAGES DU CAPE. CARVER... [1784] 26.7x34.3cm.
      folding, a French edition of Carver's 1778 map   [23] $225
CARY
   (AMERSHAM TO FINCHLEY-ROAD MAP) [1790] C19.1x12.7cm.   [12] $30
   (LONDON TO BEAKONSFIELD-ROAD MAP) [1790] C19.1x12.7cm.   [12] $27
   (LONDON TO CHALK STREET-ROAD MAP) [1790] C19.1x12.7cm.   [12] $30
   (LONDON TO HOUNDSLOW-ROAD MAP) [1790] C19.1x12.7cm.   [12] $27
   (LONDON TO RIPLEY-ROAD MAP) [1790] C19.1x12.7cm.   [12] $30
   (POTTERS BAR TO RUNDELLS-ROAD MAP) [1790] C19.1x12.7cm.   [12] $27
   (TONBRIDGE TO GODSTONE GREEN-ROAD MAP) [1790] C19.1x12.7cm.   [12] $30
   A MAP OF BRAZIL FROM THE BEST AUTHORITIES BY MR. B... [C1800] 18.6x15.9cm.
                                                                          [39] $30
   A MAP OF CHESHIRE FROM THE BEST AUTHORITIES; [1789] 39.4x51.4cm.   [24] $56
   A MAP OF DORSET-SHIRE FROM THE BEST AUTHORITIES [1789-1809] 37.5x52.1cm.
                                                                          [24] $45
   A MAP OF GLOCESTERSHIRE FROM THE BEST AUTHORITIES [1789-1805] 48.3x41.9cm.
                                                                          [24] $45
   A MAP OF PART OF THE UNITED STATES OF NORTH AMERICA EXHIBITING THE WESTERN
      TERRITORY, KENTUCKY, PENNSYLVANIA, MARYLAND, VIRGINIA, ETC. ALSO THE LAKES
      SUPERIOR, MICHIGAN, HURON, ONTARIO & ERIE [1805] 45.7x50.8cm.   [16] $250
   A MAP OF SUSSEX, FROM THE BEST AUTHORITIES... [1789-1805] 35.6x50.8cm.
                                                                          [24] $68
   A MAP OF THE EAST RIDING OF YORKSHIRE WITH AINSTY LIBERTY [1789-1805]
      41.3x51.4cm.   [24] $45
   A MAP OF WARWICKSHIRE FROM THE BEST AUTHORITIES [1789] 52.1x42.5cm.   [24] $45
   A NEW MAP OF AFRICA, FROM THE LATEST AUTHORITIES [1799-1820] 47x53.3cm.
                                                                          [24] $53
   A NEW MAP OF AMERICA [1806] 45.7x52.1cm.
      without centerfold, from "New Universal Atlas"   [16] $140
   A NEW MAP OF AMERICA FROM THE LATEST AUTHORITIES BY JOHN CARY [1808]
      45.7x52.1cm.   [3] $145
   A NEW MAP OF CHINA, FROM THE LATEST AUTHORITIES [1801] 41.9x51.4cm.   [3] $85
   A NEW MAP OF NORTH AMERICA [1806] 45.7x52.1cm.   [16] $150
   A NEW MAP OF NORTH AMERICA FROM THE LATEST AUTHORITIES BY JOHN CARY, ENGRAVER.
      1806 [1806] 45.7x52.1cm.   [8] $180
   A NEW MAP OF NOVA SCOTIA, NEWFOUNDLAND &C. FROM THE LATEST AUTHORITIES [1811]
      45.5x51.5cm.   [39] $95
   A NEW MAP OF NOVA SCOTIA, NEWFOUNDLAND &C. FROM THE LATEST AUTHORITIES BY JOHN
      CARY, ENGRAVER 1807. LONDON: PUBLISHED BY J. CARY...DECR. 1ST 1807 [1807]
      50.8x61cm. 1st state   [7] $225
   A NEW MAP OF PART OF THE UNITED STATES [1811] 45.1x51.4cm.   [32] $125
   A NEW MAP OF PART OF THE UNITED STATES OF NORTH AMERICA, CONTAINING THE
      CAROLINAS AND GEORGIA, ALSO THE FLORIDAS AND PART OF THE BAHAMA ISLANDS
      &C...APRIL 28, 1811 [1812] 51.8x45.7cm.   [25] $191
   A NEW MAP OF PART OF THE UNITED STATES OF NORTH AMERICA, CONTAINING THE
      CAROLINAS AND GEORGIA, ALSO THE FLORIDAS... [1806] 45.7x51.8cm.   [33] $185
   A NEW MAP OF PART OF THE UNITED STATES OF NORTH AMERICA, EXHIBITING THE WESTERN
      TERRITORY...BY JOHN CARY, LONDON, JUNE 1ST 1805 [1805] 45.7x51.1cm.
                                                                          [35] $350

82

CARY (continued)

A NEW MAP OF RUTLANDSHIRE, DIVIDED INTO HUNDREDS... [1801] 48.3x54cm.
  slight foxing   [24] $55
A NEW MAP OF THE UNITED STATES OF AMERICA [1806] 44.5x49.5cm.   [16] $110
A NEW MAP OF THE UNITED STATES OF NORTH AMERICA, EXHIBITING THE WESTERN
  TERRITORY, KENTUCKY, PENNSYLVANIA, MARYLAND, VIRGINIA &C...PUBLISHED BY J.
  CARY, ENGRAVER & MAP SELLER NO. 181 STRAND APRIL 21, 1811 [1812]
  50.8x45.7cm. watermark dated 1812   [25] $191
A NEW MAP OF UPPER & LOWER CANADA [1807] 45.7x57.2cm.   [16] $140
A PLAN OF THE RIVER ST. LAURENCE, FROM SILLERY TO THE FALL OF MONTMERENCE, WITH
  THE OPERATIONS OF THE SIEGE OF QUEBEC; UNDER THE COMMAND OF VICE ADML.
  SAUNDERS & MAJR. GENL. WOLFE, 5TH SEPT., 1759 [1780] 19.1x24.1cm. [27] $135
A PLAN OF THE RIVER ST. LAWRENCE, FROM SILLERY TO THE FALL OF MONTMERENCI, WITH
  THE OPERATIONS OF THE SIEGE OF QUEBEC, UNDER THE COMMAND OF VICE ADML.
  SAUNDERS & MAJR. GEN. WOLFE, 5TH SEPT. 1759. J. CARY, SCULPT. [1801]
  18.4x23.5cm. accompanied by 10 pages of text   [25] $99
CAMBRIDGESHIRE [1789-1828] C14x8.9cm.   [14] $15
DORSETSHIRE [1789-1828] C14x8.9cm.   [14] $12
ENGLAND & WALES [1789-1828] C14x8.9cm. from "Cary's Traveller's Companion,
  or, a Delineation of the Turnpike Roads of England and Wales"   [14] $12
LEICESTERSHIRE [1789-1828] C14x8.9cm.   [14] $13
MEXICO [1813] 29.2x23.5cm.   [19] $175
OXFORDSHIRE [1789-1828] C14x8.9cm.   [14] $13
SOMERSETSHIRE [1789-1828] C14x8.9cm.   [14] $13
THE WEST INDIES, AND GULF OF MEXICO. ENGRAV'D BY J. CARY. PUBLISH'D BY JAS.
  MACGOWAN & WM. DAVIES, FEBY. 24, 1781 [1781] 34.6x22.9cm.   [25] $68
THE WESTERN HEMISPHERE and THE EASTERN HEMISPHERE [1808] C51.4x88.3cm. 2
  maps joined, dimensions are overall, dated Aug. 1, 1799 & Aug. 1, 1801, from
  "New Universal Atlas," 1808, minor offsetting & minor staining in margins
                                                                                   [7] $300

CASE
MAP OF THE SEAT OF WAR TO ACCOMPANY THE AMERICAN CONFLICT [1865] 66x92.7cm.
  by O.D. Case, Hartford, folds reinforced, encapsulated   [20] $140
CASSINI
L'AMERIQUE... [1788] 33x45.7cm.   [16] $2200
LE ISOLE DELLA SONDA, MOLUCCHE, ET FILIPPINES... [1797] 47.5x34.5cm. [31] $229
CATESBY
CAROLINAE FLORIDAE NEC NON INSULARUM BAHAMENSIUM... [1755] 42.5x57.8cm.
  from Seligmann's German edition of Catesby   [17] $1250
CATLIN
A CHART SHEWING THE MOVES OF THE MANDANS & THE PLACE OF THEIR EXTINCTION
  [1841] 21.7x13.2cm.   [39] $25
U. STATES' INDIAN FRONTIER IN 1840 SHEWING THE POSITIONS OF THE TRIBES THAT
  HAVE BEEN REMOVED WEST OF THE MISSISSIPPI [1841] 21.7x13.2cm.   [39] $25
CELLARIUS
COELI STELLATI CHRISTIANI HAEMISPHAERIUM PRIUS [1660-1708] 43.2x50.8cm. long
  tear affecting engraved surface repaired, 2 short tears in margins [7] $300
COELISTALLATI CHRISTIANI HAEMISPHAERUM POSTERIUS [1660] 44.5x52.1cm.
  from 1st edition   [15] $1600
CORPORUM COELESTIUM MAGNITUDINES [1660-1708] 41.9x50.8cm.
  centerfold separation repaired   [7] $350
HAEMISPHAERIUM STELLATUM BOREALE ANTIQUUM [1660-1708] 43.2x50.8cm.
  separation at lower centerfold repaired, centerfold browned, soiling[7] $350
HAEMISPHAERIUM STELLATUM BOREALE CUM SUBIECTO HAEMISPHAERIO TERRESTRI
  [1660-1708] 42.5x50.2cm. 2 repaired wormholes   [15] $775
HEMISPHAERIUM ORBIS ANTIQUI, CUMZONIS, CIRCULIS, ET SITU POPULORUM DIVERSO
  [1660-1708] 41.9x50.8cm.
  centerfold browned, damage caused by pigment repaired   [7] $300
HYPOTHESIS PTOLEMAICA SIVE COMMUNIS PLANETARUM MOTUS PER ECCENTRICOS, ET
  EPICYCLOS DEMENSTRANS [1660-1708] 43.2x50.8cm.   [7] $425

CELLARIUS (continued)

ORBIUM PLANETARUM TERRAM COMPLECTENTIUM SCENOGRAPHIA [1660-1708] 43.2x50.8cm.
tear in margin at centerfold repaired [7] $425

PLANISPHAERIUM COPERNICANUM SIVE SYSTEMA UNIVERSE TOTIUS CREATI EX HYPOTHESI
COPERNICANA IN PLANO EXHIBITUM [1660-1708] 43.2x50.8cm. lower centerfold
repaired, tear in margin affecting 2 cm. of engraved surface [7] $525

PLANISPHAERIUM PTOLEMAICUM SIVE MACHINA ORBIUM MUNDI EX HYPOTHESI PTOLEMAICA IN
PLANO DISPOSITA [1660-1708] 41.9x49.5cm. [15] $550

THEORIA SOLIS PER ECCENTRICUM SINE EPICYCLO [1660-1708] 43.2x50.8cm.
lower centerfold repaired, waterstains in lower margin [7] $350

TYCHONIS BRAHE CALCULUS, PLANETARUM CURSUS ET ALTITUDINES OBOCULOS PONENS
[1660-1708] 41.9x50.8cm. centerfold browned, minor soiling in margins
[7] $325

TYPUS ASPECTUUM, OPPOSITIONUM ET CON IUNCTIONUM ETZ IN PLANETIS [1660-1708]
43.2x50.8cm. lower margin stained, centerfold split [7] $375

TYPUS ASPECTUUM, OPPOSITIONUM ET CON IUNCTIONUM ETZIN PLANETIS [1660]
43.2x52.1cm. from 1st edition [15] $900

CHABERT

CARTE REDUITE DES COSTES DE L'ACADIE DE L'ISLE ROYALE ET DE LA PARTIE
MERIDIONALE DE L'ISLE DE TERRE-NEUVE...OBSERVATIONS EN 1750-51 [C1765]
23.5x57.2cm. [3] $140

CARTE REDUITE DES COTES DE L'ACADIE [C1751] 55.9x85.7cm.
from "Hydrographie Francoise" [30] $203

PLAN DE LA BAIE DE GABARUS SITUEE A LA COTE S.E. DE L'ISLE ROYALE... [1779]
58.4x39.4cm. [3] $135

CHAMBERS

CENTRAL AMERICA [C1856] 22.2x26.7cm. [3] $30

UNITED STATES... [1855] 29.2x45.7cm. W. & R. Chambers, publishers [20] $150

CHAMOUIN

ETATS UNIS ET GRANDES ANTILLES [C1815] 29.8x22.2cm. [23] $60

CHANLAIRE

1802. NO 31 DEPARTEMENT DES FORETS. [1802] 20x24cm. [18] $175

1802. NO. 6. DEPARTMENT DES FORETS...PAR P.G. CHANLAIRE. PARIS CHEZ L'AUTEUR,
RUE GEOFFROY-LANGEVIN NO 328 [1802] 19x20cm. [18] $175

DEPARTEMENT DE LA MEUSE INFERIEURE [1810] 55x62cm. [18] $105

CHAPMAN & HALL

NORTH AMERICA [1842] 38.1x30.5cm. backed, 1st edition [3] $60

SOUTH AMERICA [1842] 39.4x30.5cm. [3] $25

SOUTH EASTERN ASIA BIRMAH-CHINA-JAPAN [1848] 31.8x40.6cm. [3] $30

UNITED STATES GENERAL MAP [1848] 34.3x42.5cm. backed [3] $50

CHARLEVOIX

PLAN DE JEDO [1736] 33x32.4cm. [3] $200

PLAN DE PORT ET DE LA VILLE DE NANGASAKE [1783] 26.5x34.5cm. [31] $107

CHASTENET-PUISEGUR

CARTE REDUITE DES DEBOUQUEMENTS DE ST. DOMINGUE LEVEE, DRESSEE ET PUBLIEE PAR
ORDRE DU ROI...OBSERVATIONS FAITES SUR LA CORVETTE LE VAUTOUR EN 1784 [1787]
61x91.4cm. [3] $245

CHATELAIN

CARTE CONTENANT LE ROYAUME DU MEXIQUE ET LA FLORIDA [C1720] 40.3x51.8cm.
one minor crease [8] $550

CARTE CONTENANT LE ROYAUME DU MEXIQUE ET LA FLORIDE... [1732] 40.6x52.1cm.
light offsetting, from Vol. 6 of "Atlas Historique..." [27] $600

CARTE DU CANADA OU DE LA NOUVELLE FRANCE, & DES DECOUVERTES QUI Y ONT ETE
FAITES DRESSEE SUR LES OBSERVATIONS LE PLUS NOUVELLES, & SUR DIVERS MEMOIRES
TANT MANUSCRITS QU'IMPRIMEZ [1719] 40.5x52cm. [21] $467

CARTE DU CANADA OU DE LA NOUVELLE FRANCE, & DES DECOUVERTES QUI Y ONT ETE
FAITES, DRESSEE SUR LES OBSERVATIONS LES PLUS NOUVELLES, & SUR DIVERS
MEMOIRES TANT MANUSCRITS QU'IMPRIMEZ [1719] 40.6x52.1cm.
upper margin stained [7] $650

CARTE PARTICULIERE DU FLEUVE SAINT LOUIS DRESSEE SUR LES LIEUX AVEC LES NOMS
DES SOUVAGES DU PAIS... [1719] 36.8x45.7cm.
browning at centerfold, from "Atlas Historique" [7] $700

CARTE TRES CURIEUSE DE LA MER DU SUD [1719] 81.3x139.7cm.
   on 4 sheets, dimensions are overall   [15] $3900
MAPPE-MONDE... [C1720] 33.5x45.5cm.   [4] $337
MAPPEMONDE... [C1719] 22.9x43.8cm.   [32] $400
NOUVELLE CARTE DE L'AMERIQUE SEPTENTRIONALE DRESSEE SUR LES PLUS NOUVELLES
   OBSERVATIONS... [1721] 48.3x61cm. right margin restored   [3] $365
NOUVELLE CARTE DES DIX-SEPT PROVINCES DES PAYS-BAS [C1715] 46x56cm. [18] $105
NOUVELLE CARTE DU GOUVERNEMENT DIVIL D'ANGETERRE A ET DE CELUY DE LA VILLE DE
   LONDRES [1708] 34.9x45.7cm.   [24] $79
NOUVELLE CARTE POUR CONDUIRE A L'ASTRONOMIE ET LA GEOGRAPHIQUE ET POUR FAIRE
   CONOITRE LES DIFFERENS SISTEMES DU MONDE, AVEC DIVERSES OBSERVATIONS [1739]
   50.8x62.2cm. margins slightly ragged   [7] $525
SUCCESSION DES EMPEREURS DU JAPON AVEC UNE DESCRIPTION DU MEUTRE DE L'EMPEREUR
   CUBO ET LA RECEPTION DES AMBASSADEURS HOLLANDOIS... [1719] 38.1x50.8cm.
                                        [3] $285

CHILD
A MAP OF THE COUNTRY OF THE HOTTENTOTS, TOWARDS THE CAPE OF GOOD HOPE [C1750]
   24.5x37cm.   [4] $145
PROSPECT OF THE CAPE OF GOOD HOPE (VIEW) [C1750] 21x15cm.   [4] $99

CHIQUET
ESTATS DE LA COURONNE DE SUEDE [1719] C16.5x22cm.   [4] $114
ISLE ET ROYAUME DE CANDIE [1719] C16.5x22cm.   [4] $91
L'AFRIQUE [1719] 17x23cm.   [4] $137
L'AMERIQUE MERIDIONALE [1719] 17x22cm.   [4] $114
LA GRECE [1719] C16.5x22cm.   [4] $91
LE ROYAUME DE DANEMARK [1719] C16.5x22cm.   [4] $114
LE ROYAUME DE FRANCE [1719] C16.5x22cm.   [4] $45
LE ROYAUME DE NORWEGE [1719] C22x16.5cm.   [4] $114
LES ISLES ET COSTE DE LA DALMATIE [1719] C16.5x22cm.   [4] $91
LES ROYAUMES D'ANGLETERRE, D'ECOSSE ET D'IRLANDE [1719] 16.5x22.5cm.
   list of monarchs on each side   [4] $114
LES XVII PROVINCES DES PAYS-BAS [1719] C16.5x22cm.   [4] $114

CITTI
A MAP OF THE VIRGINIA CENTRAL RAILROAD, WEST OF THE BLUE RIDGE, AND THE
   PRELIMINARY SURVEYS, WITH A PROFILE OF THE GRADES [C1868] 47x71.1cm.
   folding lithograph published by Louis F. Citti, Richmond [27] $100

CLAESZ
VARE ALBEELDINGE VAN HET LEGER...MAURITIUS VAN NASSAU...TOT
   WATERVLIET...1605...T'AMSTERDAM, BY CORNELIS CLAESSZ, OPT WATER INT
   SCHRIJFBOECK [C1605] 29x38cm. text in Dutch & French   [18] $351

CLARK
DIAGRAM OF THE STATE OF MISSOURI; SAINT LOUIS [1849] 45.1x56.5cm.
   folding   [22] $95

CLOUET
CARTE D'AMERIQUE, DIVISEE EN SES PRINCIPAUX PAYS, DRESSEE SUR LES MEMOIRES LES
   PLUS RECENTS, ET SUR DIFFERENTS VOYAGES, ET ASSAJETTIE AUX OBSERVATIONS
   ASTRONOMIQUES...PAR MR. L'ABBE CLOUET DE L'ACADEMIE ROYALE DE ROUEN [1788]
   94x124.5cm. on 4 sheets joined, dimensions are overall, extensively
   restored, some loss of surface, backed on cloth, with original rollers, a
   wall map, one of four wall maps of continents published by Clouet in 1788
                                        [7] $4100
DE L'AMERIQUE EN GENERAL [1787] 31.8x55.2cm. backed   [3] $135
DEFINITIONS GEOGRAPHIE SIGNIFIE DESCRIPTION DE LA TERRE COROGRAPHIE [1772]
   31.8x25.4cm.   [3] $90

CLUVER
AMERICA [C1638] 21x25.4cm. "H. Mosling sc."   [3] $125
AMERICAE SIVE INDIAE OCCIDENTALIS TABULA GENERALIS [1629] 12.7x12.7cm.
                                        [3] $95
TYPUS ORBIS TERRARUM [C1696] 16x30.5cm.   [4] $245
VETERIS ET NOVAE BRITANNIAE [C1696] 21.5x26cm.   [4] $145

COCHIN

COURTRAY EN FLANDRE. N. COCHIN FECIT (VIEW) [C1650] 13.5x50cm.   [18] $175
DIXMUNDE EN FLANDRE (VIEW) [1647] 14.5x50cm.   [18] $140
FURNES (VIEW) [1646] 15x50cm.   [18] $140
MONMEDI EN LUXEMBOURG (VIEW) [C1658] 14.5x50cm.   [18] $105
THIONVILLE EN LUXEMBOURG. N COCHIN SCULP. (PANORAMIC VIEW) [C1650] 16x50cm.
                                                                        [18] $351
YPRES EN FLANDRE (VIEW) [C1650] 17x51cm.   [18] $140

COLBURN

CITY OF PANAMA FROM THE SEA (VIEW) [1843] 12.1x17.8cm.   [3] $30
FORT GEORGE, ASTORIA (VIEW) [1843] 12.1x17.1cm.   [3] $35
VIEW OF ARSENAL & LIGHT HOUSE SITKA, NEW ARCKANGEL [1843] 12.1x19.1cm.
                                                                        [3] $35
VIEW OF HONOLULU, OAHU, SANDWICH ISLANDS [1843] 12.1x19.1cm.   [3] $35

COLLINS

(ISLE OF MAN) [C1738] 43.8x55.9cm.   [13] $214
(ISLE OF WIGHT) [C1738] 45.7x57.2cm.   [12] $145
(MORAY FIRTH) [1693-1753] 44.5x55.9cm.   [24] $134
A NEW & EXACT SURVEY OF THE RIVER DEE OR CHESTER WATER [C1738] 43.8x57.2cm.
                                                                       [13] $176
A NEW AND CORRECT CHART OF THE HARBOUR OF CORKE BY THE REVD. J. LINDSAY [1759]
    43.8x52.1cm.   [13] $160
HOLY ISLAND STAPLES AND BARWICK...DEDICATED TO CAPT. WILL DAVIES VICE ADMIRALL
    TO THE RT. HONOURABLE TO THE EARLE OF TORRINGTON... [1693] 44.5x55.9cm.
                                                                       [24] $61
MILFORD HAVEN [C1738] 44.5x56.5cm.   [13] $160
THE ISLANDS OF SCILLY [1693] 45.1x55.9cm. 1st issue on heavy paper   [24] $459
THIS CHART OF KINGSLAE HARBOUR...BY CAPT. GREENVILE COLLINS [C1693-1720]
    44.5x57.2cm.   [13] $153

COLNETT

VIEW OF JAMES' ISLAND ONE OF THE GALAPAGOS/CHATHAM ISLAND AT STEPHENS
    BAY/CHATHAM ISLE [1798] 16.5x26.7cm. 3 views on one sheet   [3] $65

COLTON

(ARKANSAS) [1853-55] 31.8x39.4cm.   [27] $40
(CALIFORNIA) [1855] 39.4x33cm. 1st ed., accompanied by a page of text
                                                                       [27] $75
(IOWA) [1855] 31.8x39.4cm. accompanied by a page of text   [27] $45
(KANSAS) [1866-72] 41.9x61cm. dated 1866, published 1872   [27] $60
ALABAMA [1855] 40x33cm. 1st ed.   [3] $40
CANADA WEST OR UPPER CANADA [C1860] C32x39cm.   [21] $38
CITY OF BALTIMORE [1857] 30.5x36.8cm.   [10] $25
COLTON'S CONNECTICUT WITH PORTIONS OF NEW YORK & RHODE ISLAND [1855-59]
    32.5x40cm. some waterstaining, tear just to border   [21] $28
COLTON'S JAPAN NIPPON, KIUSIU, SIKOK... [1865] 33x40.6cm.   [3] $55
COLTON'S MAP OF THE OIL DISTRICT OF PENNSYLVANIA, COMPRISING PART OF THE
    COUNTIES OF CRAWFORD, VENANGO AND WARREN. PREPARED BY H.S. PLUMB, C.E.
    PUBLISHED 1865 BY J.H. COLTON, NEW YORK [1865] 80x72.7cm.
    backed with rice paper, some browning at folds   [33] $650
COLTON'S MEXICO [1854] 33x39.4cm. margins reinforced   [19] $55
COLTON'S NEW MAP OF THE STATE OF TEXAS [C1855-60] 40.6x62.2cm.
    wrapped with transparent plastic   [20] $175
COLTON'S TERRITORIES OF NEW MEXICO AND UTAH [1855-59] 31.8x39.4cm.
    dated 1855, published 1859   [27] $90
COLTON'S TERRITORY OF ALASKA (RUSSIAN AMERICA) CEDED BY RUSSIA TO THE UNITED
    STATES [1881] 33x43.2cm.   [11] $35
COLTON'S TEXAS COMPILED FROM J. DE CORDOVA'S LARGE MAP [C1855-60] 40.6x61.6cm.
    margins chipped   [19] $165
COLTON'S WASHINGTON AND OREGON [1862] 33x40.6cm.   [9] $45
EAST CANADA OR LOWER CANADA AND NEW BRUNSWICK [C1859] C32x39cm.   [21] $36
GENERAL MAP SHOWING THE COUNTRIES EXPLORED & SURVEYED BY THE U.S. & MEXICAN
    BOUNDARY COMMISSION IN THE YEARS 1850, 51, 52 & 53. J.H. COLTON, N.Y. [1854]
    38.1x48.6cm. repaired   [20] $225

COLTON (continued)

GEOLOGICAL MAP OF MISSISSIPPI [1855-60] 40.6x33cm. "Eng. W. Hilgard, State
   Geologist," from "Report on the Geology and Agriculture of the State of
   Mississippi"   [27] $75
GEORGETOWN AND THE CITY OF WASHINGTON CAPITAL OF UNITED STATES [1855]
   30.5x40.6cm. 1st ed.   [3] $40
GUIDE THROUGH OHIO, MICHIGAN, INDIANA, ILLINOIS, MISSOURI, WISCONSIN, IOWA,
   MINNESOTA, NEBRASKA & KANSAS [1856] 50.8x68.6cm. folding, minor separations
   at folds, from C.W. Dana, "The Garden of the World, or the Great West"
                                                                   [23] $115
ILLINOIS [1855] 40.6x33cm. 1st ed.   [3] $35
INDIAN TERRITORY, DRAWN FROM MAPS & SURVEYS FURNISHED BY THE ENGINEER BUREAR,
   WAR DEPARTMENT, U.S. [1871] 31.8x39.4cm.   [27] $150
INDIANA [1855] 40x33cm.   [3] $25
IOWA [1855] 32.4x40.6cm. 1st ed.   [3] $30
J.H. COLTON'S MAP SHOWING THE OIL REGION OF WEST VIRGINIA...1865 [1865]
   52.7x44.8cm. backed with rice paper, minor stains & repairs at folds
                                                                   [36] $225
LOUISIANA [1854] 33x40cm. 1st ed.   [3] $40
MAP OF THE UNITED STATES, THE BRITISH PROVINCES, MEXICO... [1854]
   86.4x109.2cm. linen backed, folding   [20] $350
NEBRASKA AND KANZAS [1855] 31.8x40.6cm.   [10] $60
NEBRASKA AND KANZAS [1855] 32.4x40cm. 1st ed.   [3] $80
NEW BRUNSWICK, NOVA SCOTIA, NEWFOUNDLAND, AND PRINCE EDWARD ID. [1855]
   32x39cm.   [21] $36
NEW HAMPSHIRE [1855] 40x32.4cm.   [3] $30
NEW JERSEY [1855] 38.1x31.1cm.   [3] $30
NORTH CAROLINA [1855-57] 30.2x36.8cm. minor staining   [1] $30
OHIO [1855] 33x40.6cm. 1st ed.   [3] $30
TERRITORIES OF NEW MEXICO & UTAH [1855] 32.4x40cm. 1st ed.   [3] $65
TERRITORIES OF NEW MEXICO AND UTAH [1855] 30.5x40.6cm.   [10] $85
THE CITY OF LOUISVILLE, KENTUCKY/THE CITY OF NEW ORLEANS, LOUISIANA. PUBLISHED
   BY J.H. COLTON & CO... [1855] 40x33cm.   [25] $53
THE UNITED STATES OF AMERICA [1855] 38.1x65.4cm.   [3] $65
UNITED STATES OF AMERICA [1872] 41.9x73.7cm.   [3] $35
UNITED STATES OF AMERICA [1855] 39.4x66cm.   [20] $120
WASHINGTON [1853] 31.8x40.6cm.
   minor staining in lower & right margins, dated 1853 on map   [27] $75
WISCONSIN [1855] 40.6x33cm. 1st ed.   [3] $45

CONANT

VIEW OF BALTIMORE, FROM FEDERAL HILL [1850] 46.7x70.5cm. small tears in
   margins repaired, printed by Sorony & Major, New York, and published by A.
   Conant   [35] $3850

CONDER

A NEW MAP OF NORTH AMERICA AGREEABLE TO THE MOST APPROVED MAPS AND CHARTS BY
   THOS. CONDER [C1785] 33.5x37.5cm. light foxing, small tear in margin, from
   Baldwyn's "New Complete and Universal System of Geography"   [21] $142
CHART OF THE NEW ARCHIPELAGO, DISCOVER'D BY THE RUSSIANS, IN THE SEAS OF
   KAMTSCHATKA & ANADIR [1782] 15.2x20.3cm.   [3] $45
PLAN OF THE HARBOUR OF NEW YORK AND PARTS ADJACENT [C1780] 14.6x9.5cm.
                                                                   [30] $16
THE NORTHERN HEMISPHERE [C1782] 25.5x25cm.
   scuffed margins, some wear, original folds present   [21] $73
VARIOUS PLANS AND DRAUGHTS OF CITIES, TOWNS, HARBOURS &C. [C1766] 30.5x21.5cm.
                                                                   [4] $84

COOK

A CHART OF THE STRAIGHTS OF BELLISLE WITH PARTS OF THE COAST OF NEWFOUNDLAND
   AND LABRADORE [1770] 61x112cm.
   margin replaced at 2 locations, just affecting border   [5] $560
A CHART OF THE WEST COAST OF NEWFOUNDLAND [1770-79] 49x171.5cm. repaired
   tears in margins, part of blank margin replaced, slight loss of engraved
   surface   [5] $560

COOK (continued)
A GENERAL CHART OF THE ISLAND OF NEWFOUNDLAND [1775] 54.5x55.5cm.
  margin added at top & bottom, some loss of neat line   [5] $800
A GENERAL CHART: EXHIBITING THE DISCOVERIES MADE BY CAPTN. JAMES COOK IN THIS
  AND HIS TWO PRECEDING VOYAGES; WITH THE TRACKS OF THE SHIPS...BY LT. HENRY
  ROBERTS OF HIS MAJESTY'S ROYAL NAVY [C1785] 55.9x88.9cm. minor repairs
                                                    [3] $165
A VIEW OF HUAHEINE [1785] 10.8x16.5cm.   [3] $25
CARTE DES ISLES DE LA SOCIETE... [1774-85] 29x43.5cm.   [31] $22
CHART OF THE SANDWICH ISLANDS [1784] 45.1x27.3cm.   [39] $120
KAART VAN VAN DIEMENS LAND OPGIENOOMEN DOOR KAPITEIN FURNEAUX IN MAAR 1773
  [1778] 21x14cm.   [31] $114
CORNELIS
NIEUPOORT...LAMBARTUS CORNELIJ DEDICABAT [C1600] 35x45cm.
  shows the battle of Nieuport in 1600   [18] $351
CORONELLI
(EASTERN NORTH AMERICA) [1690] 60x45cm. untitled map shows eastern North
  America, and south to Brazil, one sheet of a 2 sheet map   [31] $613
(GLOBE GORE, INCLUDING MADAGASCAR) [1690] 42x26cm.
  from Coronelli's "Isolari"   [31] $114
(ICELAND) [1690] 22.9x29.8cm. title not given   [17] $285
AMERICA SETTENTRIONALE [1696] 61x90.2cm.
  on 2 sheets, dimensions are overall   [15] $3450
AMERICA SETTENTRIONALE [1688] 62.2x88.9cm.   [23] $3500
AMERICA SETTENTRIONALE COLLE NUOVE SCOPERTE SIN ALL'ANNO 1688 PIUISA NELLE SUE
  PARTI SECONDO LO STATO PRESENTE, E DESCRITTA DAL P. MRO CORONELLI M.C.
  COSMOGRAFO DELLA SERENISMA. REPUBCA: DI VENEZIA... [C1696] 61x45.7cm. on 2
  sheets, dimensions are for each, both centerfolds reinforced, minor paper
  loss just affecting engraving which has been restored in facsimile [7] $3500
AMERIQUE SEPTENTRIONALE... [1690] 60x45cm. one sheet of 2 sheet map [31] $1456
CANADA ORIENTALE NELL'AMERICA SETTENTRIONAL DESCRITTA DAL P. MIO CORONELLI M C
  COSMOGRAFO DELLA SEREN REPUBLICA DI VENETIA... [C1696] 45.7x61cm. [7] $950
CANADA ORIENTALE... [C1696] 44.5x59.7cm. minor centerfold restoration
                                            [16] $620
CARCHI, ET LIMONIA [1696] C12x16.5cm.   [31] $38
CARTA MARITTIMA DELLA COSTA LIGUSTICA... [1696-97] 40x50.8cm.
  small printer's fault   [24] $107
CHARTE MARITIMA CHE CONTENE LA COSTA SETENTRIONALE DE NEGROPONTE E LE ISOLA DA
  ESSO A TRAMONTANA COMME SCHIRO, SCHIATTA E SCOPELO/CARTE MARITIMA DEL MARE
  ARCHIPELAGO... [1690] 41x51cm.   [31] $229
CHEKIAN, E KIANGSI, PROVINCIE DELLA CHINA... [1692] 45.7x61cm.   [3] $185
CORSO DEL FIUME DELL AMAZONI, DESCRITTO DAL P. COSMOGRAFO CORONELLI, DEDICATO
  ALL'ILLUSTRISSIMO SIGNORE ALESSANDRO DE VERAZZANO NOBILE FIORENTINO [C1696]
  27.9x45.7cm. short tear in upper right margin   [7] $300
FRISLANDA SCOPERTA DA NICOLE ZENO PATRITIO VENETO CREDUTA FAULOSA... [1695]
  24.8x30.5cm.   [3] $125
IS. DI CAPRI [1695] 22x28cm.   [31] $153
ISOLA D'ISLANDA [1695] 22.9x30.5cm.   [3] $135
ISOLA D'ISLANDIA [C1670] 30x38cm.   [31] $214
ISOLA DE IAMES O'GIAMACA POSSEDUTTA DAL RE BRITANNICO DIVISA IN PARROCCHIE
  [1692] 22.2x29.2cm.   [3] $135
ISOLA DE JAMES, O GIAMAICA, PESSEDUTA DAL RE BRITANNICO DIUISA IN
  PARROCCHIE/LA SPAGNUOIA... [1696] 47x30.5cm.
  left margin discolored & narrow   [7] $110
ISOLA DEL GIAPONE E PENISOLA DI COREA [C1692] 46x61cm.   [4] $689
ISOLA DEL GIAPONE E PENISOLA DI COREA [1696] 46x61cm.
  lower centerfold repaired   [31] $728
ISOLA DI CAPO BRETON DE CANADA [1696-97] 12x16.4cm.
  with descriptive text   [39] $95
ISOLA E CITTA DI CARTAGENA NELL. AMERICA [1696-97] 21.7x12.1cm. [39] $75
ISOLE ANTILI, LA CUBA, E LA SPAGNUOLA, DESCRITTE, E DEDICATE... [1696]
  25.7x42.7cm.   [39] $15

(continued)
ISOLE ANTILLI LA CUBA, LA SPAGNUOLA, DESCRITTO E DEDICATE DAL PADRE MAESTRO
  CORONELLI... [1690] 26x43.2cm. [3] $265
ISOLE NELLE PIAGGE DELLA NUOVA SPAGNA DE CARTAGENA [1695] 38.1x29.2cm.
  text below map [3] $235
LA LOUISIANA, PARTE SETTENTRIONALLE... [C1690] 25.4x41.9cm.
  lower margin restored [32] $1250
LA LOUISIANA, PARTE SETTENTRIONALLE... [1696] 26.7x43.2cm.
  from "Atlante Veneto" [16] $800
LA SPAGNUOLA, DESCRITTA...E DEDICATA ALL'ILLUSTRISS SIG. GIUSTIMIANO LORENZO
  COCCO [1692] 22.2x29.2cm. [3] $135
MARE DEL NORD... [1696] 45x60cm. [31] $766
MARE DEL SUD DETTO ALTRIMENTI MARE PACIFICO [1696] 45.7x58.4cm. [15] $1600
MARE DEL SUD... [1690] 45x61cm. [31] $1341
NICARIA [1696] C12x16.5cm. [31] $38
PARTE DELLA NUOVA SPAGNA, O DEL MEXICO DOUE SONO LE PROVINCIE DI GUADALAIRA
  XALISCO MECOACAN E MEXICO DEDICATA ALL'ILLMO. SIGR. NICOLO DONA SU DE SRE.
  NICOLO DAL PRE. MRO. CORONELLI M.C. COSMOGRAFO DELLA SERENISSIMA REPUBLICA DI
  VENETIA [1696] 45.1x61cm. minor discoloration at centerfold [7] $300
PLANISFERO DEL MONDO NUOVO DESCRITTO DAL P. CORONELLI, COSMOGRAFO PUBLICO
  [C1696] 45.7x61cm. [15] $1200
PLANISFERO DEL MONDO NUOVO, DESCRITTO DAL P. CORONELLI, COSMOGRAFO PUBLICO
  DEDICATO ALL'ILLUSTRISSIMO, ET ECCELLENTISSIMO SIGNORE ANDREA MARCELLO
  [1695] 45.7x61.6cm. minor centerfold browning, lower margin narrow [7] $1075
PLANSIFERO DEL MONDO NUOVO... [C1690] 45.7x61cm.
  small wax stain, small repaired tear at lower centerfold [16] $1350
QUANTUNG, E FOKIEN [1690-97] 45.7x61cm. [24] $367
STALIMENE [1696] C12x16.5cm. [31] $42
STATO DI MILANO PARTE OCCIDENTALE [1691] 61x45.5cm. [4] $107
TERRE ARTICHE DESCRITTE DAL P.M. CORONELLI M.C. COSMOGRAFO DELLA SERENISS
  REPUBLICA DI VENETIA... [C1697] 45.7x61cm. [7] $1075

COTOVICUS
COLPHE ON L'ITALIA [1619] 8.5x12cm.
  from "Itinerarium Hierosolymitanum et Syriacum..." [31] $76
CORCYRA [1619] 18.5x12cm. [31] $268
CYPRI INSULAE DESCRIPTIO [1619] 17x13cm. [31] $843
MEDITERANEO E GOLF DE SETALIA [1619] 8.5x12cm. [31] $76
RHODUS [1619] 12x18cm. [31] $114

COUNT & HAMMOND
UNITED STATES... [C1838] 27.9x43.2cm.
  missing portion restored, folding [20] $65

COVENS & MORTIER
A MAP OF THE BRITISH EMPIRE IN AMERICA WITH THE FRENCH, SPANISH AND HOLLANDISH
  SETTLEMENTS ADJACENT THERETO BY HENRY POPPLE [C1737] 60x53.5cm. on 4
  sheets, dimensions are for each, plus one key map measuring 52 x 50 cm.
  [4] $2836
BELGIUM REGIUM...CARTE DES PAYS BAS CATHOLIQUES, AMSTERDAM, CHEZ JEAN COVENS ET
  CORNEILLE MORTIER [C1720] 51x60cm. [18] $105
CARTE DE L'ISLE DE LA MARTINIQUE COLONIE FRANCOISE DE L'UNE DES ISLES
  ANTILLES...AVEC DES MEMOIRES...MR. GUILL. DELISLE... [C1730] 45.7x58.4cm.
  [3] $235
CARTE DE LA LOUISIANE ET DU COURS DU MISSISSIPI [1730] 43.8x59.7cm. [36] $950
CARTE DE LA LOUISIANE ET DU COURS DU MISSISSIPI... [1730] 43.2x59.1cm.
  Dutch issue of de l'Isle's map [17] $850
CARTE DU CANADA OU DE LA NOUVELLE FRANCE [C1730] 49.5x58cm. [5] $900
CARTE DU CANADA OU DE LA NOUVELLE FRANCE ET DES DECOUVERTES...PAR GUILLAUME
  DEL'ISLE DE L'ACADEMIE ROYALE DES SCIENCES. A AMSTERDAM CHEZ JEAN COVENS ET
  CORNEILLE MORTIER GEOGRAPHES AVEC PRIVILEGE [1730] 50.2x57.2cm.
  some offsetting, Covens & Mortier version of de l'Isle's map [7] $750
CARTE GENERALS DES TREIZE ETATS UNIS... [C1785] 41.3x56.8cm.
  title also appears in Dutch, published by C. Mortier, Covens et fils [23] $750

COVENS & MORTIER (continued)

CARTE NOUVELLE DE LA COMTE DE HOLLANDE ET DE LA SEIGNEURIE D'UTRECHT. OU SONT
EXACTEMENT MARQUEE...A AMSTERDAM. CHEZ IEAN COVENS ET CORNEILLE MORTIER.
GEOGRAPHES SUR LE VYGEN-DAM [C1720] 40.5x62cm. light browning, wide margins
untrimmed, on 20 sheets, dimensions are for each sheet [18] $1756
HEMISPHERE SEPTENTRIONAL POUR VOIR PLUS DISTINCTEMENT LES TERRES ARCTIQUES
[1735] 46x46.5cm. a circular map [2] $166
JAPONIA REGNUM [C1700] 41.5x57cm. some offsetting, variant edition [31] $574
L'AMERIQUE SEPTENTRIONALE DRESSEE SUR LES OBSERVATIONS DE MR. DE L'ACADEMIE
ROYALE DES SCIENCES, & QUELQUES AUTRES, & SUR LES MEMOIRES LE PLUS RECENS PAR
G. DE L'ISLE. A AMSTERDAM: CHEZ I. COVENS & C. MORTIER. AVEC PRIVILEGE
[1730] 47x58.4cm. [7] $750
L'ASIE DIVERSEE EN SES PRINCAPALES REGIONS [C1735] 49x58cm. [2] $201
LES ENVIRONS DE LONDRES [C1745] 48.3x55.9cm.
Dutch copy of the 1741 Bowles map [12] $130
PARTIE MERIDIONALE DE MOSCOVIE DRESSEE PAR G. DE L'ISLE. A AMSTERDAM CHEZ I.
COVENS ET C. MORTIER [C1700] 50.2x61.6cm.
centerfold split at both ends, minor staining [7] $150
POLIOMETRIA BRITANNICA DAT IS STEDENMEETING VAN GROOT BRITANNIEN [C1690-1700]
48.3x58.4cm. a mileage table between British towns with a large cartouch at
upper right [12] $114
SECONDE PARTIE DE LA CRIMEE LA MER NOIRE &C. RECTIFIES PAR DIVERSES
OBSERVATIONS FAITE PAR GUILLAUME DE L'ISLE. A AMSTERDAM CHEZ JEAN COVENS ET
CORNEILLE MORTIER GEOGRAPHES [C1733] 48.9x61cm. [7] $175

COWLEY

(BEDFORDSHIRE) [1744] C14x18.4cm. [14] $27
(CAMBRIDGHSHIRE) [1744] C14x18.4cm. [14] $26
(HAMPSHIRE) [1744] C14x18.4cm. [14] $29
(NOTTINGHAMSHIRE) [1744] C14x18.4cm. [14] $24
(OXFORDSHIRE) [1744] C14x18.4cm. [14] $29
(YORKSHIRE) [1744] C14x18.4cm. [14] $32
CHARLES TOWN SOUTH CAROLINA, WITH A CHART OF THE BARS & HARBOUR [1780]
19.1x19.7cm. map by R. Cowley [3] $120

COWPERTHWAIT

GEOLOGICAL MAP OF THE U.S. [1890] 26.7x45.7cm. [19] $45

COX

POLYNESIA OR ISLANDS IN THE PACIFIC OCEAN [1853] 33x39.4cm. [3] $40
UTAH, NEW MEXICO, TEXAS, CALIFORNIA ETC... [1853] 31.8x39.4cm. backed
[3] $65

COXE

CARTE DE LA SUISSE [C1789] 49x73.5cm. from Coxe, "Switzerland" [4] $245

CRAM

(ALASKA) [1885] 24.1x31.8cm. [8] $15
(CALIFORNIA//NEVADA) [1885] 47.3x30.5cm. [8] $20
(COLORADO) [1890] 40.6x55.9cm. [27] $50
(DAKOTA//MINNESOTA & NORTH CAROLINA) [1885] 46x29.8cm. [8] $15
(FLORIDA//ALABAMA) [1885] 30.5x25.4cm. [8] $15
(ILLINOIS) [1885] 31.1x22.9cm. with additional pages of text [8] $15
(MISSOURI//IOWA) [1885] 24.1x29.8cm. [8] $20
(MONTANA) [1891] 40.6x55.9cm. [27] $50
(MONTANA//WYOMING & IDAHO) [1885] 30.5x45.7cm. [8] $35
(NEBRASKA//KANSAS) [1885] 24.1x32.1cm. [8] $20
(NEW MEXICO//COLORADO) [1885] 30.5x26cm. [8] $25
(NORTH DAKOTA) [1898] 40.6x55.9cm.
from "Cram's Standard American Railway System Atlas" [27] $45
(OREGON) [1891] 41.9x55.9cm. [27] $45
(TEXAS//ARKANSAS & INDIAN TERRITORY) [1885] 29.8x43.2cm. [8] $40
(UTAH//ARIZONA) [1885] 30.5x24.1cm. [8] $25
(WYOMING) [1891] 40.6x55.9cm. [27] $45
RAILROAD AND COUNTY MAP OF COLORADO [1883] 41.3x56.5cm. [9] $45
RAILROAD AND COUNTY MAP OF KANSAS [1883] 40.6x57.2cm. [10] $30

CRAM (continued)

RAILROAD AND COUNTY MAP OF KENTUCKY AND TENNESSEE [1885] 24.1x30.5cm.
  Virginia and West Virginia on verso [8] $20
TEXAS [1883-84] 30.5x43.2cm. [19] $50
TEXAS [1883] 29.8x43.2cm. [22] $100
TEXAS, EASTERN PART; TEXAS WESTERN PART [C1899] 104.1x67.3cm.
  on 2 sheets, dimensions are total, Reagan County not yet shown [23] $125

CRANTZ

NOVA GROENLANDIAE TABULA [1767] 17.8x25.4cm.
  backed with cloth, from David Crantz, "The History of Greenland" [23] $55
NOVA GROENLANDIAE TABULA A 59 GRADU USQUE AD 73 [1767] 17.8x25.4cm. [3] $65
THE WESTERN COAST OF GREENLAND FROM BALL'S RIVER TO ICE GLANCE [1767]
  17.1x22.9cm. [3] $55
THE WESTERN COAST OF GREENLAND, FROM BALL'S RIVER TO THE ICE GLANCE [1767]
  16.5x22.9cm.
  backed with cloth, from David Crantz, "The History of Greenland" [23] $35

CRAWFORD

MAP OF THE MEXICAN NATIONAL R.R. (LAREDO ROUTE) [1893] 61x59.7cm.
  folding [22] $85
MAP OF THE PROVIDENCE LINE & CONNECTION FOR BOSTON, PROVIDENCE...AND BRITISH
  PROVINCES [1891] 36.8x47cm. [3] $45

CREVECOEUR

ESQUISSE DU MUSKINGHUM/ESQUISSE DES RIVIERES MUSKINGHUM ET GRAND
  CASTON/ESQUISSE DE LA RIVIERE DU GRAND CASTOR [1787] 24.1x52.1cm.
  3 maps on one sheet, "pour les Lettres d'un Cultivator Ameriquain" [23] $125

CROSS

NEW BRUNSWICK & NOVA SCOTIA LAND COMPANY, MAP OF COMPANY'S TRACT OF LAND IN NEW
  BRUNSWICK [1834] 55.9x68.6cm. [3] $80

CRUCHLEY

AMERICA [1841-50] 43x33cm. some browning and splitting on centerfold [21] $36
AMERICA [1843] 46.2x34.4cm. [39] $25
CRUCHLEY'S NEW MAP OF THE WORLD ON MERCATOR'S PROJECTION SHOWING THE
  DISCOVERIES AT THE NORTH POLE AND THE NEW SETTLEMENTS IN AUSTRALIA, NEW
  ZEALAND &C. [1856] 92x165cm. folding, cloth-backed map on 28 panels with
  original cover, light soiling [39] $65
NORTH AMERICA [1840] 23.5x29.5cm. [21] $36
THE WESTERN HEMISPHERE [1841-50] 34x34cm.
  light foxing and browning along centerfold [21] $40
WEST INDIES [1861] 35.5x44.5cm. light browning & foxing [21] $36

CUMMINGS

NORTH AMERICA [1813] 20.3x26.7cm. [19] $65

D'ANVILLE

See also SANTINI
AFRIQUE [1749] 48.3x97.8cm.
  on 2 sheets, dimensions are for each, 1st issue [17] $650
AFRIQUE PUBLIEE SOUS LES AUSPICES DE MONSEIGNEUR LE DUC D'ORLEANS PREMIER
  PRINCE DU SANG...MDCC XLIX AVEC PRIVILEGE [1749] C50.8x99.1cm.
  on 2 sheets, dimensions are for each, minor soiling [7] $350
AMERIQUE MERIDIONALE [1748] 127.6x76.8cm.
  on 3 sheets, dimensions are overall [17] $550
AMERIQUE SEPTENTRIONALE PUBLIEE SOUS LES AUSPICES DE MONSEIGNEUR LE DUC
  D'ORLEANS... [1746] 83.8x86.4cm. backed, minor repairs [3] $325
AMERIQUE SEPTENTRIONALE...PAR LE SR. D'ANVILLE MDCCXLVI AVEC PRIVILEGE. A
  PARIS, CHEZ L'AUTEUR, AUX GALERIES DU LOUVRE [1761] 45.7x87.6cm. on 2
  sheets, dimensions are for each, 5th state with addition of Socorro and
  Passion Islands in the Pacific, map first issued in 1746 [7] $600
CANADA LOUISIANE ET TERRES ANGLOISES [1755] 48x56cm. [5] $600
CANADA LOUISIANE ET TERRES ANGLOISES PER LE SR. D'ANVILLE... [1755]
  39.4x64.8cm. southern sheet only [3] $110

D'ANVILLE (continued)

CARTE DE L'INDE DRESSEE POUR LA COMPAGNIE DES INDES PAR LE SR. D'ANVILLE
  SECRETAIRE DE S.A.S.MGR. LE DUC D'ORLEANS NOVEMBRE 1752 [1752]
  C48.3x104.1cm.
    4 sheets joined to form 2, dimensions are for each pair, one crease[7] $175
CARTE DE LA LOUISIANE [1732-52] 52.1x92.7cm.
  light spotting, repaired tear   [22] $550
CARTE DE LA LOUISIANE PAR LE SR. D'ANVILLE. DRESSEE EN MAI 1732, PUBLIEE EN
  1752 [1752] 52.1x92.1cm. minor repairs   [3] $325
CARTE DE LA PARTIE DE SAINT-DOMINGUE HABITEE PAR LES FRANCOIS [1731]
  23.5x30.5cm.   [3] $85
CARTE GENERALE DE LA TARTARIE CHINOISE [1732] 52x81cm.   [2] $136
LES COTES DE LA GRECE ET L'ARCHIPEL PAR LE SR. D'ANVILLE...OCTOBRE M.DCCLVI...A
  PARIS CHEZ L'AUTEUR, AUX GALERIES DE LOUVRE... [1756] 55.2x72.4cm.
  top margin narrow   [7] $125
PLAN DU PETIT GOAVE ET DE L'ACUL [1733] 16.5x20.3cm.   [3] $45
TROISIEME PARTIE DE LA CARTE D'ASIE, CONTENANT LA SIBERIE, ET QUELQUES AUTRES
  PARTIES DE LA TARTARIE...PAR LE SR. D ANVILLE...MDCCLIII AVEC PRIVILEGE
  [1753] 52.1x54.6cm. on 2 sheets, dimensions are for each   [7] $275

D'APRES DE MANNEVILLETTE

CARTE REDUITE DE L'OCEAN ORIENTAL DEPUIS LE CAP DE BONNE ESPERANCE, JUSQU'AU
  JAPON [1753-75] 56x84cm.   [13] $360
PLAN DE LA BAYE ET DU PORT DE RIO JANEIRO...VERISIE...PAR L'AUTEUR EN 1751
  [1773] 49.5x31.8cm.   [3] $95

DALRYMPLE

PLAN OF OYSTER BAY AND PART OF MARIAS ISLANDS BY CAPT. J.H. COX 1789 [1791]
  29.8x22.9cm.   [3] $65
SKETCH OF VLAMINGO ROAD ON THE EAST SIDE OF AMSTERDAM ISLAND... [1790]
  29.2x21.6cm.   [3] $75
THE WORLD IN 3 SECTIONS [1769] 28.5x46.5cm.   [39] $60

DAMPIER

A MAP OF THE MIDDLE PART OF AMERICA [1729] 15.2x29.2cm. 3 folds, 2 minor
  splits in margins, from Dampier, "A New Voyage around the World," Vol. 1,
  London 1729   [8] $150
THE GREAT AND SMALL BAY OF LE GRANDE, PART OF BRAZILE [1729] 14.6x21cm.
                                   [3] $35
THE GULF OF NICOYA, BY SOME CALL'D TH GULF OF SALINAS [1729] 16.5x21cm.
                                   [3] $85

DANCKERTS

ATLAS-TOT AMSTERDAM BY JUSTUS DANCKERS IN DE CALVERSTRAET INDE DANCBAERHEIJT
  [C1690] 48.3x25.4cm. title page showing Atlas standing on the earth
  supporting the heavens on his shoulders   [3] $165
NOUVELLE ET EXACTE CARTE DU DUCHE DE BRABANT, L'ANNEE 1635. A AMSTERDAM, CHEZ
  CORNEILLE DANKERT [1635] 38.5x48cm.   [18] $140
NOVA TOTIUS TERRARUM ORBIS TABULA [C1700] 47x55.9cm.
  minor centerfold reinforcement, light browning   [16] $2850
NOVI BELGII NOVAEQUE ANGLIAE NEC NON PENNSYLVANIAE ET PARTIS VIRGINIAE TABULA
  [1655] 45.7x54cm. 2nd state   [15] $2850
NOVI BELGII, NOVAE QUAE ANGLIAE NEC NON PENNSYLVANIAE ET PARTIS VIRGINIAE
  TABULA [C1700] 45.7x54.6cm. 2nd state of Danckerts issue   [16] $2750
NOVISSIMA ET ACCURATISSIMA TOTIUS AMERICAE DESCRIPTIO [C1680] 48.3x58.4cm.
  small separation at bottom of centerfold, narrow margins, a variant state
  based on the de Wit map, only appearing in the 1st edition of Danckerts'
  atlas, lacking "Terra Esonis"   [16] $1050
NOVISSIMA ET ACCURATISSIMA TOTIUS HUNGARIAE TABULA PAR P. DU VAL GEOGRAPHE DU
  ROY T'AMSTERDAM GEDRUCKT BY JUSTUS DANCKERS [C1696] 39.4x47.6cm.
  minor stain   [7] $350
RECENTISSIMA NOVI ORBIS SIVE AMERICAE [C1700] 49.5x58.4cm.
  minor browning, wax stain   [16] $950
REGNI HUNGARIAE, GRAECIAE, ET MOREAE... [C1680] 50.2x57.8cm.
  1st ed., 1st issue   [24] $91

DANET
AMERIQUE MERIDIONALE ET SEPTENTRIONALE [1731] 48.3x68.6cm.
  narrow margins, minor repairs at corners   [15] $1475
LA HOLLANDE OU LES PROVINCES UNIES DES PAYS BAS...AVEC LEURS CONQUESTES SUR LES
  ETATS VOISINS DU ROY CATHOLIQUE ET DE L'EMPIRE [C1720] 40x53cm. [18] $175
DAPPER
(AFRICA) [1686] 43.6x54.2cm. minor repairs, dedication cartouch blank
                                   [29] $275
(BARBARY) [1686] 26x35cm.   [29] $53
(CANARY ISLANDS) [1686] 26x35cm.   [29] $76
(CAPE VERDE ISLANDS) [1686] 26x35cm.   [29] $53
(CONGO & ANGOLA) [1686] 26x35cm.   [29] $53
(EGYPT) [1686] 26x35cm.   [29] $61
(FEZ & MOROCCO) [1686] 26x35cm.   [29] $61
(GUINEA) [1686] 26x35cm.   [29] $76
(MADAGASCAR) [1686] 26x35cm. minor spotting   [29] $53
(MALTA) [1686] 26x35cm.   [29] $153
(VALETTA, PERSPECTIVE PLAN) [1686] 26x35cm.   [29] $153
AETHIOPIA SUPERIOR VEL INTERIOR [1686] 26x35cm.   [29] $68
NEW NIEDERLAND (VIEW) [1673] 13.3x16.5cm. view of inhabitants [3] $50
VIRGINIA (VIEW) [1673] 13.3x16.5cm.   [3] $40
DARTON
A NEW CHART OF THE WORLD ON MERCATOR'S PROJECTION [1811] 23.5x35.6cm.
                                   [3] $40
A NEW MAP OF THE COUNTY OF SUFFOLK, DIVIDED INTO HUNDREDS, BY MR. THOS. DIX
  [1816-22] 34.9x44.5cm. from "A Complete Atlas of the English Counties"
                                   [13] $76
A NEW MAP OF THE COUNTY OF YORK, DIVIDED INTO ITS RIDINGS WITH THEIR
  SUBDIVISIONS, EXHIBITING THE WHOLE OF THE MAIL, DIRECT AND PRINCIPAL CROSS
  ROADS, NAVIGABLE CANALS, RIVERS &C. &C. [1820-22] 57.2x73.7cm.
  imprint shaved, from "A Complete Atlas of the English Counties" [13] $137
THE WEST INDIA ISLANDS [1821] 24.8x29.2cm.   [3] $45
DAVIES
ITALY, WITH ITS POLITICAL DIVISIONS, TOWNS, RIVERS [C1810] 45.7x96.5cm.
                                    [30] $73
DAWSON BROS.
DAWSON'S MAP OF THE DOMINION OF CANADA [1883] 55.8x82.5cm.
  folding map on 32 panels   [39] $75
DE BAR
SALT LAKE CITY (VIEW) [1872] 16.5x24.1cm.   [3] $25
DE BEAURAIN
CARTE DE LA HOLLANDE ET D'UNE PARTIE DES ETATS VOISINS, POUR SERVIR A
  L'INTELLIGENCE DE LA CAMPAGNE DE 1672 [C1760] 74x66cm.
  on 2 sheets joined, by le Chev. de Beaurain, Geogr. du Roy [18] $105
DE BELLE FOREST
BOLEDUCH. LE PLANT ET POURTRAICT DE BOLDUC UN DES VILLES CAPITALES DE BRABANT
  [1575] 29.5x34cm.   [18] $140
LE GRAND PLANT ET VRAY PORTRAIT DE LA VILLE DE BRUSSELLES [1575] 32x40cm.
                                     [18] $140
LE POURTRAICT DE LA TRES NOBLE VILLE D'ANVERS AINSI QU'ELLE SE COMPORTE A
  PRESENT [1575] 30x41cm.   [18] $140
LOUVAIN. LE POURTRAICT ET DESCRIPTION DE LA VILLE DE LOUVAIN [1575] 29x35cm.
                                     [18] $105
MALINES. LE VRAY PLANT ET POURTRAICT DE LA VILLE DE MALINES [1575] 28x34cm.
                                     [18] $105
THIONVILLE. POURTRAICT & DESCRIPTION DE THIONVILLE [1575] 12.5x15.5cm.
  with text on 31 x 20 cm page   [18] $105

DE BOUGE
CARTE CHOROGRAPHIQUE DU ROYAUME DES PAYS BAS. COMPRENANT LA DIVISION
   TERRITORIALE EN PROVINCES ET ARRONDISSEMENTS...CARTE DE LA BELGIQUE, LA FRISE
   ET BATAVIE DU TEMS DES ROMAINS...PAR LE CHEV. J.B. DE BOUGE...BRUXELLES,
   1828 [1828] 195x130cm. backed with cloth, in 20 sections   [18] $351
DE BRUYN
(AEGEAN SEA & EASTERN MEDITERRANEAN) [C1698-1714] 31.5x57.2cm.
   narrow margin at top   [29] $76
(ALEPPO, PANORAMIC VIEW) [C1698-1714] 30.5x103cm. minor repairs   [29] $153
(ALEXANDRIA, VIEW) [C1698-1714] 23.3x62.7cm.   [29] $99
(ALEXANDRIA, VIEW) [C1698-1714] 30.3x63.3cm.   [29] $114
(ARCHANGEL TO PERSIAN GULF, ROUTE MAP) [C1698-1714] 28.7x37.1cm.   [29] $38
(ARCHANGEL, VIEW) [C1698-1714] 21.5x61cm.   [29] $61
(ARCHANGEL, VIEW) [C1698-1714] 29.3x38.5cm.
   view showing shipbuilding yards   [29] $38
(ASTRAKHAN, VIEW) [C1698-1714] 21.8x63cm.   [29] $61
(BATAVIA, VIEW) [C1698-1714] 17.7x36.7cm.   [29] $53
(BETHELHEM, VIEW) [C1698-1714] 24.9x63.7cm.   [29] $183
(CAIRO, 2 VIEWS ON ONE SHEET) [C1698-1714] 28x37cm.   [29] $68
(CONSTANTINOPLE, GALATA & PERA, VIEW) [C1698-1714] 29.8x99cm.   [29] $229
(CONSTANTINOPLE, PANORAMIC VIEW) [C1698-1714] 30x190cm. minor repairs
                                                                           [29] $306
(CONSTANTINOPLE, VIEW) [C1698-1714] 23.9x31cm.   [29] $99
(GAMRON/HORMOZ, LARAK & QESHM, VIEWS) [C1698-1714] 23.2x38.2cm.   [29] $68
(ISFAHAN/MEY-DOEN, VIEWS) [C1698-1714] 21.2x38.8cm.   [29] $45
(JERUSALEM, PANORAMIC VIEW) [C1698-1714] 30.3x127cm.   [29] $689
(JOPPE, VIEW) [C1698-1714] 22x38cm.   [29] $130
(KOHM/KASJAN, VIEWS) [C1698-1714] 24.1x34.6cm.   [29] $38
(MOSCOW, PANORAMIC VIEW) [C1698-1714] 30.1x190cm.   [29] $275
(NAZERETH, VIEW) [C1698-1714] 29.5x17.8cm.   [29] $38
(PALMYRA) [C1698-1714] 27.8x63.4cm. shows ruins   [29] $68
(PERSEPOLIS, VIEW) [C1698-1714] 31.4x63.5cm.   [29] $61
(PERSEPOLIS, VIEW) [C1698-1714] 25.7x37.2cm. shows gates & columns   [29] $38
(PERSIAN GULF TO JAVA) [C1698-1714] 23.6x30.8cm.   [29] $53
(RAMA, VIEW) [C1698-1714] 23x62.5cm.   [29] $114
(RHODES, HARBOR VIEW) [C1698-1714] 23.6x63.3cm.
   galley in right foreground   [29] $153
(RHODES, HARBOR VIEW) [C1698-1714] 22.7x62.8cm.   [29] $153
(SAMACHI, VIEW) [C1698-1714] 27.1x37.6cm.   [29] $38
(SATTALIA, VIEW) [C1698-1714] 23.2x62cm. minor fault in sky area   [29] $68
(SCANDERONA/FAMAGUSTA, VIEWS) [C1698-1714] 28.1x30.8cm.   [29] $114
(SCIO, PANORAMIC VIEW) [C1698-1714] 30.5x127cm.   [29] $229
(SCUTARI & THE SERAGLIO, VIEW) [C1698-1714] 30.3x100.6cm.   [29] $229
(SIDON/JUBAIL?, VIEWS) [C1698-1714] 30x18.3cm.   [29] $38
(SMYRNA, PANORAMIC VIEW) [C1698-1714] 30x99cm.
   minor damage at paper junction, minor repairs   [29] $153
(SMYRNA, VIEW) [C1698-1714] 16.6x28.4cm.   [29] $53
(SPAHA, PANORAMIC VIEW) [C1698-1714] 30.3x191cm.   [29] $137
(STANCHIO/RHODES, VIEWS) [C1698-1714] 20.3x38cm.   [29] $84
(TIBERIAS, VIEW) [C1698-1714] 21.9x37.7cm. cut at sides   [29] $61
(TRIPOLI, VIEWS OF TOWN & HARBOUR) [C1698-1714] 28.3x39.3cm.   [29] $99
(TURRES/GALLIPOLI, VIEW) [C1698-1714] 30.3x38cm. minor repair   [29] $45
(TYRE, VIEW) [C1698-1714] 24.8x63cm.   [29] $76
(VERONIS, VIEW) [C1698-1714] 23.1x62.5cm. shows shipbuilding yards   [29] $45
ANTWERPIA (VIEW OF BATTLE) [1582] 28.5x39cm. some centerfold splitting, edge
   reinforced, published by Plantin in "La Joyeuse & Magnifique..."   [37] $200
ATREBATUM REGIONIS [1582] C24x32cm.   [18] $70
BRABANTIA [1582] C24x32cm.   [18] $105
BRABANTIA [1582] 24x32cm.   [18] $105
DESCRIPTIO GERMANIAE INFERIORIS [1582] 24x32cm.   [18] $105
FLANDRIA [1582] C24x32cm.   [18] $105

DE BRUYN (continued)

FRISIAE OCCIDENTALIS TYPUS [1582] 24x32cm.	[18]	$105
GELRIA ET ZUTFANIA [1582] 24x32cm.	[18]	$105
HANNONIAE COMITATUS [1582] C24x32cm.	[18]	$70
HOLLANDIAE TYPUS [1582] 24x32cm.	[18]	$105
LEODIENSIS EPISCOPATUS [1582] C24x32cm.	[18]	$70
LUTZENBURGENSIS DUCATUS VERISS. DESCRIPT. [1582] 23.4x31.8cm.		
no text on verso	[18]	$175
NAMURCUM COMITATUS [1582] C24x32cm.	[18]	$70
NAMURCUM COMITATUS [1582] 24x32cm.	[18]	$70
ZELANDIAE TYPUS [1582] 24x32cm.	[18]	$105

DE BRY

(BRAZIL, ARRIVAL OF NOORT, ENGRAVED SCENE) [1602] 12.5x16.8cm.		
Latin text below scene	[39]	$75
(BRAZIL, ARRIVAL OF SPEILBERGEN, ENGRAVED SCENE) [1618] 15.1x19.1cm.		
text in German below scene	[39]	$80
(CARTAGENA BEING DESTROYED BY FRENCH, ENGRAVED SCENE) [1595] 15.3x19.2cm.		
text below scene	[39]	$90
(COLOMBIA, VESPUCCI'S LANDING, ENGRAVED SCENE) [1619] 14.9x17.6cm.		
text below scene	[39]	$95
(CONCEPCION, SPEILBERGEN AT, ENGRAVED SCENE) [1620] 15.3x19.1cm.		
plus text	[39]	$85
(CUZCO, ATTEMPT BY INCAS TO RETAKE, ENGRAVED SCENE) [1596] 16.7x19.9cm.		
plus descriptive text	[39]	$80
(LIMA, ARRIVAL OF SPEILBERGEN'S FLEET, ENGRAVED SCENE) [1620] 15.4x19.1cm.		
plus descriptive text	[39]	$75
(QUINTERO, SEPILBERGEN AT, ENGRAVED SCENE) [1620] 15.3x19.1cm.		
plus text	[39]	$75
(SLAVES MINING AND SMELTING GOLD, ENGRAVED SCENE) [C1594] 15.9x19.3cm.		
plus text	[39]	$70
(TIERRA DEL FUEGO MAP) [1620] 15.4x19.1cm. plus text	[39]	$85
(WEST INDIES DISCOVERED BY COLUMBUS, ENGRAVED SCENE) [C1594] 14.4x19.4cm.		
plus descriptive text	[39]	$125
(WORLD MAP, UNTITLED) [1600] 11.5x22.5cm. on a sheet measuring 33 by 23.5		
cm., decorated with a portrait of Francis Drake	[37]	$950
(WORLD) [1619] 16.5x20.3cm. untitled double-hemisphere world on the title		
page of Part II of de Bry's issue of Schouten's voyages	[16]	$260
AMERICAE PARS MAGIS COGNITA [1629] 36.5x44cm. 2nd state, dated 1624 but		
probably appearing first in 1629 in 3rd issue of Part III, plans of "Mexico"		
and "Phernambuco" have been added, distinguishing it from 1st state	[39]	$1850
AMERICAE PARS, NUNC VIRGINIA DICTA... [C1590] 30.1x41.8cm.		
lower edge repaired	[39]	$1950
AMERICAE RETECTIO [1594] 14x19.4cm.		
allegorical scene of discovery of America, with text	[39]	$125
BORNEO INSULA [1613-33] 14x21.7cm. light browning, on a page with Latin text,		
the title appears on the island rather than in a cartouch	[12]	$58
DE SINU BAYE LA BAYE... [1599] 14x17cm.	[31]	$84
DESCRIPCION DE LAS INDIAS DEL NORTE [1623] 15.8x22.6cm.	[39]	$95
DESCRIPTIO DEL DESTRICTO DEL AUDIENCIA DEL ESPAGNOLA [1623] 19.5x21.6cm.		
	[39]	$150
F DELFINUM [C1591] 14.2x20.9cm.		
scene showing landing of French in Florida, text below	[39]	$175
FLORIDAE AMERICAE PROVINCIAE [1591] 37x45.5cm.		
some restoration to centerfold and part of ocean area	[37]	$3500
HISPANIAE NOVAE SIVE MAGNAE... [1595] 33.7x44.5cm.		
2 narrow margins, minor loss of border	[3]	$235
I. LADRONES [1631] 14x18.4cm. with text	[3]	$80
INSULAE BALY... [1599] 14x17cm.	[31]	$84
OCCIDENTALIS AMERICAE PARTIS... [C1594] 33x44cm. minor repairs, backed		
	[39]	$1950

(continued)
PUGNAINTER COLUMBUM & FRANCISCUM PORESIUM (ENGRAVED SCENE) [1594] 19.7x15.9cm.
  on a sheet of text, shows Columbus engaged in battle, from Part IV [25] $191
TABULA GEOGRAPHICA NOVA OMNIUM...REGNI GUIANA...GUALTHERO RALEGH... [1625]
  34x45.5cm.
  from 2nd ed., trimmed as issued with no left or right margins   [39] $875
DE FER
(MILAN) [1700] 22.5x33.5cm.   [4] $91
CETTE CARTE DE CALIFORNE ET DU NOUVEAUX MEXIQUE... [1700] 23x34cm.
  short tear repaired   [5] $980
ISLE DE MALTHE [1700] 37.5x52.5cm.   [31] $498
L'ASIE SUIVANT LES NOUVELLES DECOUVERTES DONT LES POINT PRINCIPAUX SONT PLACEZ
  SUR LES OBSERVATIONS DE MRS. DE L'ACADEMIE ROYALE DES SCIENCES. PAR N. DE
  FER. AVEC PRIVILEGE DU ROY. 1717 [1717] 22.9x55.2cm.
  minor tear at fold, top & side margins narrow   [7] $225
L'ISLE ST. DOMINGUE OU ESPAGNOLE DECOUVERTE EN 1492 PAR LES ESPAGNOLS DRESSEE
  SUR LES MEMOIRES DE DESSUNT MR. DE CUSSY [1715] 22.9x33cm.   [3] $90
L'ISLE ST. DOMINGUE OU ESPAGNOLE DECOUVERTE L'AN 1492...CHEZ DANIEL GENDRE DE
  L'AUTEUR SUR LE POINT N. DAME [1723] 43.2x57.8cm.   [3] $285
LA CALIFORNIE OU NOUVELLE CAROLINE [1720] 44.5x64.8cm.
  2 minor stains, minor centerfold discoloration   [16] $2500
LE PAIS D'ENTRE SAMBRE ET MEUSE ET LES ENVIRONS DE NAMUR, DINANT, CHARLES-ROY,
  MONS, ATH, BRUSSELES, LOUVAIN ET HUY. PAR N. DE FER, 1705. C. INSELIN SCULP.
  [1705] 39x50cm.   [18] $105
LE PEROU DANS L'AMERIQUE MERIDIONALE DRESSE SUR LES DIVERS RELATIONS DES
  FILIBUSTIERS ET NOUVEAUX VOYAGEURS... [1719] 48.3x57.8cm.
  minor repairs   [3] $265
LE VIEUX MEXIQUE OU NOUVELLE ESPAGNE AVEC LES COSTES DE LA FLORIDE [1705]
  22.5x33.5cm.   [5] $220
LE VIEUX MEXIQUE OU NOUVELLE ESPAGNE AVEC LES COSTES DE LA FLORIDE... [1705]
  22.9x33cm.   [9] $275
LES COSTES AUX ENVIRONS DE LA RIVIERE DE MISISIPI [1705] 22.5x33.5cm.
                                                                    [5] $300
LES ISLES DE L'AMERIQUE [1705] 22.5x33.5cm.   [5] $200
LES PROVINCES APPELEES PAIS BAS CONNUES SOUS LES NOMS DE FLANDRE ET DE
  HOLLANDE...PAR N. DE FER. PARIS, DANET, SUR LE PONT N. DAME A LA SPHERE
  ROYALE [1700-20] 53x41cm.   [18] $175
MAPPE-MONDE, OU CARTE GENERALE DE LA TERRE, DIVISEE EN DEUX HEMISPHERES SUIVANT
  LA PROJECTION LA PLUS COMMUNE OU TOUS LES POINTS PRINCIPAUX...SUR LES
  OBSERVATIONS DE MRS. DE L'ACADEMIE ROYALE DES SCIENCES...AVEC PRIVILEGE DU
  ROY 1700 [C1700] 44.5x70.5cm. centerfold separation repaired, minor stain,
  1st state, engraved by van Loon   [7] $1400
PARTIE MERIDIONALE DE LA RIVIERE MISSISIPI [1718] 47x63.5cm.
  from "Atlas ou Recueil de Cartes Geographiques"   [16] $1200
PARTIE OCCIDENTALE D'AFRIQUE [C1700] 22.5x32.5cm.   [4] $84
PLAN DE LA VILLE DE ROME [1700] 23.5x30cm.   [4] $91
PROVINCES DES PAIS BAS DIVISEES SUIVANT LES TRAITES...FAITS EN 1713, 1714 ET
  1716. ET OU LES NOUVELLES BARRIERES SONT MARQUEES. PAR N. DE FER, PARIS, CHEZ
  BENARD 1737 [1737] 47x62cm.   [18] $175
DE JODE
ANGLIAE SCOTIAE ET HIBERNIAE NOVA DESCRIPTIO [1578-93] 34.9x49.5cm.
  from the 1593 edition   [13] $1149
ANGLIAE, SCOTIAE ET HIBERNIE NOVA DESCRIPTIO [1593] 34.5x49.5cm.   [31] $1226
ASIA PARTIUM ORBIS MAXIMA [1593] 38.1x47cm.   [15] $2350
BRASILIA ET PERUVIA [1593] 36.8x41.9cm.   [15] $2600
EPISCOPATUS LEODIENSIS PROVINCIA, AUCTORE IOHANNE A SCHILDE [1578] 34x24cm.
  from 1st ed.   [18] $351
GELDRIA [1578] 36.5x48.5cm. from the first ed., several minor repairs
                                                                    [18] $260
GERMANIAE INFERIORIS, GALLIAE BELGICAE DICTAE CONTINENTIS...PER MATHIAM ZINCK
  NORICUM. IOANNES A DEUTECUM LUCAS A DEUT. FECERUNT [1578] 30.5x48.5cm.
  some restoration   [18] $351

96

DE JODE (continued)
HELVETIAE SEU SUICIAE...CHOROGRAPHIA VERA ET ELEGANS [1593] 39x52cm.
  minor restoration at lower corners in margin [2] $2107
HEMISPHERIU AB AEQUINOCTIALI LINEA AD CIRCULU POLI ARTICI/HEMISPHERIU AB
  AEQUINOCTIALI LINEA, AD CIRCULU POLI ATARTICI [1593] 33x52.1cm. [15] $6500
NOVA GUINEA FORMA & SITUS [1593] 34x21cm. [31] $4599
PALESTINAE VEL TERRAE SANCTAE TAB. II. [1593] 33x52.1cm. [15] $4700
PALESTINAE VEL TERRAE SANCTAE, TAB. I. [1593] 30.5x50.8cm. [15] $4200
TOTIUS ORBIS COGNITI UNIVERSALIS DESCRIPTIO [1593] 35.6x49.5cm.
  minor centerfold repairs [15] $5600

DE L'ISLE
  See also ALBRIZZI
  See also COVENS & MORTIER
  See also DEZAUCHE
  See also LOTTER
CARTE D'AMERIQUE [1780] 48.3x61cm. narrow top margin [22] $350
CARTE DE LA LOUISIANE ET DU COURS DU MISSISSIPPI [1718] 48.5x65cm.
  backed with archival tissue, 1st state [5] $2200
CARTE DE LA LOUISIANE ET DU COURS DU MISSISSIPPI [1718] 48.3x66cm.
  some reinforcement at folds, 1st ed. [15] $1050
CARTE DES ANTILLES FRANCOISES ET DES ISLES VOISINES [1717] 64.2x37.1cm.
  [39] $125
CARTE DES COMTEZ DE HAINAUT, DE NAMUR ET DE CAMBRESIS. PAR GUILLAUME DE
  L'ISLE...PARIS, 1706 ET AMSTERDAM, CHEZ LOUIS RENARD [C1706] 47x67cm.
  [18] $105
CARTE DES PAYS-BAS CATHOLIQUES...PARIS, CHEZ L'AUTEUR, SUR LE QUAY DE
  L'HORLOGE A L'AIGLE D'OR [1702] 49x63cm. [18] $105
CARTE DES PROVINCES UNIES DES PAYS-BAS...PAR G. DE L'ISLE, GEOGRAPHE, PARIS,
  CHEZ L'AUTEUR, 1702 [1702] 48x63cm. first state [18] $105
CARTE DU BRABANT [C1700] 64x64cm. first ed. [18] $140
CARTE DU CANADA OU DE LA NOUVELLE FRANCE ET DES DECOUVERTES QUI Y ONT ETE
  FAITES [1703-18] 49.5x64.8cm. 1st state, 3rd issue [15] $775
CARTE DU CANADA OU DE LA NOUVELLE FRANCE ET DES DECOUVERTES...PAR GUILLAUME
  DEL'ISLE DE L'ACADEMIE ROYALE DES SCIENCES ET PREMIER GEOGRAPHE DU ROY. A
  PARIS CHEZ L'AUTEUR SUR LE QUAI DE L'HORLOGE A L AIGLE D OR AVEC PRIVILEGE DE
  SA MAJTE. POUR 20 ANS 1703 [1718] 50.2x65.4cm. minor staining in right
  margin, small split in upper margin repaired, 1st state, 5th issue [7] $875
CARTES DES NOUVELLES DECOUVERTES AU NORD DE LA MER DU SUD...A PARIS, QUAY DE
  L'HORLOGE DU PALAIS, AVEC LES CARTES DE GUILL. DELISLE ET DE PHIL. BUACHE
  [1752] 45.4x63.5cm. light browning [26] $1200
HEMISPHERE OCCIDENTAL DRESSEE EN 1720 POUR L'USAGE DU ROY SUR LES OBSERVATIONS
  ASTRONOMIQUES ET GEOGRAPHIQUES...A PARIS CHEZ L'AUTEUR LE SIEUR DEL'ISLE SUR
  LE QUAY DE L'HORLOGE SOUS LE PRIVILEGE...LE 15. SEPTEMBRE 1724 [1724]
  50.8x50.8cm. top & bottom margins ragged, 1st state [7] $650
HEMISPHERE SEPTENTRIONALE POUR VOIR PLUS DISTINETEMENT LES TERRES
  ARCTIQUES...QUAY DE L'HORLOGE JUILLET 1714 [1714] 45.7x45.7cm.
  1st issue [3] $265
L'AMERIQUE MERIDIONALE DRESSEE SUR LES OBSERVATIONS... [C1702] 45.7x60cm.
  [39] $285

DE LAET
AFEELDING VAN DE CABO ST. AUGUSTIN MER HAER FORTEN (VIEW) [1644] 27.9x37.5cm.
  [3] $135
AMERICAE SIVE INDIAE OCCIDENTALIS [1633] C27.9x35.6cm. [38] $575
CHILI [1633] C27.9x35.6cm. [38] $175
FLORIDA, ET REGIONES VICINAE [1633] C27.9x35.6cm. [38] $3250
GUAIANA [1633] C27.9x35.6cm. [38] $250
MAIORES MINORES QUE INSULAE HISPANIOLA, CUBA... [1633] C27.9x35.6cm.
  [38] $575
NOVA ANGLIA NOVUM BELGIUM ET VIRGINIA [1633] C27.9x35.6cm. [38] $3200
NOVA FRANCIA ET REGIONES ADIACENTES [1633] C27.9x35.6cm. [38] $950
NOVA FRANCIA ET REGIONES ADIACENTES [1630] 27.9x35.6cm. [15] $1600

DE LAET (continued)
NOVA HISPANIA, NOVA GALICA [1633] C27.9x35.6cm.   [38] $575
PARAGUAY, O PROV. DE LA PLATA [1633] C27.9x35.6cm.   [38] $125
PERU [1633] C27.9x35.6cm.   [38] $150
PROVINCIA DE BRAZIL [1633] C27.9x35.6cm.   [38] $175
PROVINCIAE SITAE AD FRETUM MAGELLANIS ITEMQUE FRETUM LE MAIRE [1633]
   C27.9x35.6cm.   [38] $250
TIERRA FIRMA ITEM NUEVO REYNO DE GRANADA ATQUE POPAYAN [1633] C27.9x35.6cm.
                                                                        [38] $200
VENEZUALA... [1625] 28x35cm. tear in upper right blank margin   [31] $498
VENEZUELA ATQUE OCCIDENTALIS PARS NOVAE ANDALUSIAE [1633] C27.9x35.6cm.
                                                                        [38] $425
DE LETH
CARTE NOUVELLE DE LA MER DU SUD [C1730] 59.7x96.5cm.
   some reinforcements at folds   [15] $5200
LA VERITABLE DESCRIPTION DU SIEGE DE PHILIPSBOURG PAR LES FRANCOIS [C1740]
   45.7x48.3cm.   [30] $81
DE RIENZI
AMERIQUE SEPTENTRIONALE [1840] 19.1x24.8cm.   [20] $70
DE VAUGONDY
AFRIQUE DRESSEE SUR LES RELATIONS LES PLUS RECENTES, ET ASSUJETTIE AUX
   OBSERVATIONS ASTRONOMIQUES [1756] 46.4x58.4cm.
   narrow margins, one edge reinforced   [24] $61
AMERIQUE MERIDIONALE [C1750-57] 48.5x59.5cm.   [4] $107
AMERIQUE MERIDIONALE... [1750] 47x58.4cm.   [3] $165
AMERIQUE SEPTENTRIONALE [1750] 48.3x59.7cm. from "Atlas Universel"   [16] $280
AMERIQUE SEPTENTRIONALE DRESSEE SUR LES RELATIONS LES PLUS MODERNES DES
   VOYAGEURS...ET CORRIGEE EN 1775... [1775] 48.3x58.4cm. backed   [3] $385
AMERIQUE SEPTENTRIONALE DRESSEE SUR LES RELATIONS...OU SE REMARQUENT LES ETATS
   UNIS...CORRIGEE EN 1783 [1783] 48.3x58.4cm. backed   [3] $365
AMERIQUE SEPTENTRIONALE, DRESSEE, SUR LES RELATIONS LES PLUS MODERNES DES
   VOYAGEURS ET NAVIGATEURS, ET DIVISEE SUIVANT LES DIFFERENTES POSSESSIONS DES
   EUROPEENS. PAR LE SR. ROBERT DE VAUGONDY...AVEC PRIVILEGE. 1750 [1750]
   49.5x62.9cm. minor offsetting of color   [7] $525
CARTE DE L'EMPIRE D'ALLEMAGNE [C1757] C48x53cm.   [4] $107
CARTE DE L'EMPIRE D'ALLEMANGE; LES ROUTES DES POSTES [C1757] C48x53cm.
                                                                        [4] $91
CARTE DE LA CALIFORNIA SUIVANT 1. CARTE MANUSCRIT 1604... [1744] 29x38.5cm.
                                                                        [31] $268
CARTE DE LA CALIFORNIE [C1775] 29.2x38.1cm. from Diderot's Encyclopedia, 5
   maps showing various conceptions of California   [16] $380
CARTE DE LA CALIFORNIE ET DES PAYS NORD-OUEST SEPARES DE L'ASIE PAR LE DETROIT
   D'ANIAN... [C1780] 29.2x36.8cm.   [11] $175
CARTE DE LA VIRGINIE ET DU MARYLAND [C1757] 48.3x64.1cm.   [32] $500
CARTE DES CERCLES DU HAUTE ED DU BAS RHIN [C1757] C48x53cm.   [4] $137
CARTE DU DUCHE DE LUXEMBOURG [C1757] C48x53cm.   [4] $275
CARTE GENERAL DES DECOUVERTS DE L'ADMIRAL FONTE [C1775] 30.5x38.1cm.
   from Diderot's Encyclopedia   [16] $180
CARTE GENERALE DES DECOUERTES DE L'AMIRAL DE FONTE ET AUTRES NAVIGATEURS
   ESPAGNOLES, ANGLOIS ET RUSSES POUR LA RECHERCHE DU PASSAGE A LA MER DU SUD.
   PAR M. DE L'ISLE DE L'ACADAMIE ROYALE DES SCIENCES...A PARIS EN SEPTEMBRE
   1752 [1779] C27x37cm. from Diderot's Encyclopedia   [8] $175
CARTE GENERALE DES DECOUVERTES DE L'AMIRAL DE FONTE, ET AUTRES NAVIGATEURS
   ESPAGNOLS ANGLOIS ET RUSSES... [1772] 29.2x38.1cm.
   dated 1752 on the map   [11] $175
CARTE GENERALE DES DECOUVERTES DE L'AMIRAL DE FONTE...PAR THOMAS JEFFERYS...
   [C1775] 30.5x38.1cm. from Diderot's Encyclopedia   [16] $180
CARTE QUI REPRESENTE LES DIFFERENTES CONNAISSANCES QUE L'ON VUE DES TERRES
   ARCTIQUES DEPUIS 1650 JUSQU'EN 1747... [1777] 30.5x34.3cm.
   4 maps on one sheet   [3] $95
CARTES DES ROYAUMES D'ESPAGNE ET DE PORTUGAL [C1757] C48x53cm.   [4] $61

DE VAUGONDY (continued)
```
CARTES DES ROYAUMES D'ESPAGNE ET DE PORTUGAL. LES ROUTES DES POSTES [C1757]
   C48x53cm.                                                       [4]    $45
CERCLE DE BASSE SAXE [C1757] C48x53cm.                             [4]   $137
CERCLE DE FRANCONIE [C1757] C48x53cm.                             [4]   $137
CERCLE DE SOUABE [C1757] C48x53cm.                                [4]   $137
CERCLE DE WESTPHALIE [C1757] C48x53cm.                            [4]   $137
COMTE DE FLANDRES [C1757] C48x53cm.                               [4]    $76
COMTE DE HAINAULT ET DE CAMBRESIS [C1757] C48x53cm.              [4]    $45
COURS DU MISSISSIPI ET LA LOUISIANE... [1749] 21.6x16.5cm.       [3]    $95
ENVIRONS DE PARIS [C1757] C48x53cm.                              [4]    $76
ETATS DE LA COURONNE D'ARAGON [C1757] C48x53cm.                  [4]   $107
ETATS DU GRAND-SEIGNEUR EN ASIE... [C1753-57] 48x55.5cm.         [4]   $183
GERMANIA ANTIQUA [C1757] C48x53cm.                               [4]    $45
GRAECIA VETUS [C1757] C48x53cm.                                  [4]    $91
HISPANIA ANTIQUA [C1757] C48x53cm.                               [4]    $45
JUDEE OU TERRE SAINTE SOUS LES TURCS [1778] 24.1x21.6cm.         [10]   $50
L'AFRIQUE [C1756-57] 46.5x58.5cm.                                [4]   $168
L'AFRIQUE DIVISEE EN SES PRINCIPALES PARTIES, OU LES EMPIRES, LES MONARCHIES,
   LES ROYAUMES, LES ETATS, ET LES PEUPLES...PAR LE SR. ROBERT...A PARIS: CHEZ
   L'AUTEUR SUR LE QUAI DE L'HORLOGE...AVEC PRIVILEGE DU ROY 1741 [1741]
   50.8x73cm.
      top & bottom margins stained, short tear in lower margin at centerfold
                                                                 [7]   $250
L'EMPIRE DE JAPON... [1750] 48.3x53.3cm.                         [24]  $236
L'EMPIRE DU JAPON EN SEPT PRINCIPALES PARTIES... [1750] 48.3x53.3cm. [3] $275
L'EUROPE [C1757] C48x53cm.                                       [4]    $91
LA PRINCIPAUTE DE LIEGE ET LE DUCHE DE LIMBOURG [C1757] C48x53cm. [4]  $61
LE CERCLE DE BAVIERE [C1757] C48x53cm.                           [4]   $137
LE ROYAUME D'ANGLETERRE... [1753] 47.6x51.4cm.
   lower centerfold repaired & other minor repairs               [24]   $91
LE ROYAUME DE BOHEMIA [C1757] C48x53cm.                          [4]    $76
LE ROYAUME DE FRANCE [C1757] C48x53cm.                           [4]    $61
LE ROYAUME DE POLOGNE [C1757] C48x53cm.                          [4]    $91
LE TYROL [C1757] C48x53cm.                                       [4]   $107
LES PROVINCES UNIES DES PAYS-BAS... [C1750] 49x60cm.             [18]   $87
LES PROVINCES-UNIES DES PAYS-BAS [C1757] C48x53cm.               [4]   $137
LES ROYAUMES DE SUEDE ET DE NORWEGE [C1757] C48x53cm.            [4]   $137
NOUVELLE REPRESENTATION DES COTES NORD ET EST DE L'ASIE POUR SERVIR
   DE'ECLAIRCISSEMENT AUX ARTICLES DU SUPPLEMENT DE L'ENCYCLOPEDIE QUI
   CONCERNENT LE PASSAGE AUX INDES PAR LE NORD. GRAVEE SOUS LA DIRECTION DE MR.
   DE VAUGONDY EN 1772 [1779] 29.2x37.8cm. folds as issued       [21]   $73
PARTIE DE L'AMERIQUE SEPTENT QUI COMPREND LA NOUVELLE FRANCE OU LE CANADA, PAR
   LE SR. ROBERT DE VAUGONDY GEOG ORDINAIRE DU ROY. AVEC PRIVILEGE 1755 [1755]
   49.5x60.3cm.
      slight soiling in margins, inset "Supplement Pour Les Lacs Du Canada"
                                                                 [7]   $650
PARTIE DE L'AMERIQUE SEPTENT. QUI COMPREND LA NOUVELLE FRANCE OU LE CANADA
   [1755] 47.6x60.3cm.                                           [22]  $500
PARTIE DE L'AMERIQUE SEPTENT. QUI COMPREND LA NOUVELLE FRANCE OU LE CANADA. PAR
   LE SR. ROBERT DE VAUGONDY GEOG ORDINAIRE DU ROY. AVEC PRIVILEGE 1755 [1755]
   48x60cm.                                                      [21]  $394
PARTIE DE L'AMERIQUE SEPTENTRIONALE QUE COMPREND LE COURS DE L'OHIO, LA NLLE.
   ANGLETERRE...LA VIRGINIE, LA CAROLINE [1757] 47x62.2cm. 2nd ed.  [3] $375
PARTIE DE L'AMERIQUE SEPTENTRIONALE, QUI COMPREND LE COURS DE L'OHIO, LA NLLE.
   ANGLETERRE, LA NLLE YORK, LE NEW JERSEY, LA PENSYLVANIE, LE MARYLAND LA
   VIRGINIE, LA CAROLINE. PAR LE SR. ROBERT DE VAUGONDY GEOGRAPHE ORDINAIRE DU
   ROI...1755 [C1755-57] 61.6x47.6cm.                            [25]  $344
PARTIE DE L'AMERIQUE SEPTENTRIONALE, QUI COMPREND LE COURS DE L'OHIO, LA NLLE.
   ANGLETERRE, LA NLLE YORK, LE NEW JERSEY, LA PENSYLVANIE, LE MARYLAND LA
   VIRGINIE, LA CAROLINE. PAR LE SR. ROBERT DE VAUGONDY...AVEC PRIVILEGE 1755
   [1755] 49.5x62.2cm. 1st state                                 [7]   $475
```

DE VAUGONDY (continued)

PARTIE DE L'AMERIQUE SEPTENTRIONALE, QUI COMPREND LE COURS DE L'OHIO... [1755]
   47.6x62.2cm.   [35] $475
PARTIE MERIDION. DU DUCHE DE BRABANT [C1757] C48x53cm.   [4] $91
PARTIE MERIDIONALE DES ETATS DE CASTILLE [C1757] C48x53cm.   [4] $76
PARTIE MERIDIONALE DU CERCLE D'AUTRICHE [C1757] C48x53cm.   [4] $61
PARTIE MERIDIONALE DU ROYAUME DE PORTUGAL [C1757] C48x53cm.   [4] $61
PARTIE SEPTENT. QUI COMPREND LA NOUVELLE FRANCE OU LE CANADA [1755]
   47.5x60.5cm.   [5] $400
PARTIE SEPTENTRIONALE DE LA COURONNE DE CASTILLE [C1757] C48x53cm. [4] $61
PARTIE SEPTENTRIONALE DU CERCLE D'AUTRICHE [C1757] C48x53cm. [4] $137
PARTIE SEPTENTRIONALE DU DUCHE DE BRABANT [C1757] C48x53cm.   [4] $91
PARTIE SEPTENTRIONALE DU ROYAUME DE PORTUGAL [C1757] C48x53cm. [4] $61
PAYS-BAS CATHOLIQUES [1751] 59x56cm.   [18] $70
PAYS-BAS CATHOLIQUES [C1757] C48x53cm.   [4] $76
ROMANI IMPERII [C1757] C48x53cm.   [4] $61
ROYAUME D'IRLANDE [1750] 48.3x54cm.   [30] $182
ROYAUME DE DANEMARK [C1757] C48x53cm.   [4] $137
ROYAUME DE HONGRIE [C1757] C48x53cm.   [4] $76
ROYAUMES D'ESPAGNE ET DE PORTUGAL [C1757] C48x53cm.   [4] $61
ROYAUMES D'ESPAGNE ET DE PORTUGAL. LES ROUTES DE POSTES [C1757] C48x53cm.
          [4] $45
TERRE-FERME, PEROU, BRESIL PAYS DE L'AMAZON... [C1786] 24.1x27.9cm.
  backed   [3] $60
TURQUIE EUROPEENE [C1757] C48x53cm.   [4] $122

DE WIT

(BRITISH ISLES) [C1688] 47.6x55.9cm.   [17] $750
(MALTA) [1680] 44.5x53.3cm. full title not given   [17] $650
ACHAIAE NOVA & ACCURATA DESCRIPTIO [C1680-90] 38.1x55.9cm. [24] $110
BELGIUM FOEDERATUM... [1680] 31.8x45.7cm.   [17] $550
COMITATUS FLANDRIAE TABULA [C1680] 47x56cm. minor water staining [18] $140
COMITATUS NAMURCI...GEDRUCKT T'AMSTERDAM BY FREDERICK DE WIT [C1680] 47x54cm.
          [18] $140
DUCATUS GELDRIAE ET COMITATUS ZUTPHANIAE TABULA [C1680] 46.5x55.5cm. [18] $175
DUCATUS LUTZENBURGICI TABULA NUPERRIME IN LUCEM EDITA [C1680] 46.5x55.5cm.
  minor repair, 2nd state with "V" in upper-right corner   [2] $245
INSULA CANDIA EJUSQUE FORTIFICATIO [1680] 46x55.5cm.   [2] $439
INSULA CANDIA... [1680] 44.5x55.2cm. with 6 insets of towns & islands
          [17] $750
INSULA MALTA...CUM URBIBUS ET FORTALITIIS [C1680] 44.5x54cm. [2] $421
INSULARUM ARCHIPELAGI SEPTENTRIONALIS SEU MARIS AEGAEJ ACCURATA DELINEATIO
  [C1680] 47.6x57.2cm.   [24] $104
NOVA ET ACCURATA NORMANDIAE DUCATUS TABULA...EDITA A PETRO PERSOY AMSTELODAMI
  [C1680] 47x55.9cm.   [24] $91
NOVA ORBIS TABULA IN LUCEM EDITA [C1680] 47x86.4cm.   [16] $2800
NOVA TOTIUS AMERICAE DESCRIPTIO [C1670] 43.2x54.6cm.
  repairs in margin at lower corners   [15] $1800
NOVAE HISPANIAE, CHILI, PERUVIAE ET GUATIMALAE LITTORAE [1688] 49x56cm.
          [2] $333
NOVISSIMA ET ACCURATISSIMA SEPTENTRIONALIS AC MERIDINOALIS AMERICAE...PER
  FREDERICUM DE WITT AMSTELODAMI CUM PRIVILEGIO... [C1680] 49.5x58.4cm.
          [7] $1225
NOVISSIMA ET ACCURATISSIMA SEPTENTRIONALIS ET MERIDIONALIS AMERICAE [C1680]
  48.3x58.4cm. second state with altered title, Straits of Anian and "Terra
  Esonis" added   [16] $1100
NOVISSIMA ET ACCURATISSIMA TOTIUS AMERICAE DESCRIPTIO... [1670] 49.5x58.4cm.
          [16] $1000
NOVISSIMAE PRAE CAETERIS ALIIS ACCURATISSIMA REGNORUM ANGLIAE, SCOTIAE
  HIBERNIAQ TABULA [C1680] 58.4x48.3cm.   [12] $283
POLI ARCTICI, ET CIRCIMIACENTIUM TERRARUM DESCRIPTIO NOVISSIMA [C1670]
  42.9x48.9cm. minor faults, backed   [39] $525

DE WIT (continued)

POLI ARCTICI, ET CIRCUMIACENTIUM TERRARUM DESCRIPTIO NOVISSIMA PER FREDERIC DE
    WIT AMSTELODAMI [C1680] 43.2x49.5cm. some spotting & chipping in margins,
      tear in lower margin at centerfold   [7] $950
REGNUM NEAPOLIS IN QUO SUNT APRUTIUM ULTERIUS ET CITERIUS... [C1680]
    58.4x49.5cm.   [24] $79
SUYDT HOLLANDIAE [C1680] 45.5x54.5cm.   [18] $175
TABULA COMITATUS FRISIAE... [C1680] 46.5x55cm.   [18] $228
TABULA INDIAE ORIENTALIS [1680] 45.5x56cm.   [31] $1303
TERRA NOVA... [1675] 48.3x55.9cm.   [32] $650
TERRA SANCTA SIVE PROMISSIONIS, OLIM PALESTINA [C1675] 46x55cm.
    minor repair   [2] $368
TERRA SANCTA, SIVE PROMISSIONIS, OLIM PALESTINA [C1680] 45.7x55.2cm. [24] $245
TURCICUM IMPERIUM [C1690] 45.5x55.5cm.   [4] $275

DEAN & MUNDAY

MAP OF THE EASTERN TOWNSHIPS OF LOWER CANADA [1834] 24.8x40.6cm. [3] $45

DELAMARCHE

AMERIQUE OU INDES OCCIDENTALES [1792] 50.8x63.5cm.
    centerfold repaired, with an inset panel of text   [23] $150
CANADA, LOUISIANE, ETATS-UNIS [C1795] 24x28.9cm.
    early manuscript notes in margin, reissue of de Vaugondy map   [39] $95
CARTE DE L'AMERIQUE SEPTENTRIONALE ET DES ANTILLES [1844-50] 43.2x29.2cm.
    dated 1844, published in 1850 in "Atlas de Geographie..."   [27] $100
ETATS-UNIS DE L'AMERIQUE SEPTENTRIONALE AVEC LES ISLES ROYALE, DE TERRE NUEVE
    DE ST. JEAN, L'ACADIE &C. [1785] 47.4x62.7cm.   [39] $485

DEPOSITO HIDROGRAFICO

(VIRGIN ISLANDS) [1804] 58.4x90.2cm. centerfold repaired   [17] $450

DEPOT DE LA MARINE

See also BELLIN

BAYE DE L'ACUL/BAYE DAME-MARIE/PORT FRANCOIS/MOLE ST. NICOLAS/BAYE DES IROIS
    [1785] 58.4x45.1cm.   [3] $95
CARTE D'UNE PARTIE DE LA MER DE CHINE. 1798 [C1825] 69.1x49.2cm.
    margins repaired, chart by Vice Admiral Rosili   [28] $99
CARTE DE LA GONAVE, DRESSEE SUR LES OPERATIONS GEOMETRIQUES FAITES EN
    1787...PAR ORDRE DU ROI EN 1788 PAR M. DE LIEUDE DE SEPMANVILLE [1788]
    58.4x88.9cm.   [3] $160
CARTE DE LA PARTIE DE LA COTE NORD-OUEST DE L'AMERIQUE [C1825] 75x58.8cm.
    re-issued from the 1800 Paris ed. of Vancouver's voyage   [28] $229
CARTE DE LA PARTIE MERIDIONALE DE LA PRESQU'ISLE DE L'INDE QUI COMPREND L'ISLE
    DE CEYLAN. 1798 [C1825] 48.6x69.8cm. chart by Vice Admiral Rosili [28] $76
CARTE DES ARCHIPELS DES ILES SALOMON, DE LA LOUISIADE ET DE LA NOUV. LE
    BRETAGNE. 1806 [C1825] 49.3x75.5cm. chart by C.F. Beautemps-Beaupre
                   [28] $114
CARTE DES COTES DE GUZERAT, DE CONCAN ET DE CANARA. 1798 [C1825] 69x48.2cm.
    chart by Vice Admiral Rosili   [28] $53
CARTE DES COTES DE L'AMERIQUE MERIDIONALE DEPUIS LE PARALLELE 36 30' LAT. SUD
    JUSQU'AU CAP DE HORN. 1800 [C1825] 90.7x61.8cm.   [28] $153
CARTE DES ILES SANDWICH [C1825] 54.8x76.2cm.
    minor fold damage, based on Vancouver's voyage   [28] $306
CARTE GENERALE DE L'OCEAN ATLANTIQUE OU OCCIDENTAL... [1792] 60.5x89.5cm.
                   [39] $250
CARTE GENERALE DE LA MER ROUGE. 1798 [C1825] 59.5x86.5cm. on 3 sheets,
    dimensions are for each, minor staining, chart by Vice Admiral Rosili
                   [28] $245
CARTE PARTICULIERE DE LA COTE OCCIDENTALE D'ECOSSEE...PAR ORDRE DU
    CONTRE-AMIRAL DECRES...AU DEPOT GENERAL DE LA MARINE ET L'AN XII [1796]
    87.6x58.4cm. minor reinforcement   [24] $113
CARTE PARTICULIERE DU HAVRE DE BOSTON... [C1780] 58.4x87.6cm. issued by the
    Depot General des Cartes, Plans et Journaux de la Marine, based on the des
    Barres chart   [16] $800

CARTE REDUITE DE LA COTE OCCIDENTALE DE L'AMERIQUE DEPUIS 9 DE LATITUDE NORD
 JUSQU'A 7 DE LATITUDE SUD. 1821 [C1825] 84.7x56.1cm.   [28] $99
CARTE REDUITE DE LA PARTIE DE LA COTE DU CHILI COMPRISE ENTRE LE 22E ET LE 38E
 DEGRE DE LATITUDE SUD. 1821 [C1825] 84.5x56.4cm.   [28] $76
CARTE REDUITE DE LA PARTIE DE LA COTE DU PEROU COMPRISE ENTRE LE 7E ET LE 21E
 DEGRE DE LATITUDE SUD. 1821 [C1825] 84.8x55.1cm.   [28] $84
CARTE REDUITE DE LA PARTIE MERIDIONALE DE L'ILE D'HAINAN PARCOUROE EN 1817 PAR
 LA FREGATE DU ROI LA CYBELE 1819 [C1825] 42.6x57.4cm.
 light staining, chart by A. de Kergariou   [28] $45
CARTE REDUITE DES COTES ORIENTALES DE L'AMERIQUE SEPTENTRIONALE [1778]
 59.1x87.6cm. from the "Neptune Americo-Septentrionale," map by Sartine
                                                                            [23] $1000
CARTE REDUITE DES ILES DE FRANCE ET DE BOURBON. 1798, NOUVELLE EDITION, 1802
 [C1825] 58.1x87.2cm.
 minor repair, chart by Jean Baptiste Lislet-Geoffroy   [28] $130
CARTE REDUITE DES MERS DU NORD... [1776] 55.9x86.4cm.
 covers Labrador to Norway   [24] $183
CARTE REDUITE DU GOLPHE DE ST. LAURENT CONTENANT L'ISLE DE TERRE-NEUVE ET
 PARTIE DE LA COSTE DES ESQUIMAUX L'ISLE ROYALE, L'ISLE ST. JEAN ET CELLE
 D'ANTICOSTI &CA...PAR ORDRE DE M ROUILLE...AYANT DE DEPARTEMENT DE LA MARINE.
 M.DCC LIV [1754] 56.5x89.5cm. plate number 57   [7] $425
CARTE REDUITE, DES COTES DE L'ACADIE, DE L'ISLE ROYALE, ET DE LA PARTIE
 MERIDIONALE DE L'ISLE DE TERRE-NEUVE. DRESSEE SUR LES OBSERVATIONS FAITES PAR
 ORDRE DU ROY EN 1750 ET 1751. PAR MR. MARQUIS DE CHABERT CAPITAINE...
 [C1755] 58.4x87.6cm. centerfold split repaired, left margin and centerfold
 soiled, with insignia of Depot de la Marine, priced at 30 sols, composed from
 8 plates from Chabert, "Voyage"   [7] $350
COTE NORD-OUEST DE L'AMERIQUE...1E PARTIE [C1825] 76.4x61.5cm. re-issued from
 the 1800 Paris ed. of Vancouver's voyage, covers Mexico to San Francisco
                                                                            [28] $459
COTE NORD-OUEST DE L'AMERIQUE...2E PARTIE [C1825] 75.5x61cm. re-issued from
 the 1800 Paris ed. of Vancouver's voyage, covers from north of San Francisco
 to the Columbia River   [28] $183
COTE NORD-OUEST DE L'AMERIQUE...3E PARTIE [C1825] 76.8x61.3cm. minor repair,
 re-issued from the 1800 Paris ed. of Vancouver's voyage, covers Columbia
 river north to Vancouver Island   [28] $383
COTE NORD-OUEST DE L'AMERIQUE...IVE PARTIE [C1825] 74.5x61.4cm. re-issued
 from the 1800 Paris ed. of Vancouver's voyage, covers from Queen Charlotte
 Islands to Christian Sound   [28] $153
COTE NORD-OUEST DE L'AMERIQUE...VE PARTIE [C1825] 72.5x61.5cm. re-issued from
 the 1800 Paris ed. of Vancouver's voyage, covers Christian Sound to Yakutat
 Bay   [28] $153
MER DES ANTILLES ET GOLFE DU MEXIQUE. VENTS GENERAUX. DRESSE PAR CH. DE
 KERHALLET CAPITAINE DE VAISSEAU. GRAVE PAR JACOBS. DEPOT DES CARTES ET PLANS
 DE LA MARINE. NO. 1612. PRIX. 0 F-75 C [1854] 45.7x29.2cm.   [25] $58
PLAN DE LA BAIE D'YU-LIN-KAN ET DU MOUILLAGE DE SANGHIA [C1825] 42.5x57.3cm.
 chart by A. de Kergariou   [28] $45
PLAN DE LA BAIE DE GAALONG [C1825] 42.7x57.4cm.
 chart by A. de Kergariou   [28] $45
PLAN DE LA BAIE DE LYEOUNG-SOY [C1825] 42.5x57.2cm.
 chart by A. de Kergariou   [28] $45
PLAN DE LA BAIE DE NARRAGANSET DANS LA NOUVELLE ANGLETERRE [1780] 58.4x41.3cm.
                                                                            [33] $485
PLAN DU CALLAO DE LIMA/PLAN DE L'ANSE ET PORT DE VALPARAISO [C1825] 59x42.5cm.
                                                                            [28] $76
PLAN DU PORT DE BALDIVIA/PLAN DE LA RADE DE SN JUAN BAUTISTA A LA POINTE N.E.
 DE L'ILE DE JUAN FERNANDEZ. 1821 [C1825] 56.8x41.2cm.   [28] $61
PLAN DU PORT DE SN CARLOS SITUE A LA PARTIE DU NORD DE L'ILE DE CHILOE. 1821
 [C1825] 56.2x41.7cm.   [28] $61
PLAN DU PORT DES FRANCAIS 1786 [C1825] 49.7x69cm.
 minor damage, La Perouse chart re-issued   [28] $76

DEPOT DE LA MARINE (continued)

PLAN DU PORT TOULOUSE/PLAN DE LA BAIE NERICHAC [1779] 59.7x40.6cm. [3] $140
PREMIERE FEUILLE DES COTES DE LA COCHINCHINE. 1798 [C1825] 48.1x69cm.
   chart by Vice Admiral Rosili   [28] $61
SECONDE FEUILLE DES COTES DE LA COCHINCHINE. 1798 [C1825] 69.6x48.5cm.
   chart by Vice Admiral Rosili   [28] $61
SUITE DE LA CARTE REDUITE DU GOLPHE DE ST. LAURENT CONTENANT LES COSTES DE
LABRADOR DEPUIS MECATINA JUSQU'A LA BAYE DES ESQUIMAUX LE DETROIT DE
BELLE-ISLE...PAR ORDRE DE M. ROUILLE...AYANT LE DEPARTEMENT DE LA MARINE.
M.DCC LII [1753] 90.8x56.5cm.
   plate no. 58, Depot de la Marine insignia, priced at 30 sols   [7] $425
TROISIEME FEUILLE DES COTES DE LA COCHINCHINE. 1798 [C1825] 69.7x48.5cm.
   chart by Vice Admiral Rosili   [28] $61

DES BARRES

(BAY OF FUNDY, SOUTH EAST PART) [1776] 70.5x207cm. left margin somewhat
   ragged, light offsetting, untitled, "Publish'd according to Act Of Parliament
   June 5, 1776 by J.F.W. Des Barres Esq."   [7] $1300
A CHART OF DELAWAR RIVER... [C1780] 52.1x73.7cm. framed   [6] $5200
A PLAN OF THE TOWN OF NEWPORT, IN THE PROVINCE OF RHODE ISLAND. PUBLISHED
ACCORDING TO ACT, APRIL 24, 1776 BY J.F.W. DES BARRES ESQR. [1776]
52.1x73.7cm.
   light waterstain along a portion of top margin, watermarked "J.B." [25] $498
CHARLOTTE BAY. PUBLISHED ACCORDING TO ACT OF PARLIAMENT BY J.F.W. DES BARRES
ESQ. FEBY. 11TH 1776 [1776] 71.1x101.6cm. minor paper loss in margins
   repaired, folds reinforced, light offsetting   [7] $875
PORT AMHERST. PORT HALDIMAND. SURVEY'D AND PUBLISH'D ACCORDING TO ACT OF
PARLIAMENT BY J.F.W. DES BARRES ESQ. DECR 3 1775 [1775] 74.9x55.9cm.
   sepia engraving, some offsetting   [7] $775
THE HARBOUR OF CHARLES TOWN IN SOUTH-CAROLINA FROM THE SURVEYS OF SR. JAS.
WALLACE CAPTN IN HIS MAJESTYS NAVY & OTHERS WITH A VIEW OF THE TOWN FROM THE
SOUTH SHORE OF ASHLEY RIVER. PUBLISHED...NOV. 1ST 1777 BY J.F.W. DES BARRES
ESQR. [1777] 83.8x61.6cm. some separation along folds repaired, several
small section of margin replaced, with earlier view of the harbor shown as an
inset   [26] $3500

DESILVER

(FLORIDA) [1856-59] 29.2x22.9cm.
   dated 1856, published in 1859 in Baltimore   [27] $75
(ILLINOIS) [1856] 39.4x34.3cm. a later ed. with imprint "No. 714 Chesnut
   Street" rather than the earlier "No. 251 Market Street," map dated 1856,
   narrow left margin, stitch-marks repaired   [27] $75
(ILLINOIS) [1856] 39.4x33cm.   [27] $65
(KENTUCKY) [1856] 29.2x35.6cm.   [27] $60
(OHIO) [1856] 39.4x33cm.   [27] $60
(WISCONSIN) [1856] 39.4x33cm.   [27] $60
A NEW MAP OF ALABAMA WITH ITS ROADS AND DISTANCES FROM PLACE TO PLACE ALONG THE
   STAGE AND STEAM BOAT ROUTES [C1856] 29.2x36.8cm.   [9] $35
A NEW MAP OF KENTUCKY WITH ITS ROADS & DISTANCES FROM PLACE TO PLACE ALONG THE
   STAGE AND STEAMBOAT ROUTES [C1856] C32x40cm.   [21] $28
A NEW MAP OF MAINE [C1856] C40x32cm.   [21] $28
A NEW MAP OF NORTH CAROLINA WITH ITS CANALS, ROADS & DISTANCES FROM PLACE TO
   PLACE ALONG THE STAGE AND STEAM BOAT ROUTES [1856] 29.2x35.6cm.   [11] $40
A NEW MAP OF SOUTH CAROLINA [1856] 29.2x35.6cm.
   "No. 251 Market Street"   [27] $60
A NEW MAP OF THE STATE OF GEORGIA EXHIBITING IT'S INTERNAL IMPROVEMENTS, ROAD
   DISTANCES &C., BY J.H. YOUNG [1856] 33x40.6cm.   [10] $30
A NEW MAP OF THE STATE OF SOUTH CAROLINA [1859] 33x39.4cm. binding holes in
   top margin, published in 1859 in Baltimore by Cushings & Bailey, but map
   states "No. 714 Chesnut Steet, Philadelphia"   [27] $75
A NEW MAP OF THE UNITED STATES OF AMERICA [1857] 40.6x66cm.   [22] $120
CANADA WEST FORMERLY UPPER CANADA [C1856] 32x40cm.
   missing corner in margin   [21] $30

<u>DESILVER</u> (continued)
CANADA WEST FORMERLY UPPER CANADA [C1856] 32x40cm.
  missing corner in margin   [21] $30
CITY OF WASHINGTON [1856] 40.6x33cm.   [22] $90
MAP OF MINNESOTA TERRITORY [1854] C33x40.6cm.
  "Cowperthwait, Desilver & Butler. Philadelphia, 1854"   [27] $160
MAP OF MINNESOTA TERRITORY [1856] C33x40.6cm. "Charles Desilver, 151 Market
  St., Philadelphia, 1856," small spot stain   [27] $110
MAP OF MINNESOTA TERRITORY [1857] C33x40.6cm.
  "Charles Desilver, No. 714 Chesnut St., Philadelphia, 1857"   [27] $175
MAP OF MINNESOTA TERRITORY [1855] C33x40.6cm.
  "Charles Desilver, 253 Market St., Philadelphia, 1855"   [27] $135
MAP OF NEW JERSEY COMPILED FROM THE LATEST AUTHORITIES [C1856] C32x40cm.
  minor damage to border   [21] $24
MAP OF THE STATE OF TEXAS... [1856] 32.4x39.4cm.   [19] $225
MEXICO & GUATEMALA [1856] C30.5x38.1cm. foxing in margins   [19] $50
<u>DESNOS</u>
CARTE DU THEATRE DE LA GUERRE, COMPRENANT LES PAYS-BAS ET PARTIE DES PROVINCES
  UNIES AVEC L'EVE. DE LIEGE. A PARIS, CHEZ DENOS. INGENIEUR GEOGRAPHE, 1784
  [1784] 47x61cm.   [18] $70
LES DIX-SEPT PROVINCES DES PAYS-BAS [1784] 44x57cm.   [18] $105
<u>DEZAUCHE</u>
CARTE DES NOUVELLES DECOUVERTES AU NORD DE LA MER DU SUD, TANT A L'EST DE LA
  SIBERIE ET DU KAMTCHATKA, QU A L'OUEST DE LA NOUVELLE FRANCE. DRESSEE SUR LES
  MEMOIRES DE MR. DEL'ISLE PROFESSEUR ROYAL ET DE L'ACADEMIE DES SCIENCES
  [1780] 47x66.7cm. re-issue of de l'Isle map, lower margins stained, "Par Mr.
  De l'Isle...Se vend a Paris, Chez Dezauche, Rue des Noyers pres a la Rue des
  Anglois."   [7] $775
CARTE DU CANADA, QUI COMPREND LA PARTIE SEPTENTRIONALE DES ETATS-UNIS
  D'AMERIQUE...REVUE ET AUGMENTEE EN 1783. A PARIS CHEZ DEZAUCHE SUCESSEUR DES
  SRS. DEL'ISLE ET BUACHE, RUE DES NOYERS PRES CELLES DES ANGLOIS [1783]
  50.8x66cm. minor foxing in margins, 2nd state of de l'Isle's map, revised by
  Dezauche   [7] $700
CARTE DU MEXIQUE ET DES ETATS UNIS PARTIE MERIDIONALE [1783] 47x64.8cm.
                                                                [16] $380
<u>DEZOTEUX</u>
CARTE POUR SERVIR AU JOURNAL DE MR. LE MARQUIS DE CHASTELLUX [1787]
  17.8x26.7cm. folding, right margin narrow   [23] $65
CHART FOR THE JOURNAL OF MR. LE MQUIS. DE CHASTELLUX. BY MR. DEZOTEUX STAFF
  OFFICER IN THE FRENCH ARMY [1787] 18.1x23.5cm.   [39] $60
<u>DIDEROT</u>
See DE VAUGONDY
<u>DIDOT</u>
CARTES TYPO-GEOGRAPHIQUES, INVENTEES ET IMPRIMEES PAR FIRMIN DIDOT.
  FRANCE...JOS LANGLOIS, DELIN. BARBIE DU BOCAGE...A PARIS, RUE JACOB, NO 24
  [1823] 35.6x38.7cm.
  light foxing, printed with a multicolor process as a specimen [26] $675
<u>DIRECCION HIDROGRAFICA</u>
CARTA ESFERICA DE LAS ISLAS ANTILLAS CON PARTE DE LA COSTA DEL CONTINENTE DE
  AMERICA. TRABAJADA DE ORDEN DEL REY POR LOS CAPITANES DE NAVIO DE SU RT.
  ARMADA DN. COSME CHURRUCA Y DN. JOAQUIN FRANCO FIDALGO. DIRECCION
  HIDROGRAFICA [1802] 90.2x59.7cm.   [3] $295
<u>DIXON</u>
SKETCH BY COMPASS OF NORFOLK SOUND [1788] 39.7x27.8cm.   [39] $50
SKETCH BY COMPASS OF PORT BANKS... [1788] 38.1x27.9cm.
  repairs to folds   [3] $45
SKETCH BY COMPASS OF PORT MULGRAVE... [1788] 40.6x27.9cm.
  minor repairs   [3] $65
TO THE RIGHT HONORABLE THE LORDS COMMISSIONERS...THIS CHART OF THE NORTH WEST
  COAST OF AMERICA, WITH THE TRACKS OF THE KING GEORGE AND QUEEN CHARLOTTE IN
  1786 & 1787... [1788] 59.1x87.6cm.
  some reinforcements, repaired tears in margins   [26] $625

104

DIXON (continued)
  YAM BAY ONEEHEOW...1786 [1788] 19.7x27.9cm.   [3] $65
DONALDSON
  WEST MOUNTAIN MINING DISTRICT, BRIGHAM CANON... [1879-84] 29.2x30.5cm.
    folding lithographed map from Thomas Donaldson, "Public Domain" [27] $40
DORR, HOWLAND & CO.
  MASSACHUSETTS [1839] 17.8x30.5cm.   [3] $40
DOU
  T'HOOGE HEEMRAED-SCHAP VAN RHYNLAND [1687] 42x56cm. 12 double folio maps, 11
    double folio & 2 single folio sheets of arms & titles, some repaired tears &
    light browning   [18] $2107
DOWER
  See also TEESDALE
  BRITISH POSSESSIONS (NORTH AMERICA) [C1850] 20x24cm.   [21] $24
  COLUMBIA [1835] 33.7x41.3cm.   [30] $36
  MEXICO & GUATIMALA [C1835] 21x25.4cm.   [20] $100
  MEXICO & GUATIMALA [1840] 21x25.4cm.   [3] $35
  PERU & BOLIVIA [1835] 33.7x41.3cm. light browning   [30] $36
  UNITED STATES [1826] 26.7x21cm.   [3] $30
  UNITED STATES [1840] 33.7x38.1cm.   [20] $100
DRIPPS
  MAP OF NEW YORK CITY SOUTH OF 135TH STREET SHOWING NEW ARRANGEMENT DOCKS, PIERS
    AND WATER FRONTAGE... [1876] 195x66cm. on 2 sheets   [39] $125
DU SAUZET
  ANGLIA, SCOTIA ET HIBERNIA [1630-1734] 19.7x25.4cm. re-issue of the plate
    engraved by van den Keere for the Cloppenburgh edition of the
    Mercator-Hondius small atlas of 1630, without text   [12] $91
  ANGLIAE REGNUM [1630-1734] 19.7x25.4cm. re-issue of the plate engraved by van
    den Keere for the Cloppenburgh edition of the Mercator-Hondius small atlas of
    1630   [12] $82
DU VAL
  CARTE DU DUCHE DE LUXEMBOURG ET SOUVERAINETE DE SEDAN. PAR DU VAL GEOGRAPHE. A.
    PEYROUNIN FECIT. A PARIS, CHEZ PIERRE MARIETTE, RUE S. JACQUES A L'ESPERANCE.
    1646 [1646] 37.5x48.3cm.   [18] $210
  CARTE UNIVERSELLE DU MONDE...AMERIQUE SEPTEMTRIONALE [1677] 41.7x57.9cm.
    lower margin narrow   [39] $750
  L'ISLE ET ROYAUME D'IRLAND... [1685] 40.6x50.8cm. narrow top margin [24] $229
  PROVINCES UNIES DES PAIS-BAS CONNUES SOUS LE NOM DE HOLLANDE, PAR P. DU-VAL.
    PARIS, CHEZ L'AUTEUR, EN L'ISLE DU PALAIS, AU COIN DE LA RUE DE HARLAY, 1679
    [1679] 40.5x56cm.   [18] $158
DU VIVIER
  LE COMTE DE NAMUR. PAR F. DU VIVIER INGENIEUR ET GEOGRAPHE...PARIS, CHEZ LA
    VEUVE DU SR. DU VAL AU GRAND LOUIS [C1688] 42x54cm.   [18] $105
DUDLEY
  CARTA PARTICOLARE DELLA MERA INCONITA CON LA GRONLANDIA OCCIDENTALE E DELL'
    ESTOTILAND SCOP. DALL INGLESI [1641] 47x74.9cm.   [15] $1450
DUFOUR
  AMERIQUE DU SUD [1845] 90x63cm.
    folding map in 21 panels, backed with cloth   [39] $65
  CARTE GENERALE DE L'AMERIQUE DU NORD. DRESSEE PAR A.H. DUFOUR [1836-41]
    32.4x50.2cm. left margin narrow, 4 folds, from Orbigny, "Voyage Pittoresque
    dans le deus Amerique," Paris 1841   [8] $65
  CARTE GENERALE DE L'AMERIQUE DU NORD... [1836-41] 32.4x50.2cm.
    trimmed to neat line at upper left   [22] $75
DUNCAN
  RIO DE JANEIRO (VIEW) [1839] 14.6x21cm. T. Prior sc.   [3] $35
DUNN
  See also LAURIE & WHITTLE
  See also SAYER
DUPUIS
  CARTE DE LA PARTIE SEPTENTRIONALE DE LA MER DU SUD [C1790] 26x37cm. [4] $61

105

DURY

CANADA [1761] 10.5x23.5cm.
   from Dury's "New and General Atlas", folds as issued   [21] $60
NORTH AMERICA [1761] 10x12cm. "AMERIQUE SEPTEN.LE" appears along the top,
   from Dury, "New and General Atlas"   [21] $77

EDWARDS

A MAP OF THE ISLAND OF JAMAICA... [1794] 31x62.5cm.   [4] $76
A NEW MAP OF THE WEST INDIES FOR THE HISTORY OF THE BRITISH COLONIES [1794]
   69.5x113cm. on 2 sheets   [39] $175
HERGEST'S ISLANDS DISCOVERED BY THE DAEDALUS STORE SHIP, LIEUT. HERGEST
   COMMDR. [1798] 24.1x19.1cm.   [3] $40
MAP OF THE ISLAND OF BARBADOES [1794] 23.5x19.1cm.   [3] $70
PORT DICK, NEAR COOK'S INLET (VIEW) [1798] 18.4x23.5cm.   [3] $35

ELLIOTT PUBLISHING CO.

BIRDS-EYE VIEW OF AUBURN. PLACER COUNTY, CAL. [1891] 48.9x80.3cm. two repairs
   in margin, backed with rice paper, chromolithograph by Elliott Publishing
   Co., 120 Sutter St., San Francisco   [20] $585

ELLIS

A MODERN MAP OF LANCASHIRE... [1766] 24.1x19.1cm.   [24] $68
A MODERN MAP OF NORTHUMBERLAND... [1766] 24.8x19.1cm.   [24] $49
A MODERN MAP OF SUFFOLK... [1766] 19.7x24.8cm.   [24] $53
A MODERN MAP OF WORCESTERSHIRE... [1766] 25.4x19.1cm.   [24] $45
BEDFORDSHIRE [1819] C17.8x26.7cm. from "Ellis' New and Correct Atlas of
   England and Wales being An Entire New Set of County Maps"   [14] $27
CAMBRIDGESHIRE [1819] C17.8x26.7cm.   [14] $27
ESSEX [1819] C17.8x26.7cm.   [14] $27
MODERN MAP OF NORTHAMPTON-SHIRE... [1766] 25.4x19.1cm.   [24] $42
NORFOLK [1819] C17.8x26.7cm.   [14] $24
OXFORDSHIRE [1819] C17.8x26.7cm.   [14] $27
SURREY [1819] C17.8x26.7cm.   [14] $30
THE SOUTH EAST POINT OF YE ISLANDS OF RESOLUTION/A VIEW OF CAPE WALSINGHAM FROM
   THE N.E. [1748] 15x22.6cm.   [39] $50

ELWE

DE GOLF VAN MEXICO, DE EILANDEN EN HET OMLEGGENDE LAND [1792] 48x58cm.
                         [39] $320
PARTIE DE LA NOUVELLE GRANDE CARTE DES INDES ORIENTALES CONTENANT LES EMPIRES
   DE LA CHINE, DU JAPON, LES ISLES PHILIPPINES... [1792] 53x60.5cm. [2] $201

EMORY

SKETCH OF THE ACTIONS FOUGHT AT SAN PASQUAL IN UPPER CALIFORNIA BETWEEN THE
   AMERICANS AND MEXICANS, DEC. 6TH & 7TH, 1846/SKETCH OF THE PASSAGE OF THE RIO
   SAN GABRIEL, UPPER CALIFORNIA, BY THE AMERICAN...JANUARY 8TH 1847 [1848]
   45.7x59.7cm. pair of battle plans, each repeated 4 times for a total of 8
   plans on one sheet, dimensions are overall, from Major W.H. Emory, "Notes of
   a Military Reconnoissance, from Fort Leavenworth..to San Diego...," several
   minor creases, an uncut printer's sheet   [27] $175

ENGLISH PILOT

See MOUNT & PAGE

ENTICK

A NEW AND ACCURATE MAP OF NORTH AMERICA [1763] 19.7x22.9cm.
   from Entick, "General History of the Late War"   [30] $101
A NEW AND ACCURATE MAP OF THE ISLAND OF MARTINICO 1763 [1766] 17.8x23.5cm.
   fold repaired   [3] $40
PLAN OF THE RIVER ST. LAWRENCE...SIEGE OF QUEBEC [1766] 17.1x23.5cm. [30] $162

ESQUEMELING

A DESCRIPTION OF YE LAGUNA OR GULF OF BALLONA [C1684] 11.3x14cm. [39] $40
THE BAY OF PANAMA AND GULF OF BALLONA [C1684] 12.6x13.2cm.   [39] $50
THE TOWNE OF PUERTO DEL PRINCIPE TAKEN & SACKT (VIEW) [1695] 15.9x11.4cm.
                         [3] $35

ETTLING

CALIFORNIA... [1858-63] 42.5x29.8cm. from "Weekly Dispatch Atlas" [32] $60
U.S. OF N. AMERICA, SOUTH WEST SHEET [1859] 42.5x30.5cm.   [19] $75

ETTLING (continued)
  UNITED STATES (WEST SHEET) [1859] 43.2x31.8cm. browning in margin   [19] $60
  UNITED STATES OF NORTH AMERICA [1863] 43.2x31.8cm. on 2 sheets, dimensions
    are for each, map by T. Ettling from the Weekly Dispatch Atlas   [11] $100
EVERY SATURDAY
  A VIEW OF MEMPHIS [1871] 22.9x30.5cm.
    from the illustrated weekly "Every Saturday," September 23, 1871   [27] $40
FADEN
  A CHART OF THE ANTILLES, OR, CHARIBBEE, OR, CARIBS ISLANDS, WITH THE VIRGIN
    ISLES [1784] 45.7x50.8cm.   [22] $175
  A CHART OF THE COASTS OF SPAIN AND PORTUGAL, WITH THE BALEARIC ISLANDS, AND
    PART OF THE COAST OF BARBARY. BY L.S. DE LA ROCHETTE. MDCCLXXX. 2D. EDITION.
    LONDON: ENGRAVED & PUBLISHED...BY WM. FADEN...JUNE 28TH, 1780 [1780]
    53.3x72.4cm.   [7] $110
  A MAP OF AMERICA, OR THE NEW WORLD, WHEREIN ARE INTRODUCED ALL THE KNOWN PARTS
    OF THE WESTERN HEMISPHERE FROM THE MAP OF D'ANVILLE...LONDON: PUBLISHED BY W.
    FADEN, GEOGRAPHER TO THE KING...CHARING CROSS APRIL 12TH 1797 [1797]
    53.3x60.3cm. 1st state with "O rare Columbus" in clouds above cartouch
                                                                       [7] $425
  A MAP OF SOUTH CAROLINA AND A PART OF GEORGIA...FROM SURVEYS OF WM. BULL, DE
    BRAHM ETC. COLLECTED BY JOHN STUART... [1780] 134.6x121.9cm.
    on 4 sheets but lacking lower left sheet, minor repairs   [3] $325
  A MAP OF THE AUSTRIAN POSSESSIONS IN THE NETHERLANDS OR LOW COUNTRIES, WITH THE
    PRINCIPALITIES OF LIEGE AND STAVELO...LONDON: PUBLISHED BY WILLIAM FADEN,
    GEOGRAPHER TO HIS MAJESTY. JANY. 1ST 1789 [1789] 55.2x68.6cm.   [7] $175
  A MAP OF THE INHABITED PART OF CANADA FROM THE FRENCH SURVEYS; WITH THE
    FRONTIERS OF NEW YORK AND NEW ENGLAND FROM THE LARGE SURVEY BY CLAUDE JOSEPH
    SAUTHIER. ENGRAVED BY WM. FADEN, 1777. LONDON, PUBLISHED...FEBY. 25, 1777 BY
    WM. FADEN... [1777] 59.7x87.6cm. light foxing, short tears at fold
    repaired, 3rd state with dedication to Burgoyne present and table of winter
    headquarters deleted   [7] $1050
  A MAP OF THE PENINSULA OF INDIA FROM THE 19TH DEGREE NORTH LATITUDE TO CAPE
    COMORIN [1792] 40x81cm.
    on 2 sheets, dimensions are for each, small tear in margin repaired[21] $150
  A PLAN OF THE CITY AND ENVIRONS OF PHILADELPHIA [1777] 63.5x47cm.
    framed   [6] $4000
  A PLAN OF THE CITY AND ENVIRONS OF PHILADELPHIA... [1779] 61x49.2cm.
    centerfold repaired   [6] $5750
  A PLAN OF THE SURPRISE OF STONEY POINT BY A DETACHMENT OF THE AMERICAN ARMY
    COMMANDED BY GENL. WAYNE ON 15TH JULY 1779... [1784] 48.3x30.5cm.
    left part of map only   [3] $95
  CHART OF PART OF THE COAST OF LABRADORE, FROM CAPE CHARLES TO SANDWICH BAY
    SURVEY'D BY ORDER OF COMRE. BYRON, GOVERNOR OF NEWFOUNDLAND...IN 1770-71
    [1777] 43.2x61cm. upper half only, border restored   [3] $90
  CHART OF THE ISLAND OF CORSICA FROM THE TOPOGRAPHIC SURVEY MADE BY ORDER OF THE
    MARQUIS DE CURSAY WITH SEVERAL EMENDATIONS FROM BELLIN'S CHARTS [1793]
    31.8x22.2cm.   [24] $38
  CHART OF THE N.W. COAST OF AMERICA AND THE N.E. COAST OF ASIA, EXPLORED IN THE
    YEARS 1778 AND 1779. PREPARED BY LIEUT. HENY. ROBERTS...LONDON: PUBLISHED BY
    WM. FADEN...CHARING CROSS JULY 24, 1784. 2D. EDITION. PUBLISHED JANUARY 1ST.
    1794 [1794] 43.2x69.9cm.   [7] $425
  CHART OF THE NORTHWEST COAST OF AMERICA AND THE NORTHEAST COAST OF ASIA,
    EXPLORED IN THE YEARS 1778 AND 1779...LONDON...WM FADEN...2D EDITION.
    PUBLISHED JANUARY 1ST 1794 [1784-94] 39.7x67.9cm.   [26] $525
  FORT CHAMBLY [1815] 12.7x20.3cm.   [3] $40
  ISLE OF ST. DOMINGO OR HISPANIOLA [1796] 45.7x74.3cm. fold repaired [3] $135
  ITALY WITH THE ADDITION OF THE SOUTHERN PARTS OF GERMANY AS FAR AS PETTAU IN
    STIRIA; MURLAKIA, DALMATIA, THE ADJACENT COUNTRIES...LONDON PUBLISHED BY
    WILLM. FADEN...SEPTR. 12TH, 1800. 2D. EDITION DESCRIBING THE NEW DIVISIONS
    [1800] 63.5x111.1cm.
    on 2 sheets, dimensions are for each, minor offsetting   [7] $225

FADEN (continued)
MAP AND ELEVATIONS OF THE SHUBENACADIE NAVIGATION FROM HALIFAX HARBOUR TO THE
    BASIN OF MINES [1815] 12.7x32.4cm.   [3] $45
NORTHERN HEMISPHERE [1790] 36.2x34.9cm.   [3] $85
PLAN OF OSWEGO HARBOUR [1815] 21.6x12.7cm.   [3] $60
PLAN OF THE BAY, ROCK AND TOWN OF GIBRALTER, FROM AN ACTUAL SURVEY BY AN
    OFFICER WHO WAS AT GIBRALTER FROM 1769 TO 1775. WITH THE WORKS, BATTERIES,
    AND INCAMPMENT OF THE SPANISH ARMY ON THE 19TH OCTOR., 1782... [1783]
    50.8x72.4cm. tear at one side repaired   [24] $130
PLAN OF THE DIFFERENT CHANNELS LEADING FROM KINGSTON TO LAKE ONTARIO; SURVEYED
    BY JOS. BOUCHETTE 1796 [1815] 22.2x24.8cm.   [3] $100
POSITION OF THE DETACHMENT UNDER LIEUTT. COLL. BAUM AT WALMSCOCK NEAR
    BENNINGTON... [1780] 27.4x34.6cm.   [39] $175
SKETCH OF THE SURPRISE OF GERMANTOWN... [1784] 46.4x53.3cm.   [6] $3750
THE UNITED STATES OF NORTH AMERICA WITH BRITISH TERRITORIES AND THOSE OF SPAIN
    ACCORDING TO THE TREATY OF 1784 [1796] 53.3x62.9cm. backed   [3] $365
THE UNITED STATES OF NORTH AMERICA WITH THE BRITISH TERRITORIES AND THOSE OF
    SPAIN, ACCORDING TO THE TREATY OF 1784. ENGRAVED BY WM. FADEN. 1796.
    PUBLISHED AS THE ACT DIRECTS, FEBY. 11, 1796 BY WILLM. FADEN [1783-96]
    54.6x64.8cm. minor offsetting, first published in 1783, this state is the
    first to show "Tannasee Government" and "Washington, or the Federal City"
                                                                          [7] $560
THE UNITED STATES OF NORTH AMERICA: WITH THE BRITISH TERRITORIES AND THOSE OF
    SPAIN ACCORDING TO THE TREATY OF 1784... [1796] 53x63.2cm.
    lower centerfold repaired   [35] $485
FAURE
L'AMERIQUE [C1725] 17.8x14cm.
    from Buffier Geografia Universale, California as an Island   [30] $81
FENNER, SEARS & CO.
KENTUCKY AND TENNESSEE [C1831] 25.4x39.4cm.
    minor centerfold separation repaired   [23] $60
MAP OF THE STATES OF INDIANA AND OHIO, WITH PART OF MICHIGAN TERRITORY [C1831]
    24.8x39.7cm. inset map of Cincannati   [23] $50
MAP OF THE STATES OF MISSISSIPPI, LOUISIANA AND ARKANSAS TERRITORY [1832]
    41.3x26.7cm.   [3] $40
NORTH & SOUTH CAROLINA [C1831] 25.4x39.4cm.   [23] $65
FIDALGO
ENSDA. DE CARUPANO [1818] 17.8x23.5cm.   [39] $50
ENSENA. DE UNARE [1818] 17.9x23.8cm.   [39] $50
FONDEADERO DE LA GUAYRA [1818] 17x23.4cm.   [39] $65
PAMPATAR...MARGARITA [1818] 23.3x17.8cm.   [39] $60
PLANO DEL PUERTO DE NAOS Y SUS ADYACENTES-ISTMO DE PANAMA [1809] 19.1x26cm.
                                                                         [3] $95
PTO. SANTO [1818] 17.8x23.4cm.   [39] $50
PUERTO CABELLO [1818] 17.5x26.6cm.   [39] $60
FIELDING
A SOUTH WEST VIEW OF PRINCE OF WALES FORT HUDSONS BAY [1779] 12.1x16.5cm.
                                                                         [3] $40
FINDLAY
ARKANSAW [1836] 17.8x22.9cm.   [20] $70
FINLEY
INDIANA [1824] 27.9x21.6cm.   [27] $85
MAP OF MASSACHUSETTS, CONNECTICUT & RHODE ISLAND [1826] 43.2x55.2cm. [3] $135
MAP OF THE STATE OF NEW YORK PUBLISHED IN 1826 [1826] 43.2x55.2cm.
    fold repair   [3] $75
THE WORLD ON MERCATOR'S PROJECTION [1824] 22.2x28.6cm.   [3] $40
FLEURIEU
PLAN DE LA BAIE DE TCHINKITANE (LA BAIA DE GUADALUPA DES ESPAGNOLS EN 1775, ET
    NORFOLK-BAY DES ANGLAIS EN 1787) A LA COTE N.O. DE L'AMERIQUE. LEVE PAR LE
    CAP. PROSPER CHANAL 1791 [1798] 21.7x16.7cm.   [39] $60

FOOT
MAP OF THE UNITED STATES, CANADA [1799] 40x34.9cm.   [30] $81
FORSTER
CHART SHEWING THE TRACK OF THE FRENCH SHIPS THROUGH THE MOLUCCAS TO BATAVIA IN
   1768 [1777] 22.9x26.7cm. minor repairs   [3] $45
FOSTER
MAP OF THE GOLD REGION IN UPPER CALIFORNIA [1849] 12.1x22.9cm.
   folio sheet with descriptive text   [3] $35
FRANK LESLIE'S ILLUSTRATED NEWSPAPER
BELLEVUE, THE COUNTY SEAT OF SARPY COUNTY, ON THE WEST SIDE OF THE MISSISSIPPI,
   NEBRASKA TERRITORY (VIEW) [1858] 14x22.9cm.
   a view of a trading post is on the same sheet, dated June 5, 1858 [27] $25
FRANKLIN
AN OUTLINE TO SHEW THE CONNECTED DISCOVERIES OF CAPTAINS ROSS, PARRY & FRANKLIN
   IN THE YEARS 1818, 19, 20, 22 & 23 [1823] 36.9x46.3cm. with folds [39] $120
DISCOVERIES OF THE EXPEDITION UNDER THE COMMAND OF CAPTAIN FRANKLIN R.N. NEAR
   THE MOUTH OF THE MACKENZIE RIVER AND ON THE SEA COAST EAST & WEST A.D.
   1825-26 [1828] 69x128cm. with folds   [39] $160
ROUTE OF THE EXPEDITION A.D. 1825, FROM FORT WILLIAM TO THE SASKATCHAWAN RIVER;
   SURVEYED BY LIEUT. G. BACK & MR. E.N. KENDALL... [1828] 35.9x43.2cm.
   with folds   [39] $75
ROUTE OF THE EXPEDITION FROM ISLE LA CROSSE TO FORT PROVIDENCE IN 1819 & 20
   [1823] 51.4x23.5cm.   [3] $60
ROUTE OF THE EXPEDITION FROM YORK FACTORY TO CUMBERLAND HOUSE AND...TRACKS FROM
   THENCE TO ISLE A LA CROSSE IN 1819-20 [1823] 25.4x56.5cm.   [3] $60
FREZIER
CARTE REDUITE DE L'EXTREMITE DE L'AMERIQUE MERIDIONALE DANS LA PARTIE DU SUD
   [1716] 19.1x29.2cm.   [3] $145
PLAN DE LA BAYE DE LA CONCEPTION SITUEE A LA COTE DU CHILY... [1716]
   18.4x28.6cm.   [3] $65
PLAN DE LA RADE DE ARICA [1716] 17.8x29.2cm.   [3] $60
VUE DU COTE DU MOUGILAGE/PROFIL DU FORT DE VALPARAYSSO [1716] 19.1x29.2cm.
                                                                     [3] $50
FRICX
PARTIE DE L'ANGLETERRE [C1709-12] 41.9x55.9cm. one sheet of a 24 sheet map
   "Table des cartes des Pays Bas et des frontieres de France"   [12] $137
FULLARTON
ARCTIC REGIONS [1864] 45.5x31cm.   [39] $90
ARCTIC REGIONS [C1862] 46.5x31.5cm. narrow left margin   [21] $134
BRITISH GUIANA ACCORDING TO SIR ROBERT SCHOMBURGK [1850] 22.9x14cm. [3] $30
BRITISH NORTH AMERICA [1828] 20.3x25.4cm.   [3] $40
BRITISH NORTH AMERICA [C1832] 19.7x25.4cm.   [30] $121
BRITISH NORTH AMERICA [1832] 19.5x25cm.   [21] $36
BRITISH NORTH AMERICA SHEET II WEST. CANADA WITH PART OF UNITED STATES [C1862]
   41x52.5cm.   [21] $48
BRITISH NORTH AMERICA SHEET II. WEST. CANADA WITH PART OF UNITED STATES,
   COMPILED BY J. HUGH JOHNSON F.R.G.S. A FULLARTON & CO. EDINBURGH, LONDON &
   DUBLIN [C1861] 40.6x52.1cm.   [7] $175
BRITISH POSSESSIONS ON THE N.E. COAST OF SOUTH AMERICA [1860] 47x31.1cm.
                                                                     [3] $70
BRITISH WEST INDIAN POSSESSIONS, NORTHERN [1864] 44x31.5cm.   [39] $75
CHINA [1854] 43.2x53.3cm.   [3] $50
CORNWALL [1841] 19.1x24.1cm.   [24] $36
DANISH ISLANDS IN THE NORTH ATLANTIC OCEAN [1862] 46.4x30.5cm.
   2 maps on one sheet   [24] $68
ISLAND OF JAMAICA [C1858] 14x22.9cm.   [3] $20
ISLAND OF TRINIDAD/BRITISH GUYANA [1864] 46x31cm.   [39] $65
JAPAN MANDSHURIA (SHOWING THE COURSE OF THE AMUR RIVER). THE KURILE ISLES &C.
   ACCORDING TO THE BRITISH & RUSSIAN ADMIRALTY SURVEYS, KRUSENSTERN, SIEBOLD
   &C. [1860] 45.1x30.5cm.   [24] $73
MAP OF INDIAN TERRITORY AND OKLAHOMA [1890-92] 55.9x74.9cm.   [9] $100

FULLARTON (continued)
MEXICO & GUATIMALA [1832] 19.1x24.1cm.   [19] $65
NORTH AMERICA [1832] 24.5x20.5cm.   [21] $36
NORTH AMERICA [1832] 20.3x24.1cm.   [20] $60
OCEANIA, OR ISLANDS IN THE PACIFIC OCEAN, ON MERCATORS PROJECTION... [1864]
   39.6x49.9cm.   [39] $50
SOUTH AMERICA [1864] 49.5x38.6cm.   [39] $25
SOUTH AMERICA STATES. NEW GRANADA & VENEZUELA [1864] 41.2x53cm.   [39] $45
SOUTHERN PORTS & HARBOURS IN THE UNITED STATES [1864] 41.2x29.6cm.
   several maps on one sheet   [39] $60
THE ARCTIC REGIONS SHOWING THE NORTH-WEST PASSAGE AS DETERMINED BY CAP. R.
   MCCLURE... [1856] 45.7x30.5cm.   [3] $75
THE ARCTIC REGIONS, SHOWING THE NORTH-WEST PASSAGE AS DETERMINED BY CAP. R.
   MC.CLURE AND OTHER ARCTIC VOYAGERS. COMPILED BY J. HUGH JOHNSON F.R.G.S.
   [C1862] 25x25cm. narrow lower margin   [21] $36
THE SOUTH EASTERN STATES...ACCORDING TO CALVIN SMITH & TANNER [1858]
   40.6x51.4cm.   [3] $45
THE WORLD IN HEMISPHERES WITH COMPARATIVE VIEWS OF THE HEIGHTS OF THE PRINCIPAL
   MOUNTAINS AND BASINS OF THE PRINCIPAL RIVERS OF THE GLOBE BY G.H. SWANSTON
   [C1860] 41x53cm. small split at lower centerfold   [21] $101
UNITED STATES OF NORTH AMERICA [C1856] 41.3x52.7cm.   [23] $115
UNITED STATES, NORTH CENTRAL...COMPRISING MICHIGAN, ILLINOIS, WISCONSIN, IOWA,
   MINN... [1858] 40.6x50.8cm.   [3] $40
UNITED STATES...COMPRISING MICHIGAN, ILLINOIS, WISCONSIN, IOWA, MINNESOTA...
   [1859] 40.6x50.8cm.   [3] $35
UNITED STATES...SOUTH CENTRAL SECTION [C1856] 51.4x40cm.   [23] $130
WARWICKSHIRE [1841] 24.1x19.1cm.   [24] $38
GALL & INGLIS
SOUTH AMERICA [1850] 43.2x54cm.   [25] $42
UNITED STATES [1850] 43.2x52.1cm.   [25] $58
GALLE
ANTVERPIA. ANTWERPIAE CELEBERRIMI...ORBIS...DELINEATIO AEDITA PER PHILIPPUM
   GALLEUM ANNO 1581 [1581] 38x51.5cm.   [18] $702
HAERLEM. THANTWERPEN BY PHILLIPS GALLE, 1573 [C1573] 28x34cm.
   minor repairs   [18] $351
NOBILIS HANNONIAE COMITATUS DESCRIP. AUCTORE IACOBO SURHONIO MONTANO. THEODORUS
   GALLEUS EXCUDIT ANTVERPIAE. CUM PRIVILEGIJS IMP. ET REGI. MAI. AD DECENN.
   [C1610] 37x49cm. no text on verso, published separately   [18] $351
GASKELL
TEXAS [1894] 30.5x43.2cm. margins browned   [19] $45
GASTALDI
QUESTA E LA VERA DESCRITTIONE DI TUTTA LA SPAGNA... [1544] 69.2x94.6cm. on 4
   sheets, joined, dimensions are overall, minor repair, creases reinforced,
   uncolored, said to be Giacomo Gastaldi's first map   [17]$10000
GAZZETTIERE AMERICANO
CARTA RAPPRESENTANTE IL PORT DI BOSTON [1763] 21.6x17.8cm.   [16] $95
CARTA RAPPRESENTE L'ISOLA DELLA GIAMMACA [1763] 20.3x31.8cm.   [3] $110
PLANO DEL PORTO E DEGLI STABILIMENTI DI PENSACOLA [1763] 18.4x26cm.   [3] $125
PLANO DELLA CITTA DI QUEBEC [1763] 24.8x23.5cm.   [3] $90
PLANO DI PORTO BELLO [1763] 20.3x25.4cm.   [3] $70
GEDDES
MAP AND PROFILE OF THE CHAMPLAIN CANAL [1825] 19.7x49.5cm.
   some reinforcement, published in Albany, New York   [30] $48
GEMMA FRISIUS
   See APIANUS
GENTLEMAN'S MAGAZINE
(STRAITS OF MACKINAC) [1761] 24.1x31.8cm.   [17] $325
A CHART OF DELAWARE BAY AND RIVER, FROM THE ORIGINAL BY MR. FISHER OF
   PHILADELPHIA [1776-79] 17.8x22.9cm.
   fold lines as issued, from the July 1779 issue   [27] $75

GENTLEMAN'S MAGAZINE (continued)

A CHART OF DELAWARE BAY AND RIVER, FROM THE ORIGINAL BY MR. FISHER OF
PHILADELPHIA [1776-79] 23.5x18.4cm.   [22] $75

A MAP OF 100 MILES ROUND BOSTON [1775] 22.9x24.1cm.
fold lines as issued, narrow left and bottom margin   [27] $100

A MAP OF CONNECTICUT AND RHODE ISLAND, WITH LONG ISLAND SOUND, ETC. [1776]
22.9x17.1cm. from the November 1776 issue   [25] $84

A MAP OF PART OF WEST FLORIDA FROM PENSACOLA TO THE MOUTH OF THE IBERVILLE
RIVER WITH A VIEW TO SHEW SPOT FOR A SETTLEMENT ON THE MISSISSIPI [1772]
19.1x34.3cm.   [3] $110

A MAP OF PART OF WEST FLORIDA, FROM PENSACOLA TO THE MOUTH OF THE IBERVILLE
RIVER, WITH A VIEW TO SHEW THE PROPER SPOT FOR A SETTLEMENT ON THE
MISSISSIPI [1772] 18.4x34.3cm.
from the February 1772 issue, inset map of the proposed settlement   [23] $125

A MAP OF PHILADELPHIA AND PARTS ADJACENT. BY N. SCULL AND G. HEAP [1777]
33.3x29.5cm. backed with rice paper, from the December 1777 issue   [34] $285

A MAP OF THAT PART OF AMERICA WHERE A DEGREE OF LATITUDE WAS MEASURED FOR THE
ROYAL SOCIETY: BY CHA: MASON, & JERE. DIXON [1769] 16x9.5cm.
with related text, from Nov. 1769 issue   [21] $121

A MAP OF THE BRITISH AND FRENCH SETTLEMENTS IN NORTH AMERICA... [1755]
19.1x48.3cm.   [32] $85

A MAP OF THE CAPE OF GOOD HOPE [1752] 18.5x11cm.   [4] $68

A MAP OF THE COUNTRY BETWEEN CROWN POINT AND FORT EDWARD [1759] 19.1x11.4cm.
                                                                     [3] $70

A MAP OF THE COUNTRY ROUND PHILADELPHIA INCLUDING PART OF NEW JERSEY, NEW YORK,
STATEN ISLAND & LONG ISLAND [1776] 22.2x17.8cm.
from the September 1776 issue, with 1/2 page of text   [25] $99

A MAP OF THE NEW GOVERNMENTS OF EAST & WEST FLORIDA [1763] 19.1x24.8cm.
narrow left & bottom margins   [23] $100

A MAP OF THE NEW GOVERNMENTS, OF EAST & WEST FLORIDA [1762] 19.1x25.4cm.
inset map of Pensacola   [3] $125

A PLAN OF THE HARBOUR OF CHEBUCTO AND TOWN OF HALIFAX [1750] 21.6x26.7cm.
minor repairs to one fold, from the July 1750 issue, coats of arms and a
porcupine appear in the lower portion   [27] $225

A PLAN OF THE STRAITS OF ST. MARY, AND MICHILIMAKINAC TO SHEW THE SITUATION &
IMPORTANCE OF THE TWO WESTERNMOST SETTLEMENTS OF CANADA FOR THE FUR TRADE
[1751] 23.5x32.4cm.   [3] $245

AN ACCURATE MAP OF THE BRITISH EMPIRE IN NTH AMERICA AS SETTLED BY THE
PRELIMINARIES IN 1762 [C1763] 21x24.4cm.
3 folds, inset map: "A Chart of the Entrance of the Mississippi"   [8] $110

ANTARCTIC POLAR CIRCLE WITH THE COUNTRIES ADJOINING, ACCORDING TO...MR. BUACHE
[1763] 19.7x22.2cm.   [23] $85

DISCOVERIES OF ADMIRAL DE FONTE & OTHERS, BY M. DE L'ISLE [1754] 19.7x25.4cm.
                                                                     [23] $140

MAP OF POLAND WITH APPENDAGES [1772] 17.1x20.3cm.   [30] $81

MAP OF THE BLACK LEAD MINES &C. IN CUMBERLAND [1751] 19.7x24.1cm.
lower margin extended, from June 1, 1751 issue, with 3 pages of text [24] $91

MAP OF THE COUNTRY AROUND PHILADELPHIA [1778] 17.8x22.2cm.   [30] $60

MAP OF THE PROGRESS OF HIS MAJESTY'S ARMIES IN NEW YORK, DURING THE LATE
CAMPAIGN ILLUSTRATING THE ACCOUNTS PUBLISH'D IN THE LONDON GAZETTE [1776]
31.8x19.7cm. accompanied by 4 pages of text   [25] $130

OLD PT. ROYAL [1785] 17.8x31.8cm. Nov. 1785 issue   [3] $65

SKETCH OF THE COUNTRY ILLUSTRATING THE LATE ENGAGEMENT IN LONG ISLAND [1776]
31.1x19.7cm. with one page of text, from the October 1776 issue   [25] $119

THE BRITISH GOVERNMENTS IN NTH. AMERICA LAID DOWN AGREEABLE TO THE PROCLAMATION
OF OCTR. 7, 1763 [1763] 20.3x23.5cm.
trimmed just into engraved surface at bottom   [23] $90

GERSTMAYR

BOSTON [C1760] 24.1x17.8cm.
folds, sites coded by letters but no key is present   [23] $65

CHARLESTON [C1760] 24.1x17.8cm. folding   [23] $75

GIBSON

See also GENTLEMAN'S MAGAZINE

A MAP OF MARTINICO FROM THE LATEST AND BEST AUTHORITIES [1759] 19.1x24.1cm.
[3] $45

A MAP OF THE ROAD FROM LONDON TO BERWICK [C1765] 17.8x29.2cm.
strip road map
[30] $24

A MAP OF THE ROAD FROM LONDON TO HARWICH [C1765] 17.8x29.2cm.
strip road map
[30] $36

A NEW AND ACCURATE MAP OF THE EMPIRE OF CHINA FROM THE SIEUR ROBERT'S ATLAS,
WITH IMPROVEMENTS [C1760] 19.1x29.2cm.
[10] $60

A NEW AND COMPLEAT MAP OF ALL AMERICA [1763] C52.1x118.1cm. on 4 sheets
joined to form 2, dimensions are for each half, minor wear at folds, 1st
state
[16] $680

NORTHERN ITALY [C1765] 25.4x19.1cm.
[30] $16

GILLIAM

MAP OF GILLIAM'S TRAVELS IN MEXICO, INCLUDING TEXAS AND PART OF THE UNITED
STATES [1846] 48.3x47cm. light browning, tears in margins repaired [22] $75

GILMAN

THE SEVERAL STATES & TERRITORIES OF THE UNITED STATES IN SQUARE MILES & ACRES
[1848] 35.6x85.1cm. P.S. Duval Lith. Phila.
[3] $50

GILPIN

MAP OF COLORADO TERRITORY, AND NORTHERN PORTION OF NEW MEXICO SHOWING THE
SYSTEM OF PARCS [1873] 52.1x53.3cm. a folding map, from William Gilpin,
"Mission of the North American People..."
[27] $175

GLAZIER

THE "FATHER OF WATERS" [1888] 96.5x8.9cm. 5 folds, from Willard Glazier,
"Down the Great River," Philadelphia 1888
[8] $15

GOERING

MERIDA, SIERRA NEVADA (VIEW) [C1890] 20x30cm.
[39] $75

PUERTO CABELLO (VIEW) [C1890] 20.1x30.6cm.
[39] $65

THAL VON CARACAS (VIEW) [C1890] 20.3x29.8cm.
[39] $95

GOLD

CHART OF THE ISLAND OF NEWFOUNDLAND [1801] 38.7x31.8cm.
published by Bunney & Gold, London
[3] $95

CHART OF THE SUPPOSED COURSE OF THE FLORIDA STREAM. LONDON PUBLISH'D MAY 31,
1804 BY J. GOLD, 103 SHOE LANE [1798-1804] 39.4x15.9cm.
from "Naval Chronicle" with 3 pages of text
[25] $68

FISHING VILLAGE CARTHAGENA (VIEW) [1817] 12.7x22.9cm.
[3] $35

PORT ROYAL IN JAMAICA [1809] 12.7x15.9cm.
[3] $35

VIEW OF NASSAU IN THE BAHAMAS [1799] 12.7x22.9cm.
view by N. Pocock, published in London by Bunney & Gold
[3] $75

GOOS

BELGIUM, SIVE INFERIOR GERMANIA POST OMNES IN HAC FORMA, EXACTISSIME
DESCRIPTIA. AUCT. ABRAHAMO GOOS. 1621 [1621] 43x55.5cm.
[18] $1756

CUST VAN HOLLANT TUSZCHEN DE MAES ENDE TEXEL [C1666] C43x53cm.
[18] $175

DE HEERLICHEYT VAN OVER. YSSEL. [1634] 39x59.5cm.
[18] $280

DUCATUS LUTZENBURGICUS. CUM PRIVILEG. [1628] 12x17.4cm.
[18] $351

LUTZENBURGENSIS DUCATUS. JACOBO SURHONIO MONTENSI AUCTORE. PETRUS KAERIUS
CAELAVIT [1632] 18.5x25.5cm.
[18] $351

ORBIS TERRARUM NOVA ET ACCURATISSIMA TABULA [1666] 45.1x54.6cm.
[17] $4200

PASCAART VANT CANAAL BEGRYPENDE IN SICH ENGLANDT, SCHOTLANDT EN JERLANDT...
[1660] 43x53cm. two small repairs
[31] $383

PASCAARTE VANDE ZUYDER-ZEE, TEXEL ENDE VLIE-STROOM, ALS MEDE'T AMELANDER-GAT.
T'AMSTERDAM, BY PIETER GOOS OP 'T WATER INDE VERGULDE ZEE SPIEGEL. ANNO 1666
[C1666] 43x53cm.
[18] $263

PASCAERTE VANDE VLAEMSCHE, SOUTE EN CARIBESCHE EYLANDEN ALS MEDE TERRA NOVA EN
DE CUSTEN VAN NOVA FRANCIA, NOVA ANGLIA, NIEU NEDERLANDT, VENEZUELA, NUEVA
ANDALUSIA, GUIANA EN EEN GEDEELTE VAN BRAZIL [1666] 44.5x54cm.
[15] $650

PASCAERTE VANDE VLAEMSCHE, SOUTE, EN CARIBESCHE EYLANDEN, ALS MEDE TERRA NOVA,
EN DE CUSTEN VAN NOVA FRANCIA, NOVA ANGLIA, NIEU NEDERLANDT, VENEZUELA, NUEVA
ANDALUSIA, GUIANA, EN EEN GEDEELTE, VAN BRAZIL [1666] 45.1x54cm.
4 small pinholes
[7] $560

112

GOOS (continued)
PASKAERTE VAN DE ZUYDT EN NOORDT REVIER IN NIEU NEDERLANT STRECKENDE VAN CABO
    HINLOOPEN TOT RECHKEWACH [1666] 50.5x60cm. top & bottom margins narrow
                                                                    [26] $3000
PASKAERTE ZYNDE T'OOSTERDEEL VAN OOST INDIEN MET ALLES DE EYLANDEN DEER
    ONTRENDT GELEGEN VAN C. COMORIN TOT AEN JAPAN... [1666] 44x53.5cm. [31] $1418
PASKERT VAN DE ZEEUSCHE EN VLAEMSCHE KUSTEN, TONENDE ALLE DROOGHTEN, DIEPTEN,
    EN ONDIEPTEN, TUSSCHEN T'EYLANDT SCHOUWEN EN DE HOOFDEN, CURIEUSELYCK
    BESCHREVEN DOOR DIRCK DAVIDZ [C1666] 43x93.7cm.
    on 2 joined sheets, dimensions are total   [18] $263
GORDON
BOSTON WITH ITS ENVIRONS [1785-89] 22.6x32.4cm. one margin narrow [39] $75
NEW YORK ISLAND & PARTS ADJACENT [1785-89] 26.5x17cm.
    one margin narrow   [39] $60
THE JERSEYS, &C. &C. [1785-89] 26.5x17cm. one margin narrow   [39] $65
GRATTON & GILBERT
MEXICO & TEXAS [1840] 28.6x22.9cm.   [19] $100
GRAVIUS
KAART VAN DE GEHEEL WERELD [C1760] 18x29cm. on Mercator's projection [2] $52
KAART VAN DE TWEE PLATTE WARELDS BOLLEN [C1760] 17.5x30cm.
    world in 2 hemispheres   [2] $61
KAARTJE VAN HET NOORDER DEEL VAN AMERICA [C1760] 18x24.5cm.   [2] $42
GRAY
ALABAMA [1873] 36.8x30.5cm.   [27] $35
CITY OF BURLINGTON, CHITTENDEN CO. [1874] 30.5x38.1cm. from "Atlas of the
    United States," accompanied by "Principal Business Firms and Professional
    Men"   [27] $60
GRAY'S ATLAS MAP OF TEXAS [1873] 41.9x63.5cm.
    light staining in margins   [19] $110
GRAY'S GEOLOGICAL MAP OF THE U.S. BY CHARLES H. HITCHCOCK [1877] 38.1x64.8cm.
                                                                   [19] $70
GRAY'S MAP OF CALIFORNIA [1884] 68.6x40.6cm.
    with inset map of San Francisco, Washington/Oregon and Nevada on verso
                                                                   [23] $75
NEW MEXICO AND ARIZONA [1876] 29.2x38.1cm.   [9] $42
GREAT BRITAIN
COMMISSION EUROPEENE DE DELIMITATION DE LA BULGARIE. CROQUIS GENERALE DE LA
    FRONTIERE ROUMANO-BULGARE [1879] 69x400cm. on 4 sheets joined, manuscript
    title on detached board, stamp of British Government Foreign Office, compiled
    & lithographed at the Intelligence Branch of the British Quartermaster
    General's Department, litho. by J.C. Kelly   [21] $284
GREENLEAF
NORTH AND SOUTH AMERICA [1842] 29.8x32.4cm.
    from "A New Universal Atlas," Brattleboro, Vermont, light water stain
                                                                    [1] $65
OREGON TERRITORY [1842] 26.7x31.8cm.   [27] $175
GREENWOOD
(BEDFORDSHIRE) [1834] C58x69cm.   [29] $38
(CAMBRIDGESHIRE) [1834] C58x69cm. light offsetting   [29] $53
(CARDIGAN, PEMBROKE & CARMARTHEN) [1834] C58x69cm. light offsetting [29] $61
(CUMBERLAND) [1834] C58x69cm.   [29] $61
(DORSET) [1834] C58x69cm.   [29] $68
(GLOUCESTERSHIRE) [1834] C58x69cm.   [29] $91
(HERTFORDSHIRE) [1834] C58x69cm. light offsetting   [29] $68
(LANCASHIRE) [1834] C58x69cm.   [29] $130
(MIDDLESEX) [1834] C58x69cm.   [29] $91
(MONMOUTHSHIRE) [1834] C58x69cm.   [29] $53
(NORTH RIDING) [1834] C58x69cm. light offsetting   [29] $68
(NORTHUMBERLAND) [1834] C58x69cm.   [29] $68
(OXFORDSHIRE) [1834] C58x69cm.   [29] $53
(RUTLAND) [1834] C58x69cm.   [29] $45

GREENWOOD (continued)
(STAFFORDSHIRE) [1834] C58x69cm.   [29] $68
(SUSSEX) [1834] C58x69cm.   [29] $130
(WILTSHIRE) [1834] C58x69cm.   [29] $68
A MAP OF THE COUNTY OF CUMBERLAND, FROM AN ACTUAL SURVEY... [1821-30]
     61.6x68.6cm.   [24] $91
MAP OF THE COUNTY OF SOMERSET, FROM ACTUAL SURVEY MADE IN THE YEARS 1820 & 1821
     BY C. & I. GREENWOOD. LONDON PUBLISHED FOR THE PROPRIETORS BY GEORGE PRINGLE
     JUNR. 70 QUEEN STREET, CHEAPSIDE, OCTR. 1822 [1822] 134.6x182.9cm.
     mounted in sections on cloth, inset of Wells Cathedral   [7] $225
MAP OF THE COUNTY PALATINE OF CHESTER, FROM AN ACTUAL SURVEY... [1819-30]
     57.2x67.9cm. minor repairs to margins   [24] $84
GRIDLEY
A PLAN OF THE CITY & FORTIFICATIONS OF LOUISBURG TAKEN JUNE 17, 1745 AFTER
     SIEGE OF 49 DAYS.../A PLAN OF THE CITY & HARBOUR OF LOUISBURG.../GABARUS BAY
     [1758] 27.3x35.6cm.   [3] $135
GRIERSON
A DRAUGHT OF THE COAST OF GUIANA FROM THE RIVER ORONOQUE TO THE RIVER AMAZONES
     [1749] 55.2x43.8cm.
     from the pirated Dublin edition of the English Pilot   [25] $153
NORTH AMERICA ACCORDING TO THE LATEST OBSERVATIONS [1760] 14.5x16.5cm.
     plagiarized by George Grierson, Dublin publisher, from an earlier John Senex
     map, 3 tiny holes repaired   [21] $150
THE HARBOUR OF CASCO BAY AND ISLANDS ADJACENT BY CAPT. CYPRIAN SOUTHICKE.
     PRINTED AND SOLD BY GEO. GRIERSON AT THE TWO BIBLES IN ESSEX STREET DUBLIN
     [1749] 42.5x52.1cm.
     from the pirated Dublin edition of the English Pilot   [25] $214
GUICHARDIN
LIEGE (VIEW) [1582] 23x31cm.   [18] $105
GUSSEFELD
CHARTE UBER DIE XIII VEREINIGTE STAATEN VON NORD-AMERICA [1784] 44.5x57.2cm.
     minor stain at upper right   [23] $600
CHARTE VON AMERIKA AUS DER ALTESTEN NOCH UNEDIRTEN WELTCHARTE DES DIEGO RIBERO
     [1795] 66x49.5cm. minor tear in right margin, reproduction based on the 1529
     Ribero world map   [23] $160
CHARTE VON DEN VEREINIGTEN STAATEN VON NORD-AMERICA NEBST LOUISIANA [1805]
     47x68.6cm.   [23] $400
CHARTE VON WEST INDIEN NACH DER GROSSEN CHARTE DES B. EDWARDS... [1795]
     43.5x61.6cm. folding   [22] $125
GUTHRIE
A MAP OF THE UNITED STATES OF AMERICA. AGREEBLE TO THE PEACE OF 1783. ENGRAVED
     FOR GUTHRIES NEW SYSTEM OF GEOGRAPHY [1785] 39.4x35.6cm.   [25] $99
THE BRITISH COLONIES IN NORTH AMERICA, FROM THE BEST AUTHORITIES [C1785]
     33.7x33.7cm. reinforced on verso   [25] $68
THE BRITISH COLONIES IN NORTH AMERICA, FROM THE BEST AUTHORITIES [1792]
     33.7x34.3cm.   [3] $120
THE WEST INDIES ACCORDING TO THE BEST AUTHORITIES. ENGRAVED FOR GUTHRIES NEW
     SYSTEM OF GEOGRAPHY. PUBLISHED...JANUARY 1ST, 1785 BY C. DILLY & G. ROBINSON
     LONDON [1785] 53.3x28.6cm. minor repair   [25] $68
HABERMANN
VUE DE BOSTON [1776] 25.3x40.1cm.   [39] $235
VUE DE LA BASSE VILLE A QUEBECK [C1750] 25.2x39.6cm.   [39] $250
VUE DE LA PLACE CAPITALE A QUEBECK [C1750] 25.2x39.5cm.   [39] $250
HACHETTE
CARTE DES ETATS-UNIS DE L'AMERIQUE DU NORD ET MEXIQUE... [1846] 22.9x27.9cm.
                                                                    [3] $45
HADFIELD
FALKLAND ISLES [1854] 14x23cm.
     by W. Hadfield, London, shows about 200 place names   [39] $25
HALL
BRITISH NORTH AMERICA [1829] 49x51cm. light offsetting   [21] $77

114

HALL (continued)
COLOMBIA [1828] 51.6x41.7cm.   [39] $35
JAMAICA [C1841] 26x34.9cm.   [3] $65
MEXICO [C1838] 26x36.8cm.   [22] $135
MEXICO [1847] 25.4x36.8cm. inset of Guatemala   [19] $110
MEXICO [C1840] 25.4x37.1cm. inset of Guatemala   [19] $125
MEXICO [C1840] 25.4x36.8cm. top margin narrow   [22] $125
MEXICO AND CENTRAL STATES [C1843] 41x51cm. library stamp in margin   [5] $200
MEXICO AND CENTRAL STATES [C1838] 40.6x50.8cm.   [19] $160
MEXICO AND GUATIMALA CORRECTED FROM ORIGINAL INFORMATION COMMUNICATED BY SIMON
   BOURNE [1828] 41.3x51.4cm.   [3] $140
MEXICO, CALIFORNIA & TEXAS [C1850] 26x36.8cm.   [20] $100
MEXICO, CALIFORNIA & TEXAS [C1850] 26x36.8cm.   [19] $80
NORTH AMERICA [1842] 38.1x27.9cm. backed   [3] $35
NORTH AMERICA [1847] 38.1x25.4cm. minor foxing   [19] $55
NORTH AMERICA [C1838] 50.8x41.9cm.   [19] $110
UNITED STATES [C1838] 40.6x52.1cm.   [19] $150
UNITED STATES [1830] 41.9x50.8cm. from "New General Atlas"   [16] $85
WORLD ON MERCATOR'S PROJECTION [C1838] 41.9x50.2cm.   [19] $75
HALLIBURTON
PLAN OF THE HARBOUR AND FORTIFICATIONS OF LOUISBURG [1829] 9.7x17cm.   [39] $25
HALMA
TYPUS FRISIAE VETERIS...ITEMQE INSULAE BATAVORUM...DISPONENTE BERNHARDO
   SCHOTANO A STERINGA. FRANCISCUS HALMA EXCUDEBAT [1718] 48x40cm.   [18] $140
HARDESTY
MAP OF EASTERN TEXAS [1884] 33x48.3cm.   [19] $40
MAP OF NORTHWEST TEXAS AND PAN HANDLE [1884] 30.5x24.1cm.
   narrow left margin, spot in lower right margin   [19] $20
MAP OF SOUTHERN TEXAS [1884] 33x48.3cm.   [19] $35
MAP OF WESTERN TEXAS [1884] 47x30.5cm. minor spotting in margins   [19] $35
HARPER
MAP OF THE ROUTES IN NEW YORK, NEW ENGLAND & PENNSYLVANIA, DRAWN FOR THE
   NORTHERN TRAVELLER [1830] 14.1x15.4cm.   [39] $35
HARPER & BROS.
MAP OF THE UNITED STATES, AND TEXAS [C1844] 44.5x58.4cm.
   narrow left margin, tear in margin repaired   [22] $90
HARPER'S WEEKLY
(NEW YORK HARBOR, AS SEEN FROM THE BROOKLYN TOWER OF THE SUSPENSION BRIDGE,
   VIEW) [1873] 22.9x35.6cm.   [10] $25
BIRD'S-EYE VIEW OF PHILADELPHIA [1876] 49.8x74.9cm. wood engraving backed
   with rice paper, 5 cm. tear at top repaired, from supplement to Harper's
   Weekly, May 27, 1876   [34] $450
GENERAL VIEW OF THE CITY OF MONTREAL, CANADA [1860] 36x48cm.
   from August 18 issue   [21] $36
THE NEW EL DORADO IN BRITISH AMERICA [1858] 35.6x24.1cm. from July 17, 1858
   issue, with text along sides and view of Vancouver Island below   [9] $25
VIEW OF ST. THOMAS, WEST INDIES, LATELY PURCHASED BY THE UNITED STATES [1867]
   17.8x52.1cm.   [3] $30
HARREWYN
PALATIUM BRUXELLENSE DUCIS BRABANTIAE [C1700] 36x46cm.   [18] $70
HARRIS
A MAP OF THE GREAT LEVELL OF THE FENNS EXTENDING INTO YE COUNTYES OF NORFOLK,
   SUFFOLKE... [1701] 29.2x40cm.
   one margin extended, another restored where cut by binder   [24] $130
ANTIENT MEXICO (VIEW) [1744] 21x33cm.   [3] $80
PLANS OF THE OLD & NEW CITY OF PEKING YE METROPOLIS OF CHINA [1744] 34.3x21cm.
                                                                        [3] $60

HARRISON
A NEW MAP OF THE WORLD WITH THE LATEST DISCOVERIES [1788] C27.9x50.8cm.
   right margin extended   [23] $75

HARRISON (continued)

MAP OF JAMAICA PREPARED FROM THE BEST AUTHORITIES UNDER THE DIRECTION OF MAJOR
GENERAL J.R. MANN., DIRECTOR OF ROADS AND SURVEYOR GENERAL [1873] 63x159cm.
folding map in 30 panels on cloth backing, with slip case   [39] $75
MAP OF LOUISIANA FROM D'ANVILLE'S ATLAS [1788] 30.5x49.5cm.   [22] $225
NORTH AMERICA DRAWN FROM THE LATEST AND BEST AUTHORITIES [1787] 33.7x39.4cm.
tear repaired, right margin narrow   [23] $125
THE RIVER ST. LAWRENCE, ACCURATELY DRAWN FROM D'ANVILLE'S MAP PUBLISH'D UNDER
THE PARTONAGE OF THE DUKE OF ORLEANS [1791] 35.6x41.9cm.   [3] $80
THE RIVER ST. LAWRENCE, ACCURATELY DRAWN FROM D'ANVILLE'S MAP. PUBLISHED UNDER
THE PATRONAGE OF THE DUKE OF ORLEANS [1791] 33.5x42cm.
light staining at edges & minor crease   [21] $77

HAYDEN

ECONOMIC MAP OF COLORADO [1878] 64.8x89.5cm.   [11] $50

HAYWARD

PLAN OF A SURVEY FOR THE PROPOSED BOSTON AND PROVIDENCE RAIL-WAY [1828]
18.4x106cm. fold line separations & tears in margins repaired   [22] $85

HENNEPIN

A MAP OF A NEW WORLD BETWEEN NEW MEXICO AND THE FROZEN SEA... [1698]
27.1x44.5cm. minor repairs, from an English ed.   [39] $475
AMERIQUE SEPTENTRIONALIS CARTE D'UN TRES GRAND PAYS ENTRE LE NOUVEAU MEXIQUE ET
LA MER GLACIALE... [1698] 43.2x52.1cm. narrow right margin, tear in
upper-right corner repaired, folding, from 2nd ed. of Louis Hennepin,
"Nouvelle Decouverte d'un tres grande Pays Situe dans l'Amerique..." [27] $1800
CARTE D'UN TRES GRAND PAIS NOUVELLEMENT DECOUVERT DANS L'AMERIQUE
SEPTENTRIONALE ENTRE LE NOUVEAU MEXIQUE ET LA MER GLACIALE AVEC LE COURS DU
GRAND FLEUVE MESCHASIPI... [1698] 38.1x44.5cm. folding map, 10 cm. tear
upper right repaired, narrow right margin, from Louis Hennepin, "Nouvelle
Decouverte d'un tres grande Pays Situe dans l'Amerique..."   [27] $1200

HERBERSTEIN

(RUSSIA) [1551] 26x36.8cm.
published in Basle, 1551, by Sigismund Herberstein   [17] $850

HERISSON

LA MAPPE MONDE OU LE GLOBE TERRESTRE REPRESENTE EN DEUX HEMISPHERES, L'UN
ORIENTAL L'AUTRE OCCIDENTAL; OU SONT MARQUEES LES DECOUVERTES LES PLUS
RECENTES...DRESSEE PAR HERISSON. ELEVE DE MR. BONNE...A PARIS CHEZ
BASSET...AUGMENTEE IN 1823 [1823] 55.2x80cm.
minor tear repaired, dimensions are to plate mark   [25] $344
LES ETATS UNIS... [1809] 18.4x22.2cm.   [20] $100

HERRERA

DESCRIPCION DE LAS INDIAS DEL NORTE [1601] 16.5x22.5cm.   [22] $500
DESCRIPCION DEL AUDIENCIA DE LOS CHARCAS [1622] 15.2x16.5cm.   [3] $95

HEYLIN

AMERICA [1703] 36.8x42.5cm.   [3] $265

HILDBURG INSTITUT

GALVESTON IN TEXAS (VIEW) [C1850] 10.2x15.2cm.   [22] $45
NEU BRAUNFELS IN TEXAS (VIEW) [C1850] 10.2x15.2cm.   [22] $45

HILDEBRANDT

BAIE DE SAN FRANCISCO (VIEW) [1860] 16.5x24.1cm. T. Weber sc., Paris [3] $40

HILL & CO.

MAP OF THE UNITED STATES SHOWING THE FARM ANIMALS IN EACH STATE [1878]
44.5x61cm. damaged, lithographed in color, published by H.W. Hill & Co.,
Decatur, Illinois   [30] $12

HINTON

A NEW & ACCURATE MAP OF THE PRESENT SEAT OF WAR IN NORTH AMERICA, COMPREHENDING
NEW JERSEY, PHILADELPHIA, PENN. N.Y. &C. [1777] 36.8x27.9cm.   [3] $185
A NEW AND ACCURATE MAP OF THE COLONY OF MASSACHUSETTS BAY IN NORTH AMERICA FROM
A LATE SURVEY [1780] 26.7x33cm.   [3] $145
A PERSPECTIVE VIEW OF MONTREAL IN CANADA [C1775] 15.9x25.4cm.   [3] $125
MAP OF THE STATES NORTH & SOUTH CAROLINA [1832] 25.4x39.4cm.   [3] $45

116

INTON, SIMPKIN & MARSHALL

MAP OF THE STATE OF MISSOURI [1832] 25.4x36.2cm. [1] $125
MAP OF THE STATE OF NEW YORK, WITH PART OF UPPER CANADA. ENGRAVED AND PRINTED
  BY FENNER SEARS & CO. LONDON PUBLISHED APRIL 1, 1831 BY I.T. HINTON, AND
  SIMPKIN AND MARSHALL [1831] 40x24.8cm. [25] $45
MAP OF THE STATES OF ALABAMA AND GEORGIA [1831] 25.4x40cm. [3] $55
MAP OF THE STATES OF NORTH & SOUTH CAROLINA. ENGRAVED & PRINTED BY FENNER SEARS
  & CO. [1831] 24.8x40cm. [25] $58
NEW ENGLAND AND NEW YORK IN 1697 [1830-32] 19.1x24.7cm. [39] $25
NEW ENGLAND AND NEW YORK IN 1697 FROM THE "MAGNALIA AMERICANA" ENGRAVED &
  PRINTED BY FENNER, SEARS & CO. LONDON PUBLISHED NOV. 1 1830 BY I.T. HINTON, &
  SIMPKIN & MARSHALL [1830] 19.1x24.8cm. [25] $68

OGENBERG

BRABANTIA...FRANCISCUS HOGENBERGIUS IN UBIORUM METROPOLI...MDLXXXI [1581]
  36x41.5cm. cut to border, backed, published separately [18] $1053
FLANDRIA BOREALIS... [1604] 23x33.5cm. [18] $140

OGG

A CHART OF THE NORTH WEST COAST OF AMERICA & NORTH EAST COAST OF ASIA...
  [1785] 22.2x35.6cm. [3] $45
A VIEW OF BOLCHERETZK THE CAPITAL OF KAMTSCHATKA [1785] 22.9x31.8cm. [3] $35
A VIEW OF THE N.W. SIDE OF MAS A FUERA IS. [1785] 21x33cm. [3] $25
SKETCH OF THE HARBOUR OF SAMGANOODA, ON THE ISLAND OF OONALASKA...T. BOWEN,
  SCT. LONDON PUBLISHED BY ALEXR. HOGG... [1785] 20.3x32.4cm. [25] $38
THE NORTH SIDE OF LARGEST OF QUEEN CHARLOTTE'S ISLANDS [1785] 20.3x33cm. [3] $25
VIEW OF SULPHUR ISLAND [1785] 34.3x21.6cm. [3] $40

OLE

(HOLY LAND, UNTITLED) [C1660] 25.5x35cm. [4] $214
A DESCRIPTION OF THE LAND OF GOSEN, AND MOSES PASSAGE THROUGH THE DESERTS
  [C1660] 28x37cm. [4] $168
CAERNARVO COMITATUS PARS OLIM ORDOVICUM [1607] 25.4x30.5cm. 1st issue
  [24] $122
COMITATUS BERCHERIAE VULGO BARKSHYRE... [1607-37] 22.9x32.4cm. [24] $99

OMANN

See also DOPPLEMAYR

(AFRICA) [1715] 48.3x55.9cm. title not given [17] $675
AMERICA SEPTENTRIONALIS A DOMINO D'ANVILLE... [1756] 45.7x50.8cm. [23] $435
AMERICA SEPTENTRIONALIS. A DOMINO D'ANVILLE IN GALIIS EDITA NUNC IN ANGLIA
  COLONIIS IN INTERIOREM VIRGINIAM DEDUCTIS NEC NON FLUVII OHIO CURFU AUCTA
  NITISQ GEOGRAPHICIS ET HISTORICIS...SUMPTIBUS HOMANNIANORUM HEREDUM
  NORIBERGAE AO 1756 [1756] 47x50.8cm. a few spots in lower margin [7] $475
AMERICAE MAPPA GENERALIS [1746] 46x52cm. [4] $337
AMERICAE MAPPA GENERALIS... [1746] 46.6x53.6cm. [39] $350
AMPLISSIMAE REGIONIS MISSISSIPI SEU PROVINCIAE LUDOVICIANAE A R.P. LUDOVICO
  HENNEPIN, FRANCISE. MISS. IN AMERICA SEPTENTRIONALI ANNO 1687 DETECTAE, NUNC
  GALLORUM COLONIIS...EDITA A IO. BAPT. HOMANNO S.C.M. GEOGRAPHO NORIMBERGAE
  [C1745] 57.5x48.3cm. [25] $406
AMPLISSIMAE REGIONIS MISSISSIPI... [C1737] 48.3x58.4cm. 3 small stains
  [16] $700
DOMINIA ANGLORUM IN AMERICA SEPTENTRIONALI [C1740] 50x54.5cm.
  4 maps on one sheet [4] $337
DOMINIA ANGLORUM IN AMERICA SEPTENTRIONALI SPECIALIBUS MAPPIS LONDINI PRIMUM A
  MOLLIO EDITA NUNC RECUSA AB HOMANNIANIS HERED. JUNCTA EST MAPPULAE D FACIES
  EJUS REGINOIS QUAM COLONI SALISBURG INCOLUNT [1737] 55.2x49.5cm. margins
  somewhat ragged, 4 maps on one sheet, German title appears at right[7] $425
DOMINIA ANGLORUM IN AMERICA SEPTENTRIONALI... [1735] 50x55cm.
  4 maps on one sheet [31] $421
DOMINIA ANGLORUM IN AMERICA SEPTENTRIONALI... [1737] 50.8x55.9cm. narrow
  bottom margin, 4 maps on one sheet, title also appears in German [23] $345
DOMINIA ANGLORUM IN PRAECIPUS INSULIS AMERICAE [1720] 48.9x55.2cm. [3] $385
HIBERNIAE REGNUM [C1714-24] 58.4x48.3cm. [12] $114

HOMANN (continued)

MAPPA GEOGRAPHICA PROVINCIAE NOVAE EBORACI AB ANGLIS NEW YORK [1778] 71x57cm.
    on 2 sheets, joined   [5] $880
NOVA ANGLIA [C1720] 48.3x57.2cm. light browning at centerfold   [32] $750
NOVA ANGLIA [C1720] 48.3x58.4cm.   [23] $700
NOVA ANGLIA [C1725] 48.5x58.5cm.   [4] $735
PARTIE OCCIDENTALE DE LA NOUVELLE FRANCE OU DU CANADA [1755] 41.3x53.3cm.
    minor tear in margin repaired   [23] $800
PARTIE ORIENTALE DE LA NOUVELLE FRANCE OU DU CANADA PAR MR. BELLIN INGENIEUR DU
    ROY ED DE LA MARINE 1745. A PARIS CHEZ R.J. JULIEN A L'HOTEL DE SOUBIS. A
    NURMEBERG CHEZ LES HERITIERS D'HOMANN GEOGRAPHES DE S.M.J. A LONDRES CHEZ J.
    ROCQUE... [1745] 49.5x62.2cm.
    minor foxing in side margins, 2 spots in lower margin   [7] $750
PARTIE ORIENTALE DE LA NOUVELLE FRANCE OU DU CANADA, PAR MR. BELLIN INGENIEUR
    DU ROY ET DE LA MARINE POUR SERVIR A L'INTELLIGENCE DES AFFAIRES & DE L'ETAT
    PRESENT EN AMERIQUE COMMUNIQUEE AU PUBLUC PAR LES HERITIERS DE HOMAN EN L'AN
    1755 [1755] 45.7x55.9cm. centerfold tear reinforced with cardboard [7] $400
PLAN DU PORT ET VILLE DE LOUISBOURG/PLAN DE LA VILLE DE LOUISBOURG/PLAN OF THE
    TOWN OF HALIFAX IN NOVA SCOTIA [1756] 45.7x50.8cm.
    light centerfold browning, 3 charts on one sheet   [16] $520
PLANIGLOBII TERRESTRIS MAPPA UNIVERSALIS, ULTRUMQ HEMISPHAERIUM ORIENT ET
    OCCIDENTALE REPRAESENTANS EX IV. MAPPIS GENERALIBUS HASIANIS COMPOSITA ET
    ADJECTIS HEREDIBUS C.P.S.C.M. A MDCCXXXXVI...NORIMBERGENSIBUS [C1746]
    47x56.5cm.   [7] $1050
PRINCIPATUS GOTHA, COBURG ET ALTENBURG... [C1740] 48.3x55.9cm.   [24] $88
REGIONIS, QUAE EST CIRCA LONDIUM SPECIALIS REPRAESENTATIO GEOGRAPHICA [C1741]
    48.3x55.9cm. the title also appears in German; a copy of the Bowles map of
    1741, minor repair at top center   [12] $99
REGNI MEXICANI SEU NOVAE HISPANIAE... [C1730] 48.3x57.2cm.   [22] $575
REGNI SINAE VEL SINAE PROPRIE MAPA ET DESCRIPTIO GEOGRAPHICA... [1730]
    58.4x52.1cm.   [3] $145
REGNI SUECIAE IN OMNES SUAS SUBJACENTES PROVINCIAS ACCURATE DIVISI TABULA
    GENERALIS... [C1745] 48.9x29.2cm.   [24] $145
TOPOGRAPHICA REPRAESANTO BARBARICI PORTUS ET URBIS MUNITAE ORAN...DELINEATA A
    CHRISTIANO GEPHARTO. GEOMETRA, ET LUCI TRADITA AB HOMANNIANIS HEREDIBUS ANNO
    MDCCXXXII... [1732] 50.8x58.4cm. centerfold browned, minor creasing
               [7] $225
TOTIUS AFRICAE NOVA REPRAESENTATIO [1714-24] 44x47cm.
    minor reinforcement of centerfold, the issue of 1724   [14] $321
VIRGINIA, MARYLAND ET CAROLINA IN AMERICA SEPTENTRIONALI [C1740] 48.3x58.4cm.
               [16] $620
VIRGINIA, MARYLANDIA ET CAROLINA... [C1714] 48.3x57.2cm.   [22] $600

HONDIUS

See also JANSSON
See also MERCATOR

...CIVITATIS GANDAVENSIS HANC TERRITORY EIUSDEM...HENRICUS HONDIUS [C1610]
    38x47cm. centerfold reinforced   [18] $702
AFRICAE... [1641] 37.5x49.5cm.   [17] $850
AMERICA NOVITER DELINEATA [1636] 38.1x49.5cm.
    minor rust stain, light browning, from Vol. 1 of "Atlas Novus"   [16] $1000
AMERICA NOVITER DELINEATA [1634] 35.6x44.5cm. minor repair along folds,
    atypical full margins, from Vol. 1 of de Bry's Grand Voyages, newly engraved
               [16] $1200
BARBARIA [1606] 35.6x47cm. centerfold tear repaired   [7] $400
BELEGERINGHE VAN HET SLOT GENNEP DOOR...DEN PRINCE VAN ORAIGNIEN. GHEDRUCKT IN
    S'GRAVENHAGHE, TEN HUYSE VAN HENRICUS HONDIUS [1641] 31x39cm.   [18] $263
BELGII SIVE GERMANIAE INFERIORIS ACCURATISSIMA TABULA. AUCTORE HENRICO HONDIO.
    1631. AMSTELODAMI, SUMPTIBUS HENRICI HONDII [1631] 48x61cm.
    several repairs   [18] $1053
BELGII SIVE GERMANIAE INFERIORIS...TABULA. 1631 [1631] 39x50cm.   [18] $140
BELGII VETERIS TYPUS. PATRUS KAERIUS CAELAVIT [1639] 38x48cm.   [18] $70

COMITATUS MANSFELDIA [1641-42] 38.1x50.2cm. [24] $84
COMITATUS ZUTPHANIA. AUTH. NICOLAO GEILKERCKIO. [1639] 40x52.5cm.
  light staining in margins [18] $175
DESCRIPTION DE BERGEN-SUR-ZOOM...APUD JOANNEM JANSSONIUM [1639] 22.5x53.5cm.
  light staining in margins [18] $70
DESCRIPTION DU BRABANT. BRABANTIAE DUCATUS TABULA. ANNO 1629 [1639] 39x50cm.
  [18] $140
DESCRIPTION DU PAYS DE HAINAULT. COMITATUM HANNONIAE ET NAMURCI DESCRIPTIO
  [1639] 39x50cm. [18] $70
DESIGNATIO ORBIS CHRISTIANI [1614] 15.2x19.1cm.
  from "Purchas his Pilgrimes" [3] $165
EUROPA EXACTISSIME DESCRITPA [1631] 38x51cm. [2] $263
EXQUISITA & MAGNO ALIQUOT MENSIUM PERICULO LUSTRATA ET IAM RETECTA FRETI
  MAGELLANICI FACIES [1606] 35.6x46.4cm. margins stained [7] $550
FRISIA OCCIDENTALIS AUCTORIBUS ADRIANO METIO ET GERARDO FREITAG [1639]
  39x50cm. light staining in margins [18] $263
GRONINGA DOMINIUM AUCTORE BARTHOLDO WICHERINGE. EXCUDEBAT IOANNES IANSSONIS
  [1639] 38x50cm. light staining in margins [18] $263
GUIANA SIVE AMAZONUM REGIO [C1636] 37.5x49cm. [39] $175
HISPANIA NOVA [C1635] 14x18.6cm. [39] $50
HISPANIAE NOVA DESCRIPTIO, DE INTEGRO MULTIS INCOLIS, SECUNDUM HYDROGRAPHICAS,
  DESC. EMENDATA [1606] 38.1x50.8cm. margins trimmed, 1st state [7] $400
INDIA QUAE ORIENTALIS DICTUR, ET INSULAE ADIACENTES... [1633] 38x49cm.
  [31] $383
INS. CEILAN QUAE INCOLIS TENARISIN DICITUR [1606] 34.3x49.5cm.
  short tear in margin at centerfold repaired [7] $400
INSULAE INDIAE ORIENTALIS PRAECIPUA [1606-19] 34x48cm.
  issue of 1619, French text on verso [14] $498
L'EVESCHE DE LIEGE. DIOECESIS LEODIENSIS... [1639] 46x54cm. [18] $140
LA CHASTELLENIE D'IPRE. HENRICUS HONDIUS EXCUDEBAT (VIEW) [1641] 39x49cm.
  [18] $35
LA DELFLANDE ET SCHIELANDE, AVEC LES ISLES...HENRICI HONDII, 1629 [1639]
  46x55cm. light staining in margins [18] $175
LA FLANDRE GALLICANE. FLANDRIA GALLICA CONTINENS CASTELLANIAS INSULENSEM,
  DUACENSEM, ORCHIANENSEM CIVITATEM DOMINIUMQUE TORNACENSE [1639] 40x51cm.
  [18] $105
LA FLANDRE IMPERIALE ET PROPRIETAIRE [1639] 40x50cm. [18] $105
LA HOLLANDE MERIDIONALE...ZUYT HOLLAND. HENRICI HONDII, 1629 [1639] 45x55cm.
  light staining in margins [18] $175
LA HOLLANDE. COMITATUS HOLLANDIAE. HENRICI HONDII, 1629 [1639] 40x51cm.
  light staining in margins [18] $263
LA PARTIE PLUS OCCIDENTALE DE LA FLANDRE TEUTONIQUE. FLANDRIAE PARS
  OCCIDENTALIS... [1639] 40x50cm. [18] $105
LA PARTIE PLUS ORIENTALE DE LA FLANDRE TEUTONIQUE PARS FLANDRIAE ORIENTALIS...
  [1639] 40x49cm. [18] $105
LA RHEINLANDE. RHINOLANDIAE, AMSTELANDIAE...HENRICI HONDII, 1629 [1639]
  45x55cm. light staining in margins [18] $175
LA SEIGNEURIE DE MALINES. MECHLINIA DOMINIUM ET AERSCHOT DUCATUS. AUCTORE
  MICHAELE FLOR. A LANGREN. APUD IOANNEM IANSSONIUM [1639] 41x51cm. [18] $105
LA WEST-FRISE AUTREMENT DITE LA HOLLANDE SEPTENTRIONALE [1639] 45x55cm.
  light staining in margins [18] $175
LE COMTE DE DRENTE & LA SEIGNEURIE DE WESTERWOLD...CORNELI PYNACKER, 1634
  [1639] 38x49cm. light staining in margins [18] $140
LE COMTE DE NAMUR. NAMURCUM COMITATUS. 1632 [1639] 39x50cm. [18] $105
LE COMTE DE ZUTPHEN. COMITATUS ZUTPHANIA EXCUDIT JOANNES JANSSONIS [1639]
  38x49cm. light staining in margins [18] $175
LE DOMAINE D'UTRECHT. EPISCOP. ULTRAIECTINUS, 1628 [1639] 37x49cm.
  light staining in margins [18] $140
LE DUCHE DE GUELDRE. DUCATUS GELDRIAE...AUCTORE BALTHAZARO FLOR. A BERCKENRODE
  1629 [1639] 39x50cm. light staining in margins [18] $140

119

LUTZENBURG [1616] 9.7x13.3cm.   [18] $351
MAGNAE BRITANNIAE ET HIBERNIAE TABULA [1631-38] 38.1x49.5cm.   [14] $291
MAGNI MOGOLIS IMPERIUM [1636] 36.2x48.9cm.   [17] $350
MAPPA AESTIVARUM INSULARUM ALIAS BARMUDAS [1633] 39.4x51.4cm.   [15] $925
MAPPA AESTIVARUM INSULARUM ALIAS BARMUDAS DICTARUM [1633] 39x52cm.
   light browning   [2] $526
MAPPA AESTIVARUM INSULARUM... [1633] 39.4x51.4cm.   [17] $1400
MARCHIONATUS MORAVIAE AUCT I. COMENIO [C1636] 38.1x53.3cm.
   one margin reinforced   [24] $85
NOVA BRABANTIAE DUCATUS TABULA. AUCTORE JUDOCO HONDIO. DIRCK GRYP SCULPSIT
   [1630] 46.5x53.5cm.   [18] $1053
NOVA EUROPAE DESCRIPTIO AUCTORE IODOCO HONDIO [1606] 38.1x50.2cm.
   minor tears & tear into engraved surface repaired, 1st edition   [7] $1050
NOVA TOTIUS TERRARUM ORBIS GEOGRAPHICA AC HYDROGRAPHICA TABULA [1630]
   38.1x53.3cm.   [15] $3300
NOVA TOTIUS TERRARUM ORBIS GEOGRAPHICA AC HYDROGRAPHICA TABULA [1632]
   38x54.5cm.   [2] $1404
NOVA TOTIUS TERRARUM ORBIS GEOGRAPHICA AC HYDROGRAPHICA TABULA [1630-41]
   37.5x54cm.   [17] $3800
NOVA TOTIUS TERRARUM ORBIS GEOGRAPHICA AC HYDROGRAPHICA TABULA [1630]
   38.1x54.6cm. minor centerfold repairs   [16] $3200
NOVA VIRGINIAE TABULA [1636] 38.1x49.5cm.
   small wormhole not affecting printed surface   [16] $800
NOVA VIRGINIAE TABULA [1633] 38.1x50.2cm.   [23] $800
OVER-ISSEL. DITIO TRANS-ISULANA. JOANNES JANSSONIUS EXCUD. [1639] 39x49cm.
   light staining in margins   [18] $140
POLI ARCTICI... and POLUS ANTARCTICUS... [1637] 43.2x49.5cm.
   a pair of polar maps, dimensions are for each, light offsetting   [17] $2000
PREMIER QUARTIER DE BRABANT, DONT LA CAPITALE EST LOUVAIN. PARS MERIDIONALIS
   BRABANTIAE... [1639] 46x54cm.   [18] $105
PRINCIPATUS HENNENBERGENSIS [1641-42] 37.5x49.5cm.   [24] $82
QUATRIEME QUARTIER DE BRABANT. BOISLEDUC. BRABANTIAE PARS ORIENTALIS... [1639]
   46x54cm. light staining in margins   [18] $140
SANTVLIET: TABULA CASTELLI AD SANDFLIATUM...APUD IOAN. IANSSONIUM [1639]
   37x49cm. light staining in margins   [18] $105
SAXONIAE SUPERIORIS LUSATIAE MISNIAEQUE DESCRIPTIO [1641] 34.9x48.9cm.
    [24] $88
SILESIAE DUCATUS... [C1635] 38.1x48.9cm.   [24] $79
SITUS TERRAE PROMISSIONIS, S.S. BIBLIORUM INTELLIGENTIUM EXACTE APERIENS
   [1633-39] 36.8x48.3cm.   [15] $750
SITUS TERRAE PROMISSIONIS...PER CHR. ADRICHOM [C1632] 37x50cm. small
   separation in centerfold repaired, 1st state with address of H. Hondius
    [2] $263
TROISIEME QUARTIER DE BRABANT, DONT LA CAPITALE EST ANVERS ET LE MARQUISAT DU
   SAINT-EMPIRE. BRABANTIAE PARS SEPTENTRIONALIS... [1639] 47x54cm. [18] $105
TURCICI IMPERII IMAGO [1606-33] 35.6x48.3cm.   [24] $429
TURCICI IMPERII IMAGO [1606-19] 36x48cm.
   issue of 1619, French text on verso   [14] $352
TYPUS ORBIS TERRARUM [1625] 14x20.3cm.
   narrow margins, on a page of text, from Purchas, "Hakluytus Posthumus"
    [16] $350
VENEZUELA CUM PARTE AUSTRALI NOVAE ANDALUSIAE [1633] 35.6x48.9cm. [3] $400
VIRGINIAE ITEM ET FLORIDAE [C1640] 34.3x48.3cm.
   minor centerfold repair   [16] $750
WARWICUM NORTHAMTONIA HUNTINGDONIA CANTABRIGIA SUFFOLCIA OXONIUM BUCKINGHAMIA
   BEDFORDIA HARDFORDIA ESSEXIA BERCERIA MIDDELSEXIA SOUTHAMTONIA SURRIA CANTIUM
   ET SOUTHSEXIA [1595] 36.8x47cm.
   Mercator's 1595 map with Hondius' new title cartouch   [14] $130
ZE ZYPE. DE PURMER. DE WORMER. WATERLAND [1639] 35x47cm.
   light staining in margins   [18] $105

HONDIUS (continued)
ZELANDE. ZEELANDIA COMITATUS. JOANNES JANSSONIUS [1639] 39x50cm.
  light staining in margins   [18] $351
HONTER
ORBIS UNIVERSALIS DESCRIPTIO & HIBERNIA [1561] 12.7x16.5cm.
  cordiform world map, with Ireland on the verso   [16] $620
UNIVERSALIS COSMOGRAPHIA [1546-60] 12.7x16.5cm. on a page of text missing one
  corner, early color, originally published in "Rudimenta Cosmographia"
                                        [16] $800
HORNIUS
TABULA PEUTINGERIANA [1685] C39.4x50.8cm. on 4 sheets, dimensions are for
  each, minor tears in margins repaired, strip map based on a Roman map,
  published in Hornius' historical atlas, Leiden   [16] $700
HOWEN
PLAN OF OSWEGO 1727 [C1834] 26.7x36.8cm. A. Howen Lith. Baltimore, 1st
  printing of manuscript map by Chaussegros de Lery   [3] $35
HUBERTI
GROENINGHEN. PORTRAICT DE LA VILLE DE GROENINGHEN AVECQ LE CHASTEAU QUE LES
  ESTATS DES PROVINCES UNIEZ ONT FAICT BASTIR L'AN 1600...A HUBERTI EXCUDIT
  [1600] 20x27.5cm.   [18] $351
HULST (VIEW) [C1596] 20x28cm. minor repairs   [18] $140
HUY AU PAYS DE LIEGE (VIEW) [C1595] 20x27.5cm.
  legend in Flemmish & French   [18] $175
LE VRAY PORTRAICT DE LA VILLE D'OOSTENDE LAQUELLE FUT ASSIEGEE PAR LARCHIDUC LE
  5 JUILLET 1601 ET PRINSE LAN 1604 A LA FIN DE JUILLET [C1604] 20x27.5cm.
                                        [18] $140
HUGHES
MEXICO & CENTRAL AMERICA [1864] 50.8x60.3cm.   [20] $100
HULSIUS
INSULA PUNA [1603] 15.9x12.1cm.   [39] $60
LA MOCHA (ENGRAVED SCENE) [C1649] 11.7x15.6cm.   [39] $65
MANOA O DEL DORADO (VIEW) [1599] 10.5x14.1cm.   [39] $160
VAL PARYSA (VIEW) [C1649] 11.8x15.9cm.   [39] $75
HUMBOLDT
CARTE DE LA VALLEE DE MEXICO ET DES MONTAGNES VOISINES... [1811] 39.4x45.7cm.
  from "Atlas Geographique et Physique..." accompanying Humboldt's "Essai
  Politique sur le Royaume de la Nouvelle-Espagne"-on a sheet 56 x 79 cm.
                                      [27] $300
CARTE REDUITE DE LA PARTIE ORIENTALE DE LA NOUVELLE ESPAGNE DEPUIS LE PLATEAU
  DE LA VILLE DE MEXICO JUSQU'AU PORT DE LA VERACRUZ [1811] 21.6x62.2cm. from
  "Atlas Geographique et Physique..." accompanying Humboldt's "Essai Politique
  sur le Royaume de la Nouvelle-Espagne"-on a sheet 56 x 79 cm. [27] $225
CARTE REDUITE DE LA ROUTE D'ACAPULCO A MEXICO [1811] 39.4x19.1cm. from "Atlas
  Geographique et Physique..." accompanying Humboldt's "Essai Politique sur le
  Royaume de la Nouvelle-Espagne"-on a sheet 55 x 39 cm.   [27] $125
HUNTINGTON
NORTH AMERICA & WEST INDIES [1838] 27.9x23.5cm.   [19] $75
UNITED STATES, TEXAS & ...THE CANADAS [1838] 29.2x47.6cm. [19] $125
HURD
MAP OF THE CITY AND TOWN OF MANCHESTER, N.H. [1892] 40.8x68.9cm.
  2 plans on verso   [39] $30
HYDROGRAPHIC OFFICE
See ADMIRALTY
ILLUSTRATED LONDON NEWS
THE TOWN & HARBOUR OF ST. JOHN, NEW BRUNSWICK [1866] 24.1x34.3cm. [3] $25
IMBERT
CARTE DES POSSESIONS ANGLOISES DANS L'AMERIQUE SEPTENTRIONALE POUR SERVIR
  D'INTELLIGENCE A LA GUERRE [1777] 62.2x72.4cm. slight wrinkling [22] $475
IVISON & BLAKEMAN
MAP OF STANDARD TIME ADOPTED BY THE RAILWAYS OF UNITED STATES [1884]
  22.2x27.9cm. text on verso   [3] $40

IVISON & BLAKEMAN (continued)
THE UNITED STATES [1884] 27.9x43.8cm.   [3] $18
JACKSON
CHARLESTON, SOUTH CAROLINA (VIEW) [1829] 12.7x15.2cm.   [3] $40
JACOBSZ
DE CUSTEN VAN NOORWEGEN EN FINMARCKEN VAN WTWEERCLIPPEN TO AEN DE NOORT-CAAP
   [1663] 43x55cm.   [2] $263
PASCAART VANT CANAAL BEGRYPENDE IN SICH ENGELANDT, SCHOTLANDT EN IERLANDT ALS
   MEDE EEN GEDEELTE VAN FRANCRYCK [1663] 43.5x55cm. some wear   [2] $280
PASCAARTE VAN 'T WESTELYCKSTE DEEL VAN DE MIDDELLANDSCHE ZEE/PASCAARTE VAN 'T
   OOSTELYCKSTE DEEL VAN DE MIDDELLANDSCHE ZEE [1663] C40x50cm. two charts
   forming together a chart of the entire Mediterranean, dimensions are for
   each, lower corners stained   [2] $210
PASCAERTE OM ACHTER YRLANDT OM TE ZEYLEN [1663] 43.5x54.5cm. some wear
                                                                        [2] $193

PASKAERT VAN DE NOORDELIJCKSTE KUSTE VAN AMERICA VAN GROELAND DOOR DE STRAET
   DAVIS EN DE STRAET HUDSON TOT TERRA NEUF. T'AMSTERDAM, BIJ JACOB EN CASPARUS
   LOOTSMAN BEOCKVERKOOPERS OP'T WATER [C1705] 43.2x54cm.   [7] $750
JAILLOT
See also MORTIER
AMERICA SEPTENTRIONALE... [1694] 48.3x58.4cm.   [16] $1050
AMERICA SEPTENTRIONALIS... [1694] 48.3x58.4cm.   [23] $1000
AMERIQUE SEPTENTRIONALE DIVISEE EN SES PRINCIPALES PARTIES OU SONT DISTINGUES
   LES UNS DES AUTRES LES ESTATS [1679-95] 45.7x64.8cm.   [15] $1275
CARTE DES XVII PROVINCES DES PAYS BAS TIREE DE PLUSIEURS CARTES FAITES SUR LES
   LIEUX PAR CORNEILLE PYNCACKER...B. JAILLOT, GEOGRAPHE QUAY DE
   L'HORLOGE...1713 [1713] 66x82cm.   [18] $263
CARTE TOPOGRAPHIQUE DES FORTS, VILLE, CITADELLE D'ANVERS ET DE SES ENVIRONS.
   PAR LE SIEUR JAILLOT [1781] 50x69cm.   [18] $105
COMTE DE NAMUR [1689] 43x57cm.   [18] $105
ESTAT ET SEIGNEURIE DE L'EVESCHE DE LYEGE [1681] 44x57cm.   [18] $140
FLANDRE ESPAGNOLE ET FLANDRE HOLLANDOISE [1689] 43.5x56.5cm.   [18] $140
GUELDRE ESPAGNOLE OU QUARTIER DE RUREMONDE... [1674] 43x56cm.   [18] $122
JUDAEA SEU TERRA SANCTA... [1691] 58.4x83.8cm.   [17] $1400
LA BRETAGNE DIVISEE EN SES NEUF EVESCHES [1696] 48x61cm.
   side margins narrow   [2] $149
LA SEIGNEURIE D'OUEST-FRISE OU FRISE OCCIDENTALE... [1674] 43x57cm.   [18] $140
LA SEIGNEURIE D'OVER-YSSEL... [1674] 56x43cm.   [18] $122
LA SEIGNEURIE D'UTRECHT [1675] 43x56cm.   [18] $122
LA SEIGNEURIE DE GRONINGUE [1674] 44x58cm.   [18] $140
LA VELUWE, LA BETUWE ET LE COMTE DE ZUTPHEN DANS LE DUCHE DU GUELDRE... [1674]
   43x57cm.   [18] $122
LE BRABANT ESPAGNOL QUI COMPREND LES QUARTIERS DE BRUSSELLES, DE LOUVAIN ET
   PARTIE DE CELUY D'ANVERS [1684] 44x57cm.   [18] $105
LE CANADA OU PARTIE DE LA NOUVELLE FRANCE...CONTENANT LA TERRE DE LABRADOR, LA
   NOUVELLE FRANCE, LES ISLES TERRE NEUVE, DE NOSTRE DAME, &C. [1696]
   48.3x59.7cm.   [16] $750
LE COMTE DE HAYNAUT, DIVISE EN FRANCOIS ET ESPAGNOL. PAR SANSON. A PARIS, CHEZ
   H. JAILOT [1674] 43.5x57cm.   [18] $70
LE COMTE DE ZEELANDE... [1674] 43x57cm.   [18] $210
LE DUCHE DE BRABANT... [1705] 48x80cm.
   on 2 separate sheets, dimensions are for each   [18] $210
LE DUCHE DE LUCXEMBOURG DIVISE EN QUARTIER WALON ET ALLEMAND [1695] 52x62cm.
   on 4 sheets, dimensions are for each, some fold reinforcement   [18] $526
LE DUCHE DE LUXEMBOURG DIVISE EN FRANCOIS ET ESPAGNOL [1689] 43.8x57cm.
                                                                        [18] $140
LE LIMBOURG... [1674] 43.5x57cm.   [18] $122
LES DIX-SEPT PROVINCES DES PAYS-BAS...PARIS [1709] 44x57cm.   [18] $122
LES PROVINCES DES PAYS-BAS CATHOLIQUES... [1707] 47x65cm.   [18] $70

JAILLOT (continued)

MAPPE-MONDE GEO-HYDROGRAPHIQUE, OU DESCRIPTION GENERALE DU GLOBE TERRESTRE ET
AQUATIQUE, EN DEUX PLANS-HEMISPHERES...PAR LE SR. SANSON, GEOGRAPHE ORDINAIRE
DU ROY, 1695. DEDIE AU ROY...A PARIS CHEZ H. JAILLOT...CORDIER, SCULPSIT
[1695] 47x66cm. centerfold tear repaired, some spotting in margins, last two
digits in date are in manuscript   [7] $1250
MAPPEMONDE [1696] 49.5x61cm.   [16] $1200
PARTIE MERIDIONALE DU COMTE DE HOLLANDE [1700] 44x57cm.   [18] $140
PARTIE SEPTENTRIONALE DU COMTE DE HOLLANDE... [1674] 43.5x58cm.   [18] $122
PROVINCES UNIES DES PAYS-BAS. PARIS, JAILLOT D'APRES SANSON, 1700. CORDIER
SCULPT. [1700] 47x65cm.   [18] $105

JAMES

PLAN OF THE OPERATIONS OF THE BRITISH & AMERICAN FORCES BELOW NEW ORLEANS ON
THE 8TH OF JAN. 1815 [1818] 50.8x19.7cm. from W. James, "A Full and Correct
Account of the Late War between Great Britain and the United States," London
                                                                    [3] $125

JANSSON

See also HONDIUS
See also MERCATOR
See also VALK & SCHENK
AETHIOPIE SUPERIOR VEL INTERIOR VULGO ABISSINORUM SIVE PRESBITERI IOANNIS
IMPERIUM [C1640] 38.1x49.5cm.   [24] $245
AMERICA SEPTENTRIONALIS [1636] 47x54.6cm. light browning   [16] $1150
AMERICA SEPTENTRIONALIS [C1638] 46.5x55cm.
backed with thin paper, 2nd state with Jansson's name in cartouch   [2] $1317
AMERICA SEPTENTRIONALIS [1666] 54x46cm.   [31] $1341
AMSTELODAMI CELEBERRIMI HOLLANDIAE EMPORII DELINEATIO NOVA [1657] 42.5x54cm.
top & bottom centerfold reinforced   [24] $574
BELGII NOVI, ANGLIAE NOVAE ET PARTIS VIRGINIAE [C1694] 44.5x55.9cm.
3rd state of the first issue, published by P. Schenk & G. Valk   [16] $1400
BRITANNIA...HEPTARCHIA [1652] 41.9x52.7cm.   [17] $900
CANTIUM VERNACULE KENT [C1650] 38.5x50cm.   [4] $536
CHINA VETERIBUS SINARUM REGIO NUNC INCOLIS TAME DICTA [C1650] 40.5x49.5cm.
                                                                    [2] $280
COMITATIS CANTABRIGIENSIS VERNACULE CAMBRIDGE SHIRE [1646] 41.3x51.4cm.
lower centerfold repaired   [24] $421
COMITATUS DORCESTRIA. VULGO ANGLICE DORSET SHIRE [1646] 37.5x49.5cm. [24] $321
CUBA INSULA/HISPANIOLA INSULA/INS. JAMAICA/INS. S. JOANNIS/I.S. MARGARETA
[C1630] 14.5x18cm.   [5] $100
DUCATUS LUTZENBURGENSIS NOVA ACCURATA DESCRIPTIO [1639] 39.5x50cm.
light browning   [18] $245
HIBERNIA... [1636] 33.7x47cm. on 2 sheets, dimensions are for each [17] $750
HISPANIAE NOVAE NOVA DESCRIPTIO [C1630] 13.5x19cm.   [5] $100
HUNTINGDONENSIS COMITATUS HUNTINGTON SHIRE [1646] 39.4x49.5cm.   [24] $237
INS. CEILAN QUAE INCOLIS TENARISIN DICITUR [1606-39] 34.5x49.5cm. [13] $160
INSULA BORNEO ET OCCIDENTALIS PART CELIBIS CUM ADJACENTIBUS INSULIS [1657]
41.9x52.1cm. corner of blank margin replaced, centerfold repaired [24] $150
INSULAE BALEARIDES... [1636] 38.1x49.5cm.   [17] $375
INSULAE MELITAE VULGO MALTE NOVA ET ACCURATA DESCRIPTIO [1650] 41x50.5cm.
minor browning in fold   [2] $368
INSULAE SARDINIAE NOVA ET ACCURATA DESCRIPTIO [C1660] 41x51cm.
from Spanish ed.   [2] $166
INSULARUM BRITANNICARUM ACURATA DELINEATIO [C1650] 39x50.5cm.   [4] $268
JUDAEAE SEU TERRAE ISRAELIS TABULA GEOGRAPHICA... [1653] 35.6x48.3cm.
                                                                    [17] $750
MAR DEL NORT and MAR DI AETHIOPIA [1650] 43.2x55.9cm. a pair of maps, one
showing the North Atlantic, the other the South Atlantic, light browning,
dimensions are for each   [17] $1400
MERVINIA; ET MONTGOMERIA COMITATUS [1646] 38.1x49.5cm. 1st issue   [24] $145
MONA INSULA VULGO ANGLESEY/MONA INSULA: VULGO THE ISLE OF MAN/VECTIS INSULA
ANGLICE THE ISLE OF WIGHT [C1646-59] 50.2x55.9cm.   [12] $283

MONA INSULA VULGO ANGLESEY/MONA INSULA: VULGO THE ISLE OF MAN/VECTIS INSULA
  ANGLICE THE ISLE OF WIGHT [1646-59] 50.2x55.9cm.
    the issue of 1659, French text on verso, 3 maps on one sheet   [14] $283
MOSCOVIAE PARS AUSTRALIS AUCTORE ISACCO MASSA [C1680] 38.7x50.8cm.
    margins stained, creasing, published by Jansson's heir Waesberger   [7] $175
NOVA ANGLIA NOVUM BELGIUM ET VIRGINIA [C1640] 38.7x50.2cm.   [32] $1250
NOVA ANGLIA NOVUM BELGIUM ET VIRGINIA. AMSTELODAMI JOHANNES JANSSONIUS EXCUDIT
  [C1636-47] 38.7x50.2cm. browned, 1st state   [7] $1300
NOVA ANGLIA, NOVUM BELGIUM ET VIRGINIA [C1640] 38.1x50.8cm.   [15] $1200
NOVA ANGLIA, NOVUM BELGIUM, ET VIRGINIA [1636] 38.7x50.8cm.
    moderate browning, early state with heart-shaped cartouch   [23] $1100
NOVA ANGLIA, NOVVUM BELGIUM ET VIRGINIA. AMSTELODAMI JOHANNES JANSSONIUS.
  EXCUDIT [1636] 38.7x50.8cm. from the Latin ed. of 1636   [25] $651
NOVA BARBARIAE DESCRIPTIO [1638] 35.6x51.4cm.   [17] $450
NOVA ET ACCURATA POLI ARCTICI ET TERRARUM CIRCUM IACENTIUM DESCRIPTIO [C1645]
  40.6x52.1cm.   [7] $825
NOVA ET ACCURATA POLI ARCTICI ET TERRARUM CIRCUM IACENTIUM DESCRIPTIO [1637]
  41x52.5cm. light browning, some pigment damage to paper repaired   [21] $467
NOVA ET ACCURATA POLI ARCTICI ET TERRARUM CIRCUM IACENTIUM DESCRIPTIO.
  AMSTELODAMI, APUD IOANNEM IANSSONIUM [1637-50] 41x52.7cm.   [25] $574
NOVA ET ACCURATA POLI ARCTICI ET TERRARUM CIRCUMIACENTIUM DESCRIPTIO [C1636]
  40.6x53.3cm.   [15] $950
NOVA VIRGINIAE TABULA [C1630] 13x19cm.   [5] $160
ORBIS TERRARUM VETERIBUS COGNITI TYPUS GEOGRAPHICUS [1741] 40.6x50.8cm.
    centerfold tear repaired, some paper loss at lower margin, one pinhole
    affecting engraved surface, from "Description exacte de l'Univers...,"
    published by Pieter de Hondt, The Hague, 1741, first published by Jannson
                                                                        [7] $600
ORCADUM ET SCHETLANDIAE INSULARUM ACCURATISSIMA DESCRIPTIO [1646] 37.5x48.9cm.
                                                                        [24] $222
RUSSIA VULGO MOSCOVIA DICTAE, PARTES SEPTENTRIONALIS ET ORIENTALIS. AUCTORE
  ISACCO MASSA. APUD JANSSONIO-WAESBERGIOS [C1680] 41.9x53.3cm.
    margins stained, creasing, published by Jansson's heir Waesberger   [7] $175
SCOTIA... [1636] 41.9x54.6cm.   [17] $575
SEPTENTRIONALIUM TERRARUM DESCRIPT. [C1630] 14.5x20cm.   [5] $120
SITUS TERRAE PROMISSIONIS. S.S. BIBLIORUM INTELLIGENTIAM EXACTE APERIENS
  [1658] 36.8x49.5cm.   [17] $850
SITUS TERRAE PROMISSIONIS...PER CHR. ADRICHOM [1632] 37.5x50cm.
    minor staining at fold, address of Jansson   [2] $263
SUTHSEXIA VERNACULE SUSSEX [1646-52] 38.1x47.6cm.
    centerfold reinforced, issue of 1652, Dutch text on verso   [14] $383
SUTHSEXIA: VERNACULE SUSSEX [C1650] 38.5x51cm.   [4] $490
TABULA MAGELLANICA QUA TIERRAE DEL FUEGO CUM CELEBERRIMIS FREITIS A F.
  MAGELLANO [1658] 40.6x53.3cm.   [3] $295
VIRGINIA ITEM ET FLORIDAE AMERICAE PROVINCIARUM NOVA DESCRIPTIO [1673]
  18.7x25.7cm. from a plate originally in Mercator's atlas of 1630, verso
  blank, small tear in right margin   [1] $240
JANVIER
L'AMERIQUE DIVISEE PAR GRANDS ETATS [1762] 30.5x44.5cm.   [23] $145
L'AMERIQUE DIVISEE PAR GRANDS ETATS...CHEZ LATTRE... [1783] 31.1x45.1cm.
  backed   [3] $185
L'AMERIQUE SEPTENTRIONALE DIVISEE EN SES PRINCIPAUX ETATS PAR LE SR. JANVIER
  GEOGRAPHE, PARIS CHEZ LATTRE GRAVEUR, RUE ST. JACQUES 1762 [1762]
  30.5x44.5cm.   [3] $190
L'AMERIQUE SEPTENTRIONALE... [1762] 30.5x44.5cm.   [32] $200
PARTIE SEPTENTRIONALE DES PAYS BAS COMPRENANT LES ETATS GENERAUX DES PROVINCES
  UNIES. PAR LE SR. JANVIER, GEOGRAPHE, P. CHOFFARD FECIT [1760] 48x66cm.
    the word "Roy" cut out, otherwise fine   [18] $105
JEFFERYS
See also LAURIE & WHITTLE

A CHART OF PART OF THE COAST OF LABRADORE, FROM GRAND POINT TO SHECATICA.
SURVEYED BY MICHAEL LANE IN 1768. AND ENGRAVED BY THOMAS JEFFERYS...LONDON
PRINTED FOR R. SAYER AND I. BENNETT N. 53 IN FLEET-STREET, 10 MAY 1770
[1775] 50.2x52.1cm. side margins narrow, several tears in margin just
touching engraved area, from "The North-America Pilot for Newfoundland"
[7] $300

A GENERAL CHART OF THE ISLAND OF NEWFOUNDLAND WITH THE ROCKS &
SOUNDINGS...LONDON: PUBLISHED ACCORDING TO THE ACT OF PARLIAMENT 10TH MAY
1775. BY THOMAS JEFFERYS GEOGRAPHER TO THE KING. PRINTED FOR ROBT. SAYER &
JNO. BENNETT... [1775] 54.6x56.8cm. lower margin reinforced, 2nd state,
from "The North-American Pilot for Newfoundland, Labradore"   [7] $560

A MAP OF CANADA AND THE NORTH PART OF LOUISIANA WITH THE ADJACENT COUNTRYS. BY
THOS. JEFFERYS, GEOGRAPHER TO HIS ROYAL HIGHNESS THE PRINCE OF WALES [1760]
30.5x53.3cm. 1st state   [7] $525

A MAP OF SOUTH AMERICA CONTAINING TIERRA-FIRMA, GUYANA, NEW GRANADA,
AMAZONIA...AND PATAGONIA FROM MR. D'ANVILLE... [1779] 69.9x116.8cm.
on 2 sheets, backed   [3] $235

A MAP OF THE ISLAND OF ST. JOHN IN THE GULF OF ST. LAURENCE DIVIDED INTO
COUNTRIES & PARISHES AND THE LOTS AS GRANTED BY GOVERNMENT...PUBLISHED 12TH.
MAY 1794, BY LAURIE & WHITTLE, 53, FLEET STREET, LONDON [1794] 38.1x71.1cm.
in 1776 this map by Holland was revised by Jefferys, adding proprietors'
names & removing the cartouch, later issued unchanged by Laurie & Whittle
[7] $575

A MAP OF THE MOST INHABITED PART OF NEW ENGLAND CONTAINING THE PROVINCES OF
MASSACHUSETTS BAY AND NEW HAMPSHIRE WITH COLONIES CONECTICUT & RHODE
ISLAND... [1774] 102.9x48.3cm. right 2 sheets only, backed   [3] $185

A NEW MAP OF NOVA SCOTIA, AND CAPE BRETON ISLAND, WITH THE ADJACENT PARTS OF
NEW ENGLAND AND CANADA...PUBLISHED ACCORDING TO ACT OF PARLIAMENT BY THOS.
JEFFERYS...PRINTED & SOLD BY R. SAYER & J. BENNETT, NO. 53 IN FLEET STREET,
15 JUNE 1775 [1775] 47.6x61.6cm.
tear in margin repaired, a few surface abrasions   [7] $650

A PLAN OF PORT ROYAL IN SOUTH CAROLINA. SURVEY'D BY CAPN. JOHN GASCOIGNE
[1773] 71.5x58.2cm.   [39] $650

AN EXACT CHART OF THE RIVER ST. LAURENCE, FROM FORT FRONTENAC TO QUEBEC [1775]
59x95cm.   [5] $340

AN EXACT CHART OF THE RIVER ST. LAURENCE, FROM FRONTENAC TO THE ISLAND OF
ANTICOSTI...THIS CHART IS MOST HUMBLY INSCRIBED BY...THOS. JEFFERYS. LONDON,
PRINTED FOR ROBT. SAYER...AS THE ACT DIRECTS 25 MAY 1775 [1775] 59.7x94cm.
4th state of Jefferys' chart   [7] $650

AN INDEX MAP TO THE FOLLOWING SIXTEEN SHEETS, BEING A COMPLEAT CHART OF THE
WEST INDIES [1775] 37.8x62.9cm.   [22] $250

CHART CONTAINING PART OF THE ICY SEA WITH THE ADJACENT COAST OF ASIA & AMERICA
[1775] 45.7x53.3cm. fold repaired   [3] $100

CHART OF SOUTH AMERICA, COMPREHENDING THE WEST INDIES... [1753] 53.5x60.5cm.
original issue   [39] $140

GRENADA DIVIDED INTO ITS PARISHES [1794] 46.5x61.5cm.   [4] $183

MARTINICO, ONE OF THE CARIBEE ISLANDS...ACCORDING TO THE OBSERVATIONS OF MR.
HOUEL... [1768] 34.5x36.7cm.   [39] $85

NORTH AMERICA FROM THE FRENCH OF MR D'ANVILLE IMPROVED WITH THE BACK
SETTLEMENTS OF VIRGINIA AND COURSE OF OHIO ILLUSTRATED WITH GEOGRAPHICAL AND
HISTORICAL REMARKS. LONDON PRINTED FOR ROBT. SAWYER IN FLEET STREET AND THOS.
JEFFERYS... [C1768] 47.6x55.2cm. centerfold tear repaired, 2nd state with
updated information on Treaty of Paris, Quebec is now named, and the
reference to "French Encroachments" is still present   [7] $525

PLAN OF AMELIA ISLAND IN EAST FLORIDA.../VIEW OF ENTRANCE INTO ST. MARY'S
RIVER [1770] 50.8x61cm.   [3] $385

PLAN OF PORT ROYAL LAGUNA, COMMONLY CALLED THE LOGWOOD CREEKS [C1768]
20.1x27.4cm.   [39] $55

PLAN OF THE CITY OF SAN DOMINGO [1762] 19.1x26.7cm. 1st ed.   [3] $85

PLAN OF THE TOWN AND HARBOUR OF SAN JUAN DE PUERTO RICO [1762] 21x29.8cm.
1st ed.   [3] $100

JEFFERYS (continued)

PLAN OF THE TOWN OF BASSETERRE THE CAPITAL OF GUADELOUPE FROM AN AUTHENTIC
   SURVEY [1760] 32.4x23.5cm. [3] $90
PLAN OF THE TOWN, ROAD AND HARBOUR OF CHAGRE [1762] 26.7x20.3cm.
   1st ed. [3] $80
PLAN OF ZISAPATA BAY [1762] 22.2x29.2cm. 1st ed. [3] $45
RUATAN OR RATTAN, SURVEYED BY LIEUT. HENRY BARNSLEY WITH IMPROVEMENTS [1775]
   45.7x61cm. [3] $135
THE ISLAND OF SABLE LIES IN LAT... [1770] 28.6x36.8cm. [3] $140
THE VIRGIN ISLANDS FROM ENGLISH AND DANISH SURVEYS [1775] 45.7x61cm. [22] $350

JOHNSON

(GEORGIA AND ALABAMA) [1863-64] 38.7x55.6cm. [8] $20
AUSTRALIA AND THE EAST INDIES [1867] 58x43cm. light browning [31] $38
CALIFORNIA ALSO UTAH, NEVADA, COLORADO, NEW MEXICO & ARIZONA [1864]
   43.2x59.7cm. [3] $90
JOHNSON'S MEXICO [1867] 29.2x36.8cm. [19] $50
JOHNSON'S MEXICO [1870] 27.9x39.4cm. [19] $35
JOHNSON'S NEBRASKA DAKOTA, MONTANA AND KANSAS [1865] 31.8x39.4cm. [11] $45
JOHNSON'S NEBRASKA, DAKOTA, COLORADO & KANSAS [1863] 31.8x39.4cm. [9] $45
JOHNSON'S NEBRASKA, DAKOTA, COLORADO, IDAHO & KANSAS [1864] 31.8x39.4cm.
    [9] $45
JOHNSON'S NEBRASKA, DAKOTA, IDAHO AND MONTANA [1868] 43.2x58.4cm. [10] $65
JOHNSON'S NEW MAP OF TEXAS [1862] 39.4x59.7cm. [19] $150
JOHNSON'S NEW MAP OF THE STATE OF TEXAS [1864] 41.9x62.2cm.
   fold reinforced [19] $135
JOHNSON'S NEW MAP OF THE STATE OF TEXAS [1863] 41.9x62.2cm.
   lower fold reinforced, 4 cm. tear in blank region repaired [23] $160
JOHNSON'S NEW MAP OF THE STATE OF TEXAS [C1863-64] 41.9x62.2cm.
   stains in margins [20] $130
JOHNSON'S NEW MILITARY MAP OF THE U.S. SHOWING THE FORTS, MILITARY POSTS...
   [1861-62] 41.3x56.5cm. narrow margins [20] $95
JOHNSON'S ONTARIO, OF THE DOMINION OF CANADA [1867] 42.5x58.5cm. [21] $28
JOHNSON'S TEXAS [C1880] 43.2x59.7cm. lower fold reinforced [22] $150
JOHNSON'S TEXAS [1866-83] 43.2x58.4cm. [20] $95
JOHNSON'S TEXAS [C1880] 43.2x59.7cm. minor reinforcement in lower fold, this
   map is dated 1866, but counties created in 1876 appear, the Texas & Pacific
   Railroad spans the state [23] $130
JOHNSON'S TEXAS [C1881] 43.2x59.7cm. on this state the Texas and New Orleans
   Railroad links San Antonio with El Paso [23] $130
JOHNSON'S TEXAS [1866] 43.2x58.4cm. [23] $110
JOHNSON'S TEXAS [1866-67] 39.4x55.2cm. [19] $120
JOHNSON'S TEXAS [1866] 42.5x58.4cm. margins dark [20] $120
JOHNSON'S UNITED STATES [1864] 42.5x57.8cm. [3] $65

JOHNSON & BROWNING

CALIFORNIA TERRITORIES OF NEW MEXICO & UTAH [1860] 43.2x62.2cm. [3] $95
JAPAN NIPPON, KIUSIU, SIKOK... [1862] 33x38.7cm. [3] $50

JOHNSON & WARD

(ARKANSAS, MISSISSIPPI AND LOUISIANA) [1864] 36.2x43.8cm. [8] $20
(CALIFORNIA WITH UTAH, NEVADA, COLORADO, NEW MEXICO & ARIZONA) [1864]
   42.5x59.1cm. minor split repaired [8] $45
(DELAWARE & MARYLAND) [1864] 32.4x40cm. [8] $20
(FLORIDA) [1863-64] 30.5x38.4cm. minor foxing [8] $25
(ILLINOIS) [1864] 58.4x43.2cm. [8] $25
(IOWA AND NEBRASKA) [1864] 43.2x58.7cm. [8] $20
(KENTUCKY & TENNESSEE) [1864] 43.2x61cm. [8] $30
(MINNESOTA & DAKOTA) [1864] 31.8x39.7cm. [8] $25
(MISSOURI & KANSAS) [1864] 43.2x58.4cm. [8] $30
(NEBRASKA, DAKOTA, COLORADO, IDAHO & KANSAS) [1863] 31.8x39.4cm. [27] $45
(NEBRASKA, DAKOTA, COLORADO, IDAHO & KANSAS) [1864] 31.8x38.1cm. [8] $40
(NEBRASKA, DAKOTA, COLORADO, MONTANA & KANSAS) [1865] 31.8x39.4cm. [27] $60
(NORTH AND SOUTH CAROLINA) [1862-64] 43.2x59.1cm.
   vignettes and inset of Charleston [8] $20

JOHNSON & WARD (continued)
```
(WASHINGTON, OREGON & IDAHO) [1864] 31.8x39.4cm.                          [8]    $20
GEORGETOWN AND THE CITY OF WASHINGTON [1864] 31.8x39.4cm.                 [8]    $25
JOHNSON'S CALIFORNIA, TERRITORIES OF NEW MEXICO AND UTAH [1863] 43.2x61cm.
                                                                        [23]   $150
JOHNSON'S MEXICO [1866] 29.2x36.8cm.                                    [19]    $50
JOHNSON'S MEXICO [1862] 29.2x36.8cm.                                    [19]    $60
JOHNSON'S NEW MAP OF THE STATE OF TEXAS [1860] 41.9x62.2cm.
  lower fold reinforced, tear in blank area repaired                    [22]   $150
JOHNSON'S NEW MAP OF THE STATE OF TEXAS [1865] 41.9x62.2cm.             [23]   $145
JOHNSON'S NEW MAP OF THE STATE OF TEXAS [1864] 41.9x36.8cm.
  minor spotting                                                        [8]    $65
JOHNSON'S NEW MEXICO [1862-64] 29.2x36.8cm.                             [19]    $50
JOHNSON'S NEW MILITARY MAP OF THE U.S. SHOWING THE FORTS, MILITARY POSTS &C.
  [1861-62] 41.3x56.5cm.                                                [19]   $100
JOHNSON'S NEW MILITARY MAP OF THE U.S... [1861-64] 40.6x57.8cm.         [19]    $90
JOHNSON'S NORTH AMERICA [1863] 55.9x43.2cm.                             [23]    $70
JOHNSON'S WASHINGTON AND OREGON [1860] 31.1x39.4cm.                     [3]     $50
JOHNSON'S WASHINGTON AND OREGON [1863] 31.8x40cm.                       [23]    $75
NEBRASKA, DAKOTA, COLORADO, & KANSAS [1863] 31.8x39.4cm.                [23]    $65
```
JOHNSTON
```
AUSTRALIA [C1868] 32.5x43cm.                                            [4]     $61
BASIN OF THE NORTH ATLANTIC OCEAN [1881] 44x57cm.                       [39]    $45
CANADA BY A.K. JOHNSTON F.R.G.S. [1850] 50x60.5cm.                      [21]    $69
CHART OF THE WORLD ON MERCATORS PROJECTION SHOWING THE DIRECTION OF THE OCEAN
  CURRENTS, WITH THE ROUTES AND DISTANCES BETWEEN PRINCIPAL PORTS [1881]
  44x57.1cm.                                                           [39]    $45
CHINA [1844] 49.5x61cm.                                                 [10]    $45
CHINA [1846] 50.2x61cm. backed                                         [3]     $60
DOMINION OF CANADA (EAST CENTRAL SHEET) BY KEITH JOHNSTON F.R.S.E. [1884]
  C32.5x42.5cm.                                                        [21]    $20
DOMINION OF CANADA (EASTERN SHEET) NEW BRUNSWICK, NOVA SCOTIA, PRINCE EDWARD
  ID. CAPE BRETON ID. AND NEWFOUNDLAND BY KEITH JOHNSTON F.R.S.E. [1884]
  C32.5x42.5cm.                                                        [21]    $16
DOMINION OF CANADA (EASTERN SHEET) SHOWING NEW BRUNSWICK, NOVA SCOTIA, PRINCE
  EDWARD ID. CAPE BRETON ID. AND NEWFOUNDLAND BY KEITH JOHNSTON F.R.S.E.
  [C1870]  C42.5x55.5cm.                                               [21]    $36
DOMINION OF CANADA (WEST CENTRAL SHEET) BY T.B. JOHNSTON [1884]  C32.5x42.5cm.
                                                                        [21]    $28
DOMINION OF CANADA (WESTERN SHEET) [1861] 43.8x57.2cm.
  from "Royal Atlas"                                                    [30]    $81
DOMINION OF CANADA (WESTERN SHEET) [1881] 44x57.2cm.                    [39]    $30
DOMINION OF CANADA (WESTERN SHEET) BY KEITH JOHNSTON. F.R.S.E. [C1870]
  C42.5x55.5cm.                                                        [21]    $36
DOMINION OF CANADA SHOWING NEW BRUNSWICK & NOVA SCOTIA, WITH PRINCE EDWARD ID.
  CAPE BRETON ID. AND NEWFOUNDLAND [1881] 44.1x57cm.                    [39]    $30
NEW ZEALAND [C1865] 42.5x32.4cm.                                       [24]    $58
NORTH AMERICA [C1864] 57.5x44cm.                                        [21]    $24
NORTH POLAR CHART [1881] 42.6x32.3cm.                                   [39]    $45
PROVINCE OF CANADA (EASTERN SHEET) NEW BRUNSWICK, NOVA SCOTIA, PRINCE EDWARD
  ID. CAPE BRETON ID. AND NEWFOUNDLAND [C1864]  C44x57.5cm.            [21]    $20
PROVINCE OF CANADA (EASTERN SHEET) NEW BRUNSWICK, NOVA SCOTIA, PRINCE EDWARD
  ID. CAPE BRETON ID. AND NEWFOUNDLAND BY KEITH JOHNSTON F.R.S.E. [C1870]
  C42.5x55.5cm.                                                        [21]    $36
PROVINCE OF CANADA (EASTERN SHEET), NEW BRUNSWICK, NOVA SCOTIA, PRINCE EDWARD
  ID., CAPE BRETON ID, AND NEWFOUNDLAND [1863] 44.5x57.2cm.            [27]    $75
PROVINCE OF CANADA (WESTERN SHEET) [C1864]  C44x57.5cm.                [21]    $20
PROVINCE OF CANADA (WESTERN SHEET) [1863] 44.5x57.2cm. minor foxing    [27]    $75
PROVINCE OF CANADA (WESTERN SHEET) BY KEITH JOHNSTON. F.R.S.E. [1861]
  C42.5x55.5cm.                                                        [21]    $36
THE WORLD IN HEMISPHERES [1881] 29.5x57cm.                             [39]    $35
```

JOHNSTON (continued)
THE WORLD IN HEMISPHERES WITH COMPARATIVE VIEWS OF THE HEIGHTS OF THE PRINCIPAL
    MOUNTAINS AND LENGTHS OF THE PRINCIPAL RIVERS ON THE GLOBE BY A.K. JOHNSTON
    F.R.G.S. [1843] 52x60cm. narrow bottom margin   [21] $113
THE WORLD... [1844] 50.8x61cm.   [10] $125
UNITED STATES AND TEXAS [C1844] 49.5x61cm.   [9] $225
UNITED STATES AND TEXAS [1844] 49.5x61cm.
    from W. & A.K. Johnston, "National Atlas"   [27] $350
UNITED STATES AND TEXAS [C1843-44] 49.5x62cm.   [5] $280
UNITED STATES OF NORTH AMERICA (EASTERN STATES) [1881] 57.2x44.2cm.   [39] $30
UNITED STATES OF NORTH AMERICA (EASTERN STATES) [C1864] 57.5x44cm.   [21] $48
VAN DIEMAN'S LAND OR TASMANIA [C1844] 50x60cm.   [13] $122
WEST INDIA ISLANDS AND CENTRAL AMERICA [1888] 44.2x57.2cm.   [39] $30
KANE
CHART EXHIBITION THE DISCOVERIES OF THE SECOND AMERICAN GRINNELL EXPEDITION IN
    SEARCH OF SIR JOHN FRANKLIN BY E.K. KANE [1853-56] 28.5x45.5cm.
    minor wear at folds, backed with archival tissue   [21] $77
KELLY
BRITISH COLONIES IN NORTH AMERICA [C1832] 19x24cm.   [21] $30
BRITISH COLONIES OF NORTH AMERICA [1815] 19.7x24.8cm.   [3] $35
CANADA [C1840] 20x25cm.   [21] $20
NEW SOUTH WALES [1830-41] 19.5x24.5cm.   [31] $27
KEPOHONI
AMERIKA HUIPUIA [1839] 25.4x41.3cm. light spotting, printed at a missionary
    school in Hawaii run by Rev. Lorrin Andrews, Kepohoni was the engraver,
    engraved for the Lahainulana School Atlas of 1840   [23] $3000
KEYSER
L'ILE DE TERRE NEUVE ET LE GOLFE DE SAINT LAURENT [1715] 20.3x30.5cm.
    from Bernard, "Recueil de Voyages au Nord"   [30] $142
KEYSTONE PUBLISHING CO.
BIRD'S-EYE VIEW OF ANDERSONVILLE PRISON FROM THE SOUTH-EAST [1890]
    35.6x48.3cm. chromolithograph, minor creases   [27] $150
KILBOURN
A MAP OF OHIO, BY JOHN KILBOURN, COLUMBUS, JANUARY 1821 [1821] 31.1x30.5cm.
    folding, margins trimmed close, from "The Ohio Gazetteer," 1821 [23] $80
KINGMAN BROS.
MAP OF CLEAR CREEK TOWNSHIP [1879] 39.4x31.9cm.
    2 views of farms on verso   [39] $20
MAP OF DALLAS TOWNSHIP-MAP OF HUNTINGTON TOWNSHIP [1879] 39.7x65.7cm.
                                                                     [39] $40
MAP OF HUNTINGTON COUNTY [1879] 41x32.1cm.
    court house & infirmary on verso   [39] $20
MAP OF JACKSON TOWNSHIP [1879] 39.4x31.9cm. 3 views of farms on verso
                                                                     [39] $20
MAP OF THE CITY OF HUNTINGTON [1879] 65.4x84.7cm.   [39] $95
NEW RAIL ROAD MAP OF THE UNITED STATES [1879] 39.8x66.8cm.   [39] $40
KINGSBURY
WESTERN TERRITORY [1836] 49.5x88.9cm. folding map, not formally titled,
    "Western Territory" is written across body of map, from Lieut. J.P.
    Kingsbury, "Journal of the Expedition of Dragoons, Under the Command of
    Colonel Henry P. Dodge...1835"   [27] $375
KIP
BEDFORD... [1607-37] 27.3x33.7cm.   [24] $99
BRECKNOC COMITATUS PARS OLIM SILURUM [1607-37] 26.7x31.8cm.   [24] $73
CUMBRIA SIVE CUMBERLANDIA... [1607-10] 28.6x31.8cm.   [24] $99
DENBIGH COMITATUS PARS OLIM ORDOVICUM [1610-37] 26.7x31.8cm.   [24] $76
DENBIGH COMITATUS PARS OLIM ORDOVICUM [1607] 26.7x31.8cm. 1st issue   [24] $99
LINCOLNIAE COMITATUS UBI OLIM INSEDERUNT CORITANI... [1607-10] 29.8x34.9cm.
    narrow margins, minor reinforcements   [24] $107
MERIONETH COMITATUS OLIM PARS ORDIWICUM [1607] 26.7x32.4cm.   [24] $64
MONTGOMERY COMITATUS QUI OLIM PARS ORDOVICUM [1607-37] 26.7x31.8cm.   [24] $64

KIP (continued)
NORFOLCIAE COMITATUS QUEM... [1607-37] 26.7x38.7cm.
  right margin restored   [24] $130
NOTINGAMIAE COMITATUS OLIM PART CORITANIORUM [1607-10] 26x31.1cm.   [24] $104
PENBROK COMITATUS OLIM PARS DEMETARUM [1607-37] 27.9x34.3cm.
  small loss of engraved surface   [24] $91
RADNOR COMITATUS QUEM SILVRES OLIM INCOLUERUNT [1607-37] 27.3x32.4cm.
                                                                             [24] $55
RUTLANDIAE... [1607-10] 28.6x21.6cm.   [24] $73
STAFFORDIAE COMITATUS PARS... [1607-37] 26.7x37.5cm.   [24] $104
SUSSEXIA SIVE SOUTHSEX, OLIM PARS REGNORUM [1607-37] 22.2x40.3cm.
  narrow left margin   [14] $214
SUSSEXIA... [1607-37] 22.2x38.7cm. right & left margins restored   [24] $176
WILTONIAE... [1607-37] 27.9x35.6cm.   [24] $107
KIRCHER
MAPPA FLUXUS ET REFLUXUS... [1678] 34.3x41.1cm.   [39] $425
SCHEMA CORPORIS SOLARIS PROUT AB AUTHORE ET P. SCHEINERO. ROMAE ANNO 1635
  OBSERVATUM SUIT [1665] 37x42cm. shows the sun   [37] $325
SYSTEMA IDEAL QUO EXPRIMITUR, AQUARUM PER CANALES HYDRAGOGOS SUBTERRANEOS...
  [1665] 36.5x41.5cm. lower right repaired, shows underground water flows
                                                                             [37] $500
SYSTEMA IDEALE PYROPHYLACIORUM SUBTERRANEORUM QUORUM MONTES VULCANI... [1665]
  37x42cm. shows the earth in cross-section, with lava tubes & volcanoes
                                                                             [37] $500
TABULA FLUXUS REFLUXUX, RATIONES IN MARI ANGLICO... [1678] 19.5x19.7cm.
                                                                             [39] $75
TABULA GEOGRAPHICO-HYDROGRAPHICA MOTUS OCEANI, CURRENTES, ABYSSOS, MONTES
  IGNIUOMOS... [1678] 33.7x55.2cm.   [39] $385
TABULA QUA HYDROPHYLACIUM... [1678] 20.4x34.2cm.
  a world map showing the ocean currents   [39] $140
KITCHIN
(MEXICO & NEW MEXICO, PART OF) [1755] 62.2x27.9cm.
  damaged, from "Postlethwayt's Dictionary of Commerce"   [30] $4
A GENERAL MAP OF NORTH AMERICA FROM THE BEST AUTHORITIES [C1788] 19x22.5cm.
  light spotting   [21] $89
A MAP OF NEW ENGLAND AND NOVA SCOTIA; WITH PART...CANADA & NEW
  BRITAIN...ISLANDS OF NEW FOUNDLAND, CAPE BRETON &C... [1758] 27.3x33.7cm.
                                                                             [3] $125
A NEW AND ACCURATE MAP OF EAST AND WEST FLORIDA DRAWN FROM THE BEST
  AUTHORITIES [C1763] 17.8x22.9cm.   [3] $120
A NEW AND ACCURATE MAP OF THE BRITISH DOMINIONS IN AMERICA, ACCORDING TO THE
  TREATY OF 1763, DIVIDED INTO THE SEVERAL PROVINCES [C1766] 52.7x62.9cm.
                                                                             [3] $435
A NEW AND CORRECT PLAN OF THE CITIES OF LONDON, WESTMINSTER, AND SOUTHWARK...
  [1773] 44x68cm.   [4] $337
A NEW CHART OF THE RIVER ST. LAWRENCE [1759] 18.4x25.4cm.   [30] $81
A NEW IMPROVED MAP OF CORNWALL FROM THE BEST SURVEYS... [C1785] 51.4x68.6cm.
                                                                             [13] $222
A NEW IMPROVED MAP OF OXFORDSHIRE... [1749-55] 71.1x52.1cm.   [24] $114
A NEW MAP OF DEVON SHIRE... [1764] 19.1x24.8cm.   [24] $61
A NEW MAP OF HAMP SHIRE DRAWN FROM THE BEST AUTHORITIES [1764] 19.1x25.4cm.
                                                                             [24] $58
A NEW MAP OF HARTFORDSHIRE... [1764] 19.7x24.8cm.   [24] $61
A NEW MAP OF NORFOLK... [1764] 19.7x25.4cm.   [24] $45
A NEW MAP OF NORTHHAMPTON SHIRE... [1764] 25.4x19.1cm.   [24] $42
A NEW MAP OF NOTTINGHAMSHIRE... [1764] 25.4x19.7cm.   [24] $30
A NEW MAP OF THE BRITISH DOMINIONS IN NORTH AMERICA...SETTLED BY PROCLAMATION,
  OCTOBER 7, 1763 [1763] 23.5x30.5cm. margins narrow   [32] $85
A NEW MAP OF THE BRITISH EMPIRE IN NORTH AMERICA DRAWN FROM THE LATEST
  AUTHORITIES BY THOS. KITCHIN GEOGR. HYDROGRAPHER TO HIS MAJESTY [1782]
  33x37cm. minor repairs, from Millar's "New Complete & Universal System of
  Geography"   [21] $117

A NEW MAP OF THE CHEROKEE NATION WITH THE NAMES OF THE TOWNS &
  RIVERS...ENGRAVED FROM AN INDIAN DRAUGHT [1760] 17.8x22.9cm.   [3] $225
A NEW MAP OF THE PROVINCE OF QUEBEC [1764] 17.1x21cm.   [30] $89
A NEW MAP OF THE PROVINCE OF QUEBEC IN NORTH AMERICA DRAWN FROM THE BEST
  AUTHORITIES [1764] 17.1x21.6cm.   [3] $110
A NEW MAP OF THE UNITED STATES OF NTH. AMERICA. DRAWN FROM THE LATEST
  AUTHORITIES... [1795] 34.3x38.1cm. minor repairs   [3] $135
A PLAN OF FORT EDWARD AND ITS ENVIRONS ON HUDSON'S RIVER [1772] 28.2x25.7cm.
     [39] $125
AN ACCURATE MAP OF BRECKNOCK SHIRE. DRAWN FROM AN ACTUAL SURVEY WITH VARIOUS
  IMPROVEMENTS... [1754] 34.3x50.8cm. upper margin restored, 1st issue
     [24] $61
AN ACCURATE MAP OF CARMARTHEN SHIRE. DRAWN FROM AN ACTUAL SURVEY, WITH VARIOUS
  IMPROVEMENTS... [1754] 34.3x52.1cm.
  separated from another map below, lower margin replaced   [24] $76
BRITISH DOMINIONS IN AMERICA. DRAWN FROM THE LATEST AND BEST AUTHORITIES BY
  THOS KITCHIN, HYDROGRAPHER TO HIS MAJESTY [C1771] 34.5x38cm.
  folds, small tear repaired, offsetting, laid down for mounting   [21] $93
LA VERA CRUZ OR ST. JUAN DE ULUA [1768] 17.8x11.4cm.   [3] $65
LAKE ONTARIO [1772] 22.2x25.4cm. from Mant's History   [30] $182
LOUISIANA, AS FORMERLY CLAIMED BY FRANCE, NOW CONTAINING PART OF BRITISH
  AMERICA TO THE EAST & SPANISH AMERICA TO THE WEST OF THE MISSISSIPPI [C1778]
  17.8x22.9cm.   [16] $85
LOUISIANA...& SPANISH AMERICA [1765] C17.8x22.9cm.   [20] $175
MAP OF SOUTH AMERICA [1777] 44.5x32.5cm.   [39] $50
MAP OF THE GULF OF MEXICO, THE ISLANDS AND COUNTRIES ADJACENT [1777]
  31.5x48.9cm.   [39] $55
MEXICO OR NEW SPAIN IN WHICH THE MOTIONS OF CORTES MAY BE TRACED [1777]
  29.2x38.1cm.   [3] $145
MEXICO OR NEW SPAIN... [1777] C38.1x27.9cm.   [20] $200
NEW MAP OF THE ISLE OF MAN... [1764] 25.4x19.1cm.   [24] $58
NORTH AMERICA DRAWN FROM THE LATEST & BEST AUTHORITIES BY THOS. KITCHIN
  [C1780] 34x37cm. small tear repaired, laid down for mounting   [21] $101
NORTH AMERICA DRAWN FROM THE LATEST AND BEST AUTHORITIES [1787] 33.7x39.4cm.
  right margin narrow, tear repaired   [22] $125
NORTH AMERICA... [1759] 14.6x19.4cm.   [20] $85
PLAN OF FORT PITT OR PITTSBOURG [1772] 24x25.3cm.   [39] $35
PLAN OF THE LAND BETWEEN LAKE CHAMPLAIN AND FORT EDWARD ON THE HUDSON [1772]
  26.5x16.5cm.   [39] $65
SOUTH AMERICA [1755] 37.5x74.3cm. Plate III, the southern part of South
  America, from "Postlethwayt's Dictionary of Commerce," London 1766, some
  staining & damage   [30] $36
THE BRITISH ISLANDS AND PRIVILEGES IN THE WEST INDIES [1744] 17.8x29.8cm.
     [30] $101

KRAYENHOFF

CARTE GENERALE DE LA HOLLANDE AVEC LES ROUTES DE POSTES. 1810 [1810] 76x92cm.
  in 4 sections backed with cloth   [18] $140
CHORO-TOPOGRAPHISCHE KAART DER NOORDELYKE PROVINCIEN VAN HET KONIGRYK DER
  NEDERLANDEN, UITGEVOERD AAN HET TOPOGRAPHISCHEN BUREAU VAN DEZEN STAAT...
  [C1820] 87x96cm. on 9 sheets, dimensions are for each sheet, with an index
  sheet 44 x 77 cm.   [18] $702

KREFFELDT

EGENTLICKE BESCHRYVINGE DES ISELSTROOMS, SAMPT ITTELICKE OMLIGGENDE STEEDEN
  UNDE VLECKEN, DOOR MART. KAROL KREFFELDT [C1580] 13.5x35.5cm.
  trimmed to neat line   [18] $1053

KRUIKIUS

T'HOOGE HEEMRADSCHAP VAN DELFLAND MET ALLE DE STEDEN, DORPEN, AMBACHTEN...
  [1712] 50x59cm. on 25 sheets with 2 title sheets, dimensions are for each
  sheet, margins untrimmed   [18] $1756

LA FEUILLE
L'AMERIQUE MERIDIONALE [1710] 14x19.1cm. from "Atlas Portatif" [30] $69
LE ROYAUME D'ESPAGNE AVEC SES CONFINS [1710] 14.6x21.6cm.
  16 coats of arms at sides, some separation at folds [30] $40

LA HONTAN
A GENERAL MAP OF NEW FRANCE COM. CALL'D CANADA [1703] 21.6x33.3cm. 4 folds,
  from La Hontan, "New Voyages to North America...," London 1703 [8] $290
ATAQUE DE QUEBEC [1703] 11.4x16.5cm. [3] $90
CARTE GENERALE DE CANADA A PETIT POINT [1706] 8.9x14cm. [30] $121
NEW FOUND LAND. H. MOLL, FECIT. [1703] 16.2x10.8cm.
  from La Hontan, "New Voyages to North America...," London 1703 [8] $75
THE ATTACK OF QUEBEC [1703] 10.5x16.5cm.
  from La Hontan, "New Voyages to North America...," London 1703 [8] $45
THE GREAT BAY OF PLACENTIA [1703] 16.2x10.2cm.
  from La Hontan, "New Voyages to North America...," London 1703 [8] $45

LA PEROUSE
See also ROBINSON
CARTE D'UNE PARTIE DU GRAND OCEAN A L'E ET S.E. DE NOUVELLE GUINEE [1798]
  24x37cm. [31] $42
CARTE DES COTES DE L'AMERIQUE ET DE L'ASIE DEPUIS LA CALIFORNIE JUSQU'A
  MACAO... [1797] 50.2x68.6cm. [3] $175
CHART OF THE DISCOVERIES TO THE NORTH OF JAPAN INCLUDING JESO, STATEN IS. &
  COMPANY'S LAND EXPLORED IN 1787 BY THE BOUSSOLE [1798] 38.1x48.3cm.
  [3] $80
PARTIE DE LA MER DU SUD COMPRISE ENTRE LES PHILLIPPINES ET LA CALIFORNIA
  [1797] 48.9x67.3cm. [3] $75

LABAT
CARTE DE L'ISLE DE SAINT CHRISTOPHLE SITUEE A 17 DEGREZ 30 MINUTES DE LAT.
  SEPTENTRIONALE [1724] 13.3x24.1cm. [3] $65

LADIES REPOSITORY
(LOUISVILLE, KENTUCKY, VIEW) [1854] 12.7x20.3cm. [10] $25
(NEW BEDFORD, MASSACHUSETTS, VIEW) [1854] 12.7x17.8cm. [10] $25
(NEW ORLEANS, VIEW) [1854] 11.4x18.4cm. [10] $25
(PITTSBURGH AND ALLEGHENY, VIEW) [1854] 10.8x18.4cm. [10] $25
(PORTLAND, MAINE, VIEW) [C1854] 11.4x20.3cm. [10] $25
(RICHMOND, VIRGINIA, VIEW) [1854] 10.8x19.1cm. [10] $25

LAFRERI SCHOOL
ANTVERPIAE CIVITATIS BELGICAE TOTO ORBE COGNITI ET CELEBRATI SIMULACRUM
  [C1560] 32x42.8cm. anonymous, based on Cock's 1557 plan of Antwerp [18] $1053
DISIGNO DELL'ISOLA... [C1560] 30.5x44.5cm. shows Djerba Island, with a battle
  in progress between Christian & Turkish navies [17] $2000
IL VERO DISEGNO DEL MIRABILE ASSEDIO DELLA FORTISSIMA CITA DE ANVERSA FATTO
  DAL...ALEXANDRO FARNESE...DEL 27 AGOSTO 1585. G.R. FORM. [1585] 37.5x50cm.
  [18] $1053

LANGENES
HISPANIOLA [C1601] 10.2x13.3cm. minor repairs [3] $95

LANGLOIS
1695. LE BOMBARDEMENT DE LA VILLE DE BRUXELLES CAPITALE DES PAYS-BAS PAR
  L'ARMEE DU ROI SOUS MR. LE MARECHAL DUC DE VILLEROY...15E AOUT 1695...
  [1695] 88x57cm.
  from the Grand Almanach Royal, many views & scenes shown [18] $702

LASOR A VAREA
CUSCO (BIRD'S EYE PLAN) [1713] 8.9x14cm. [3] $45
IAMAICA [1713] 11.4x14.6cm. in "Universus Terrarum" [3] $95
ISOLA DI CENGO CYTHERA [1700] 15.5x21cm. [31] $91
S. GIOVANNI [1713] 11.4x15.2cm. from "Universus Terrarum Orbis" [3] $100

LATTRE
CARTE DE L'OCEAN ATLANTIQUE [C1780] 49.5x63cm. [5] $300
LA GRENADE DIVISEE PAR QUARTIERS AVEC SES PORTS ET MOUILLAGES D'APRES CELL
  LEVEE PAR ORDRE DU GOUVERNEUR SCOTT... [1779] 43.8x59.1cm. [3] $295

LAURENT
CARTE DES ISLES KOURILES D'APRES LA CARTE RUSSE DRESSEE ET GRAVEE PAR LAURENT
[C1753] 24.1x26.7cm.   [3] $125
LAURIE & WHITTLE
See also JEFFERYS
A GENERAL MAP OF THE WORLD OR TERRAQUEOUS GLOBE [1794] 104.1x121.9cm. on 4
sheets joined to form 2, dimensions are overall, the Dunn world map with
numerous printed notes   [16] $750
A NEW AND CORRECT MAP OF THE BRITISH COLONIES IN NORTH AMERICA... [1794]
48.3x67.3cm.   [16] $320
A NEW AND GENERAL MAP OF THE MIDDLE DOMINIONS BELONGING TO THE UNITED STATES OF
AMERICA [1794] 48.3x66cm.   [22] $500
A NEW AND GENERAL MAP OF THE MIDDLE DOMINIONS BELONGING TO THE UNITED STATES OF
AMERICA, VIZ VIRGINIA, MARYLAND, THE DELAWARE COUNTIES, PENNSYLVANIA, NEW
JERSEY, ETC. WITH THE ADDITION OF NEW YORK AND THE GREATEST PART OF NEW
ENGLAND...1794 [1808] 48.3x66cm.   [8] $350
A NEW CHART OF THE EAST COAST OF ENGLAND FROM FLAMBOROUGH HEAD TO THE ENTRANCE
OF BOSTON DEEPS WITH THE COURSE OF THE RIVER HUMBER FROM HULL TO THE SEA...
[1794] 69.2x49.5cm.   [24] $99
A NEW MAP OF NORTH AMERICA WITH THE WEST INDIA ISLANDS DIVIDED ACCORDING TO
PRELIMINARY ARTICLES OF PEACE SIGNED AT VERSAILLES...1783, WHEREIN ARE
DISTINGUISHED THE UNITED STATES... [1794] 99.1x115.6cm.
on 2 sheets, dimensions are overall, backed   [3] $475
A NEW MAP OF NORTH AMERICA... [1794] 101.6x116.8cm.
on 4 sheets joined to form two, some offsetting   [32] $950
A NEW MAP OF SCOTLAND COMPILED FROM ACTUAL SURVEYS & REGULATED BY THE LATEST
ASTRONOMICAL OBSERVATIONS [1807] 62.9x48.3cm. some reinforcement   [24] $79
A NEW MAP OF THE WHOLE CONTINENT OF AMERICA DIVIDED INTO THE NORTH AND SOUTH
AND WEST INDIES...COMPILED FROM MR. D'ANVILLE'S MAPS OF THAT CONTINENT...FROM
THE ORIGINAL MATERIALS OF GOVERNOR POWNALL MP [1794] C52.1x118.1cm.
on 4 sheets joined to form 2, dimensions are for each half   [16] $680
A PLAN OF RISTAGOUCHE HARBOUR, IN CHALEUR BAY, SURVEYED IN 1760, BY THE KING'S
SHIP NORWICH. PUBLISHED 12TH MAY, 1794 BY LAURIE & WHITTLE, 53, FLEET STREET
LONDON [1794] 34.3x51.4cm. narrow margins, a later state of this map
                                                                      [7] $225
A VIEW OF THE PALACE OF CHANTILLI TAKEN FROM THE ORANGERY [1794] 24.1x41.3cm.
minor soiling   [24] $73
ANTIGUA, SURVEYED BY ROBERT BAKER, SURVEYOR GENERAL OF THE ISLAND: ENGRAVED AND
IMPROVED BY THOMAS JEFFERYS [1794] 46.4x61.7cm.   [39] $145
JAMAICA FROM THE LATEST SURVEYS; IMPROVED AND ENGRAVED BY THOMS JEFFERYS
[1810] 46x61.2cm.   [39] $95
PLAN OF THE ISLE OF TRINIDAD, FROM ACTUAL SURVEYS MADE IN THE YEAR 1797 [1800]
49x64.1cm. 1st ed.   [39] $155
ST. CHRISTOPHERS, OR ST. KITTS, SURVEYED BY ANTHONY RAVELL...ENGRAVED BY THOMAS
JEFFERYS [1794] 46.7x61.7cm.   [39] $135
LAW
LOUISIANA BY DE RIVIER MISSISIPPI [C1720] 19.1x15.2cm. John Law founded the
Compagnie de la Louisiane ou l'Occident in 1717, this map was part of a
publication to promote the Mississippi Scheme, the title is in Dutch & a coat
of arms bearing the legend "Het Wapen van de Compagnie" appears at the left
                                                                      [16] $360
LAWSON
A MAP OF THE ENGLISH PLANTATIONS IN AMERICA [1718] 17.8x18.4cm.
from Lawson, "History of North Carolina"   [3] $120
LE CLERC
DINANT VILLE CELEBRE DE L'EVECHE DE LIEGE... [C1675] 44x38cm.
from "Conquetes de Louis XIV"   [18] $175
DOESBURG. VILLE TRES FORTE DU COMTE DE ZUTPHEN... [1672] 44x38cm.
from "Conquetes de Louis XIV"   [18] $175
GAND, CAPITALE DU COMTE DE FLANDRES & LA PLUS GRANDE VILLE DES PAIS BAS...
(VIEW) [1685] 39x33.5cm. from "Conquetes de Louis XIV"   [18] $175

132

LE CLERC (continued)

GANDE (VIEW) [C1685] 43x33.5cm. from "Conquetes de Louis XIV" [18] $175
HUY. VILLE DU DIOCESE DE LIEGE SUR LA MEUSE... [C1675] 44x37cm.
   from "Conquetes de Louis XIV" [18] $175
LA BATAILLE DE SENEFFE... [1674] 44x37cm.
   from "Conquetes de Louis XIV" [18] $105
MASTRICH (VIEW) [1673] 44x33cm. from "Conquetes de Louis XIV" [18] $298
UTRECHT. CAPITALE DE LA PROVINCE D'UTRECHT, C'EST APRES AMSTERDAM LA PLUS BELLE
   VILLE DES HOLLANDAIS... (VIEW) [1672] 44x37cm.
   from "Conquetes de Louis XIV" [18] $263
YPRES. GRAND VILLE RICHE & MARCHANDE... (VIEW) [C1680] 42x36cm.
   from "Conquetes de Louis XIV" [18] $140

LE ROUGE

(PENNSYLVANIA) [1778] 66x130.8cm.
   3 sheets joined, dimensions are overall [17] $1500
A MAP OF THE MOST INHABITED PART OF NEW ENGLAND... [1777] 50x96cm.
   a French copy of the Jefferys map [4] $1226
AMERIQUE MERIDIONALE [1748] 20.3x27.3cm. [3] $60
AMERIQUE SEPTENTRIONALE AVEC LES ROUTES, DISTANCES EN MILES, VILLAGES ET
ETABLISSMENTS FRANCOIS ET ANGLOIS PAR LE DOCTEUR MITCHEL TRADUIT DE
L'ANGLOISE A PARIS PAR LE ROUGE INGR GEOGRAPHE DU ROY RUE DES GRAND AUGUSTINS
1756 [1777] 43.2x49.5cm. on 8 sheets, dimensions are for each, margins torn
& repaired, occasionally affecting engraved surface, a few spots in margins,
one sheet with repairs in margin & upper right corner, 2nd state, 1st issue
of this copy of the Mitchell map [7] $5200
AMERIQUE SUIVANT LE R.P. CHARLEVOIX JTE. MR. DE LA CONDAMINE, ET PLUSIEURS
AUTRES NOUVLE. OBSERVATIONS [1746] 48.9x63.5cm. [23] $1000
CARTE DU JAPAN ET DE LA COREE... [1746] 21.5x27.5cm. [31] $107
CARTE TOPOGRAPHIQUE DES ENVIRONS DE CHARLEROY JUSQU'A PHILIPPEVILLE. PAR LE
   ROUGE, INGR. GEOGRAPHE [1746] 63x48cm. [18] $70
ISLE DE ST. DOMINGUE [1748] 20.3x27.9cm. backed [3] $60
LA BARBADE UNE DES ANTILLES AUX ANGLOIS DIVISEE PAR PAROISSES/ISLE ST.
   CHRISTOPHLE [1746] 27.9x21cm. [3] $110
LA BERMUDE AUX ANGLOIS.../LA JAMAIQUE AUX ANGLOIS [1746] 20.3x27.3cm. [3] $110
LA HOLLANDE OU LES VII PROVINCES UNIES [1746] 49x58cm. [18] $122
LA JAMAIQUE.../LA BERMUDE [1746] 20x27cm. [39] $120
LA MARTINIQUE UNE DES ANTILLES FRANCOISES DE L'AMERIQUE DRESSEE SUR LES
   NOUVELLES OBSERVATIONS... [1753] 48.3x63.5cm. [3] $285
LA PENNSYLVANIE EN TROIS FEUILLES... [C1777] 66x132.1cm. on 3 sheets,
dimensions are overall, published in "Atlas Ameriquais Septentrionale,"
Paris, but this copy may have been sold separately [16] $1250
LE BRABANT [1746] 63x51cm. [18] $105
LES XVII PROVINCES DITES LES PAYS-BAS, PAR ET CHEZ LE SR. LE ROUGE [1742]
   50x57cm. [18] $105
MAPPE MONDE QUI COMPREND LES NOUVELLES DECOUVERTES FAITES JUSQUA CE JOUR
[1748] 21.9x29.5cm. from "Atlas Nouveau Portatif" [34] $300
PLAN DE BOSTON, AVEC LES SONDES ET LES DIRECTIONS POUR LA NAVIGATION. TRADUIT
   DE L'ANGLAIS [1778] 50.8x85.1cm. [22] $950
TOPOGRAPHIE DE LA ZELANDE EN 9 FEUILLES. PARIS, RUE DES GRANDS AUGUSTINS, PRES
   LE PANIER FLEURY [1748] 46x56cm. on 9 sheets, dimensions are for each [18] $1053
VIRGINIA, MARYLAND EN DEUX FEUILLES PAR FRY ET JEFFERSON [1777] 67.3x101.6cm. [15] $1800
VIRGINIE, MARYLAND EN 2 FEUILLES PAR FRY ET JEFFERSON [1777] 67x98.7cm. [35] $1250
VIRGINIE, MARYLAND... [1777] 67.9x98.4cm.
   French edition of the Fry & Jefferson map [17] $1800

LEIGH

ANGLESEY [1820-25] C7.6x12.1cm. from Samuel Leigh, "New Pocket Road-Book of
   England, Wales, and part of Scotland" [13] $12

LEIGH (continued)
CAMBRIDGESHIRE [1820-25] C7.6x12.1cm.   [13] $13
CUMBERLAND [1820-25] C7.6x12.1cm.   [13] $13
DURHAM [1820-25] C7.6x12.1cm.   [13] $12
GLAMORGANSHIRE [1820-25] C7.6x12.1cm.   [13] $12
ISLE OF WIGHT [1820-25] C7.6x12.1cm.   [13] $15
LINCOLNSHIRE [1820-25] C7.6x12.1cm.   [13] $13
NORTHUMBERLAND [1820-25] C7.6x12.1cm.   [13] $13
OXFORDSHIRE [1820-25] C7.6x12.1cm.   [13] $13
SUSSEX [1820-25] C7.6x12.1cm.   [13] $15
LEVANTO
CARTA MARITIMA DEL LEVANTE [1664] 40.6x50.8cm. minor centerfold repair,
    repaired hole upper right, from Levanto's "Specchio del Mare"   [15] $850
LEVASSEUR
AMERIQUE MERIDIONALE [1847-61] 43.2x28.6cm.
    edition of 1861 with imprint of Lemercier added   [25] $58
AMERIQUE SEPTENTRIONALE [1847] 28x43cm.
    from "Atlas Universel Illustre"   [21] $93
AMERIQUE SEPTENTRIONALE [C1840] 27.9x43.2cm.   [20] $120
AMERIQUE SEPTENTRIONALE [1847-61] 43.2x28.3cm.
    edition of 1861 with the imprint of Lemercier added   [25] $76
PLANISPHERE [1845] 26.7x47cm. backed   [3] $60
LEWIS
See also CAREY
THE BRITISH POSSESSIONS IN NORTH AMERICA [1809] 38.7x43.8cm.
    deacidified, state 3   [30] $182
THE STATE OF MARYLAND, FROM THE BEST AUTHORITIES [1795] 28.5x41.9cm.
    1st state   [39] $160
THE STATE OF NORTH CAROLINA FROM THE BEST AUTHORITIES... [1795] 27.8x46.8cm.
    1st state   [39] $140
THE STATE OF SOUTH CAROLINA: FROM THE BEST AUTHORITIES... [1795] 38.9x44.3cm.
    1st state   [39] $175
THE STATE OF VIRGINIA FROM THE BEST AUTHORITIES [1794-1801] 34.9x49.8cm.
    lightly browned, repaired tear, backed with cloth   [22] $140
LEWIS & ARROWSMITH
DELAWARE [1812] 25.4x20.3cm.
    from Arrowsmith & Lewis, "New and Elegant General Atlas"   [27] $65
MISSISSIPPI TERRITORY [1812] C25.4x20.3cm.   [27] $150
SPANISH DOMINIONS IN NORTH AMERICA [1804] 20.3x24.8cm.
    lower margin ragged & narrow   [19] $100
VIRGINIA. S. LEWIS DEL. [1812] 20x25.1cm.   [8] $35
LIEFRINCK
LUTZENBOURG. LUTZENBURGUM...URBS... [1582] 23.3x31.5cm.
    no text on verso   [18] $263
LINSCHOTEN
(AFRICA, EAST COAST & MADAGASCAR) [1595-1620] C40x50cm.   [31] $919
(WEST AFRICA, ARABIA, INDIA) [1596] 38.7x52.7cm. some fold wear   [26] $800
IEHOVA [1596] 8.5x12.3cm. title page from Linschoten's "Itinerario" with
    double hemisphere world map by Hondius   [39] $220
VERA EFFIGIES ET DELINEATIO INSULAE HELENAE... [1599] 61x48.3cm.   [24] $183
LIZARS
CHART OF THE ATLANTIC OCEAN [C1828] 48.9x41.3cm.   [3] $40
CHART OF THE WORLD ON MERCATOR'S PROJECTION [C1830] 53.3x80cm.
    short tear repaired, minor wear along folds   [16] $100
CHINA [C1828] 39.4x44.5cm.   [3] $55
MAP OF UNITED STATES AND CANADA [1828] 32.4x27.9cm.   [30] $69
NORTH AMERICA BRITISH POSSESSIONS [C1842] 53.5x42cm.
    upper margin somewhat frayed   [21] $89
UNITED STATES [1831] 40.6x50.8cm.   [23] $175

LODGE
A MAP OF THAT PART OF AMERICA WHICH WAS THE PRINCIPAL SEAT OF WAR IN 1756
[C1756] 21.6x33cm. minor repairs   [3] $125
A MAP OF THE BRITISH AND FRENCH SETTLEMENTS IN NORTH AMERICA [1755]
27.9x38.7cm.   [32] $125
A NEW AND ACCURATE MAP OF THE PROVINCE OF NOVA SCOTIA IN NORTH AMERICA, FROM
THE LATEST OBSERVATIONS [C1778] 28.6x33cm.   [3] $125
A NEW MAP OF STAFFORDSHIRE FROM THE LATEST AUTHORITIES. J. LODGE, SCULP. LONDON
PUBLISHED AS THE ACT DIRECTS MARCH 31ST. 1790 BY R. BUTTERS NO. 79, FLEET
STREET [1790] 32.4x26cm. 1st issue   [24] $41
AN EXACT MAP OF NOVA SCOTIA NEWFOUNDLAND...1777 [1778] 21x25.4cm.   [30] $73
AN EXACT MAP OF THE PROVINCE OF QUEBEC WITH PART OF NEW YORK & NEW ENGLAND FROM
THE LATEST SURVEYS [C1790] 20.6x26.5cm.   [39] $55
LONDON MAGAZINE
A MAP OF GUADELOUPE ONE OF THE CARIBBY ISLANDS IN THE WEST INDIES SUBJECT TO
FRANCE [C1760] 12.1x17.8cm.   [3] $35
A MAP OF SUCH PARTS OF GEORGIA AND SOUTH CAROLINA AS TEND TO ILLUSTRATE THE
PROGRESS AND OPERATIONS OF THE BRITISH ARMY &C. [1780] 18.4x23.5cm.
from the May 1780 ed.   [22] $120
A MAP OF THE COLONIES OF CONNECTICUT AND RHODE ISLAND... [1758] 17.8x22.9cm.
narrow right margin, from April 1758 issue   [23] $110
A MAP OF THE EASTERN PART OF THE PROVINCE OF NEW YORK; WITH PART OF NEW JERSEY
[1756] 21.6x16.5cm.   [23] $100
A MAP OF THE FIVE GREAT LAKES WITH PART OF PENNSYLVANIA, NEW YORK, CANADA AND
HUDSONS BAY TERRITORIES &C. [1755] 21x26cm.
from the September 1755 issue   [35] $125
A NEW AND ACCURATE MAP OF EAST AND WEST FLORIDA... [1765] 17.8x22.2cm.
from the March 1765 issue   [23] $100
A NEW MAP OF THE RIVER MISSISSIPI, FROM THE SEA TO BAYAGOULAS [1761]
17.8x24.1cm. from the March 1761 ed.   [22] $110
A NEW MAP OF THE RIVER MISSISSIPPI FROM THE SEA TO BAYAGOULAS [C1770]
17.8x24.1cm.   [16] $90
A NEW MAP, OF THE ONLY USEFUL AND FREQUENTED PART OF NEW FOUND LAND [C1760]
17.8x24.5cm.   [39] $65
A PLAN OF THE LATE SIEGE OF HAVANNA, AND MOOR'S CASTLE & THEIR ENVIRONS.
ENGRAV'D FOR THE LONDON MAGAZINE [1763] 18.4x10.8cm.
from the March 1763 issue   [25] $41
A PLAN OF THE TOWN AND CITADEL OF FORT ROYAL IN MARTINICO [1762] 19.1x24.8cm.
                                                                  [3] $75

AN ACCURATE MAP OF THE EAST PART OF ENGLAND WITH THE PARTS OF HOLLAND AND
FLANDERS BORDERING ON THE GERMAN OCEAN [1760] 35.6x26.7cm.
narrow margin on right reinforced   [11] $35
ISLAND OF BARBADOS/ISLAND OF ST. LUCIA/ISLAND OF ST. VINCENT/CHART OF PART OF
THE WINDWARD IS. [1764] 24.8x19.1cm. May 1764 issue   [3] $50
LOUISIANA, AS FORMERLY CLAIMED BY FRANCE, NOW CONTAINING PART OF BRITISH
AMERICA TO THE EAST & SPANISH AMERICA TO THE WEST OF THE MISSISSIPI...
[1765] 17.8x22.9cm. fold lines as issued, from the June 1765 issue [27] $135
NOVA SCOTIA DRAWN FROM SURVEYS BY T. KITCHIN [1749] 10.8x17.1cm.   [3] $55
PLAN OF THE GENERAL ATTACK UPON THE ISLAND OF GUADELOUPE [1759] 11.4x17.8cm.
                                                                  [3] $40
PLAN OF THE TOWN & FORT OF GRENADA. BY M. DE CAYLUS, ENGINEER GENERAL OF THE
FRENCH ISLANDS [1762] 22.2x17.8cm. inset map of the island   [23] $40
THE SOUTHERN PART OF THE PROVINCE OF NEW YORK: WITH PART OF THE ADJOINING
COLONIES [1778] 24.8x18.4cm. from the March 1778 issue   [23] $100
LONDON NEWS
SACRAMENTO GENERAL VIEW [1850] 12.7x22.9cm. October 1850   [3] $25
SALT LAKE CITY UTAH (VIEW) [1869] 24.1x35.6cm.   [3] $30
SITKA, THE RUSSIAN POSSESSION ON THE NORTH WEST COAST OF AMERICA (VIEW) [1855]
10.2x21.6cm.   [3] $30
THE TOWN OF BASSETERRE, GUADELOUPE (VIEW) [1865] 17.8x23.5cm.   [3] $30

LONGMAN
SKETCH DISTINGUISHING THE PARTS OF NORTH EAST AMERICA BEST ADAPTED TO THE
  SETTLEMENT OF EUROPEAN EMIGRANTS [C1820] 18.7x11.1cm.   [39] $35
SPANISH NORTH AMERICA [1818] 24.8x39.4cm.
  fold repaired, right margin extended   [22] $75
VIEW OF ROSEAU, IN THE ISLAND OF DOMINICA. ENGRAVED BY GEORGE COOKE. LONDON
  PUBLISHED BY LONGMAN, HURST, REES, ORME & BROWN. PATERNOSTER ROW, SEPTR. 1,
  1812 [1812] 19.1x12.7cm. tear in right margin repaired   [25] $49
VIEW OF THE ISLAND OF ST. THOMAS, TAKEN FROM HAVENSICHT. ENGRAVED FROM A LARGE
  PRINT BY PERMISSION OF MESSRS. BOYDELL & CO. LONDON PUBLISHED BY LONGMAN,
  HURST, REES, ORME & BROWN, PATERNOSTER ROW, JULY 1, 1812 [1812] 20.3x15.2cm.
                            [25] $73

LOOTSMAN
See JACOBSZ

LOTTER
A MAP OF THE MOST INHABITED PART OF NEW ENGLAND CONTAINING THE PROVINCES OF
  MASSACHUSETS BAY AND NEW HAMPSHIRE WITH THE COLONIES OF CONECTICUT AND RHODE
  ISLAND [1779] 104x98.5cm. tear in lower section repaired, lower right
  corner repaired with small loss of surface; Lotter's copy of the Jefferys
  map   [2] $878
A MAP OF THE PROVINCES OF NEW-YORK AND NEW-JERSEY, WITH A PART OF PENNSYLVANIA
  AND THE PROVINCE OF QUEBEC [1777] 74.9x55.9cm.   [22] $750
A NEW AND CORRECT MAP OF NORTH AMERICA WITH THE WEST INDIA ISLANDS, DIVIDED
  ACCORDING TO THE TREATY OF PEACE 20TH JAN. 1783...PARTICULARLY DISTINGUISHED
  THE THIRTEEN PROVINCES WHICH COMPOSE THE UNITES STATES... [1784]
  50.8x57.2cm. top right sheet only   [3] $285
A PLAN OF THE CITY AND ENVIRONS OF PHILADELPHIA [1777] 59.7x45.7cm. a missing
  portion about 8 x 2 cm. has been restored, affecting part of border and
  letter "A" in title, a copy of the Scull & Heap map   [23] $650
A PLAN OF THE CITY AND ENVIRONS OF PHILADELPHIA [1777] 34.3x45.7cm.
  copied from Faden's plan, with view of State House   [16] $800
AMERICA MERIDIONALIS... [1772] 45.6x58.2cm.   [39] $145
AMERICA SEPTENTRIONALIS [C1755] 45.5x58cm.   [5] $440
AMERICA SEPTENTRIONALIS CONCINNATUS JUXTA OBSERVATIONES...APUD TOBIAM LOTTER
  [1772] 45.7x58.4cm.   [3] $475
CARTE DE L'OCEAN PACIFIQUE AU NORD DE L'EQUATEUR, ET DES COTES QUI LE BORNENT
  DES DEUX COTES: D'APRES LES DERNIERES DECOUVERTES FAITES PAR LES ESPAGNOLS,
  LES RUSSES ET LES ANGLOIS, JUSQU'EN 1780. PUBLIEE PAR TOBIE CONRAD LOTTER A
  AUGSBOURG [1781] 48.9x56.5cm. margins ragged & slightly discolored, map
  based on 1780 Kitchin chart published in Gentleman's Magazine   [7] $875
CARTE NOUVELLE DE L'AMERIQUE ANGLOISE CONTENANT TOUT CE QUE LES ANGLOIS
  POSSEDENT SUR LE CONTINENT DE L'AMERIQUE SEPTENTRIONALE [C1770] 49.5x62.2cm.
                            [15] $775
CARTE NOUVELLE DE L'AMERIQUE ANGLOISE CONTENANT TOUT CE QUE LES ANGLOIS
  POSSEDENT...LE CANADA...NOUVELLE ANGLETERRE...AVEC LA FLORIDE [C1776]
  59.7x48.9cm.   [3] $465
LE ROYAUME DE FRANCE ET LES CONQUETES DE LOUIS GRAND [C1760] 45.7x57.2cm.
  numerous plans & notes appear in an elaborate border, contemporary color of
  central map, but border is uncolored   [17] $675
LIVONIAE ET CURLANDIAE DUCATUS CUM INSULIS ADJACENTIB. [C1746] 48.9x57.2cm.
  narrow margins   [24] $91
PARTIE ORIENTALE DE LA NOUVELLE FRANCE OU DU CANADA AVEC L'ISLE DE TERRE-NEUVE
  ET DE NOUVELLE ECOSSE ACADIE ET NOUV. ANGLETERRE AVEC FLEUVE DE ST
  LAWRENCE... [1750] 57.2x49.5cm.   [16] $500
PENNSYLVANIA, NOVA JARSEY ET NOVA YORK CUM REGIONIBUS [C1760] 55.9x48.3cm.
                            [16] $650
RECENS EDITA TOTIUS NOVI BELGII IN AMERICA SEPTENTRIONALI... [1757]
  49.8x58.2cm.   [39] $1250

LOWIZIO
SPECIMEN TRIGESINAE SEXTAE PARTIS EX GLOBO TERRESTRIUM... [1749] 82.5x16.5cm.
  browning on one fold, apparently a broadside or specimen, showing a globe
  gore including the West Indies for a globe apparently never made   [26] $725

LUCAS
ALABAMA [1823] 27.9x22.2cm.	[26]	$75
ALABAMA [1823] C22.9x29.2cm.	[34]	$95
ANTIGUA [1823] C22.9x29.2cm.	[34]	$85
BAHAMA'S [1823] 24.8x28.6cm.	[34]	$145
BARBADOS [1823] C22.9x29.2cm.	[34]	$75
CONNECTICUT [1823] C22.9x29.2cm.	[34]	$85
CUBA [1823] 29.2x43.8cm. offsetting	[34]	$85
CURACAO [1823] C22.9x29.2cm.	[34]	$75
DELAWARE [1823] 27.3x21.6cm. light staining	[26]	$60
DELAWARE [1823] C22.9x29.2cm.	[34]	$85
DOMINICA [1823] C22.9x29.2cm.	[34]	$65
GRENADA [1823] C22.9x29.2cm.	[34]	$75
GUADALOUPE [1823] C22.9x29.2cm.	[34]	$65
HAYTE OR ST. DOMINGO [1823] 30.2x47.6cm. offsetting	[34]	$75
ILLINOIS [1823] C22.9x29.2cm.	[34]	$95
ILLINOIS [1823] 30.2x22.2cm.	[26]	$85
INDIANA [1823] 27.9x22.2cm.	[26]	$90
INDIANA [1823] C22.9x29.2cm.	[34]	$95
JAMAICA [1823] C22.9x29.2cm.	[34]	$85
KENTUCKY [1823] 29.5x48.9cm.	[34]	$125
KENTUCKY [1823] 29.2x48.3cm.	[27]	$250
LOUISIANA [1823] 27.3x43.5cm. offsetting	[34]	$125
MARTINIQUE [1823] C22.9x29.2cm.	[34]	$65
MARYLAND [1823] 28.6x49.5cm. offsetting	[34]	$125
MEXICO [1823] C22.9x29.2cm.	[34]	$85
MICHIGAN TER. [1823] 22.9x30.5cm.	[34]	$145
MISSISSIPPI [1823] C22.9x29.2cm.	[34]	$95
MISSISSIPPI [1823] 29.2x22.9cm.	[26]	$75
NEW HAMPSHIRE [1823] C22.9x29.2cm.	[34]	$85
NEW YORK [1823] 29.8x46.4cm. offsetting	[34]	$95
NORTH AMERICA [1823] C22.9x29.2cm.	[34]	$85
NORTH CAROLINA [1823] 27.9x48.3cm. offsetting	[26]	$75
OHIO [1823] C22.9x29.2cm.	[34]	$95
PENNSYLVANIA [1823] 28.6x45.1cm.	[26]	$65
PENNSYLVANIA [1823] 27.9x45.1cm.	[34]	$95
PORTO RICO [1823] C22.9x29.2cm.	[34]	$75
RHODE ISLAND [1823] C22.9x29.2cm.	[34]	$75
SOUTH CAROLINA [1823] C22.9x29.2cm.	[34]	$95
SOUTH CAROLINA [1823] 24.4x27.9cm.	[26]	$75
ST. CHRISTOPHERS [1823] C22.9x29.2cm.	[34]	$85
ST. LUCIA [1823] C22.9x29.2cm.	[34]	$65
ST. VINCENT [1823] C22.9x29.2cm.	[34]	$75
TOBAGO [1823] C22.9x29.2cm.	[34]	$65
TRINIDAD [1823] C22.9x29.2cm.	[34]	$75
VERMONT [1823] C22.9x29.2cm.	[34]	$85
VERMONT [1823] 27.3x22.2cm.	[26]	$60
VIRGIN ISLANDS &C. [1823] 22.9x30.8cm.	[34]	$145
VIRGINIA [1823] 31.1x47.6cm. light offsetting	[26]	$75
VIRGINIA [1823] 31.1x47.6cm.	[34]	$125
WEST INDIES [1823] C22.9x29.2cm.	[34]	$65

LYELL
GEOGNOSTISCHE KARTE DER VEREINIGTEN STAATEN, CANADA &C. [1846] 38.1x49.5cm. 2
  cm. tear into right border, light stain near title, folding map, lithographed
  in color, from German ed. of Charles Lyell, "Travels in North America"
    [27] $125

MACGREGOR
MAP OF THE ARGENTINE REPUBLIC SHEWING THE LINE OF RAILWAY BETWEEN ROSARIO &
    CORDOVA [1864] 38.1x45.7cm. published by M. MacGregor, London   [3] $55
MACKENZIE
DOMINION OF CANADA [C1889] 22x27cm.   [21] $12
NORTH POLAR REGIONS WITH RESULTS OF LATEST EXPLORATIONS [C1878] 29.5x23cm.
    [21] $12
RIVERS, MOUNTAINS [C1866] 24.5x30.5cm.
    minor splits at ends of centerfold   [21] $28
MACKINLAY
NEW BRUNSWICK, NOVA SCOTIA [1886] 123x158cm.
    on 2 folding sheets, 72 panels, with slip case   [39] $185
MACLURE & MACDONALD
MAP OF THE BOUNDARY DIFFERENCES [1840] 18.4x26cm.
    illustrates the Maine boundary dispute by color, published in Glasgow
    [30] $101
MACPHERSON
SPANISH DOMINIONS IN N. AMERICA [1821] 18.4x24.1cm.
    map by A. MacPherson, published by Sherwood, Neely & Jones, London [19] $85
MAFFEIUS
INDIARUM ORIENTALIUM OCCIDENTALIUMQUE DESCRIPTIO, DEDICATA PET. MAFFEI
    HISTORIAE HARUM VERISSIMAE [C1589] 25.4x49.5cm.
    right margin added, from "Historiarum Indicarum"   [15] $2250
MAGGI
STATI UNITI D'AMERICA RIDOTTA DELLA CARTA PUBBLICATA A NUOVA YORK [1840]
    33x27.9cm. published in Turin   [3] $45
MAGINI
See PTOLEMY
MAGNUS
UNION MILITARY CHART [1861] 57.5x68.3cm. backed with cloth, Charles Magnus &
    Co. of New York & Liverpool published other similar composite maps, in this
    case consisting of a U.S. railroad map, and smaller maps of Virginia &
    Maryland, military movements, and views of the Capitol &c   [33] $175
MALLET
AMERIQUE MERIDIONALE [1686] 15.2x10.2cm.   [3] $40
CARTHAGENE (VIEW) [1683] 20.3x10.2cm.   [3] $40
CONTINENT ARCTIQUE [1683-1720] 14.5x11cm.   [21] $77
CUSCO [1683] 17.8x10.2cm.   [3] $30
DE FERO DE SCHELAND, ORKNAY ET HEBRIDES [1683] 20x14.5cm.   [31] $45
DE JERSEY ET DE GARNESEY [1683] 20x14.5cm.   [31] $68
DER GRUNDRISS VON DER STAT DESS HEYL DOMINICUS...LA VILLE DE SAN DOMINGO
    [1686] 17.8x11.4cm.   [3] $40
DT DE MAGELLAN [1686] 10.2x15.2cm.   [9] $35
GROENLANDE [1683-1720] 15x10.5cm.   [21] $69
GUINEE [1683] 14x10.2cm.   [9] $45
I DE ST HELENE (VIEW OF PORT) [1683] 20x14.5cm.   [31] $22
I. D HISPANIOLA ET P. RICO [1683] 20x14.5cm.   [31] $42
I. DE GUAVANHI OU DE ST. SALVADOR [1683] 20x14.5cm.   [31] $22
IE. D'HORN [1683] 20x14.5cm.   [31] $22
IS. COCOS [1683] 20x14.5cm.   [31] $15
IS. DE CUBA ET DE JAMAICA [1683] 20x14.5cm.   [31] $53
IS. DE MAN D'ANGLESEY [1683] 20x14.5cm.   [31] $61
ISLE D IRLANDE [1683] 20x14.5cm.   [31] $38
ISLE DE CAYENNE [1683] 20x14.5cm.   [31] $38
ISLE DE CAYENNE (VIEW) [1683] 15.2x10.2cm.   [3] $30
ISLE DE STE. HELENE (VIEW OF WHOLE ISLAND) [1683] 20x14.5cm.   [31] $38
ISLE DE TERRE NEUVE [1683] 20x14.5cm.   [31] $114
ISLE DE WIGH [1683] 20x14.5cm.   [31] $55
ISLE DE ZOCOTORA [1683] 20x14.5cm.   [31] $15
ISLES ACORES [1683] 20x14.5cm.   [31] $30
ISLES CANARIES [1683] 20x14.5cm.   [31] $38

ISLES CARIBES [1683] 20x14.5cm.	[31]	$76
ISLES DE MADAGASCAR DITE DE ST. LAURENS [1683] 20x14.5cm.	[31]	$15
ISLES DE MADERA [1683] 20x14.5cm.	[31]	$45
ISLES DE SALOMON [1683] 20x14.5cm.	[31]	$91
ISLES DES CANARIES ET DU CAP VERD [1683] 20x14.5cm.	[31]	$15
ISLES DES LARRON [1683] 15.2x9.5cm. 1st ed.	[3]	$45
ISLES DU CAP-VERD [1683] 20x14.5cm.	[31]	$38
ISLES DU CAP-VERD [1683] 10.2x15.2cm.	[9]	$40
ISLES DU JAPON [1683] 15.2x10.2cm.	[3]	$135
ISLES LUCAYES [1683] 20x14.5cm.	[31]	$76
LE PLAN DE L'ISLE DE ST. JAN ET PTO RICO [1683] 20x14.5cm.	[31]	$38
MEXIQUE-DE STADT MEXICO [1683] 15.2x10.2cm.	[3]	$45
MONTAGNE DE POTOSI [1683] 10.2x15.2cm.	[9]	$35
NOUVEAU MEXIQUE ET CALIFORNIE [1683] 11x14cm.	[31]	$268
PAIS QUI SONT AUX ENVIRONS DE LA RIVIERE DE LA PLATA ET DU PAIS... [1686] 16.5x10.2cm.	[3]	$35
PARTIE DE LA TERRE FERME DE L'INDIE OU L'EMPIRE DU MOGOL [1683] 10.2x14cm.	[10]	$35
ST. AUGUS. DE FLORIDE (VIEW) [1683] 14.6x10.8cm.	[25]	$91
ST. THOMAS [1683] 20x14.5cm.	[31]	$15
SYSTEME DE L'UNIVERS SELON TICHO [1683] 10.2x14cm.	[10]	$35

MALTE-BRUN

(BOSTON, VIEW) [1834] 14x20.3cm.	[10]	$30
AMERIQUE RUSSE, NOUVELLE BRETAGNE ET CANADA [1836] 22.2x32.4cm.	[3]	$35
AMERIQUE SEPTENTRIONALE [1836] 22.2x30.5cm.	[3]	$35
CARTE DES ETATS-UNIS D'AMERICA [1836] 22.9x29.8cm. backed	[3]	$40

MANTE

A SKETCH OF THE CHEROKEE COUNTRY [1772] 27.3x40cm. lower margin extended, J. Lodge sc., from Thomas Mante, "The history of the late war in North America," London	[3]	$365

MARCY

MAP OF THE COUNTRY BETWEEN...ARKANSAS & NEW MEXICO...EXPLORED IN 1849, 50, 51 & 52... [1854] 68.6x149.9cm. on 2 sheets joined	[20]	$300
MAP OF THE COUNTRY UPON THE UPPER RED RIVER EXPLORED IN 1852 [1854] 41.3x85.7cm.	[20]	$160

MARIETTE

COMITATUS FLANDRIAE NOVA TABULA. PARIS, PIERRE MARIETTE, RUE ST-JACQUES A L'ENSEIGNE DE ESPERANCE [C1640] 39x50.5cm.	[18]	$140

MARSHALL

PLAN OF THE COUNTRY FROM FROGS PT. TO COTTON RIVER SHEWING...THE AMERICAN & BRITISH ARMIES FROM THE 12TH OCTOBER 1776 UNTIL THE ENGAGEMENT ON THE WHITE PLAINS... [1806] 43.2x21.6cm. minor repairs, R. Phillips, London	[3]	$70
THEATRE DES OPERATIONS DE L'ARMEE DU NORD, ET DESERT QUE LE GENERAL ARNOLD TRAVERSE EN MARCHANT CONTRE QUEBEC [1807] 25.4x21.6cm.	[3]	$75

MARTIN

THE FIRST PRINCIPLES OF GEOGRAPHY AND ASTRONOMY MADE EASY BY INSPECTION IN A NEW PROJECTION OF THE GLOBE OF THE EARTH & DELINEATION OF THE VARIOUS PARTS & PHAENOMENA OF THE SOLAR SYSTEM [1758] 30.5x59.7cm. margins worn, small hole in engraved border, a double-hemisphere world map with text around each hemisphere, separately published for 1 shilling & sixpence by B. Martin	[16]	$240

MARZOLLA

AUSTRALIA OCCIDENTALE ET ISOLA DI VAN-DIEMEN [1848] 42.5x50cm.	[31]	$38

MAST, CROWELL & KIRKPATRICK

MAP OF TEXAS [1897] 32.4x50.2cm. edge browned	[19]	$35
MAP OF TEXAS [1890] 32.4x50.2cm. repairs, browning in margin	[19]	$35

MATHER

GEOLOGICAL MAP OF LONG & STATEN ISLANDS WITH THE ENVIRONS OF NEW YORK, BY W.W. MATHER...FROM THE TOPOGRAPHICAL SURVEYS OF J. CALVIN SMITH, ENDICOTT, NEW YORK, 1842. [1842] 11.4x64.8cm. folding, inset: Map of New-York Island	[23]	$300

MATTHEWS, NORTHRAP CO.
MAP OF THE NEW YORK CENTRAL LINES [1898] 19.7x39.4cm.   [3] $25
SOUTHERN STATES-WESTERN SECTION [C1890] 21.6x27.9cm. foxed   [19] $15
THE THOUSAND ISLANDS OF ST. LAWRENCE RIVER REACHED BY THE RICHELIEU & ONTARIO
   NAVIGATION CO. [1898] 22.2x39.4cm.   [3] $35
MCGREGOR
CHART EXHIBITION THE BRITISH POSSESSIONS IN NORTH AMERICA; THE ATLANTIC,
   BRITISH ISLES &C. WITH THE PROPOSED TRACKS OF THE PROJECTED TRANS-ATLANTIC
   STEAM NAVIGATION [1833] 16.7x38.8cm.   [39] $45
MAP EXHIBITING THE HARBOUR OF HALIFAX AND THE SHUBENACADIE CANAL... [1833]
   11.5x32.1cm.   [39] $35
MAP OF CAPE BRETON... [1833] 11.6x19.9cm.   [39] $25
MAP OF NEWFOUNDLAND... [1833] 12x15.6cm.   [39] $20
MAP OF NOVA-SCOTIA FROM LATE SURVEYS... [1833] 19.3x24.1cm.   [39] $30
MAP OF PRINCE EDWARD ISLAND IN THE GULF OF ST. LAWRENCE... [1833] 11x17.1cm.
                                                                       [39] $25
MAP OF THE BRITISH NORTH AMERICAN PROVINCES AND ADJOINING STATES [1833]
   39.4x67.4cm.   [39] $85
MAP OF THE HARBOUR AND THREE RIVERS OF PICTOU, AND THE POSITION OF THE ALBION
   MINES... [1833] 19.5x15.5cm.   [39] $30
MAP OF THE HARBOUR CITY AND ENVIRONS OF MONTREAL... [1833] 18.3x22.5cm.
                                                                       [39] $30
MAP OF THE HARBOUR CITY AND ENVIRONS OF QUEBEC... [1833] 18.5x22.3cm.
                                                                       [39] $35
MAP OF THE HARBOUR OF SYDNEY AND BRIDPORT AND THE POSITION OF THE GENERAL
   MINING COMPANY'S COAL MINES... [1833] 18.9x23.5cm.   [39] $30
MAP OF THE PROVINCES OF NEW BRUNSWICK AND PART OF LOWER CANADA... [1833]
   19.8x23.5cm.   [39] $35
MAP OF THE RIVER ST. LAURENCE AND TRIBUTARIES EXHIBITING THE SIGNEURIES &C.
   FROM QUEBEC TO THE BOUNDARY OF UPPER CANADA... [1833] 11.5x16.3cm. [39] $20
MAP OF UPPER CANADA EXHIBITING THE DISTRICTS & COUNTIES... [1833] 12x20.3cm.
                                                                       [39] $25
PLAN OF PLACE D'ARMES AND ST. JAMES STREET AT MONTREAL FOR THE ELUCIDATION OF
   THE EVENTS OF THE 21ST MAY 1832 [1833] 17.5x23.1cm.   [39] $45
PLAN OF THE HARBOUR OF LOUISBURG, AND THE TOWN & FORTIFICATIONS WHEN IT
   SURRENDERED TO THE BRITISH FORCES [1833] 11.5x15cm.   [39] $25
MCINTYRE
THE WORLD FROM THE BEST AUTHORITIES [C1773] 20x31.5cm.
   folds worn, minor staining at edges, backed with archivists tissue [21] $56
MEARS
A PLAN OF PORT EFFINGHAM IN BERKLEY'S SOUND [1790] 19.1x23.5cm.
   minor repairs   [3] $65
A PLAN OF PORT EFFINGHAM IN BERKLEY'S SOUND... [1791] 18.7x23.3cm.
   one margin narrow   [39] $45
A PLAN OF THE SEA OTTER HARBOUR AND ST. PATRICKS BAY TAKEN BY CAPT. JAMES
   HANNA... [1791] 23.7x19cm. one margin narrow   [39] $40
A SKETCH OF PORT COX IN THE DISTRICT OF WICANANISH [1791] 23.7x19cm.
   one margin narrow   [39] $40
A SKETCH OF PORT COX IN THE DISTRICT OF WICANANISH [1790] 19.1x19.1cm.
   minor repairs   [3] $45
A SKETCH OF RAFT-COVE, TAKEN BY MR. FUNTER, MASTER OF THE NORTH WEST
   AMERICAN... [1791] 24x19.4cm.   [39] $35
A VIEW OF OTTER SOUND... [1791] 24.2x19.2cm. one margin narrow   [39] $35
A VIEW OF PORT MEARES [1791] 23.6x18.8cm.   [39] $30
NOOTKA SOUND-PORT EFFINGHAM... [1790] 19.7x31.8cm.   [3] $40
MEGAREY
NEWBURG (VIEW) [1820-25] 35.6x53.7cm. aquatint by J. Hill after William G.
   Wall, No. 14 in "The Hudson River Portfolio" published by Henry I. Megarey,
   NY   [33] $1500
MEISNER
DIR NATUR IST SPARSAM CUSCO IN WEST INDIEN (VIEW) [1627] 10.2x14cm. [3] $85

MEISNER (continued)
LUTZENBURG (VIEW) [1625] 9.6x14.6cm.   [18] $263
MELISH
BALLSTON & SARATOGA SPRINSG, CITY OF ALBANY, AND ADJACENT COUNTRY [1822]
    16.5x10.4cm.   [39] $25
BALTIMORE, ANNAPOLIS AND ADJACENT COUNTRY [1822] 16.3x10.3cm.   [39] $25
BOSTON AND ADJACENT COUNTRY [1822] 16.6x10cm.   [39] $25
CHARLESTON, AND ADJACENT COUNTRY [1822] 16.7x10.3cm.   [39] $25
MAP OF THE NATIONAL ROAD BETWEEN CUMBERLAND AND WHEELING [1815] 15.2x28.6cm.
                                                                       [3] $65
MAP OF THE SEAT OF WAR IN NORTH AMERICA [C1813-15] 40x55.2cm. repaired tears,
    small loss of text repaired, "Second Edition with Additions & Improvements.
    Entered as the Act Directs, and Published by John Melish, Philadelphia"
                                                                       [7] $350
NEW-YORK AND ADJACENT COUNTRY [1822] 16.2x10.4cm.   [39] $25
OUTLET OF COLUMBIA RIVER [1822] 16.7x9.7cm.   [39] $30
PHILADELPHIA AND ADJACENT COUNTRY [1822] 16.4x10.4cm.   [39] $25
ST. LOUIS AND ADJACENT COUNTRY [1822] 16.6x10.2cm.   [39] $25
UNITED STATES OF AMERICA [1821] 42.5x54cm.
    minor stains, centerfold repaired, engraved by B. Tanner   [19] $200
UNITED STATES OF AMERICA... [1820] 43.2x54cm.
    narrow margins, some centerfold repairs & stains   [19] $225
UNITED STATES OF AMERICA... [1818] 41.3x49.5cm.
    folding, margin repaired   [19] $500
VIEW OF THE COUNTRY ROUND THE FALLS OF NIAGARA [1816] 16.7x10.3cm.   [39] $45
MERCATOR
See also HONDIUS
See also JANSSON
MERCATOR (FOLIO)
AFRICA STUDIO ET INDUSTRIA G.M. IUNIORIS [C1630] 38.5x46.5cm.   [2] $298
AMERICA SIVE INDIA NOVA [C1587] 38.1x45.7cm.   [15] $2800
AMERICA SIVE INDIA NOVA... [1595] 36.8x46.4cm.   [17] $3800
AMERICA SIVE INDIA NOVA...IN COMPENDIUM REDACTA PER MICHAELEM MERCATOREM
    DUYSBURGENSEM [1632] 37.5x47cm.   [2] $1404
AMERICAE SIVE INDIA NOVA AD MAGNAE GERARDI MERCATORIS AVI UNIVERSALIS
    IMITATIONEM... [C1623] 37x46.5cm.   [5] $2400
ANGLESEY/WIGHT VECTIS OLIM/GARNESAY/IARSAY [1606] 31.8x43.2cm.
    minor spotting   [7] $350
ANGLESEY/WIGHT VECTIS OLIM/GARNESAY/IARSAY [C1595-38] 35.6x43.2cm.
    a later reissue by Jansson of Mercator's 1595 map   [14] $245
ASIA EX MAGNA DESCRIPTIONE...DESUMPTA STUDIO G.M. IUNIORIS [1632] 38x47cm.
                                                                       [2] $421
CAMBRIAE TYPUS AUCTORE HUMFREDO LHUYDO, DENBIGIENSE CAMBROBRITANNO, PETRUS
    KAERIUS CAELA. [1606-33] 36.8x49.5cm.   [14] $383
CAMBRIAE TYPUS. AUCTORE HUMFREDO LHUYDO [C1573] 36.8x49.5cm.   [12] $298
CANDIA CUM INSULIA ALIQUOT CIRCA GRAECIAM [1606] 33.7x47.6cm.   [7] $225
CYPRUS INS. [C1632] 35.5x49.5cm. minor staining in margins   [2] $509
CYPRUS INS. [C1630] 35.5x49.5cm.   [4] $490
EUROPA, AD MAGNAE EUROPAE GERARDI MERCATORIS IMITATIONEM, RUMOLDI MERCATORIS
    CURA EDITA [C1612] 38.5x47cm.   [2] $263
EXQUISITA & MAGNO ALIQUOT MENSIUM PERICULO LUSTRATA ET IAM RETECTA FRETI
    MAGELLANICI [1606] 34.9x45.7cm. moderate browning   [17] $750
FRANCE PICARDIE CHAMPAIGNE CUM REGIONIBUS ADIACENTIBUS [1606] 35.6x40cm.
    margins browned   [7] $175
GRAECIA [C1612] 36x47.5cm.   [2] $228
HABES HIC NOVAM & ACCURATISSIMAM DESCRIPTIONEM TRACTUS ILLIUS FLANDRIAE...
    [C1620] 37x52cm.   [18] $263
HANNONIA NAMURCUM COMITATUS. PAR GERARDUM MERCATOREM [C1585] 35x46cm.
                                                                       [18] $70
INSULAE INDAE ORIENTALIS PRAECIPUAE... [1606-30] 34.3x47cm.   [24] $421
JAPONIA [1606-19] 34.3x44.5cm.   [15] $1350

LATIUM NUNC COMPAGNA DI ROMA [1606] 36.8x72.4cm.
   minor stain, margins somewhat ragged   [7] $200
LEODIENSIS DIOECESIS TYPUS [1606] 33.5x48cm.
   early state, before inclusion into atlas of 1606, no text on verso [18] $351
RUSSIA CUM CONFINIJS [1606] 35.6x48.3cm.
   centerfold split repaired, inset: Russiae Pars Amphiscta   [7] $425
SCOTIA REGNUM [1606] 34.9x40.6cm. browned, centerfold tear repaired [7] $325
SEPTENTRIONALIUM TERRARUM DESCRIPTIO [C1620] 37x39.5cm.   [2] $860
SEPTENTRIONALIUM TERRARUM DESCRIPTIO. PER GERARDUM MERCATOREM CUM PRIVILEGIO
   [1595-1602] 36.8x39.4cm. centerfold repaired, several pinholes, 1st state
   with signature "I" and 28 lines of text on verso   [7] $1050
SICILIAE REGNUM [1595] 33.7x48.3cm.   [9] $175
TERRA SANCTA QUAE IN SACRIS TERRA PROMISSIONIS OL: PALESTINA [1606-07]
   35.6x49.5cm.   [24] $383
VIRGINIAE ITEM ET FLORIDA [1606-19] 34.3x48.3cm.   [23] $1250
VIRGINIAE ITEM ET FLORIDAE AMERICAE PROVINCIARUM, NOVA DESCRIPTIO [1606]
   34.5x49cm.   [2] $632
VIRGINIAE ITEM ET FLORIDAE AMERICAE... [1606] 34.2x48.3cm.
   worm holes at lower centerfold repaired   [39] $520
WESTMORLANDIA, LANCASTRIA, CESTRIA...CUM INSULIS MANIA ET ANGLESEY [1595-1628]
   36.8x41.9cm. French text on verso   [14] $84

MERCATOR (SMALL)

AMERICAE DESCRIPTIO [1634] 14.6x19.7cm.   [30] $182
AUSTRIA ARCHIDUCATUS [1630] 14x19.1cm.   [10] $60
HONDIUS HIS MAP OF CYPRUS [1621] 14x18.5cm.   [31] $91
HONDIUS, HIS MAP OF ICELAND [1621] 13x18.5cm.   [31] $99
INDIA ORIENTALIS [C1610] 14.5x18.5cm.   [4] $53
JAPAN I. [1625] 14x17.1cm. from Purchas, with text in English [3] $135
NOVA VIRGINIAE TABULA [1630-32] 18.4x25.4cm.   [22] $250
NOVA VIRGINIAE TABULA PETRUS KAERIUS CAELAVIT [C1630] 13.3x19.1cm. [9] $180
TRIER ET LUTZEBORG [1608] 13.7x18.2cm.   [18] $351
VIRGINIA ET FLORIDA [1635] 15.2x19.1cm. 1st English ed.   [3] $125
VIRGINIAE ITEM ET FLORIDAE [1673] 19.1x25.4cm.
   a slightly larger engraving than that first appearing in "Atlas Minor"
                                         [16] $220

MERCATOR-HONDIUS

See MERCATOR

MERIAN

(ACAPULCO, ENGRAVED SCENE OF DUTCH FLEET) [1630] 15x17.5cm. [39] $120
(JUAN FERNANDEZ ISLANDS, L'HERMITE'S FLEET) [1630] 12.3x18cm. [39] $75
(MATANZAS BAY, ENGRAVED SCENE) [1630] 15.1x17.5cm.   [39] $135
(MEXICO CITY) [1630] 15.1x17.6cm.   [39] $125
AMERICA NOVITER DELINEATA [C1640] 27.3x35.6cm. later color, inset,
   "Septentrionalisimas Americae parties Groenlandiam"   [7] $650
EROBERUNG DER VESTUNG PROVANCON ZU PORTO CALVO IN BRASILIA... [C1630] 27x35cm.
   library stamp   [39] $150
GENEVE. GENSS (VIEW) [C1628] 23x34cm.   [4] $367
HUUM. HOY. (VIEW) [1648] 19x36cm.   [18] $140
IERUSALEM [C1640] 20.3x33cm.   [15] $550
INSULAE BALEARIDES ET PYTIUSAE [1645] 28x37cm.   [31] $130
LEODIUM. LEIGE. LUTICH (BIRD'S EYE VIEW) [1648] 28.5x37.5cm. [18] $105
LEODIUM. LIEGE. LUTICH. (PANORAMIC VIEW) [1648] 22x33cm.   [18] $140
NAMURCUM COMITATUS [C1650] 25.5x33.5cm.   [18] $52
NOVA TOTIUS TERRARUM ORBIS GEOGRAPHICA AC HYDROGRAPHICA TABULA [C1638]
   26.7x35.6cm. world map based on Blaeu   [16] $650
NOVA TOTIUS TERRARUM ORBIS GEOGRAPHICA AC HYDROGRAPHICA TABULA [C1650]
   26x35.5cm.   [37] $1200
PROSP. DER STATT NAMUR [C1650] 14x36cm.   [18] $35
TRAIECTUR. UTRECHT (BIRD'S EYE VIEW) [1648] 21x31cm.   [18] $70
VALLETTA CITTA NOVA DI MALTA (VIEW) [C1628] 27.5x35cm.   [4] $306

METELLUS
MARIS PACIFICI VULGO MAR DEL ZUR [C1598] 20.3x27.9cm.   [15] $1400

MEYER
MAINE, NEW HAMPSHIRE, MASSACHUSETTS, VERMONT, CONNECTICUT & RHODE I. [1846]
  26.7x19.7cm.   [22] $35
N. & S. CAROLINA, GEORGIA & FLORIDA [1850] 25.4x19.4cm.   [22] $35
NEUESTE KARTE VON OHIO [1845] 37.1x30.2cm. from "Meyer's Handatlas"   [34] $95
NEW YORK, PENSYLVANIA, MARYLAND, NEW JERSEY, DELAWARE & VIRGINIA [1850]
  26.7x19.7cm.   [22] $35
ROCK ISLAND CITY (VIEW) [C1850] 10.2x15.2cm.
  from Hermann J. Meyer "Universum"   [27] $40
WHEELING IN VIRGINIA (VIEW) [C1850] 11.4x15.2cm.
  from Hermann J. Meyer, "Universum"   [27] $45

MICHAULT
COSTES ET RIVIERES DE VIRGINIE, DE MARILAND ET DE NOUVELLE ANGLETERE [1674]
  19.1x24.1cm. from "Le Recueil de Divers Voyages," inset map: "L'Isle De
  Terre Neuve"   [7] $400

MIDDLETON
A VIEW OF THE NEW DISCOVERED ISLAND OF ULIETEA WITH SOME OF ITS INHABITANTS, &
  A DOUBLE CANOE [1778] 17.8x27.3cm.   [3] $40

MIGEON
OCEANIE... [1874] 28.5x38cm.   [31] $58

MILLAR
THE MOST SURPRISING CATARACT OF NIAGARA IN CANADA (VIEW) [1779] 19.1x28.6cm.
                                                                        [3] $65

MILTON & CHEADLE
GENERAL MAP OF BRITISH NORTH AMERICA, SHOWING THE ROUTE OF LORD MILTON & DR.
  CHEADLE IN 1862-3 [1866] 18.9x27.3cm.   [39] $50

MITCHELL
(ARIZONA AND NEW MEXICO) [1874-75] 28.3x35.6cm.   [8] $25
(ARKANSAS) [1847] 36.8x29.2cm.   [27] $55
(ARKANSAS) [1850] 36.8x29.2cm.   [27] $45
(CALIFORNIA) [1874-75] 54x35.6cm. split at fold repaired   [8] $25
(CHICAGO) [1874-75] 34.6x27.9cm. wards 1,2,9, 17-20 colored pink   [8] $25
(COLORADO) [1887] 27.9x36.8cm.   [27] $50
(COLORADO, WYOMING, DAKOTA & MONTANA) [1874-75] 49.5x35.6cm.   [8] $30
(GEORGIA AND ALABAMA) [1874-75] 26.7x34cm.   [8] $15
(GEORGIA) [1850-54] 35.6x29.2cm. dated 1850, probably 1854 ed.   [27] $50
(IOWA AND MISSOURI) [1874-75] 54.3x36.2cm.   [8] $15
(KANSAS AND NEBRASKA) [1875] 35.6x54.3cm.   [8] $25
(KANSAS, NEBRASKA & COLORADO) [1861-65] 29.2x35.6cm.   [8] $30
(KENTUCKY AND TENNESSEE) [1875] 36.2x54cm.   [8] $25
(MILWAUKEE) [1873-75] 34.9x26cm.   [8] $15
(MINNESOTA) [1874-75] 35.6x29.2cm.   [8] $20
(MISSISSIPPI) [1847] 35.6x29.2cm.   [27] $55
(MISSOURI) [1847] 40.6x33cm.   [27] $60
(NEW ORLEANS) [1874-75] 23.2x27.6cm.   [8] $15
(NEW YORK & BROOKLYN) [1874-75] 33.7x52.7cm.   [8] $20
(NORTHWESTERN AMERICA) [1872-75] 29.2x35.6cm.   [8] $20
(OREGON, WASHINGTON, IDAHO & PART OF MONTANA) [1874-75] 27x34cm.   [8] $20
(ST. LOUIS) [1874-75] 34.9x27.6cm.   [8] $35
A NEW MAP OF ARKANSAS WITH ITS CANALS, ROADS & DISTANCES [1848] 36.8x29.8cm.
                                                                        [3] $45
A NEW MAP OF THE STATES OF TEXAS, CALIFORNIA... [1850-52] 63.5x59.1cm.
  browned, a wall map   [20] $350
CANADA WEST [C1847] 30.5x40.6cm.   [30] $52
CHILI, PARAGUAY, THE ARGENTINE CONFEDERATION AND URUGUAY [1873] 25.4x20.3cm.
                                                                        [3] $20
COUNTY AND TOWNSHIP MAP OF OREGON AND WASHINGTON [1882] 50.8x36.8cm. [32] $35
COUNTY MAP OF ARKANSAS, MISSISSIPPI AND LOUISIANA [1874-75] 53x34.9cm.
                                                                        [8] $15

COUNTY MAP OF COLORADO, WYOMING, DAKOTA, MONTANA [1875] 49.5x36.8cm. [11] $50
COUNTY MAP OF FLORIDA [1874-75] 26.7x34cm.   [8] $15
COUNTY MAP OF ILLINOIS [1871-72] 34.3x27.3cm. inset of Springfield [8] $20
COUNTY MAP OF TEXAS [1867] 27.9x34.3cm.   [22] $110
COUNTY MAP OF TEXAS [1860] 27.3x34cm. 1st ed. of this version   [19] $120
COUNTY MAP OF TEXAS [1860] 27.3x34cm.   [20] $125
COUNTY MAP OF TEXAS [1873-75] 35.6x54cm. inset of Galveston & Vicinity
                                                                   [8] $45
COUNTY MAP OF TEXAS [1870] 26.7x34.3cm.   [23] $115
COUNTY MAP OF TEXAS [1872] 26.7x34.3cm.   [23] $115
COUNTY MAP OF TEXAS [1866-67] C22.9x30.5cm.   [19] $100
COUNTY MAP OF THE STATE OF TEXAS [1884] 35.6x53.3cm.   [22] $115
COUNTY MAP OF THE STATE OF TEXAS [1873-75] 35.6x53.3cm.   [19] $70
COUNTY MAP OF THE STATE OF TEXAS [1873] 35.6x53.3cm.   [20] $110
COUNTY MAP OF THE STATE OF TEXAS [1882] 35.6x53.3cm.   [32] $70
COUNTY MAP OF THE STATE OF TEXAS, SHOWING ALSO PORTIONS OF THE ADJOINING STATES
  AND TERRITORIES [1879] 35.6x54.6cm. same as 1878 issue, but with more
  railroads, including a spur reaching Denton   [23] $135
COUNTY MAP OF THE STATE OF TEXAS, SHOWING ALSO PORTIONS OF THE ADJOINING STATES
  AND TERRITORIES [1878] 35.6x54.6cm.   [23] $135
COUNTY MAP OF UTAH AND NEVADA [1867] 29.2x35.6cm.   [11] $50
MAP OF KANSAS, NEBRASKA, AND COLORADO...DACOTAH [1867] 29.2x35.6cm. [9] $45
MAP OF LOUISIANA, TEXAS, ARKANSAS, AND INDIAN TERRITORY [1881-90] 20.6x26.7cm.
  spotted   [19] $20
MAP OF MEXICO, CENTRAL AMERICA, & WEST INDIES [1860-65] 30.5x50.2cm. [19] $60
MAP OF MEXICO... [1866-67] 29.2x50.2cm.   [19] $55
MAP OF NORTH AMERICA...& RECENT DISCOVERIES IN POLAR REGIONS [1870]
  35.6x27.9cm.   [3] $30
MAP OF OREGON, WASHINGTON, IDAHO AND PART OF MONTANA [1871] 26.7x34.3cm.
                                                                   [3] $30
MAP OF OREGON, WASHINGTON, IDAHO, AND PART OF MONTANA [1867] 27.9x34.3cm.
                                                                   [9] $35
MAP OF TEXAS FROM THE MOST RECENT AUTHORITIES [1850] 31.1x38.1cm.
  light browning   [22] $265
MAP OF THE STATE OF TEXAS [1858-59] 20.3x26.7cm.   [19] $80
MAP OF THE STATE OF TEXAS [1852-56] 20.3x26.7cm.   [19] $85
MAP OF THE STATE OF TEXAS [1852] 20.3x26.7cm. 1st issue of new edition
                                                                   [19] $100
MAP OF THE STATE OF TEXAS [1846-48] 26.7x20.3cm.   [19] $150
MAP OF THE STATE OF TEXAS [1852-57] 20.3x26.7cm.   [19] $80
MAP OF THE STATE OF TEXAS [1852-55] 20.3x26.7cm. small spot stain [19] $90
MAP OF THE STATE OF TEXAS [1858-66] 20.3x26.7cm. minor spotting   [19] $65
MAP OF THE STATE OF TEXAS [1858-63] 20.6x26.7cm.
  worn, foxing in margins   [19] $65
MAP OF THE STATE OF TEXAS [1858] 20.3x26.7cm.
  tear in upper right margin, new edition for 1858   [19] $75
MAP OF THE STATE OF TEXAS [1852-54] C20.3x26.7cm.   [20] $90
MAP OF THE STATE OF TEXAS [1846-51] 26.7x20.3cm.   [19] $100
MAP OF THE STATE OF TEXAS [1852-54] 20.3x26.7cm. small spot stain [19] $90
MAP OF THE STATE OF TEXAS [1852-55] C20.3x26.7cm. similar to 1854 ed. but
  Fts. Belknap, Chadbourne, McKavett, Territt, Clark & Phantom Hill are added,
  spotting in margins   [20] $80
MAP OF THE STATES OF CALIFORNIA THE TERRITORIES OF OREGON & UTAH... [1845-50]
  39.4x33cm.   [9] $145
MAP OF THE UNITED STATES AND TERRITORIES, TOGETHER WITH CANADA &C. [1865]
  33.7x53.3cm.   [10] $45
MAP OF THE UNITED STATES ENGRAVED TO ILLUSTRATE MITCHELL'S SCHOOL AND FAMILY
  GEOGRAPHY [1852] 26.4x42.5cm.   [36] $145
MAP OF THE WORLD ON THE MERCATOR PROJECTION... [1871] 36.2x45.7cm. [3] $30
MEXICO & GUATEMALA [1850-51] 30.5x38.1cm.   [19] $55

MITCHELL'S MAP OF ILLINOIS EXHIBITING ITS INTERNAL IMPROVEMENTS...PUBLISHED BY
    S.A. MITCHELL [1838] 38.1x31.8cm.
    backed with rice paper, printed in blue ink & colored in outline   [36] $145
MITCHELL'S NATIONAL MAP OF THE AMERICAN REPUBLIC... [1843] 92.7x115.6cm.
    original shellac & rollers   [19] $275
NORTH AMERICA [1848] 39.4x32.4cm.   [3] $65
NORTH AMERICA SHOWING ITS POLITICAL DIVISIONS AND RECENT DISCOVERIES IN THE
    POLAR REGIONS [1874-75] 34.6x27cm.   [8] $20
NORTHWESTERN AMERICA SHOWING THE TERRITORY CEDED BY RUSSIA TO THE UNITED
    STATES [1872] 29.2x36.8cm.   [27] $30
ONTARIO IN COUNTIES [1867-69] 27x34.3cm.   [8] $20
PLAN OF BALTIMORE [1874-75] 24.1x27.9cm.   [8] $15
PLAN OF BOSTON [1874-75] 33.3x52.7cm.   [8] $20
PLAN OF CINCINNATI AND VICINITY [1867] 26.7x28.6cm.   [3] $28
PLAN OF PHILADELPHIA [1870] 27.9x33cm.   [3] $30
PLAN OF THE CITY OF WASHINGTON, THE CAPITOL OF UNITED STATES OF AMERICA
    [1874-75] 27.6x34cm.   [8] $20
TERRITORY OF MONTANA [1878] 36.2x26.7cm.   [9] $40
TEXAS [1865-80] 20.3x27cm.   [19] $40
TEXAS [C1865-87] 20.3x26.7cm. one worn spot   [20] $25
TEXAS [C1865] 21x27cm.   [22] $60
TEXAS [1865-86] 20.3x27cm.   [19] $30
TEXAS [1865-68] 20.6x27cm.   [19] $60
UNITED STATES AND TERRITORIES [1874-75] 34.3x54cm.   [8] $25

MITCHELL, JOHN

A MAP OF THE BRITISH AND FRENCH DOMINIONS IN NORTH AMERICA WITH THE ROADS,
    DISTANCES, LIMITS, AND EXTENT OF THE SETTLEMENTS...VERY HUMBLE SERVANT JOHN
    MITCHELL [C1755] 134.6x193.7cm. this is the lower-left quarter only of the
    Mitchell map, dimensions are for the complete map, minor wrinkling [1] $850

MOFFAT

BRITISH NORTH AMERICAN PROVINCES [1833] 39.4x67.3cm. repaired & backed
    [30] $162
CHART OF NORTH ATLANTIC OCEAN WITH TRACKS OF THE SHIPPING TO WEST INDIES
    [1815] 53.3x62.9cm.   [3] $85

MOLL

(SOUTHERN HEMISPHERE, TRADEWINDS) [1723] 15.2x48.3cm.
    from "Complete Geographer"   [30] $36
(WEST INDIES) [C1710] 58.4x101cm.   [17] $1250
A MAP OF AMERICA [C1730] 27x18.5cm.   [4] $137
A MAP OF CHILI, PATAGONIA, PART OF LA PLATA ETC. BY H. MOLL GEOGRAPHER
    [1729-45] 17.8x25.4cm.   [25] $45
A MAP OF MEXICO OR NEW SPAIN, FLORIDA NOW CALLED LOUISIANA, AND PART OF
    CALIFORNIA & C. [C1717] 17.8x25.4cm. corner of margin missing   [22] $160
A MAP OF NEW FRANCE CONTAINING CANADA, LOUISIANA & C. IN NTH. AMERICA ACCORDING
    TO THE PATENT GRANTED...TO MONSIEUR CROZAT DATED 14TH SEP. 1712, REGISTERED
    IN PARLIAMENT OF PARIS THE 24TH OF SAME MONTH [1712] 18.4x25.4cm. [3] $245
A MAP OF THE BAY OF CAMPECHY [1717] 14.8x27.9cm.   [39] $45
A MAP OF THE NORTH POLE WITH ALL THE TERRITORIES THAT LIE NEAR IT, KNOWN TO
    US... [1729] 20.3x27.9cm.   [3] $85
A MAP OF THE WEST INDIES & C. MEXICO OR NEW SPAIN, ALSO YE TRADE WINDS AND YE
    SEVERAL TRACTS MADE BY YE GALLEONS & FLOTA... [1729] 20.3x26.7cm. [3] $95
A MAP OF THE WEST INDIES OR THE ISLANDS OF AMERICA IN THE NORTH SEA... [1711]
    59x102cm.   [39] $750
A MAP OF THE WORLD SHEWING THE COURSE OF MR. DAMPIER'S VOYAGE ROUND IT: FROM
    1679 TO 1691. H. MOLL FECIT [1729] 16.2x29.2cm. minor splits on the 2 fold
    lines, some wrinkling on one of them, from Dampier, "A New Voyage Around the
    World," Vol. 1, London 1729   [8] $125
A MAP OF THE WORLD. SHEWING THE COURSE OF MR. DAMPIERS VOYAGE ROUND IT: FROM
    1679 TO 1691 [1717] 16x29.2cm.   [39] $85

MOLL (continued)

A NEW & EXACT MAP OF THE COASTS, COUNTRIES AND ISLANDS WITHIN YE LIMITS OF
YE SOUTH SEA COMPANY, FROM YE RIVER ARANOCA TO TERRA DEL FUEGO, AND FROM
THENCE THROUGH YE SOUTH SEA, TO YE NORTH PART OF CALIFORNIA...HERMAN MOLL,
LONDON 1711 [1711] 64.8x49.2cm. light browning at folds, the main map of
South America contains several inset maps, and 3 additional maps appear above
it   [33] $385
A NEW & EXACT MAP OF THE COASTS, COUNTRIES AND ISLANDS WITHIN YE LIMITS OF YE
SOUTH SEA COMPANY... [C1711] 66x48.3cm.
title is for main map, 3 smaller maps appear along the top   [17] $725
A NEW AND CORRECT MAP OF SCOTLAND & THE ISLES... [1725] 30.5x27.9cm. [24] $91
A NEW GENERALL CHART FOR THE WEST INDIES OF E. WRIGHTS PROJECTION VUL MERCATORS
CHART [C1703] 45.6x48cm.
small tear repaired, J. Seller & C. Price, London   [12] $176
A NEW MAP OF IRELAND... [1714-32] 101.6x61cm.   [24] $306
A NEW MAP OF NEW FOUNDLAND, NEW SCOTLAND, THE ISLES OF BRETON, ANTICOSTE, ST.
JOHNS & WITH THE FISHING BANKS [1741] 18.4x26cm.   [3] $120
A NEW MAP OF NEWFOUND LAND, THE ISLES OF BRETON, ANTICOSTI, ST. JOHNS &
TOGETHER WITH THE FISHING BANKS [1716] 17.8x25.4cm.   [3] $135
A NEW MAP OF NEWFOUNDLAND, NEW SCOTLAND... [1723] 18.4x26cm.
from "Complete Geographer"   [30] $162
A NEW MAP OF NORTH AMERICA ACCORDING TO THE NEWEST OBSERVATIONS [1709-45]
17.8x24.8cm.   [22] $175
A NEW MAP OF THE ISLAND OF BARBADOES, CONTAINING ALL YE PARISHES AND PRINCIPAL
PLANTATIONS...TOGETHER WITH YE FORTS, LINES, BATTERIES, ROADS &C. [C1716]
18.4x25.4cm.   [3] $110
A NEW MAP OF YE ISTHMUS OF DARIEN IN AMERICA... [1710] 29.8x48.3cm. [3] $165
A PLAN OF PORT ROYAL HARBOUR IN CAROLINA WITH PROPOSED FORTS [1729]
20.3x25.4cm.   [3] $100
A PLAN OF THE PORT ROYAL HARBOUR IN CAROLINA [C1729-63] 27x20cm. the numeral
"52" is present, appearing in later editions of 1732, 1736, 1763 [1] $175
AMERICA [1723] 17.1x19.1cm. from "Complete Geographer"   [30] $203
AMERICA [C1710] 17.1x18.4cm. on a sheet measuring about 33 x 20 cm., left
margin trimmed and extended   [23] $150
AMERICA BY H. MOLL GEOGRAPHER [C1729-32] 26.4x19.7cm.
from "Atlas Minor"   [34] $225
ASIA [1723] 17.1x19.1cm.   [30] $60
ASIA MINOR [1723] 17.8x20.3cm.   [30] $60
BEDFORDSHIRE [1724] C19.1x30.5cm. 1st issue, from "A New Description of
England and Wales, With the Adjacent Islands"   [14] $53
BRAZIL [1723] 16.5x18.4cm.   [30] $81
CANAAN, PALESTINE [1723] 22.2x17.8cm.   [30] $142
CAROLINA BY H. MOLL [C1729] 19.1x27.9cm. backed   [3] $110
CHILI, MAGELLANS-LAND [1723] 16.5x18.4cm.   [30] $101
CHINA [1723] 17.1x19.1cm.   [30] $121
CORSICAE ANTIQUA DESCRIPTIO/SARDINAE ANTIQUA DESCRIPTIO [1717] 26x10.5cm.
                                                                   [31] $45
DENMARK [1723] 17.1x19.1cm.   [30] $89
EAST INDIES [1723] 17.1x19.1cm.   [30] $101
ESSEX [1724] C19.1x30.5cm.   [14] $45
EUROPE [1723] 16.5x18.4cm.   [30] $52
FLANDERS OF SPANISH NETHERLANDS [1723] 17.1x19.1cm.   [30] $48
FLANDERS OR THE SPANISH NETHERLANDS WITH YE ARCHBISHOPRICK OF CAMBRESIS AND
BISHOPRICK OF LYEGE [1732] 17.8x25.4cm.   [11] $25
FLORIDA CALLED BY YE FRENCH LOUISIANA [C1725] 20.3x27.9cm.
from "Atlas Minor"   [16] $160
FRANCE [1723] 16.5x18.4cm.   [30] $32
GERMANY [1723] 19.1x19.1cm.   [30] $97
GREAT TARTARY/THE ISLE OF JAPON [1723] C17.1x18.4cm.   [30] $89
GULF OF AMAPALLA ALIAS FONSECA [1717] 16.5x21.2cm.   [39] $45
HUNGARY [1723] 17.8x19.1cm.   [30] $40

146

MOLL (continued)

I.O. WIGHT [1724] C19.1x30.5cm.	[14]	$45
INDIA OR THE MOGUL'S EMPIRE [1723] 17.1x19.1cm.	[30]	$121
IRELAND [1723] 18.4x17.8cm.	[30]	$97
ITALY [1723] 18.4x18.4cm.	[30]	$60
MEXICO OR NEW SPAIN [1723] 16.5x18.4cm.	[30]	$81
MONMOUTHSHRIRE [1724] C19.1x30.5cm.	[14]	$42
MOSCOVIA OR RUSSIA [1723] 16.5x17.8cm.	[30]	$52
NEW ENGLAND, NEW YORK, NEW JERSEY AND PENSILVANIA [C1730] 20x27.5cm.	[5]	$200
NORTH WALES [1724] 20.3x31.8cm.	[24]	$42
OXFORDSHIRE [1724] C19.1x30.5cm.	[14]	$45
PERSIA [1723] 17.1x19.1cm.	[30]	$81
PERU AND THE AMAZONES COUNTRY [1723] 17.1x19.1cm.	[30]	$81
PLAN OF STRASBURG [1723] 8.9x13.3cm.	[30]	$16
POLAND [1723] 17.8x19.7cm.	[30]	$97
RIO DE LA PLATA [1723] 16.5x18.4cm.	[30]	$81
SAVOY & PIEDMONT [1723] 21.6x18.4cm.	[30]	$52
SCANDINAVIA [1723] 14x19.1cm.	[30]	$32
SCOTLAND [1723] 17.8x17.8cm.	[30]	$73
SEVEN PROVINCES OF THE UNITED NETHERLANDS [1723] 17.1x19.1cm.	[30]	$89
SOUTH AMERICA, ACCORDING TO THE NEWEST AND MOST EXACT OBSERVATIONS...		
[1710-15] 58x97cm.	[39]	$300
SPAIN & PORTUGAL [1723] 15.9x18.4cm.	[30]	$32
SWEDEN & NORWAY [1723] 17.1x18.4cm.	[30]	$89
SWITZERLAND [1723] 17.8x19.1cm.	[30]	$89
TERRA FIRMA AND THE CARIBBE ISLANDS [1723] 15.9x19.1cm.	[30]	$60
TERRA FIRMA. GUIANA AND THE ANTILLES ISLANDS [C1729] 17.8x25.4cm.	[23]	$70
THE ENGLISH EMPIRE IN AMERICA [1723] 21.6x17.8cm.	[30]	$162
THE GALLAPAGOS ISLANDS DISCOVERED BY CAPT. JOHN EATON [1717] 13.8x13cm.		
	[39]	$65
THE GREAT RIVER MARANON OR THE AMASONS GEOGRAPHICALLY DESCRIBED BY SAMUEL		
FRITZ, MISSIONER ON SAID RIVER [C1714] 15.9x36.2cm.	[3]	$95
THE ISLAND OF JAMAICA [C1729] 20.3x27.9cm.	[23]	$80
THE ISLAND OF ST. CHRISTOPHERS [C1729] 17.8x25.4cm.		
with maps of Antigua and the West Indies on the same sheet	[23]	$75
THE ISLE OF CALIFORNIA, NEW MEXICO, LOUISIANE, RIVER MISISIPI AND THE LAKES OF		
CANADA [1723] 16.5x18.4cm.	[30]	$162
THE ISLE OF CALIFORNIA. NEW MEXICO. LOUISIANE. THE RIVER MISISIPI AND THE		
LAKE'S OF CANADA... [C1701] 16.2x18.4cm. faint stain at upper right		
	[34]	$225
THE ISLE OF WIGHT/SCILLY ISLANDS/HOLY ISLAND/FAIRN ISLANDS AND STAIPLES &C.		
[1724-39] 20.3x31.8cm.	[24]	$45
THE KINGDOM OF ENGLAND [1723] 18.4x18.4cm.	[30]	$89
THE WORLD IN PLANISPHERE [1709] 16.5x19.1cm. from "Atlas Manuale"	[30]	$182
TO THE RIGHT HONORABLE JOHN LORD SOMMERS THIS MAP OF NORTH AMERICA ACCORDING TO		
YE NEWEST & MOST EXACT OBSERVATIONS [1720] 57.8x96.5cm.		
some browning at centerfold, some reinforcements	[15]	$1450
TURKY IN ASIA [1723] 17.1x19.1cm.	[30]	$81
TURKY IN EUROPE [1723] 17.1x19.1cm.	[30]	$73
VIRGINIA AND MARYLAND [C1730] 27x20cm.	[4]	$114
VIRGINIA AND MARYLAND BY H. MOLL GEOGRAPHER [C1732-45] 26.7x20.3cm.		
small wormhole in lower margin	[27]	$175
WARWICKSHIRE [1724] C19.1x30.5cm.	[14]	$42
WESTMORLAND [1724] 19.7x32.4cm.	[24]	$41
WILTSHIRE... [1724-47] 31.1x19.1cm.	[24]	$58

MONIN & FREMIN

ETATS UNIS [1836] 19.1x24.1cm.	[20]	$75
MEXIQUE [1836] 19.1x24.1cm.	[19]	$75
OCEANIE [1836] 34x25cm.	[31]	$53

MONK

NEW MAP OF N. AMERICA... [1852] C152.4x152.4cm. by Jacob Monk, Baltimore, a
wall map with the lower portion in poor condition [20] $250
NEW MAP OF...NORTH AMERICA EXHIBITING THE UNITED STATES & TERRITORIES...
[1854] 157.5x147.3cm. linen backed, with original wood ferrules, some cracks
in shellac, blank margins ragged [19] $500

MORDEN

...NEW MAP OF THE CHIEF RIVERS, BAYES, CREEKS, HARBOURS AND SETTLEMENTS IN
SOUTH CAROLINA ACTUALLY SURVEYED... [C1695] 48.3x55.9cm.
small wax stain, 2 small rust stains [16] $2500
A MAP OF THE WESTERN ISLANDS [1688] 12.7x14.6cm.
backed, left margin narrow, from "Geography Rectified" [3] $65
A NEW AND CORRECT MAP OF NORTH-WALES [1722] 35.6x43.2cm.
2nd ed., 1st issue, re-engraved by A. Johnston [24] $55
A NEW MAP OF CAROLINA [C1700] 12.7x12.7cm. on a page of text, some soiling,
first appearing in 1688 in "Geography Rectified" [16] $85
A NEW MAP OF HUNGARY BY ROBT. MORDEN [1693] 12.1x14cm. [11] $35
A NEW MAP OF NEW ENGLAND AND NEW YORK [1688] 12.7x14.6cm. [3] $95
A NEW MAP OF THE ENGLISH EMPIRE IN AMERICA. VIZ VIRGINIA, MARYLAND, CAROLINA,
NEW YORK, NEW JARSEY, NEW ENGLAND, PENNSYLVANIA, NEWFOUNDLAND, NEW FRANCE...
[C1695] 49.5x58.4cm. minor creasing [16] $2000
A NEW MAP OF YE WORLD BY ROBT MORDEN [C1680] 5.8x9.2cm.
from "Geography Rectified" [13] $168
A NEW MAP OF YE WORLD BY ROBT. MORDEN [1680-88] 9.2x15.6cm.
from Morden "Geography Rectified" [34] $225
AMERICA BY R. MORDEN [1680-88] 10.5x12.4cm. from "Geography Rectified"
[34] $250
AMERICA BY R. MORDEN [1693] 10.8x12.7cm. [11] $165
ARMENIA & GEORGIA COMANIA &C BY ROBT. MORDEN [1693] 13.3x11.4cm. [11] $40
BARK SHIRE [1695] 35.6x41.9cm. 1st issue [24] $76
BUCKINGHAMSHIRE [1695] 41.9x34.9cm. [24] $76
CAMBRIDGE SHIRE [1695] 41.9x35.6cm. 1st issue [24] $76
CHINA A NEW DESCRIPTION... [1684] 14x13.3cm. [3] $50
EPISCOPATUS DUNELMENSIS VULGO THE BISHOPRIC OF DURHAM BY ROBT. MORDEN [1695]
36.8x41.9cm. 1st issue [24] $64
HERTFORDSHIRE BY ROBT. MORDEN [1695-1722] 36.2x44.5cm. [24] $91
INSULA JAMAICAE [1688] 11.4x12.7cm. from "Geography Rectified" [3] $100
NEW MEXICO [C1700] 11.5x13cm. on a sheet with text [4] $214
NORFOLK BY ROBT. MORDEN [1695] 37.5x57.8cm.
upper left corner replaced, 1st issue [24] $72
NORTHAMPTONSHIRE [1695-1722] 35.6x41.3cm. [24] $49
NOTTINGHAM SHIRE [1695-1772] 34.9x41.9cm. [24] $58
OXFORD SHIRE [1695-1753] 41.9x35.6cm. [24] $76
POLAND BY ROBT. MORDEN [1693] 10.2x12.7cm. on a page with text [9] $45
SHROPSHIRE [1695] 36.2x41.9cm. [24] $68
SUFFOLK [1695] 35.6x41.3cm. 1st issue [24] $67
THE COUNTY PALATINE OF CHESTER... [1695] 34.3x41.3cm. [24] $131
THE COUNTY PALATINE OF LANCASTER... [1695] 41.9x36.2cm. 1st issue [24] $130
WESTMORLAND [1695] 35.6x41.9cm. [24] $68
WILLIAM CAMDEN CLARENCEUX OBIJT AO.D. 1623. AETATIS SUCE LXXIII. R. WHITE
SCULP. (PORTRAIT) [1695] 29.2x19.1cm.
frontispiece to Camden's "Britannia" of 1695 [25] $33

MORDEN & BERRY

TO CAPT. JOHN WOOD THIS MAP OF THE WORLD...IS HUMBLY DEDICATED [1676]
49x101cm. on 2 sheets, dimensions are overall, lower margins narrow &
repaired, 1st state before addition of "Pensilvania" & "N. Jersey," published
by Robert Morden & William Berry, 4 complete copies of this state are said to
be known [2] $4390

MORGAN

MAP: SHOWING INDIAN RESERVATIONS WITHIN THE LIMITS OF THE U.S. [1889]
53.3x83.8cm. [20] $65

1ORRISON & WEST
NORTH AMERICA [C1810] 24.5x19.5cm. engraved by Menzies   [21] $36

1ORSE
A CORRECT MAP OF GEORGIA WESTERN TERRITORY [1797] 17.8x15.2cm.
   light browning, offsetting, from "The American Gazetteer," Boston [1] $125
A MAP OF GEORGIA ALSO THE TWO FLORIDAS FROM THE BEST AUTHORITIES [1796]
   19.1x31.1cm. backed, map engraved by Amos Doolittle, from Morse, "Universal
   Geography," Thomas & Andrews, Boston 1796   [1] $120
A MAP OF GEORGIA, ALSO THE TWO FLORIDAS [1796] 18.7x31.1cm.
   narrow left margin, minor tears repaired   [22] $75
A MAP OF NORTH CAROLINA FROM THE BEST AUTHORITIES [1794] 22.2x42.5cm.
   Published in London by J. Stockdale   [3] $130
A MAP OF THE DISTRICT OF MAINE WITH NEW BRUNSWICK & NOVA SCOTIA [1796]
   18.4x23.5cm.   [3] $110
A MAP OF THE STATES OF NEW HAMPSHIRE AND VERMONT BY J. DENISON [1796]
   19.1x23.5cm.   [9] $60
ALABAMA, MISSISSIPPI AND LOUISIANA [1825] 19.1x24.4cm.   [8] $35
CANADA [1825] 20.5x25cm. light foxing   [21] $52
CANADA [1825] 20x24.8cm.   [8] $40
CITY OF NEW YORK 1842 [C1842] 38.1x30.5cm.   [3] $25
ILLINOIS [1844] 35.6x27.9cm.   [3] $40
ILLINOIS & MISSOURI [1825] 25.1x19.1cm. with 1 page index   [8] $50
KENTUCKY & TENNESSEE [1825] 19.1x25.4cm. with a page of index   [8] $45
MAINE, NEW HAMPSHIRE & VERMONT [1825] 20x25.1cm. with an index page   [8] $20
MAP OF NORTH AND SOUTH CAROLINA [1796] 19.1x23.5cm. two narrow margins
                                                                     [22] $100
MAP OF THE DISTRICT OF MAINE, PART OF MASSACHUSETTS [1802] 30.5x19.7cm.
   separation along fold repaired, from the 4th edition of Morse's geography
                                                                     [23] $75
MAP OF THE STATE OF NEW YORK [1796] 19.1x24.1cm. narrow left margin, thin
   spot in blank area, from the 3rd edition of Morse's geography   [23] $75
MAP OF THE WORLD FROM THE BEST AUTHORITIES [1796] 18.4x34.9cm. small thin
   spot, light spotting, from 3rd edition of "The America Universal Geography"
                                                                     [23] $95
MASSACHUSETTS AND RHODE ISLAND [1843] 30.5x37.5cm.   [3] $30
MASSACHUSETTS, RHODE ISLAND & CONNECTICUT [1825] 20x24.8cm.
   with an index page   [8] $20
NEW JERSEY [1841] 35.6x27.9cm.   [3] $45
NEW YORK [1825] 20x24.4cm. inset of New York & Vicinity   [8] $30
NORTH AMERICA [1825] 24.4x20cm.
   from Morse, "New Universal Atlas," New Haven 1825   [8] $50
NORTH AMERICA SHOWING ALL THE NEW DISCOVERIES 1797 [1797] 19.1x21.6cm.
   narrow margin, wrinkled, backed with cloth   [19] $45
NORTH AMERICA... [1796] 19.1x21.6cm. some foxing   [19] $75
NORTH CAROLINA [1843] 31.8x42.5cm.   [3] $35
NORTH CAROLINA, SOUTH CAROLINA AND GEORGIA [1825] 19.7x24.8cm.
   from "A New Universal Atlas of the World"   [1] $50
NORTH CAROLINA, SOUTH CAROLINA AND GEORGIA [1825] 19.7x25.4cm.
   inset of Charleston & vicinity, with a page of index   [8] $35
NOVA-SCOTIA, NEW BRUNSWICK &C [1843] 38.1x30.5cm. by S.E. Morse   [3] $35
OHIO & INDIANA [1825] 19.1x25.1cm. with a page of index   [8] $25
PACIFIC OCEAN [1825] 19.7x24.4cm. with 1 page index   [8] $20
PENNSYLVANIA & NEW JERSEY [1825] 19.1x25.1cm.
   with a page of index, inset of Philadelphia & Vicinity   [8] $25
PENNSYLVANIA DRAWN FROM THE BEST AUTHORITIES [1796] 19.1x33.7cm. minor wear,
   minor spotting, from the 3rd edition of Morse, "American Universal
   Geography"   [23] $75
RHODE ISLAND AND CONNECTICUT... [1802] 19.1x33cm.
   from the 4th ed. of Morse, "American Universal Geography"   [11] $60
UNITED STATES [1825] 25.4x41.9cm. minor discoloration at fold   [8] $75
VIRGINIA [1843] 30.5x39.4cm.   [3] $30

MORSE (continued)
WEST INDIES [1825] 19.7x24.8cm. with a page of index   [8] $30
MORSE & BREESE
ARKANSAS [C1844] 30.5x37.8cm.   [8] $50
ARKANSAS [1844] 30.5x38.1cm.   [3] $40
KENTUCKY AND TENNESSEE [1845] 30.5x41.9cm.   [3] $30
MAINE [1843] 38.1x30.5cm.   [3] $30
MEXICO [1844] 30.5x41.9cm.   [3] $70
MICHIGAN [1844] 32.4x38.1cm.   [3] $45
NEW YORK [1842] 30.5x38.1cm.   [3] $30
NORTH AMERICA [1842] 38.1x31.1cm.   [3] $45
OREGON [1844] 27.3x35.6cm.   [3] $95
PENNSYLVANIA [1843] 30.5x40cm.   [3] $40
WEST INDIA ISLANDS [1844] 30.5x35.6cm.   [3] $25
WISCONSIN SOUTHERN PART [1845] 31.8x39.4cm.   [3] $45
MORTIER
See also JAILLOT
(DIEPPE TO ROUEN, SEA CHART) [1693] 58.4x47cm.
  engraved by de Hooghe, full title not given   [17] $750
(GOLD COAST TO CONGO, SEA CHART) [1700] 57.2x43.2cm.
  full title not given   [17] $450
AMERIQUE SEPTENTRIONALE [1700] 54x87.5cm. centerfold reinforced   [5] $700
AMERIQUE SEPTENTRIONALE [1700] C57.2x87.6cm. from "Atlas Nouveau"   [16] $1650
AMERIQUE SEPTENTRIONALE DIVISEE EN SES PRINCIPALES PARTIES...A AMSTERDAM CHEZ
  PIERRE MORTIER [1700] 55.9x86.4cm.   [15] $1600
ASIA MINOR [C1700] 38.1x52.1cm. from "Atlas Nouveau"   [16] $200
CARTE DE L'ENTREE DE LA TAMISE AVEC LES BANCS [1693] 45.1x88.9cm.
  an 18th century issue   [24] $183
CARTE DE LA MANCHE [C1700] C57.2x86.4cm. from "Atlas Nouveau"   [16] $380
CARTE DES COTES DE L'ASIE SUR L'OCEAN CONTENANT LES BANC ISLES ET COSTES
  ETC... [1700] 56x87cm.   [31] $843
CARTE DES INDES ET DE LA CHINE [C1700] C57.2x86.4cm.
  from "Atlas Nouveau"   [16] $380
CARTE DES ISLES D'ACORES... [1700] 50.2x54cm.
  from "Suite de Neptune Francais"   [17] $425
CARTE GENERAL DE LA CAROLINE... [C1696] 56.2x46.4cm.
  small repaired tear into left neat line   [35] $850
CARTE GENERALE DE LA CAROLINE [1700] 57.2x47cm. from "Atlas Nouveau" [16] $1000
CARTE GENERALE DU MONDE, OU DESCRIPTION DU MONDE TERRESTRE & AQUATIQUE [C1696]
  39.7x46.7cm. title given appears at upper left, at upper right the title
  appears in Dutch, five circular diagrams near the top convey geographic and
  celestial concepts   [17] $1100
CARTE MARINE DES ENVIRONS DE L'ISLE D'OLERON A L'USAGE DES ARMEES DU ROY DE LA
  GRANDE BRETAGNE...CHEZ P. MORTIER 1693 [1693] 58.4x47cm.
  right margin extended, on heavy paper   [24] $183
CARTE MARITIME DEPUIS LA RIVIERE DE BORDEAUX JUSQUES A ST. SEBASTIEN A L'USAGE
  DES-ARMEES DU ROY DE LA GRANDE BRETAGNE... [1693] 57.8x47cm.
  narrow right margin, on heavy paper   [24] $229
CARTE MARITIME DES ENVIRONS DE DIEPPE DEPUIS PONT ASSELANE JUSQUES AU HAVRE DE
  GRACE...1693 [1693] 58.4x47cm. on heavy paper   [24] $214
CARTE NOUVELLE DE L'AMERIQUE ANGLOISE CONTENANT LA VIRGINIE, MARY-LAND,
  CAROLINE, PENNSYLVANIA NOUVELLE IORCK: N. IARSEY N. FRANCE, ET LES TERRES
  NOUVELLEMENT DECOUVERTE PAR LE SIEUR S A AMSTERDAM CHEZ PIERRE MORTIER
  LIBRAIRE... [C1692-1700] 60.3x91.4cm.
  minor creasing at centerfold, inset of Charleston Harbor   [7] $1400
CARTE NOUVELLE DU CREMASCO [C1700] 47x39.4cm. from "Atlas Nouveau"   [16] $180
CARTE NOUVELLE DU PADOUAN [C1700] C57.2x86.4cm. from "Atlas Nouveau"
                                                                             [16] $180
CARTE PARTICULIERE DE ISTHMUS OU DARIEN...CARTAGENE [C1700] C57.2x86.4cm.
  from "Atlas Nouveau," minor damage caused by pigment repaired   [16] $320

MORTIER (continued)

CARTE PARTICULIERE DE L'AMERIQUE SEPTENTRIONALE OU SONT COMPRES LE DETROIT DE
  DAVIDS, LE DETROIT DE HUDSON... [1700]   C57.2x87.6cm.
  from "Atlas Nouveau"   [16] $700
CARTE PARTICULIERE DE LA CAROLINE [1700] 48.3x61cm.
  from "Atlas Nouveau"   [16] $1250
CARTE PARTICULIERE DE VIRGINIE, MARYLAND, PENNSILVANIE, LA NOUVELLE IARSEY
  ORIENT ET OCCIDENTALE...A AMSTERDAM CHEZ P. MORTIER [C1700] 51.4x80cm.
  slight creasing along centerfold   [26] $1500
CARTE PARTICULIERE DE VIRGINIE, MARYLAND, PENNSILVANIE, LA NOUVELLE JARSEY
  ORIENT ET OCCIDENTALE [1700]   C57.2x87.6cm. from "Atlas Nouveau"   [16] $2500
CARTE PARTICULIERE DES POSTES DE FRANCE [C1700]   C57.2x86.4cm.
  from "Atlas Nouveau"   [16] $200
COMTE DE NAMUR [C1700]   C57.2x86.4cm. from "Atlas Nouveau"   [16] $150
DAUPHINE [C1700]   C57.2x86.4cm. from "Atlas Nouveau"   [16] $190
DES POSTES DE L'ITALIE [C1700]   C57.2x86.4cm. from "Atlas Nouveau" [16] $225
DUCHE ET LEGATION DE FERRARE [C1700]   C57.2x86.4cm.
  from "Atlas Nouveau," minor pigment damage repaired   [16] $200
ESTATS DE L'EGLISE ET DE TOSCANE [C1700]   C57.2x86.4cm.
  from "Atlas Nouveau"   [16] $180
ESTATS DE POLOGNE [C1700]   C57.2x86.4cm. from "Atlas Nouveau"   [16] $240
FRISE OCCIDENTALE [C1700] 43.2x58.4cm. from "Atlas Nouveau"   [16] $180
GOUVERNEMENT GENERALE DE CHAMPAGNE [C1700]   C57.2x86.4cm.
  from "Atlas Nouveau"   [16] $240
GRAND TARTARIE [C1700]   C57.2x86.4cm. from "Atlas Nouveau"   [16] $240
GUELDRE ESPAGNOL [C1700] 43.2x58.4cm. from "Atlas Nouveau"   [16] $120
GUIENNE ET GASCOIGNE [C1700] 48.3x59.7cm. from "Atlas Nouveau"   [16] $180
IUDEA SEU TERRA SANCTA [C1700]   C57.2x86.4cm. from "Atlas Nouveau" [16] $480
L'AFRIQUE [C1700]   C57.2x86.4cm. from "Atlas Nouveau"   [16] $550
L'ALSACE [C1700]   C57.2x86.4cm. from "Atlas Nouveau"   [16] $190
L'AMERIQUE MERIDIONALE [C1700]   C57.2x86.4cm. from "Atlas Nouveau" [16] $400
L'ARCHIDUCHE D'AUSTRICHE [C1700]   C57.2x86.4cm. from "Atlas Nouveau" [16] $250
L'ASIE [C1700]   C57.2x86.4cm. from "Atlas Nouveau"   [16] $380
L'EMPIRE DU GRAND SEIGNEUR DES TURCS [C1700]   C57.2x86.4cm.
  from "Atlas Nouveau"   [16] $350
L'ESPAGNE [C1700]   C57.2x86.4cm.
  from "Atlas Nouveau," short tear repaired   [16] $550
L'ETAT DE LA REPUBLIQUE DE VENISE [C1700]   C57.2x86.4cm.
  from "Atlas Nouveau"   [16] $190
L'EUROPE [C1700]   C57.2x86.4cm. from "Atlas Nouveau"   [16] $240
L'EVERSCHE DE LIEGE [C1700]   C57.2x86.4cm. from "Atlas Nouveau" [16] $300
L'ISLE D'ISCHIA DANS LE VOISINAGE DE NAPLES [1705] 38x48cm.   [31] $268
L'ISLE DAUPHINE [C1700]   C57.2x86.4cm. from "Atlas Nouveau"   [16] $210
L'ISLE ET ROYAUME DE SARDAGNE [C1700]   C57.2x86.4cm.
  from "Atlas Nouveau"   [16] $150
L'ITALIE [C1700]   C57.2x86.4cm. from "Atlas Nouveau"   [16] $240
LA LORRAINE [C1700]   C57.2x86.4cm. from "Atlas Nouveau"   [16] $150
LA MER ROUGE [C1700]   C57.2x86.4cm. from "Atlas Nouveau"   [16] $240
LA MOREE [C1700]   C57.2x86.4cm. from "Atlas Nouveau"   [16] $225
LA RUSSIE BLANCHE OU MOSCOVIE [C1700]   C57.2x86.4cm.
  from "Atlas Nouveau"   [16] $150
LA SCANDINAVIE [C1700]   C57.2x86.4cm. from "Atlas Nouveau"   [16] $360
LA SEIGNEURIE D'UTRECHT [C1700] 43.2x58.4cm. from "Atlas Nouveau" [16] $180
LA SICILE [C1700]   C57.2x86.4cm. from "Atlas Nouveau"   [16] $180
LA VELUWE, LA BETUWE... [C1700]   C57.2x86.4cm. from "Atlas Nouveau" [16] $270
LE BRETAGNE [C1700]   C57.2x86.4cm. from "Atlas Nouveau"   [16] $300
LE CANADA OU PARTIE DE LA NOUVELLE FRANCE... [1700]   C57.2x87.6cm.
  from "Atlas Nouveau"   [16] $1000
LE COMTE DE FLANDRE [C1700]   C57.2x86.4cm. from "Atlas Nouveau" [16] $240
LE COMTE DE HOLLANDE [C1700]   C57.2x86.4cm. from "Atlas Nouveau" [16] $240
LE COMTE DE ZEELANDE [C1700]   C57.2x86.4cm. from "Atlas Nouveau" [16] $400

MORTIER (continued)

LE DUCHE DE BRABANT. PARTIE MERIDIONALE [C1700] C57.2x86.4cm.
from "Atlas Nouveau" [16] $240
LE DUCHE DE BRABANT. PARTIE SEPTENTRIONALE [C1700] C57.2x86.4cm.
from "Atlas Nouveau" [16] $340
LE DUCHE DE LUXEMBOURG [C1700] C57.2x86.4cm. from "Atlas Nouveau" [16] $420
LE DUCHE DE MILAN [C1700] C57.2x86.4cm. from "Atlas Nouveau" [16] $225
LE GOUVERNEMENT GENERALE DE L'ISLE DE FRANCE [C1700] C57.2x86.4cm.
from "Atlas Nouveau" [16] $130
LE LIMBOURG [C1700] 43.2x55.9cm. from "Atlas Nouveau" [16] $180
LE ROYAUME D'ECOSSE [C1700] C86.4x57.2cm. from "Atlas Nouveau" [16] $260
LE ROYAUME D'IRLAND [C1700] C86.4x57.2cm.
from "Atlas Nouveau," right margin narrow & extended [16] $420
LE ROYAUME DE DANEMARK [C1700] C57.2x86.4cm. from "Atlas Nouveau" [16] $360
LE ROYAUME DE FRANCE [C1700] C57.2x86.4cm. from "Atlas Nouveau" [16] $200
LE ROYAUME DE HONGRIE [C1700] C57.2x86.4cm. from "Atlas Nouveau" [16] $150
LE ROYAUME DE SIAM [C1700] C86.4x57.2cm. from "Atlas Nouveau" [16] $350
LES DESERTS D'EGYPTE [C1700] C57.2x86.4cm. from "Atlas Nouveau" [16] $420
LES DIX-SEPT PROVINCES DES PAYS-BAS [C1700] C86.4x57.2cm.
from "Atlas Nouveau" [16] $150
LES DUCHES DE STIRIE, DE CARINTHIE, DE CARNIOLE [C1700] C57.2x86.4cm.
from "Atlas Nouveau" [16] $180
LES ISLES BRITANNIQUES [C1700] C57.2x86.4cm. from "Atlas Nouveau" [16] $380
LES MONTAGNES DES ALPES [C1700] C57.2x86.4cm. from "Atlas Nouveau" [16] $250
LES MONTS PYRENEES [C1700] C57.2x86.4cm. from "Atlas Nouveau" [16] $150
LES PROVINCES DES PAYS-BAS CATHOLIQUES [C1700] C57.2x86.4cm.
from "Atlas Nouveau" [16] $180
LUCQUES OU LUCA...PIERRE MORTIER [1704] 41.3x52.1cm. [24] $88
MAPPE-MONDE GEO-HYDROGRAPHIQUE DESCRIPTION GENERALE DU GLOBE TERRESTRE...
[C1700] 55.9x96.5cm. narrow margins, margins added, minor wax stains, minor
centerfold repairs [16] $3000
MER DE SUD OU PACIFIQUE CONTENANT L'ISLE DE CALIFORNIA [1700] 59.7x73.7cm.
offsetting in left margin [15] $3700
MER MEDITERRANE [C1700] C57.2x86.4cm.
from "Atlas Nouveau," narrow side margins extended [16] $460
OCCIDENTALIOR REGNI ANGLIAE DISTRICTUS COMPREHENDENS PRINCIPATUM WALLIAE ET
GLOCESTRIAE DUCATUM [C1680-1700] 58.4x48.3cm.
Mortier issue of this de Wit map [12] $226
OOST FRISE OU LE COMTE D'EMBDEN [C1700] 43.2x58.4cm.
from "Atlas Nouveau" [16] $210
ORBIS VETUS, ET ORBIS VETERIS ULTRAQUE CONTINENS, TERRARUM & TRACTUS ARCTICU,
ET ANTARCTICUS EX PLATONE. THEOPOMPO, SIVE AELIANO MANILIO, STRABONE, &C.
AUCTORE N. SANSON...AMSTELODAMI APUD P. MORTIER CUM PRIVILEGIO [C1705]
40x54.6cm. outer margins wormed [7] $775
ORIENTALIOR DISTRICTUS REGNI ANGLIAE...CANTIUM...RUTLANDIAQ [C1680-1700]
58.4x48.3cm. Mortier issue of this de Wit map [12] $237
PARTE OCCIDENTALE D'UNE PARTIE D'ASIE OU SONT LES ISLES DE ZOCOTORA, DE
L'AMIRANTE... [1692] 59.1x86.4cm. two tears in side margins, another title
"CARTE PARTICULIERE..." appears at the lower right [24] $306
PARTIE DU DUCHE DE MILAN [C1700] C57.2x86.4cm. from "Atlas Nouveau" [16] $225
PARTIE ORIENTALE DE L'AMERIQUE ANGLOISE [1700] C57.2x87.6cm.
from "Atlas Nouveau" [16] $1500
PLAN DE LA VILLE DE VIENNE [C1700] C57.2x86.4cm. from "Atlas Nouveau"
[16] $420
PLAN DE LA VILLE, CITE, UNIVERSITE ET FAUBOURGS DE PARIS [C1700]
C57.2x86.4cm. from "Atlas Nouveau," minor damage from pigment repaired
[16] $480
PRINCIPAUTE DE CATALOGNE [C1700] C57.2x86.4cm.
from "Atlas Nouveau," light browning [16] $380
PRINCIPAUTE DE TRANSILVANIE [C1700] C57.2x86.4cm.
from "Atlas Nouveau" [16] $120

MORTIER (continued)

ROMA [C1700] C57.2x86.4cm. from "Atlas Nouveau" [16] $460
SITUS TERRAE CANAAN [C1700] C57.2x86.4cm. from "Atlas Nouveau" [16] $740
TERRITOIRE DE VERONE [C1700] C57.2x86.4cm. from "Atlas Nouveau" [16] $180
THEATRE DE LA GUERRE DES COURONNES DU NORD [C1700] 47x58.4cm.
   from "Atlas Nouveau" [16] $180
TRACTUS REGNI ANGLIAE SEPTENTRION. IN QUO DUCATUS EBORACENSIS...ET LANCASTRIAE
   CUM MONA INSULA [C1680-1700] 48.3x58.4cm.
   Mortier issue of this de Wit map [12] $229

MOULE

ESSEX [1836-50] 21x26.7cm. [24] $45
HERTFORDSHIRE [1836-50] 21x26.7cm. [24] $61
WESTMORELAND [1832] 20.3x26.7cm. minor repair [30] $28
YORKSHIRE WEST RIDING [1837] 19.7x26.7cm. [30] $52
YORKSHIRE, WEST RIDING [1836-50] 20.3x26.7cm. [24] $61

MOUNT & PAGE

(ENGLISH CHANNEL) [1746] 49.5x58.4cm. title not given [17] $650
A CHART OF THE COASTS OF IRELAND AND PART OF ENGLAND [1747] 43.8x53.3cm.
   with owner's signature [17] $550
A CHART SHOWING PART OF THE SEA COAST OF NEW FOUNDLAND FROM YE BAY OF BULLS TO
   LITTLE PLACENTIA EXACTLY AND CAREFULLY LAYD DOWN BY JOHN GAUDY [1758]
   44.5x55.9cm. waterstains in margins, inset map: "A Draught of the Harbour of
   Trepassey in Newfoundland" [7] $600
A CORRECT CHART OF THE CARIBBEAN ISLANDS... [C1758] 43.8x53.3cm.
   minor repairs [3] $135
A DRAUGHT OF THE WEST END OF THE ISLAND OF PORTO RICO AND ISLAND OF ZACHEE
   [C1740] 48.3x59.1cm. [3] $145
A DRAUGHT OF VIRGINIA [1737] 45.7x58.4cm.
   minor restoration, map by Tiddeman [16] $1000
A DRAUGHT OF VIRGINIA...BY MARK TIDDEMAN. SOLD BY W. & I. MOUNT & T. PAGE ON
   TOWER HILL LONDON [C1732-51] 45.4x58.1cm. narrow margins, plate 1, state 2,
   with scrollwork around cartouch and other alterations [25] $306
A LARGE DRAUGHT OF THE ISLAND ANTEGUA [C1728-94] 26x32.5cm.
   based on the John Thornton chart of 1704 [12] $130
A NEW AND CORRECT CHART OF THE NORTH PART OF AMERICA FROM NEW FOUND LAND TO
   HUDSON'S BAY. SOLD BY W. & I. MOUNT & T. PAGE ON TOWER HILL LONDON [C1755]
   43.2x55.9cm. some staining, short repaired tear in margin [7] $425
AN EXACT DRAUGHT OF THE GULF OF DARIEN & THE COAST TO PORTO BELLO WITH PANAMA
   IN THE SOUTH SEA & THE SCOTCH SETTLEMENT IN CALLEDONIA [C1745] 43.2x54cm.
   [3] $325
BARBADOS [C1728-94] 29x25.5cm. light browning, woodcut coastal profiles of
   the edition of 1789 are printed below the chart, title appears on the island
   [12] $145
BERMUDAS [1728-94] 22x29cm.
   with sailing directions, title appears on the island [12] $199
THE HARBOUR OF CASCO BAY AND ISLANDS ADJACENT. BY CAPT. CYPRIAN SOUTHICKE. EM.
   BOWEN, SCULPT. PRINTED FOR & SOLD BY RICHD. MOUNT, THO. PAGE AND COMPANY ON
   TOWER HILL LONDON 1720 [1732] 43.2x53.3cm.
   from the 1732 ed. of "The English Pilot, The Fourth Book" [25] $176
THE SEA COAST OF ITALY FROM CAPE DELLE MELLE TO MOUNT ARGENTATO WITH THE ISLAND
   OF CORSICA [1740] 40x52.1cm. top and bottom centerfold repaired, from the
   set of charts originally published by John Seller in 1671 and reissued by
   John & Samuel Thornton [24] $99
THE SEA COAST OF LANGUEDOC PROVENCE AND PART OF ITALY, FROM CAPE DRAGON TO CAPE
   DELLE MELLE [C1732] 40.6x52.1cm. [24] $88
VIRGINIA, MARYLAND, PENNSILVANIA, EAST AND WEST NEW JERSEY [1689] 50.8x78.7cm.
   [15] $1450

MULLER

(CANARY ISLANDS) [1692] 6.5x7.5cm. [31] $45
CEILAN [1692] 6.5x7.5cm. descriptive text below map [31] $38
INSULAE ANTILLES [1692] 6.5x8cm. text below map [31] $68

MULLER (continued)

INSULAE MALDIVES [1692] 6.5x7.5cm. descriptive text below map [31] $22
INSULAE MOLOCCAE [1692] 6.5x7.5cm. descriptive text below map [31] $27
INSULAE SONDAE [1692] 6.5x7.5cm. descriptive text below map [31] $27
JAPAN [1692] 6.5x7.5cm. descriptive text below map [31] $76
NOUVELLE CARTE DES DECOUVERTES FAITES PAR DES VAISSEAUX RUSSIENS AUX COTES
 INCONNUES DE L'AMERIQUE SEPTENTRIONALE AVEC LES PAIS ADIACENTS...A ST.
 PETERSBOURG A L'ACADEMIE DES SCIENCES 1784 [1784] 50.2x66.7cm. various
 editions of this map were published from 1754 to 1784 with updated
 information [7] $875
NOUVELLE CARTE DES DECOUVERTES...RUSSIENS [1758-73] 45.7x63.5cm. margins
 somewhat ragged, 1773 revision by von Stahlin of Muller's map, with part of
 Alaska now detached from the mainland, and the Aleutians no longer a
 peninsula, with 4 old manuscript notes [23] $750
TERRAE ARCTICA [1692] 6.5x7.5cm. [31] $76

MUNSTER

(HOLY LAND) [C1560] 26.5x17cm. [4] $137
(NETHERLANDS) [C1545-59] 20.3x14cm. [24] $91
AMERICAE SIVE NOVI ORBIS, NOVA DESCRIPTIO [C1588-1628] 30.5x36cm. later
 version of the America map, a title in German appears above the top border
 [5] $1100
ANGLIAE DESCRIPTIO [1572] 26.7x34.3cm.
 minor worming in margins, first issued in 1540 [16] $420
BASLE [C1549-60] 25.5x35cm. [4] $275
BERNE (VIEW) [C1549-60] 21x30cm. French text below [4] $214
BESCHREIBUNG ENGELLANTS UND SCHOTTLANDTS [C1578] 25.4x16.5cm.
 woodcut executed for the 1578 edition [13] $160
CYPRUS [1550] 9.5x11cm. [31] $73
DAS HEILIG JUDISCH LANDT... [1544] 26.7x33cm. browned, some ink marks
 [17] $650
DE INSULIS BRITANNICIS, ALBIONE QUAE EST... [1550] 8x13cm. [31] $38
DE NOVIS INSULIS [C1550] 10.2x14.6cm.
 bird's eye view of Caribbean Islands [32] $125
DELL' ISOLE DELLA BRETTAGNE, DELL' ALBIO [1558] 7.5x13.5cm. [31] $53
DIE ERST GENERAL TAFEL [C1588-1628] 31x36cm. 2 small repaired wormholes,
 later version of world map based on Ortelius [5] $980
DIE ERST GENERAL TAFEL DIE RESCHREIBUNG UND DEN CIRKEL DES GANTZEN ERDTRICHS
 UND MEERS INNHALTENDE [C1588] 31.1x36.2cm. backed on conservators' paper,
 the later version of Munster's world map based on Ortelius [23] $700
DU LAC DE LEMAN (VIEW) [C1565] 15x16cm. French text below [4] $91
ENGELLANDT, MIT DEM ANSTOSSENDEN REICH SCHOTTLANDT, SO VORZEITEN ALBION UND
 BRITANNIA HABEN GEHEISSEN [1588-1628] 30.5x35.6cm.
 woodcut map newly engraved for the later editions [13] $298
FRIBURG IM BRISGEW (VIEW) [C1549-60] 19.5x36cm. French text below [4] $183
FRISE ORIENTALE [C1565] 20x17cm. French text above [4] $68
INDIA EXTREMA [C1550] 25.4x34.3cm.
 the earlier version of Asia with a large fish in the Indian Ocean [14] $298
L'ISLE DE CYPRE [C1565] 10x15cm. French text below [4] $76
LA TABLES DES ISLES NEUVUES [C1540] 25.4x34.3cm. shows N. & S. America
 [15] $2000
LONDINUM... [C1598] 23x36.5cm. [4] $444
NOU GRECIA... [1540] 25.4x34.3cm. shows modern Greece [17] $450
S.M. ANNO AETATIS SUAE 60 (PORTRAIT) [1559] 16.2x13.3cm. on the verso of the
 title page to "Cosmogrphiae universalis," accompanied by the last leaf with
 imprint [25] $114
TABULA NOVARUM INSULARUM [C1555] 27.9x34.3cm. shows N. & S. America [16] $2000
TABULA NOVARUM INSULARUM... [C1544] 25.5x34cm. shows America [39] $1050
TYPUS ORBIS UNIVERSALIS [1540-72] 26.7x36.8cm. shows the world [15] $1450
TYPUS ORBIS UNIVERSALIS [C1550] 27.9x36.8cm. 2nd state, cut by Kandel
 [16] $1250

MURPHY & CO.
MAP OF BALTIMORE PREPARED FOR THE STRANGER'S GUIDE IN BALTIMORE. MURPHY & CO.
  PUBLISHERS. 1876. WM. SIDES, SURVEYOR. LITH. BY A. HOEN & CO...ENTERED
  ACCORDING TO THE ACT OF CONGRESS, IN THE YEAR 1871, BY JOHN W. WOODS...
  [1876] 28.6x52.7cm.   [25] $53
MURRAY
CHART OF THE DISCOVERIES & ROUTE OF HIS MAJESTY'S SHIPS HECLA & GRIPER ON
  SEARCH OF A NORTH WEST PASSAGE... [1821] 34.9x94.6cm.   [3] $145
SKETCH OF NORTH AMERICA SHEWING THE PROPOSED ROUTES OF CAPT. BACK [1853]
  24.8x30.5cm. backed, Bradbury Lith., London   [3] $30
SURVEY OF WINTER HARBOUR MELVILLE ISLAND JUNE 1820. J. WALKER, SCULPT.
  PUBLISHED BY JOHN MURRAY...LONDON JUNE 1821 [1821] 24.1x17.1cm.   [25] $30
THE VIRGIN ISLANDS SHEWING THE SET OF THE TIDE [1835] 19.1x41.9cm.   [3] $65
NATIONAL GEOGRAPHIC SOCIETY
MAP OF THE VALLEY OF THE ORINOCO RIVER [1896] 26x40.6cm.
  from February 1896 issue   [30] $4
NEELE
CARACCAS AND GUYANAS [1814] 19.1x24.1cm.   [3] $30
MAP OF THE CITY OF QUEBEC [1792] 20x20.5cm.
  from Trusler, "The Habitable World Described..."   [21] $77
NORTH AMERICA [C1840] 43.8x53.3cm. minor repair, trimmed   [30] $69
SOUTH AMERICA [1796] 23.5x19.1cm. right margin narrow   [30] $36
UNITED STATES OF AMERICA [1797] 19.7x24.1cm.   [30] $36
NEPTUNE FRANCOIS
See also DEPOT DE LA MARINE
See also JAILLOT
NEWBERY
CAVENDISH PLUNDERS & BURNS PAITA [1773] 10.2x15.2cm.
  J. June sc., London, a view of the city burning   [3] $35
NICOLOSI
(JAPAN) [1661] 38.5x44.5cm. from Nicolosi's "Geografico"   [31] $344
(PHILIPPINES) [1661] 38x44cm. untitled, from Nicolosi's "Geographico"
                                                                        [31] $498
(WESTERN HEMISPHERE) [1661] 54x42cm. from Nicolosi's "Geografico"   [31] $1149
ITALIA SECUNDUM DOMINATUS DESCRIPTA PER IOANNEM BAPTISTAM NICOLOSIUM. S.T.D.
  [C1660] 40x45.7cm.
  minor foxing, minor browning at centerfold, a gore of northern Russia
                                                                        [7] $200
NOLIN
LA PARTIE MERIDIONALE DES PAYS-BAS, CONNUE SOUS LE NOM DE FLANDRE...PAR LE P.
  CORONELLI, CORRIGEE PAR LE SR. DE TILLEMONT [1690] 44.5x60cm.   [18] $140
LE COMTE DE HAYNAUT...LE COMTE DE CAMBRESIS...PAR I.B. NOLIN [1696] 46x57cm.
                                                                        [18] $105
LES PROVINCES UNIES OU LA PARTIE SEPTENTRIONALE DES PAYS-BAS CONNUE SOUS LE NOM
  DE HOLLANDE. PARIS, NOLIN, 1690. H. VAN LOON SCULPT. [1690] 46x60cm.
                                                                        [18] $140
LIEGE ET PARTIE DE L'EVESCHE DE LIEGE [C1695] 21x46.5cm.
  a plan with a map of the surrounding region   [18] $70
NORDEN
MIDDLESEX OLIMA TRINOBANTIBUS HABITATA [1607-37] 27.3x26cm.
  lower margin extended, minor overinking by printer   [24] $130
NORWOOD
GEOLOGICAL MAP OF PARTS OF MINNESOTA AND WISCONSIN, DESIGNED TO SHOW PORTIONS
  OF THE ROCK FORMATIONS NOW CONCEALED BY DRIFT BY J.G. NORWOOD [1852]
  25.4x19.1cm.   [11] $25
NUREMBERG CHRONICLE
See SCHEDEL
NUTTALL, FISHER & DIXON
STATES OF AMERICA [1814] 19.1x22.9cm.   [9] $50
OGILBY
(ROAD MAP, BAGSHOT-SALISBURY) [1675] 31.8x47cm. right margin extended
                                                                       [24] $168

OGILBY (continued)
```
(ROAD MAP, BRISTOL-BANBURY) [1675-98] 33x45.1cm.                      [24]   $107
(ROAD MAP, BRISTOL-LUDLOW) [1675] 34.3x43.2cm. 1st issue              [24]   $107
(ROAD MAP, BURTON FERRY-ST. DAVIDS) [1675-98] 33x44.5cm.             [24]    $99
(ROAD MAP, CHELMSFORD-SAFFRON WALDEN) [1675] 33x42.5cm.              [24]   $107
(ROAD MAP, GLOUCESTER-MONTGOMERY) [1675] 31.8x43.2cm.                [24]    $91
(ROAD MAP, HUNTINGDON-IPSWICH) [1675] 32.4x45.7cm. 1st issue         [24]   $114
(ROAD MAP, KING'S LYNN-HARWICH) [1675] 34.3x43.8cm. 1st issue        [24]   $114
(ROAD MAP, LONDON TO NEWHAVEN) [1695-98] 34.3x43.2cm.                [13]   $130
(ROAD MAP, LONDON-NEW SHORHAM) [1675-98] 34.3x43.2cm.                [24]   $229
(ROAD MAP, TALYBONT-HOLYWELL) [1675] 34.3x44.5cm. 1st issue          [24]    $91
(ROAD MAP, WINCHESTER-CREWKERNE) [1675] 31.8x43.8cm. 1st issue       [24]   $122
AMERICA [1671] 27.9x15.2cm. allegorical titlepiece                   [3]    $80
CUSCO [1671] 26.7x35.6cm.                                            [3]   $120
NOVA VIRGINIAE TABULA [1671] 29.2x35.6cm.                           [33]   $600
NOVUM AMSTERODAMUM [1670-71] 12.7x16.5cm.
    on a sheet approximately 41 x 25 cm., with text                 [23]   $225
PAGUS HISPANORUM IN FLORIDA (VIEW) [1671] 26.7x35.6cm.
    minor repairs, shows St. Augustine                              [3]   $235
TRUXILLO (VIEW) [1671] 28.6x34.3cm.                                  [3]   $110
TRUXILLO (VIEW) [1670] 27.2x33.8cm.                                 [39]    $55
URBIS DOMINGO IN HISPANIOLA [1670] 28.6x35.1cm.                     [39]    $75
VENEZUELA CUM PARTE AUSTRALI NOVAE ANDALUSIAE [1667] 28.5x35.5cm.   [39]   $195
VIRGINIAE PARTIS AUSTRALIS, ET FLORIDAE PARTIS ORIENTALIS... [1673]
    28.9x35.4cm.                                                   [39]   $395
YUCATAN CONVENTUS JURIDICI HISPANIAE NOVAE PARS OCCIDENTALIS, ET GUATIMALA
    CONVENTUS JURIDICUS [1671] 28.3x35.6cm. centerfold reinforced  [25]   $114
```
OLNEY
```
MAP OF TEXAS [1844-49] 26.7x21.6cm.                                 [19]   $125
MAP OF THE UNITED STATES, CANADA, TEXAS & PART MEXICO [1844] 27.3x44.5cm.
    minor repairs                                                   [3]    $65
```
ORTELIUS (FOLIO)
```
(TITLE PAGE TO "PARERGON") [1592] 35.6x22.9cm.                      [15]   $285
ABRAHAM PATRIARCHAE PEREGRINATIO ET VITA [1590-92] 35.6x45.7cm.     [15]  $1750
AEVI VETERIS TYPUS GEOGRAPHICUS [1606] 31.8x44.5cm.
    minor browning, English text on verso                          [16]   $500
AEVI VETERIS, TYPUS GEOGRAPHICUS [1590] 30.5x43.5cm.                [4]    $398
AMERICAE SIVE NOVE ORBIS, NOVA DESCRIPTIO [1587-1603] 35.6x48.3cm. from the
    1603 Latin edition, later version of this map without the South American
    bulge                                                          [23]  $2500
AMERICAE SIVE NOVE ORBIS, NOVA DESCRIPTIO [1587] 35.6x48.3cm. minor
    offsetting of color, from the French 1587 edition, later version of this map
    without the South American bulge                               [23]  $2500
AMERICAE SIVE NOVI•ORBIS'NOVA DESCRIPTIO [1587] 35.6x48.3cm.
    light offsetting, 2nd version with no bulge in S. America coast [15]  $2750
AMERICAE SIVE NOVI ORBIS, NOVA DESCRIPTIO [1588] 36x48cm. centerfold
    reinforced, tear in engraved surface repaired, later version with bulge in
    South America removed                                          [7]   $2600
AMERICAE SIVE NOVI ORBIS, NOVA DESCRIPTIO [1587-1601] 35.5x48.5cm.
    3rd version of this map                                        [5]   $3000
ANGLIAE REGNI FLORENTISSIMI [1601] 38.1x47cm. first published in 1573
                                                                   [16]   $450
ANGLIAE, SCOTIAE ET HIBERNIAE [1598] 34.3x49.5cm. margins narrow   [16]   $630
ANGLIAE, SCOTIAE ET HIBERNIAE SIVE BRITANNICAR: INSULARUM DESCRIPTIO [1570]
    34.3x49.5cm.                                                   [17]  $1000
ANGLIAE, SCOTIAE ET HIBERNIAE, BRITANNICAE INSULAE... [1573] 34.5x49.5cm.
                                                                   [31]   $452
ANGLIAE, SCOTIAE, ET HIBERNIAE, SIVE BRITANNICAR: INSULARUM DESCRIPTIO [1598]
    34.3x49.5cm. light browning, centerfold browning               [26]   $375
ASIAE NOVA DESCRIPTIO [1570] 36.8x48.3cm.                          [17]  $1500
```

ATREBATUM REGIONIS VERA DESCRIPTIO. JOHANNE SURHONIO MONTENSI AUCTORE
   [1584-1606] 37.5x48.9cm.
   upper corners reinforced, English text on verso   [24] $122
AUSTRIAE DUCATUS CHOROGRAPHIA, WOLFGANGO LAZIO AUCTORE [1598] 34x47cm.
                                                                      [26] $275
BRABANTIAE...DESCRIPTIO. JACOBO A DAVENTRIA AUCT [1570] 36.5x50cm.   [18] $280
BRABANTIAE...DESCRIPTIO. JACOBO A DAVENTRIA AUCT [1570] 36.5x50cm.
   no text on verso, issued before inclusion in atlas   [18] $351
BRITANNICARUM INSULARUM TYPUS [1595] 36.8x52.1cm.   [16] $480
CALETENSIUM ET BONONI ENSIUM DITIONIS ACCURATA DELINATIO/VEROMANDUORUM EORUM
   QUE CONFINIUM EXACTISSIMA DISCRIPTIO. IOHANNE SURHONIO AUCTORE [C1592]
   33.7x48.3cm.   [7] $250
CAMBRIAE TYPUS [1579] 38.1x49.5cm.
   margins narrow & repaired, wormhole just affecting border, 1st state[16] $420
CRETA... [1584] 33.7x48.3cm. shows Crete, Corsica & Sardinia   [17] $475
CULIACANAE AMERICAE REGIONIS DESCRIPTIO/HISPANIOLA, CUBAE ALIARUMQUE
   INSULARUM...DELINEATIO [1580] 36x50cm.   [2] $368
CULIACANAE AMERICAE.../HISPANIOLAE, CUBAE ALIARUM QUE INSULARUM... [1578]
   45x50cm.   [31] $459
CYPRI INSULAE NOVA DESCRIPT [C1580] 36x50cm.   [2] $439
DESCRIPTIO GERMNAIAE INFERIORIS [C1570] 38x51cm.   [18] $351
ERYN, HIBERNIAE BRITANNICAE INSULAE, NOVA DESCRIPTIO. IRLANDT [1573]
   35.6x48.3cm.   [13] $298
EUROPAE [1574] 34x46cm.   [26] $550
EUROPAE [1570] 34.3x46.4cm.   [24] $306
FLANDRIA GERARDUS MERCATOR RUPELMANDANUS DESCRIBEBAT [1570] 38x50cm.
   no text on verso, issued before inclusion in atlas   [18] $351
FLANDRIA GERARDUS MERCATOR RUPELMANDANUS DESCRIBEBAT [1570] 38x50cm. [18] $280
FRISIA OCCIDENTALIS, 1579... [C1570] 36x49cm.   [18] $351
GALLIAE REGNI POTENTISS. NOVA DESCRIPTIO, IOANNE IOLIVETO AUCTORE [1592]
   35x50.5cm.   [2] $140
GELRIAE, CLIVIAE... [C1570] 37x50cm.   [18] $280
GERMANIA [1570] 36.2x50.2cm.   [17] $850
GRAECIAE UNIVERSAE SECUNDUM HODIERNUM SITUM NEOTERICA DESCRIPTIO [1598]
   36.2x50.8cm.   [26] $400
GRAECIAE UNIVERSAE SECUNDUM HODIERNUM SITUM NEOTERICA DESCRIPTIO [1570]
   36.2x51.4cm.   [17] $850
HELVETIAE DESCRIPTIO AEGIDIO TSCHUDI AUCT. [1574] 34.5x45.5cm.   [2] $421
HIBERNIAE BRITANNICAE INSULAE, NOVA DESCRIPTIO... [1573] 49x34.5cm. [31] $344
HIBERNIAE... [1598] 35.6x48.3cm. margins narrow   [16] $420
HISPALENSIS CONVENTUS DELINEATIO... [1579] 34.3x45.7cm.   [17] $575
HISPANIAE NOVAE SIVE MAGNAE RECENS ET VERA DESCRIPTIO [1579] 35x50.5cm.
                                                                      [2] $193
HOLLANDIAE...NOVA DESCRIPTIO... [1570] 35x48.7cm.   [18] $421
HOLLANDIAE...NOVA DESCRIPTIO... [1570] 35x48.7cm.   [18] $351
HUNGARIAE DESCRIPTIO. WOLFGANGO LAZIO AUCT... [1570-84] 34.9x49.5cm.
   several small wormholes repaired   [24] $104
INDIAE ORIENTALIS [1603] 34x48cm.   [31] $613
INDIAE ORIENTALIS INSULARUMQUE ADIACENTIUM TYPUS [1574] 35x50cm.   [2] $421
INSULARUM ALIQUOT MARIS MEDITERRANEI [1584] 33.7x48.9cm.
   shows Mediterranean islands   [17] $475
ISLANDIA [1589] 34x49cm. repaired wormhole   [2] $790
ISLANDIA [1598] 33.7x48.9cm.   [26] $1600
JAPONIAE INSULAE DESCRIPTIO [C1595-1602] 35.5x48.5cm.   [4] $1226
LA FLORIDA/GUASTECAN REG./PERUVIAE AURIFERAE REGIONIS TYPUS [C1584] 33x46.4cm.
   minor browning in margin   [23] $1000
LA FLORIDA/PERUVIAE AURIFERAE REGIONIS TYPUS/GUASTECAN REG. [1584] 33x45.7cm.
                                                                     [15] $1350
LEODIENSIS DIOCESIS TYPUS [1584] 38x49cm.   [18] $245
LEODIENSIS DIOCESIS TYPUS [1584] 38x49cm.
   no text on verso, issued before inclusion in atlas   [18] $351

ORTELIUS (FOLIO) (continued)

LUTZENBURGENSIS DUCATUS VERISS DESCRIPT. IACOBO SURHONIO MONTANO AUCTORE
[1592] 36.7x49.5cm. fold reinforced   [18] $280
LUTZENBURGENSIS DUCATUS VERISS. DESCRIPT. IACOBO SURHONIO MONTANO AUCTORE
[1592] 36.5x49cm.   [2] $316
MARIS PACIFICI (QUOD VULGO MAR DEL ZUR) CUM REGIONIBUS CIRCUMIACENTIBUS,
INSULISQUE IN CODEM PASSIM SPARIS, NOVISSIMA DESCRIPTIO...1589 [C1590]
37.5x50.8cm.   [7] $2600
MARIS PACIFICI... [1589] 34.3x49.5cm.   [17] $2800
NAMURCUM, COMITATUS. IOES. SURHON DESCRIB. 1579 [1579] 39x51cm.
no text on verso, issued before inclusion in atlas   [18] $210
NAMURCUM, COMITATUS. IOES. SURHON DESCRIB. 1579 [1579] 39x51cm.   [18] $175
NATOLIAE, QUAE OLIM ASIA MINOR, NOVA DESCRIPTIO. AEGYPTI RE CENTOR DE SCRIPTO.
CARTHAGINIS CELEBERRIMI SINUS TYPUS [C1570] 29.2x48.9cm.
minor browning in margins   [7] $325
NOBILIS HANNONIAE COMITATUS DESCRIP. AUCTORE IACOBO SURHONIO MONTANO [1579]
37x49cm.   [18] $140
OOST ENDE WEST VRIESLANDTS, 1568... [1570] 34x51cm.   [18] $351
PALAESTINA SIVE TOTIUS TERRAE PROMISSIONIS NOVA DESCRIPTIO [1570] 34.5x46.5cm.
                                                                       [2] $403
PICARDIAE BELGICAE REGIONIS DESCRIPTIO. JOANNE SURHONIO AUCTORE [1579-1606]
33x50.5cm. English text on verso   [24] $130
PICARDIAE, BELGICAE REGIONIS DESCRIPTIO. IOANNE SURHONIO AUCTORE. CUM IMP. ET
REG PRIVILEGIO DECENN. 1579. [C1592] 33x50.8cm.   [7] $225
POICTOU. PICTONUM VICINARUM QUE REGIONUM FIDISS DESCRIPTIO. AUCTORE NOBILI DUO
PETRO ROGIERO... [C1592] 36.2x50.2cm.   [7] $225
POLONIAE, LITUANIAEQ. DESCRIPTIO. AUCTORE WENCESLAV GODRECCIO; ET CORRECTORE
ANDREA POGRABIO PILSNENSI [1598] 36.8x48.3cm.   [26] $450
PORTUGALLIAE QUE OLIM LUSITANIA... [1598] 33.7x50.2cm.   [26] $275
PRESBITERI IOHANNIS, SIVE ABISSINORUM IMPERII DESCRIPTIO [1598] 36.8x43.5cm.
                                                                       [26] $450
REGNI BOHEMIAE DESCRIPTIO [1570-84] 33x50.8cm.   [24] $99
ROMANIAE, (QUAE OLIM THRACIA DICTA) VICINORUMQ REGIONUM, UTI BULGARIAE,
WALCHIAE, SYRSIAE, ETC. DESCRIPTIO, AUCTORE IACOBO CASTALDO. CUM PRIVILEGIO
DECENNALI... [1592] 36.8x50.8cm.   [7] $250
RUSSIAE, MOSCOVIAE ET TARTARIAE DESCRIPTIO AUCTORE ANTONIO IENKENSONO ANGLO...
[1598] 34.9x44.5cm.   [26] $475
RUSSIAE... [1570] 35.6x44.5cm.   [17] $750
SCHLAVONIAE, CROATIAE, CARNIAE, ISTRIAE, BOSNIAE... [1570-1606] 33x45.7cm.
upper corners reinforced, English text on verso   [24] $119
SCOTIAE TABULA [C1602] 35.5x47.5cm.   [4] $383
SCOTIAE TABULA [1592] 36.8x48.3cm.   [16] $390
SEPTENTRIONALIUM REGIONUM DESCRIP. [1603] 35.9x48.9cm.   [26] $1350
SEPTENTRIONALIUM REGIONUM DESCRIP. [1570] 36.2x49.5cm.
minor offsetting, minor repair   [17] $850
SEPTENTRIONALIUM REGIONUM DESCRIP. [C1579] 36.5x49cm.   [4] $843
TARTARIAE [1608] 34.3x47cm. light browning   [32] $850
TARTARIAE SIVE MAGNI CHAMI REGNI [1570] 33.7x47cm.   [17] $1500
TARTARIAE SIVE MAGNI CHAMI REGNI TYPUS [1570] 34.9x47cm.
minor browning at centerfold   [23] $1100
TARTARIAE SIVE MAGNI CHAMI REGNI TYPUS [C1603] 35.5x47cm.   [4] $689
TARTARIAE SIVE MAGNI CHAMI REGNI TYPUS [1574] 35x47.5cm.   [2] $526
TARTARIAE SIVE MAGNI CHAMI REGNI TYPUS CONTINET HEC TABULA OEM TARTARIUM, CUM
RELIQUA ASIA ORIENTSARIORIS USQ, OCEANU EUOM PARTE, MAGNO CHAMO OBEDIENTE...
[1612] 34.9x47cm. margins ragged, minor browning   [7] $1175
TERRA SANCTA A PETRO LAICSTAIN PERLUSTRATA...ET A CHR. SCHROT IN TABULAM
REDACTA [1584] 36.5x50.5cm.   [2] $421
TERRA SANCTA, A PETRO LAICSTAIN PERLUSTRATA, ET AB EIUS ORE ET SCHEDIA A
CHRISTIANO SCHROT IN TABULAM REDACTA [1584] 36.8x50.8cm.   [26] $1000
TERRA SANCTA... [1584] 36.8x49.5cm.   [17] $1600
TYPUS ORBIS TERRARUM [1587] 35.6x49.5cm.
early version with clouds in border   [15] $3200

ORTELIUS (FOLIO) (continued)

TYPUS ORBIS TERRARUM [1606] 34.3x49.5cm.
  minor centerfold repairs, English text on verso   [16] $2500
TYPUS ORBIS TERRARUM [1570-87] 33x48.9cm. from the French 1587 edition
                                    [23] $3000
TYPUS ORBIS TERRARUM [1587-1612] 36x49cm.
  lower centerfold reinforced, second version of Ortelius world map [5] $2600
UTRIUSQUE FRISIORUM REGIONIS NOVISS: DESCRIPTIO 1686 [1586-1606] 34.3x50.8cm.
  minor repairs to margins, English text on verso   [24] $245
VALENTIAE REGNI... [1584] 34.3x49.5cm.   [17] $525
ZELANDICARUM INSULARUM EXACTISSIMA ET NOVA DESCRIPTIO, AUCTORE D. IACOBO A
  DAVENTRIA [1570] 33.5x46.7cm.   [18] $351
ZELANDICARUM INSULARUM EXACTISSIMA ET NOVA DESCRIPTIO, AUCTORE D. IACOBO A
  DAVENTRIA [1570] 33.5x46.7cm.
  trial proof published before the first atlas, no text   [18] $702

ORTELIUS (MINIATURE)
AEGYPTUS [1609] 8.9x11.4cm.   [9] $35
AMERICA SIVE NOVUS ORBIS [1603] 7.6x10.2cm.   [10] $275
ANGLIA [1577] 11x8cm. framed   [31] $58
CANDIA [1603] 7.6x10.8cm.   [11] $40
CHINA REGIO ASIE [1603] 7.6x10.2cm.   [10] $70
CORSICAE [1609] 8.5x12.5cm.   [31] $42
HELVETIA [1603] 7.6x10.2cm.   [10] $50
HIBERNIA [1603] 7.6x10.2cm.   [10] $50
IAPONIA INSULA. [1603] 7.6x10.2cm.   [10] $70
ISCHIA [1609] 8.5x12.5cm.   [31] $42
LUTZEBURG [1601] 8.1x10.5cm.   [18] $351
PRESBITERI IOHANNIS SIVE ABISSINORUM IMPERIUM [C1600] 7.6x10.2cm. [10] $50
SARDINIA [1609] 8.5x12.5cm.   [31] $38
SEPTEMTRIONALES REG. [1603] 7.6x10.2cm.   [10] $65
SICILIAE [1609] 8.5x12.5cm.   [31] $42
TARTARIAE SIVE MAGNI CHAMI REGNI TYPUS [1595] 7.6x10.8cm.   [11] $150

OTTENS
AMERICA GEDRUCKT TOT AMSTERDAM BY R AND J OTTENS OP DEN NIEWE DRUK UIT DER
  WERELDT KAART [1740] 135x170cm.
  fair condition, as typical of wall maps   [31] $3832
AMERIQUE SEPTENTRIONALE DIVISEE EN SES PRINCIPALES PARTIES. PRESENTE A
  MONSEIGNEUR LE DUC DE BOURGOGNE. PAR...H. JAILLOT. A AMSTERDAM CHEZ R. & J.
  OTTENS [C1740-50] 48.3x58.4cm.
  ends of centerfold reinforced, embossed library stamp at upper right[7] $1075
CARTE DES POSSESSIONS ANGLOISES & FRANCOISES DU CONTINENT DE L'AMERIQUE
  SEPTENTRIONALE. KAART VAN DE ENGELSCHE EN FRANSCHE BEZITTENGEN IN HET VASTE
  LANDE VAN NOORD AMERICA, 1755. A AMSTERDAM CHEZ R. ET J. OTTENS, GEOGRAPHES
  [1755] 45.7x57.2cm.
  minor spotting in margin, minor restoration of "explication" portion[7] $525
CARTE MARINE DE LA MER CASPIENE LEVEE SUIVANT LES ORDRES DE S.M. CZARIENNE, PAR
  MR. CARL VANVERDEN EN 1719, 1720, ET 1724. ET REDUITE AU MERDIEN DE PARIS PAR
  GUILLAUME DELISLE...A AMSTERDAM PAR REINER OTTENS EN 1723 [1723]
  88.9x60.3cm.   [7] $475
CARTE NOUVELLE DE TOUT L'EMPIRE DE LA GRANDE RUSSIE DANS L'ESTAT OU IL S'EST
  TROUVE A LA MORT DE PIERRE LE GRAND. DRESSEE SUR DES OBSERVATIONS TOUTES
  NOUVELLS...AVEC PRIVILEGE. A AMSTERDAM [1726] 47.6x65.4cm.
  based on a map by Strahlenberg   [7] $400
DUCATUM LIVONIA ET CURLANDIA... [C1755] 48.5x58cm.   [4] $68
HEMISPHERE SEPTENTRIONALE and HEMISPHERE MERIDIONALE [C1745] 45.7x60.3cm. a
  pair of polar maps, dimensions are for each, a reissue of de l'Isle's maps
                                   [17] $1200
LE CANADA OU PARTIE DE LA NOUVELLE FRANCE DANS L'AMERIQUE SEPTENTRIONALE,
  CONTENANT LA TERRE DE LABRADOR, LA NOUVELLE FRANCE, LES ISLES DE TERRE
  NEUVE...H. IALLOT A AMSTERDAM CHEZ R. & J. OTTENS [C1740] 47x59.7cm.
                                   [7] $775

OWEN
GEOLOGICAL CHART OF PART OF IOWA, WISCONSIN, AND ILLINOIS [1844] 58.4x45.7cm.
narrow left margin, from David Dale Owen, "Report of a Geological
Exploration of Part of Iowa, Wisconsin, and Illinois, Made...in the...year
1839"   [27] $75
OWEN & BOWEN
BEDFORDSHIRE [1720-64] C17.8x11.4cm.
from J. Owen & E. Bowen, "Britannia Depicta"   [14] $24
CAMBRIDGESHIRE [1720-64] C17.8x11.4cm.   [14] $26
HAMPSHIRE [1720-64] C17.8x11.4cm.   [14] $26
HERTFORDSHIRE [1720-64] C17.8x11.4cm.   [14] $27
NOTTINGHAMSHIRE [1720-64] C17.8x11.4cm.   [14] $21
OXFORDSHIRE [1720-64] C17.8x11.4cm.   [14] $24
RADNORSHIRE [1720-64] C17.8x11.4cm.   [14] $12
YORKSHIRE E.R. [1720-64] C17.8x11.4cm.   [14] $27
YORKSHIRE W.R. [1720-64] C17.8x11.4cm.   [14] $29
PARKE
SAN FRANCISCO BAY TO THE PLAINS OF LOS ANGELES FROM EXPLORATIONS & SURVEYS
UNDER DIRECTION OF JEFFERSON DAVIS, SEC. OF WAR...DRAWN BY H. CUSTER [1855]
71.8x88.3cm. map by J.G. Parke   [3] $95
PARKER
MAP OF OREGON TERRITORY [1838] 35.6x57.5cm. backed with rice paper, folds
reinforced, minor repairs, from Samuel Parker "Journal of an Exploring Tour
Beyond the Rocky Mountains"   [33] $350
MAP OF OREGON TERRITORY [1838] 35.6x55.9cm. narrow right margin, small piece
of border scale missing, minor tear into map repaired   [22] $225
PARRY
CHART OF HUDSON'S STRAIT & SIR THOS. ROWE'S WELCOME, SHEWING THE TRACK &
DISCOVERIES OF H.M.S. GRIPER [1825] 18.4x36.8cm.   [23] $60
GENERAL CHART SHEWING THE TRACK OF H.M. SHIPS FURY AND HECLA, ON A VOYAGE FOR
THE DISCOVERY OF A NORTH WEST PASSAGE, AD. 1821-22-23 [1824] 25.4x59.7cm.
                                                                    [23] $70
GENERAL CHART SHEWING THE TRACK OF HMS HECLA & GRIPER, FROM THE ORKNEYS TO
MELVILLE ISLAND, NORTH GEORGIA [1821] 25.4x61cm. 1st ed.   [3] $85
PAYNE
THE STATE OF CAROLINA FROM THE BEST AUTHORITIES 1799 [1799] 18.7x21.3cm.
from "Payne's Geography," New York, light staining, two vertical folds
                                                                     [1] $75
THE STATE OF PENNSYLVANIA FROM THE LATEST SURVEYS 1800 [1800] 18.4x26cm.
J. Low, N.Y., publisher   [3] $60
PEABODY & CO.
MAP OF THE CITY OF NEW YORK [C1834] 38.7x30.5cm. backed   [3] $25
PELHAM
SNUG CORNER COVE IN PRINCE WILLIAM'S SOUND [1808] 14x19.7cm.
from C. Pelham, "The World"   [25] $15
PENDLETON
VIEW OF PORTLAND IN 1832, TAKEN FROM FORT PREBLE, ON PURPOODUCK POINT
[1831-33] 15.2x34.3cm. backed with rice paper, traces of original folds,
view of Portland, Maine, lithographed by Pendleton's Lithography, Boston for
William Willis, "The History of Portland, Maine"   [36] $165
PERELLE
LIEGE 1693 (PANORAMIC VIEW) [C1700] 17x50cm.   [18] $175
LUXEMBOURG (VIEW) [C1670] 11x15cm. engraved by A. Perelle   [18] $140
PERTHES
ETHNOGRAPHISCHE KARTE VON NORDAMERIKA [1846] 37.1x39.7cm.   [22] $140
VEREIN-STAATEN VON NORD-AMERICA MIT AUSNAHME FLORIDAS UND DER WESTLICHEN
TERRITORIEN [1869] 34.9x39.4cm.   [3] $50
PETRI
See MUNSTER
PHILIP
CANADA, NOVA SCOTIA & NEW BRUNSWICK &C. [C1852] 50x60.5cm.   [21] $77

PHILIP (continued)
    ISLANDS IN THE ATLANTIC [1853] 49.5x59.7cm. 4 maps on one sheet   [24] $76
    THE WORLD ON MERCATOR'S PROJECTION [1852] 50.8x61cm.   [3] $50
    UNITED STATES INCLUDING CALIFORNIA, TEXAS &C. [1851] 52.1x61cm. backed
                                                                             [3] $115
PHILLIPS
    CHART OF BEHRING'S STRAIT, UPON MERCATOR'S PROJECTION [1821] 19.7x19.7cm.
                                                                             [3] $50
    VIEW OF THE ISLE OF ST. THOMAS [C1806] 12.1x16.5cm.   [3] $60
PICQUET
    NOUVELLE CARTE DU POLE ARTIQUE [C1785] 17.8x20.3cm. folding   [23] $50
    STATE OF NEW YORK [1806] 20.3x24.1cm. folding   [23] $55
PIGOT & CO.
    ESSEX [1831] 22.2x34.9cm.   [24] $58
PINKERTON
    BRITISH POSSESSIONS IN NORTH AMERICA [1814] 50.8x68.6cm.   [16] $160
    BRITISH POSSESSIONS IN NORTH AMERICA. FROM MR. ARROWSMITH'S MAP OF NORTH
        AMERICA... [1814] 50x69.5cm.   [21] $154
    NORTH AMERICA [1812] 50.8x71.1cm. backed   [3] $160
    SOUTH AMERICA [1811] 68.6x49.5cm.   [3] $80
    SPANISH DOMINIONS IN NORTH AMERICA MIDDLE PART [1811] 50.8x69.9cm.
        backed   [3] $85
    SPANISH DOMINIONS IN NORTH AMERICA, SOUTHERN PART [1811] 50.8x69.9cm.
        backed, minor repairs   [3] $80
    SPANISH DOMINIONS IN NORTH AMERICA. MIDDLE PART. PINKERTON'S MODERN ATLAS.
        DRAWN UNDER THE DIRECTION OF MR. PINKERTON BY L. HERBERT. NEELE, SCULPT.
        LONDON PUBLISHED SEPTR. 1ST 1811, BY CADELL & DAVIES...& LONGMAN, HURST,
        REES, & BROWN... [1811] 50.8x69.9cm.   [25] $91
    THE WORLD ON MERCATOR'S PROJECTION [1812] 69.9x50.8cm.
        on 2 sheets, dimensions are for each   [3] $125
    UNITED STATES OF AMERICA NORTHERN PART [1810] 51.4x69.9cm.   [3] $150
    UNITED STATES OF AMERICA SOUTHERN PART [1809] 52.1x69.9cm.   [3] $165
PITT
    TAVARICA CHERSONESUS, HODIE PRZCOPSCA, ET GAZARA DICTUR. EXCUDEBANT JANSSONIO
        WAESBERGII, ET MOSES PITT [C1680] 38.1x49.5cm.   [7] $175
PLANCIUS
    ORBIS TERRARUM TYPUS DE INTEGRO MULTIS IN LOCIS EMENDATUS [C1590] 27.9x50.8cm.
                                                                             [15] $2600
    ORBIS TERRARUM TYPUS... [1594] 40.6x56.5cm. repaired, margins restored
                                                                             [32] $6500
PLUCHE
    MAPPEMONDE POUR LA CONCORDE DE LA GEOGRAPHIE [1785] 14x27cm.
        minor offsetting   [23] $85
POIRSON
    AMERIQUE SEPTENTRIONALE, PAR J.B. POIRSON, 1830 [1830] 22x31.5cm.
        from "Traite Elementaire de Geographie"   [21] $36
    CARTE DES DEUX FLORIDES ET DE LA LOUISIANE INFERIEURE... [1807] 40.4x67cm.
        without margins as issued   [39] $235
    CARTE DES DEUX FLORIDES ET DE LA LOUISIANE INFERIEURE... [1807] 40.6x66cm.
        left margin trimmed for binding into book, small tear repaired, from Robin,
        "Voyages dans l'Interieur de la Louisiane..."   [23] $225
    PARTIE SEPTENTRIONALE DE L'OCEAN PACIFIQUE OU L'ON A MARQUE LES DISCOUVERTES ET
        LES ROUTES DE MRS. DE LA PEROUSE ET COOK. PAR J.B. POIRSON INGENIEUR
        GEOGRAPHE [C1824] 38.7x49.5cm. 2 short tears in upper margin   [7] $300
POLITICAL MAGAZINE
    A CHART OF THE ISLAND OF JAMAICA, WITH BAYS, HARBOURS, ROCKS, SOUNDINGS &C.
        [1780] 25.6x37.8cm.   [39] $45
    A DRAUGHT OF THE HARBOURS OF PORT ROYAL AND KINGSTON, IN JAMAICA WITH THE
        FORTIFICATIONS CORRECTLY LAID DOWN... [1782] 26x36.5cm.
        includes 1/2 page of descriptive text   [39] $65

161

A GENERAL CHART EXHIBITING THE DISCOVERIES MADE BY CAPTN. JAMES COOK IN THIS
AND HIS TWO PRECEEDING VOYAGES; WITH THE TRACKS OF THE SHIPS UNDER HIS
COMMAND [1784] 54.6x88.9cm. folding map, backed, tear into right border,
several minor defects along folds repaired, dated December 1784   [27] $350

A MAP AND CHART OF THOSE PARTS OF THE BAY OF CHESAPEAK, YORK AND JAMES RIVERS
WHICH ARE AT PRESENT THE SEAT OF WAR [1781] 25.6x37.9cm.
with 4 pages of text   [39] $70

A MAP OF EAST AND WEST FLORIDA, GEORGIA AND LOUISIANA...THE GULF OF MEXICO WITH
THE TRACT OF THE SPANISH GALLEONS... [1781] 27.3x36.7cm.
with half-page of text   [39] $45

A MAP OF MEXICO OR NEW SPAIN... [1781] 27.7x36.5cm.
with 5 pages of related text   [39] $45

A MAP OF SOUTH AMERICA DRAWN FROM THE LATEST AND BEST AUTHORITIES [1780]
27.3x29cm. with 6 pages of related text   [39] $45

A MAP OF THE DUTCH SETTLEMENTS OF SURINAM, DEMERARY, ISSEQUIBO, BERBICES, AND
THE ISLANDS OF CURASSO, ARUBA, BONAIRE, &C... [1781] 26.9x36.9cm.
with 3 1/2 pages of related text   [39] $45

A MAP OF THE ENGLISH, FRENCH, SPANISH, DUTCH & DANISH ISLANDS IN THE WEST
INDIES, TAKEN FROM AN IMPROVED MAP OF THE GEOGRAPHER TO THE KING OF FRANCE
WITH THE TRACK OF THE LAST WEST INDIA FLEET, THROUGH THE WINDWARD PASSAGE
[1781] 27x36.1cm. with 3 pages of related text   [39] $40

A MAP OF THE ISLANDS OF ST. LUCIA AND MARTINIQUE...THE STATION OF THE FRENCH
FLEETS IN THE WEST INDIES; AND TO ILLUSTRATE THE LATE ENGAGEMENT BETWEEN SIR
SAML. HOOD AND THE COUNT DE GRASSE [1781] 37.4x27.2cm.
with 3 1/2 pages of related text   [39] $55

A MAP OF THE PROVINCE OF MASSACHUSETTS BAY, AND COLONY OF RHODE ISLAND, WITH
PART OF CONNECTICUT, NEW HAMPSHIRE AND VERMONT [1782] 27.6x37.2cm. [39] $65

A NEW & ACCURATE MAP OF THE PROVINCE OF CANADA IN NORTH AMERICA... [1782]
25.4x33.4cm.   [39] $75

A NEW AND ACCURATE CHART OF THE HARBOUR OF BOSTON IN NEW ENGLAND IN NORTH
AMERICA [1782] 22.3x16.6cm. with half-page of text   [39] $40

A NEW AND ACCURATE MAP OF NORTH CAROLINA, AND PART OF SOUTH CAROLINA, WITH THE
FIELD OF BATTLE BETWEEN EARL CORNWALLIS AND GENERAL GATES [1780]
27.4x38.2cm. with 4 pages of text   [39] $55

A NEW AND ACCURATE MAP OF THE CHIEF PARTS OF SOUTH CAROLINA AND GEORGIA FROM
THE BEST AUTHORITIES [1780] 27.4x37.4cm.   [39] $50

A NEW AND ACCURATE MAP OF THE PROVINCE OF NEW YORK AND PART OF THE JERSEYS, NEW
ENGLAND AND CANADA, SHEWING THE SCENES OF OUR MILITARY OPERATIONS DURING THE
PRESENT WAR. ALSO THE NEW ERECTED STATE OF VERMONT [1782] 37.1x27.4cm.
with 2 1/2 pages of related text   [39] $70

A NEW AND ACCURATE MAP OF VIRGINIA AND PART OF MARYLAND AND PENNSYLVANIA
[1780] 27.2x37.6cm. with some text   [39] $55

A NEW AND CORRECT MAP OF NORTH AMERICA IN WHICH THE PLACES OF THE PRINCIPAL
ENGAGEMENTS DURING THE PRESENT WAR ARE ACCURATELY INSERTED [1780]
27.6x38.1cm. 6 pages of text included   [39] $60

A NEW AND CORRECT MAP OF NORTH AMERICA IN WHICH THE PLACES OF THE PRINCIPAL
ENGAGEMENTS DURING THE PRESENT WAR ARE ACCURATELY INSERTED. AND THE
BOUNDARIES AS SETTLED BY TREATY IN 1783 CLEARLY MARKED [1783] 27.6x37.9cm.
1/4 page of text included   [39] $85

A NEW AND EXACT MAP OF THE ISLAND OF ANTIGUA IN AMERICA...WITH THE DIVISIONS,
BOUNDARIES; AND A PLAN OF ENGLISH HARBOUR [1782] 27.6x37cm.
with half-page of text   [39] $75

A NEW MAP OR CHART IN MERCATORS PROJECTION OF THE WESTERN OR ATLANTIC OCEAN...
[1781] 39.4x51.7cm.   [39] $185

A PLAN OF CHARLES TOWN THE CAPITAL OF SOUTH CAROLINA, WITH THE HARBOURS,
ISLANDS AND FORTS; THE ATTACK ON FORT SULIVAN... [1780] 13.5x28.6cm.
with some text   [39] $55

AN ACCURATE MAP OF THE ISLAND OF BARBADOES IN WHICH THE DIFFERENT PARISHES ARE
LAID DOWN; WITH A PLAN OF BRIDGE TOWN AND CARLISLE BAY [1781] 28.3x36.7cm.
with 1 page of related text   [39] $120

AN ACCURATE MAP OF THE ISLAND OF ST. CHRISTOPHERS, FROM AN ACTUAL SURVEY,
    SHEWING THE PARISHES, CHURCHES, AND RIVERS; ALSO THE BAYS, ROCKS, SHOALS AND
    SOUNDINGS... [1782] 27.5x36.6cm. with text describing the map   [39] $55
CAPE FEAR RIVER, WITH THE COUNTIES ADJACENT, AND THE TOWNS OF BRUNSWICK AND
    WILMINGTON, AGAINST WHICH LORD CORNWALLIS DETACHED PART OF HIS ARMY, THE 17TH
    OF JANUARY LAST [1781] 23.9x17.8cm. with 2 pages of text   [39] $45
CHART AND PLAN OF THE HARBOUR OF NEW YORK & THE COUNY. ADJACENT FROM SANDY HOOK
    TO KINGSBRIDGE, COMPREHENDING THE WHOLE OF NEW YORK & STATEN ISLAND...
    [1781] 41.9x24.3cm. with 2 pages of related text   [39] $70
MAP OF THE ISLANDS OF MARTINICO, DOMINICO, GUARDALUPE, ST. CHRISTOPHERS &C.
    SHEWING THE PLACE OF ADML. RODNEY'S LATE VICTORY OVER THE FRENCH FLEET
    [1782] 23.7x27.7cm. with half-page of text   [39] $45
NEW AND ACCURATE CHART OF HUDSON'S BAY, IN NORTH AMERICA [1782] 17.5x22.6cm.
    with text   [39] $65
PLAN OF THE TOWN AND HARBOUR OF ST. AUGUSTIN IN EAST FLORIDA [1783] 16.7x24cm.
                                                                        [39] $45
THE DUTCH ISLANDS OF ST. EUSTATIA, SABA, AND ST. MARTINS; THE FRENCH ISLAND OF
    ST. BARTHOLOMEW; THE ENGLISH ISLAND OF ST. CHRISTOPHERS, NEVIS AND
    ANGUILA... [1781] 26.5x20.9cm. with half-page of text   [39] $45
THE ISLAND OF ST. DOMINGO, CALLED BY THE SPANIARDS, HISPANIOLA, SUBJECT TO
    FRANCE AND SPANI... [1783] 33x47.2cm. with 4 pages of related text   [39] $30
WEST INDIES, WITH THE HARBOUR & FORT OF OMOA... [1780] 29.2x64.2cm.
    with 4 pages of related text   [39] $75

POPPLE
(SHEET 7 FROM HIS LARGE MAP SHOWING COAST FROM CAPE BRETON TO RHODE ISLAND)
    [1733] 48.9x68.2cm. minor restorations   [39] $350
(SHEET 15 FROM HIS LARGE MAP SHOWING EASTERN HISPANIOLA, PUERTO RICO, ETC.)
    [1733] 48.6x68cm.   [39] $175
(SHEET 16 FROM HIS LARGE MAP SHOWING 5 PANELS OF WEST INDIAN HARBORS) [1733]
    48.6x29.5cm.   [39] $95
A MAP OF THE BRITISH EMPIRE IN AMERICA [1733] 52.1x49.5cm.
    the index sheet to Popple's 20 sheet map of America   [16] $1200

PORCACCHI
CORFU [1572-1620] 10.5x14.5cm. Latin text below map   [31] $130
DESCRITTIONE DEL L'ISOLA ET TERRA DI SANTA CROCE, OVERO MONDO NUOVO
    [1672-1612] 10.2x14cm.
    on a sheet with text, measuring about 28 x 19 cm., shows North America
                                                                        [23] $325
DESCRITTIONE DEL MAPPAMONDO [1572-1612] 10.2x14.6cm.
    on a sheet about 28 x 19 cm. with text, a world map within an oval   [23] $275
DISCORSE INTORNO ALLA CARTA DA NIVIGARE [C1572] 11.4x14.6cm.   [3] $175
DISCORSO INTORNO ALLA CARTA DA NAVIGARE [1590] 10.2x14cm.
    a chart of the world, Latin text below   [30] $264
DISCORSO INTORNO ALLA CARTA DA NAVIGARE [1572-1612] 10.2x14cm. on a sheet
    about 28 x 19 cm. with text, shows the world with rhumb-lines   [23] $285
IRLANDA [C1572-90] 12.4x14cm. on a page of text   [12] $58
ISLANDIA [C1576] 10.5x14.5cm. on a page with Italian text   [4] $114
MAIORICA [C1605] 10.5x14.5cm. on a page with text   [4] $99
MALTA [C1605] 10.5x14.5cm. on a page with text   [4] $114
MONDO NUOVO [1572] 10.2x14.3cm. from "L'Isole Piu Famose del Mondo"   [34] $285
MONDO NUOVO [C1605] 10.5x14.5cm.
    on a page of Italian text, accompanied by an additional sheet of text
                                                                        [4] $268
S. GIOVANNI [1590] 10.2x14cm.   [3] $110
TEMISTITAN [C1605] 10.5x14.5cm. shows Mexico City on a sheet of text,
    accompanied by another sheet of text   [4] $130

PORTLOCK
SKETCH OF MCLEOD'S HARBOUR ON THE WEST SIDE OF MONTAGU I... [1789] 30x29.5cm.
                                                                        [39] $50

PORTLOCK (continued)

SKETCH OF PORT ETCHES, SITUATED 5 LEAGUES NNE OF CAPE HINCHINGBROOK; TOGETHER
    WITH A SKETCH OF BROOKS HARBOUR [1789] 20.3x29.5cm.   [39] $45

PREVOST D'EXILES

See also BELLIN

CARTE DU GROENLAND DRESSEE ET GRAVEE PAR LAURENT [1770] 19.7x25.4cm. [3] $75
CARTE DU KAMTSCHATKA DRESSEE ET GRAVEE PAR LAURENT [1756] 52.1x29.8cm.
                                                                       [3] $65

PRICE

SOUTH AMERICA CORRECTED FROM THE OBSERVATIONS COMMUNICATED TO THE ROYAL
    SOCIETY'S... [C1700] 89.5x64.5cm. ragged edges, backed   [39] $135

PTOLEMY

See also MERCATOR
See also MUNSTER

PTOLEMY (1482-86 ULM)

DECIMA EUROPE TABULA [1486] 38.7x54cm. shows Greece   [17] $6800
DUODECIMA ASIE TABULA [1486] 29.2x39.4cm. shows Ceylon   [17] $2000
TABULA MODERNA FRANCIE [1486] 38.7x54.6cm. minor centerfold repair, lower
    margin narrow, shows France, Belgium & Switzerland   [17] $4500
TERCIA AFFRICE TABULA [1486] 30.5x55.9cm. original color, repaired   [17] $4000

PTOLEMY (1511 VENICE)

PRIMA EUROPAE TABULA//SECUNDA EUROPAE TABULA/(PTOLEMAIC WORLD) [1511]
    40.6x53.3cm. centerfold repaired, top & bottom margins narrow, printed in 2
    colors, 2 extra leaves attached to reverse so that the untitled Ptolemaic
    world map and "Secunda Europae Tabula" (Spain) are also present plus half of
    the map of France   [16] $3600

PTOLEMY (1513-20 STRASSBURG)

DECIMA ASIAE TABULA [1513]   C36.8x55.9cm. includes India   [26] $300
LOTHARINGIE DUCATUS [1513]   C36.2x26cm.
    printed in 3 colors, probably the 2nd map so printed   [26] $2000
NONA ASIAE TABULA [1513]   C40x48.3cm.
    minor centerfold repair, includes Pakistan, Iran, Afghanistan   [26] $200
OCTAVA ASIE TABULA [1513]   C35.6x38.1cm.
    light staining, includes central Asia   [26] $175
QUARTA ASIAE TABULA [1513]   C38.7x53.3cm.
    15 cm. tear mended, includes Holy Land & Mesopotamia   [26] $1000
QUINTA ASIE TABULA [1513]   C36.5x50.8cm. shows Persia   [26] $250
SECONDA ASIAE TABULA [1513]   C36.8x40.6cm. shows Sarmatia   [26] $200
SEPTIMA ASIE TABULA [1513]   C33.7x53.3cm. shows Scythia   [26] $250
SEPTIME EUROPE TABULA [1513]   C31.8x55.9cm. shows Sardinia & Sicily   [26] $400
SEXTA ASIE TABULA [1513]   C31.8x55.9cm.
    right side somewhat faint, shows Arabia   [26] $1000
TABULA MODERNA BOSSINE SERVICE GRETIAE ET SCLAVONIE (GREECE) [1513]
    C41.6x54.3cm.   [26] $950
TABULA MODERNA ET NOVA HISPANIE [1513] 41.3x55.9cm.
    contemporary color, dark blue ocean & green mountains   [17] $1800
TABULA MODERNA INDIAE [1513] 40.6x50.8cm.
    minor wormholes at centerfold   [15] $2600
TABULA MODERNA PRIME PARTIS APHRICAE [1513]   C43.8x57.2cm.
    long vertical crease with separations repaired   [26] $950
TABULA MODERNA TERRA SANCTE [1513] 33x55.9cm.
    wormholes near centerfold repaired   [15] $4450
TABULA NEOTERICA CRETE SIVE CENDIE INSULE [1513]   C38.7x53cm.   [26] $1000
TABULA SECONDA AFRICAE (LIBYA) [1513]   C34.3x54.6cm.   [26] $300
TERTI AFRICAE TABULA [1513]   C34.3x53.3cm. shows Egypt   [26] $300
UNDECIMA ASIAE TABULA [1513]   C36.8x42.5cm. shows India & Burma   [26] $250

PTOLEMY (1522-41 STRASSBURG)

(PTOLEMAIC WORLD, UNTITLED) [1522-25] 30.5x45.7cm.   [15] $1700
(TAPROBANA WITH SOUTHERN TIP OF INDIA) [1535] 27.9x45.7cm.
    minor repairs in margins, tear near centerfold repaired   [24] $306

PTOLEMY (1522-41 STRASSBURG) (continued)

ASIA TABULA SECUNDA CONTINET SARMATIAM ASIATICAM [1541] 30.5x36.2cm.
   browning at centerfold, worming in upper margin at centerfold   [7] $200
ASIAE TABULA QUINTA CONTINENTUR ASSYRIA, MEDIA, SUSTANA, PERSIS, PARTHIA...
   [1541] 30.5x45.7cm. light browning, several short tears at centerfold
                                                                   [7] $200
ORBIS TYPUS UNIVERSALIS IUXTA HYDROGRAPHORUM TRADITIONEM EXACTISSIME DEPICTA
   [1522-41] 31.8x47cm. "Tabula orbis cum descriptione ventorum" appears above
   the map, the title given appears within the upper border   [15] $2450
TABULA MODERNA INDIA ORIENTALIS ET MERIDIONALIS [1522-41] 27.9x40.6cm.
                                                            [15] $1275
TABULA NOVA ANGLIAE & HIBERNIAE [1541] 28.6x41.3cm.   [14] $758
TABULA NOVA PARTIS AFRICAE (SOUTH AFRICA) [1541] 30.5x42.5cm.
   minor staining   [26] $750
TABULA NOVA PARTIS AFRICAE (WEST AFRICA) [1541] 27.9x40cm.   [26] $450
TABULA NOVA TERRA SANCTAE [1522-41] 24.1x40.6cm.   [15] $1600
TABULA NOVA TOTIUS ORBIS [1522-41] 27.9x45.7cm.   [15] $1900
TABULA OCTAVA ASIAE CONTINET SCYTHIAM EXTRA IMAUM MONTEM, & SERICAM [1541]
   30.5x34.9cm. foxed   [7] $200
TABULA QUARTA ASIA [1522-41] 30.5x45.7cm.   [15] $1300
TABULA SUPERIORIS INDIAE ET TARTARIAE MAJORIS [1522-41] 27.9x33cm.   [15] $1400
TERRA NOVA [1522-41] 29.2x38.1cm. sometimes called the "Admiral's map"
                                                             [15] $3200
TYPUS ORBIS DESCRIPTIONE PTOLEMAI [1541] 31.8x45.7cm.
   the Ptolemaic world   [16] $1200

PTOLEMY (1548 VENICE)

ANGLIAE E HIBERNIA NOVA [1548] 12x17cm.   [31] $229
DALMACIA NOVA TABULA [1548] 12.7x17.1cm.   [7] $90
FLANDRIA, BARBANTIA E HOLANDA NOVA [1548] 12.7x17.1cm.   [7] $90
GALLIA NOVA TABULA [1548] 13.3x17.1cm.   [7] $90
GERMANIA NOVA TABULA MDXXXXII [1548] 12.7x17.1cm. stained   [7] $90
GRAETIA NOVA TABULA [1548] 12.7x17.1cm.   [7] $90
HISPANIA NOVA TABULA [1548] 13.3x17.1cm. margins stained   [7] $90
INDIA TERCERA NOVA TABULA [1548] 12.7x16.5cm.   [15] $675
ITALIA NOVA TAVOLA [1548] 12.7x17.1cm.
   faint impression, margins soiled   [7] $90
NUEVA HISPANIA TABULA NOVA [1548] 13x16.8cm. minor staining   [26] $1800
NUEVA HISPANIA TABULA NOVA [1548] 12.7x16.5cm.   [15] $1900
PIAMONTE NOVA TAV. [1548] 13.3x17.1cm.   [7] $90
POLONIA ET HUNGARIA NOVA TABULA [1548] 13.3x17.1cm. browned   [7] $90
SICILIA SARDINIA NOVA TABULA [1548] 13.3x17.1cm. a few spots   [7] $90
TABULA ASIAE VI [1548] 12.7x17.1cm.
   waterstain in lower margin, shows Arabia   [7] $90
TABULA EUROPAE I [1548] 12x17cm.   [31] $229
TABULA EUROPAE II [1548] 13.3x17.1cm.   [7] $90
TABULA EUROPAE III [1548] 13.3x16.5cm.   [7] $90
TABULA EUROPAE IX [1548] 12.7x17.1cm. waterstain in lower margin   [7] $90
TABULA EUROPAE IX [1548] 13.3x17.1cm. waterstain in lower margin   [7] $90
TABULA EUROPAE V [1548] 13.3x17.1cm. minor waterstain in upper margin
                                                             [7] $90
TABULA EUROPAE VI [1548] 13.3x17.1cm. minor waterstaining in margins [7] $90
TABULA EUROPAE VII [1548] 13.3x17.1cm.
   faint impression, spotting in margins   [7] $90
TABULA EUROPAE VIII [1548] 13.3x17.1cm.   [7] $90
TIERRA NOVA (SOUTH AMERICA) [1548] 13.3x17.1cm.   [26] $475
TIERRA NUEVA [1548] 12.7x16.5cm. shows northeastern North America   [15] $1850
UNIVERSALE NOVA [1548] 12.7x16.5cm. small wormhole in centerfold   [15] $950

PTOLEMY (1561-99 VENICE)

AFRICA MINOR NUOVA TAVOLA [1561] 17.8x24.1cm.   [24] $42
ANGLIA ET HIBERNIA NOVA [1561] C18x25cm.   [31] $45
ANGLIA ET HIBERNIA NOVA [C1561-64] 17.8x24.8cm. Italian text on verso
                                                             [13] $176

PTOLEMY (1561-99 VENICE) (continued)

CARTA MARINA NUOVA TAVOLA [1561-99] 17.8x24.1cm.	[34]	$450
FLANDRIA, BRABANTIA ET HOLANDA NUOVA [1561-62] 20x25cm.	[18]	$140
GRAETIA NUOVA TAVOLA [1561] 17.8x24.1cm.	[24]	$53
ISOLA CUBA NOVA [1574] 16x25cm.	[31]	$68
ISOLA CUBA NOVA [1599] 19.7x24.8cm.	[3]	$135
MARMARICA NUOVA TAVOLA [1561] 17.8x24.1cm.	[9]	$60
MARMARICA NUOVA TAVOLA [1561-74] 17.8x24.1cm. wormholes repaired	[24]	$38
NATOLIA NUOVA TAVOLA [1561] 17.8x24.8cm.	[24]	$39
NUEVA HISPANIA TABULA NOVA [1561] 17.8x24.1cm.		
faint impression at lower right & light stain	[9]	$425
NUEVA HISPANIA TABULA NOVA [1599] 19.1x26cm.	[23]	$390
ORBIS DESCRIPTIO [1561] 18.4x26.7cm.	[23]	$375
ORBIS DESCRIPTIO [1561] 19x26cm.	[37]	$450
ORBIS DESCRIPTIO [1561] 16.5x25.4cm.	[16]	$350
PERSIA NUOVA TAVOLA [1561] 45.7x62.2cm.	[24]	$45
SEPTENTRIONALIUM PARTIUM NOVA TABULA [1561] 17.8x24.1cm.		
minor browning in margins	[7]	$400
TABULA APHRICAE II [1574] 16x25cm.	[31]	$22
TABULA ASIA XII [1574] 19x24cm. includes a view of an elephant	[31]	$45
TABULA EUROPAE X [1561] 18.4x25.4cm.	[24]	$41
TABULAE EUROPAE I [1561] 18x25cm.	[31]	$45
TAVOLA NUOVA D'ITALIA [1561] 18.4x24.1cm.	[24]	$42
TAVOLA NUOVA DI SARDIGNA ET DI SICILIA [1561] 17.8x24.8cm.	[24]	$36
TAVOLA NUOVA DI SCHIAVONIA [1561] 17.8x24.1cm.	[24]	$38
TERRA NOVA [1561] 17.9x24.6cm. shows South America	[39]	$175
TIERRA NUEVA [1561] 19.1x26cm. shows northeastern America	[23]	$425
TIERRA NUEVA [1574] 19x26cm.	[31]	$421
TIERRA NUEVA [1561] 17.8x24.8cm.		
light browning, shows northeastern North America	[7]	$650

PTOLEMY (1578-1730 MERCATOR)

EUR. X TAB. [1578-1730] 35x46cm. shows Greece, decorated with a fish	[4]	$137
TAB. XII ASIAE, TAPROBANUM... [1695] 34.3x35.6cm.	[24]	$114

PTOLEMY (1596-1621 MAGINI)

AMERICA [1596] 12.7x16.5cm.	[27]	$350
AMERICA [1598] 12.7x17.1cm.	[17]	$385
AMERICA [1620] 13.3x17.8cm.		
on a sheet measuring about 29 x 20 cm. with text	[23]	$225
AMERICA [1620] 13.3x17.8cm. on a sheet of text	[22]	$225
ASIA [C1596] C13.5x17.5cm. on a page with Italian text	[4]	$68
BELGIUM, SUE GERMANIA INFERIOR [C1596] C13.5x17.5cm.		
on a page with Italian text	[4]	$114
CANDIA INSULA, OLIM CRETA [C1596] C13.5x17.5cm.		
on a page with Italian text	[4]	$68
CORSICAE ISOLA, OLIM CYRNUS [1620] 34x45cm. centerfold slightly worn	[31]	$229
EUROPE [C1596] C13.5x17.5cm. on a page with Italian text	[4]	$53
FORUM IULII, ET HISTRIA [C1596] C13.5x17.5cm.		
on a page with Italian text	[4]	$30
GALLIAE REGNUM [C1596] C13.5x17.5cm. on a page with Italian text	[4]	$38
GERMANIA [C1596] C13.5x17.5cm. on a page with Italian text	[4]	$68
INDIA ORIENTALIS [C1596] C13.5x17.5cm. on a page with Italian text	[4]	$68
ITALIA [C1596] C13.5x17.5cm. on a page with Italian text	[4]	$45
LATIUM [C1596] C13.5x17.5cm. on a page with Italian text	[4]	$45
LOMBARDIA ET MARCHIA TARUISINA [C1596] C13.5x17.5cm.		
on a page with Italian text	[4]	$45
MARCA ANCONAE [C1596] C13.5x17.5cm. on a page with Italian text	[4]	$22
NATOLIA OLIM ASIA MINOR [C1596] C13.5x17.5cm.		
on a page with Italian text	[4]	$45
NEOPOLITANUM REGNUM [C1596] C13.5x17.5cm. on a page with Italian text		
	[4]	$22
ORBIS TERRAE COMPENDIOSA DESCRIPTIO [1596-98] 16.5x24.5cm.		
on sheet measuring 29.5 x 19.5 cm.	[37]	$650

PTOLEMY (1596-1621 MAGINI) (continued)
ORBIS TERRAE COMPENDIOSA DESCRIPTIO [C1598] 16x24cm.   [5] $400
ORBIS TERRAE... [1598] 15.9x24.1cm. the world in 2 hemispheres   [17] $450
PALAESTINA, VEL TERRA SANCTA [C1596] C13.5x17.5cm.
   on a page with Italian text   [4] $137
PEDEMONTIUM, MONSSERRATUS ET LIGURIA [C1596] C13.5x17.5cm.
   on a page with Italian text   [4] $45
PERSIAE REGNUM [C1596] C13.5x17.5cm. on a page with Italian text   [4] $84
PORTUGALLIAE REGNUM [C1596] C13.5x17.5cm. on a page with Italian text
                                                                                [4] $61
PTOLEMAEI TYPUS [C1598] 13.5x17.5cm.
   the Ptolemaic world on a sheet of text   [4] $137
SARDINIA/SCILIA [C1596] C13.5x17.5cm. on a page with Italian text   [4] $38
TABULA ASIAE XII [C1596] C13.5x17.5cm. on a page with Italian text   [4] $68
TARTARIAE IMPERIUM [C1598] 12.5x17cm.   [5] $140
TARTARIAE IMPERIUM [1620] 14x17.8cm. on a sheet of text   [22] $170
TAVOLA DELLA GRAN GERMANIA, QUARTA DELL'EUROPA. TABULA EUROPAE IIII [1598]
   12.7x16.5cm. on a sheet 29 x 20 cm   [9] $85
TURCICI IMPERII [C1596] C13.5x17.5cm. on a page with Italian text   [4] $122
TUSCIA [C1596] C13.5x17.5cm. on a page with Italian text   [4] $45
UNIVERSI ORBIS DESCRIPTIO [C1598] 13.5x17.5cm. on a page of text   [4] $214
UNIVERSI ORBIS... [1598] 13x17.8cm. the world in oval projection   [17] $425
UNIVERSI...NAVIGANTIUM [1598] 13x17.1cm.
   the world in "Carta Marina" style   [17] $385

PURCHAS
See also HONDIUS
See also MERCATOR
(NEW ENGLAND & NEW FRANCE, UNTITLED) [1625] 25x34cm.
   tear into left margin, backed with cloth   [37] $1500
GOLFE OF CANADA [1625] 25x34.5cm.   [39] $1475
VIRGINIA ET FLORIDA [C1625-26] 14.6x18.4cm. on a page of text, above the neat
   line is a second title, "Hondius his map of Florida"   [1] $250
VIRGINIA ET FLORIDA [1625] 15.2x17.8cm. on a page of text   [16] $240

QUAD
ANGLIAE REGNI FLORENTISSIMI... [1600] 17.8x26.7cm.
   from "Europae totius terrarum partis...descriptio," Cologne   [16] $300
ASIA PARTIU ORBIS MAXIMA MDXCVIII [1600] 53.3x74.9cm.   [13] $429
NAMURCUM...NAMEN. COLONIE EXC. IOHAN BUSSM [C1589] 19x26.5cm.
   German text on verso   [18] $175
POLUS ARCTICUS SIVE TRACT SEPTENTRIONALIS [1608] 21.6x27.9cm.   [15] $775
POLUS ARCTICUS SIVE TRACT, SEPTENTRIONALIS. COLONIAE, EX OFFICINA TYPOGRAPHICA
   JANI BUSSEMECHERS [1600] 21.6x27.9cm.
   minor browning in margins, "77" on verso   [7] $1300
TYPUS ORBIS TERRARUM, AD IMITATIONEM UNIVERSALIS GERHARDI MERCATORIS [1608]
   21.6x31.1cm.   [15] $2000

RADEFELD
BRITISCHES, NORD-AMERICA GEZEICHNET NACH AUFNAHME DER HUDSONS-BAY [1847]
   21.6x26cm. backed   [3] $35

RAIGNAULD
DESCRIPTION DE LA CITE, VALETTE [1629] 20x14cm.   [31] $84
ISLE DE CIPRE [1629] 19x26.5cm.   [31] $766

RAMSAY
EQUISSE DES OPERATIONS DU SIEGE DE CHARLESTON CAPITALE DE LA CAROLINA
   MERIDIONALE, EN 1780 [1787] 36.8x29.2cm. light waterstain, side margins
   narrow, from a 1787 French ed. of David Ramsay's map of 1785   [1] $200

RAMUSIO
(BRAZIL) [C1550] 26.7x36.5cm. faint centerfold staining   [26] $600
IL CUSCHO CITTA PRINCIPALE DELLA PROVINCIA DEL PERU [C1550] 26.7x36.8cm.
   faint centerfold staining   [26] $250
LA NUOVA FRANCIA [1556] 26.7x36.8cm.   [15] $1600

<u>RAMUSIO</u> (continued)
LA NUOVA FRANCIA [C1556] 26.7x36.8cm. a woodcut first issued in 1556, this
    impression is from a second block cut to replace the first, which was
    destroyed; the second block is identifiable by the presence of several willow
    trees   [7] $2100
LA TERRA DE HOCHELAGA NELLA NOVA FRANCIA [C1550] 26.7x36.8cm.
    faint centerfold staining   [26] $900
LA TERRA DE HOCHELEGA NELLA NOVA FRANCIA [C1556] 26.7x35.6cm. a woodcut first
    issued in 1556, this impression is from a second block cut to replace the
    first, which was destroyed; the second block is identifiable by the presence
    of several willow trees   [7] $1300
LA TERRA DE HOCHELEGA NELLA NOVA FRANCIA [1556] 26.7x36.8cm. [15] $900
NUOVA FRANCIA [1556] 26.7x37.5cm. narrow margins   [32] $1950
PARTE DE LA FRICA (WEST AFRICA) [C1550] 26.7x36.8cm.
    faint centerfold staining   [26] $350
SUMATRA [C1550] 26.7x36.8cm. faint staining   [26] $150
UNIVERSALE DELLE PARTE DEL MONDO NUOVAMENTE RITROVATA [1556] 26.7x26.7cm.
    printed in a circular border   [15] $950
<u>RAND MCNALLY</u>
KANSAS [1889] 48.3x66cm. creases reinforced on verso, copyright 1888,
    apparently issued separately, advertising for 1889 ed. of Business Atlas and
    Shippers' Guide on verso   [27] $75
MONTANA [1898] 31.8x48.3cm.   [27] $40
NORTH DAKOTA [1889-91] 34.3x57.2cm. dated 1889, published 1891 [27] $45
TEXAS [1895] 23.5x31.8cm.   [19] $30
TEXAS [1893] 23.5x31.8cm.   [19] $30
TEXAS & INDIAN TERRITORY [1889] 31.8x24.1cm.   [19] $35
UTAH [1883] 49.5x33cm.   [27] $45
<u>RAPIN</u>
See TINDAL
<u>RAPKIN</u>
See TALLIS
<u>RATELBAND</u>
KAARTE VAN DE GOLF VAN MEXICO EN HET ZUYD-AMERICA WAAR IN PORTO-BELLO EN PANAMA
    AANG EWEZEN WERDEN [1735] 18.4x30.5cm.
    four folds, one repaired, published by Johannes Ratelband, Amsterdam[1] $150
<u>RAU</u>
NORWICH, CONN. (VIEW) [C1867] 41.9x74.9cm. bird's eye view & 3 smaller scenes
    on one sheet, chromolithograph by H. Knecht, printed by Jacob Rau, 381 Pearl
    St., New York   [34] $1500
<u>RAWLINGS</u>
ST. PAUL, MINNESOTA...(VIEW) [1865] 11.4x18.4cm.   [3] $25
<u>REICHARD</u>
DER NOERDLICHE THEIL DES GROSSEN WELT MEERES...WEIMAR IM VERLAGE DES L.
    INDUSTRIE COMPTOIX... [1803] 50.2x66.7cm.   [26] $275
DER NOERDLICHE THEIL DES GROSSEN WLT MEERES NACH DEN NEUESTEN BESTIMMUNGEN UND
    ENTDECKUNGEN VON C.G. REICHARD. WEIMAR IM VERLAGE DES L. INDUSTRIE COMPTOIX
    [C1820] 50.2x66.7cm. side margins narrow, paper weak in spots   [7] $350
NORDLICHER THEIL DER VEREINIGTEN STAATEN [1817] 27.9x33.7cm.
    margins soiled   [22] $90
<u>RENNER</u>
BOSTON & BUNKER HILL VON DER OSTSEITE (VIEW) [C1850] 18.7x28.6cm.
    published by J.C. Renner, Nuremberg, after William H. Bartlett   [33] $250
<u>ROBERTS</u>
THE EMPIRE OF CHINA WITH ITS PRINCIPAL DIVISIONS DRAWN FROM THE SURVEYS MADE BY
    THE JESUITS [1778] 48.3x62.9cm.   [3] $135
<u>ROBINSON</u>
(SANDWICH ISLANDS) [1798] 50x38.5cm.
    from "Atlas du Voyage de La Perouse", 2 maps on one sheet   [5] $540
CARTE DES COTES DE L'AMERIQUE ET DE L'ASIE [1798] 38.5x50cm.
    from "Atlas du Voyage de La Perouse"   [5] $200

ROBINSON (continued)
CARTE DU GRAND OCEAN, OU MER DU SUD [1798] 36x49cm.
  from "Atlas du Voyage de La Perouse"   [5] $200
CARTE GENERAL D'UNE PARTIE DE LA COTE DU NORD OUEST DE L'AMERIQUE [1798]
  49.5x38cm.   [5] $240
CHART FOR THE JOURNAL OF MR. LE MARQUIS DE CHASTELLUX BY MR. DEZOTEUX...OF THE
  FRENCH ARMY [1787] 17.8x26cm.   [3] $95
CHART OF THE COAST OF AMERICA & ASIA FROM CALIFORNIA TO MACAO ACCORDING TO THE
  DISCOVERIES MADE IN 1786 & 1787 BY THE BOUSSOLE & ASTROLABE [1798]
  38.7x48.9cm.   [3] $135
CHART OF THE NORTH WEST COAST OF AMERICA EXPLORED BY THE BOUSSOLE & ASTROLABE
  IN 1786 [1798] 38.7x49.5cm. 3rd sheet   [3] $115
CHART OF THE NORTHWEST COAST OF AMERICA. EXPLORED BY THE BOUSSOLE, AND
  ASTROLABE IN 1786. 1ST. SHEET. PUBLISHED...NOVR. 1ST. 1798 BY G.G. AND J.
  ROBINSON...LONDON [1798] 35.9x48.6cm.
  light staining, some reinforcements on reverse   [25] $38
COTE DU NORD-OUEST DE L'AMERIQUE RECONNUE PAR LES FREGATES FRANCAISES LA
  BOUSSOLE ET L'ASTROLABE EN 1786 [1798] 36x49.5cm.
  from "Atlas du Voyage de La Perouse"   [5] $240
MAP OF NORTH AMERICA [1829-41] 23.8x20.3cm.   [19] $70
MAP OF NORTH AMERICA... [1844] 26.7x21.6cm.   [19] $70
MAP OF NORTH AMERICA... [1844-49] 26.7x21.6cm.   [19] $60
MAP OF TEXAS [1844-49] 26.7x21.6cm.
  published by D.F. Robinson, Hartford   [20] $125
MAP OF THE UNITED STATES [1828-41] 25.4x43.2cm.   [19] $120
MAP OF THE UNITED STATES [1837] 25.4x42.5cm.   [19] $120
NORTH AMERICA [1837] 23.5x20.3cm.   [19] $65
NORTH AMERICA... [1844-49] 26.7x21.6cm.
  published by D.F. Robinson, Hartford   [20] $65
PLAN DE L'ENTREE DU PORT DE BUCARELLI [1798] 38.5x50cm.
  from "Atlas du Voyage de La Perouse"   [5] $80
PLAN DE LA BAIE DE MONTEREY [1798] 25x36.3cm.
  from "Atlas du Voyage de La Perouse"   [5] $200
PLAN DU PORT DE ST DIEGO/PLAN DU PORT ET DU DEPARTEMENT DE ST BLAS [1798]
  36.5x24.5cm. from "Atlas du Voyage de La Perouse"   [5] $300
PLAN DU PORT DE ST FRANCOIS [1798] 36.5x24.5cm.
  from "Atlas du Voyage de La Perouse"   [5] $440
PLAN DU PORT DES FRANCAIS [1798] 37x50cm.
  from "Atlas du Voyage de La Perouse"   [5] $80
PLAN OF PORT DES FRANCAIS ON THE NORTH WEST COAST OF AMERICA...BY THE BOUSSOLE
  & ASTROLABE. PUBLISHED...NOVR. 1ST. 1798 BY G.G. & J. ROBINSON...LONDON
  [1798] 37.1x49.5cm.   [25] $53
PLAN OF PORT S. DIEGO IN CALIFORNIA...SURVEY 1782/PORT & DEPARTMENT OF S. BLAS
  SURVEY... [1798] 36.8x24.1cm.   [3] $95
PLAN OF THE BAY OF CONCEPTION IN CHILI... [1798] 25.4x36.8cm.   [3] $40
PLAN OF THE BAY OF MONTEREY SITUATE IN NORTH CALIFORNIA [1798] 25.4x37.5cm.
                                                                    [3] $100
PLAN OF THE PORT AND DEPARTMENT OF S. BLAS...SURVEY IN NOV. 1777/PORT OF S.
  DIEGO IN CALIFORNIA [1798] 36.8x24.1cm.   [3] $95
VIEW OF THE ANCHORAGES OF THE VESSELS AT THE ISLAND OF MOWEE [1798]
  22.2x32.4cm.   [3] $65
VIEWS OF NORTH WEST COAST OF AMERICA EXPLORED BY THE BOUSSOLE IN 1786. 2ND
  SHEET [1798] 22.9x29.2cm.   [3] $35
VIEWS OF THE NORTHWEST COAST OF AMERICA EXPLORED BY THE ASTROLABE IN 1786. 3RD
  SHEET [1798] 22.9x29.2cm. 6 profiles   [3] $35
ROCQUE
(ORKNEY ISLES, SUTHERLANDSHIRE, CATHNES-SHIRE) [1764] C9.5x12.7cm. from "A
  Collection of Plans of the Principal Cities of Great Britain and Ireland," A.
  Dury, London   [14] $15
A PLAN OF BOSTON IN THE COUNTY OF LINCOLN [1764] C9.5x12.7cm.   [14] $38

ROCQUE (continued)

A PLAN OF THE CITIES OF LONDON & WESTMINSTER AND THE BOROUGH OF SOUTHWARK, &C.
[1764] C9.5x12.7cm. 2 sheets [14] $53
A PLAN OF THE CITY AND SUBURBS OF BATH [1764] C9.5x12.7cm. [14] $38
A PLAN OF THE CITY AND SUBURBS OF BRISTOL [1764] C9.5x12.7cm. [14] $42
A PLAN OF THE PALACE, GARDENS & TOWN OF KENSINGTON [1764] C9.5x12.7cm.
[14] $38

ROGERS

HOTCHKISS' GEOLOGICAL MAP OF VIRGINIA AND WEST VIRGINIA. THE GEOLOGY BY PROF.
W.B. ROGERS, CHIEFLY FROM THE VIRGINIA STATE SURVEY, 1835-41 'WITH LATER
OBSERVATIONS IN SOME PARTS' [1884-85] 33x50.8cm. folding lithograph,
overprinted with red lines, from William Barton Rogers, "Reprint of the
Annual Reports and Other Papers, on the Geology of the Virginias," D.
Appleton & Co., New York 1884, "Copyright 1885..." on map [27] $50

ROLLOS

AN ACCURATE MAP OF NORTH AMERICA DRAWN FROM THE SIEUR ROBERT, WITH
IMPROVEMENTS [C1760] 19x29cm. minor spot in ocean [21] $77
AN ACCURATE MAP OF NORTH AMERICA FROM THE LATEST IMPROVEMENTS AND REGULATED BY
ASTRONOMICAL OBSERVATIONS [C1780] 18.7x29.2cm. [8] $120
AN ACCURATE MAP OF NORTH AMERICA... [C1779] 17.1x17.5cm. [22] $75
AN ACCURATE MAP OF THE WORLD... [1759] 14.6x27.9cm.
narrow right margin [22] $100
THE KINGDOM OF BOHEMIA [C1770] 22.9x27.9cm. [30] $81

ROSS

A COPY OF THE TRACING OF THE ICY BARRIER ATTACHED TO THE ARCTIC CONTINENT
DISCOVERED BY THE UNITED STATES EXPLORING EXPEDITION 1840... [1847]
19.5x96cm. [39] $125

ROSSI

IL DUCATO DI MEKLENBURGO CHE E PARTE DELLA BASSO SASSONIA...IL TUTTO PRESSO DA
GIACO CANTELLI, GEOGO DEL SERMO DI MODENA...DI GIO GIACO DE ROSSI EN
ROMA...1692 [1692] 43.2x57.8cm. from "Mercurio Geografico" [7] $400
L'AMERICA SETTENTRIONALE [1687] 39.4x54.6cm. light impression in places,
faint stain in top margin, 2nd edition of a map first appearing in 1677,
based on the Sanson map of 1669 [16] $1100
L'AMERICA SETTENTRIONALE. NUOVAMENTE CORRETTA ET ACCRESCIUTA SECONDO LE
RELATIONI PIU MODERNE DA GUGLIELMO SANSONE GEOGRAFO DI S.M. CHRISTIANISA. E
DATA IN LUCE DA GIO. GIACOMO DE ROSSI, IN ROMA NELLA SUA STAMPERIA ALLA PACE,
L'ANNO 1677 [1677] 41x56cm. light browning [21] $642
L'ISOLE BRITANNICHE... [1677] 41x51cm. slight centerfold wear [31] $91

ROYAL GEOGRAPHICAL SOCIETY

MAP OF SIKKIM [1881] 21.6x22.9cm. lithographed color [30] $4

RUSSELL

A GENERAL MAP OF NORTH AMERICA DRAWN FROM THE BEST SURVEYS [1794] 37x47cm.
light creasing, from Winterbottam, "An Historical, Geographical and
Philosophical View of the American United States," 1795 [21] $126
A VIEW OF THE CITY OF MEXICO [1778] 15.2x20.3cm. [3] $50
BRITISH COLONIES IN NORTH AMERICA FROM THE BEST AUTHORITIES [1800]
19.1x22.9cm. backed [3] $35
MAP OF THE SOUTHERN PART OF THE UNITED STATES OF AMERICA [1798] 19.7x38.7cm.
top margin chipped, 1 cm. tear into map [1] $95
MAP OF THE SOUTHERN STATES OF AMERICA COMPREHENDING MARYLAND, VIRGINIA,
KENTUCKY, TERRITORY STH. OF THE OHIO, NORTH CAROLINA, TENNESSEE GOVERNMENT,
SOUTH CAROLINA & GEORGIA [1795] 36.8x49.5cm. [3] $160
MAP OF THE STATE OF KENTUCKY; WITH ADJOINING TERRITORIES [1794] 38x45cm.
backed [39] $165
MAP OF THE STATE OF KENTUCKY; WITH THE ADJOINING TERRITORIES [1794]
37.5x45.1cm. light browning, repaired tear, right margin narrow [22] $275
NORTH AMERICA FROM THE BEST AUTHORITIES [1798] 19.1x22.9cm. [3] $35
STATES OF AMERICA FROM THE BEST AUTHORITIES [C1792] 19.1x22.9cm. [3] $60

SANSON

See also MORTIER

AMERIQUE MERIDIONALE PAR N. SANSON GEOGRAPHE ORDN. DU ROY REVUE ET CHANGE...PAR
  G. SANSON [1669] 40x55.9cm. backed   [3] $265
AMERIQUE SEPTENTRIONALE [1656] 38.1x55.9cm.
  1st printed map to indicate all 5 great lakes   [15] $2900
AMERIQUE SEPTENTRIONALE [1657] 20.3x27.9cm.
  from 1st ed. of "L'Amerique en Plusieurs Cartes...," minor soiling [27] $375
ATLANTIS INSULA [1668] 40x56cm.   [4] $536
AUDIENCE DE GUATIMALA PAR N. SANSON D'ABBEVILLE GEOGR. ORDIN DU ROY [C1683]
  17.8x27.9cm.   [3] $120
AUDIENCE DE MEXICO PAR N. SANSON D'ABBEVILLE GEOGR. ORDIN. DU ROY [C1678]
  16.5x27.3cm.   [3] $125
CARTE GENERALE DES ROYAUME D'ANGLETERRE, ESCOSSE ET IRLANDE [1646]
  39.4x51.4cm.   [11] $225
CEYLON ET LES MALDIVES [1656-67] 19x16cm.   [31] $61
CHAMPAIGNE ET BRIE, ETC. [C1664] 40x49.5cm.   [24] $91
CHURFURSTENTHUM, UND MARCH BRANDEBURG [1679] 30.5x48.9cm.
  minor wormhole repairs in margins, title also given in French   [24] $91
DESTROIT DE MAGELLAN, TERRE ET ISLES MAGELLANICQUES [C1700] 19.1x24.1cm.
                              [30] $101
GEOGRAPHIAE SACRAE TABULA [C1700] 19.7x27.9cm.   [30] $81
HAUTE ETHIOPE...ET LE ZANGUEBAR [1655] 40x50.5cm.   [4] $122
ISLES BRITANNIQUE... [1646] 23x18cm.   [31] $38
L'ASIE [C1700] 19.7x27.3cm.   [30] $69
L'INDE...L'EMPIRE DU GRAND MOGOL... [1654] 33.7x54cm.   [17] $300
L'INDE...L'EMPIRE DU GRAND MOGOL... [1654] 34.3x54cm.   [24] $73
LA CHINE ROYAUME [1656] 41.3x53.3cm.   [17] $750
LA CHINE ROYAUME. A PARIS: CHEZ PIERRE MARIETTE, RUE S. IACQUE A L'ESPERANCE,
  AVECQ PRIVILEGE DU ROY. POUR VINGT ANS 1656 [1656] 41.9x53.3cm.   [7] $425
LE NOUVEAU MEXIQUE ET LA FLORIDE: TIREES DE DIVERSE CARTES ET RELATIONS [1656]
  31.1x54.3cm.   [15] $2900
LE PARAGUAY [C1700] C21x27.3cm.   [30] $81
LES ISLES ANTILLES &C. ENTRE LESQUELLES SONT LUCAYES ET LES CARIBES [1703]
  38.7x55.2cm. backed   [3] $250
LES ISLES ANTILLES... [C1700] C21x30.5cm.   [30] $121
LES ISLES MOLUCQUES; CELEBES GILOLO, &C... [1683] 18.4x24.1cm.   [24] $64
LES ISLES MOLUCQUES [1656-67] 19x16cm.   [31] $30
LES ISLES PHILIPPINES/ISLAS DE LOS LADRONES... [1656-67] 19x16cm.   [31] $53
LES ISLES PHILIPPINES/ISLAS DE LOS LANDRONES OU ISLE DE LARRONS. A DE WINTER,
  SCULP. PAR LE SR. SANSON D'ABBEVILLE... [1683] 24.4x19.1cm.   [25] $61
LES PROVINCES DES PAY-BAS CATHOLIQUES VULGAIREMENT CONNUES SOUS LE NOM
  FRANDRE...PAR LES SRS SANSON...1690...R. MICHAUT SCRIPSIT [1690] 44x59cm.
                              [18] $105
MAPPE-MONDE OU CARTE GENERALE DU GLOBE TERRESTRE, REPRESENTE EN DEUX
  PLAN-HEMISPHERES [C1665] 14.6x16.5cm.   [34] $300
NOVUS ORBIS POTIUS ALTERA CONTINENS SIVE ATLANTIS INSULA... [1699]
  39.7x55.9cm. minor browning at fold, minor spotting in upper margin[23] $475
PARTIE DE LITHUANIE OU SONT LES PALATINATS DE POLOCZK, WITEPSK, MSEISLAW, ET
  PARTIE DE MINSK. AVEC LE DUCHE DE SMOLENSKO [1665] 42.5x54.6cm.   [24] $79
PICARDIE ET LES PAYS BAS CATHOLIQUES... [1648] 37x52cm. first ed.   [18] $105
PRESQU'ISLE DE L'INDE... [1652] 19.1x24.1cm.   [24] $33
PROVINCES UNIES DES PAYS-BAS. PAR N. SANSON D'ABBEVILLE. GEOGR. DU ROY. 1648
  [1648] 41x51cm. lower margin narrow   [18] $70
ROYAUME D'ANNAN COMPRENENT LES ROYAUMES DE TUMKIN ET DE LA COCHINCHINE...
  [C1650-70] 43.2x31.1cm.   [24] $99
SUMATRA, JAVA, BORNEO, &C. [C1700] 19.5x25cm.   [4] $84
TERRE FERME OU SONT LES GOVERNATIONS OU GOUVERNEMENS DE TERRE FERME, CARTAGENE,
  STA. MARTHE... [1656] 39.8x53.8cm.   [39] $235
TURCOMANIE GEORGIE COMMANIE [1653] 19.1x23.5cm.   [24] $41

SANTINI

CARTE DES ENVIRONS DE LA MER-NOIRE OU SE TROUVENT L'UKRAYNE LA PETITE TARTRIE, ET LES CONFINS DE LA RUSSIE EUROPEENE...PAR LE SR. ROBERT DE VAUGONDY GEOG. A VENISE CHE FRANCOIS SANTINI... [C1784] 49.5x64.1cm. minor stain at lower edge [7] $110

CARTE DES NOUVELLES DECOUVERTES AU NORD DE LA MER DU SUD... [1776] 44.5x62.2cm. Santini's version of the de l'Isle-Buache map of 1752 [23] $675

CARTE DU MEXIQUE ET DU NOUVELLE ESPAGNE [1799] 45x58.5cm. [5] $200

CARTE GENERALE DU CANADA, DE LA LOUISIANE, DE LA FLORIDE, DE LA CAROLINE, DE LA VIRGINIE, DE LA NOUVELLE ANGLETERRE ETC. PAR LE SR. D'ANVILLE A VENISE PAR P. SANTINI 1766 [1766] 48.9x66cm. centerfold discolored [7] $425

CARTE GENERALE DU CANADA, DE LA LOUISIANE...FLORIDE, CAROLINE...VIRGINIE DE LA NOUVELLE ANGLETERRE EC [1776] 47.6x64.8cm. [22] $350

L'AMERIQUE DIVISEE EN SES PRINCIPAUX ETATS ASSUJETTIE AUX OBSERVATIONS ASTRONOMIQES. PAR LE SR. JANVIER GEOGRAPHE. A VENISE CHEZ FRANCOIS SANTINI RUE STE. JUSTINE PRES LA DITE EGLISE [1784] 48.3x66cm. [7] $400

L'EMPIRE DE LA CHINE AVEC LA TARTARIE CHINOISE [1779] 48x54cm. map by Bonne, shows Japan [2] $96

PARTIE MERIDIONALE DE LA LOUISIANE, AVEC LA FLORIDE, LA CAROLINE ET LA VIRGINIE... [1776] 47.8x57.5cm. [39] $320

PARTIE OCCIDENTALE DU CANADA ET SEPTENTRIONALE DE LA LOUISIANE AVEC UNE PARTIE DE LA PENSILVANIE PAR LE SR. D'ANVILLE...A VENISE PAR P. SANTINI 1775 [1775] 48.3x58.4cm. [7] $475

PARTIE OCCIDENTALE DU CANADA... [1775] 48.3x56.5cm. [32] $400

PARTIE ORIENTALE DU CANADA AVEC LA NOUVELLE ANGLETERRE, L'ACADIE, ET LA TERRE-NEUVE [C1780] 48.3x58.4cm. dated 1776, from "Atlas Universel...," Venice, based on the de Vaugondy map [16] $420

ROYAUME D'IRLANDE [1778-83] 47.6x53.3cm. [30] $150

SAYER

A NEW CHART OF HARWICH HARBOUR WITH THE ROLLING GROUND, FELSTOW ROAD, GOLDERMORES AND FLATS OF THE NAZE... [1778] 48.3x48.9cm. minor repair in margin [24] $114

COURSE OF THE RIVER MISSISSIPPI FROM THE BALISE TO FORT CHARTRES; TAKEN ON AN EXPEDITION TO THE ILLINOIS, IN THE LATTER END OF THE YEAR 1765 BY LIEUT ROSS... [1775] 112x34.5cm. light offsetting, on 2 sheets, joined [5] $1200

PLYMOUTH SOUND, HAMOAZE AND CATWATER SURVEYED IN 1786 [1786-91] 69.9x51.4cm. [24] $99

SAYER & BENNETT

A DRAUGHT OF THE GUT OF CANSO BETWEEN NOVA SCOTIA AND CAPE BRETON ISLAND SURVEYED BY THE KING'S SHIPS IN 1761 [1775] 34.3x51.4cm. insets of Port Dauphin & Cow Bay [3] $150

A GENERAL MAP OF THE NORTHERN BRITISH COLONIES IN AMERICA. WHICH COMPREHENDS THE PROVINCES OF QUEBEC, THE GOVERNENT OF NEWFOUNDLAND, NOVA-SCOTIA, NEW ENGLAND AND NEW-YORK...PRINTED FOR ROBT. SAYER & JNO. BENNETT...14TH, AUGUST 1776 [1776] 49.5x66cm. side margins narrow, tears at folds repaired, minor offsetting, from "American Military Pocket Atlas" [7] $700

A MAP OF PHILADELPHIA... [1775] 71.1x137.2cm. map by William Scull [6] $2750

A NEW MAP OF NORTH AMERICA, WITH THE WEST INDIA ISLANDS, DIVIDED ACCORDING TO THE PRELIMINARY ARTICLES OF PEACE, SIGNED AT VERSAILLES, 20 JAN. 1783...LONDON PRINTED FOR ROBT. SAYER AND JNO. BENNETT...AUGUST 15TH. 1783 [C1755-83] 117.5x50.8cm. 4 sheets joined to form 2, dimensions are for each pair, 2nd state of the 1783 edition, the articles from the 1763 treaty being replaced by some from the 1783 treaty [25] $590

A NEW MAP OF THE PROVINCE OF QUEBEC, ACCORDING TO THE ROYAL PROCLAMATION, OF THE 7TH. OF OCTOBER 1763, FROM THE FRENCH SURVEYS CONNECTED WITH THOSE MADE AFTER THE WAR...PRINTED FOR ROBT. SAYER AND JOHN BENNETT...16TH FEBRUARY 1776 [1776] 50.8x70.5cm. centerfold tear repaired, 1st state [7] $1225

A SEA CHART OF THE ATLANTIC OCEAN BETWEEN THE EQUATOR AND LATITUDE 36 NORTH [1777] 49x139cm. may connect with adjoining sheets to form a larger map [39] $135

SAYER & BENNETT (continued)

CHART, CONTAINING THE COASTS OF CALIFORNIA, NEW ALBION, AND RUSSIAN DISCOVERIES
   TO THE NORTH; WITH THE PENINSULA OF KAMTSCHATKA, IN ASIA, OPPOSITE
   THERETO...PUBLISHED ACCORDING TO ACT OF PARLIAMENT 10 JUNE 1775, BY R. SAYER
   & J. BENNETT... [1775] 45.7x111.1cm. on 2 sheets joined, dimensions are
   overall, separations at folds in margins repaired, minor offsetting[7] $650
NORTH AMERICA WITH WEST INDIES WHEREIN ARE DISTINGUISHED THE UNITED STATES AND
   ALL THE POSSESSIONS BELONGING TO THE EUROPEAN POWERS [1783] 30.5x44.5cm.
   backed   [3] $465

SCHEDEL

(WORLD MAP) [1493] 31x43cm. minor damage at centerfold from stitching
   [2] $2985

(WORLD) [1493] 31.8x44.5cm.
   minor repairs in margins, centerfold restoration   [16] $3800
BASILEA (PANORAMIC VIEW) [1493] 24.8x52cm.
   woodcut, narrow margins on all sides   [2] $245

SCHENK

(ALEXANDRIA, VIEW) [1702] C21x25.4cm. one margin narrow	[24]	$153
(ALGIERS, VIEW) [1702] C21x25.4cm.	[24]	$214
(AMARA, VIEW) [1702] C21x25.4cm.	[24]	$183
(ARZILIE, VIEW) [1702] C21x25.4cm.	[24]	$153
(AUGSBURG, VIEW) [1702] C21x25.4cm.	[24]	$229
(BANDEL, VIEW) [1702] C21x25.4cm.	[24]	$229
(CAIRO, VIEW) [1702] C21x25.4cm.	[24]	$214
(COCHIN, VIEW) [1702] C21x25.4cm.	[24]	$214
(DERBENT, VIEW) [1702] C21x25.4cm.	[24]	$183
(DUNKIRK, VIEW) [1702] C21x25.4cm.	[24]	$214
(GAMRON, VIEW) [1702] C21x25.4cm.	[24]	$214
(GIGERI, DJIDJELLI, VIEW) [1702] C21x25.4cm.	[24]	$153
(GOA, VIEW) [1702] C21x25.4cm.	[24]	$183
(INNESBRUCK, VIEW) [1702] C21x25.4cm.	[24]	$229
(JERUSALEM, VIEW) [1702] C21x25.4cm.	[24]	$283
(LEIDEN, VIEW) [1702] C21x25.4cm.	[24]	$214
(LEIPSIG, VIEW) [1702] C21x25.4cm.	[24]	$199
(LINZ, VIEW) [1702] C21x25.4cm.	[24]	$214
(LORETTO, VIEW) [1702] C21x25.4cm.	[24]	$153
(MAGDEBURG, VIEW) [1702] C21x25.4cm.	[24]	$199
(MAINZ, VIEW) [1702] C21x25.4cm.	[24]	$229
(MANTUA, VIEW) [1702] C21x25.4cm.	[24]	$199
(MESSINA, VIEW) [1702] C21x25.4cm.	[24]	$214
(MIDDELEBURG, VIEW) [1702] C21x25.4cm.	[24]	$229
(NAMUR, VIEW) [1702] C21x25.4cm.	[24]	$214
(PASSAU, VIEW) [1702] C21x25.4cm.	[24]	$229
(PRAGUE, VIEW) [1702] C21x25.4cm.	[24]	$229
(RIGA, VIEW) [1702] C21x25.4cm.	[24]	$229
(ROTTERDAM, VIEW) [1702] C21x25.4cm.	[24]	$306
(SALE, VIEW) [1702] C21x25.4cm.	[24]	$183
(SLOBITTEN, VIEW) [1702] C21x25.4cm.	[24]	$122
(SMYRNA, VIEW) [1702] C21x25.4cm.	[24]	$153
(SULTANIA, VIEW) [1702] C21x25.4cm.	[24]	$153
(SURAT, VIEW) [1702] C21x25.4cm.	[24]	$183
(TANGIER, VIEW) [1702] C21x25.4cm.	[24]	$183
(TRIER, VIEW) [1702] C21x25.4cm.	[24]	$229
(TUNIS, VIEW) [1702] C21x25.4cm. small tear in margin	[24]	$183
(VIENNA, VIEW) [1702] C21x25.4cm.	[24]	$229

DIVERSA ORBIS TERRAE...IN PLANUM ORTHOGRAPHICA PROJECTIO [1706] 51x59cm.
   backed with paper   [2] $965
HUNGARIAE [1717] 50.8x57.2cm.   [30] $203
IUDEA, SEU TERRA SANCTA QUAE HEBRAEORUM SIVE ISRAELITARUM... [C1700]
   48.3x58.4cm. backed with tissue, several brown spot stains   [24] $245

PLANSIPHAERIUM COELESTE HYPOTHESIS PTOLEMAICA. EX FORMIS PETRI SCHENCK
AMSTELAEDAMI. CUM PRIV: ORD: HOLL: ET WEST-FRISIAE [C1705] 50.8x57.2cm.
a celestial chart   [7] $1050

SCHERER

AFRICA AB AUCTORE NAURAE SUIS DOTIBUS INSTRUCTA GEOGRAPHICE EXHIBITA [C1700]
23x33cm.   [12] $114
ANGLIA SCOTIA HIBERNIA 1699 [C1700] 22.9x34.3cm.   [12] $122
ARCHIPELAGI AMERICANI DELINEATIO GEOGRAPHICA [C1702] C22x35cm.   [39] $165
ARCHIPELAGI AMERICANI DELINEATIO GEOGRAPHICA [C1700] 23x33cm.   [12] $122
ASIAE PARS AUSTRALIS INSULAE INDICAE CUM SUIS NATURAE DOTIBUS [C1700] 22x33cm.
     [12] $160
ASIAE STATUS NATURALIS DEXTERA DEI OMNIPOTENTIS PERFECT 'GEOGRAPHICE DESIGNAT'
ANNO M.D.C.D. [C1700] 22x33cm.   [12] $145
BEATAM MEDICENT OMNES GENERATIONES [C1703] 23x35cm. a world map   [13] $344
CUM SUO APPARATU VOLUCRUM ET QUADRUPEDUM A MDCC [C1700] 22x33cm.
shows North America   [12] $298
DANIA POMERANIA DVC MECHLE BURGICUS 1699 [C1700] 23x33cm.   [12] $107
DELINEATIO NOVA ET VERA PARTIS AUSTRALIS NOVI MEXICI CUM AUSTRALI PARTE INSULAE
CALIFORNIAE [1702] 23.5x35cm.   [2] $298
FUGURA NATURALIS AMERICAE AUSTRALIS... [1702-10] 22.4x34.9cm.   [39] $95
HISPANIAE ET LUSITANIAE COMPLURA PIA LOCA IMMACULATAE VIRGINAE DICATA...1699
[C1703] 28.5x36cm.   [13] $84
IMAGO TOTIUS ORBIS TERRAQUEI CUM SUO APPARATU AB AUCTORE NATURAE IN SUAS PARTES
DISTRIBUTI. GEOGRAPHICA EXHIBITA. ANNO MDCC [C1700] 23x33cm.
a north polar projection of the entire world   [12] $298
INSULAE INDICAE CUM TERRIS CIRCUMVICINIS [1710] 23x35cm.   [31] $229
REGIONUM CIRCUMPOLARIUM LAPPONIAE ISLANDIAE ET GROENLANDIAE NOVA ET VETERIS
DESCRIPTIO GEOGRAPHICA 1701 [C1703] 29x36cm.   [13] $229
RELIGIONIS CATHOLICAE AUSTRALI AMERICAE IMPLANTATAE DESCRIPTIO GEOGRAPHICA
[1702-10] 21.7x34.2cm.   [39] $145
REPRAESENTATIO GEOGRAPHICA ITINERIS NAVIS VICTORIAE...1522 [1702] 23x35.5cm.
world map showing Magellan's voyage   [2] $263
SOCIETAS IESU PER UNIVERSAM MUNDUM DIFFUSA [1702] 23.5x35.5cm.
world map on a polar projection   [2] $245
SUECIA NORUEGIA RUSSIA MOSCOVE TICA 1699 [C1700] 23x33cm.   [12] $99
TOTIUS ASIAE CONTINENS CUM PRAECIPUS INSULIS EIDEM ANNEXIS [C1700] 22x33cm.
     [12] $122
TYPUS TOTIUS ORBIS TERRAQUEI GEOGRAPHICE DELINEATUS ET AD USUM GLOBO MATERIALI
SUPER INDUCENDUS [1700] 22x35cm. a set of globe gores for a globe 10.5 cm.
in diameter, a cartouch gives a second title, "Globus geographicus novus anno
1700 construct Monachii"   [2] $421
UTRIUSQ TARTARIAE EUROPAE ET ASIATICAE DELINEATIO/INSULARUM INDICARU & TERRA
AUSTRALIA... [1710] 23.5x18cm.   [31] $153

SCHOMBURGK

MAP 5 TO ILLUSTRATE ROUTE FOLLOWED FROM PIRARA TO TORONG [1848] 31.5x22.9cm.
     [39] $20
MAP 6 TO ILLUSTRATE ROUTE FOLLOWED BETWEEN "OUR VILLAGE" AND TORONG [1848]
22.9x25.3cm.   [39] $20

SCHONBERG

SCHONBERG'S MAP OF MEXICO [1866] 37.5x58.4cm.   [20] $85

SCHOOLCRAFT

MAP OF THE INDIAN TERRITORIES WEST OF MISSOURI AND ARKANSAS, COMPILED AND DRAWN
BY S. EASTMAN, CAPT. U.S. ARMY 1853 [1854] 20.3x28.6cm.
from Schoolcraft "History of the Indian Tribes"   [9] $60

SCHOUTEN

CAERTE VANDE NIEUWE PASSAGIE BEZUYDEN DE STRATE MAGELLANI... [C1648]
15.5x22.6cm.   [39] $95

SCHRADER

MAP OF ASHLAND [C1857] 50.8x66cm. minor soiling, creasing, fold damage,
backed with linen, a real estate map lithographed by "Th. Schrader" of St.
Louis   [27] $275

CHRAEMBL
GENERALKARTE VON NORDAMERICA SAMT DEN WESTINDISCHEN INSELN [1788]
   99.1x114.3cm. on 4 sheets joined, folded, some wear at fold intersections,
   minor loss of surface, minor foxing, based on the map by Pownall   [23] $675

COT'S MAGAZINE
A MAP OF THE COUNTRY ROUND PHILADELPHIA INCLUDING PART OF NEW JERSEY, NEW YORK,
   STATEN ISLAND & LONG ISLAND [1776] 17.1x23.5cm. narrow top margin [22] $90
A MAP OF THE COUNTRY ROUND PHILADELPHIA INCLUDING PART OF NEW JERSEY, NEW YORK,
   STATEN ISLAND & LONG ISLAND [1776] 17.8x21.6cm.
   folding map, from September 1776 issue   [27] $135
THIRTY-MILES ROUND BOSTON [1775] 25.4x26cm.
   folds, minor offsetting, 4 cm. tear into map repaired   [23] $175

COTT

CONNECTICUT [1795] 15.2x18.4cm. light staining	[26]	$75
DELAWARE [1795] 18.4x15.2cm. minor staining	[26]	$70
GEORGIA [1800] 15.9x18.4cm.	[11]	$70
KENTUCKY [1795] 15.2x18.4cm.	[26]	$80
MASSACHUSETTS [1795] 15.2x18.4cm. 1st state	[30]	$77
N.W. TERRITORY [1795-1800] 15.2x17.8cm.	[9]	$80
NEW JERSEY [1795] 18.4x15.2cm.	[26]	$75
NEW YORK [1795] 15.2x18.4cm. light offsetting	[26]	$75
NORTH CAROLINA [1795] 15.2x18.4cm.	[26]	$75
PENNSYLVANIA [1795] 15.2x18.4cm. light browning at fold	[26]	$75
SOUTH CAROLINA [1795] 15.2x18.4cm. minor staining	[26]	$70
TENNASSEE [1800] 15.2x19.1cm.	[9]	$60
VIRGINIA [1795] 15.2x18.4cm. some spotting	[26]	$75

SDUK (SOCIETY FOR THE DIFFUSION OF USEFUL KNOWLEDGE)
BOSTON WITH CHARLESTOWN AND ROXBURY. UNDER THE SUPERINTENDENCE OF THE SOCIETY
   FOR THE DIFFUSION OF USEFUL KNOWLEDGE. ENGRAVED BY B.R. DAVIES. LONDON
   CHARLES KNIGHT & CO... [1847] 29.5x37.1cm.   [25] $58
CALCUTTA [1842] 40.5x31cm.   [21] $24
CENTRAL AMERICA I [1842] 30.5x39.4cm.   [19] $75
CENTRAL AMERICA II [1842] 31.1x39.4cm. upper margin repaired [19] $160
CENTRAL AMERICA II [1842] 31.1x39.4cm.   [20] $195
CENTRAL AMERICA II, INCLUDING TEXAS, CALIFORNIA... [C1843] 31.8x39.4cm.
                                      [23] $160
CIRCUMJACENT THE POLE [C1844] 25x25cm.   [21] $28
ISLANDS IN THE ATLANTIC. ENGRAVED BY J. & C. WALKER. PUBLISHED BY BALDWIN &
   CRADOCK 47 PATERNOSTER ROW JUNE 1ST. 1836. FOR THE SOCIETY FOR THE DIFFUSION
   OF USEFUL KNOWLEDGE [1836] 39.7x33cm. narrow margins as issued [25] $42
MADRID [1831] 30.5x36.8cm.   [24] $49
NORTH AMERICA [1843] 38.1x30.5cm.   [19] $90
NORTH AMERICA [1843-44] 38.1x30.5cm.   [20] $75
NORTH AMERICA [1843-44] 38.1x30.5cm.   [8] $85
NORTH AMERICA SHEET IX PARTS OF MISSOURI, ILLINOIS, AND INDIANA [1833]
   29.5x37cm.   [21] $32
NORTH AMERICA SHEET VI NEW-YORK, VERMONT, MAINE, NEW-HAMPSHIRE, MASSACHUSETTS,
   CONNECTICUT, RHODE-ISLAND, AND NEW-JERSEY [1832] 35x31cm.   [21] $36
NORTH AMERICA SHEET VII PENNSYLVANIA, NEW JERSEY, MARYLAND, DELAWARE, COLUMBIA
   AND PART OF VIRGINIA [C1840] 37x31.5cm.   [21] $36
NORTH AMERICA SHEET VIII OHIO, WITH PARTS OF KENTUCKY AND VIRGINIA [1833]
   35.5x31.5cm.   [21] $32
NORTH AMERICA SHEET XV [C1857] 32x39cm. covers the U.S. southwest [4] $76
NORTH AMERICA, SHEET IV... [1846] 30.5x38.1cm.   [10] $50
NORTH AMERICA, SHEET XV, UTAH, NEW MEXICO, TEXAS, CALIFORNIA &C. AND THE
   NORTHERN STATES OF MEXICO [1853] 31.1x39.4cm.   [10] $135
PARIS. PUBLISHED BY BALDWIN & CRADOCK...APRIL 1ST. 1834 [1834] 38.7x52.1cm.
                                      [7] $150
SOUTH AMERICA. SHEET 1. ECUADOR, GRANADA, VENEZUELA, AND PARTS OF BRAZIL AND
   GUYANA...JANY. 15TH. 1842... [1842] 40.6x31.1cm.   [25] $38
THE ANTILLES OR WEST-INDIA ISLANDS...LONDON EDWARD STANFORD... [1873]
   38.7x30.8cm.   [25] $42

SDUK (SOCIETY FOR THE DIFFUSION OF USEFUL KNOWLEDGE) (continued)
```
THE AUSTRALIAN COLONIES [1855] 39x69cm.                               [31]    $53
THE ISLANDS OF NEW ZEALAND [1838-73] 38.1x31.8cm.                     [24]    $68
WESTERN HEMISPHERE [1842] 33x33cm. backed                            [3]    $30
```
SEALE
```
A MAP OF NORTH AMERICA [1747] 36.8x46.4cm. light stain in lower margin
                                                                     [32]   $450
A MAP OF NORTH AMERICA [C1745] 36.8x45.7cm.
  from "Mr Tindal's Continuation of Rapin's History of England"      [16]   $550
A MAP OF NORTH AMERICA... [1745] 36.8x47cm.                          [19]   $300
A MAP OF SOUTH AMERICA WITH ALL THE EUROPEAN SETTLEMENTS... [1740] 47x36.8cm.
                                                                     [3]    $95
A PLAN OF THE TOWN OF PAYTA IN THE KINGDOM OF SANTA FEE [C1749] 21.6x38.1cm.
                                                                     [30]    $20
WEST AFRICA 1753 [1766] 38.1x47cm.
  damaged, from "Postlethwayt's Dictionary"                          [30]    $40
```
SELIGMANN
```
ITINERA VARIA AUCTORIS [C1753] 25.4x20.3cm. sometimes called "the beetle
map," with two large beetles in the North Sea, from G. Edwards, "A Natural
History of Uncommon Birds," 1743-51                                  [13]    $68
```
SELLER
```
A CHART OF THE ISLANDS CORFU, PASHCU AND ANTIPASCHU [1677] 39.5x52.5cm.
                                                                     [2]   $131
A GENERAL CHART OF THE WEST INDIA'S [1675] 42.8x53.5cm.
  a large elephant occupies Africa                                   [39]   $875
A GENERALL CHART OF THE NORTHERN SEAS DESCRIBING THE SEA COAST AND ISLANDS FROM
FRANCE TO GREENELAND [C1680-1700] 41.5x52.5cm.                       [12]   $222
A MAPP OF THE WORLD SHEWING WHAT A CLOCK IT IS IN ANY PART OF THE WORLD, AND TO
KNOW WHERE THE PEOPLE ARE RISEING... [1685] 12.7x15.2cm.             [3]   $100
A NEW GENERALL CHART FOR THE WEST INDIES OF E. WRIGHT'S PROJECTION...MERCATOR'S
CHART BY JER. SELLER. & CH. PRICE HYDROGRAPHERS TO THE QUEEN AT THE HERMITAGE
STAIRS, LONDON 1703 [1703] 45.7x57.2cm.                             [3]   $335
ANGLESEA ISLAND [1693-1787]  C11.4x14cm.
  from "Supplement to the Antiquities of England and Wales"          [30]    $32
BEDFORDSHRIRE [1693-1787]  C11.4x14cm.                               [30]    $32
BERWICKSHIRE [1693-1787]  C11.4x14cm.                                [30]    $40
BISHORPICK OF DURHAM [1693-1787]  C11.4x14cm.                        [30]    $24
BRECKNOCKSHIRE [1693-1787]  C11.4x14cm.                              [30]    $32
BUCKINGHAMSHIRE [1693-1787]  C11.4x14cm.                             [30]    $56
CAMBRIDGESHIRE [1695]  C11.4x15.2cm.                                 [12]    $30
CAMBRIDGESHIRE [1693-1787]  C11.4x14cm.                              [30]    $56
CARMARTHENSHIRE [1693-1787]  C11.4x14cm.                             [30]    $32
CHESHIRE [1693-1787]  C11.4x14cm.                                    [30]    $65
CORNWALL [1693-1787]  C11.4x14cm.                                    [30]    $65
CUMBERLAND [1693-1787]  C11.4x14cm.                                  [30]    $32
DERBYSHIRE [1695]  C11.4x15.2cm.                                     [12]    $27
DERBYSHIRE [1693-1787]  C11.4x14cm.                                  [30]    $32
DEVONSHIRE [1693-1787]  C11.4x14cm.                                  [30]    $56
DORSETSHIRE [1693-1787]  C11.4x14cm.                                 [30]    $52
ESSEX [1693-1787]  C11.4x14cm.                                       [30]    $56
FLINTSHIRE [1695]  C11.4x15.2cm.                                     [12]    $16
FLINTSHIRE [1693-1787]  C11.4x14cm.                                  [30]    $24
GLAMORGANSHIRE [1695]  C11.4x15.2cm.                                 [12]    $22
HAMPSHIRE [1693-1787]  C11.4x14cm.                                   [30]    $40
HEREFORDSHIRE [1693-1787]  C11.4x14cm.                               [30]    $40
HERTFORDSHIRE [1693-1787]  C11.4x14cm.                               [30]    $40
IRELAND [C1690] 44.5x53.3cm.
  trimmed to plate mark, titled in large letters on the map itself   [13]   $298
ISLE OF GUERNSEY [1693-1787]  C11.4x14cm.                            [30]    $48
ISLE OF JERSEY [1693-1787]  C11.4x14cm.                              [30]    $48
ISLE OF MAN [1693-1787]  C11.4x14cm.                                 [30]    $48
```

```
 ISLE OF WIGHT [1693-1787] C11.4x14cm.                                        [30]    $56
 LANCASHIRE [1693-1787] C11.4x14cm.                                           [30]    $40
 LEICESTERSHIRE [1693-1787] C11.4x14cm.                                       [30]    $32
 LINCOLNSHIRE [1695] C11.4x15.2cm.                                            [12]    $27
 LINCOLNSHIRE [1693-1787] C11.4x14cm.                                         [30]    $40
 MERIONETHSHIRE [1693-1787] C11.4x14cm.                                       [30]    $32
 MIDDLESEX [1693-1787] C11.4x14cm.                                            [30]    $56
 MIDDLESEX [1695] C11.4x15.2cm.                                               [12]    $38
 MONTGOMERYSHIRE [1693-1787] C11.4x14cm.                                      [30]    $24
 NORFOLK [1693-1787] C11.4x14cm.                                              [30]    $40
 NORTHUMBERLAND [1693-1787] C11.4x14cm.                                       [30]    $40
 NOTTINGHAMSHIRE [1693-1787] C11.4x14cm.                                      [30]    $40
 OXFORDSHIRE [1695] C11.4x15.2cm.                                             [12]    $27
 PEMBROKESHIRE [1693-1787] C11.4x14cm.                                        [30]    $56
 RADNORSHIRE [1693-1787] C11.4x14cm.                                          [30]    $24
 RUTLANDSHIRE [1693-1787] C11.4x14cm.                                         [30]    $24
 SCOTLAND [1695] C11.4x15.2cm.                                                [12]    $30
 SHROPSHIRE [1695] C11.4x15.2cm.                                              [12]    $22
 SHROPSHIRE [1693-1787] C11.4x14cm.                                           [30]    $32
 STAFFORDSHIRE [1695] C11.4x15.2cm.                                           [12]    $24
 STAFFORDSHIRE [1693-1787] C11.4x14cm.                                        [30]    $32
 SUFFOLK [1693-1787] C11.4x14cm.                                              [30]    $40
 SURRY [1693-1787] C11.4x14cm.                                                [30]    $56
 SUSSEX [1693-1787] C11.4x14cm.                                               [30]    $40
 THE COASTS OF ENGLAND & FRANCE FROM THE START, TO THE ISLES OF SILLY, & FROM
   ISLE DE BASS TO USHANT [C1690] 50.8x38.1cm.                                [13]   $298
 WARWICKSHIRE [1693-1787] C11.4x14cm.                                         [30]    $40
 WESTMORELAND [1693-1787] C11.4x14cm.                                         [30]    $40
 WILTSHIRE [1693-1787] C11.4x14cm.                                            [30]    $52
 WORCESTERSHIRE [1693-1787] C11.4x14cm.                                       [30]    $40
```

SENEX

```
A CHART OF THE COAST OF BRAZIL IN AMERICA: WITH PARTS OF THE CARIBBE ISLANDS
  [C1720] 49.5x117cm. minor faults                                           [39]   $130
A MAP OF LOUISIANA AND OF THE RIVER MISSISSIPI [1721] 48.9x58.4cm.           [19]  $1250
A MAP OF LOUISIANA AND OF THE RIVER MISSISSIPI [1721] 49.5x57.2cm.           [16]   $600
A MAP OF THE WORLD SHEWING THE COURSE OF CAPT. COOK'S VOYAGE ROUND THE SAME
  [1712] 15.9x28.9cm. the "Cook" referred to is Edward Cooke                 [39]    $75
A MAP OF TURKY, ARABIA AND PERSIA...REVISED BY I. SENEX [C1720] 47x56.5cm.
                                                                             [14]   $183
A NEW AND CORRECT MAP OF THE TEN SPANISH PROVINCES... [1714] 62.9x94cm.
                                                                             [24]   $283
A NEW MAP OF IRELAND FROM THE LATEST OBSERVATIONS BY JOHN SENEX [1720-21]
  58.4x47cm.                                                                 [13]   $145
A NEW MAP OF THE ENGLISH EMPIRE IN AMERICA, VIZ. VIRGINIA, NEW YORK, MARYLAND,
  NEW JARSEY, CAROLINA, NEW ENGLAND [1719] 50.5x60cm.
  insets of Boston Harbor and of eastern North America                       [2]  $1317
A NEW MAP OF VIRGINIA, MARYLAND AND THE IMPROVED PARTS OF PENNSYLVANIA AND NEW
  JERSEY [1719] 48.3x54.6cm. engraved in 1719, published in 1721 is "A New
  General Atlas of the World"                                                [16]   $800
NEW MAP OF THE ENGLISH EMPIRE IN AMERICA VIZ VIRGINIA MARYLAND CAROLINA
  PENNSYLVANIA NEW YORK NEW IARSEY NEW ENGLAND NEWFOUNDLAND NEW FRANCE &C
  REVISED BY ION. SENEX 1719... [1721] 50.2x59.1cm.
  some loss near right border repaired, from Senex, "Atlas"                   [7]   $750
NORTH AMERICA ACCORDING TO THE LATEST OBSERVATIONS... [C1710] 15.2x17.8cm.
                                                                              [3]   $135
POLAND AND OTHER COUNTRIES BELONGING TO THAT CROWNE ACCORDING TO THE NEWEST
  OBSERVATION 1719 [1721] 47x28.6cm.                                         [24]    $76
SOUTH AMERICA CORRECTED FROM OBSERVATIONS COMMUNICATED TO THE ROYAL
  SOCIETY...BY JOHN SENEX & JOHN MAXWELL [1710] 94x58.4cm.                    [3]   $250
```

SEUTTER
(JERUSALEM) [C1730] 57.2x49.5cm.   [15] $625
(SCANDINAVIA) [C1740] 48.9x57.2cm. full title not given   [17] $750
ACCURATA DELINEATIO CELEBERRIMAE REGIONIS LUDOVICIANAE VEL GALLICE LOUISANAE
   OT. CANADAE ET FLORIDAE ADPELLATIONE IN SEPTEMTRIONALI AMERICA DESCRIPAE QUOE
   HODI NOMINE FLUMINIS MISSIPPI...MATTHAEI SEUTTERI, CHALCOG. AUGUSTON.
   [C1740] 48.9x55.9cm. margins slightly ragged   [7] $1400
ACCURATA DELINEATIO CELEBERRIMAE REGIONIS LUDOVICIANAE VEL GALLICE LOUISIANE AT
   CANADA ET FLORIDAE...MATTHAEI SEUTTERI [C1740] C49x56cm.
   2 small brown spots, occasional faint underlining with pencil   [8] $900
AMERICA MERIDIONALIS, PER SUA REGNA... [C1740] 19.7x25.7cm.   [39] $95
BOHEMIA REGNUM JUXTA XII. CIRCULOS DIVISUM, CUM COMITATU GLACENSI ET DITIONE
   EGRANA, NEC NON CONFINIBUS PROVINCIIS IN MAPPA GEOGRAPHICA ACCURATISSIME
   DELINEATUM PER MATTHAEUM SEUTTER... [C1734] 48.9x57.2cm.
   minor crease, short tear in lower margin at centerfold   [7] $275
DIVERSI GLOBI TERR-AQUEI [C1725] 50x58cm.
   side margins and lower centerfold reinforced   [5] $1200
DIVERSI GLOBI IRR-AQUEI... [C1734-40] 49.5x57.2cm.
   15 cm. separation in lower centerfold repaired, backed   [27] $1500
DIVERSI GLOBI TERR-AQUI STATIONE VARIANTE ET VISU INTERCEDENTE... [C1727]
   50x58.2cm.   [39] $975
INSULAE JAMAICAE [1730-42] 49.5x59cm.   [31] $459
LUXEMBOURG, UNE FORTERESSE TRES-CELEBRE DE LA DUCHE DE CETTE NOM... [1725-30]
   49.5x57cm.   [18] $702
NOVUS ORBIS SIVE AMERICA [C1725] 50x57.5cm. side margins reinforced   [5] $1400
NOVUS ORBIS SIVE AMERICA MERIDIONALIS ET SEPTENTRIONALIS, PER SUA REGNA,
   PROVINCIAS ET INSULAS IUXTA OBSERVATIONES ET DESCRIPTIONES RE, CENTISS.
   DIVISA ET ADORNATA CURA ET OPERA. MATTH. SEUTTER, SAC. CAES. MAJ. GEOGR. AUG.
   VIND. [C1730] 49.5x58.4cm.
   centerfold separation repaired, minor browning in margins   [7] $1075
PENSYLVANIA NOVA JERSEY ET NOVA YORK CUM REGIONIBUS AD FLUVIUM DELEWARE IN
   AMERICA SITIS, NOVA DELINEATIONE OB OCULOS POSITA... [C1750] 55.9x48.9cm.
   left margin repaired affecting engraved surface, narrow margins   [26] $750
RECENS EDITA TOTIUS NOVI BELGII, IN AMERICA SEPTENTRIONALI... [C1730]
   49.5x57.2cm. minor tears in margins, light spotting, 3rd state   [16] $1250
REGIO CANAAN... [1725] 48.9x56.5cm.   [17] $950

SILVER
A VIEW OF THE TOWN AND CASTLE OF ST. AUGUSTINE AND THE ENGLISH CAMP BEFORE IT
   JUNE 20, 1740 BY THOS. SILVER [1742] 29.2x16.5cm.   [3] $175

SILVESTRE
VEUE ET PERSPECTIVE DE MOMMEDY. ISRAEL SULVESTRE DELIN. ET SCULPSIT 1669
   (VIEW) [1669] 37x98cm. 1st state   [18] $263

SIMONS
DEVONSHIRE [1635] 10.2x10.2cm. J. Jenner issue of 1643   [24] $64

SMITH
A CHART OF THE NORTHERN OCEAN, BETWEEN SCOTLAND & CAPE FAREWEL [1748]
   29.3x44.5cm.   [39] $110
A NEW MAP OF THE COUNTY OF CAMBRIDGE, DIVIDED INTO HUNDREDS [1821]
   50.2x45.1cm. folding, backed with cloth, with original slip case   [30] $48
A NEW MAP OF THE COUNTY OF OXFORD DIVIDED INTO HUNDREDS [1801] 51.4x45.7cm.
   folding, backed with cloth   [30] $44
AMERICA [1820] 35.6x26.7cm.   [3] $45
CHART ILLUSTRATIVE OF THE VOYAGES AND TRAVELS OF CAPTAINS ROSS, PARRY AND
   FRANKLIN [C1832] 26x35cm.   [21] $73
COLOMBIA [1849] 37.5x26.7cm.   [25] $42
MAP OF THE COUNTRIES ROUND THE NORTH POLE [1823] 30.5x27.9cm.   [3] $45
NORTH AMERICA [1808] 26.7x35.6cm.   [20] $95
NORTH AMERICA [1816] 22x35cm. light browning   [21] $69
THE WORLD ON MERCATOR'S PROJECTION [1826] 36.8x57.2cm.   [3] $45
UNITED STATES [1808] 27.9x36.8cm.   [3] $65
UNITED STATES [C1830] 35.6x57.2cm.   [19] $95

SMITH (continued)
UPPER AND LOWER CANADA [1826] 26x35cm. from "The General Atlas"   [21] $36
MOLLETT
A NEW MAP OF NORTH AMERICA FROM THE LATEST DISCOVERIES, 1761. J. SPILBURY,
    SCULP. ENGRAVED FOR THE CONTINUATION OF DR. SMOLLETTS HISTORY OF ENGLAND
    [1761] 38.1x27.9cm. one margin restored   [25] $68
SMYTH
MISSION OF SAN CARLOS, AND BAY OF CARMEL, UPPER CALIFORNIA (VIEW) [C1840]
    11.1x19.6cm.   [39] $30
SANTA BARBARA-UPPER CALIFORNIA (VIEW) [C1840] 11x17.8cm.   [39] $30
THE MISSION OF SAN FRANCISCO, UPPER CALIFORNIA (VIEW) [C1840] 11x17.5cm.
                                                                    [39] $30
SOLINUS
(ASIA, WITH PART OF AFRICA AND N.W. AMERICA, UNTITLED) [1538] 24.1x33cm.
                                                                    [15] $1450
SPEED
(ANGLESEY & CAERNARVONSHIRE) [1627] C8.6x12cm.   [28] $53
(BEDFORDSHIRE) [1627] C8.6x12cm.   [28] $30
(BERKSHIRE) [1627] C8.6x12cm.   [28] $38
(BUCKINGHAMSHIRE) [1627] C8.6x12cm.   [28] $45
(CAITHNESS & ORKNEYS) [1627] C8.6x12cm.   [28] $53
(CAMBRIDGESHIRE) [1627] C8.6x12cm.   [28] $38
(CHESHIRE) [1627] C8.6x12cm. weak impression at right   [28] $45
(CONNAUGHT) [1627] C8.6x12cm.   [28] $30
(CORNWALL) [1627] C8.6x12cm.   [28] $84
(DENBIGHSHIRE & FLINTSHIRE) [1627] C8.6x12cm.   [28] $30
(DERBYSHIRE) [1627] C8.6x12cm.   [28] $53
(DEVONSHIRE) [1627] C8.6x12cm.   [28] $76
(DORSET) [1627] C8.6x12cm.   [28] $53
(DURHAM) [1627] C8.6x12cm. trimmed close at one point   [28] $38
(ENGLAND) [1627] C8.6x12cm.   [28] $38
(ENGLAND, SCOTLAND & IRELAND) [1627] C12.1x15.2cm.
    folding, small cut at one side   [28] $76
(ESSEX) [1627] C8.6x12cm.   [28] $61
(GLAMORGANSHIRE) [1627] C8.6x12cm.   [28] $76
(GLOUCESTERSHIRE) [1627] C8.6x12cm. old inked notation   [28] $53
(HAMPSHIRE) [1627] C8.6x12cm.   [28] $76
(HEBRIDES ETC.) [1627] C8.6x12cm.   [28] $30
(HEREFORDSHIRE) [1627] C8.6x12cm.   [28] $30
(HERTFORDSHIRE) [1627] C8.6x12cm.   [28] $45
(HOLY ISLAND, GUERNSEY, FARNE & JERSEY) [1627] C8.6x12cm.   [28] $53
(HUNTINGDONSHIRE) [1627] C8.6x12cm.   [28] $38
(IRELAND) [1627] C8.6x12cm.   [28] $61
(ISLE OF MAN) [1627] C8.6x12cm.   [28] $84
(ISLE OF WIGHT) [1627] C8.6x12cm.   [28] $61
(KENT) [1627] C8.6x12cm.   [28] $91
(LANCASHIRE) [1627] C8.6x12cm.   [28] $91
(LEICESTERSHIRE) [1627] C8.6x12cm. minor staining   [28] $38
(LEINSTER) [1627] C8.6x12cm.   [28] $61
(LINCOLNSHIRE) [1627] C8.6x12cm.   [28] $53
(MIDDLESEX) [1627] C8.6x12cm.   [28] $84
(MONMOUTHSHIRE) [1627] C8.6x12cm.   [28] $38
(MONTGOMERYSHIRE & MERIONETHSHIRE) [1627] C8.6x12cm.   [28] $30
(MUNSTER) [1627] C8.6x12cm.   [28] $45
(NORFOLK) [1627] C8.6x12cm.   [28] $45
(NORTHAMPTONSHIRE) [1627] C8.6x12cm.   [28] $45
(OXFORDSHIRE) [1627] C8.6x12cm.   [28] $45
(PEMBROKESHIRE) [1627] C8.6x12cm. text shows through   [28] $45
(RADNORSHIRE, BRECKNOCKSHIRE, CARDIGANSHIRE & CARMARTHENSHIRE) [1627]
    C8.6x12cm.   [28] $38
(RUTLAND) [1627] C8.6x12cm.   [28] $38

(SCOTLAND) [1627] C8.6x12cm.	[28]	$61
(SCOTLAND, EASTERN) [1627] C8.6x12cm.	[28]	$38
(SCOTLAND, SOUTHERN) [1627] C8.6x12cm.	[28]	$61
(SCOTLAND, SOUTHWESTERN) [1627] C8.6x12cm.	[28]	$45
(SHROPSHIRE) [1627] C8.6x12cm.	[28]	$30
(SOMERSET) [1627] C8.6x12cm.	[28]	$53
(STAFFORDSHIRE) [1627] C8.6x12cm. light staining	[28]	$45
(STRANAVERNE) [1627] C8.6x12cm.	[28]	$38
(SUFFOLK) [1627] C8.6x12cm.	[28]	$45
(SURREY) [1627] C8.6x12cm.	[28]	$91
(SUSSEX) [1627] C8.6x12cm. printing smudged	[28]	$76
(ULSTER) [1627] C8.6x12cm.	[28]	$53
(WALES) [1627] C8.6x12cm.	[28]	$84
(WARWICKSHIRE) [1627] C8.6x12cm. notation in old ink	[28]	$61
(WESTMORLAND & CUMBERLAND) [1627] C8.6x12cm.	[28]	$45
(WILTSHIRE) [1627] C8.6x12cm.	[28]	$53
(WORCESTERSHIRE) [1627] C8.6x12cm.	[28]	$45
(YORKSHIRE) [1627] 12.1x16.5cm. folding map, repaired	[28]	$99

A MAP OF JAMAICA.../BARBADOS [1676] 38x50cm.   [5] $540
A MAP OF JAMAICA/BARBADOS [1676] 49.5x38.1cm. 1st ed., "Sold by Thomas
  Bassett in Fleetstreet, and Richard Chiswell in St. Pauls Church yard"
                                                                           [25] $651
A MAP OF NEW ENGLAND AND NEW YORK [C1676] 38x50cm.
  centerfold reinforced, small part of blank margin replaced   [5] $1400
A MAP OF NEW ENGLAND AND NEW YORK [1676] C38.7x47.6cm.   [38] $1850
A MAP OF NEW ENGLAND AND NEW YORK [1676] 38.1x50.8cm.
  2 worm holes in margins   [16] $1800
A MAP OF RUSSIA [1676] C38.7x47.6cm.   [38] $450
A MAP OF VIRGINIA AND MARYLAND [C1676] 38x49.5cm.
  centerfold reinforced   [5] $1100
A MAP OF VIRGINIA AND MARYLAND [1676] C38.7x47.6cm.   [38] $1850
A MAP OF VIRGINIA AND MARYLAND [1676] 39.4x48.3cm.   [15] $1100
A MAPP OF THE SOMMER ISLANDS ONCE CALLED THE BERMUDAS... [1676] C38.7x47.6cm.
  trimmed at top   [38] $750
A NEW AND ACCURAT MAP OF THE WORLD [1626] 39.4x50.8cm.
  minor splits repaired, narrow margins, 1st ed.   [15] $3700
A NEW AND ACCURAT MAP OF THE WORLD [1646] 8.9x15.2cm.   [16] $220
A NEW AND ACCURAT MAP OF THE WORLD DRAWNE ACCORDING TO YE TRUEST DESCRIPTIONS
  LATEST DISCOVERIES PE. KAERIUS CAELAVIT 1646 [1646] 9x12cm.   [13] $160
A NEW AND ACCURAT MAP OF THE WORLD. DRAWNE ACCORDING TO YE TRUEST DESCRIPTIONS
  LATEST DISCOVERIES. PE. KAERIUS, CAELAVIT 1646 [1646] 8.6x12.1cm.   [25] $145
A NEW AND ACCURAT MAP OF THE WORLD... [1676] C38.7x47.6cm.   [38] $3750
A NEW DESCRIPTION OF CAROLINA [1676] 37.5x50.8cm. centerfold repaired
                                                                          [32] $1100
A NEW DESCRIPTION OF CAROLINA [1676] 37.5x51.1cm.   [1] $1400
A NEW DESCRIPTION OF CAROLINA [1676] 37.5x50.8cm.   [39] $750
A NEW DESCRIPTION OF CAROLINA [1676] C38.7x47.6cm.   [38] $1750
A NEW DESCRIPTION OF CAROLINA... [1676] 37.8x50.5cm.
  minor repairs in margins, lower centerfold repaired   [35] $950
A NEW MAP OF THE EAST INDIA [1676] C38.7x47.6cm. top margin narrow   [38] $1200
A NEW MAP OF THE ROMAN EMPIRE... [1676] C38.7x47.6cm.   [38] $550
A NEW MAPPE OF YE XVII PROVINCES OF LOW GERMANIE... [1676] C38.7x47.6cm.
                                                                          [38] $450
A NEWE MAPE OF GERMANY... [1676] C38.7x47.6cm.   [38] $700
A NEWE MAPE OF POLAND [1676] C38.7x47.6cm. several light spot stains
                                                                          [38] $650
A NEWE MAPE OF TARTARY... [1676] C38.7x47.6cm.   [38] $850
AFRICAE... [1676] C38.7x47.6cm.   [38] $1600
AMERICA [1626] 38.1x50.8cm.   [15] $2900

AMERICA, WITH THOSE KNOWN PARTS IN THAT UNKNOWNE WORLD... [1676] 40.6x50.8cm.
  minor centerfold repair   [16] $2400
AMERICA... [1676] C38.7x47.6cm. faint impression   [38] $2200
ANGLESEY ANTIENTLY CALLED MONA [1676] C38.7x47.6cm.   [38] $450
ASIA WITH THE ISLANDS ADJOINING... [1676] C38.7x47.6cm.   [38] $1500
BARBADOS [1676] 8.9x12.7cm.   [3] $115
BARKSHIRE DESCRIBED [1676] C38.7x47.6cm. minor wrinkling   [38] $550
BEDFORD SHIRE... [1676] C38.7x47.6cm. tears repaired   [38] $475
BEDFORDSHIRE AND THE SITUATION OF BEDFORD DESCRIBED WITH THE ARMES OF THOS
  HONORABLE FAMILYES THAT HAVE BORNE YE TITLES OF DUKES AND EARLES THEREOF
  [1610-76] 38.1x50.8cm.   [24] $375
BOHEMIA... [1676] C38.7x47.6cm.   [38] $575
BREKNOKE... [1676] C38.7x47.6cm.   [38] $475
BRITAIN AS IT WAS DIVIDED...HEPTARCHY [1676] C38.7x47.6cm.
  minor wrinkling   [38] $375
BRITAIN... [1610-1767] 38.1x50.8cm. the Heptarchy map with decorative panels
  on each side, English text on verso   [13] $728
BUCKINGHAM BOTH SHYRE, AND SHIRE... [1676] C38.7x47.6cm.
  minor wrinkling, repair of tear in margin   [38] $625
CAERMARDEN... [1676] C38.7x47.6cm. portion of lower margin replaced [38] $450
CAERNARVON BOTH SHYRE AND SHYRETOWNE WITH THE ANCIENT CITIE BANGOR DESCRIBED
  [1610-1715] 38.1x50.8cm. narrow margins, Henry Overton issue of c1715
                                             [24] $321
CAERNARVON... [1676] C38.7x47.6cm.   [38] $450
CAMBRIDGSHIRE DESCRIBED... [1676] C38.7x47.6cm.   [38] $850
CANAAN [1651] 38.1x52.1cm.   [15] $1750
CANAAN [1676] C38.7x47.6cm. minor wrinkling   [38] $1200
CARDIGAN SHYRE... [1676] C38.7x47.6cm.   [38] $475
CAROLINA [1675] 8.9x12.4cm.
  two small light stains, top margin narrow, from Speed's "Epitome" [1] $180
CORNWALL [1676] C38.7x47.6cm. one wrinkle   [38] $850
CUMBERLAND... [1676] C38.7x47.6cm.   [38] $550
DARBIESHIRE DESCRIBED 1666 [1676] C38.7x47.6cm.   [38] $450
DENBIGH SHIRE [1676] C38.7x47.6cm.   [38] $475
DENBIGHSHIRE [1610-27] 38.1x50.8cm. Jodocus Hondius Caelavit   [24] $337
DEVONSHIRE... [1676] C38.7x47.6cm. minor wrinkling   [38] $750
DORSETSHYRE... [1676] C38.7x47.6cm. minor wrinkling at centerfold [38] $750
ESSEX DEVIDED INTO HUNDREDS... [1676] C38.7x47.6cm.   [38] $650
EUROP... [1676] C38.7x47.6cm.   [38] $1250
FLINT... [1676] C38.7x47.6cm.   [38] $450
FRANCE... [1676] C38.7x47.6cm. centerfold separation repaired   [38] $250
GLAMORGAN SHYRE [1676] C38.7x47.6cm.   [38] $450
GLOCESTERSHIRE CONTRIVED INTO THRE SEVERALL HUNDREDS & THOSE AGAIN INTO FOURE
  PRINCIPALL DIVISIONS [1611-76] 38.1x49.5cm.
  the Bassett & Chiswell issue of 1676   [14] $383
GLOCHESTERSHIRE... [1676] C38.7x47.6cm. minor crease   [38] $525
GLOUCESTERSHIRE CONTRIVED INTO THIRTY THRE SEVERALL HUNDREDS...THE CITIE OF
  GLOCESTER & BRISTOWE DISCRIBED WITH THE ARMES OF...YE...EARLES & DUKES
  THEREOF [1610-16] 38.1x51.4cm. 2 margins reinforced, 1614-16 issue [24] $528
GREECE [C1676] 39.5x51cm. small stain   [4] $337
GREECE [1627] 8x12.5cm.   [31] $58
GREECE [1676] C38.7x47.6cm. repair in lower portion   [38] $675
HANTSHIRE... [1676] C38.7x47.6cm.   [38] $650
HEBRIDES INSULAE [1627] 8x12.5cm.   [31] $58
HEREFORDSHIRE... [1676] C38.7x47.6cm.   [38] $525
HOLY ISLAND/GARNSEY/FARNE/JARSEY [1676] C38.7x47.6cm.   [38] $250
HOLY ISLAND/GARNSEY/FARNE/JARSEY [1627] 8x12.5cm.   [31] $76

SPEED (continued)

HUNTINGTON BOTH SHIRE AND SHIRE TOWNE WITH THE ANCIENT CITIE ELY DESCRIBED
   [1611-1779] 38.1x49.5cm. the 1770 issue by C. Dicey & Co., with the
   engraving touched-up and altered, Bassett & Chiswell imprint erased, but 1738
   date of Overton issue still shown at bottom right   [14] $229
HUNTINGTON... [1676] C38.7x47.6cm. chip in margin replaced   [38] $550
ITALIA... [1676] C38.7x47.6cm.   [38] $575
JAMAICA [1676] 8.9x12.7cm.   [3] $110
JAMAICA/BARBADOS [1676] C38.7x47.6cm.   [38] $900
KENT WITH HER CITIES AND HER EARLES... [1676] C38.7x47.6cm.   [38] $750
LEICESTER BOTH COUNTYE AND CITIE DESCRIBED [1611-1770] 38.1x50.8cm. printed
   on thin gray paper, no text on verso, backed with cloth, the C. Dicey & Co.
   issue with Dicey imprint at lower left   [14] $229
LEICESTERSHIRE... [1676] C38.7x47.6cm.   [38] $650
MARIONETHSHIRE DESCRIBED 1610 [1676] C38.7x47.6cm.   [38] $475
MIDDLE-SEX DESCRIBED [1676] C38.7x47.6cm.
   centerfold separation repaired   [38] $850
MIDLE-SEX, DESCRIBED WITH THE MOST FAMOUS CITIES OF LONDON AND WESTMINSTER
   [1610-76] 38.1x50.8cm. lower centerfold repaired   [24] $521
MONTGOMERY SHIRE [1676] C38.7x47.6cm. small spot stain   [38] $475
NORFOLK A COUNTIE FLORISHING & POPULOUS DESCRIBED AND DEVIDED WITH THE ARMES OF
   SUCH NOBLE FAMILIES AS HAVE BORNE THE TITLES THEREOF [C1611-76] 39.4x50.8cm.
   new plate engraved by John Goddard, replacing the earlier plate which had
   deteriorated, this copy dating perhaps to 1665, English text   [13] $344
NORFOLK A COUNTIE FLORISHING & POPULOUS DESCRIBED AND DEVIDED WITH THE ARMS OF
   SUCH NOBLE FAMILIES AS HAVE BORNE THE TITLES THEREOF [1611-76] 38.1x50.2cm.
   the new plate engraved by John Goddard   [14] $321
NORFOLK A COUNTIE FLORISHING & POPULOUS... [1676] C38.7x47.6cm.
   tear in margin repaired   [38] $550
NORTHAMPTON SHIRE [1676] C38.7x47.6cm.   [38] $575
NORTHUMBERLAND [1676] C38.7x47.6cm.   [38] $550
OXFORDSHIRE... [1676] C38.7x47.6cm.   [38] $850
PEMBROKSHYRE... [1676] C38.7x47.6cm.   [38] $550
RUTLANDSHIRE... [1676] C38.7x47.6cm.   [38] $450
SHROPSHYRE... [1676] C38.7x47.6cm.   [38] $475
SOMERSET SHIRE... [1676] C38.7x47.6cm.   [38] $850
SPAINE... [1676] C38.7x47.6cm.   [38] $450
STAFFORD COUNTIE AND TOWNE WITH THE ANCIENT CITIE LICHFIELD DESCRIBED
   [1610-76] 38.1x50.8cm.   [24] $344
STAFFORD COUNTIES AND TOWNE... [1676] C38.7x47.6cm.   [38] $500
SUFFOLKE DESCRIBED AND DIVIDED INTO HUNDREDS [1676] C38.7x47.6cm.   [38] $575
SUFFOLKE DESCRIBED AND DIVIDED INTO HUNDREDS, THE SITUATION OF THE FAYRE TOWNE
   IPSWICH SHEWED, WITH THE ARMS OF THE MOST NOBLE FAMILIES THAT HAVE BEEN
   EITHER DUKES OR EARLES BOTH OF THAT COUNTIE AS ALSO OF CLARE [1611-76]
   38.1x50.8cm. the issue of 1676   [14] $298
SURREY DESCRIBED AND DIVIDED INTO HUNDREDS [1610-76] 38.1x51.4cm.
   the issue of 1676   [14] $521
SURREY... [1676] C38.7x47.6cm. light spotting   [38] $750
SUSSEX... [1676] C38.7x47.6cm. wear on part of neat line   [38] $750
THE BISHOPRICK AND CITIE OF DURHAM [1676] C38.7x47.6cm.   [38] $550
THE BISHOPRICK AND CITIE OF DURHAM. ARE TO BE SOLD BY HENRY OVERTON AT THE
   WHITE HORSE WITHOUT NEWGATE LONDON [1610-1743] 38.1x48.3cm. margins added,
   small blue mark on compass, issued by Henry Overton in 1743   [24] $283
THE COUNTIE AND CITIE OF LYNCOLNE... [1676] C38.7x47.6cm.   [38] $575
THE COUNTIE OF LEINSTER... [1676] C38.7x47.6cm.   [38] $550
THE COUNTIE OF NOTTINGHAM... [1676] C38.7x47.6cm.   [38] $675
THE COUNTIE OF RADNOR... [1676] C38.7x47.6cm.   [38] $475
THE COUNTIE OF WESTMORELAND... [1676] C38.7x47.6cm.   [38] $550
THE COUNTY OF WARWICK... [1676] C38.7x47.6cm. minor crease   [38] $575
THE COUNTYE OF MONMOUTH... [1676] C38.7x47.6cm.   [38] $550
THE COUNTYE PALATINE OF CHESTER... [1676] C38.7x47.6cm.   [38] $550

SPEED (continued)

THE COUNTYE PALATINE OF LANCASTER... [1676] C38.7x47.6cm.	[38]	$650
THE INVASIONS OF ENGLAND AND IRELAND... [1676] C38.7x47.6cm.		
accompanied by 4 pages of text	[38]	$550
THE ISLE OF MAN [1676] C38.7x47.6cm.	[38]	$550
THE ISLE OF WIGHT [1627] 8x12.5cm.	[31]	$64
THE KINGDOME OF CHINA [1676] C38.7x47.6cm.	[38]	$1100
THE KINGDOME OF DENMARKE [1676] 39.4x50.8cm.	[17]	$1250
THE KINGDOME OF DENMARKE... [1676] C38.7x47.6cm. 3 light stain spots		
	[38]	$575
THE KINGDOME OF ENGLAND [1627] 8x12.5cm.	[31]	$84
THE KINGDOME OF ENGLAND [1676] C38.7x47.6cm.		
minor wrinkling, light spotting	[38]	$275
THE KINGDOME OF ENGLAND [1610-76] 38.1x51.4cm. issue of 1676	[14]	$398
THE KINGDOME OF IRELAND [1627] 8x12.5cm.	[31]	$84
THE KINGDOME OF IRELAND... [1676] C38.7x47.6cm.		
centerfold separation repaired	[38]	$650
THE KINGDOME OF PERSIA... [1676] C38.7x47.6cm.		
small chip in lower margin replaced	[38]	$650
THE MAPE OF HUNGARI... [1676] C38.7x47.6cm.	[38]	$475
THE NORTH AND EAST RIDINGE OF YORKSHIRE [1676] C38.7x47.6cm.	[38]	$575
THE NORTH AND EAST RIDINS OF YORKSHIRE [1610-17] 38.7x51.4cm.		
the 1627 issue	[14]	$298
THE PROVINCE OF CONNAUGH... [1676] C38.7x47.6cm.	[38]	$550
THE PROVINCE OF MOUNSTER [1676] C38.7x47.6cm.	[38]	$550
THE PROVINCE OF ULSTER [1676] C38.7x47.6cm.	[38]	$475
THE TURKISH EMPIRE [1676] C38.7x47.6cm. one spot stain	[38]	$1200
THE TURKISH EMPIRE [1626] 39.4x50.8cm.	[17]	$850
THE WEST RIDINGE OF YORKESHYRE... [1676] C38.7x47.6cm.	[38]	$575
WALES [1676] C38.7x47.6cm.	[38]	$550
WIGHT ISLAND [1676] C38.7x47.6cm.	[38]	$625
WILSHIRE [1676] C38.7x47.6cm. minor spotting, wrinkle near centerfold		
	[38]	$500
WILTSHIRE [1610-76] 38.1x50.8cm.	[13]	$329
WORCESTERSHIRE DESCRIBED [1676] C38.7x47.6cm. minor creasing	[38]	$550
YORK SHIRE [1676] C38.7x47.6cm.	[38]	$575
YORKSHIRE [C1743] 38.5x51cm. Henry Overton issue, no text on verso	[4]	$421

SPEER

A PLAN OF CAPE NICHOLA MOLE...ISLAND OF HISPANIOLA [1771] 25.4x25.4cm.		
	[3]	$65

SPILBERGEN

NOVA TOTIUS ORBIS TERRARUM DESCRIPTIO [1619] 31.4x44.1cm.		
by Joris van Spilbergen, Leyden	[17]	$1800

STANFORD

BRITISH COLUMBIA, VANCOUVER ISLAND &C. [1859] 33.5x38.5cm.		
minor foxing, small tears in margin	[21]	$52
BRITISH NORTH AMERICA SHEET II, WEST. CANADA WITH PART OF UNITED STATES.		
COMPILED BY J. HUGH JOHNSON, F.R.G.S. ENGRAVED AT STANFORD'S GEOGRAPHICAL		
ESTABLISHMENT, 6 CHARING CROSS, LONDON [1854-62] 40.6x52.7cm.	[25]	$61
JAMAICA [C1880] 48x61cm. folding map in 18 panels, backed with cloth	[39]	$35
THE BAHAMAS [1884] 50.2x65.4cm.		
sectioned, mounted on cloth in boards as issued	[3]	$85

STEDMAN

A MAP OF SURINAM [1791] 19.8x44.1cm.	[39]	$75
A PLAN OF THE ACTION AT BUNKERS HILL, ON THE 17TH OF JUNE 1775 [1794] 49x43cm.		
with the overlay, restored, backed with tissue	[5]	$600
A PLAN OF THE OPERATIONS OF THE KING'S ARMY UNDER THE COMMAND OF GE. SIR		
WILLIAM HOWE, K.B. IN NEW YORK AND EAST NEW JERSEY, AGAINST THE AMERICAN		
FORCES COMMANDED BY GENERAL WASHINGTON... [1794] 73.5x49.5cm.		
left margin added	[5]	$600
PLAN OF THE BATTLE FOUGHT NEAR CAMDEN AUGUST 16TH 1780 [1794] 21.2x18.9cm.		
	[39]	$175

STEDMAN (continued)

PLAN OF THE POSITION WHICH THE ARMY UNDER LT GEN. BURGOINE TOOK AT SARATOGA ON
   THE 10TH OF SEPTEMBER 1777 [1794] 22x47.5cm.   [5] $200
PLAN OF THE SEIGE OF CHARLESTOWN IN SOUTH CAROLINA [1794] 25.5x30cm. [5] $200
PLAN OF THE SEIGE OF YORK TOWN IN VIRGINIA [1794] 27.5x32.5cm.   [5] $200
PLAN OF THE SIEGE OF CHARLESTOWN IN SOUTH CAROLINA [1794] 25.3x29.7cm.
   margins narrow   [39] $75
PLAN OF THE SIEGE OF YORK TOWN IN VIRGINIA [1794] 27.4x32.3cm.   [39] $175
PLAN OF THE SIEGE OF YORK TOWN IN VIRGINIA [1794] 29.2x31.9cm.
   one margin trimmed   [39] $145
POSITION OF THE ENGLISH & FRENCH FLEETS IMMEDIATELY PREVIOUS TO THE ACTION ON
   5TH SEPT. 1781 [1794] 21.6x25.4cm.   [3] $115
STEUDNER

AMSTERDAM (VIEW) [C1690] 19x33cm.   [18] $351
STEVENS

FORT SMITH-ARKANSAS (VIEW) [1859] 14.8x21.9cm.   [39] $35
FORT VANCOUVER W.T. (VIEW) [1859] 15.2x22.8cm.   [39] $50
SAINT PAUL M.T. (VIEW) [1859] 15.1x22.7cm.   [39] $40
STOCKDALE

A MAP OF PENNSYLVANIA FROM THE BEST AUTHORITIES [1794] 17.8x22.9cm. [3] $65
A MAP OF THE COUNTRY BETWEEN ALBEMARLE SOUND AND LAKE ERIE, COMPREHENDING THE
   WHOLE OF VIRGINIA, MARYLAND, DELAWARE AND PENNSYLVANIA [1787] 59.1x59.4cm.
   trimmed to just within neat line at right, remargined, from Thomas Jefferson,
   "Notes on the State of Virginia" published by J. Stockdale, London [35] $850
A MAP OF THE STATES OF VIRGINIA, NORTH CAROLINA, SOUTH CAROLINA AND GEORGIA,
   COMPREHENDING THE SPANISH PROVINCES OF EAST AND WEST FLORIDA: EXHIBITING THE
   BOUNDARIES AS FIXED BY THE LATE TREATY OF PEACE... [1792] 31.1x36.8cm.
                                        [22] $225
A NEW MAP OF UPPER & LOWER CANADA [1798] 17.8x22.9cm.   [3] $55
AN EYE SKETCH OF THE FALLS OF NIAGARA [1798] 16.5x22.9cm. folding [22] $55
SKETCH OF MCLEOD'S HARBOUR, THE WEST SIDE OF MONTAGU IS. [1789] 31.8x30.5cm.
                                        [3] $45
SKETCH OF PORTLOCK'S & GOULDING'S HARBOURS ON NORTH WEST COAST OF AMERICA
   [1789] 31.8x33cm. minor repairs   [3] $40
VIEW OF BETHLEHEM-A MORAVIAN SETTLEMENT [1798] 16.5x22.9cm.
   narrow right margin, light browning   [22] $65
VIEW OF PART OF THE SOUTH SIDE OF THE ISLAND SAPAN, ONE OF THE LADRONE ISLES
   [1789] 17.1x21.6cm. minor repair   [3] $75
STOPIUS

EXACTISSIMA FLANDRIAE DESCRIPTIO...AD CORDATUM LECTOREM N. STOPIUS. VENETIJS,
   1559 [1559] 49.8x41.6cm.   [18] $1404
STROBRIDGE & CO.

PEORIA, ILL. 1874. (VIEW) [1874] 66.7x94cm. tears in margin repaired, drawn
   by F. Dirkson, chromolithograph by Strobridge & Co., Cincinnati, views of
   various buildings above & below main view   [34] $850
STUART

TEXAS, NEW MEXICO & INDIAN TY. [1866-77] 21.6x27.3cm.   [19] $30
SUDLOW

THE WORLD WITH THE LATEST DISCOVERIES [C1795] 25.4x49.5cm.
   narrow top margin   [23] $90
UNIVERSALIS TABULA IUXTA PTOLEMAEUM [C1785] 27.3x43.8cm.
   Ptolemaic world map from Anderson "History of Commerce"   [30] $81
SWINSTON

ARKANSAS, LOUISIANA & MISSISSIPPI [1884] 27.3x21.6cm.
   by W. Swinston or W. Swinton, published by Ivison, New York   [3] $18
ILLINOIS [1884] 45.7x27.9cm.   [3] $20
MARYLAND & DELAWARE [1884] 27.9x43.2cm.   [3] $20
NEW JERSEY [1884] 26.7x16.5cm.   [3] $18
PACIFIC STATES & THE TERRITORIES [1884] 27.9x20.3cm.   [3] $20
RHODE ISLAND [1884] 27.9x22.2cm.   [3] $20
SOUTHERN STATES WESTERN DIVISION [1884] 22.9x27.9cm.   [3] $25

SWINSTON (continued)
VERMONT & NEW HAMPSHIRE [1884] 35.6x27.9cm.   [3] $20
TALLIS
AFRICA [1850-54] C20x25cm.   [14] $38
ANCIENT PALESTINE [1850-54] C20x25cm.   [14] $30
ARABIA [1850-54] C20x25cm.   [14] $22
ASIA [1851] 25.4x32.4cm.   [30] $60
ASIA MINOR [1850-54] C20x25cm.   [14] $18
AUSTRALIA [1850-54] C20x25cm.   [14] $76
AUSTRIA [1850-54] C20x25cm.   [14] $22
BELGIUM [1850-54] C20x25cm.   [14] $15
BOSTON. THE ILLUSTRATIONS DRAWN, & ENGRAVED BY J. WATKINS. THE PLAN, DRAWN &
   ENGRAVED BY J. RAPKIN. THE LONDON PRINTING AND PUBLISHING COMPANY [C1850-65]
   32.4x26cm. a late edition of this map   [25] $67
BRAZIL [1851] C34.3x26.7cm. "London & New York" 2nd state, 1st issue
                                                                 [25] $53
BRAZIL [1850-54] C20x25cm.   [14] $15
BRITISH AMERICA [1851] 25.4x33cm.   [27] $60
BRITISH AMERICA [1850-54] C20x25cm.   [14] $45
BRITISH AMERICA [C1850} C26x32cm.   [21] $73
BRITISH AMERICA [1851] 25.8x32.8cm.   [39] $60
BRITISH AMERICA [C1865] C34.3x26.7cm.
   "The London Printing and Publishing Company" 3rd state, 1st issue [25] $82
BRITISH AMERICA [1850] C34.3x26.7cm.
   "London, Edinburgh & Dublin" 1st state, 1st issue   [25] $70
BRITISH GUAYANA [1850-54] C20x25cm.   [14] $22
BRITISH GUYANA [1851] C34.3x26.7cm.
   "London & New York" 2nd state, 2nd issue having 5 vignettes   [25] $38
BRITISH GUYANA [1851] C34.3x26.7cm.
   "London & New York" 2nd state, 1st issue having 4 vignettes   [25] $38
BRITISH INDIA [1850-54] C20x25cm.   [14] $16
BRITISH ISLES [1850-54] C20x25cm.   [14] $58
BRITISH POSSESSIONS IN THE MEDITERRANEAN [1851] 34.9x25.4cm.   [30] $52
CABOOL, THE PUNJAB... [1850-54] C20x25cm.   [14] $12
CENTRAL AMERICA [1851] C34.3x26.7cm.
   "London & New York" 2nd state, 1st issue   [25] $38
CENTRAL AMERICA (GUATEMALA) [1850-54] C20x25cm.   [14] $12
CEYLON [1850-54] C20x25cm.   [14] $27
CHANNEL ISLANDS [1850-54] C20x25cm.   [14] $30
CHILI AND LA PLATA [1850-54] C20x25cm.   [14] $12
CHILI AND LA PLATA [1851] C34.3x26.7cm.
   "London & New York" 2nd state, 1st issue   [25] $38
CHINA [1850-54] C20x25cm.   [14] $38
DENMARK [1850-54] C20x25cm.   [14] $27
EAST CANADA [1850-54] C20x25cm.   [14] $42
EAST CANADA & NEW BRUNSWICK [1851] 25.4x33cm.   [3] $65
EAST CANADA AND NEW BRUNSWICK [1851] 26.7x34.3cm.   [30] $134
EAST CANADA AND NEW BRUNSWICK [1850] C34.3x26.7cm.
   "London, Edinburgh & Dublin" 1st state, 1st issue   [25] $76
EAST CANADA AND NEW BRUNSWICK [1851] C34.3x26.7cm.
   "London & New York" 2nd state, 1st issue   [25] $67
EAST CANADA AND NEW BRUNSWICK [1850] 25.6x33.5cm. 1st state & issue [39] $80
EAST CANADA, AND NEW BRUNSWICK [1851] C26x32cm.   [21] $65
EASTERN HEMISPHERE [1850-54] C20x25cm.   [14] $53
EASTERN HEMISPHERE/WESTERN HEMISPHERE [1851] C26x32cm.
   two separate sheets, dimensions are for each   [21] $142
EGYPT [1850-54] C20x25cm.   [14] $22
ENGLAND AND WALES [1850-54] C20x25cm.   [14] $53
ENGLAND AND WALES... [1850] 34.3x26cm.   [24] $45
EUROPE [1850-54] C20x25cm.   [14] $38
FALKLAND ISLANDS AND PATAGONIA [1851] C34.3x26.7cm.
   "London & New York" 2nd state, 1st issue   [25] $38

FALKLAND ISLANDS AND PATAGONIA [1850-54] C20x25cm.	[14]	$12
FALKLAND ISLANDS AND PATAGONIA [1851] 34.9x25.4cm.	[30]	$81
FRANCE [1850-54] C20x25cm.	[14]	$18
GERMANY [1850-54] C20x25cm.	[14]	$38
GIBRALTAR, MALTA AND IONIAN ISLES [1850-54] C20x25cm.	[14]	$30
GREECE [1850-54] C20x25cm.	[14]	$18
HOLLAND [1850-54] C20x25cm.	[14]	$22
HUNGARY [1850-54] C20x25cm.	[14]	$22
INDEPENDENT TARTARY [1850-54] C20x25cm.	[14]	$13
INDEPENDENT TARTARY [1851] 25.4x33cm.	[30]	$32
IRELAND [1850-54] C20x25cm.	[14]	$38
ISLANDS IN THE ATLANTIC [1850-54] C20x25cm.	[14]	$36
ISLANDS IN THE INDIAN OCEAN [1850-54] C20x25cm.	[14]	$15
ISLANDS OF THE ATLANTIC [1851] 35x24.5cm.	[31]	$61
ISTHMUS OF PANAMA [1851] 26x33cm.	[30]	$48
ISTHMUS OF PANAMA [1850-54] C20x25cm.	[14]	$12
JAMAICA [1850-54] C20x25cm.	[14]	$22
JAMAICA [1851] C34.3x26.7cm. "London & New York" 2nd state, 1st issue	[25]	$58
JAMAICA [1851] 26.7x34.9cm.	[30]	$81
JAMAICA [1851] 26x34.3cm.	[3]	$55
JAPAN & COREA [1850] 26x33.7cm. backed	[3]	$75
JAPAN AND KOREA [1850-54] C20x25cm.	[14]	$30
MALAY ARCHIPELAGO [1850-54] C20x25cm.	[14]	$58
MEXICO [C1850] 25.4x33cm.	[19]	$125
MEXICO, CALIFORNIA & TEXAS [1849] 26.7x33cm. 1st issue	[3]	$90
MEXICO, CALIFORNIA & TEXAS [C1850] 24.8x32.4cm.	[20]	$140
MEXICO, CALIFORNIA AND TEXAS [C1851] 25.4x33cm.	[22]	$150
MEXICO, CALIFORNIA AND TEXAS [1850] 25.4x33cm. minor browning at centerfold	[23]	$145
MEXICO, CALIFORNIA AND TEXAS [1850-54] C20x25cm.	[14]	$45
MODERN PALESTINE [1850-54] C20x25cm.	[14]	$27
NATAL [1850-54] C20x25cm.	[14]	$12
NEW SOUTH WALES [1850-54] C20x25cm.	[14]	$73
NEW ZEALAND [1851] 35.6x26cm.	[30]	$73
NEW ZEALAND [1850-54] C20x25cm.	[14]	$73
NEWFOUNDLAND AND NOVA SCOTIA [1851] C34.3x26.7cm. "London & New York" 2nd state, 1st issue, 3 vignettes including one included in lower border	[25]	$91
NORTH AMERICA [1850-54] C20x25cm.	[14]	$53
NORTH AMERICA [1851] C26x32cm.	[21]	$73
NORTH AMERICA [1851] 35.6x24.1cm.	[30]	$101
NORTH AMERICA [1849] 35.6x24.1cm.	[3]	$65
NORTH AMERICA [1850] C34.3x26.7cm. "London, Edinburgh & Dublin" 1st state, 1st issue	[25]	$84
NORTH AMERICA [C1850] 35.6x23.8cm.	[20]	$110
NORTH AMERICA [1851] 35.6x24.1cm.	[9]	$85
NORTH AMERICA [C1850] C32x26cm.	[19]	$100
NORTHERN AFRICA [1850-54] C20x25cm.	[14]	$15
NORTHERN INDIA [1850-54] C20x25cm.	[14]	$16
NORTHERN ITALY [1850-54] C20x25cm.	[14]	$12
NOVA SCOTIA AND NEWFOUNDLAND [C1865] C34.3x26.7cm. "The London Printing and Publishing Company" 3rd state, 1st issue	[25]	$52
NOVA SCOTIA AND NEWFOUNDLAND [1851] C34.3x26.7cm. "London & New York" 2nd state, 2nd issue with 5 vignettes including one incorporated in lower border	[25]	$61
NOVA SCOTIA AND NEWFOUNDLAND [1851] C26x32cm.	[21]	$73
NOVA SCOTIA... [1850-54] C20x25cm.	[14]	$38
OVERLAND ROUTE TO INDIA [1850-54] C20x25cm.	[14]	$12
PART OF SOUTH AUSTRALIA [C1851] 33.5x24.5cm.	[4]	$91
PERSIA [1850-54] C20x25cm.	[14]	$15

```
PERU & BOLIVIA [1851]  C34.3x26.7cm.
   "London & New York" 2nd state, 1st issue                      [25]    $38
PERU & BOLIVIA [1850] 35.6x25.4cm.                               [3]     $30
PERU AND BOLIVIA [1850-54]  C20x25cm.                            [14]    $12
POLYNESIA [1850-54]  C20x25cm.                                   [14]    $15
POLYNESIA OR ISLANDS IN THE PACIFIC OCEAN [1851] 26x35.6cm.      [30]    $48
PRUSSIA [1850-54]  C20x25cm.                                     [14]    $22
RUSSIA IN ASIA [1850-54]  C20x25cm.                              [14]    $18
RUSSIA IN EUROPE [1850-54]  C20x25cm.                            [14]    $18
SCOTLAND [1850-54]  C20x25cm.                                    [14]    $45
SCOTLAND [1850-51] 36.2x25.4cm.                                  [24]    $49
SOUTH AMERICA [1850] 35.6x24.1cm.                                [3]     $50
SOUTH AMERICA [1850-54]  C20x25cm.                               [14]    $45
SOUTH AMERICA [1850]  C34.3x26.7cm.
   "London, Edinburgh & Dublin" 1st state, 1st issue             [25]    $53
SOUTH AUSTRALIA [1850-54]  C20x25cm.                             [14]    $42
SOUTHERN AFRICA (CAPE COLONY) [1850-54]  C20x25cm.               [14]    $22
SOUTHERN INDIA [1850-54]  C20x25cm.                              [14]    $16
SOUTHERN ITALY [1850-54]  C20x25cm.                              [14]    $12
SPAIN AND PORTUGAL [1850-54]  C20x25cm.                          [14]    $18
SWEDEN AND NORWAY [1850-54]  C20x25cm.                           [14]    $30
SWITZERLAND [1850-54]  C20x25cm.                                 [14]    $30
SYRIA [1850-54]  C20x25cm.                                       [14]    $18
THE WORLD [1850-54]  C20x25cm.                                   [14]    $38
THE WORLD ON MERCATOR'S PROJECTION [1850] 26.7x35.6cm.           [3]     $50
THE WORLD ON MERCATOR'S PROJECTION [1851]  C26x32cm.             [21]    $69
THE WORLD ON MERCATOR'S PROJECTION, SHEWING THE VOYAGES OF CAPTAIN COOK...
   [1851] 22.2x31.8cm.                                           [22]   $100
THIBET, MONGOLIA AND MANDCHOURIA [1851] 25.4x33cm.               [30]    $32
THIBET, MONGOLIA... [1850-54]  C20x25cm.                         [14]    $12
TURKEY IN ASIA [1850-54]  C20x25cm.                              [14]    $18
TURKEY IN EUROPE [1850-54]  C20x25cm.                            [14]    $12
UNITED STATES [1851]  C34.3x26.7cm.
   "London & New York" 2nd state, 1st issue                      [25]    $73
UNITED STATES [C1850] 22.2x30.5cm. light browning, Texas shown in large
   pre-1850 configuration, possibly an earlier state of this map [20]   $120
UNITED STATES [1850-54]  C20x25cm.                               [14]    $52
UNITED STATES [C1850] 24.1x33.7cm.                               [19]   $125
UNITED STATES [C1850] 22.2x30.5cm.                               [20]   $125
UNITED STATES [C1850] 24.1x31.8cm. light spotting                [16]    $85
UNITED STATES [1851]  C26x32cm.                                  [21]    $97
VAN DIEMEN'S LAND [1850-54]  C20x25cm.                           [14]    $58
VENEZUELA, NEW GRANADA, EQUADOR, AND THE GUYANAS [1851]  C34.3x26.7cm.
   "London & New York" 2nd state, 1st issue                      [25]    $49
VENEZUELA, NEW GRANADA... [1850-54]  C20x25cm.                   [14]    $12
VICTORIA OR PORT PHILLIP [1850-54]  C20x25cm.                    [14]    $58
WEST CANADA [1850]  C34.3x26.7cm.
   "London, Edinburgh & Dublin" 1st state, 1st issue             [25]    $68
WEST CANADA [1851]  C26x32cm.                                    [21]    $73
WEST CANADA [1850-54]  C20x25cm.                                 [14]    $38
WEST CANADA [1850] 24.8x32.8cm.                                  [39]    $70
WEST CANADA [1851] 25.4x33cm.                                    [30]   $134
WEST CANADA [1851]  C34.3x26.7cm.
   "London & New York" 2nd state, 1st issue                      [25]    $68
WEST CANADA [C1851] 25x33cm.                                     [4]     $68
WEST INDIA ISLANDS [1850-54]  C20x25cm.                          [14]    $45
WEST INDIES [C1865]  C34.3x26.7cm.
   "The London Printing and Publishing Company" 3rd state, 1st issue [25] $53
WESTERN AFRICA [1850-54]  C20x25cm.                              [14]    $22
WESTERN AFRICA [1851] 25.4x35.6cm.                               [30]    $36
```

TALLIS (continued)
WESTERN AUSTRALIA [1850-54] C20x25cm.   [14] $76
WESTERN AUSTRALIA [C1851] 34x24cm.   [4] $107
WESTERN HEMISPHERE [1851] C34.3x26.7cm.
  "London & New York" 2nd state, 1st issue   [25] $53
WESTERN HEMISPHERE [1850-54] C20x25cm.   [14] $53
WESTERN HEMISPHERE [1851] 24.1x34.9cm.   [32] $120

TANNER
(ALABAMA) [1836] 33.7x26.7cm.   [26] $50
(GEORGIA) [1833] 33x27.3cm. minor stains   [26] $75
(ILLINOIS) [1836] 33.7x26.7cm.   [26] $75
(LOUISIANA) [1833] 27.3x33.7cm.   [26] $75
(MISSISSIPPI) [1836] 33x26.7cm.   [26] $50
(MISSOURI) [1836] 33x26.7cm. stain at upper right   [26] $50
(NEW JERSEY) [1834] 35.6x29.2cm.   [26] $75
(NEW YORK) [1833] 27.3x32.4cm.   [26] $45
(OHIO) [1836] 33x26.7cm.   [26] $50
(VIRGINIA) [1836] 27.3x33cm.   [26] $45
A NEW MAP OF THE WORLD ON THE GLOBULAR PROJECTION [1836] 22.9x33.7cm.
                                                                                 [3] $60

CITY OF WASHINGTON [1836] 29.2x36.8cm.
  from Henry Tanner, "Universal Atlas"   [27] $110
CONNECTICUT [1834-36] 29.2x35.6cm. map dated 1834, published in 1836 in "New
  Universal Atlas," upper margin narrow, minor foxing   [27] $75
LOUISIANA [1839] 26.7x34.3cm.   [27] $125
MAP OF TEXAS FROM THE MOST RECENT AUTHORITIES [1845] 30.5x37.5cm.   [22] $400
MARYLAND AND DELAWARE [1836] 26.7x34.3cm.   [27] $90
MASSACHUSETTS AND RHODE ISLAND [1846] 30.5x39.5cm.
  folding, with covers   [39] $35
MEXICO & GUATEMALA [1834] 29.2x36.2cm. 1st ed.   [3] $135
NEW JERSEY [1834-42] 35.6x29.2cm.
  dated 1834 in lower margin, 1841 in title, published in 1842   [27] $70
NORTH AMERICA [1836] 37.1x30.2cm.   [26] $200
NORTH AMERICA [C1836-43] 38.4x32.1cm.   [33] $125
PENNSYLVANIA [1833-36] 26.7x34.3cm.
  dated 1833, published 1836 in "Universal Atlas"   [27] $75
PERU & BOLIVIA [1838] 30.5x35.6cm.   [3] $35
PHILADELPHIA [1836] 35.6x29.2cm.   [3] $75
THE WORLD ON MERCATOR'S PROJECTION [1823] 46.4x53.3cm.   [3] $125

TARDIEU
CARTE DES ETATS-UNIS DE L'AMERIQUE SEPTENTRIONALE COPIEE ET GRAVEE SUR CELLE
  D'ARROWSMITH... [1802] 122x142cm. relaid onto 4 linen sheets, in 60 panels,
  several worm holes filled, with original slip case, 1st ed.   [39] $725
OCEANIQUE ORIENT [1840] 22x30cm.   [31] $84

TARLETON
PLAN OF THE SIEGE OF CHARLESTOWN IN SOUTH CAROLINA [1787] 25.5x29.6cm.
  special edition on separate sheets, wide margins   [39] $155

TASSIN
CARTE GENERALE DES DIX ET SEPT PROVINCES DES PAYS-BAS [1634] 37x52cm.
                                                                                 [18] $175

TAVERNIER
CARTE GENERALE DES DIX SEPT PROVINCES DES PAIS BAS. PARIS, PAR M.
  TAVERNIER...EN LISLE DU PALAIS A LA SPHERE ROYALLE, 1661 [1661] 30x37cm.
                                                                                 [18] $105

CARTE GENERALE DES DIXSEPT PROVINCES DES PAIS-BAS...PAR M. TAVERNIER, GRAVEUR
  ET IMPRIMEUR DU ROY...A LA SPHERE ROYALLE, 1640 [1640] 53x41.5cm.   [18] $175

TEESDALE
See also DOWER
A COMPARATIVE VIEW OF THE HEIGHTS OF THE PRINCIPAL MOUNTAINS AND LENGTHS OF THE
  PRINCIPAL RIVERS IN THE WORLD [C1834] 40.5x32.5cm.
  small splits in margin at centerfold   [21] $60

TEESDALE (continued)
```
AMERICA [1834] 41.9x33.7cm.                                         [3]    $45
AMERICA. DRAWN & ENGRAVED BY J. DOWER...LONDON PUBLISHED BY HENRY TEESDALE &
   CO. 302 HIGH HOLBORN, MARCH 1831 [1832] 41.3x33.7cm.           [25]    $64
BRAZIL. DRAWN & ENGRAVED BY J. DOWER...LONDON PUBLISHED BY HENRY TEESDALE &
   CO...1831 [1831-32] 41.3x33.7cm.                               [25]    $70
CANADA, NEW BRUNSWICK AND NOVA SCOTIA [1838] 40x32cm.
   from "New General Atlas"                                       [21]    $52
CHINA AND JAPAN [1845] 33x43.2cm.                                  [3]    $35
MEXICO AND GUATIMALA [1845] 33x40.6cm.                            [22]   $175
MEXICO AND GUATIMALA [C1852] 33.7x40.6cm.                         [11]    $90
PERU AND BOLIVIA [1831] 41.3x33.7cm.                              [25]    $39
THE WORLD ON MERCATOR'S PROJECTION [1842] 34.3x41.3cm.             [3]    $40
THE WORLD ON MERCATOR'S PROJECTION. DRAWN AND ENGRAVED BY J. DOWER...LONDON
   PUBLISHED BY HENRY TEESDALE & CO. 302 HIGH HOLBORN, MARCH 1831 [1832]
   33.7x41.3cm. watermarked "J. Whatman 1832"                    [25]    $49
UNITED STATES [C1842] 34.3x40.6cm.                                 [3]    $60
UNITED STATES [1831] 33.7x40.6cm.                                 [25]    $42
```
TEGG
```
ASIA FROM THE BEST AUTHORITIES [1823] 19.7x23.5cm.
   from "Brook's Gazetteer"                                       [30]    $20
EUROPE, FROM THE BEST AUTHORITIES [1823] 23.5x22.9cm.             [30]    $12
NORTH AMERICA FROM THE BEST AUTHORITIES [1823] 19.7x22.9cm.       [30]    $32
SOUTH AMERICA FROM THE BEST AUTHORITIES [1823] 19.7x23.5cm.       [30]    $16
WEST INDIES FROM THE BEST AUTHORITIES [1823] 19.1x23.5cm.         [30]   $243
```
THOMAS, COWPERTHWAIT & CO.
```
(ALABAMA) [1850-54] 36.2x29.2cm.                                   [8]    $35
(ARKANSAS) [1850-54] 36.5x29.8cm.                                  [8]    $35
(CALIFORNIA AND THE TERRITORIES OF OREGON, WASHINGTON UTAH & NEW MEXICO)
   [1853-54] 39.4x31.8cm.                                         [8]    $60
(FLORIDA) [1850-54] 36.5x29.5cm.                                   [8]    $40
(GEORGIA) [1850-54] 35.6x29.2cm.                                   [8]    $40
(ILLINOIS) [1850-54] 39.4x33cm.                                    [8]    $45
(INDIANA) [1850-54] 35.2x28.9cm. inset of Wabash & Erie Canal      [8]    $40
(IOWA) [1850-54] 33x40.6cm.                                        [8]    $35
(KENTUCKY) [1850-54] 29.2x35.2cm.                                  [8]    $35
(LOUISIANA) [1850-54] 29.5x36.2cm. inset of New Orleans            [8]    $30
(MAINE) [1850-54] 38.1x30.5cm.                                     [8]    $30
(MARYLAND AND DELAWARE) [1850-54] 29.2x36.8cm.                     [8]    $30
(MASSACHUSETTS AND RHODE ISLAND) [1850-54] 29.2x36.8cm.            [8]    $30
(MICHIGAN) [1850-54] 36.8x29.5cm.                                  [8]    $35
(MINNESOTA TERRITORY) [1850-54] 33.7x40.6cm.                       [8]    $75
(MISSISSIPPI) [1850-54] 35.2x29.5cm.                               [8]    $35
(MISSOURI) [1850-54] 33x40.6cm.                                    [8]    $45
(NEW HAMPSHIRE & VERMONT) [1850-54] 37.5x30.5cm.                   [8]    $30
(NEW JERSEY) [1850-54] 37.8x31.8cm.                                [8]    $35
(NEW YORK) [1854] 40.6x26cm.                                       [8]    $40
(NORTH AMERICA) [1850-54] 39.4x32.4cm.                             [8]    $40
(NORTH CAROLINA) [1850-54] 29.2x35.2cm.                            [8]    $45
(OHIO) [1850-54] 40x33cm.                                          [8]    $35
(PENNSYLVANIA) [1853-54] 29.2x36.2cm.                              [8]    $25
(PHILADELPHIA) [1854] 39.7x32.4cm.                                 [8]    $25
(SOUTH CAROLINA) [1850-54] 28.9x35.6cm. inset of Charleston        [8]    $35
(TENNESSEE) [1850-54] 36.2x38.7cm.                                 [8]    $70
(TEXAS) [1850-54] 32.4x40cm. minor damage in lower margin          [8]    $75
(VIRGINIA) [1850-54] 29.2x34.9cm.
   inset: Profile of the Chesapeake & Ohio Canal                  [8]    $35
(WISCONSIN) [1850-54] 40.3x33.7cm.                                 [8]    $35
A NEW MAP OF ARKANSAS WITH THE CANALS, ROADS & DISTANCES [1850] 36.8x29.2cm.
                                                                  [3]    $40
A NEW MAP OF GEORGIA [1850] 35.6x29.2cm.                           [3]    $45
```

A NEW MAP OF LOUISIANA WITH...DISTANCES ALONG STAGE & STEAMBOAT ROUTES [1850]
   29.2x36.8cm.   [3] $45
A NEW MAP OF NEW YORK WITH ITS CANALS, ROADS & DISTANCES [1850] 29.2x35.6cm.
        [3] $35
A NEW MAP OF PENNSYLVANIA WITH ITS CANALS, RAILROADS &C. [1850] 30.5x35.6cm.
        [3] $45
A NEW MAP OF SOUTH CAROLINA WITH ITS CANALS, ROADS & DISTANCES [1850]
   29.2x35.6cm.   [3] $35
A NEW MAP OF TENNESSEE WITH ITS ROADS & DISTANCES AMONG STAGE & STEAM BOAT
   ROUTES [1850] 27.9x39.4cm.   [3] $40
A NEW MAP OF THE UNITED STATES [1850-54] 40.6x66.7cm.   [8] $85
A NEW MAP OF THE UNITED STATES OF AMERICA BY J.H. YOUNG [1850] 40.6x67.3cm.
   minor repairs   [3] $85
A NEW MAP OF THE WORLD ON THE GLOBULAR PROJECTIONS [1850-54] 24.1x36.2cm.
        [8] $50
BRAZIL [1850] 38.1x31.8cm.   [3] $30
CANADA EAST FORMERLY LOWER CANADA [1850-54] 31.1x39.4cm.   [8] $35
CANADA WEST FORMERLY UPPER CANADA [1850-54] 31.8x39.4cm.   [8] $35
CHILI, LA PLATA & URUGUAY [1850] 38.1x31.8cm.   [3] $30
CITY OF WASHINGTON [1850-54] 31.8x39.7cm.   [8] $25
MAP OF MINNESOTA TERRITORY [1850] 33x40.6cm.   [3] $60
MAP OF NEW HAMPSHIRE & VERMONT [1850] 38.1x30.5cm.   [3] $30
MAP OF THE STATE OF CALIFORNIA, THE TERRITORIES OF OREGON & UTAH, & PART OF NEW
   MEXICO [1851] 40x33cm.   [3] $95
MAP OF THE STATE OF OHIO [1850] 39.4x33cm.   [3] $40
MEXICO AND GUATEMALA [1850] 30.5x38.1cm.   [10] $35
SOUTH AMERICA [1851] 39.4x32.4cm. minor repairs   [3] $30

THOMSON

A CHART OF THE DISCOVERIES OF CAPTAINS ROSS, PARRY & FRANKLIN, IN THE ARCTIC
   REGIONS, IN THE YEARS 1818, 1819, 1820, 1821 & 1822 [C1827] 49.5x58.4cm.
   minor foxing, inset: Capt. Franklin's Journey from Coppermine River, To The
   Head Of Bathurst Inlet, & Return By Hood's River   [7] $300
A COMPARATIVE VIEW OF THE HEIGHTS OF THE PRINCIPAL MOUNTAINS AND OTHER
   ELEVATIONS IN THE WORLD [C1814] 50.5x63.5cm.   [4] $68
ATLANTIC ISLANDS [1816] 50.2x59.7cm.   [3] $75
ATLANTIC ISLANDS [1814] 50.8x59.7cm.   [3] $70
BARBADOS [1816] 50.8x30.5cm. left margin restored   [3] $45
CANADA [C1819-32] 18x23.5cm.   [21] $36
CANADA AND NOVA SCOTIA [1814] 48x60cm. fold reinforced   [21] $130
CANADA AND NOVA SCOTIA. DRAWN AND ENGRAVED FOR THOMSON'S NEW GENERAL ATLAS
   1814 [1814] 48.9x59.7cm. tear in lower margin at centerfold repaired
        [7] $225
CARACAS AND GUIANA [1814] 49.5x59.1cm. narrow, soiled lower margin [32] $75
CARACCAS AND GUIANA. ENGD. BY J. MOFFAT... [1817] 50.2x59.7cm. [25] $49
CHART OF THE BAHAMA ISLANDS/THE BERMUDAS OR SUMMER ISLANDS/ISLAND OF CUBA
   [1817-28] 50x58.6cm.   [39] $95
CHART OF THE NORTHERN PASSAGE BETWEEN ASIA & AMERICA [C1817] 50x59cm.
        [4] $183
CHART OF THE NORTHERN PASSAGE BETWEEN ASIA & AMERICA. DRAWN & ENGRAVED FOR
   THOMSON'S NEW GENERAL ATLAS 1816 [1816] 49.5x58.4cm.
   margins ragged, severals short tears repaired   [7] $300
COREA AND JAPAN [1817] 49.5x63.5cm.   [3] $145
HYDROGRAPHICAL CHART OF THE WORLD ON WRIGHT OR MERCATOR'S PROJECTION WITH
   TRACKS...CIRCUMNAVIGATORS [1814] 44.5x50.8cm.   [3] $120
JAMAICA [1814] 41.9x59.7cm. lower margin ragged   [32] $135
NORTH AMERICA [1814] 50.2x60.3cm.   [3] $110
NORTH AMERICA. N.R. HEWITT SC., 10 BROAD STR. BLOOMSBY. LONDON. DRAWN AND
   ENGRAVED FOR THOMSONS NEW GENERAL ATLAS 1814 [1814-17] 59.1x49.5cm.
   watermarked "J. Whatman 1815"   [25] $99
NORTHERN PROVINCES OF THE UNITED STATES [1817] 49.5x59.1cm. [3] $135

THOMSON (continued)

NORTHERN PROVINCES OF THE UNITED STATES [1817] 49.5x58.4cm. [32] $140
NORTHERN PROVINCES OF THE UNITED STATES [1817] 49.5x59cm.
   light offsetting [21] $117
POLAR REGIONS [C1819] 18x24cm. from Wyld, "A General Atlas" [21] $52
PORTO RICO & VIRGIN ISLANDS [1814] 23.5x61cm. [3] $75
PORTO RICO AND VIRGIN ISLES/HAITI HISPANIOLA OR ST. DOMINGO...FEBY. 1815
   [1817] 61x50.8cm. no centerfold [25] $58
SOUTHERN PROVINCES OF THE UNITED STATES [1817] 49.5x58.4cm. [3] $145
SOUTHERN PROVINCES OF UNITED STATES [1817] 49.5x58.4cm. [3] $145
SPANISH NORTH AMERICA [1814-17] 62.2x50.8cm. bottom margin narrow, 2 cm.
   separation of lower centerfold repaired, minor discoloration, dated 1814,
   published in 1817 in "New General Atlas" [27] $325
THE COURSE OF THE RIVER ST. LAURENCE, FROM LAKE ONTARIO, TO MANICOUAGAN POINT.
UNITED STATES OF AMERICA [1817] 43.8x62.9cm. [7] $250
UNITED STATES OF AMERICA AND THE COURSE OF THE RIVER ST. LAURENCE FROM LAKE
   ONTARIO TO MANICOUAGAN POINT [1817] 41.5x23cm. light foxing & browning
      [21] $105
WESTERN HEMISPHERE [1815] 52.1x50.8cm. from "General Atlas" [30] $142

THORNTON

A CHART OF THE COAST OF BARBARIA WITH THE WESTERN, CANARIA, & CAPE DE VERD,
   ISLES. BY SAML. THORNTON AT THE SIGN OF ENGLAND SCOTLAND AND IRELAND IN THE
   MINORIES LONDON [C1706] 41.9x54.6cm.
   small hole repaired, an early issue [24] $130
A LARGE DRAUGHT OF THE NORTH PART OF CHINA SHOWING ALL THE PASSAGES AND
   CHANNELS INTO THE HARBOUR OF CHUSAN [1706] 53x87cm.
   water staining of upper portion, creases, separately published [2] $333
A LARGE DRAUGHT OF THE NORTH PART OF CHINA: SHEWING ALL THE PASSAGES OF AND
   CHANELLS INTO THE HARBOUR OF CHUSAN. BY SAML. THORNTON, HYDROGR. AT THE
   ENGLAND, SCOTLAND AND IRELAND IN THE MINORIES LONDON [1716] 52.1x86.4cm.
   an early issue [24] $268

TINDAL

AETH, A STRONG, FRONTIER TOWN IN BRABANT [1732-51] 38.1x48.3cm. [30] $60
ALLIED & ENEMY TROOP MOVEMENTS IN THE ENVIRONS OF DENAIN [1732-51]
   38.1x48.3cm. [30] $130
ALLIED INTRENCHMENT COVERING THE SIEGE OF DOUAY [1732-51] 38.1x48.3cm.
      [30] $97
PLAN OF THE BATTLE OF ECKEREN [1732-51] 38.1x48.3cm. [30] $97
PLAN OF THE BATTLE OF MALPLAQUET [1732-51] 38.1x48.3cm. [30] $81
PLAN OF THE CITY AND FORTIFICATIONS OF NAMUR [1732-51] 38.1x48.3cm. [30] $89
PLAN OF THE CITY OF BARCELONA [1732-51] 38.1x48.3cm. [30] $81
PLAN OF THE CITY OF DENDERMONDE [1732-51] 38.1x48.3cm. [30] $97
PLAN OF THE CITY OF DOWAY [1732-51] 38.1x48.3cm. [30] $89
PLAN OF THE CITY OF MONS [1732-51] 38.1x48.3cm. [30] $89
PLAN OF THE CITY OF YPRES [1732-51] 38.1x48.3cm. [30] $81
PLAN OF THE COUNTRY & CAMPS OF ALMANAR [1732-51] 38.1x48.3cm. [30] $81
PLAN OF THE SIEGE OF CARDONA [1732-51] 38.1x48.3cm. [30] $81
PLAN OF THE SIEGE OF MENIN [1732-51] 38.1x48.3cm. [30] $81
SIEGE OF BETHUNE [1732-51] 38.1x48.3cm. [30] $81
SIEGE OF CITY OF AIRE, FORT ST. FRANCIS AND ST. VENANT [1732-51] 38.1x48.3cm.
      [30] $89

TIRION

See also ALBRIZZI
ALGEMEENE KAART VAN DE WESTINDISCHE EILANDEN [1765] 36.8x47cm. [3] $130
CARTHAGENA INDE SPAANSCHE WEST INDIEN [1766] 18.4x26cm. [3] $65
DE STADT EN HAVEN VAN PORTO BELLO [1767] 17.8x25.4cm. [3] $50
GEZIGT VAN'T SPAANSCHE VELK PENSACOLA...IN DE GOLF VAN MEXIKO...VAN DE RIVIER
   MISISIPPI [1758] 16.5x25.4cm. [3] $125
GRONDVLAKTE VAN NIEUW ORLEANS DE HOOFDSTAD VAN LOUISIANA/DE UITLOOP VAN DE
   RIVIER MISSISSIPPI/DE OOSTELIJKE INGANG VAN DE MISSISSIPPI [1767] 34x45.5cm.
      [2] $210

TIRION (continued)

HET WESTINDISCH EILAND MARTENIQUE... [1763] 30.5x36.8cm.   [3] $65
HOOFSTAD EN HAVEN VAN'T EILAND PORTO RICO IN DE WESTINDIEN [1767] 17.8x26cm.
                                                                                   [3] $60
KAART VAN HET WESTELYK GEDEELTE VAN NIEUW MEXICO EN VAN CALIFORNIA [1765]
    32.4x34.9cm. light offsetting   [35] $550
NIEUWE KAART VAN HET WESTELYKSTE DEEL DE WEERELD [1754] 33x35.6cm.   [3] $150
NIEUWE KAART VAN HET WESTELYKSTE DEEL DER WEERELD... [1754] 34.3x35.6cm.
    right margin narrow   [27] $175
PLAN VAN DE HAVEN CARTHAGENA [1766] 17.8x30.5cm.   [3] $60
QUEBEK, DE HOOFSTAD VAN KANADA; AAN DE RIVIER VAN ST. LAURENS: DOOR DE
    ENGELSCHEN BELEGERD EN BY VERDRAG BEMAGTIGD, IN'T JAAR 1759 [1769]
    33x43.2cm. inset: De Rivier boren Quebek   [7] $300
TEGENWOORDIGE STAAT VAN DE WESTINDISCHE EILANDEN EN NOOD AMERICA [1768]
    16.5x10.2cm.
    a small map surrounded by a cornucopia, flora, and mythical figures[11] $90
TOMS

THIS PLAN OF THE HARBOURS, TOWNS AND FORTS OF PORTO BELLO TAKEN BY EDWARD
    VERNON ESQR...22D NOVEMBER 1739... [1740] 43.2x58.4cm.   [3] $325
TORBETT

PROPOSED CANAL FROM BAY VERT TO CUMBERLAND BASON [C1830] 10.2x17.8cm.
    by C.W. Torbett, London   [3] $30
PROPOSED CANAL FROM ST. PETER'S BAY TO BRAS D'OR LAKE [1830] 10.8x17.8cm.
                                                                                   [3] $25
TORNIELLO

SITUS PARTIUM PRAECIPUARUM TOTIUS ORBIS TERRARUM [1610] 44.5x38.1cm. woodcut
    world map based on Ortelius, a late state, re-engraved with some names added
                                                                                  [16] $1200
TORRENTE

MAPA DE LAS PROVINCIAS DE VENEZUELA Y DEL REINO DE SANTA FE [1831] 24.5x32cm.
                                                                                  [39] $55
TRAMEZINI

DESCRIPTIO TOTIUS GALLIAE BELGICAE. PYRRHO LIGORIO NEAPOLIT. AUCTORE. ROMAE
    MDLVIII. MICHAELIS TRAMEZINI FORMIS...SEBASTIANUS DE REGIBUS CLODIENSIS
    INCIDEBAT [1558] 37.5x49cm.
    Italian ed. of the lost map of Boileau de Buillon   [18] $1053
HOLLANDIAE BATAVOR VETERIS INSULAE ET LOCORUM ADIACENTIUM EXACTA DESCRIPTIO
    MICHAELIS TRAMEZINI FORMIS...MDLVIII [1558] 37.5x52cm.
    Italian version of the 1540 van Deventer map   [18] $1404
TREMAINE

TREMAINE'S MAP OF THE COUNTY OF PRINCE EDWARD, UPPER CANADA, TORONTO, 1863.
    COMPILED BY JOHN FERRIS WARD...DRAWN...BY ARTHUR W. KEDDIE. ENGRAVED AND
    PRINTED AT TREMAINE'S MAP ESTABLISHMENT, 79 FRONT STREET,
    TORONTO...PUBLISHED...BY GEO. C. TREMAINE [1863] 154.9x125.1cm.
    backed with cloth as issued, some splits, holes & loss of surface [7] $300
TRUTCH

MAP OF BRITISH COLUMBIA COMPILED FROM THE MAP OF THE PROVINCE RECENTLY
    PREPARED...WITH EDITIONS... [1874] 15.2x62.2cm.   [3] $65
TUNISON

SOUTH DAKOTA [1891] 25.4x31.8cm.   [27] $35
TYSON

GEOLOGICAL RECONNOISSANCES IN CALIFORNIA [1850] 29.2x38.1cm. a folding map,
    left upper margin trimmed, some spotting, from Philip Tyson, "Geology and
    Topography of California"   [27] $110
U.S.

"T" SKETCH OF PUBLIC SURVEYS IN NEW MEXICO, TO ACCOMPANY REPORT OF THE SURVEYOR
    GENERAL, 1856 [1856] 56.5x81.9cm.
    some browning, repairs, several ink spots   [19] $60
A DIAGRAM OF A PORTION OF OREGON TERRITORY. OREGON CITY OCT. 20, 1851. JOHN B.
    PRESTON, SURVEYOR GENERAL [1851] 89.5x34.9cm. 9 folds   [8] $40
A DIAGRAM OF PUBLIC SURVEYS IN OREGON [1863] 45.7x59.7cm.
    a few tears at folds   [32] $50

A PLAT EXHIBITING THE STATE OF SURVEYS IN THE STATE OF FLORIDA WITH
   REFERENCES...JOHN WESCOTT...1854 [1854] 56.5x63.5cm.   [3] $60
A PLAT EXHIBITING THE STATE OF THE SURVEYS IN THE STATE OF FLORIDA...SURVEYOR
   GENERAL'S OFFICE, ST. AUGUSTINE SEPT. 30TH, 1851 [1851] 55.9x63.5cm.
   7 folds   [8] $40
ANACAPA ISLAND IN SANTA BARBARA CHANNEL [1854] 15.2x24.1cm.
   Bien & Sterner Lith. N.Y.   [3] $25
ASHTABULA HARBOR, OHIO [1854] 32.4x54.6cm.   [3] $40
BASE LINE & BOUNDARY BETWEEN KANSAS & NEBRASKA [1854] 45.7x30.5cm.
   by the Surveyor General   [3] $45
BIRDS EYE VIEW OF FORT LYON-COL. [1875] 16.9x22.1cm.   [39] $30
COOCHETOPA PASS TO THE WASATCH MOUNTAINS [1861] 78.7x57.8cm.
   splits & browning at folds, small stain   [32] $25
DIAGRAM OF ST. AUGUSTINE LAND DISTRICT SHEWING THE TOWNSHIPS IN WHICH SWAMPLAND
   EXISTS... [1856] 21.6x17.8cm. Sen. Doc. 34th Congress   [3] $20
DIAGRAM OF THE STATE OF MISSOURI. OFFICE OF THE SURVEYOR GENERAL FOR THE STATES
   OF ILLINOIS & MISSOURI SAINT LOUIS, NOV. 17TH, 1851. M. LEWIS CLARK, SURVEYOR
   GENERAL [1851] 45.1x55.2cm. 7 folds   [8] $35
FORT D.A. RUSSELL, W.T. GENERAL PLAN [1875] 20.8x16.1cm.   [39] $30
FORT GIBSON, INDIAN TERRITORY, GENERAL PLAN OF POST 1874 [1875] 18.2x20.4cm.
    [39] $30
FORT LARAMIE, WYOMING TERRITORY. GENERAL PLAN OF POST, 1874 [1875]
   16.5x21.7cm.   [39] $30
FORT LEAVENWORTH, KANSAS [1875] 16.3x20.8cm.   [39] $30
FORT MCKAVETT, TEXAS. GENERAL PLAN OF POST 1874 [1875] 17.1x21.8cm. [39] $30
FORT RANDALL, DAKOTA TERRITORY 1873 [1875] 21.4x17.2cm.   [39] $30
FORT SILL, INDIAN TERRITORY-GENERAL PLAN OF THE POST 1874 [1875] 18x21.4cm.
    [39] $30
FORT SMITH TO THE RIO GRANDE [1861] 55.2x128.3cm.
   splits & browning at folds   [32] $35
GENERAL MAP OF EXPLANATIONS AND SURVEYS IN CALIFORNIA [1861] 60.3x44.5cm.
   on 2 sheets, joined, splits & browning at folds   [32] $45
GENERAL PLAN OF FORT BUFORD, DAKOTA TERRITORY 1874 [1875] 17.5x19cm. [39] $30
GRAND RIVER HARBOR, OHIO [1854] 25.4x43.8cm.   [3] $35
GREAT SALT LAKE TO THE HUMBOLDT MOUNTAINS [1861] 52.1x45.1cm.
   splits & browning at folds   [32] $50
HARBOR OF DUBUQUE [1854] 35.6x27.9cm. one margin narrow   [3] $30
HARBOR OF MANITOWOC WISCONSIN [1854] 31.1x33cm.   [3] $30
HUMBOLDT MOUNTAINS TO THE MUD LAKES [1861] 52.1x45.1cm.
   splits & browning at folds   [32] $40
INDIAN TERRITORY [1876] 61x81.3cm.
   several pinholes repaired at fold intersections   [27] $135
MAP AND PROFILE OF THE CANADA DE LAC UVAS [1861] 55.2x75.6cm.
   splits & browning at folds   [32] $20
MAP AND PROFILE OF THE TEJON PASS [1861] 55.9x83.8cm.
   left margin trimmed, splits & browning at folds   [32] $20
MAP OF BUFFALO HARBOR, N.Y. [1854] 27.3x36.2cm.   [3] $35
MAP OF LOUISIANA REPRESENTING THE SEVERAL LAND DRISTRICTS... [1854]
   39.4x41.9cm. by the Surveyor General   [3] $35
MAP OF OREGON TERRITORY WEST OF THE CASCADE MOUNTAINS [1855] 44.5x26.7cm.
   light browning at folds   [11] $50
MAP OF PASSES IN THE SIERRA NEVADA [1861] 76.8x50.2cm.
   splits & browning at folds   [32] $30
MAP OF PUBLIC SURVEYS IN CALIFORNIA [1861] 89.5x76.2cm.
   a few tears at folds   [32] $40
MAP OF PUBLIC SURVEYS IN CALIFORNIA [1855] 91.4x78.7cm.
   a few tears at folds   [32] $40

MAP OF TEXAS AND THE COUNTRIES ADJACENT. WASHINGTON, FOR THE STATE DEPARTMENT
[1844] 53.3x81.9cm. folding, with original paper wrapper & portion of a red
wax seal, formerly the property of Sen. John Brown Francis of Rhode Island,
published by order of the U.S. Senate in connection with the annexation of
Texas   [23] $2250

MAP OF THE ARKANSAS SURVEYING DISTRICT SHOWING THE EXTENT OF PUBLIC
SURVEYS...30TH SEPTEMBER 1851. SURVEYOR'S OFFICE, LITTLE ROCK, OCT. 20TH
1851 [1851] 38.7x42.5cm. 4 folds   [8] $25

MAP OF THE DEPARTMENT OF THE COLUMBIA... [1885] 80x102.9cm. without crease
marks, an earlier version was issued in 1881, this ed. is "2nd Edition,
Revised June 1st, 1885"   [27] $225

MAP OF THE GENERAL GOVERNMENT ROADS IN THE TERITORY OF MINNESOTA [1854]
45.7x31.8cm. minor repair   [3] $40

MAP OF THE TERRITORY OF THE UNITED STATES FROM THE MISSISSIPPI TO THE PACIFIC
OCEAN... [1861] 107.3x116.8cm. on 2 sheets, joined, one tear, splits &
browning at folds, left margin trimmed   [32] $400

MAP OF THE U.S. & TERRITORIES SHOWING THE EXTENT OF THE PUBLIC
SURVEYS...GENERAL LAND OFFICE, 1870 [1870] 71.8x142.2cm.
foxing & repairs on folds, "Fred Mayer & Sons, N.Y."   [19] $325

MAP OF THE U.S. AND THEIR TERRITORIES BETWEEN THE MISSISSIPPI AND THE PACIFIC
OCEAN AND PART OF MEXICO [1857] 51.4x58.4cm. minor creases, repair in
margin, from "Report of the U.S. and Mexican Boundary Survey," Washington,
1857   [19] $125

MAP OF THE U.S. EXHIBITING THE PROGRESS MADE IN THE GEOLOGIC SURVEY...1884-5
[1886] 43.8x71.8cm. Julius Bien, N.Y.   [19] $60

MAP OF THE U.S.A. SHOWING THE BOUNDARIES OF THE UNION & CONFEDERATE
GEOGRAPHICAL DIVISIONS & DEPARTMENTS, DEC. 31, 1863 [1891-95] 42.5x70.5cm.
                                                                [19] $85

MAP OF THE U.S.A. SHOWING THE BOUNDARIES OF THE UNION AND CONFEDERATE
GEOGRAPHICAL DIVISIONS AND DEPARTMENTS, DEC. 31, 1864 [1891-95] 42.5x70.5cm.
                                                                [19] $85

MAP OF THE WESTERN MILITARY DEPARTMENTS, OF THE UNITED STATES, SHOWING MILITARY
POSTS AND PRINCIPAL ROUTES [1875] 29.4x34cm.   [39] $35

MAP SHOWING THE LOCATION OF PUEBLOS IN NEW MEXICO [1890-94] 22.9x34.3cm.
from "Indians Taxed" volume of 11th Census, Washington, 1894   [27] $40

MICHIGAN [1878] 77.5x63.5cm.
unfolded, two-color lithograph, minor wrinkling in margin   [27] $135

MISSISSIPPI RIVER AND ENVIRONS [1802] 21.6x42.5cm.
minor repairs in margins, map engraved by Alexander Lawson   [23] $50

MISSOURI TO THE MOUTH OF TRAP CREEK [1861] 78.7x57.8cm.
splits & browning at folds   [32] $25

MOUTH OF GALIEN RIVER MICHIGAN [1854] 49.5x77.5cm.   [3] $45

MUD LAKES TO THE PACIFIC OCEAN [1861] 52.1x44.5cm.
tear into map, splits & browning at folds   [32] $30

NORTHERN BOUNDARY OF CALIFORNIA TO THE COLUMBIA RIVER [1861] 68.6x58.4cm.
splits & browning at folds   [32] $45

OUTLET OF THE SOUTH CHANNEL OF RIVER ST. CLAIR [1854] 40x48.3cm. [3] $30

PLAN FOR THE ALTERATION OF THE STREETS AROUND THE CAPITAL SUBMITTED BY B.
FRENCH ESQ. [1854] 27.9x24cm.   [3] $25

PLAN OF KENOSHA HARBOR WISCONSIN [1854] 33x50.8cm.   [3] $30

PLAN OF NORTH CUT AT MILWAUKEE [1854] 43.2x31.8cm. minor repairs [3] $60

PLAN OF RACINE HARBOR [1854] 27.3x31.8cm.   [3] $40

PLAN OF RINGOLD BARRACKS, TEXAS [1875] 21.7x17.3cm.   [39] $30

PLATE LIV. MAP OF TEXAS & PART OF NEW MEXICO COMPILED...1857 [1891-95]
41.3x68.6cm. folds browned & repaired   [19] $100

POST AT BROWNSVILLE, TEXAS [1875] 21.1x16.1cm.   [39] $30

PROGRESS MAP OF THE UNITED STATES GEOGRAPHICAL SURVEYS WEST OF THE 100TH
MERIDIAN [1880] 40.6x55.9cm. waterstain upper margin, folding   [19] $90

RIO COLORADO OF THE WEST, MAP NO. 1 [1858-61] 37.5x88.9cm. light browning at
folds, minor wear at one fold, from Lt. Joseph C. Ives, "Report upon the
Colorado River of the West"   [23] $75

RIO COLORADO OF THE WEST, MAP NO. 2 [1858-61] 37.5x88.9cm. light browning at
   folds, minor wear at one fold, from Lt. Joseph C. Ives, "Report upon the
   Colorado River of the West"   [23] $80
RIO GRANDE TO THE PACIFIC [1861] 55.9x127cm.
   left margin trimmed, splits & browning at folds   [32] $45
RIVIERE DES LACS TO THE ROCKY MOUNTAINS [1861] 62.2x92.7cm.
   splits & browning at folds   [32] $35
ROCKY MOUNTAINS TO PUGET SOUND [1861] 62.2x91.4cm.
   splits & browning at folds   [32] $45
ROUTE NEAR 32ND PARALLEL. MAP & PROFILE NO.1. FROM THE RED RIVER TO THE RIO
   GRANDE; FROM EXPLORATION AND SURVEYS MADE UNDER THE DIRECTION OF THE HON.
   JEFFERSON DAVIS, SEC. OF WAR...1854-56 [1861] 54x144.8cm.
   folding map, some folds repaired   [20] $400
SAN FRANCISCO BAY TO NORTHERN BOUNDARY OF CALIFORNIA [1861] 68.6x58.4cm.
   splits & browning at folds   [32] $45
SANTA FE CROSSING TO THE COOCHETOPA PASS [1861] 79.4x59.1cm.
   left margin narrow, splits & browning at folds   [32] $20
SKETCH OF HURON HARBOUR SHOWING THE EXTENT OF REPAIRS MADE IN 1853 [1854]
   45.1x61cm.   [3] $35
SKETCH OF MONROE HARBOR SHOWING THE EXTENT OF REPAIRS MADE IN 1854... [1854]
   39.4x57.2cm. one margin trimmed   [3] $30
SKETCH OF THE LEAD MINE DISTRICT IN WASHINGTON COUNTY, MISSOURI TERRITORY
   [1816] 47x39.4cm. by the General Land Office   [3] $85
SKETCH OF THE PUBLIC SURVEYS IN IOWA. DUBUQUE OCT. 24, 1851. GEORGE B. SARGENT,
   SURV. GENL. [1851] 44.5x56.5cm.
   7 folds, small hole in blank area of bottom of map   [8] $20
SKETCH OF THE PUBLIC SURVEYS IN MICHIGAN [1854] 54x55.9cm.
   one margin narrow, by the Surveyor General   [3] $30
SKETCH OF THE PUBLIC SURVEYS IN MICHIGAN. DETROIT OCT. 21, 1851. CHARLES NOBLE,
   SURVEYOR GENERAL [1851] 54.6x54cm. 8 folds   [8] $20
SKETCH OF THE PUBLIC SURVEYS IN WISCONSIN & TERRITORY OF MINNESOTA [1854]
   44.5x53.3cm. by the Surveyor General   [3] $40
SODUS BAY, WAYNE CO. N.Y. [1854] 39.4x31.8cm.   [3] $20
ST. PAUL TO RIVIERE DES LACS [1861] 62.2x92.7cm.
   splits & browning at folds   [32] $30
STATE OF NEVADA [1876] 80x61cm.
   minor browning at folds, and pinholes at fold intersections repaired   [27] $100
STATE OF OREGON [1884] 58.4x76.2cm.   [32] $60
SURVEY OF HARBOR OF CLEVELAND, OHIO [1854] 26x45.1cm.   [3] $25
TERRITORY OF ARIZONA [1896] 52.1x43.2cm.   [27] $75
TERRITORY OF ARIZONA [1899] 52.1x43.2cm.   [27] $75
THAT PART OF DISTURNELL'S TREATY MAP IN THE VICINITY OF THE RIO GRANDE AND
   SOUTHERN BOUNDARY OF NEW MEXICO... [1851] 21.6x26.7cm.
   folding, "Senate Ex. Doc. 32d. Congress 2d Session"   [27] $85
TRAP CREEK TO THE SANTA FE CROSSING [1861] 78.7x59.7cm.   [32] $25
U.S. PACIFIC RAIL ROAD EXP. & SURVEY WAR DEPARTMENT: GEOLOGICAL MAP OF THE
   ROUTE EXPLORED BY LIEUT. A.W. WHIPPLE CORPS OF TOPL. ENGRS. NEAR THE PARALLEL
   OF 35 NORTH LATITUDE FROM THE MISSISSIPPI RIVER TO THE PACIFIC OCEAN
   1853-1854... [1859] 19.9x93.2cm.   [39] $80
VALLEY OF GREEN RIVER TO THE GREAT SALT LAKE [1861] 52.1x45.1cm.
   splits & browning at folds   [32] $40
WESTERN TERRITORY [1836] 50.2x88.9cm. repaired tear, small hole, map by Lt.
   Enoch Steen of the Henry Dodge expedition   [23] $375

U.S. COAST SURVEY

(MONOMOY AND NANTUCKET SHOALS TO MUSKEGET CHANNEL) [1860] 95.3x67.3cm.
   light browning on folds, pinholes at intersections of folds   [27] $75
(MUSKETEG CHANNEL TO BUZZARD'S BAY AND ENTRANCE TO VINEYARD SOUND) [1860]
   95.3x67.3cm.
   light browning on folds, pinholes at intersections of folds   [27] $125
...MAGNETIC DECLINATION ISOGONIC LINES FOR THE YEAR 1870 [1867] 35x50cm.
                                                                          [39] $20

A MAP OF THE VICINITY OF MONTEREY BAY, CALIFORNIA, TO ACCOMPANY A REPORT ON THE
   PHYSICAL GEOGRAPHY AND GEOLOGY OF THE COAST [1855] 17.8x25.4cm.   [9] $15
BARNEGAT INLET-NEW JERSEY [1867] 43.9x36.7cm.   [39] $25
CAPE LOOKOUT SHOALS [1867] 57x44cm.   [39] $20
CHARLESTON HARBOR AND ITS APPROACHES [1867] 79.5x81cm.   [39] $60
EASTERN END OF DEER ISLAND... [1867] 42.9x44.6cm.   [39] $25
ECLIPSE HARBOUR LABRADOR [1860] 38.1x31.8cm.   [3] $25
ENTRANCE TO CAPE FEAR RIVER-NORTH CAROLINA [1867] 78x65.5cm.
   inset of "Frying Pan Shoals"   [39] $55
GALVESTON ENTRANCE, TEXAS [1853] 34.3x43.2cm.
   light browning at fold, trimmed at lower left for binding   [23] $75
GENERAL CHART OF DELAWARE AND CHESAPEAKE BAYS AND THE SEA COAST FROM CAPE MAY
   TO CAPE HENRY [1867] 78.7x63.3cm.   [39] $60
KENNEBEC AND SHEEPCOT RIVERS, MAINE [1867] 97.5x59cm. folds reinforced
   [39] $75
KOOS BAY-OREGON [1867] 49.5x65cm.   [39] $30
MISSISSIPPI CITY HARBOUR [1857] 40.6x43.2cm.   [3] $40
MOUTH OF THE COLUMBIA RIVER... [1851] 43.2x67.9cm.
   a few tears at folds   [32] $75
NANTUCKET HARBOR [1867] 35.9x43.7cm.   [39] $55
NEW YORK BAY AND HARBOR, NEW YORK [1867] 77.5x67.6cm. backed   [39] $95
PACIFIC COAST FROM POINT PINOS TO BODEGA HEAD, CALIFORNIA [1867] 98x71.5cm.
   [39] $50
PORT OF PROVIDENCE-RHODE ISLAND [1867] 48.9x39.2cm.   [39] $35
PORT TOWNSHEND WASHINGTON TERR...1858 [C1858] 36.2x29.2cm.   [3] $35
PRELIMINARY CHART OF GALVESTON BAY [1855] 49.5x42.2cm.
   minor fold repairs, browning   [19] $75
PRELIMINARY CHART OF NORTH EDISTO RIVER [1856] 45.1x35.6cm.
   minor repairs   [3] $30
PRELIMINARY SURVEY OF OCRACOKE INLET NORTH CAROLINA... [1857] 45.1x36.8cm.
   minor repairs   [3] $30
PRELIMINARY SURVEY OF POINT REYES AND DRAKE'S BAY CALIFORNIA [1855]
   21.6x24.8cm.   [3] $55
RECONNAISANCE OF PORT GAMBLE WASH. TERR. 1856 [C1856] 30.5x22.2cm.   [3] $30
RECONNAISSANCE OF THE S.E. END OF SAN CLEMENTE ISLAND CALIFORNIA [1856]
   30.5x47.6cm.   [3] $35
SEA COAST OF THE UNITED STATES FROM CAPE SMALL POINT MAINE TO CAPE COD, MASS.
   [1867] 92.5x80.5cm. backed   [39] $65
SKETCH A SHOWING THE PROGRESS OF THE SURVEY...FROM 1832 TO 1865 [1867]
   44.4x69.1cm.   [39] $25
SKETCH I SHOWING THE PROGRESS OF THE SURVEY IN SECTION NO. 9 FROM 1848 TO 1855
   [1855] 18.4x54cm. fold reinforced, browning   [19] $55
SKETCH I SHOWING THE PROGRESS OF THE SURVEY IN SECTION NO. 9, 1848 TO 52
   [C1853] 19.1x28.6cm. on thin paper, with triangulation lines   [23] $20
SKETCH OF SOUTH FARALLON ISLAND [1855] 33x32.4cm. minor repairs   [3] $30
SKETCH OF THE GULF OF MEXICO SHOWING LINES OF DEEP SEA SOUNDINGS AND PROFILES
   OF BOTTOM [1855] 38.1x71.1cm. folds reinforced, browning   [19] $40
SKETCH SHOWING THE PROGRESS OF THE SURVEY ON THE ATLANTIC GULF OF MEXICO AND
   PACIFIC COAST OF THE UNITED STATES [1867] 61x61cm.   [39] $25
ST. GEORGE'S RIVER AND MUSCLE RIDGE CHANNEL-MAINE [1867] 95.6x65.7cm.
   backed   [39] $75
STELLACOOM HARBOR WASHINGTON TERRITORY-BY W. FAIRFAX [1858] 30.5x39.4cm.
   [3] $35
THE HARBOR OF HOLMES' HOLE... [1847] 26x35.9cm.   [33] $90

U.S. EXPLORING EXPEDITION
LOW ARCHIPELAGO OR PAUMOTU GROUP [C1841] 21.6x29.2cm.   [30] $20

UNIVERSAL MAGAZINE
A NEW & ACCURATE MAP OF THE PROVINCES OF SOUTH CAROLINA IN NORTH AMERICA
   [1779] 33x27.9cm.   [3] $135

A NEW AND ACCURATE MAP OF NEW JERSEY... [1780] 31.8x26.7cm.
   minor offsetting, folds, from June 1780 issue   [23] $120
A NEW AND ACCURATE MAP OF NORTH AMERICA [1763] 26x34.3cm.
   narrow margins, tear in margin repaired   [23] $100
A NEW AND ACCURATE MAP OF NORTH CAROLINA IN NORTH AMERICA [1779] 26.7x35.6cm.
                                                                    [1] $150
A NEW AND ACCURATE MAP OF QUEBEC AND ITS BOUNDARIES; FROM A LATE SURVEY [1781]
   26.7x31.8cm. minor repairs   [3] $120
A NEW AND ACCURATE MAP OF THE PRESENT WAR IN NORTH AMERICA [1757] 27.9x36.8cm.
   lower margin narrow, tear repaired, folds   [23] $95
A NEW AND ACCURATE MAP OF THE PROVINCE OF GEORGIA IN NORTH AMERICA [1779]
   32.4x27.3cm. folding, light offsetting, from April 1779 ed.   [22] $150
A NEW AND ACCURATE MAP OF THE PROVINCE OF SOUTH CAROLINA IN NORTH AMERICA
   [1779] 33x27.9cm. folding map, 3 small spots   [27] $200
A NEW AND ACCURATE MAP OF THE PROVINCE OF SOUTH CAROLINA... [1779] 33x27.9cm.
   folding, minor offsetting, from the June 1779 issue   [23] $150
A NEW AND ACCURATE MAP OF THE PROVINCE OF VIRGINIA IN NORTH AMERICA [1779]
   27.9x34.3cm. narrow margin at right, margin added, fold lines present
                                                                    [16] $140
A PERSPECTIVE VIEW OF PENSACOLA [1764] 14.6x24.8cm. folding   [23] $140
A VIEW OF THE CITY OF BOSTON THE CAPITAL OF NEW ENGLAND [1775] 26.7x15.2cm.
   dimensions are to plate mark, from the March 1775 issue, accompanied by 6
   pages of text   [25] $191
AN ACCURATE MAP OF CANADA, WITH THE ADJACENT COUNTRIES; EXHIBITING THE LATE
   SEAT OF WAR BETWEEN THE ENGLISH & FRENCH IN THOSE PARTS. UNIVERS. MAG. J.
   HINTON, NEWGATE STREET. R.W. SEALE, DEL. ET SCULP. [1761] 26x34.3cm. minor
   stain, paper at lower-right cut out by binder has been restored, accompanied
   by 6 pages of text   [25] $114
AN ACCURATE MAP OF NEW YORK IN NORTH AMERICA [1780] 33.7x27cm.
   light browning   [23] $130
AN EXACT PLAN OF THE CITY, FORTIFICATIONS & HARBOUR OF HAVANA... [1762]
   26x34.3cm. trimmed at lower right for binding   [23] $45
MARTINICO... [1759] 36.8x34.9cm. trimmed at lower right for binding [23] $50
THE CANARY ISLANDS & A DRAUGHT OF THE FOUNTAIN TREE IN THE ISLAND OF FERRO
   [1748] 18.5x22.5cm.   [31] $183

VALDOR
VERA ET EXACTA DEXCRIPTIO SPA VICI ARDUENNE CUM VICINIS MONTIBUS SYLVIS ET
   PRATIS J. VALDOR FECIT 1603 [1603] 29x39cm.
   backed on old paper, legends in Latin, Italian & French   [18] $351
VALENTINE'S MANUAL
NEW YORK IN 1792 (VIEW) [1850] 29.8x46.4cm. backed with rice paper, side
   margins extended, from D.T. Valentine, "Manual of the Corporation of the City
   of New York, 1850," lithographed by G. Haywood   [34] $165
VALENTYN
(PHILIPPINES) [1724-26] 31x39cm.
   untitled, from Valentyn's "Oud et Niew Oost Indien"   [31] $306
ANTHONY VAN DIEMANS LAND/HET VASTE LANDT BEZUYDEN DEN KLIPPIGEN HOEK/HET STATEN
   LANDT BEZUYDEN DEN KLIPPIGEN HOEK [C1711] 29x17cm.
   2 views & one map on one sheet, engraved by F. Ottens   [13] $130
VALK
AMERICA AUREA PARS ALTERA MUNDI [C1706] 48.3x59.7cm.
   shows the western hemisphere   [23] $1300
ORBIS TERRARUM NOVA ET ACCURATA TABULA [C1690] 48.5x57cm.
   lower centerfold restored   [37] $1900
VALK & SCHENK
A GENERAL PLOTT AND DESCRIPTION OF THE FENNES... [C1633-1700] 43.2x54.6cm.
   reissue of the Hondius plate of 1633   [12] $76
CANTIUM VERNACULE KENT [C1644-1700] 38.1x49.5cm.
   reissue of the Jansson plate   [12] $275
DUCATUS EBORACENSIS. ANGLICE YORKSHIRE [C1636-1700] 38.1x49.5cm.
   a reissue of the Jansson plate   [12] $214

HOLY ILAND/GARNSEY/FARNE/IARSEY [1705] 40x51cm.   [31] $536
INDIA QUAE ORIENTALIS DICTUR... [1700] 39x46cm.   [31] $536
INSULAE AMERICANAE IN OCEANO SEPTENTRIONALI CUM TERRIS ADIACENTIBUS [C1710]
    37.5x51.4cm.   [15] $425
NOVIS ET ACCURATA JAPANIAE TERRAE ESONIS [C1700] 45x54.5cm.   [31] $728
NOVISSIMA ISLANDIAE TABULA [C1695] 37.5x48.3cm.   [17] $750
OXONIUM COMITATUS VULGO OXFORD SHIRE [C1644-1700] 38.1x49.5cm.
    reissue of the Jansson plate   [12] $291
SOMERSETTENSIS COMITATUS: SOMERSET SHIRE [C1646-1700] 36.8x48.3cm.
    late issue of Jansson plate, no text on verso   [13] $252

VAN ADRICHEM
IERUSALEM ET SUBURBIA EIUS... [C1590] 51.4x74.9cm.
    narrow margins, some folds reinforced, by Christian van Adrichem   [15] $1475

VAN DEN HOEYE
THOFF VAN NASSOUWE. EXCUDEBAT ROMBOUTIUS HOEYUS (VIEW) [C1650] 39x52cm.
    trimmed to border, minor repairs to centerfold, based on the plate by de Jode
    published about 1595   [18] $526

VAN DEN KEERE
BEEMSTRA. AGRI BIEMSTRANI, 1617... [1617] 36.5x47cm.   [18] $263
BELGICARUM PROVINCIARUM NOVA DESCRIPTIO [1625] 25x33.5cm.   [18] $210
BELGII VETERIS TYPUS. PETRUS KAERIUS CELAVIT ET EXCUD. AMSTELODA [1617]
    37.5x49cm.   [18] $280
BRABANTIA DUCATUS, MACHLINIAE URBIS DOMINIUM. PETRUS KAERIUS CAELAVIT [C1610]
    35x50cm.   [18] $526
BRABANTIAE DESCRIPTIO [1625] 23.5x31.5cm.   [18] $105
CELEBERRIMI FLANDRIAE COMITATUS TYPUS [1608] 33x48cm.
    minor repairs in margini   [18] $280
COMITATUS ZUTPHANIA. 1617 [1617] 37x48cm.   [18] $421
DITIO TRANSISULANA... [1617] 37x48.5cm.   [18] $421
FLANDRIA PETRUS KAERIUS CAELAVIT [1625] 23x31cm.   [18] $105
FRISIAE OCCIDENTALIS TYPUS [1625] 23x31cm.   [18] $105
GELDRIA ET TRANSISULANA [1617] 37x49cm.   [18] $351
GELRIA ET ZUTFANIA [1625] 23x31cm.   [18] $105
GRAEFSCHAPPE VAN HOLLANDT [1625] 26x36.5cm.   [18] $140
HANNONIA [1625] 23.5x31cm.   [18] $70
HEREFORD SHIRE [1599-1646] 8.3x12.1cm.   [24] $36
HOLLANDIAE COMITATUS. HOLLANDIA...DELINEATIO. AMSTELODAMI PETRUS
    KAERIUS-EXCUDEBAT. ANNO 1617 [1617] 37.5x51.5cm. several minor repairs
                                                                       [18] $702
LEODIENSIS EPISCOPATUS [1625] 23.5x31cm.   [18] $70
LIMBURGENSIS DUCATUS, 1616 [1617] 37x48.5cm.   [18] $351
LUTZENBURG [1609] 8.7x12.2cm.   [18] $351
LUTZENBURGENSIS DUCATUS VERISS. DESCRIPT. IACOBO SUHONIO MONTANO AUCTORE.
    PETRUS KAERIUS CAELAVIT [1625] 23.3x31cm.   [18] $175
NAMURCUM COMITATUS. IOES. SURHON DESCR. AMSTERDAM, P. KAERIUS EXCUDIT, 1607
    [1607] 38x50cm.   [18] $280
NAMURCUM COMITATUS. PETRUS KAERIUS CAELAVIT [1625] 23.5x31cm.   [18] $70
NOBILIS HANNONIAE COM. DESCRIPTIO. P. KAERIUS EXCUDIT 1616 [1616] 37x48cm.
    minor repairs in margin   [18] $351
NOVA DESCRIPTIO ORIENTALIS ET OCCIDENTALIS FRISIAE...ANNO 1617 [1617] 37x49cm.
                                                                       [18] $526
NOVUS XVII INFERIORIS GERMANIAE PROVINCIARUM TYPUS. DE INTEGRO MULTIS IN LOCIS
    EMENDATUS A PETRO KAERIO. ANNO 1617 [1617] 38x49.5cm.   [18] $526
TYPUS FRISIAE ORIENTALIS...AUTHORE UBBONE. P. KEER. EXC. [1622] 39.5x50cm.
                                                                       [18] $421
ULTRAIECTUM DOMINIUM, 1616... [1617] 36.5x47cm.   [18] $421
ULTRAIECTUM DOMINIUM, 1616... [1617] 36.5x47cm.
    without text on verso, minor repairs in margins   [18] $351
ZELANDIAE COMITATUS... [1617] 35x47cm.   [18] $526

VAN DEN KEERE (continued)

ZELANDIAE COMITATUS... [1617] 35x47cm. no text on verso, no Kaerius
  signature, probably issued separately before publication in the atlas
                                                                   [18] $702
ZELANDIAE TYPUS [1625] 23.5x31.5cm.   [18] $140
ZIPA. AGRI ZUPANI NOVA DESCRIPTIO. 1617 [1617] 37.5x48cm.   [18] $245

VAN DER AA

AMERICA IN PRAECIPUAS...IPSIUS PARTES DISTRIBUTA AD OBSERVATIONES ACADEMIAE
  REGIAE SCIENTIARUM... [1714] 49.5x66cm.   [26] $2400
L'AMERIQUE SELON LES NOUVELLES OBSERVATIONS DE MSSRS DE L'ACADEMI DES
  SCIENCES... [C1706] 47x66cm.   [15] $1500
L'AMERIQUE... [1713] 49.5x66cm. light browning   [16] $2200
L'IRLANDE SUIVANT LES NOUVELLES OBSERVATIONS [1729] 25.4x38.1cm. [13] $130
LA CHINE, SUIVANT LES NOUVELLES OBSERVATIONS [1714-20] 39.5x32.5cm.
  set in a separately printed frame, from "La Galerie Agreable du Monde"
                                                      [13] $114
LA FLORIDE [1729] 22.9x30.5cm.   [19] $275
LA FLORIDE... [1714-29] 33.3x40.3cm.
  a printed frame-like border surrounds the map   [33] $550
LES ISLES BRITANNIQUES SUIVANT LES NOUVELLES OBSERVATIONS [1729] 25.4x38.1cm.
                                                     [13] $160
NOUVELLE CARTE DE L'AMERIQUE [1729] 43.2x53.3cm.   [16] $1100
NOUVELLE CARTE DE L'AMERIQUE [1729] 43.2x53.3cm.   [33] $1250
NOVA DELINEATIO TOTIUS ORBIS TERRARUM PER PETRUM VANDER AA [C1710] 26.5x35cm.
                                                     [37] $875
POTOSI (VIEW) [1708] 28.6x35.6cm.   [3] $125
VIRGINIE, GRANDE REGION DE L'AMERIQUE SEPTENTRIONALE [1729] 28.9x35.6cm.
                                                    [33] $650

VAN DER HAGEN

(LEYDEN, PANORAMIC VIEW) [1675] 35x176cm.
  several small tears, on 3 sheets joined   [18] $1756

VAN DOETECUM

TOTIUS ORBIS COGNITI UNIVERSALIS DESCRIPTIO [C1605] 30x50.5cm.
  three minor paper flaws   [4] $2146

VAN KEULEN

ARCHIPELAGISCHE EYLANDEN [C1730] 50.5x58cm.   [2] $114
NIEUWE AFTEEKENING VAN...DE STAD ENKHUISEN INDE ZUYDER ZEE...P.E. INV. GETEKENT
  DOOR IAN BELKMEER. UYTGEGEVEN TOT AMSTERDAM BY GERARD VAN KEULEN, AEN DE NIEU
  WEN BRUG [C1700] 51x59cm. folding   [18] $210
NIEUWE PLATTE PASKAART VAN DE STRAAT DAVIDS, VAN 67 GRAADE TOT 73 GRAADE
  NOORDER BREETEN, OF VAN DE ZUYD BAY TOT VERBY DE VROUWE EYLANDEN: ALLES
  NAAUKEURIG AFGETEEKENT DOOR SCHIPPER LAURENS FEYKES HAAN...GERARD VAN
  KUELEN...MET PRIVILEGIE [1728] 59.7x100.3cm.   [25] $298
PAS KAART VAN DE GOLFF VAN MEXICO DOOR VOOGT GEOMETRA... [C1695] 50.8x58.4cm.
  bottom margin narrow, two small holes in engraved area   [26] $1500
PAS KAART VAN DE KUST VAN CAROLINA [C1680] 50.8x58.4cm.   [15] $1500
PAS KAART VAN DE KUST VAN CAROLINA TUSSCHEN C. DE CANAVERAL EN C. HENRY DOOR
  C.I. VOOGT GEOMETRA [C1690] 51.8x58.7cm. the numeral "18" appears at both
  lower corners putting the date sometime after 1690   [1] $1400
PAS KAART VAN DE KUST VAN CAROLINA... [1695] 51.8x52.7cm.
  reinforced where color has made paper brittle   [26] $1250
PAS KAART VAN DE ZEE KUSTEN VAN VIRGINIA TUSSCHEN C HENRY EN T HOOGE LAND VAN
  RENSELAARS HOEK DOOR VOOGHT GEOMETRA. T AMSTERDAM BY JOHANNIS VAN KEULEN...
  [C1695] 51.1x57.8cm.
  reinforced where color has made paper brittle, some offsetting [26] $1250
PAS KAART VAN DE ZUYD-KUST VAN ESPANJOLA MET...NUEVO REYNE DE GRENADA...
  [C1681] 52.1x58.4cm.   [3] $235
PAS KAART VAN WEST INDIES... [C1680] 50.8x58.4cm.   [15] $1900
PAS-KAART VANDE ZEE KUSTEN...NIEW ENGELAND... [1695] 51.4x58.4cm. [17] $1250

VAN KEULEN (continued)
PAS-KAART VANDE ZEE-KUSTEN, VAN, TERRA NOVA...FRANCIA NOVA CANADA EN
ACADIE...AMSTERDAM BY JOHANNES VAN KEULEN... [C1687] 50.8x58.4cm. short
tears along top margin repaired, waterstains in margins, 2nd state with
number engraved at lower right   [7] $1225

VAN LOCHOM
L'AMERIQUE [1646] 38.1x49.5cm. wear along old folds, from "Le Monde ou la
Description Generale de Ses Quatre Parties"   [16] $1100

VAN LOON
IMPERII SINARUM NOVA DESCRIPTIO. AUCTORE JOH VAN LOON [1658] 47x52.7cm.
1st issue   [24] $229
ORBIS TERRARUM NOVA ET ACCURATISSIMA TABULA [1666] 44.5x53.3cm.   [15] $2650
ORBIS TERRARUM NOVA ET ACCURATISSIMA TABULA, AUCTORE IOANNE A LOON [1666]
44.5x53.3cm. pinhole in engraved surface, small tears in left margin, lower
centerfold repaired, numeral "1" in lower-right corner   [7] $3000

VANCOUVER
PARTIE DE LA COTE NORD-OUEST DE L'AMERIQUE [1800] 43.8x34.3cm.
reduced version from French edition of Vancouver's voyages   [30] $162
THE TOWN OF VALPARAISO ON THE COAST OF CHILI [1798] 17.8x22.9cm.   [3] $30
VILLAGE OF ALMANDRAL IN THE BAY OF VALPARAISO... [1798] 19.1x23.5cm.
minor repair   [3] $30

VANDERMAELEN
AMER. SEP. IIE SOUTHAMPTON. NO 17 [1825] 48.3x61cm. light foxing   [3] $75
AMER. SEPT. DETROIT D'HUDSON NO. 18 [1825] 48.3x55.9cm.
backed, light foxing   [3] $85
AMER. SEPT. PARTIE DU LABRADOR NO. 29 [1825] 48.3x58.4cm.   [3] $40
NOUVELLE CALIFORNIE [1827] 47x57.2cm. minor spotting   [27] $300
PARTIE DE L'ILE DE TERRE NEUVE NO. 37 [1825] 48.3x61cm. minor spotting
    [3] $75
PARTIE DE LA NOUVELLE BRETAGNE [1827] 47x55.9cm. "AMER. SEP. No. 33" [27] $275
PARTIE DU MEXIQUE NO. 47 [1825] 45.7x55.9cm.   [3] $225
PARTIE DU MEXIQUE NO. 65 [1827] 45.7x53.3cm.   [3] $90

VARELA Y ULLOA
CARTA ESFERICA DE LA COSTA DE AFRICA DESDE CO BOJADOR HASTA CO VERDE E YSLAS
ADJACENTES. PRESENTADA AL REY...POR DN. ANTONIO VALDES... [1787]
64.8x54.6cm.   [3] $95

VARLE
CARTE DE LA PARTIE FRANCOIS DE ST. DOMINGUE FAITE PAR BELLIN INGR. DE LA MARINE
ET DEPUIS AUGMENTE PAR VARLE [1814] 37.5x48.3cm. backed   [3] $145

VERBIEST
HET NOORDER DEEL VAN T'GRAEFSCHAP VLEANDREN...T'ANTWERPEN, GEDRUCKT BIJ PEETER
VERBIST OP DE LOMBAERDE VEST IN AMERICA. ANNO 1644 [1644] 40x48cm.
no text on verso   [18] $351

VIRTUE
BRITISH COLUMBIA, VANCOUVER ISLAND, AND THE VALLEY OF THE SASKATCHEWAN [C1880]
22.9x30.6cm.   [39] $35
CANADA [C1840] 18.5x24.5cm.   [21] $13
THE BRITISH COLONIES IN NORTH AMERICA [C1860] 25x35cm.
poor condition, 1st state, from Smollett, "History of England"   [21] $12
THE BRITISH COLONIES IN NORTH AMERICA... [1868] 22.3x30.5cm.   [39] $30

VISSCHER
See also SCHENK
See also VALK & SCHENK
AMSTELODAMI VETERIS ET NOVISSIMAE URBIS ACCURATISSIMA DELINEATIO. GETEECKENT
ENDE OP T'PAPIER GEBRACHT DOOR DANIEL STALPAERT STADTS ARCHITEC.'T AMSTELDAM
GEDRUCKT BY NICOLAS VISSCHER [C1676] 49x57cm.   [18] $351
BELGII REGII TABULA, IN QUA OMNES PROVINCIAE AB HISPANIS AD ANNUM 1684
POSSESSAE...PER NICOLAUM VISSCHER [1684] 47x54cm.   [18] $140
BELGIUM FOEDERATUM [1689] 47x57cm.   [18] $263
BRABANTIAE DUCATUS CUM ADJACENTIBUS PROVINCIIS [C1670] 60x51cm.
left margin trimmed to border   [18] $263

VISSCHER (continued)

CARTE NOUVELLE CONTENANT LA PARTIE D'AMERIQUE LA PLUS SEPTENTRIONALE, OU SONT
EXACTEMENT DECRITES LES PROVINCES SUIVANTES COMME LE CANADA OU NOUVELLE
FRANCE, LA NOUVELLE ECOSSE LA NOUVELLE ANGLETERRE...PER NICOLAS VISSCHER AVEC
PRIVILEGE... [C1685-1700] 59.7x48.3cm.   [7] $650
CARTE VAN T'VRYE...EEN GEDEELTE VAN VLAENDEREN...DOOR C.I. VISSCHER. H. HONDIUS
EXCUD. [C1620] 38x42cm.   [18] $351
COMITATUS FLANDRIA. T'AMSTERDAM GEDRUCKT BIJ CLAES JANSS VISSCHER INDE
CALVERSTRAAT IN DE VISSCHER [1630] 46x56.5cm. side margins trimmed [18] $702
COMITATUS HANNONIAE [C1670] 47x58cm.   [18] $140
COMITATUS HANNONIAE TABULA... [C1690] 46.4x58.4cm.   [24] $76
COMITATUS NAMURCI... [C1670] 47x57cm.   [18] $245
COMITATUS ZELANDIAE NOVA DESCRIPTIO ANNO 1645. N. VISSCHER EXCUDEBAT [1645]
47x56cm.   [18] $1229
COMITATUS ZELANDIAE... [1689] 47x57cm.   [18] $351
DE STOEL DES OORLOGS IN ITALIEN... [C1690] 59.1x73.7cm.
margins repaired, fold reinforced   [24] $130
DOMINII FRISIAE TABULA... [1689] 48x57cm.   [18] $298
DUCATUS GELDRIAE ET ZUTPHANIAE [1689] 47x57cm.   [18] $263
DUCATUS LUTZENBURGI NOVISSIMA ET ACCURATISSIMA DELINEATIO [1677-79] 46x56cm.
                                                                         [18] $263
FLANDRIAE COMITATUS... [C1670] 47x56cm.   [18] $280
GRONINGA DOMINIUM. ANNO 1621 [1621] 37x48cm.   [18] $351
GRONINGAE ET OMLANDIAE DOMINIUM... [1689] 47x57cm.   [18] $298
HOLLANDIAE COMITATUS [1689] 75x56cm.   [18] $35
INSULAE AMERICANAE [C1680] 46x56cm.   [5] $600
INSULAE AMERICANAE [C1680] 46.5x56cm. minor repairs in margin   [2] $263
INSULAE AMERICANAE... [1698] 45.7x55.2cm.   [17] $1000
JAMAICA, AMERICA SEPTENTRIONALE AMPLA INSULA... [1680] 51x58cm.   [31] $582
LEODIENSIS EPISCOPATUS...PER NICOLAUM VISSCHER AMST. BAT. [C1670] 46.5x56.5cm.
                                                                         [18] $263
L!MBURGI...VALCKENBURGI NOVA DESCRIPTIO [1689] 47x57cm.   [18] $263
MARCHIONATUS SACRI ROMANI IMPERII. CL. J. VISSCHER EXCUDEBAT. NICOLAUS
JANSENIUS PISCATOR [C1650] 46x56cm.   [18] $526
MARCHIONATUS SACRI ROMANI IMPERII. CL. J. VISSCHER EXCUDIT ANNO 1624 [1624]
38.5x49.5cm. no text on verso   [18] $526
NOVA TABULA GEOGRAPHICA COMPLECTENS BOREALIOREM AMERICAE PARTEM: IN QUA EXACTE
DELINEATAE SUNT CANADA SIVE NOVA FRANCIA, NOVA SCOTIA, NOVA ANGLIA, NOVUM
BELGIUM, PENSYLVANIA, VIRGINIA...A NICOLAO VISSCHER... [C1685-1700]
59.7x48.3cm. centerfold reinforced, lower portion somewhat stained [7] $950
NOVISSIMA ET ACCURATISSIMA TOTIUS AMERICAE DESCRIPTIO [1670] 43.2x59.1cm.
                                                                         [23] $1500
ORBIS TERRARUM TABULA RECENS EMENDATA ET IN LUCEM EDITA PER N. VISSCHER
[C1660] 30.5x47.5cm. lower centerfold reinforced, from a Dutch Bible
                                                                         [37] $1200
ORBIS TERRARUM TABULA RECENS EMENDATA ET IN LUCEM EDITA PER N. VISSCHER [1679]
30.5x47cm.   [15] $1600
OVER-YSSEL... [1689] 44x57cm.   [18] $263
PORTUGALLIAE ET ALGARBIAE REGNA [C1680] 46x56.5cm. light browning   [2] $140
TERRA SANCTA SIVE PROMISSIONIS, OLIM PALAESTINA [1659] 46.5x56cm.
minor stains in margins, slight wear   [2] $333
ULTRAIECTINI DOMINI... [1689] 47x57cm.   [18] $263
ULTRAJECTUM DOMINIUM [1624] 36.5x47cm. no text on verso   [18] $280
XVII PROVINCIARUM GERMANIAE INFERIORIS DELINEATIO [1689] 47x57cm.   [18] $263

VIVIEN

CARTE DE LA PARTIE SEPTENTRIONALE DU NOUVEAU MONDE QU'SONT COMPRISES LES
POSSESSIONS ANGLAISES DE L'AMERIQUE DU NORD [1825] 26.7x45.7cm.   [8] $55

VON REILLY

KARTE VON DER INSELWELT POLYNESIEN...1795 [1795] 47x64cm.   [31] $728

VRIENTS

LIMBURGENSIS DUCATUS TABULA NOVA, EXUSA SUMPTIBUS IOAN. BAPTISTAE VRINTS...
  [1613] 40x48.5cm. folds & margins reinforced   [18] $702
TORNACI NERVORUM EPISCOPATUS PERANTIQUUS TOTAQ. TORNACESII DITIO...IOAN.
  BAPTISTA VRIENTIUS ANTVERP...ANTVERPIAE 1610. NONIS MARTIJ. [1610]
  37x48.5cm. no folds   [18] $1404
VRAIJE DESCRIPTION DE L'ASSIEGEMENT D'ANVERS PAR LE...PRINCE DE PARME ETC. SUR
  LA RIVIERE DE L'ESCAULT ENTRE CALLOO ET OIRDAM L'AN 1585. IOANNES BAPTISTA
  VRINTS EXCUDIT [1585] 37.5x44cm.
  cut to border, legend is in Spanish, Italian & French   [18] $702

WAGHENAER

(LAREDO TO LLANES, SEA CHART) [1583] 34.3x50.8cm.
  full title not given, repaired   [17] $1250
BESCHRIJVINGHE DER ZEE CUSTEN VANT LANDT VAN ARGARBE... [1583] 32.4x50.8cm.
         [24] $536
DIE ZEE CUSTEN VAN BISCAIJEN... [1583] 33x50.8cm.   [24] $459
ZEE CARTE VAN PORTUGAL... [1583] 33x50.8cm.   [24] $689

WAGNER & MCGUIGAN

SURVEY OF THE MOUTH OF CLINTON RIVER, MICHIGAN MADE IN 1853 [1851]
  29.2x37.5cm.   [3] $25

WALCH

AUSTRALIEN (SUDLAND) AUCH POLYNESIEN ODER INSELWELT, INSGEMEIN DER FUNFTE
  WELTTHEIL GENANNT [1824] 49.5x62.5cm.   [13] $191

WALKER

A PLAN OF LONDON AND ITS ENVIRONS [1834-35] 38.1x47cm.
  margin restored, minor tears   [24] $122
BRITISH POSSISSIONS IN NORTH AMERICA [1836] 31.1x43.2cm.
  from Montgomery Martin, "History of the British Colonies"   [30] $142
CITY OF MONTREAL 1830 [C1830] 20.3x23.5cm.   [3] $100
HUNTINGDONSHIRE [1837-50] 39.4x31.8cm.   [24] $33
NORTH AMERICA XIV FLORIDA [1853] 38.1x30.5cm.   [3] $85
SURREY [1835] 32.4x39.4cm.   [24] $76

WALLING & GRAY

KANSAS AND THE TERRITORIES OF ARIZONA, COLORADO, NEW MEXICO, UTAH AND INDIAN
  TERRITORY [1872] 41.9x64.8cm.   [11] $70

WALLING, TACKABURY & CO.

MADISON, DANE COUNTY [1876] 40.6x29.2cm.
  from "Atlas of Wisconsin," map of Green Bay on verso   [27] $45

WALLIS & REID

ANGLESEY [1820] C10.8x6.4cm.   [12] $7
BUCKINGHAMSHIRE [1820] C10.8x6.4cm. from "The Panorama: or, Traveller's
  Instructive Guide; through England And Wales"   [12] $10
CAMBRIDGESHIRE [1820] C10.8x6.4cm.   [12] $12
CARMARTHENSHIRE [1820] C10.8x6.4cm.   [12] $6
CORNWALL [1820] C10.8x6.4cm.   [12] $13
DEVONSHIRE [1820] C10.8x6.4cm.   [12] $10
ESSEX [1820] C10.8x6.4cm.   [12] $10
GLAMORGANSHIRE [1820] C10.8x6.4cm.   [12] $7
HEREFORDSHIRE [1820] C10.8x6.4cm.   [12] $7
LINCOLNSHIRE [1820] C10.8x6.4cm.   [12] $10
NORFOLK [1820] C10.8x6.4cm.   [12] $9
NOTTINGHAMSHIRE [1820] C10.8x6.4cm.   [12] $7
OXFORDSHIRE [1820] C10.8x6.4cm.   [12] $10
PEMBROKESHIRE [1820] C10.8x6.4cm.   [12] $7
SOMERSETSHIRE [1820] C10.8x6.4cm.   [12] $10
SURREY [1820] C10.8x6.4cm.   [12] $13
WESTMORLAND [1820] C10.8x6.4cm.   [12] $10

WATSON

NEW RAILROAD AND DISTANCE MAP OF KENTUCKY AND TENNESSEE [1877] 31.8x40.6cm.
  from Gaylord Watson, "New Commercial, County and Railroad Atlas of the
  U.S...   [27] $50

WEIGEL
FACIES POLI ARCTICI ADIACENTIUMQUE EI REGIONUM EX RECENTISSIMIS ITINERARIIS
   DELINEATA CURA CHRISTOPHORI WEIGELII, NORIB. [C1740] 31.8x35.6cm.
  minor discoloration at centerfold   [7] $400
INSULAE ANTILLAE FRANCICAE SUPERIORIS CUM VICINIS INSULIS... [1720] 33x35.6cm.
  minor stain in margin   [3] $165
KARTE VON AUSTRALIEN ODER POLYNESIEN...BIS 1789 ENTWORDEN IM JAHR 1792 [1792]
  46.5x66cm.   [31] $574
NOVI ORBIS SIVE TOTIUS AMERICAE... [C1712] 27.5x34.3cm.   [39] $250

WEIMAR GEOGRAPHISCHES INSTITUT
CHART VAN DEN INSELN TRINIDAD, TABAGO AND MARGARETHA... [1816] 21.9x40.3cm.
                                            [39] $95
CHARTE VON NORD-AMERICA PRAG...1818 [1818] 41.9x29.8cm. backed   [3] $100
KENTUCKY [1819] 16.5x36.2cm. narrow left margin   [23] $65
OHIO [1819] 23.5x21cm. narrow left margin, small hole   [23] $70
VEREINIGTE STAATEN VON NORD-AMERIKA [1839] 22.9x29.8cm. backed [3] $65

WELD
A PLAN OF THE CITY OF QUEBEC [1799] 17.5x24cm.
  laid down, from same plate as used in 1771 by J. Andrews   [21] $73

WELLER
AUSTRALIA [C1860] 30.5x43cm.   [4] $45
BRITISH COLUMBIA/VANCOUVER ISLAND [C1860] 43x30.5cm.   [4] $61
CALIFORNIA, UTAH, LR. CALIFORNIA AND NEW MEXICO [C1860] 43x30.5cm. [4] $68
ESTANCIA DE SAN JORGE URUGUAY [1880] 21.6x24.8cm. lithographed color [30] $4
MAP OF KHORASAN AND NEIGHBOURING COUNTRIES [1881] 62.2x82.5cm.
  lithographed color   [30] $16
MAP OF THE GREAT SALT LAKE AND ADJACENT COUNTY IN THE TERRITORY OF UTAH (WITH)
   THE GREAT SALT LAKE (MORMON) CITY AND SURROUNDING COUNTRY [1863]
  43.8x30.5cm. minor stain   [22] $75
NEW SOUTH WALES [C1860] 43x30.5cm.   [4] $45
NORTH AMERICA [1854] 31.8x24.8cm.   [3] $25
THE EMPIRE OF JAPAN WITH PART OF THE CONTINENT OF ASIA SHOWING...NEW BOUNDARY
   BETWEEN RUSSIAN & CHINESE TERRITORIES [C1850] 43.2x30.5cm.   [3] $35
VICTORIA [C1860] 30.5x43cm.   [4] $45
WESTERN AUSTRALIA/SOUTH AUSTRALIA [C1860] 31x43cm.   [4] $45

WELLS
A NEW MAP OF PRESENT ASIA DEDICATED TO HIS HIGHNESS WILLIAM DUKE OF GLOUCESTER
  [C1700] 37.5x50.8cm.   [7] $175
A NEW MAP OF SOUTH AMERICA, SHEWING ITS GENERAL DIVISIONS... [1700-04]
  36.3x48.8cm.   [39] $285
ORBIS TERRARUM COGNITUS [C1700] 8.5x16cm.   [39] $50
PRESENT ASIA... [C1700] 36.8x50.8cm. minor repairs in margins [24] $76

WERNER
DAS REICH MEXICO [1830] 19.1x26cm. published in Leipzig   [23] $80
GEBEIT MISSOURI. GEBEIT OREGAN [1830] 19.7x26.7cm.   [23] $75

WEST SHORE
GENERAL VIEW OF INDEPENDENCE [1887] 12.7x20.3cm.
  lithographed view from "West Shore," published in Portland, Oregon [27] $25

WHYMPER
SAN FRANCISCO, CALIFORNIA, FROM THE BAY (VIEW) [1868] 18.4x34.9cm.
  view by F. Whymper, London   [3] $35
SITKA OR NEW ARCHANGEL (VIEW) [1868] 16.5x24.1cm.   [3] $35

WILCOCKE
PLAN OF THE CITY OF BUENOS AYRES [1807] 18.9x10.9cm.   [39] $60

WILD
(BOSTON VIEW) [C1840] 31.8x48.3cm. lithographed by Louis Le Breton, printed
  by Auguste Bry, published by Wild, Paris   [34] $1750

WILKES
BERKSHIRE [1801-28] C23.5x19.1cm.   [12] $22
CAMBRIDGESHIRE [1801-28] C23.5x19.1cm.   [12] $22
ESSEX [1801-28] C23.5x19.1cm.   [12] $22

WILKES (continued)
  GLOUCESTERSHIRE [1801-28] C23.5x19.1cm.   [12] $22
  MIDDLESEX [1801-28] C23.5x19.1cm.   [12] $24
  MONMOUTHSHIRE [1801-28] C23.5x19.1cm.   [12] $18
  RUTLANDSHIRE [1801-28] C23.5x19.1cm.   [12] $19
  SHROPSHIRE [1801-28] C23.5x19.1cm.   [12] $18
WILKINSON
  A MAP OF THE UNITED STATES OF AMERICA, WITH PART OF THE ADJOINING PROVINCES
     FROM THE LATEST AUTHORITIES [1794] 21.6x26.7cm.   [3] $75
WILLDEY
  A NEW & EXACT MAP OF GERMANY... [C1717] 63.5x93.3cm.   [24] $229
WILLIAMS
  BRITISH COLONIES IN NORTH AMERICA [C1830] 22.3x30.8cm.   [39] $30
  MAP OF THE SOUTHERN & SOUTHWESTERN STATES [1849-57] 30.5x44.5cm.   [19] $55
WILLIAMSON
  GENERAL MAP OF EXPLORATION & SURVEYS IN CALIFORNIA UNDER DIRECTION OF JEFFN.
     DAVIS SEC. OF WAR...ASSISTED BY LT. PARKE & ISAAC SMITH-1853 [1853]
     184.2x61cm. light browning   [3] $135
  MAP AND PROFILE OF THE CANADA DE LAS UVAS; FROM EXPLORATIONS...BY LT. J. PARKE
     [1853] 55.9x76.2cm. browning at fold   [3] $45
WOLFF
  GAND. LE RESA ALLI ALLEATI DELLA CITTA DI GANDA, CAPITALE DELLA FLANDRA...AO
     1709... [C1715] 46x38cm. left margin trimmed, one corner repaired [18] $175
WOODBRIDGE
  PHYSICAL MAP OF THE UNITED STATES [1843-45] 29.2x42.5cm. fold repaired
                                                                     [19] $65
  POLITICAL MAP OF NORTH AMERICA [1843-45] C21.6x26.7cm.   [19] $70
  POLITICAL MAP OF NORTH AMERICA... [1843] 21.6x26.7cm.
     published by Wm. Woodbridge, Hartford   [20] $95
  POLITICAL MAP OF THE UNITED STATES, MEXICO... [1843-45] 27.3x45.7cm.
     minor spotting, fold & margin repaired   [19] $75
  POLITICAL MAP OF THE UNITED STATES, MEXICO... [C1845-48] 27.3x45.7cm.
                                                                     [19] $100
WYLD
  A MAP OF IRELAND DIVIDED INTO PROVINCES AND COUNTIES, SHOWING THE GREAT AND
     CROSS ROADS [C1830-52] 69.9x53.3cm. the issue of 1852   [14] $68
  A NEW MAP OF THE PROVINCE OF LOWER CANADA, DESCRIBING ALL THE SEIGNEURIES,
     TOWNSHIPS, GRANTS OF LAND, &C...BY SAMUEL HOLLAND...TO WHICH IS ADDED A PLAN
     OF THE RIVERS SCOUDIAC...SURVEYED IN 1796, 97, AND 98...LONDON, PUBLISHED BY
     JAMES WYLD [C1843] 57.2x87cm.
     a few tears at folds repaired, margins somewhat ragged   [7] $475
  CHART OF THE WORLD ON MERCATOR'S PROJECTION [C1812] 30.5x45.1cm.   [3] $75
  MAP OF COLOMBIA, AND BRITISH GUYANA, INCLUDING THE STATES OF NEW GRANADA,
     VENEZUELA & ECUADOR [1845] 22.2x27.9cm.   [25] $53
  MAP OF NORTH AMERICA EXHIBITING THE RECENT DISCOVERIES GEOGRAPHICAL & NAUTICAL
     BY J.W. GEOGRAPHER [1838] 47.6x36.2cm.   [3] $125
  MAP OF THE BRITISH POSSESSIONS IN NORTH AMERICA [1833] 22.5x27cm. [21] $40
  MAP OF THE GOLD REGIONS OF THE FRAZER RIVER AND THE WASHINGTON TERRITORY ON THE
     WESTERN COAST OF AMERICA [1858] 41.9x35.6cm.   [22] $150
  MAP OF THE WEST INDIA & BAHAMA ISLANDS WITH THE ADJACENT COASTS OF YUCATAN,
     HONDURAS, CARACAS &C. [1829] 52.7x76.8cm.   [3] $175
  NORTHERN HEMISPHERE [1838] 58.4x58.4cm.   [3] $90
  SKETCH OF THE NORTH EASTERN BOUNDARY BETWEEN GREAT BRITAIN AND THE UNITED
     STATES AS SETTLED BY TREATY AUGT. 1842. PUBLISHED. SEPT. 29TH. 1842. BY JAS.
     WYLD... [1842] 24.1x32.4cm. in sections & backed with cloth as issued
                                                                     [7] $250
  SKETCH OF THE NORTH EASTERN BOUNDARY BETWEEN GREAT BRITAIN AND THE UNITED
     STATES AS SETTLED BY TREATY AUGT. 9TH 1842 [1842] 23.9x32.7cm.
     on 8 panels   [39] $85
  THE UNITED STATES OF NORTH AMERICA WITH THE BRITISH TERRITORIES [1841]
     54x64cm. centerfold crease, on thick paper   [21] $134

WYLD (continued)

THE UNITED STATES OF NORTH AMERICA WITH THE BRITISH TERRITORIES [1838]
  53.3x64.8cm.   [3] $145
  WESTERN HEMISPHERE [1839] 78.7x78.7cm. h   [3] $130

WYTFLIET

UTRIUSQUE HEMISPHEREIO DELINEATIO [1597] 22.9x28.6cm.   [15] $700

YOUNG

FROM THE NORTHERN BOUNDARY OF CALIFORNIA TO THE COLUMBIA RIVER FROM
  EXPLORATIONS & SURVEYS UNDER DIRECTION OF JEFF. DAVIS SEC. OF WAR BY LT. R.S.
  WILLIAMSON & LT. H.S. ABBOT [1855] 69.9x58.4cm.   [3] $120

ZATTA

(JAMAICA, FOGL. IX) [1778] C30.5x40.6cm.   [32] $200
(LAKE MICHIGAN, FOGL. IV) [1778] C30.5x40.6cm.   [32] $85
(LAKE SUPERIOR, FOGL. I) [1778] C30.5x40.6cm.   [32] $210
(MID-ATLANTIC, FOGL. VIII) [1778] C30.5x40.6cm.   [32] $250
(MIDWEST, LOWER, FOGL. VII) [1778] C30.5x40.6cm.   [32] $240
(NEW ENGLAND & EASTERN CANADA, FOGL. VI) [1778] C30.5x40.6cm.   [32] $275
(SOUTHEAST COAST, FOGL. XI) [1778] C30.5x40.6cm.   [32] $225
AMERICA DIVISA NE SUOL PRINCIPALI STATI DI NUOVA PROJEZIONE [1776] 31.1x40cm.
                                          [3] $180
AMERICA SETTENTRIONALE DIVIDA NE' SUOI PRINCIPALI STATI [C1785] 31.5x41.5cm.
                                          [2] $166
EMISFERO TERRESTRE SETTENTRIONALE TAGLIATO SU L'EQUATORE [1778] 32x41cm.
  some centerfold browning   [21] $150
IL CANADA, LE COLONIE INGLESI, CON LA LOUIGIANA E FLORIDA [1778] 31x41cm.
  2 wormholes repaired   [2] $172
IL MARYLAND IL JERSEY MERIDIONALE LA DELAWARE, E LA PARTE ORIENTALE DELLA
  VIRGINIA E CAROLINA SETTENTRIONALE [1778] 33x43.2cm. backed   [3] $175
IL PAESE DE SELVAGGI OUTAGAMIANI MASCOUTENSI ILLINESI... [1778] 33x42.5cm.
                                          [3] $185
IL PAESE DE' SELVAGGI OUTAGAMIANI, MASCOUTENSI, ILLINESI, E PARTE DELLA VI
  NAZIONI [1778] 31.8x41.9cm.   [22] $250
IL PAESE DE' SELVAGGI OUTAUACESI, E KILISTINESI INTORNO AL LAGO SUPERIORE
  [1778] 31.8x41.9cm.   [22] $220
IL PAESE DE' SELVAGGI OUTAUCE SI, E KILISTINE SI INTORNO AL LAGO SUPERIORE
  [1778] 33x43.8cm. minor browning at centerfold, inset: "Supplemento Alla
  Florida Orientale"   [7] $350
IL REGNI DI SUEZIA, DANIMARCA E NORVEGA [1781] 30.5x40.6cm.   [30] $81
ISOLE ANTILLE, CUBA, ANTIGUA, BARBADOS... [1776] 33x42cm.   [39] $120
ISOLE FILIPPINE [1776] 40.5x31cm.   [31] $153
L'ACADIA, LE PROVINCIE DI SAGADAHOOK E MAIN, LA NUOVA HAMPSHIRE, LA RHODE
  ISLAND, E PARTE DI MASSACHUSETT E CONNECTICUT [1778] 31.8x41.9cm. [22] $230
L'AMERICA [1775] 32x40.5cm.   [2] $166
L'AMERICA DIVISA NE SUOI PRINCIPALI STATI [1776-88] 30.5x40.6cm.
  from "Atlante Novissimo"   [30] $313
L'AMERICA DIVISA NE SUOI PRINCIPALI STATI DI NUOVA PROJEZIONE. VENEZIA 1776.
  PRESSO ANTONIO ZATTA CON PRIVILEGIO DELL'ECEMO SENATO [1776] 30.5x40.6cm.
                                          [7] $300
LA BAJA D'HUDSON TERRA DI LABRADOR E GROENLANDIA CON LE ISOLE ADIACENTI DI
  NUOVA PROJEZIONE. VENEZIA 1778 PRESSO ANTONIO ZATTA CON PRIVILEGIO DELL'ECCMO
  SENATO [C1799] 31.8x41.3cm. from "Atlante Novissimo"   [7] $400
LA BAJA D'HUDSON... [1778] 30x40.5cm.   [4] $168
LA PARTIE OCCIDENTALE DELLA NUOVA FRANCIA O CANADA [1778] 33.7x43.8cm.
                                          [7] $350
LA PENSILVANIA, LA NUOVA YORK, IL JERSEY SETTENTRIOLE: CON LA PARTIE
  OCCIDENTALE DEL CONNECTICUT, MASSACHUSETTS BAYE E L'IROCHESIA. FOGL. V.
  [1778] 33.7x43.8cm.   [7] $350
LA REPUBBLICA D'OLLANDA [1776] 41x31cm.   [4] $130
LA SUEZIA [1781] 41.9x31.8cm.   [30] $101
LE COLONIE UNITE DELL' AMERICA SETTENTR. DI NUOVE PROJEZIONE... [1778]
  31.8x41.9cm. on 12 sheets, dimensions are for each, minor centerfold splits
  on some sheets   [15] $1575

ZATTA (continued)

LE COLONIE UNITE DELL' AMERICA SETTENTRIONALE [1778] 32x42.5cm.
  set of 12 sheets, dimensions are for each   [5] $2000
LE ISOLE DI TERRA NUOVA E CAPO BRETON [1778] 42x32cm.   [2] $96
LE ISOLE DI TERRA NUOVA E CAPO BRETON [1778] 43.2x31.8cm.   [30] $243
LE ISOLE DI TERRA NUOVA E CAPO BRETON DI NUOVA PROJEZIONE. VENEZIA 1778 PRESSO
  ANTONIO ZATTA CON PRIVILEGIO DEL ECCMO SENATO [1778] 43.2x34.3cm. [7] $400
LUIGIANA INGLESE, COLLA PARTE OCCIDENTALE DELLA FLORIDA, DELLA GIORGIA, E
  CAROLINA MERIDIONALE [1778] 33x41.9cm.   [3] $185
MESSICO OU VERO NUOVA SPAGNA CHE CONTIENE EL NUOVO MESSICO-LA CALIFORNIA...
  [1785] 31.1x40.6cm. minor repairs   [3] $180
MESSICO...IL NUOVO MESSICO, LA CALIFORNIA... [1785] 31x41cm. · [2] $131
NUOVE SCOPERTE FATTA NEL 1765, E 69 NEL MARE DEL SUD [1776] 30x40cm. [31] $574
NUOVE SCOPERTE...MARE DEL SUD [1776] 30x40cm.   [12] $383
PARTE ORIENTALE DELLA FLORIDA DE LA GIORGIA E CAROLINA MERIDIONALE [1778]
  33x42.5cm. backed   [3] $175
PARTE ORIENTALE DELLA FLORIDA, DELLA GEORGIA, E CAROLINA MERIDIONALE [1778]
  31.8x41.9cm.   [22] $225
PARTIE ORIENTALE DEL CANADA, NUOVA SCOZIA SETTENTRIONALE, E PARTE DI LABRADOR.
  FOGL. III. [1778] 33.7x43.8cm.   [7] $350
REGNI D'ARACAN DEL PEGU DI SIAM DI CAMBOGE E DI LAOS [1783] 39.5x32cm.
                                     [4] $114
STABILIMENTI DE FRANCESI INGLESI E SPAGNUOLI NELLE ISOLE ANTILLE... [1785]
  31.8x41.9cm.   [3] $140

ZIEGLER

(CYPRUS, VIEW) [1532] 23x34.5cm.
  margins slightly trimmed, from "Quae intus Continentum Syria..." [31] $1034
(HOLY LAND) [1532] 22.9x35.6cm.   [15] $1400

ALPHABETICAL INDEX
TO MAP TITLES

(ACAPULCO, ENGRAVED SCENE OF DUTCH FLEET)	15.0 X 17.5 CM	MERIAN
(AEGEAN SEA & EASTERN MEDITERRANEAN)	31.5 X 57.2 CM	DE BRUYN
(AFRICA)	43.6 X 54.2 CM	DAPPER
(AFRICA)	48.3 X 55.9 CM	HOMANN
(AFRICA, EAST COAST & MADAGASCAR)	40.0 X 50.0 CM	LINSCHOTEN
(ALABAMA)	33.7 X 26.7 CM	TANNER
(ALABAMA)	36.2 X 29.2 CM	THOMAS, COWPERTHWAI...
(ALASKA)	24.1 X 31.8 CM	CRAM
(ALEPPO, PANORAMIC VIEW)	30.5 X 103.0 CM	DE BRUYN
(ALEXANDRIA, VIEW)	23.3 X 62.7 CM	DE BRUYN
(ALEXANDRIA, VIEW)	30.3 X 63.3 CM	DE BRUYN
(ALEXANDRIA, VIEW)	21.0 X 25.4 CM	SCHENK
(ALGIERS, VIEW)	21.0 X 25.4 CM	SCHENK
(ALOST, PLAN)	30.0 X 45.0 CM	BRAUN & HOGENBERG
(AMARA, VIEW)	21.0 X 25.4 CM	SCHENK
(AMERICA ON A HEMISPHERE)	12.4 X 10.9 CM	APIANUS
(AMERSFOORT, PLAN & VIEW)	30.0 X 45.0 CM	BRAUN & HOGENBERG
(AMERSHAM TO FINCHLEY-ROAD MAP)	19.1 X 12.7 CM	CARY
(AMSTERDAM, PLAN)	30.0 X 45.0 CM	BRAUN & HOGENBERG
(ANGLESEY & CAERNARVONSHIRE)	8.6 X 12.0 CM	SPEED
(ANVERS, PLAN)	30.0 X 45.0 CM	BRAUN & HOGENBERG
(ARCHANGEL TO PERSIAN GULF, ROUTE MAP)	28.7 X 37.1 CM	DE BRUYN
(ARCHANGEL, VIEW)	29.3 X 38.5 CM	DE BRUYN
(ARCHANGEL, VIEW)	21.5 X 61.0 CM	DE BRUYN
(ARIZONA AND NEW MEXICO)	28.3 X 35.6 CM	MITCHELL
(ARKANSAS)	31.8 X 39.4 CM	COLTON
(ARKANSAS)	36.8 X 29.2 CM	MITCHELL
(ARKANSAS)	36.8 X 29.2 CM	MITCHELL
(ARKANSAS)	36.5 X 29.8 CM	THOMAS, COWPERTHWAI...
(ARKANSAS, LOUISIANA, MISSISSIPPI, INDIAN TY. & EAST TEXAS)	26.7 X 21.6 CM	BURGESS
(ARKANSAS, MISSISSIPPI AND LOUISIANA)	36.2 X 43.8 CM	JOHNSON & WARD
(ARNHEM/VENLO/GELDERN/RUREMONDE, PLAN)	30.0 X 45.0 CM	BRAUN & HOGENBERG
(ARZILIE, VIEW)	21.0 X 25.4 CM	SCHENK
(ASIA, WITH PART OF AFRICA AND N.W. AMERICA, UNTITLED)	24.1 X 33.0 CM	SOLINUS
(ASTRAKHAN, VIEW)	21.8 X 63.0 CM	DE BRUYN
(AUGSBURG, VIEW)	21.0 X 25.4 CM	SCHENK
(BANDEL, VIEW)	21.0 X 25.4 CM	SCHENK
(BARBARY)	26.0 X 35.0 CM	DAPPER
(BATAVIA, VIEW)	17.7 X 36.7 CM	DE BRUYN
(BAY OF FUNDY, SOUTH EAST PART)	70.5 X 207.0 CM	DES BARRES
(BEDFORDSHIRE)	17.1 X 19.1 CM	BOWEN
(BEDFORDSHIRE)	11.4 X 11.4 CM	BOWEN
(BEDFORDSHIRE)	14.0 X 18.4 CM	COWLEY
(BEDFORDSHIRE)	58.0 X 69.0 CM	GREENWOOD
(BEDFORDSHIRE)	8.6 X 12.0 CM	SPEED
(BERGEN OP ZOOM, PLAN)	30.0 X 45.0 CM	BRAUN & HOGENBERG
(BERKSHIRE)	17.1 X 19.1 CM	BOWEN
(BERKSHIRE)	8.6 X 12.0 CM	SPEED
(BETHELHEM, VIEW)	24.9 X 63.7 CM	DE BRUYN
(BOLSWARD/STAVEREN/HARLINGEN/HINGE/DELOPEN, PLANS)	30.0 X 45.0 CM	BRAUN & HOGENBERG
(BOSTON VIEW)	31.8 X 48.3 CM	WILD
(BOSTON, VIEW)	14.0 X 20.3 CM	MALTE-BRUN
(BRAZIL)	26.7 X 36.5 CM	RAMUSIO
(BRAZIL, ARRIVAL OF NOORT, ENGRAVED SCENE)	12.5 X 16.8 CM	DE BRY
(BRAZIL, ARRIVAL OF SPEILBERGEN, ENGRAVED SCENE)	15.1 X 19.1 CM	DE BRY
(BRECKNOCKSHIRE)	11.4 X 11.4 CM	BOWEN
(BRIELLE, VIEW)	30.0 X 45.0 CM	BRAUN & HOGENBERG
(BRITISH ISLES)	47.6 X 55.9 CM	DE WIT
(BRUGES, PLAN)	30.0 X 45.0 CM	BRAUN & HOGENBERG
(BRUXELLES, PLAN)	30.0 X 45.0 CM	BRAUN & HOGENBERG
(BUCKINGHAMSHIRE)	11.4 X 11.4 CM	BOWEN
(BUCKINGHAMSHIRE)	8.6 X 12.0 CM	SPEED
(CAIRO, 2 VIEWS ON ONE SHEET)	28.0 X 37.0 CM	DE BRUYN

(CAIRO, VIEW)	21.0 X 25.4 CM	SCHENK
(CAITHNESS & ORKNEYS)	8.6 X 12.0 CM	SPEED
(CALIFORNIA AND THE TERRITORIES OF OREGON, WASHINGTON UTAH & NEW MEXIC	39.4 X 31.8 CM	THOMAS, COWPERTHWAI...
(CALIFORNIA WITH UTAH, NEVADA, COLORADO, NEW MEXICO & ARIZONA)	42.5 X 59.1 CM	JOHNSON & WARD
(CALIFORNIA)	39.4 X 33.0 CM	COLTON
(CALIFORNIA)	54.0 X 35.6 CM	MITCHELL
(CALIFORNIA//NEVADA)	47.3 X 30.5 CM	CRAM
(CAMBRIDGESHIRE)	11.4 X 11.4 CM	BOWEN
(CAMBRIDGESHIRE)	58.0 X 69.0 CM	GREENWOOD
(CAMBRIDGESHIRE)	8.6 X 12.0 CM	SPEED
(CAMBRIDGHSHIRE)	14.0 X 18.4 CM	COWLEY
(CANARY ISLANDS)	26.0 X 35.0 CM	DAPPER
(CANARY ISLANDS)	6.5 X 7.5 CM	MULLER
(CAPE VERDE ISLANDS)	26.0 X 35.0 CM	DAPPER
(CARDIGAN, PEMBROKE & CARMARTHEN)	58.0 X 69.0 CM	GREENWOOD
(CARTAGENA BEING DESTROYED BY FRENCH, ENGRAVED SCENE)	15.3 X 19.2 CM	DE BRY
(CHARLEMONT/AVESNES/LANDRECY/BEAUMONT, PLANS)	30.0 X 45.0 CM	BRAUN & HOGENBERG
(CHESHIRE)	28.0 X 38.0 CM	CAMDEN
(CHESHIRE)	8.6 X 12.0 CM	SPEED
(CHICAGO)	34.6 X 27.9 CM	MITCHELL
(COCHIN, VIEW)	21.0 X 25.4 CM	SCHENK
(COLOMBIA, VESPUCCI'S LANDING, ENGRAVED SCENE)	14.9 X 17.6 CM	DE BRY
(COLORADO)	40.6 X 57.2 CM	ASHER & ADAMS
(COLORADO)	40.6 X 55.9 CM	CRAM
(COLORADO)	27.9 X 36.8 CM	MITCHELL
(COLORADO, WYOMING, DAKOTA & MONTANA)	49.5 X 35.6 CM	MITCHELL
(CONCEPCION, SPEILBERGEN AT, ENGRAVED SCENE)	15.3 X 19.1 CM	DE BRY
(CONGO & ANGOLA)	26.0 X 35.0 CM	DAPPER
(CONNAUGHT)	8.6 X 12.0 CM	SPEED
(CONSTANTINOPLE, GALATA & PERA, VIEW)	29.8 X 99.0 CM	DE BRUYN
(CONSTANTINOPLE, PANORAMIC VIEW)	30.0 X 190.0 CM	DE BRUYN
(CONSTANTINOPLE, VIEW)	23.9 X 31.0 CM	DE BRUYN
(CORNWALL)	8.6 X 12.0 CM	SPEED
(CUMBERLAND)	17.1 X 19.1 CM	BOWEN
(CUMBERLAND)	58.0 X 69.0 CM	GREENWOOD
(CUZCO, ATTEMPT BY INCAS TO RETAKE, ENGRAVED SCENE)	16.7 X 19.9 CM	DE BRY
(CYPRUS, VIEW)	23.0 X 34.5 CM	ZIEGLER
(DAKOTA//MINNESOTA & NORTH CAROLINA)	46.0 X 29.8 CM	CRAM
(DELAWARE & MARYLAND)	32.4 X 40.0 CM	JOHNSON & WARD
(DELFT, PLAN)	30.0 X 45.0 CM	BRAUN & HOGENBERG
(DENBIGHSHIRE & FLINTSHIRE)	8.6 X 12.0 CM	SPEED
(DERBENT, VIEW)	21.0 X 25.4 CM	SCHENK
(DERBYSHIRE)	28.0 X 38.0 CM	CAMDEN
(DERBYSHIRE)	8.6 X 12.0 CM	SPEED
(DEVENTER, PLAN)	30.0 X 45.0 CM	BRAUN & HOGENBERG
(DEVONSHIRE)	28.0 X 38.0 CM	CAMDEN
(DEVONSHIRE)	8.6 X 12.0 CM	SPEED
(DIEPPE TO ROUEN, SEA CHART)	58.4 X 47.0 CM	MORTIER
(DORDRECHT, BIRD'S EYE VIEW)	30.0 X 45.0 CM	BRAUN & HOGENBERG
(DORDRECHT, PANORAMIC VIEW)	30.0 X 45.0 CM	BRAUN & HOGENBERG
(DORSET)	58.0 X 69.0 CM	GREENWOOD
(DORSET)	8.6 X 12.0 CM	SPEED
(DUNKIRK, VIEW)	21.0 X 25.4 CM	SCHENK
(DURHAM)	8.6 X 12.0 CM	SPEED
(EASTERN NORTH AMERICA)	60.0 X 45.0 CM	CORONELLI
(EGYPT)	26.0 X 35.0 CM	DAPPER
(ENGLAND)	8.6 X 12.0 CM	SPEED
(ENGLAND, SCOTLAND & IRELAND)	12.1 X 15.2 CM	SPEED
(ENGLISH CHANNEL)	49.5 X 58.4 CM	MOUNT & PAGE
(ENGLISH COLONIES)	51.4 X 75.6 CM	BRION DE LA TOUR
(ENKHUIZEN, BIRD'S EYE VIEW)	30.0 X 45.0 CM	BRAUN & HOGENBERG
(ESSEX)	28.0 X 38.0 CM	CAMDEN
(ESSEX)	8.6 X 12.0 CM	SPEED

(FEZ & MOROCCO)	26.0 X 35.0 CM	DAPPER
(FINLAND)	43.2 X 52.7 CM	BLAEU
(FLINTSHIRE)	11.4 X 11.4 CM	BOWEN
(FLORIDA)	29.2 X 22.9 CM	DESILVER
(FLORIDA)	30.5 X 38.4 CM	JOHNSON & WARD
(FLORIDA)	36.5 X 29.5 CM THOMAS, COWPERTHWAI...	
(FLORIDA//ALABAMA)	30.5 X 25.4 CM	CRAM
(GAMRON, VIEW)	21.0 X 25.4 CM	SCHENK
(GAMRON/HORMOZ, LARAK & QESHM, VIEWS)	23.2 X 38.2 CM	DE BRUYN
(GAND, PLAN)	30.0 X 45.0 CM	BRAUN & HOGENBERG
(GEORGIA AND ALABAMA)	38.7 X 55.6 CM	JOHNSON
(GEORGIA AND ALABAMA)	26.7 X 34.0 CM	MITCHELL
(GEORGIA)	35.6 X 29.2 CM	MITCHELL
(GEORGIA)	33.0 X 27.3 CM	TANNER
(GEORGIA)	35.6 X 29.2 CM THOMAS, COWPERTHWAI...	
(GIGERI, DJIDJELLI, VIEW)	21.0 X 25.4 CM	SCHENK
(GLAMORGANSHIRE)	28.0 X 38.0 CM	CAMDEN
(GLAMORGANSHIRE)	8.6 X 12.0 CM	SPEED
(GLOBE GORE, INCLUDING MADAGASCAR)	42.0 X 26.0 CM	CORONELLI
(GLOUCESTERSHIRE)	11.4 X 11.4 CM	BOWEN
(GLOUCESTERSHIRE)	58.0 X 69.0 CM	GREENWOOD
(GLOUCESTERSHIRE)	8.6 X 12.0 CM	SPEED
(GOA, VIEW)	21.0 X 25.4 CM	SCHENK
(GOLD COAST TO CONGO, SEA CHART)	57.2 X 43.2 CM	MORTIER
(GOUDA, BIRD'S EYE VIEW)	30.0 X 45.0 CM	BRAUN & HOGENBERG
(GOUDA, VIEW)	18.0 X 48.0 CM	BRAUN & HOGENBERG
(GRONINGEN, BIRD'S EYE VIEW)	30.0 X 45.0 CM	BRAUN & HOGENBERG
(GRONINGEN/BROUWERSHAVEN/GORCUM, VIEWS)	30.0 X 45.0 CM	BRAUN & HOGENBERG
(GUINEA)	26.0 X 35.0 CM	DAPPER
(HAARLEM, BIRD'S EYE VIEW)	30.0 X 45.0 CM	BRAUN & HOGENBERG
(HAINAUT, ARMORIAL)	30.0 X 45.0 CM	BRAUN & HOGENBERG
(HAMPSHIRE)	28.0 X 38.0 CM	CAMDEN
(HAMPSHIRE)	14.0 X 18.4 CM	COWLEY
(HAMPSHIRE)	8.6 X 12.0 CM	SPEED
(HEBRIDES ETC.)	8.6 X 12.0 CM	SPEED
(HEREFORDSHIRE)	17.1 X 19.1 CM	BOWEN
(HEREFORDSHIRE)	8.6 X 12.0 CM	SPEED
(HERTFORDSHIRE)	28.0 X 38.0 CM	CAMDEN
(HERTFORDSHIRE)	58.0 X 69.0 CM	GREENWOOD
(HERTFORDSHIRE)	8.6 X 12.0 CM	SPEED
(HOLY ISLAND, GUERNSEY, FARNE & JERSEY)	8.6 X 12.0 CM	SPEED
(HOLY LAND)	26.5 X 17.0 CM	MUNSTER
(HOLY LAND)	22.9 X 35.6 CM	ZIEGLER
(HOLY LAND, UNTITLED)	25.5 X 35.0 CM	HOLE
(HUNTINGDONSHIRE)	8.6 X 12.0 CM	SPEED
(HUY, VIEW)	30.0 X 45.0 CM	BRAUN & HOGENBERG
(ICELAND)	22.9 X 29.8 CM	CORONELLI
(IDAHO MONTANA, WESTERN PORTION)	57.2 X 40.6 CM	ASHER & ADAMS
(ILLINOIS)	31.1 X 22.9 CM	CRAM
(ILLINOIS)	39.4 X 33.0 CM	DESILVER
(ILLINOIS)	39.4 X 34.3 CM	DESILVER
(ILLINOIS)	58.4 X 43.2 CM	JOHNSON & WARD
(ILLINOIS)	33.7 X 26.7 CM	TANNER
(ILLINOIS)	39.4 X 33.0 CM THOMAS, COWPERTHWAI...	
(INDIANA)	35.2 X 28.9 CM THOMAS, COWPERTHWAI...	
(INNESBRUCK, VIEW)	21.0 X 25.4 CM	SCHENK
(IOWA AND MISSOURI)	54.3 X 36.2 CM	MITCHELL
(IOWA AND NEBRASKA)	43.2 X 58.7 CM	JOHNSON & WARD
(IOWA)	31.8 X 39.4 CM	COLTON
(IOWA)	33.0 X 40.6 CM THOMAS, COWPERTHWAI...	
(IRELAND)	8.6 X 12.0 CM	SPEED
(ISFAHAN/MEY-DOEN, VIEWS)	21.2 X 38.8 CM	DE BRUYN
(ISLE OF MAN)	43.8 X 55.9 CM	COLLINS

(ISLE OF MAN)	8.6 X 12.0 CM	SPEED
(ISLE OF WIGHT)	45.7 X 57.2 CM	COLLINS
(ISLE OF WIGHT)	8.6 X 12.0 CM	SPEED
(JAMAICA, FOGL. IX)	30.5 X 40.6 CM	ZATTA
(JAPAN)	38.5 X 44.5 CM	NICOLOSI
(JERUSALEM)	74.9 X 48.3 CM	BRAUN & HOGENBERG
(JERUSALEM)	57.2 X 49.5 CM	SEUTTER
(JERUSALEM, PANORAMIC VIEW)	30.3 X 127.0 CM	DE BRUYN
(JERUSALEM, VIEW)	21.0 X 25.4 CM	SCHENK
(JOPPE, VIEW)	22.0 X 38.0 CM	DE BRUYN
(JUAN FERNANDEZ ISLANDS, L'HERMITE'S FLEET)	12.3 X 18.0 CM	MERIAN
(KAMPEN, BIRD'S EYE VIEW)	30.0 X 45.0 CM	BRAUN & HOGENBERG
(KAMPEN, PANORAMIC VIEW)	30.0 X 45.0 CM	BRAUN & HOGENBERG
(KANSAS AND NEBRASKA)	35.6 X 54.3 CM	MITCHELL
(KANSAS)	41.9 X 61.0 CM	COLTON
(KANSAS, NEBRASKA & COLORADO)	29.2 X 35.6 CM	MITCHELL
(KENT)	11.4 X 11.4 CM	BOWEN
(KENT)	8.6 X 12.0 CM	SPEED
(KENTUCKY & TENNESSEE)	43.2 X 61.0 CM	JOHNSON & WARD
(KENTUCKY AND TENNESSEE)	36.2 X 54.0 CM	MITCHELL
(KENTUCKY)	29.2 X 35.6 CM	DESILVER
(KENTUCKY)	29.2 X 35.2 CM	THOMAS, COWPERTHWAI...
(KOHM/KASJAN, VIEWS)	24.1 X 34.6 CM	DE BRUYN
(LAKE MICHIGAN, FOGL. IV)	30.5 X 40.6 CM	ZATTA
(LAKE SUPERIOR, FOGL. I)	30.5 X 40.6 CM	ZATTA
(LANCASHIRE)	58.0 X 69.0 CM	GREENWOOD
(LANCASHIRE)	8.6 X 12.0 CM	SPEED
(LAREDO TO LLANES, SEA CHART)	34.3 X 50.8 CM	WAGHENAER
(LEEUWARDEN/FRANEKER, PLANS)	30.0 X 45.0 CM	BRAUN & HOGENBERG
(LEICESTERSHIRE & RUTLAND)	17.1 X 19.1 CM	BOWEN
(LEICESTERSHIRE)	8.6 X 12.0 CM	SPEED
(LEIDEN, VIEW)	21.0 X 25.4 CM	SCHENK
(LEINSTER)	8.6 X 12.0 CM	SPEED
(LEIPSIG, VIEW)	21.0 X 25.4 CM	SCHENK
(LEYDEN, PANORAMIC VIEW)	35.0 X 176.0 CM	VAN DER HAGEN
(LEYDEN, PLAN)	30.0 X 45.0 CM	BRAUN & HOGENBERG
(LIEGE, VIEW)	30.0 X 45.0 CM	BRAUN & HOGENBERG
(LIER, PLAN)	30.0 X 45.0 CM	BRAUN & HOGENBERG
(LIMA, ARRIVAL OF SPEILBERGEN'S FLEET, ENGRAVED SCENE)	15.4 X 19.1 CM	DE BRY
(LIMBURG, VIEW)	30.0 X 45.0 CM	BRAUN & HOGENBERG
(LINCOLNSHIRE)	8.6 X 12.0 CM	SPEED
(LINZ, VIEW)	21.0 X 25.4 CM	SCHENK
(LONDON TO BEAKONSFIELD-ROAD MAP)	19.1 X 12.7 CM	CARY
(LONDON TO CHALK STREET-ROAD MAP)	19.1 X 12.7 CM	CARY
(LONDON TO HOUNDSLOW-ROAD MAP)	19.1 X 12.7 CM	CARY
(LONDON TO RIPLEY-ROAD MAP)	19.1 X 12.7 CM	CARY
(LORETTO, VIEW)	21.0 X 25.4 CM	SCHENK
(LOUISIANA)	27.3 X 33.7 CM	TANNER
(LOUISIANA)	29.5 X 36.2 CM	THOMAS, COWPERTHWAI...
(LOUISVILLE, KENTUCKY, VIEW)	12.7 X 20.3 CM	LADIES REPOSITORY
(LOUVAIN, PLAN)	30.0 X 45.0 CM	BRAUN & HOGENBERG
(LOUVAIN, VIEW)	13.0 X 47.0 CM	BRAUN & HOGENBERG
(MAASTRICHT, PANORAMIC VIEW)	30.0 X 45.0 CM	BRAUN & HOGENBERG
(MAASTRICHT, PLAN)	30.0 X 45.0 CM	BRAUN & HOGENBERG
(MADAGASCAR)	26.0 X 35.0 CM	DAPPER
(MAGDEBURG, VIEW)	21.0 X 25.4 CM	SCHENK
(MAINE)	38.1 X 30.5 CM	THOMAS, COWPERTHWAI...
(MAINZ, VIEW)	21.0 X 25.4 CM	SCHENK
(MALINES, PLAN)	30.0 X 45.0 CM	BRAUN & HOGENBERG
(MALINES, VIEW)	13.0 X 47.0 CM	BRAUN & HOGENBERG
(MALTA)	26.0 X 35.0 CM	DAPPER
(MALTA)	44.5 X 53.3 CM	DE WIT
(MANTUA, VIEW)	21.0 X 25.4 CM	SCHENK

(MARYLAND AND DELAWARE)	29.2 X 36.8 CM	THOMAS, COWPERTHWAI...
(MASSACHUSETTS AND RHODE ISLAND)	29.2 X 36.8 CM	THOMAS, COWPERTHWAI...
(MATANZAS BAY, ENGRAVED SCENE)	15.1 X 17.5 CM	MERIAN
(MESSINA, VIEW)	21.0 X 25.4 CM	SCHENK
(MEXICO & NEW MEXICO, PART OF)	62.2 X 27.9 CM	KITCHIN
(MEXICO CITY)	15.1 X 17.6 CM	MERIAN
(MICHIGAN)	36.8 X 29.5 CM	THOMAS, COWPERTHWAI...
(MID-ATLANTIC, FOGL. VIII)	30.5 X 40.6 CM	ZATTA
(MIDDELBURG, BIRD'S EYE VIEW)	30.0 X 45.0 CM	BRAUN & HOGENBERG
(MIDDELEBURG, VIEW)	21.0 X 25.4 CM	SCHENK
(MIDDLESEX)	28.0 X 38.0 CM	CAMDEN
(MIDDLESEX)	58.0 X 69.0 CM	GREENWOOD
(MIDDLESEX)	8.6 X 12.0 CM	SPEED
(MIDWEST, LOWER, FOGL. VII)	30.5 X 40.6 CM	ZATTA
(MILAN)	22.5 X 33.5 CM	DE FER
(MILWAUKEE)	34.9 X 26.0 CM	MITCHELL
(MINNESOTA & DAKOTA)	31.8 X 39.7 CM	JOHNSON & WARD
(MINNESOTA TERRITORY)	33.7 X 40.6 CM	THOMAS, COWPERTHWAI...
(MINNESOTA)	35.6 X 29.2 CM	MITCHELL
(MISSISSIPPI)	35.6 X 29.2 CM	MITCHELL
(MISSISSIPPI)	33.0 X 26.7 CM	TANNER
(MISSISSIPPI)	35.2 X 29.5 CM	THOMAS, COWPERTHWAI...
(MISSOURI & KANSAS)	43.2 X 58.4 CM	JOHNSON & WARD
(MISSOURI)	40.6 X 33.0 CM	MITCHELL
(MISSOURI)	33.0 X 26.7 CM	TANNER
(MISSOURI)	33.0 X 40.6 CM	THOMAS, COWPERTHWAI...
(MISSOURI//IOWA)	24.1 X 29.8 CM	CRAM
(MONMOUTHSHIRE)	58.0 X 69.0 CM	GREENWOOD
(MONMOUTHSHIRE)	8.6 X 12.0 CM	SPEED
(MONOMOY AND NANTUCKET SHOALS TO MUSKEGET CHANNEL)	95.3 X 67.3 CM	U.S. COAST SURVEY
(MONS, PLAN)	30.0 X 45.0 CM	BRAUN & HOGENBERG
(MONS, VIEW)	15.0 X 48.0 CM	BRAUN & HOGENBERG
(MONTANA)	40.6 X 55.9 CM	CRAM
(MONTANA//WYOMING & IDAHO)	30.5 X 45.7 CM	CRAM
(MONTGOMERYSHIRE & MERIONETHSHIRE)	8.6 X 12.0 CM	SPEED
(MONTGOMERYSHIRE)	11.4 X 11.4 CM	BOWEN
(MORAY FIRTH)	44.5 X 55.9 CM	COLLINS
(MOSCOW, PANORAMIC VIEW)	30.1 X 190.0 CM	DE BRUYN
(MUNSTER)	8.6 X 12.0 CM	SPEED
(MUSKETEG CHANNEL TO BUZZARD'S BAY AND ENTRANCE TO VINEYARD SOUND)	95.3 X 67.3 CM	U.S. COAST SURVEY
(NAMUR, PLAN)	30.0 X 45.0 CM	BRAUN & HOGENBERG
(NAMUR, VIEW)	30.0 X 45.0 CM	BRAUN & HOGENBERG
(NAMUR, VIEW)	21.0 X 25.4 CM	SCHENK
(NAZERETH, VIEW)	29.5 X 17.8 CM	DE BRUYN
(NEBRASKA, DAKOTA, COLORADO, IDAHO & KANSAS)	31.8 X 39.4 CM	JOHNSON & WARD
(NEBRASKA, DAKOTA, COLORADO, IDAHO & KANSAS)	31.8 X 38.1 CM	JOHNSON & WARD
(NEBRASKA, DAKOTA, COLORADO, MONTANA & KANSAS)	31.8 X 39.4 CM	JOHNSON & WARD
(NEBRASKA//KANSAS)	24.1 X 32.1 CM	CRAM
(NETHERLANDS)	20.3 X 14.0 CM	MUNSTER
(NEW BEDFORD, MASSACHUSETTS, VIEW)	12.7 X 17.8 CM	LADIES REPOSITORY
(NEW ENGLAND & EASTERN CANADA, FOGL. VI)	30.5 X 40.6 CM	ZATTA
(NEW ENGLAND & NEW FRANCE, UNTITLED)	25.0 X 34.0 CM	PURCHAS
(NEW HAMPSHIRE & VERMONT)	37.5 X 30.5 CM	THOMAS, COWPERTHWAI...
(NEW JERSEY)	35.6 X 29.2 CM	TANNER
(NEW JERSEY)	37.8 X 31.8 CM	THOMAS, COWPERTHWAI...
(NEW MEXICO//COLORADO)	30.5 X 26.0 CM	CRAM
(NEW ORLEANS)	23.2 X 27.6 CM	MITCHELL
(NEW ORLEANS, VIEW)	11.4 X 18.4 CM	LADIES REPOSITORY
(NEW YORK & BROOKLYN)	33.7 X 52.7 CM	MITCHELL
(NEW YORK HARBOR, AS SEEN FROM THE BROOKLYN TOWER OF THE SUSPENSION BR	22.9 X 35.6 CM	HARPER'S WEEKLY
(NEW YORK)	27.3 X 32.4 CM	TANNER
(NEW YORK)	40.6 X 26.0 CM	THOMAS, COWPERTHWAI...
(NIJMEGEN, PANORAMIC VIEW)	30.0 X 45.0 CM	BRAUN & HOGENBERG

(NIJMEGEN, PLAN)	30.0 X	45.0 CM	BRAUN & HOGENBERG
(NORFOLK)	8.6 X	12.0 CM	SPEED
(NORTH AMERICA)	39.4 X	32.4 CM	THOMAS, COWPERTHWAI...
(NORTH AND SOUTH CAROLINA)	43.2 X	59.1 CM	JOHNSON & WARD
(NORTH CAROLINA)	29.2 X	35.2 CM	THOMAS, COWPERTHWAI...
(NORTH DAKOTA)	40.6 X	55.9 CM	CRAM
(NORTH RIDING)	58.0 X	69.0 CM	GREENWOOD
(NORTHAMPTONSHIRE)	8.6 X	12.0 CM	SPEED
(NORTHUMBERLAND)	28.0 X	38.0 CM	CAMDEN
(NORTHUMBERLAND)	58.0 X	69.0 CM	GREENWOOD
(NORTHWEST AMERICA)	14.8 X	9.6 CM	CAMPANIUS HOLME
(NORTHWESTERN AMERICA)	29.2 X	35.6 CM	MITCHELL
(NOTTINGHAMSHIRE)	11.4 X	11.4 CM	BOWEN
(NOTTINGHAMSHIRE)	17.1 X	19.1 CM	BOWEN
(NOTTINGHAMSHIRE)	28.0 X	38.0 CM	CAMDEN
(NOTTINGHAMSHIRE)	14.0 X	18.4 CM	COWLEY
(OHIO)	39.4 X	33.0 CM	DESILVER
(OHIO)	33.0 X	26.7 CM	TANNER
(OHIO)	40.0 X	33.0 CM	THOMAS, COWPERTHWAI...
(OREGON)	41.9 X	55.9 CM	CRAM
(OREGON, WASHINGTON, IDAHO & PART OF MONTANA)	27.0 X	34.0 CM	MITCHELL
(ORKNEY ISLES, SUTHERLANDSHIRE, CATHNES-SHIRE)	9.5 X	12.7 CM	ROCQUE
(OXFORDSHIRE)	11.4 X	11.4 CM	BOWEN
(OXFORDSHIRE)	28.0 X	38.0 CM	CAMDEN
(OXFORDSHIRE)	14.0 X	18.4 CM	COWLEY
(OXFORDSHIRE)	58.0 X	69.0 CM	GREENWOOD
(OXFORDSHIRE)	8.6 X	12.0 CM	SPEED
(PALMYRA)	27.8 X	63.4 CM	DE BRUYN
(PASSAU, VIEW)	21.0 X	25.4 CM	SCHENK
(PEMBROKESHIRE)	8.6 X	12.0 CM	SPEED
(PENNSYLVANIA)	66.0 X	130.8 CM	LE ROUGE
(PENNSYLVANIA)	29.2 X	36.2 CM	THOMAS, COWPERTHWAI...
(PERSEPOLIS, VIEW)	31.4 X	63.5 CM	DE BRUYN
(PERSEPOLIS, VIEW)	25.7 X	37.2 CM	DE BRUYN
(PERSIAN GULF TO JAVA)	23.6 X	30.8 CM	DE BRUYN
(PHILADELPHIA)	39.7 X	32.4 CM	THOMAS, COWPERTHWAI...
(PHILIPPEVILLE/MARIEBOURG/CHIMAY/WALCOURT, PLANS)	30.0 X	45.0 CM	BRAUN & HOGENBERG
(PHILIPPINES)	38.0 X	44.0 CM	NICOLOSI
(PHILIPPINES)	31.0 X	39.0 CM	VALENTYN
(PITTSBURGH AND ALLEGHENY, VIEW)	10.8 X	18.4 CM	LADIES REPOSITORY
(PORTLAND, MAINE, VIEW)	11.4 X	20.3 CM	LADIES REPOSITORY
(POTTERS BAR TO RUNDELLS-ROAD MAP)	19.1 X	12.7 CM	CARY
(PRAGUE, VIEW)	21.0 X	25.4 CM	SCHENK
(PTOLEMAIC WORLD, UNTITLED)	30.5 X	45.7 CM	PTOLEMY (1522-41 ST...
(QUINTERO, SEPILBERGEN AT, ENGRAVED SCENE)	15.3 X	19.1 CM	DE BRY
(RADNORSHIRE, BRECKNOCKSHIRE, CARDIGANSHIRE & CARMARTHENSHIRE)	8.6 X	12.0 CM	SPEED
(RAMA, VIEW)	23.0 X	62.5 CM	DE BRUYN
(RHODES, HARBOR VIEW)	23.6 X	63.3 CM	DE BRUYN
(RHODES, HARBOR VIEW)	22.7 X	62.8 CM	DE BRUYN
(RICHMOND, VIRGINIA, VIEW)	10.8 X	19.1 CM	LADIES REPOSITORY
(RIGA, VIEW)	21.0 X	25.4 CM	SCHENK
(ROAD MAP, BAGSHOT-SALISBURY)	31.8 X	47.0 CM	OGILBY
(ROAD MAP, BRISTOL-BANBURY)	33.0 X	45.1 CM	OGILBY
(ROAD MAP, BRISTOL-LUDLOW)	34.3 X	43.2 CM	OGILBY
(ROAD MAP, BURTON FERRY-ST. DAVIDS)	33.0 X	44.5 CM	OGILBY
(ROAD MAP, CHELMSFORD-SAFFRON WALDEN)	33.0 X	42.5 CM	OGILBY
(ROAD MAP, GLOUCESTER-MONTGOMERY)	31.8 X	43.2 CM	OGILBY
(ROAD MAP, HUNTINGDON-IPSWICH)	32.4 X	45.7 CM	OGILBY
(ROAD MAP, KING'S LYNN-HARWICH)	34.3 X	43.8 CM	OGILBY
(ROAD MAP, LONDON TO NEWHAVEN)	34.3 X	43.2 CM	OGILBY
(ROAD MAP, LONDON-NEW SHORHAM)	34.3 X	43.2 CM	OGILBY
(ROAD MAP, TALYBONT-HOLYWELL)	34.3 X	44.5 CM	OGILBY
(ROAD MAP, WINCHESTER-CREWKERNE)	31.8 X	43.8 CM	OGILBY

213

(ROTTERDAM, BIRD'S EYE VIEW)	30.0 X 45.0 CM	BRAUN & HOGENBERG
(ROTTERDAM, VIEW)	19.0 X 48.0 CM	BRAUN & HOGENBERG
(ROTTERDAM, VIEW)	21.0 X 25.4 CM	SCHENK
(RUSSIA)	26.0 X 36.8 CM	HERBERSTEIN
(RUTLAND)	58.0 X 69.0 CM	GREENWOOD
(RUTLAND)	8.6 X 12.0 CM	SPEED
(S'HERTOGENBOSCH, BIRD'S EYE VIEW)	30.0 X 45.0 CM	BRAUN & HOGENBERG
(S'HERTOGENBOSCH, VIEW)	11.0 X 49.0 CM	BRAUN & HOGENBERG
(SALE, VIEW)	21.0 X 25.4 CM	SCHENK
(SAMACHI, VIEW)	27.1 X 37.6 CM	DE BRUYN
(SANDWICH ISLANDS)	50.0 X 38.5 CM	ROBINSON
(SATTALIA, VIEW)	23.2 X 62.0 CM	DE BRUYN
(SCANDERONA/FAMAGUSTA, VIEWS)	28.1 X 30.8 CM	DE BRUYN
(SCANDINAVIA)	48.9 X 57.2 CM	SEUTTER
(SCIO, PANORAMIC VIEW)	30.5 X 127.0 CM	DE BRUYN
(SCOTLAND)	8.6 X 12.0 CM	SPEED
(SCOTLAND, EASTERN)	8.6 X 12.0 CM	SPEED
(SCOTLAND, SOUTHERN)	8.6 X 12.0 CM	SPEED
(SCOTLAND, SOUTHWESTERN)	8.6 X 12.0 CM	SPEED
(SCUTARI & THE SERAGLIO, VIEW)	30.3 X 100.6 CM	DE BRUYN
(SHEET 7 FROM HIS LARGE MAP SHOWING COAST FROM CAPE BRETON TO RHODE I	48.9 X 68.2 CM	POPPLE
(SHEET 15 FROM HIS LARGE MAP SHOWING EASTERN HISPANIOLA, PUERTO RICO,	48.6 X 68.0 CM	POPPLE
(SHEET 16 FROM HIS LARGE MAP SHOWING 5 PANELS OF WEST INDIAN HARBORS)	48.6 X 29.5 CM	POPPLE
(SHROPSHIRE)	8.6 X 12.0 CM	SPEED
(SIDON/JUBAIL?, VIEWS)	30.0 X 18.3 CM	DE BRUYN
(SLAVES MINING AND SMELTING GOLD, ENGRAVED SCENE)	15.9 X 19.3 CM	DE BRY
(SLOBITTEN, VIEW)	21.0 X 25.4 CM	SCHENK
(SLUYS, PLAN)	30.0 X 45.0 CM	BRAUN & HOGENBERG
(SMYRNA, PANORAMIC VIEW)	30.0 X 99.0 CM	DE BRUYN
(SMYRNA, VIEW)	16.6 X 28.4 CM	DE BRUYN
(SMYRNA, VIEW)	21.0 X 25.4 CM	SCHENK
(SNEECK/DOCCUM/SLOTEN/ILSTEN)	30.0 X 45.0 CM	BRAUN & HOGENBERG
(SOMERSET)	8.6 X 12.0 CM	SPEED
(SOMERSETSHIRE)	17.1 X 19.1 CM	BOWEN
(SOUTH CAROLINA)	28.9 X 35.6 CM	THOMAS, COWPERTHWAI...
(SOUTHEAST COAST, FOGL. XI)	30.5 X 40.6 CM	ZATTA
(SOUTHERN HEMISPHERE, TRADEWINDS)	15.2 X 48.3 CM	MOLL
(SPAHA, PANORAMIC VIEW)	30.3 X 191.0 CM	DE BRUYN
(ST. LOUIS)	34.9 X 27.6 CM	MITCHELL
(STAFFORDSHIRE)	11.4 X 11.4 CM	BOWEN
(STAFFORDSHIRE)	28.0 X 38.0 CM	CAMDEN
(STAFFORDSHIRE)	58.0 X 69.0 CM	GREENWOOD
(STAFFORDSHIRE)	8.6 X 12.0 CM	SPEED
(STANCHIO/RHODES, VIEWS)	20.3 X 38.0 CM	DE BRUYN
(STRAITS OF MACKINAC)	24.1 X 31.8 CM	GENTLEMAN'S MAGAZINE
(STRANAVERNE)	8.6 X 12.0 CM	SPEED
(SUFFOLK)	8.6 X 12.0 CM	SPEED
(SULTANIA, VIEW)	21.0 X 25.4 CM	SCHENK
(SURAT, VIEW)	21.0 X 25.4 CM	SCHENK
(SURREY)	8.6 X 12.0 CM	SPEED
(SUSSEX)	58.0 X 69.0 CM	GREENWOOD
(SUSSEX)	8.6 X 12.0 CM	SPEED
(TANGIER, VIEW)	21.0 X 25.4 CM	SCHENK
(TAPROBANA WITH SOUTHERN TIP OF INDIA)	27.9 X 45.7 CM	PTOLEMY (1522-41 ST...
(TENNESSEE)	36.2 X 38.7 CM	THOMAS, COWPERTHWAI...
(TEXAS)	32.4 X 40.0 CM	THOMAS, COWPERTHWAI...
(TEXAS//ARKANSAS & INDIAN TERRITORY)	29.8 X 43.2 CM	CRAM
(TIBERIAS, VIEW)	21.9 X 37.7 CM	DE BRUYN
(TIERRA DEL FUEGO MAP)	15.4 X 19.1 CM	DE BRY
(TIRLEMONT, PLAN)	30.0 X 45.0 CM	BRAUN & HOGENBERG
(TITLE PAGE TO "PARERGON")	35.6 X 22.9 CM	ORTELIUS
(TONBRIDGE TO GODSTONE GREEN-ROAD MAP)	19.1 X 12.7 CM	CARY
(TOURNAY, PLAN)	30.0 X 45.0 CM	BRAUN & HOGENBERG

214

(TRIER, VIEW)	21.0 X 25.4 CM	SCHENK
(TRIPOLI, VIEWS OF TOWN & HARBOUR)	28.3 X 39.3 CM	DE BRUYN
(TUNIS, VIEW)	21.0 X 25.4 CM	SCHENK
(TURRES/GALLIPOLI, VIEW)	30.3 X 38.0 CM	DE BRUYN
(TYRE, VIEW)	24.8 X 63.0 CM	DE BRUYN
(ULSTER)	8.6 X 12.0 CM	SPEED
(UTAH)	40.6 X 57.2 CM	ASHER & ADAMS
(UTAH//ARIZONA)	30.5 X 24.1 CM	CRAM
(UTRECHT, PLAN)	30.0 X 45.0 CM	BRAUN & HOGENBERG
(VALETTA, PERSPECTIVE PLAN)	26.0 X 35.0 CM	DAPPER
(VERONIS, VIEW)	23.1 X 62.5 CM	DE BRUYN
(VIENNA, VIEW)	21.0 X 25.4 CM	SCHENK
(VIRGIN ISLANDS)	58.4 X 90.2 CM	DEPOSITO HIDROGRAFICO
(VIRGINIA)	27.3 X 33.0 CM	TANNER
(VIRGINIA)	29.2 X 34.9 CM	THOMAS, COWPERTHWAI...
(WALES)	8.6 X 12.0 CM	SPEED
(WARWICKSHIRE)	28.0 X 38.0 CM	CAMDEN
(WARWICKSHIRE)	8.6 X 12.0 CM	SPEED
(WASHINGTON, OREGON & IDAHO)	31.8 X 39.4 CM	JOHNSON & WARD
(WEST AFRICA, ARABIA, INDIA)	38.7 X 52.7 CM	LINSCHOTEN
(WEST INDIES DISCOVERED BY COLUMBUS, ENGRAVED SCENE)	14.4 X 19.4 CM	DE BRY
(WEST INDIES)	58.4 X 101.0 CM	MOLL
(WESTERN HEMISPHERE)	54.0 X 42.0 CM	NICOLOSI
(WESTMORLAND & CUMBERLAND)	8.6 X 12.0 CM	SPEED
(WILTSHIRE)	11.4 X 11.4 CM	BOWEN
(WILTSHIRE)	58.0 X 69.0 CM	GREENWOOD
(WILTSHIRE)	8.6 X 12.0 CM	SPEED
(WISCONSIN)	39.4 X 33.0 CM	DESILVER
(WISCONSIN)	40.3 X 33.7 CM	THOMAS, COWPERTHWAI...
(WORCESTERSHIRE)	28.0 X 38.0 CM	CAMDEN
(WORCESTERSHIRE)	8.6 X 12.0 CM	SPEED
(WORLD MAP)	31.0 X 43.0 CM	SCHEDEL
(WORLD MAP, UNTITLED)	11.5 X 22.5 CM	DE BRY
(WORLD)	16.5 X 20.3 CM	DE BRY
(WORLD)	31.8 X 44.5 CM	SCHEDEL
(WYOMING)	40.6 X 57.2 CM	ASHER & ADAMS
(WYOMING)	40.6 X 55.9 CM	CRAM
(YORKSHIRE E. RIDING)	28.0 X 38.0 CM	CAMDEN
(YORKSHIRE W. RIDING)	28.0 X 38.0 CM	CAMDEN
(YORKSHIRE)	14.0 X 18.4 CM	COWLEY
(YORKSHIRE)	12.1 X 16.5 CM	SPEED
(YPRES, PLAN)	30.0 X 45.0 CM	BRAUN & HOGENBERG
(ZUTPHEN, PLAN)	30.0 X 45.0 CM	BRAUN & HOGENBERG
(ZWOLLE, BIRD'S EYE VIEW)	30.0 X 45.0 CM	BRAUN & HOGENBERG
...CIVITATIS GANDAVENSIS HANC TERRITORY EIUSDEM...HENRICUS HONDIUS	38.0 X 47.0 CM	HONDIUS
...MAGNETIC DECLINATION ISOGONIC LINES FOR THE YEAR 1870	35.0 X 50.0 CM	U.S. COAST SURVEY
...NEW MAP OF THE CHIEF RIVERS, BAYES, CREEKS, HARBOURS AND SETTLEMENT	48.3 X 55.9 CM	MORDEN
1695. LE BOMBARDEMENT DE LA VILLE DE BRUXELLES CAPITALE DES PAYS-BAS P	88.0 X 57.0 CM	LANGLOIS
1802. NO 31 DEPARTEMENT DES FORETS.	20.0 X 24.0 CM	CHANLAIRE
1802. NO. 6. DEPARTMENT DES FORETS...PAR P.G. CHANLAIRE. PARIS CHEZ L'	19.0 X 20.0 CM	CHANLAIRE
A CARICATURE OF ENGLAND AND WALES	13.0 X 9.5 CM	ANON
A CARICATURE OF IRELAND	13.0 X 9.5 CM	ANON
A CHART OF DELAWAR RIVER...	52.1 X 73.7 CM	DES BARRES
A CHART OF DELAWARE BAY AND RIVER FROM THE ORIGINAL BY MR. FISHER OF P	18.4 X 23.5 CM	ANON
A CHART OF DELAWARE BAY AND RIVER, FROM THE ORIGINAL BY MR. FISHER OF	23.5 X 18.4 CM	GENTLEMAN'S MAGAZINE
A CHART OF DELAWARE BAY AND RIVER, FROM THE ORIGINAL BY MR. FISHER OF	17.8 X 22.9 CM	GENTLEMAN'S MAGAZINE
A CHART OF HUDSON'S STRAITS AND BAY ACCORDING TO THE DISCOVERIES MADE	34.2 X 29.3 CM	ANON
A CHART OF PART OF THE COAST OF LABRADORE, FROM GRAND POINT TO SHECATI	50.2 X 52.1 CM	JEFFERYS
A CHART OF THE ANTILLES, OR, CHARIBBEE, OR, CARIBS ISLANDS, WITH THE V	45.7 X 50.8 CM	FADEN
A CHART OF THE COAST OF BARBARIA WITH THE WESTERN, CANARIA, & CAPE DE	41.9 X 54.6 CM	THORNTON
A CHART OF THE COAST OF BRAZIL IN AMERICA: WITH PARTS OF THE CARIBBE I	49.5 X 117.0 CM	SENEX
A CHART OF THE COASTS OF IRELAND AND PART OF ENGLAND	43.8 X 53.3 CM	MOUNT & PAGE
A CHART OF THE COASTS OF SPAIN AND PORTUGAL, WITH THE BALEARIC ISLANDS	53.3 X 72.4 CM	FADEN

215

MAP OF GEORGIA, ALSO THE TWO FLORIDAS	18.7 X 31.1 CM	MORSE
MAP OF GLOCESTERSHIRE FROM THE BEST AUTHORITIES	48.3 X 41.9 CM	CARY
MAP OF GUADELOUPE ONE OF THE CARIBBY ISLANDS IN THE WEST INDIES SUBJ	12.1 X 17.8 CM	LONDON MAGAZINE
MAP OF IRELAND ACCORDING TO THE BEST AUTHORITIES	38.1 X 34.3 CM	CAREY
MAP OF IRELAND DIVIDED INTO PROVINCES AND COUNTIES, SHOWING THE GREA	69.9 X 53.3 CM	WYLD
MAP OF JAMAICA.../BARBADOS	38.0 X 50.0 CM	SPEED
MAP OF JAMAICA/BARBADOS	49.5 X 38.1 CM	SPEED
MAP OF LOUISIANA AND OF THE RIVER MISSISSIPI	49.5 X 57.2 CM	SENEX
MAP OF LOUISIANA AND OF THE RIVER MISSISSIPI	48.9 X 58.4 CM	SENEX
MAP OF MARCO POLO'S VOYAGES & TRAVELS IN THE 13TH CENTURY THROUGH A	20.3 X 30.5 CM	ANON
MAP OF MARTINICO FROM THE LATEST AND BEST AUTHORITIES	19.1 X 24.1 CM	GIBSON
MAP OF MEXICO OR NEW SPAIN, FLORIDA NOW CALLED LOUISIANA, AND PART O	17.8 X 25.4 CM	MOLL
MAP OF MEXICO OR NEW SPAIN...	27.7 X 36.5 CM	POLITICAL MAGAZINE
MAP OF NEW ENGLAND AND NEW YORK	38.7 X 47.6 CM	SPEED
MAP OF NEW ENGLAND AND NEW YORK	38.0 X 50.0 CM	SPEED
MAP OF NEW ENGLAND AND NEW YORK	38.1 X 50.8 CM	SPEED
MAP OF NEW ENGLAND AND NOVA SCOTIA; WITH PART...CANADA & NEW BRITAIN	27.3 X 33.7 CM	KITCHIN
MAP OF NEW FRANCE CONTAINING CANADA, LOUISIANA & C. IN NTH. AMERICA	18.4 X 25.4 CM	MOLL
MAP OF NORTH AMERICA	36.8 X 46.4 CM	SEALE
MAP OF NORTH AMERICA	36.8 X 45.7 CM	SEALE
MAP OF NORTH AMERICA...	36.8 X 47.0 CM	SEALE
MAP OF NORTH CAROLINA FROM THE BEST AUTHORITIES	22.2 X 42.5 CM	MORSE
MAP OF OHIO, BY JOHN KILBOURN, COLUMBUS, JANUARY 1821	31.1 X 30.5 CM	KILBOURN
MAP OF PALESTINE	41.9 X 26.0 CM	APPLETON
MAP OF PART OF THE UNITED STATES OF NORTH AMERICA EXHIBITING THE WES	45.7 X 50.8 CM	CARY
MAP OF PART OF WEST FLORIDA FROM PENSACOLA TO THE MOUTH OF THE IBERV	19.1 X 34.3 CM	GENTLEMAN'S MAGAZINE
MAP OF PART OF WEST FLORIDA, FROM PENSACOLA TO THE MOUTH OF THE IBER	18.4 X 34.3 CM	GENTLEMAN'S MAGAZINE
MAP OF PENNSYLVANIA FROM THE BEST AUTHORITIES	17.8 X 22.9 CM	STOCKDALE
MAP OF PHILADELPHIA AND PARTS ADJACENT. BY N. SCULL AND G. HEAP	33.3 X 29.5 CM	GENTLEMAN'S MAGAZINE
MAP OF PHILADELPHIA...	71.1 X 137.2 CM	SAYER & BENNETT
MAP OF RUSSIA	38.7 X 47.6 CM	SPEED
MAP OF SOUTH AMERICA CONTAINING TIERRA-FIRMA, GUYANA, NEW GRANADA, A	69.9 X 116.8 CM	JEFFERYS
MAP OF SOUTH AMERICA DRAWN FROM THE LATEST AND BEST AUTHORITIES	27.3 X 29.0 CM	POLITICAL MAGAZINE
MAP OF SOUTH AMERICA WITH ALL THE EUROPEAN SETTLEMENTS...	47.0 X 36.8 CM	SEALE
MAP OF SOUTH CAROLINA AND A PART OF GEORGIA...FROM SURVEYS OF WM. BU	134.6 X 121.9 CM	FADEN
MAP OF SUCH PARTS OF GEORGIA AND SOUTH CAROLINA AS TEND TO ILLUSTRAT	18.4 X 23.5 CM	LONDON MAGAZINE
MAP OF SURINAM	19.8 X 44.1 CM	STEDMAN
MAP OF SUSSEX, FROM THE BEST AUTHORITIES...	35.6 X 50.8 CM	CARY
MAP OF THAT PART OF AMERICA WHERE A DEGREE OF LATITUDE WAS MEASURED	16.0 X 9.5 CM	GENTLEMAN'S MAGAZINE
MAP OF THAT PART OF AMERICA WHICH WAS THE PRINCIPAL SEAT OF WAR IN 1	21.6 X 33.0 CM	LODGE
MAP OF THE AUSTRIAN POSSESSIONS IN THE NETHERLANDS OR LOW COUNTRIES,	55.2 X 68.6 CM	FADEN
MAP OF THE BAY OF CAMPECHY	14.8 X 27.9 CM	MOLL
MAP OF THE BRITISH AND FRENCH DOMINIONS IN NORTH AMERICA WITH THE RO	134.6 X 193.7 CM	MITCHELL, JOHN
MAP OF THE BRITISH AND FRENCH SETTLEMENTS IN NORTH AMERICA	27.9 X 38.7 CM	LODGE
MAP OF THE BRITISH AND FRENCH SETTLEMENTS IN NORTH AMERICA...	19.1 X 48.3 CM	GENTLEMAN'S MAGAZINE
MAP OF THE BRITISH AND FRENCH SETTLEMENTS IN NORTH AMERICA: (PART TH	19.1 X 48.6 CM	BOWEN
MAP OF THE BRITISH EMPIRE IN AMERICA	52.1 X 49.5 CM	POPPLE
MAP OF THE BRITISH EMPIRE IN AMERICA WITH THE FRENCH, SPANISH AND HO	60.0 X 53.5 CM	COVENS & MORTIER
MAP OF THE BRITISH PLANTATIONS CANADA FLORIDA	10.8 X 13.3 CM	BOWEN
MAP OF THE CAPE OF GOOD HOPE	18.5 X 11.0 CM	GENTLEMAN'S MAGAZINE
MAP OF THE CARACAS	31.8 X 51.4 CM	CAREY
MAP OF THE COLONIES OF CONNECTICUT AND RHODE ISLAND...	17.8 X 22.9 CM	LONDON MAGAZINE
MAP OF THE COUNTRIES SITUATE ABOUT THE NORTH POLE AS FAR AS THE 50TH	26.0 X 25.4 CM	CAREY
MAP OF THE COUNTRY BETWEEN ALBEMARLE SOUND AND LAKE ERIE, COMPREHEND	59.1 X 59.4 CM	STOCKDALE
MAP OF THE COUNTRY BETWEEN CROWN POINT AND FORT EDWARD	19.1 X 11.4 CM	GENTLEMAN'S MAGAZINE
MAP OF THE COUNTRY OF THE HOTTENTOTS, TOWARDS THE CAPE OF GOOD HOPE	24.5 X 37.0 CM	CHILD
MAP OF THE COUNTRY ROUND PHILADELPHIA INCLUDING PART OF NEW JERSEY,	17.8 X 21.6 CM	SCOT'S MAGAZINE
MAP OF THE COUNTRY ROUND PHILADELPHIA INCLUDING PART OF NEW JERSEY,	22.2 X 17.8 CM	GENTLEMAN'S MAGAZINE
MAP OF THE COUNTRY ROUND PHILADELPHIA INCLUDING PART OF NEW JERSEY,	17.1 X 23.5 CM	SCOT'S MAGAZINE
MAP OF THE COUNTY OF CUMBERLAND, FROM AN ACTUAL SURVEY...	61.6 X 68.6 CM	GREENWOOD
MAP OF THE DISCOVERIES MADE BY CAPT. WM. DAMPIER IN THE ROEBUCK IN 1	20.0 X 32.0 CM	BOWEN
MAP OF THE DISCOVERIES MADE BY CAPTS. COOK & CLERKE IN THE YEARS 177	19.1 X 27.9 CM	CAREY
MAP OF THE DISCOVERIES MADE BY CAPTS. COOKE & CLERKE IN THE YEARS 17	20.3 X 29.8 CM	CAREY

Title	Dimensions	Source
A MAP OF THE DISTRICT OF MAINE WITH NEW BRUNSWICK & NOVA SCOTIA	18.4 X 23.5 CM	MORSE
A MAP OF THE DUTCH SETTLEMENTS OF SURINAM, DEMERARY, ISSEQUIBO, BERBIC	26.9 X 36.9 CM	POLITICAL MAGAZINE
A MAP OF THE EAST RIDING OF YORKSHIRE WITH AINSTY LIBERTY	41.3 X 51.4 CM	CARY
A MAP OF THE EASTERN PART OF THE PROVINCE OF NEW YORK; WITH PART OF NE	21.6 X 16.5 CM	LONDON MAGAZINE
A MAP OF THE ENGLISH PLANTATIONS IN AMERICA	17.8 X 18.4 CM	LAWSON
A MAP OF THE ENGLISH, FRENCH, SPANISH, DUTCH & DANISH ISLANDS IN THE W	27.0 X 36.1 CM	POLITICAL MAGAZINE
A MAP OF THE FIVE GREAT LAKES WITH PART OF PENNSYLVANIA, NEW YORK, CAN	21.0 X 26.0 CM	LONDON MAGAZINE
A MAP OF THE FRENCH PART OF ST. DOMINGO	39.4 X 49.5 CM	CAREY
A MAP OF THE GREAT LEVELL OF THE FENNS EXTENDING INTO YE COUNTYES OF N	29.2 X 40.0 CM	HARRIS
A MAP OF THE INHABITED PART OF CANADA FROM THE FRENCH SURVEYS; WITH TH	59.7 X 87.6 CM	FADEN
A MAP OF THE ISLAND OF JAMAICA...	31.0 X 62.5 CM	EDWARDS
A MAP OF THE ISLAND OF ST. JOHN IN THE GULF OF ST. LAURENCE DIVIDED IN	38.1 X 71.1 CM	JEFFERYS
A MAP OF THE ISLAND OF TOBAGO DRAWN FROM AN ACTUAL SURVEY	19.1 X 24.1 CM	BOWEN
A MAP OF THE ISLANDS OF ST. LUCIA AND MARTINIQUE...THE STATION OF THE	37.4 X 27.2 CM	POLITICAL MAGAZINE
A MAP OF THE MIDDLE PART OF AMERICA	15.2 X 29.2 CM	DAMPIER
A MAP OF THE MOST INHABITED PART OF NEW ENGLAND CONTAINING THE PROVINC	63.5 X 52.0 CM	BOWLES
A MAP OF THE MOST INHABITED PART OF NEW ENGLAND CONTAINING THE PROVINC	102.9 X 48.3 CM	JEFFERYS
A MAP OF THE MOST INHABITED PART OF NEW ENGLAND CONTAINING THE PROVINC	104.0 X 98.5 CM	LOTTER
A MAP OF THE MOST INHABITED PART OF NEW ENGLAND...	50.0 X 96.0 CM	LE ROUGE
A MAP OF THE NEW GOVERNMENTS OF EAST & WEST FLORIDA	19.1 X 24.8 CM	GENTLEMAN'S MAGAZINE
A MAP OF THE NEW GOVERNMENTS, OF EAST & WEST FLORIDA	19.1 X 25.4 CM	GENTLEMAN'S MAGAZINE
A MAP OF THE NORTH POLE WITH ALL THE TERRITORIES THAT LIE NEAR IT, KNO	20.3 X 27.9 CM	MOLL
A MAP OF THE PENINSULA OF INDIA FROM THE 19TH DEGREE NORTH LATITUDE TO	40.0 X 81.0 CM	FADEN
A MAP OF THE PROVINCE OF MASSACHUSETTS BAY, AND COLONY OF RHODE ISLAND	27.6 X 37.2 CM	POLITICAL MAGAZINE
A MAP OF THE PROVINCES OF NEW-YORK AND NEW-JERSEY, WITH A PART OF PENN	74.9 X 55.9 CM	LOTTER
A MAP OF THE RAILROADS IN THE UNITED STATES...	99.1 X 106.7 CM	ANDREWS
A MAP OF THE ROAD FROM LONDON TO BERWICK	17.8 X 29.2 CM	GIBSON
A MAP OF THE ROAD FROM LONDON TO HARWICH	17.8 X 29.2 CM	GIBSON
A MAP OF THE SOURCES OF THE COLORADO & BIG SALT LAKE, PLATTE, YELLOW-S	41.9 X 39.4 CM	BONNEVILLE
A MAP OF THE SOUTH POLE WITH TRACK OF HIS MAJESTY'S SLOOP RESOLUTION I	22.9 X 21.6 CM	BOWEN
A MAP OF THE STATES OF NEW HAMPSHIRE AND VERMONT BY J. DENISON	19.1 X 23.5 CM	MORSE
A MAP OF THE STATES OF VIRGINIA, NORTH CAROLINA, SOUTH CAROLINA AND GE	31.1 X 36.8 CM	STOCKDALE
A MAP OF THE UNITED STATES OF AMERICA, WITH PART OF THE ADJOINING PROV	21.6 X 26.7 CM	WILKINSON
A MAP OF THE UNITED STATES OF AMERICA. AGREEBLE TO THE PEACE OF 1783.	39.4 X 35.6 CM	GUTHRIE
A MAP OF THE UNITED STATES OF NORTH AMERICA	121.9 X 141.0 CM	ARROWSMITH
A MAP OF THE VICINITY OF MONTEREY BAY, CALIFORNIA, TO ACCOMPANY A REPO	17.8 X 25.4 CM	U.S. COAST SURVEY
A MAP OF THE VIRGINIA CENTRAL RAILROAD, WEST OF THE BLUE RIDGE, AND TH	47.0 X 71.1 CM	CITTI
A MAP OF THE WEST INDIES & C. MEXICO OR NEW SPAIN, ALSO YE TRADE WINDS	20.3 X 26.7 CM	MOLL
A MAP OF THE WEST INDIES OR THE ISLANDS OF AMERICA IN THE NORTH SEA...	59.0 X 102.0 CM	MOLL
A MAP OF THE WESTERN ISLANDS	12.7 X 14.6 CM	MORDEN
A MAP OF THE WESTERN PARTS OF THE COLONY OF VIRGINIA	19.7 X 12.1 CM	BALDWIN
A MAP OF THE WHOLE CONTINENT OF AMERICA. PARTICULARLY SHEWING THE BRIT	49.8 X 54.3 CM	BOWLES
A MAP OF THE WORLD SHEWING THE COURSE OF CAPT. COOK'S VOYAGE ROUND THE	15.9 X 28.9 CM	SENEX
A MAP OF THE WORLD SHEWING THE COURSE OF MR. DAMPIER'S VOYAGE ROUND IT	16.2 X 29.2 CM	MOLL
A MAP OF THE WORLD. SHEWING THE COURSE OF MR. DAMPIERS VOYAGE ROUND IT	16.0 X 29.2 CM	MOLL
A MAP OF TURKY, ARABIA AND PERSIA...REVISED BY I. SENEX	47.0 X 56.5 CM	SENEX
A MAP OF VIRGINIA AND MARYLAND	39.4 X 48.3 CM	SPEED
A MAP OF VIRGINIA AND MARYLAND	38.0 X 49.5 CM	SPEED
A MAP OF VIRGINIA AND MARYLAND	38.7 X 47.6 CM	SPEED
A MAP OF WARWICKSHIRE FROM THE BEST AUTHORITIES	52.1 X 42.5 CM	CARY
A MAPP OF ALL THE WORLD	57.2 X 87.6 CM	BERRY
A MAPP OF HANTSHIRE	30.5 X 25.4 CM	BLOME
A MAPP OF HUNTINGDON SHIRE WITH ITS HUNDREDS...	31.8 X 25.4 CM	BLOME
A MAPP OF ITALY...	29.8 X 39.4 CM	BLOME
A MAPP OF STAFFORD SHIRE WITH ITS HUNDREDS...	33.0 X 23.5 CM	BLOME
A MAPP OF THE COUNTIES OF LEICESTER AND RUTLAND...	53.3 X 68.6 CM	BLOME
A MAPP OF THE COUNTY OF DARBYE WITH ITS HUNDREDS...	31.8 X 25.4 CM	BLOME
A MAPP OF THE COUNTY OF RUTLAND WITH ITS HUNDREDS	21.6 X 27.9 CM	BLOME
A MAPP OF THE SOMMER ISLANDS ONCE CALLED THE BERMUDAS...	38.7 X 47.6 CM	SPEED
A MAPP OF THE WORLD SHEWING WHAT A CLOCK IT IS IN ANY PART OF THE WORL	12.7 X 15.2 CM	SELLER
A MAPP OF WORCESTER SHIRE WITH ITS HUNDREDS...	26.7 X 32.4 CM	BLOME
A MAPP OF YE COUNTY OF LINCOLNE, WTH ITS DIVISIONS & HUNDREDS: OR WAPO	33.0 X 26.7 CM	BLOME
A MERCATOR CHART OF THE WORLD	33.0 X 44.0 CM	BOWEN

A MODERN MAP OF LANCASHIRE...	24.1 X 19.1 CM	ELLIS
A MODERN MAP OF NORTHUMBERLAND...	24.8 X 19.1 CM	ELLIS
A MODERN MAP OF SUFFOLK...	19.7 X 24.8 CM	ELLIS
A MODERN MAP OF WORCESTERSHIRE...	25.4 X 19.1 CM	ELLIS
A NEW & ACCURATE CHART OF THE WESTERN OR ATLANTIC OCEAN DRAWN FROM THE	21.6 X 26.7 CM	BOWEN
A NEW & ACCURATE MAP OF ASIA. DRAWN FROM ACTUAL SURVEYS...BY EMMAN. BO	35.6 X 42.5 CM	BOWEN
A NEW & ACCURATE MAP OF CHINA. DRAWN FROM SURVEYS MADE BY THE JESUIT M	34.3 X 41.9 CM	BOWEN
A NEW & ACCURATE MAP OF LOUISIANA...	34.3 X 41.9 CM	BOWEN
A NEW & ACCURATE MAP OF SPAIN AND PORTUGAL	35.6 X 43.2 CM	BOWEN
A NEW & ACCURATE MAP OF THE ISLANDS OF HISPANIOLA AND PORTO RICO...	17.1 X 41.9 CM	BOWEN
A NEW & ACCURATE MAP OF THE PRESENT SEAT OF WAR IN NORTH AMERICA, COMP	36.8 X 27.9 CM	HINTON
A NEW & ACCURATE MAP OF THE PROVINCE OF CANADA IN NORTH AMERICA...	25.4 X 33.4 CM	POLITICAL MAGAZINE
A NEW & ACCURATE MAP OF THE PROVINCES OF NORTH & SOUTH CAROLINA, GEORG	34.9 X 43.2 CM	BOWEN
A NEW & ACCURATE MAP OF THE PROVINCES OF SOUTH CAROLINA IN NORTH AMERI	33.0 X 27.9 CM	UNIVERSAL MAGAZINE
A NEW & ACCURATE MAP OF TURKEY IN ASIA. ARABIA, &C. DRAWN FROM THE BES	34.9 X 42.5 CM	BOWEN
A NEW & EXACT MAP OF GERMANY...	63.5 X 93.3 CM	WILLDEY
A NEW & EXACT MAP OF THE COASTS, COUNTRIES AND ISLANDS WITHIN YE LIMIT	64.8 X 49.2 CM	MOLL
A NEW & EXACT MAP OF THE COASTS, COUNTRIES AND ISLANDS WITHIN YE LIMIT	66.0 X 48.3 CM	MOLL
A NEW & EXACT SURVEY OF THE RIVER DEE OR CHESTER WATER	43.8 X 57.2 CM	COLLINS
A NEW AND ACCURAT MAP OF THE WORLD	8.9 X 15.2 CM	SPEED
A NEW AND ACCURAT MAP OF THE WORLD	39.4 X 50.8 CM	SPEED
A NEW AND ACCURAT MAP OF THE WORLD DRAWNE ACCORDING TO YE TRUEST DESCR	9.0 X 12.0 CM	SPEED
A NEW AND ACCURAT MAP OF THE WORLD. DRAWNE ACCORDING TO YE TRUEST DESC	8.6 X 12.1 CM	SPEED
A NEW AND ACCURAT MAP OF THE WORLD...	38.7 X 47.6 CM	SPEED
A NEW AND ACCURATE CHART OF THE HARBOUR OF BOSTON IN NEW ENGLAND IN NO	22.3 X 16.6 CM	POLITICAL MAGAZINE
A NEW AND ACCURATE CHART OF THE WEST INDIES WITH THE ADJACENT COASTS O	36.5 X 44.0 CM	BOWEN
A NEW AND ACCURATE CHART OF THE WESTERN OR ATLANTIC OCEAN DRAWN FROM T	21.5 X 26.5 CM	BOWEN
A NEW AND ACCURATE MAP OF ALL THE KNOWN WORLD	31.5 X 53.5 CM	BOWEN
A NEW AND ACCURATE MAP OF ALL THE KNOWN WORLD	31.0 X 53.0 CM	BOWEN
A NEW AND ACCURATE MAP OF AMERICA	34.3 X 44.5 CM	BOWEN
A NEW AND ACCURATE MAP OF EAST AND WEST FLORIDA DRAWN FROM THE BEST AU	17.8 X 22.9 CM	KITCHIN
A NEW AND ACCURATE MAP OF EAST AND WEST FLORIDA...	17.8 X 22.2 CM	LONDON MAGAZINE
A NEW AND ACCURATE MAP OF NEW JERSEY...	31.8 X 26.7 CM	UNIVERSAL MAGAZINE
A NEW AND ACCURATE MAP OF NEW SOUTH WALES, WITH NORFOLK AND LORD HOWE'	29.2 X 24.1 CM	CAREY
A NEW AND ACCURATE MAP OF NORTH AMERICA	19.7 X 22.9 CM	ENTICK
A NEW AND ACCURATE MAP OF NORTH AMERICA	26.0 X 34.3 CM	UNIVERSAL MAGAZINE
A NEW AND ACCURATE MAP OF NORTH CAROLINA IN NORTH AMERICA	26.7 X 35.6 CM	UNIVERSAL MAGAZINE
A NEW AND ACCURATE MAP OF NORTH CAROLINA, AND PART OF SOUTH CAROLINA,	27.4 X 38.2 CM	POLITICAL MAGAZINE
A NEW AND ACCURATE MAP OF QUEBEC AND ITS BOUNDARIES; FROM A LATE SURVE	26.7 X 31.8 CM	UNIVERSAL MAGAZINE
A NEW AND ACCURATE MAP OF SCOTLAND COMPILED FROM SURVEYS, AND THE MOST	31.8 X 22.2 CM	BOWEN
A NEW AND ACCURATE MAP OF THE BRITISH DOMINIONS IN AMERICA, ACCORDING	52.7 X 62.9 CM	KITCHIN
A NEW AND ACCURATE MAP OF THE CHIEF PARTS OF SOUTH CAROLINA AND GEORGI	27.4 X 37.4 CM	POLITICAL MAGAZINE
A NEW AND ACCURATE MAP OF THE COLONY OF MASSACHUSETTS BAY IN NORTH AME	26.7 X 33.0 CM	HINTON
A NEW AND ACCURATE MAP OF THE EMPIRE OF CHINA FROM THE SIEUR ROBERT'S	19.1 X 29.2 CM	GIBSON
A NEW AND ACCURATE MAP OF THE ISLAND OF JAMAICA	34.0 X 42.5 CM	BOWEN
A NEW AND ACCURATE MAP OF THE ISLAND OF MARTINICO 1763	17.8 X 23.5 CM	ENTICK
A NEW AND ACCURATE MAP OF THE PRESENT WAR IN NORTH AMERICA	27.9 X 36.8 CM	UNIVERSAL MAGAZINE
A NEW AND ACCURATE MAP OF THE PROVINCE OF GEORGIA IN NORTH AMERICA	32.4 X 27.3 CM	UNIVERSAL MAGAZINE
A NEW AND ACCURATE MAP OF THE PROVINCE OF NEW YORK AND PART OF THE JER	37.1 X 27.4 CM	POLITICAL MAGAZINE
A NEW AND ACCURATE MAP OF THE PROVINCE OF NOVA SCOTIA IN NORTH AMERICA	28.6 X 33.0 CM	LODGE
A NEW AND ACCURATE MAP OF THE PROVINCE OF SOUTH CAROLINA IN NORTH AMER	33.0 X 27.9 CM	UNIVERSAL MAGAZINE
A NEW AND ACCURATE MAP OF THE PROVINCE OF SOUTH CAROLINA...	33.0 X 27.9 CM	UNIVERSAL MAGAZINE
A NEW AND ACCURATE MAP OF THE PROVINCE OF VIRGINIA IN NORTH AMERICA	27.9 X 34.3 CM	UNIVERSAL MAGAZINE
A NEW AND ACCURATE MAP OF VIRGINIA AND PART OF MARYLAND AND PENNSYLVAN	27.2 X 37.6 CM	POLITICAL MAGAZINE
A NEW AND COMPLEAT MAP OF ALL AMERICA	52.1 X 118.1 CM	GIBSON
A NEW AND CORRECT CHART OF THE HARBOUR OF CORKE BY THE REVD. J. LINDSA	43.8 X 52.1 CM	COLLINS
A NEW AND CORRECT CHART OF THE NORTH PART OF AMERICA FROM NEW FOUND LA	43.2 X 55.9 CM	MOUNT & PAGE
A NEW AND CORRECT MAP OF NORTH AMERICA IN WHICH THE PLACES OF THE PRIN	27.6 X 38.1 CM	POLITICAL MAGAZINE
A NEW AND CORRECT MAP OF NORTH AMERICA IN WHICH THE PLACES OF THE PRIN	27.6 X 37.9 CM	POLITICAL MAGAZINE
A NEW AND CORRECT MAP OF NORTH AMERICA WITH THE WEST INDIA ISLANDS, DI	101.6 X 114.3 CM	BOWEN
A NEW AND CORRECT MAP OF NORTH AMERICA WITH THE WEST INDIA ISLANDS, DI	50.8 X 57.2 CM	LOTTER
A NEW AND CORRECT MAP OF NORTH-WALES	35.6 X 43.2 CM	MORDEN
A NEW AND CORRECT MAP OF SCOTLAND & THE ISLES...	30.5 X 27.9 CM	MOLL

A NEW AND CORRECT MAP OF THE BRITISH COLONIES IN NORTH AMERICA...	48.3 X 67.3 CM	LAURIE & WHITTLE
A NEW AND CORRECT MAP OF THE COAST OF AFRICA...WITH EXPLANATORY NOTES	48.3 X 57.2 CM	BOWLES
A NEW AND CORRECT MAP OF THE TEN SPANISH PROVINCES...	62.9 X 94.0 CM	SENEX
A NEW AND CORRECT PLAN OF THE CITIES OF LONDON, WESTMINSTER, AND SOUTH	44.0 X 68.0 CM	KITCHIN
A NEW AND EXACT MAP OF THE ISLAND OF ANTIGUA IN AMERICA...WITH THE DIV	27.6 X 37.0 CM	POLITICAL MAGAZINE
A NEW AND GENERAL MAP OF THE MIDDLE DOMINIONS BELONGING TO THE UNITED	48.3 X 66.0 CM	LAURIE & WHITTLE
A NEW AND GENERAL MAP OF THE MIDDLE DOMINIONS BELONGING TO THE UNITED	48.3 X 66.0 CM	LAURIE & WHITTLE
A NEW CHART OF HARWICH HARBOUR WITH THE ROLLING GROUND, FELSTOW ROAD,	48.3 X 48.9 CM	SAYER
A NEW CHART OF THE EAST COAST OF ENGLAND FROM FLAMBOROUGH HEAD TO THE	69.2 X 49.5 CM	LAURIE & WHITTLE
A NEW CHART OF THE RIVER ST. LAWRENCE	18.4 X 25.4 CM	KITCHIN
A NEW CHART OF THE WORLD ON MERCATOR'S PROJECTION	23.5 X 35.6 CM	DARTON
A NEW DESCRIPTION OF CAROLINA	37.5 X 50.8 CM	SPEED
A NEW DESCRIPTION OF CAROLINA	37.5 X 51.1 CM	SPEED
A NEW DESCRIPTION OF CAROLINA	37.5 X 50.8 CM	SPEED
A NEW DESCRIPTION OF CAROLINA	38.7 X 47.6 CM	SPEED
A NEW DESCRIPTION OF CAROLINA...	37.8 X 50.5 CM	SPEED
A NEW GENERALL CHART FOR THE WEST INDIES OF E. WRIGHT'S PROJECTION...M	45.7 X 57.2 CM	SELLER
A NEW GENERALL CHART FOR THE WEST INDIES OF E. WRIGHTS PROJECTION VUL	45.6 X 48.0 CM	MOLL
A NEW IMPROVED MAP OF CORNWALL FROM THE BEST SURVEYS...	51.4 X 68.6 CM	KITCHIN
A NEW IMPROVED MAP OF OXFORDSHIRE...	71.1 X 52.1 CM	KITCHIN
A NEW MAP OF AFRICA, FROM THE LATEST AUTHORITIES	47.0 X 53.3 CM	CARY
A NEW MAP OF ALABAMA WITH ITS ROADS AND DISTANCES FROM PLACE TO PLACE	29.2 X 36.8 CM	DESILVER
A NEW MAP OF AMERICA	45.7 X 52.1 CM	CARY
A NEW MAP OF AMERICA FROM THE LATEST AUTHORITIES BY JOHN CARY	45.7 X 52.1 CM	CARY
A NEW MAP OF AMERICA SEPTENTRIONALE...	38.1 X 54.6 CM	BLOME
A NEW MAP OF ARKANSAS WITH ITS CANALS, ROADS & DISTANCES	36.8 X 29.8 CM	MITCHELL
A NEW MAP OF ARKANSAS WITH THE CANALS, ROADS & DISTANCES	36.8 X 29.2 CM	THOMAS, COWPERTHWAI...
A NEW MAP OF CAROLINA	12.7 X 12.7 CM	MORDEN
A NEW MAP OF CHINA, FROM THE LATEST AUTHORITIES	41.9 X 51.4 CM	CARY
A NEW MAP OF DEVON SHIRE...	19.1 X 24.8 CM	KITCHIN
A NEW MAP OF GEORGIA	35.6 X 29.2 CM	THOMAS, COWPERTHWAI...
A NEW MAP OF GEORGIA WITH PART OF CAROLINA, FLORIDA AND LOUISIANA	35.6 X 47.0 CM	BOWEN
A NEW MAP OF HAMP SHIRE DRAWN FROM THE BEST AUTHORITIES	19.1 X 25.4 CM	KITCHIN
A NEW MAP OF HARTFORDSHIRE...	19.7 X 24.8 CM	KITCHIN
A NEW MAP OF HUNGARY BY ROBT. MORDEN	12.1 X 14.0 CM	MORDEN
A NEW MAP OF IRELAND FROM THE LATEST OBSERVATIONS BY JOHN SENEX	58.4 X 47.0 CM	SENEX
A NEW MAP OF IRELAND...	101.6 X 61.0 CM	MOLL
A NEW MAP OF KENTUCKY WITH ITS ROADS & DISTANCES FROM PLACE TO PLACE A	32.0 X 40.0 CM	DESILVER
A NEW MAP OF LOUISIANA WITH...DISTANCES ALONG STAGE & STEAMBOAT ROUTES	29.2 X 36.8 CM	THOMAS, COWPERTHWAI...
A NEW MAP OF MAINE	40.0 X 32.0 CM	DESILVER
A NEW MAP OF NEW ENGLAND AND NEW YORK	12.7 X 14.6 CM	MORDEN
A NEW MAP OF NEW FOUNDLAND, NEW SCOTLAND, THE ISLES OF BRETON, ANTICOS	18.4 X 26.0 CM	MOLL
A NEW MAP OF NEW YORK WITH ITS CANALS, ROADS & DISTANCES	29.2 X 35.6 CM	THOMAS, COWPERTHWAI...
A NEW MAP OF NEWFOUND LAND, THE ISLES OF BRETON, ANTICOSTI, ST. JOHNS	17.8 X 25.4 CM	MOLL
A NEW MAP OF NEWFOUNDLAND, NEW SCOTLAND...	18.4 X 26.0 CM	MOLL
A NEW MAP OF NORFOLK...	19.7 X 25.4 CM	KITCHIN
A NEW MAP OF NORTH AMERICA	45.7 X 52.1 CM	CARY
A NEW MAP OF NORTH AMERICA ACCORDING TO THE NEWEST OBSERVATIONS	17.8 X 24.8 CM	MOLL
A NEW MAP OF NORTH AMERICA AGREEABLE TO THE MOST APPROVED MAPS AND CHA	33.5 X 37.5 CM	CONDER
A NEW MAP OF NORTH AMERICA FROM THE LATEST AUTHORITIES BY JOHN CARY, E	45.7 X 52.1 CM	CARY
A NEW MAP OF NORTH AMERICA FROM THE LATEST DISCOVERIES, 1761. J. SPILB	38.1 X 27.9 CM	SMOLLETT
A NEW MAP OF NORTH AMERICA WITH THE WEST INDIA ISLANDS DIVIDED ACCORDI	99.1 X 115.6 CM	LAURIE & WHITTLE
A NEW MAP OF NORTH AMERICA, WITH THE WEST INDIA ISLANDS, DIVIDED ACCOR	117.5 X 50.8 CM	SAYER & BENNETT
A NEW MAP OF NORTH AMERICA...	101.6 X 116.8 CM	LAURIE & WHITTLE
A NEW MAP OF NORTH CAROLINA WITH ITS CANALS, ROADS & DISTANCES FROM PL	29.2 X 35.6 CM	DESILVER
A NEW MAP OF NORTHHAMPTON SHIRE...	25.4 X 19.1 CM	KITCHIN
A NEW MAP OF NOTTINGHAMSHIRE...	25.4 X 19.7 CM	KITCHIN
A NEW MAP OF NOVA SCOTIA	17.8 X 26.7 CM	ANON
A NEW MAP OF NOVA SCOTIA, AND CAPE BRETON ISLAND, WITH THE ADJACENT PA	47.6 X 61.6 CM	JEFFERYS
A NEW MAP OF NOVA SCOTIA, NEWFOUNDLAND &C. FROM THE LATEST AUTHORITIES	45.5 X 51.5 CM	CARY
A NEW MAP OF NOVA SCOTIA, NEWFOUNDLAND &C. FROM THE LATEST AUTHORITIES	50.8 X 61.0 CM	CARY
A NEW MAP OF PART OF THE UNITED STATES	45.1 X 51.4 CM	CARY
A NEW MAP OF PART OF THE UNITED STATES OF NORTH AMERICA, CONTAINING TH	51.8 X 45.7 CM	CARY

Title	Size	Maker
A NEW MAP OF PART OF THE UNITED STATES OF NORTH AMERICA, CONTAINING TH	45.7 X 51.8 CM	CARY
A NEW MAP OF PART OF THE UNITED STATES OF NORTH AMERICA, EXHIBITING TH	45.7 X 51.1 CM	CARY
A NEW MAP OF PENNSYLVANIA WITH ITS CANALS, RAILROADS &C.	30.5 X 35.6 CM	THOMAS, COWPERTHWAI...
A NEW MAP OF PRESENT ASIA DEDICATED TO HIS HIGHNESS WILLIAM DUKE OF GL	37.5 X 50.8 CM	WELLS
A NEW MAP OF RUTLANDSHIRE, DIVIDED INTO HUNDREDS...	48.3 X 54.0 CM	CARY
A NEW MAP OF SCOTLAND COMPILED FROM ACTUAL SURVEYS & REGULATED BY THE	62.9 X 48.3 CM	LAURIE & WHITTLE
A NEW MAP OF SOUTH AMERICA FROM THE LATEST AUTHORITIES	53.3 X 42.5 CM	CAREY
A NEW MAP OF SOUTH AMERICA, SHEWING ITS GENERAL DIVISIONS...	36.3 X 48.8 CM	WELLS
A NEW MAP OF SOUTH CAROLINA	29.2 X 35.6 CM	DESILVER
A NEW MAP OF SOUTH CAROLINA WITH ITS CANALS, ROADS & DISTANCES	29.2 X 35.6 CM	THOMAS, COWPERTHWAI...
A NEW MAP OF STAFFORDSHIRE FROM THE LATEST AUTHORITIES. J. LODGE, SCUL	32.4 X 26.0 CM	LODGE
A NEW MAP OF TENNESSEE WITH ITS ROADS & DISTANCES AMONG STAGE & STEAM	27.9 X 39.4 CM	THOMAS, COWPERTHWAI...
A NEW MAP OF THE BRITISH DOMINIONS IN NORTH AMERICA...SETTLED BY PROCL	23.5 X 30.5 CM	KITCHIN
A NEW MAP OF THE BRITISH EMPIRE IN NORTH AMERICA DRAWN FROM THE LATEST	33.0 X 37.0 CM	KITCHIN
A NEW MAP OF THE CHEROKEE NATION WITH THE NAMES OF THE TOWNS & RIVERS.	17.8 X 22.9 CM	KITCHIN
A NEW MAP OF THE COUNTY OF CAMBRIDGE, DIVIDED INTO HUNDREDS	50.2 X 45.1 CM	SMITH
A NEW MAP OF THE COUNTY OF OXFORD DIVIDED INTO HUNDREDS	51.4 X 45.7 CM	SMITH
A NEW MAP OF THE COUNTY OF SUFFOLK, DIVIDED INTO HUNDREDS, BY MR. THOS	34.9 X 44.5 CM	DARTON
A NEW MAP OF THE COUNTY OF YORK, DIVIDED INTO ITS RIDINGS WITH THEIR S	57.2 X 73.7 CM	DARTON
A NEW MAP OF THE EAST INDIA	38.7 X 47.6 CM	SPEED
A NEW MAP OF THE ENGLISH EMPIRE IN AMERICA, VIZ. VIRGINIA, NEW YORK, M	50.5 X 60.0 CM	SENEX
A NEW MAP OF THE ENGLISH EMPIRE IN AMERICA. VIZ VIRGINIA, MARYLAND, CA	49.5 X 58.4 CM	MORDEN
A NEW MAP OF THE ISLAND OF BARBADOES, CONTAINING ALL YE PARISHES AND P	18.4 X 25.4 CM	MOLL
A NEW MAP OF THE KINGDOM OF HUNGARY AND OF THE COUNTRIES, PROVINCES &C	64.8 X 100.3 CM	BOWLES
A NEW MAP OF THE PROVINCE OF LOWER CANADA, DESCRIBING ALL THE SEIGNEUR	57.2 X 87.0 CM	WYLD
A NEW MAP OF THE PROVINCE OF QUEBEC	17.1 X 21.0 CM	KITCHIN
A NEW MAP OF THE PROVINCE OF QUEBEC IN NORTH AMERICA DRAWN FROM THE BE	17.1 X 21.6 CM	KITCHIN
A NEW MAP OF THE PROVINCE OF QUEBEC, ACCORDING TO THE ROYAL PROCLAMATI	50.8 X 70.5 CM	SAYER & BENNETT
A NEW MAP OF THE RIVER MISSISSIPI, FROM THE SEA TO BAYAGOULAS	17.8 X 24.1 CM	LONDON MAGAZINE
A NEW MAP OF THE RIVER MISSISSIPPI FROM THE SEA TO BAYAGOULAS	17.8 X 24.1 CM	LONDON MAGAZINE
A NEW MAP OF THE ROMAN EMPIRE...	38.7 X 47.6 CM	SPEED
A NEW MAP OF THE STATE OF GEORGIA EXHIBITING IT'S INTERNAL IMPROVEMENT	33.0 X 40.6 CM	DESILVER
A NEW MAP OF THE STATE OF SOUTH CAROLINA	33.0 X 39.4 CM	DESILVER
A NEW MAP OF THE STATES OF TEXAS, CALIFORNIA...	63.5 X 59.1 CM	MITCHELL
A NEW MAP OF THE UNITED STATES	40.6 X 66.7 CM	THOMAS, COWPERTHWAI...
A NEW MAP OF THE UNITED STATES OF AMERICA	44.5 X 49.5 CM	CARY
A NEW MAP OF THE UNITED STATES OF AMERICA	40.6 X 66.0 CM	DESILVER
A NEW MAP OF THE UNITED STATES OF AMERICA BY J.H. YOUNG	40.6 X 67.3 CM	THOMAS, COWPERTHWAI...
A NEW MAP OF THE UNITED STATES OF NORTH AMERICA, EXHIBITING THE WESTER	50.8 X 45.7 CM	CARY
A NEW MAP OF THE UNITED STATES OF NTH. AMERICA. DRAWN FROM THE LATEST	34.3 X 38.1 CM	KITCHIN
A NEW MAP OF THE WEST INDIES FOR THE HISTORY OF THE BRITISH COLONIES	69.5 X 113.0 CM	EDWARDS
A NEW MAP OF THE WHOLE CONTINENT OF AMERICA DIVIDED INTO THE NORTH AND	52.1 X 118.1 CM	LAURIE & WHITTLE
A NEW MAP OF THE WORLD ON THE GLOBULAR PROJECTION	22.9 X 33.7 CM	TANNER
A NEW MAP OF THE WORLD ON THE GLOBULAR PROJECTIONS	24.1 X 36.2 CM	THOMAS, COWPERTHWAI...
A NEW MAP OF THE WORLD WITH THE LATEST DISCOVERIES	27.9 X 50.8 CM	HARRISON
A NEW MAP OF UPPER & LOWER CANADA	45.7 X 57.2 CM	CARY
A NEW MAP OF UPPER & LOWER CANADA	17.8 X 22.9 CM	STOCKDALE
A NEW MAP OF VIRGINIA, MARYLAND AND THE IMPROVED PARTS OF PENNSYLVANIA	48.3 X 54.6 CM	SENEX
A NEW MAP OF YE ISTHMUS OF DARIEN IN AMERICA...	29.8 X 48.3 CM	MOLL
A NEW MAP OF YE WORLD BY ROBT MORDEN	5.8 X 9.2 CM	MORDEN
A NEW MAP OF YE WORLD BY ROBT. MORDEN	9.2 X 15.6 CM	MORDEN
A NEW MAP OR CHART IN MERCATORS PROJECTION OF THE WESTERN OR ATLANTIC	39.4 X 51.7 CM	POLITICAL MAGAZINE
A NEW MAP OR CHART OF THE WESTERN OR ATLANTIC OCEAN...SHEWING THE COUR	35.6 X 29.8 CM	BOWEN
A NEW MAP, OF THE ONLY USEFUL AND FREQUENTED PART OF NEW FOUND LAND	17.8 X 24.5 CM	LONDON MAGAZINE
A NEW MAPPE OF YE XVII PROVINCES OF LOW GERMANIE...	38.7 X 47.6 CM	SPEED
A NEW PROJECTION OF THE WESTERN HEMISPHERE OF THE EARTH ON A PLANE (SH	24.0 X 22.5 CM	BOWEN
A NEW...MAP OF PERSIA, WITH THE ADJACENT COUNTRIES...	34.3 X 41.9 CM	BOWEN
A NEWE MAPE OF GERMANY...	38.7 X 47.6 CM	SPEED
A NEWE MAPE OF POLAND	38.7 X 47.6 CM	SPEED
A NEWE MAPE OF TARTARY...	38.7 X 47.6 CM	SPEED
A PERSPECTIVE VIEW OF MONTREAL IN CANADA	15.9 X 25.4 CM	HINTON
A PERSPECTIVE VIEW OF PENSACOLA	14.6 X 24.8 CM	UNIVERSAL MAGAZINE
A PLAN OF BOSTON IN THE COUNTY OF LINCOLN	9.5 X 12.7 CM	ROCQUE

Title	Dimensions	Author
A PLAN OF CAPE NICHOLA MOLE...ISLAND OF HISPANIOLA	25.4 X 25.4 CM	SPEER
A PLAN OF CAPTAIN CARVERS TRAVELS IN THE INTERIOR PARTS OF NORTH AMERI	26.7 X 34.3 CM	CARVER
A PLAN OF CHARLES TOWN THE CAPITAL OF SOUTH CAROLINA, WITH THE HARBOUR	13.5 X 28.6 CM	POLITICAL MAGAZINE
A PLAN OF FORT EDWARD AND ITS ENVIRONS ON HUDSON'S RIVER	28.2 X 25.7 CM	KITCHIN
A PLAN OF LONDON AND ITS ENVIRONS	38.1 X 47.0 CM	WALKER
A PLAN OF PORT EFFINGHAM IN BERKLEY'S SOUND	19.1 X 23.5 CM	MEARS
A PLAN OF PORT EFFINGHAM IN BERKLEY'S SOUND...	18.7 X 23.3 CM	MEARS
A PLAN OF PORT ROYAL HARBOUR IN CAROLINA WITH PROPOSED FORTS	20.3 X 25.4 CM	MOLL
A PLAN OF PORT ROYAL IN SOUTH CAROLINA. SURVEY'D BY CAPN. JOHN GASCOIG	71.5 X 58.2 CM	JEFFERYS
A PLAN OF RISTAGOUCHE HARBOUR, IN CHALEUR BAY, SURVEYED IN 1760, BY TH	34.3 X 51.4 CM	LAURIE & WHITTLE
A PLAN OF THE ACTION AT BUNKERS HILL, ON THE 17TH OF JUNE 1775	49.0 X 43.0 CM	STEDMAN
A PLAN OF THE CITIES OF LONDON & WESTMINSTER AND THE BOROUGH OF SOUTHW	9.5 X 12.7 CM	ROCQUE
A PLAN OF THE CITY & FORTIFICATIONS OF LOUISBURG TAKEN JUNE 17, 1745 A	27.3 X 35.6 CM	GRIDLEY
A PLAN OF THE CITY AND ENVIRONS OF PHILADELPHIA	63.5 X 47.0 CM	FADEN
A PLAN OF THE CITY AND ENVIRONS OF PHILADELPHIA	59.7 X 45.7 CM	LOTTER
A PLAN OF THE CITY AND ENVIRONS OF PHILADELPHIA	34.3 X 45.7 CM	LOTTER
A PLAN OF THE CITY AND ENVIRONS OF PHILADELPHIA...	61.0 X 49.2 CM	FADEN
A PLAN OF THE CITY AND SUBURBS OF BATH	9.5 X 12.7 CM	ROCQUE
A PLAN OF THE CITY AND SUBURBS OF BRISTOL	9.5 X 12.7 CM	ROCQUE
A PLAN OF THE CITY OF LIMA	16.5 X 24.1 CM	ANDREWS
A PLAN OF THE CITY OF QUEBEC	17.5 X 24.0 CM	WELD
A PLAN OF THE FORT AND BAY OF FRONTENAC WITH THE ADJACENT COUNTRY	10.8 X 17.8 CM	BALDWIN
A PLAN OF THE HARBOUR OF CHEBUCTO AND TOWN OF HALIFAX	21.6 X 26.7 CM	GENTLEMAN'S MAGAZINE
A PLAN OF THE LATE SIEGE OF HAVANNA, AND MOOR'S CASTLE & THEIR ENVIRON	18.4 X 10.8 CM	LONDON MAGAZINE
A PLAN OF THE OPERATIONS OF THE KING'S ARMY UNDER THE COMMAND OF GE. S	73.5 X 49.5 CM	STEDMAN
A PLAN OF THE PALACE, GARDENS & TOWN OF KENSINGTON	9.5 X 12.7 CM	ROCQUE
A PLAN OF THE PORT ROYAL HARBOUR IN CAROLINA	27.0 X 20.0 CM	MOLL
A PLAN OF THE RIVER ST. LAWRENCE, FROM SILLERY TO THE FALL OF MONTMERE	19.1 X 24.1 CM	CARY
A PLAN OF THE RIVER ST. LAWRENCE, FROM SILLERY TO THE FALL OF MONTMERE	18.4 X 23.5 CM	CARY
A PLAN OF THE SEA OTTER HARBOUR AND ST. PATRICKS BAY TAKEN BY CAPT. JA	23.7 X 19.0 CM	MEARS
A PLAN OF THE STRAITS OF ST. MARY, AND MICHILIMAKINAC TO SHEW THE SITU	23.5 X 32.4 CM	GENTLEMAN'S MAGAZINE
A PLAN OF THE SURPRISE OF STONEY POINT BY A DETACHMENT OF THE AMERICAN	48.3 X 30.5 CM	FADEN
A PLAN OF THE TOWN AND CITADEL OF FORT ROYAL IN MARTINICO	19.1 X 24.8 CM	LONDON MAGAZINE
A PLAN OF THE TOWN OF NEWPORT, IN THE PROVINCE OF RHODE ISLAND. PUBLIS	52.1 X 73.7 CM	DES BARRES
A PLAN OF THE TOWN OF PAYTA IN THE KINGDOM OF SANTA FEE	21.6 X 38.1 CM	SEALE
A PLAT EXHIBITING THE STATE OF SURVEYS IN THE STATE OF FLORIDA WITH RE	56.5 X 63.5 CM	U.S.
A PLAT EXHIBITING THE STATE OF THE SURVEYS IN THE STATE OF FLORIDA...S	55.9 X 63.5 CM	U.S.
A SEA CHART OF THE ATLANTIC OCEAN BETWEEN THE EQUATOR AND LATITUDE 36	49.0 X 139.0 CM	SAYER & BENNETT
A SKETCH BY COMPASS OF THE COAST OF THE PROMONTORY OF SHAN-TUNG WITH T	68.6 X 49.5 CM	BARROW
A SKETCH OF PORT COX IN THE DISTRICT OF WICANANISH	23.7 X 19.0 CM	MEARS
A SKETCH OF PORT COX IN THE DISTRICT OF WICANANISH	19.1 X 19.1 CM	MEARS
A SKETCH OF RAFT-COVE, TAKEN BY MR. FUNTER, MASTER OF THE NORTH WEST A	24.0 X 19.4 CM	MEARS
A SKETCH OF THE CHEROKEE COUNTRY	27.3 X 40.0 CM	MANTE
A SOUTH WEST VIEW OF PRINCE OF WALES FORT HUDSONS BAY	12.1 X 16.5 CM	FIELDING
A VIEW OF BOLCHERETZK THE CAPITAL OF KAMTSCHATKA	22.9 X 31.8 CM	HOGG
A VIEW OF CUMBERLAND BAY AT THE ISLAND JUAN FERNANDES	20.3 X 34.3 CM	ANSON
A VIEW OF HUAHEINE	10.8 X 16.5 CM	COOK
A VIEW OF MEMPHIS	22.9 X 30.5 CM	EVERY SATURDAY
A VIEW OF OTTER SOUND...	24.2 X 19.2 CM	MEARS
A VIEW OF PORT MEARES	23.6 X 18.8 CM	MEARS
A VIEW OF THE CITY OF BOSTON THE CAPITAL OF NEW ENGLAND	26.7 X 15.2 CM	UNIVERSAL MAGAZINE
A VIEW OF THE CITY OF MEXICO	15.2 X 20.3 CM	RUSSELL
A VIEW OF THE N.W. SIDE OF MAS A FUERA IS.	21.0 X 33.0 CM	HOGG
A VIEW OF THE NEW DISCOVERED ISLAND OF ULIETEA WITH SOME OF ITS INHABI	17.8 X 27.3 CM	MIDDLETON
A VIEW OF THE PALACE OF CHANTILLI TAKEN FROM THE ORANGERY	24.1 X 41.3 CM	LAURIE & WHITTLE
A VIEW OF THE S.W. SIDE OF TENIAN	20.3 X 50.2 CM	ANSON
A VIEW OF THE TOWN AND CASTLE OF ST. AUGUSTINE AND THE ENGLISH CAMP BE	29.2 X 16.5 CM	SILVER
A...CHART OF THE WORLD...	33.0 X 45.7 CM	BOWEN
ABRAHAM PATRIARCHAE PEREGRINATIO ET VITA	35.6 X 45.7 CM	ORTELIUS
ACCURATA DELINEATIO CELEBERRIMAE REGIONIS LUDOVICIANAE VEL GALLICE LOU	48.9 X 55.9 CM	SEUTTER
ACCURATA DELINEATIO CELEBERRIMAE REGIONIS LUDOVICIANAE VEL GALLICE LOU	49.0 X 56.0 CM	SEUTTER
ACHAIAE NOVA & ACCURATA DESCRIPTIO	38.1 X 55.9 CM	DE WIT
ADIRONDACK MOUNTAINS	14.6 X 20.0 CM	BAEDEKER

Title	Dimensions	Maker
AEGYPTUS	8.9 X 11.4 CM	ORTELIUS
AETH, A STRONG, FRONTIER TOWN IN BRABANT	38.1 X 48.3 CM	TINDAL
AETHIOPIA INFERIOR...	38.1 X 49.5 CM	BLAEU
AETHIOPIA SUPERIOR VEL INTERIOR	26.0 X 35.0 CM	DAPPER
AETHIOPIA SUPERIOR VEL INTERIOR; VULGO ABISSINORUM SIVE PRESBITERI IOA	38.7 X 50.8 CM	BLAEU
AETHIOPIE SUPERIOR VEL INTERIOR VULGO ABISSINORUM SIVE PRESBITERI IOAN	38.1 X 49.5 CM	JANSSON
AEVI VETERIS TYPUS GEOGRAPHICUS	31.8 X 44.5 CM	ORTELIUS
AEVI VETERIS, TYPUS GEOGRAPHICUS	30.5 X 43.5 CM	ORTELIUS
AFBELDINGE VAN'T ZEER VERMAARDE EILAND GEKS-KOP	28.6 X 22.9 CM	ANON
AFEELDING VAN DE CABO ST. AUGUSTIN MER HAER FORTEN (VIEW)	27.9 X 37.5 CM	DE LAET
AFRICA	20.0 X 25.0 CM	TALLIS
AFRICA AB AUCTORE NAURAE SUIS DOTIBUS INSTRUCTA GEOGRAPHICE EXHIBITA	23.0 X 33.0 CM	SCHERER
AFRICA MINOR NUOVA TAVOLA	17.8 X 24.1 CM	PTOLEMY (1561-99 VE...
AFRICA STUDIO ET INDUSTRIA G.M. IUNIORIS	38.5 X 46.5 CM	MERCATOR
AFRICAE...	37.5 X 49.5 CM	HONDIUS
AFRICAE...	38.7 X 47.6 CM	SPEED
AFRIQUE	48.3 X 97.8 CM	D'ANVILLE
AFRIQUE DRESSEE SUR LES RELATIONS LES PLUS RECENTES, ET ASSUJETTIE AUX	46.4 X 58.4 CM	DE VAUGONDY
AFRIQUE PUBLIEE SOUS LES AUSPICES DE MONSEIGNEUR LE DUC D'ORLEANS PREM	50.8 X 99.1 CM	D'ANVILLE
AGGER CHANNEL-DENMARK	19.7 X 19.1 CM	BLUHME
ALABAMA	35.6 X 28.6 CM	BRADFORD
ALABAMA	35.6 X 29.2 CM	BRADFORD
ALABAMA	40.0 X 33.0 CM	COLTON
ALABAMA	36.8 X 30.5 CM	GRAY
ALABAMA	27.9 X 22.2 CM	LUCAS
ALABAMA	22.9 X 29.2 CM	LUCAS
ALABAMA, MISSISSIPPI AND LOUISIANA	19.1 X 24.4 CM	MORSE
ALGEMEENE KAART VAN DE WESTINDISCHE EILANDEN	36.8 X 47.0 CM	TIRION
ALLIED & ENEMY TROOP MOVEMENTS IN THE ENVIRONS OF DENAIN	38.1 X 48.3 CM	TINDAL
ALLIED INTRENCHMENT COVERING THE SIEGE OF DOUAY	38.1 X 48.3 CM	TINDAL
AMER. SEP. IIE SOUTHAMPTON. NO 17	48.3 X 61.0 CM	VANDERMAELEN
AMER. SEPT. DETROIT D'HUDSON NO. 18	48.3 X 55.9 CM	VANDERMAELEN
AMER. SEPT. PARTIE DU LABRADOR NO. 29	48.3 X 58.4 CM	VANDERMAELEN
AMERCICA SETTENTRIONALE	61.0 X 90.2 CM	CORONELLI
AMERICA	61.0 X 47.6 CM	ARROWSMITH
AMERICA	21.0 X 25.4 CM	CLUVER
AMERICA	43.0 X 33.0 CM	CRUCHLEY
AMERICA	46.2 X 34.4 CM	CRUCHLEY
AMERICA	36.8 X 42.5 CM	HEYLIN
AMERICA	13.3 X 17.8 CM	MAGINI
AMERICA	17.1 X 19.1 CM	MOLL
AMERICA	17.1 X 18.4 CM	MOLL
AMERICA	27.9 X 15.2 CM	OGILBY
AMERICA	13.3 X 17.8 CM	PTOLEMY (1596-1621 ...
AMERICA	12.7 X 16.5 CM	PTOLEMY (1596-1621 ...
AMERICA	12.7 X 17.1 CM	PTOLEMY (1596-1621 ...
AMERICA	35.6 X 26.7 CM	SMITH
AMERICA	38.1 X 50.8 CM	SPEED
AMERICA	41.9 X 33.7 CM	TEESDALE
AMERICA AUREA PARS ALTERA MUNDI	48.3 X 59.7 CM	VALK
AMERICA BY H. MOLL GEOGRAPHER	26.4 X 19.7 CM	MOLL
AMERICA BY R. MORDEN	10.5 X 12.4 CM	MORDEN
AMERICA BY R. MORDEN	10.8 X 12.7 CM	MORDEN
AMERICA DAS MITTERNACHTIGE	32.4 X 41.9 CM	BAUMGARTEN
AMERICA DAS MITTERNACHTIGE NACH DER ZEICHNUNG DES HERRN WILHELM DELISL	31.8 X 41.3 CM	BAUMGARTEN
AMERICA DIVISA NE SUOL PRINCIPALI STATI DI NUOVA PROJEZIONE	31.1 X 40.0 CM	ZATTA
AMERICA GEDRUCKT TOT AMSTERDAM BY R AND J OTTENS OP DEN NIEWE DRUK UIT	135.0 X 170.0 CM	OTTENS
AMERICA IN PRAECIPUAS...IPSIUS PARTES DISTRIBUTA AD OBSERVATIONES ACAD	49.5 X 66.0 CM	VAN DER AA
AMERICA MERIDIONALIS, PER SUA REGNA...	19.7 X 25.7 CM	SEUTTER
AMERICA MERIDIONALIS...	45.6 X 58.2 CM	LOTTER
AMERICA NOVITER DELINEATA	35.6 X 44.5 CM	HONDIUS
AMERICA NOVITER DELINEATA	38.1 X 49.5 CM	HONDIUS
AMERICA NOVITER DELINEATA	27.3 X 35.6 CM	MERIAN

223

AMERICA SEPTENTRIONALE...	48.3 X 58.4 CM	JAILLOT
AMERICA SEPTENTRIONALIS	54.0 X 46.0 CM	JANSSON
AMERICA SEPTENTRIONALIS	47.0 X 54.6 CM	JANSSON
AMERICA SEPTENTRIONALIS	46.5 X 55.0 CM	JANSSON
AMERICA SEPTENTRIONALIS	45.5 X 58.0 CM	LOTTER
AMERICA SEPTENTRIONALIS A DOMINO D'ANVILLE...	45.7 X 50.8 CM	HOMANN
AMERICA SEPTENTRIONALIS CONCINNATUS JUXTA OBSERVATIONES...APUD TOBIAM	45.7 X 58.4 CM	LOTTER
AMERICA SEPTENTRIONALIS. A DOMINO D'ANVILLE IN GALIIS EDITA NUNC IN AN	47.0 X 50.8 CM	HOMANN
AMERICA SEPTENTRIONALIS...	48.3 X 58.4 CM	JAILLOT
AMERICA SETTENTRIONALE	62.2 X 88.9 CM	CORONELLI
AMERICA SETTENTRIONALE	62.2 X 88.9 CM	CORONELLI
AMERICA SETTENTRIONALE COLLE NUOVE SCOPERTE SIN ALL'ANNO 1688 PIUISA N	61.0 X 45.7 CM	CORONELLI
AMERICA SETTENTRIONALE DIVIDA NE' SUOI PRINCIPALI STATI	31.5 X 41.5 CM	ZATTA
AMERICA SIVE INDIA NOVA	38.1 X 45.7 CM	MERCATOR
AMERICA SIVE INDIA NOVA...	36.8 X 46.4 CM	MERCATOR
AMERICA SIVE INDIA NOVA...IN COMPENDIUM REDACTA PER MICHAELEM MERCATOR	37.5 X 47.0 CM	MERCATOR
AMERICA SIVE NOVUS ORBIS	7.6 X 10.2 CM	ORTELIUS
AMERICA, N.W. COAST: STRAIT OF JUAN DE FUCA	95.7 X 63.0 CM	ADMIRALTY
AMERICA, WITH THOSE KNOWN PARTS IN THAT UNKNOWNE WORLD...	40.6 X 50.8 CM	SPEED
AMERICA. DRAWN & ENGRAVED BY J. DOWER...LONDON PUBLISHED BY HENRY TEES	41.3 X 33.7 CM	TEESDALE
AMERICA. LONDON, PUBD. 15 FEBY. 1840 BY J. ARROWSMITH, 10 SOHO SQUARE	63.5 X 53.3 CM	ARROWSMITH
AMERICA...	38.7 X 47.6 CM	SPEED
AMERICAE DESCRIPTIO	14.6 X 19.7 CM	MERCATOR
AMERICAE MAPPA GENERALIS	46.0 X 52.0 CM	HOMANN
AMERICAE MAPPA GENERALIS...	46.6 X 53.6 CM	HOMANN
AMERICAE NOVA TABULA	40.6 X 55.9 CM	BLAEU
AMERICAE NOVA TABULA	40.6 X 54.6 CM	BLAEU
AMERICAE NOVA TABULA	41.0 X 55.6 CM	BLAEU
AMERICAE NOVA TABULA	40.6 X 55.2 CM	BLAEU
AMERICAE NOVA TABULA	41.5 X 56.0 CM	BLAEU
AMERICAE NOVA TABULA AUCT. GUILJELMO BLAEUW	41.3 X 55.9 CM	BLAEU
AMERICAE PARS MAGIS COGNITA	36.5 X 44.0 CM	DE BRY
AMERICAE PARS, NUNC VIRGINIA DICTA...	30.1 X 41.8 CM	DE BRY
AMERICAE RETECTIO	14.0 X 19.4 CM	DE BRY
AMERICAE SIVE INDIA NOVA AD MAGNAE GERARDI MERCATORIS AVI UNIVERSALIS	37.0 X 46.5 CM	MERCATOR
AMERICAE SIVE INDIAE OCCIDENTALIS	27.9 X 35.6 CM	DE LAET
AMERICAE SIVE INDIAE OCCIDENTALIS TABULA GENERALIS	12.7 X 12.7 CM	CLUVER
AMERICAE SIVE NOVI ORBIS NOVA DESCRIPTIO	35.6 X 48.3 CM	ORTELIUS
AMERICAE SIVE NOVI ORBIS, NOVA DESCRIPTIO	30.5 X 36.0 CM	MUNSTER
AMERICAE SIVE NOVI ORBIS, NOVA DESCRIPTIO	35.5 X 48.5 CM	ORTELIUS
AMERICAE SIVE NOVI ORBIS, NOVA DESCRIPTIO	35.6 X 48.3 CM	ORTELIUS
AMERICAE SIVE NOVI ORBIS, NOVA DESCRIPTIO	36.0 X 48.0 CM	ORTELIUS
AMERICAE SIVE NOVI ORBIS...	35.6 X 48.3 CM	ORTELIUS
AMERIKA HUIPUIA	25.4 X 41.3 CM	KEPOHONI
AMERIQUE DU SUD	90.0 X 63.0 CM	DUFOUR
AMERIQUE MERIDIONALE	127.6 X 76.8 CM	D'ANVILLE
AMERIQUE MERIDIONALE	48.5 X 59.5 CM	DE VAUGONDY
AMERIQUE MERIDIONALE	20.3 X 27.3 CM	LE ROUGE
AMERIQUE MERIDIONALE	43.2 X 28.6 CM	LEVASSEUR
AMERIQUE MERIDIONALE	15.2 X 10.2 CM	MALLET
AMERIQUE MERIDIONALE ET SEPTENTRIONALE	48.3 X 68.6 CM	DANET
AMERIQUE MERIDIONALE PAR N. SANSON GEOGRAPHE ORDN. DU ROY REVUE ET CHA	40.0 X 55.9 CM	SANSON
AMERIQUE MERIDIONALE...	47.0 X 58.4 CM	DE VAUGONDY
AMERIQUE OU INDES OCCIDENTALES	50.8 X 63.5 CM	DELAMARCHE
AMERIQUE RUSSE, NOUVELLE BRETAGNE ET CANADA	22.2 X 32.4 CM	MALTE-BRUN
AMERIQUE SEPTENTRIONALE	18.4 X 21.6 CM	ANON
AMERIQUE SEPTENTRIONALE	22.2 X 29.2 CM	BELLIN
AMERIQUE SEPTENTRIONALE	21.2 X 31.8 CM	BONNE
AMERIQUE SEPTENTRIONALE	21.6 X 31.8 CM	BONNE
AMERIQUE SEPTENTRIONALE	21.6 X 31.8 CM	BONNE
AMERIQUE SEPTENTRIONALE	19.1 X 24.8 CM	DE RIENZI
AMERIQUE SEPTENTRIONALE	48.3 X 59.7 CM	DE VAUGONDY
AMERIQUE SEPTENTRIONALE	28.0 X 43.0 CM	LEVASSEUR

AMERIQUE SEPTENTRIONALE	43.2 X 28.3 CM	LEVASSEUR
AMERIQUE SEPTENTRIONALE	27.9 X 43.2 CM	LEVASSEUR
AMERIQUE SEPTENTRIONALE	22.2 X 30.5 CM	MALTE-BRUN
AMERIQUE SEPTENTRIONALE	54.0 X 87.5 CM	MORTIER
AMERIQUE SEPTENTRIONALE	57.2 X 87.6 CM	MORTIER
AMERIQUE SEPTENTRIONALE	38.1 X 55.9 CM	SANSON
AMERIQUE SEPTENTRIONALE	20.3 X 27.9 CM	SANSON
AMERIQUE SEPTENTRIONALE AVEC LES ROUTES, DISTANCES EN MILES, VILLAGES	43.2 X 49.5 CM	LE ROUGE
AMERIQUE SEPTENTRIONALE DIVISEE EN SES PRINCIPALES PARTIES OU SONT DIS	45.7 X 64.8 CM	JAILLOT
AMERIQUE SEPTENTRIONALE DIVISEE EN SES PRINCIPALES PARTIES. PRESENTE A	48.3 X 58.4 CM	OTTENS
AMERIQUE SEPTENTRIONALE DIVISEE EN SES PRINCIPALES PARTIES...A AMSTERD	55.9 X 86.4 CM	MORTIER
AMERIQUE SEPTENTRIONALE DRESSEE SUR LES RELATIONS LES PLUS MODERNES DE	48.3 X 58.4 CM	DE VAUGONDY
AMERIQUE SEPTENTRIONALE DRESSEE SUR LES RELATIONS...OU SE REMARQUENT L	48.3 X 58.4 CM	DE VAUGONDY
AMERIQUE SEPTENTRIONALE PUBLIEE SOUS LES AUSPICES DE MONSEIGNEUR LE DU	83.8 X 86.4 CM	D'ANVILLE
AMERIQUE SEPTENTRIONALE, DRESSEE, SUR LES RELATIONS LES PLUS MODERNES	49.5 X 62.9 CM	DE VAUGONDY
AMERIQUE SEPTENTRIONALE, PAR J.B. POIRSON, 1830	22.0 X 31.5 CM	POIRSON
AMERIQUE SEPTENTRIONALE...	60.0 X 45.0 CM	CORONELLI
AMERIQUE SEPTENTRIONALE...PAR LE SR. D'ANVILLE MDCCXLVI AVEC PRIVILEGE	45.7 X 87.6 CM	D'ANVILLE
AMERIQUE SEPTENTRIONALIS CARTE D'UN TRES GRAND PAYS ENTRE LE NOUVEAU M	43.2 X 52.1 CM	HENNEPIN
AMERIQUE SUIVANT LE R.P. CHARLEVOIX JTE. MR. DE LA CONDAMINE, ET PLUSI	48.9 X 63.5 CM	LE ROUGE
AMPLISSIMAE REGIONIS MISSISSIPI SEU PROVINCIAE LUDOVICIANAE A R.P. LUD	57.5 X 48.3 CM	HOMANN
AMPLISSIMAE REGIONIS MISSISSIPI...	48.3 X 58.4 CM	HOMANN
AMSTELODAMI CELEBERRIMI HOLLANDIAE EMPORII DELINEATIO NOVA	42.5 X 54.0 CM	JANSSON
AMSTELODAMI VETERIS ET NOVISSIMAE URBIS ACCURATISSIMA DELINEATIO. GETE	49.0 X 57.0 CM	VISSCHER
AMSTERDAM (VIEW)	19.0 X 33.0 CM	STEUDNER
AN ACCURATE MAP OF BRECKNOCK SHIRE. DRAWN FROM AN ACTUAL SURVEY WITH V	34.3 X 50.8 CM	KITCHIN
AN ACCURATE MAP OF CAMBRIDGESHIRE DIVIDED INTO ITS HUNDREDS	72.4 X 52.1 CM	BOWEN
AN ACCURATE MAP OF CANADA, WITH THE ADJACENT COUNTRIES; EXHIBITING THE	26.0 X 34.3 CM	UNIVERSAL MAGAZINE
AN ACCURATE MAP OF CARMARTHEN SHIRE. DRAWN FROM AN ACTUAL SURVEY, WITH	34.3 X 52.1 CM	KITCHIN
AN ACCURATE MAP OF ENGLAND & WALES WITH THE PRINCIPAL ROADS FROM THE B	36.8 X 33.0 CM	CAREY
AN ACCURATE MAP OF HINDOSTAN OR INDIA FROM THE BEST AUTHORITIES	40.0 X 40.6 CM	CAREY
AN ACCURATE MAP OF NEW YORK IN NORTH AMERICA	33.7 X 27.0 CM	UNIVERSAL MAGAZINE
AN ACCURATE MAP OF NORTH AMERICA DRAWN FROM THE SIEUR ROBERT, WITH IMP	19.0 X 29.0 CM	ROLLOS
AN ACCURATE MAP OF NORTH AMERICA FROM THE LATEST IMPROVEMENTS AND REGU	18.7 X 29.2 CM	ROLLOS
AN ACCURATE MAP OF NORTH AMERICA...	15.2 X 20.3 CM	BOWEN
AN ACCURATE MAP OF NORTH AMERICA...	17.1 X 17.5 CM	ROLLOS
AN ACCURATE MAP OF THE BRITISH EMPIRE IN NTH AMERICA AS SETTLED BY THE	21.0 X 24.4 CM	GENTLEMAN'S MAGAZINE
AN ACCURATE MAP OF THE COUNTY OF LANCASTER DIVIDED INTO ITS HUNDREDS..	67.9 X 52.1 CM	BOWEN
AN ACCURATE MAP OF THE COUNTY OF SUFFOLK DIVIDED INTO ITS HUNDREDS	52.1 X 69.9 CM	BOWEN
AN ACCURATE MAP OF THE COUNTY PALATINE OF CHESTER DIVIDED INTO ITS HUN	53.3 X 69.2 CM	BOWEN
AN ACCURATE MAP OF THE EAST PART OF ENGLAND WITH THE PARTS OF HOLLAND	35.6 X 26.7 CM	LONDON MAGAZINE
AN ACCURATE MAP OF THE ISLAND OF BARBADOES	35.0 X 42.5 CM	BOWEN
AN ACCURATE MAP OF THE ISLAND OF BARBADOES IN WHICH THE DIFFERENT PARI	28.3 X 36.7 CM	POLITICAL MAGAZINE
AN ACCURATE MAP OF THE ISLAND OF BARBADOS DRAWN FROM ACTUAL SURVEY...	42.5 X 34.9 CM	BOWEN
AN ACCURATE MAP OF THE ISLAND OF ST. CHRISTOPHERS, FROM AN ACTUAL SURV	27.5 X 36.6 CM	POLITICAL MAGAZINE
AN ACCURATE MAP OF THE WEST INDIES DRAWN FROM THE LATEST AUTHORITIES	34.3 X 41.9 CM	BOWEN
AN ACCURATE MAP OF THE WORLD LAID DOWN FROM THE MOST APPROVED MAPS AND	15.2 X 26.0 CM	BOWEN
AN ACCURATE MAP OF THE WORLD...	14.6 X 27.9 CM	ROLLOS
AN EXACT CHART OF ALL THE COUNTRIES THROUGH WHICH CAPT. BEHRING TRAVEL	17.8 X 32.4 CM	BOWEN
AN EXACT CHART OF THE RIVER ST. LAURENCE, FROM FORT FRONTENAC TO QUEBE	59.0 X 95.0 CM	JEFFERYS
AN EXACT CHART OF THE RIVER ST. LAURENCE, FROM FRONTENAC TO THE ISLAND	59.7 X 94.0 CM	JEFFERYS
AN EXACT DRAUGHT OF THE GULF OF DARIEN & THE COAST TO PORTO BELLO WITH	43.2 X 54.0 CM	MOUNT & PAGE
AN EXACT MAP OF NOVA SCOTIA NEWFOUNDLAND...1777	21.0 X 25.4 CM	LODGE
AN EXACT MAP OF THE PROVINCE OF QUEBEC WITH PART OF NEW YORK & NEW ENG	20.6 X 26.5 CM	LODGE
AN EXACT PLAN OF THE CITY, FORTIFICATIONS & HARBOUR OF HAVANA...	26.0 X 34.3 CM	UNIVERSAL MAGAZINE
AN EYE SKETCH OF THE FALLS OF NIAGARA	16.5 X 22.9 CM	STOCKDALE
AN INDEX MAP TO THE FOLLOWING SIXTEEN SHEETS, BEING A COMPLEAT CHART O	37.8 X 62.9 CM	JEFFERYS
AN OUTLINE TO SHEW THE CONNECTED DISCOVERIES OF CAPTAINS ROSS, PARRY &	36.9 X 46.3 CM	FRANKLIN
ANACAPA ISLAND IN SANTA BARBARA CHANNEL	15.2 X 24.1 CM	U.S.
ANCIENT FORTIFICATION ON THE MISSOURI/GREAT FALLS OF COLUMBIA RIVER	10.1 X 17.4 CM	ANON
ANCIENT PALESTINE	20.0 X 25.0 CM	TALLIS
ANGLESEA ISLAND	11.4 X 14.0 CM	SELLER
ANGLESEY	7.6 X 12.1 CM	LEIGH

ANGLESEY	10.8 X	6.4 CM	WALLIS & REID
ANGLESEY ANTIENTLY CALLED MONA	38.7 X	47.6 CM	* SPEED
ANGLESEY/WIGHT VECTIS OLIM/GARNESAY/IARSAY	31.8 X	43.2 CM	MERCATOR
ANGLESEY/WIGHT VECTIS OLIM/GARNESAY/IARSAY	35.6 X	43.2 CM	MERCATOR
ANGLIA	11.0 X	8.0 CM	ORTELIUS
ANGLIA ET HIBERNIA NOVA	18.0 X	25.0 CM PTOLEMY (1561-99 VE...
ANGLIA ET HIBERNIA NOVA	17.8 X	24.8 CM PTOLEMY (1561-99 VE...
ANGLIA SCOTIA HIBERNIA 1699	22.9 X	34.3 CM	SCHERER
ANGLIA, SCOTIA ET HIBERNIA	19.7 X	25.4 CM	DU SAUZET
ANGLIAE DESCRIPTIO	26.7 X	34.3 CM	MUNSTER
ANGLIAE E HIBERNIA NOVA	12.0 X	17.0 CM PTOLEMY (1548 VENICE)
ANGLIAE REGNI FLORENTISSIMI	38.1 X	47.0 CM	ORTELIUS
ANGLIAE REGNI FLORENTISSIMI...	17.8 X	26.7 CM	QUAD
ANGLIAE REGNUM	19.7 X	25.4 CM	DU SAUZET
ANGLIAE SCOTIAE ET HIBERNIAE NOVA DESCRIPTIO	34.9 X	49.5 CM	DE JODE
ANGLIAE, SCOTIAE ET HIBERNIAE	34.3 X	49.5 CM	ORTELIUS
ANGLIAE, SCOTIAE ET HIBERNIAE SIVE BRITANNICAR: INSULARUM DESCRIPTIO	34.3 X	49.5 CM	ORTELIUS
ANGLIAE, SCOTIAE ET HIBERNIAE, BRITANNICAE INSULAE...	34.5 X	49.5 CM	ORTELIUS
ANGLIAE, SCOTIAE ET HIBERNIE NOVA DESCRIPTIO	34.5 X	49.5 CM	DE JODE
ANGLIAE, SCOTIAE, ET HIBERNIAE, SIVE BRITANNICAR: INSULARUM DESCRIPTIO	34.3 X	49.5 CM	ORTELIUS
ANNIS SQUAM	10.2 X	17.8 CM	BLUNT
ANTARCTIC POLAR CIRCLE WITH THE COUNTRIES ADJOINING, ACCORDING TO...MR	19.7 X	22.2 CM	GENTLEMAN'S MAGAZINE
ANTHONY VAN DIEMANS LAND/HET VASTE LANDT BEZUYDEN DEN KLIPPIGEN HOEK/H	29.0 X	17.0 CM	VALENTYN
ANTIENT MEXICO (VIEW)	21.0 X	33.0 CM	HARRIS
ANTIGUA	22.9 X	29.2 CM	LUCAS
ANTIGUA, SURVEYED BY ROBERT BAKER, SURVEYOR GENERAL OF THE ISLAND: ENG	46.4 X	61.7 CM	LAURIE & WHITTLE
ANTVERPIA (PLAN)	46.0 X	78.0 CM	BRAUN & HOGENBERG
ANTVERPIA. ANTHERPIAE CELEBERRIMI...ORBIS...DELINEATIO AEDITA PER PHIL	38.0 X	51.5 CM	GALLE
ANTVERPIAE CIVITATIS BELGICAE TOTO ORBE COGNITI ET CELEBRATI SIMULACRU	32.0 X	42.8 CM	LAFRERI SCHOOL
ANTWERPIA (VIEW OF BATTLE)	28.5 X	39.0 CM	DE BRUYN
ARABIA	20.0 X	25.0 CM	TALLIS
ARACHAN & PEGU	8.9 X	13.3 CM	BERTIUS
ARCHIPELAGI AMERICANI DELINEATIO GEOGRAPHICA	25.0 X	35.0 CM	SCHERER
ARCHIPELAGI AMERICANI DELINEATIO GEOGRAPHICA	23.0 X	33.0 CM	SCHERER
ARCHIPELAGISCHE EYLANDEN	50.5 X	58.0 CM	VAN KEULEN
ARCTIC REGIONS	46.5 X	31.5 CM	FULLARTON
ARCTIC REGIONS	45.5 X	31.0 CM	FULLARTON
ARCTIC REGIONS AND BRITISH AMERICA CONTAINING ALL DISCOVERIES IN ARCTI	41.9 X	55.9 CM	BARTHOLOMEW
ARCTIC REGIONS AND BRITISH AMERICA. CONTAINING ALL THE DISCOVERIES IN	42.0 X	56.0 CM	BLACK
ARIZONA AND NEW MEXICO	36.8 X	55.9 CM	BRADLEY
ARKANSAS	35.6 X	27.9 CM	BRADFORD
ARKANSAS	35.6 X	29.2 CM	BRADFORD
ARKANSAS	30.5 X	37.8 CM	MORSE & BREESE
ARKANSAS	30.5 X	38.1 CM	MORSE & BREESE
ARKANSAS, LOUISIANA & MISSISSIPPI	27.3 X	21.6 CM	SWINSTON
ARKANSAW	17.8 X	22.9 CM	FINDLAY
ARMENIA & GEORGIA COMANIA &C BY ROBT. MORDEN	13.3 X	11.4 CM	MORDEN
ASHER & ADAMS' PART OF QUEBEC	56.5 X	40.5 CM	ASHER & ADAMS
ASHTABULA HARBOR, OHIO	32.4 X	54.6 CM	U.S.
ASIA	17.1 X	19.1 CM	MOLL
ASIA	13.5 X	17.5 CM PTOLEMY (1596-1621 ...
ASIA	25.4 X	32.4 CM	TALLIS
ASIA EX MAGNA DESCRIPTIONE...DESUMPTA STUDIO G.M. IUNIORIS	38.0 X	47.0 CM	MERCATOR
ASIA FROM THE BEST AUTHORITIES	19.7 X	23.5 CM	TEGG
ASIA MINOR	17.8 X	20.3 CM	MOLL
ASIA MINOR	38.1 X	52.1 CM	MORTIER
ASIA MINOR	20.0 X	25.0 CM	TALLIS
ASIA NOVITER DELINEATA	40.6 X	55.9 CM	BLAEU
ASIA PARTIU ORBIS MAXIMA MDXCVIII	53.3 X	74.9 CM	QUAD
ASIA PARTIUM ORBIS MAXIMA	38.1 X	47.0 CM	DE JODE
ASIA TABULA SECUNDA CONTINET SARMATIAM ASIATICAM	30.5 X	36.2 CM PTOLEMY (1522-41 ST...
ASIA WITH THE ISLANDS ADJOINING...	38.7 X	47.6 CM	SPEED
ASIAE NOVA DESCRIPTIO	36.8 X	48.3 CM	ORTELIUS

ASIAE PARS AUSTRALIS INSULAE INDICAE CUM SUIS NATURAE DOTIBUS	22.0 X	33.0 CM	SCHERER
ASIAE STATUS NATURALIS DEXTERA DEI OMNIPOTENTIS PERFECT 'GEOGRAPHICE D	22.0 X	33.0 CM	SCHERER
ASIAE TABULA QUINTA CONTINENTUR ASSYRIA, MEDIA, SUSTANA, PERSIS, PARTH	30.5 X	45.7 CM	PTOLEMY (1522-41 ST...
ATAQUE DE QUEBEC	11.4 X	16.5 CM	LA HONTAN
ATLANTIC ISLANDS	50.8 X	59.7 CM	THOMSON
ATLANTIC ISLANDS	50.2 X	59.7 CM	THOMSON
ATLANTIC OCEAN	36.2 X	43.8 CM	BOWEN
ATLANTIS INSULA	40.0 X	56.0 CM	SANSON
ATLAS-TOT AMSTERDAM BY JUSTUS DANCKERS IN DE CALVERSTRAET INDE DANCBAE	48.3 X	25.4 CM	DANCKERTS
ATREBATUM REGIONIS	24.0 X	32.0 CM	DE BRUYN
ATREBATUM REGIONIS VERA DESCRIPTIO. JOHANNE SURHONIO MONTENSI AUCTORE	37.5 X	48.9 CM	ORTELIUS
AUDIENCE DE GUATIMALA PAR N. SANSON D'ABBEVILLE GEOGR. ORDIN DU ROY	17.8 X	27.9 CM	SANSON
AUDIENCE DE MEXICO PAR N. SANSON D'ABBEVILLE GEOGR. ORDIN. DU ROY	16.5 X	27.3 CM	SANSON
AUSTRALIA	32.5 X	43.0 CM	JOHNSTON
AUSTRALIA	20.0 X	25.0 CM	TALLIS
AUSTRALIA	30.5 X	43.0 CM	WELLER
AUSTRALIA AND THE EAST INDIES	58.0 X	43.0 CM	JOHNSON
AUSTRALIA OCCIDENTALE ET ISOLA DI VAN-DIEMEN	42.5 X	50.0 CM	MARZOLLA
AUSTRALIEN (SUDLAND) AUCH POLYNESIEN ODER INSELWELT, INSGEMEIN DER FUN	49.5 X	62.5 CM	WALCH
AUSTRIA	20.0 X	25.0 CM	TALLIS
AUSTRIA ARCHIDUCATUS	14.0 X	19.1 CM	MERCATOR
AUSTRIAE DUCATUS CHOROGRAPHIA, WOLFGANGO LAZIO AUCTORE	34.0 X	47.0 CM	ORTELIUS
BAHAMA'S	24.8 X	28.6 CM	LUCAS
BAIE DE SAN FRANCISCO (VIEW)	16.5 X	24.1 CM	HILDEBRANDT
BALLSTON & SARATOGA SPRINSG, CITY OF ALBANY, AND ADJACENT COUNTRY	16.5 X	10.4 CM	MELISH
BALTIMORE	28.6 X	35.6 CM	BRADFORD
BALTIMORE	35.6 X	29.2 CM	BRADFORD
BALTIMORE, ANNAPOLIS AND ADJACENT COUNTRY	16.3 X	10.3 CM	MELISH
BARBADOS	22.9 X	29.2 CM	LUCAS
BARBADOS	29.0 X	25.5 CM	MOUNT & PAGE
BARBADOS	8.9 X	12.7 CM	SPEED
BARBADOS	50.8 X	30.5 CM	THOMSON
BARBARIA	35.6 X	47.0 CM	HONDIUS
BARK SHIRE	35.6 X	41.9 CM	MORDEN
BARKSHIRE DESCRIBED	38.7 X	47.6 CM	SPEED
BARNEGAT INLET-NEW JERSEY	43.9 X	36.7 CM	U.S. COAST SURVEY
BASE LINE & BOUNDARY BETWEEN KANSAS & NEBRASKA	45.7 X	30.5 CM	U.S.
BASILEA (PANORAMIC VIEW)	24.8 X	52.0 CM	SCHEDEL
BASIN OF THE NORTH ATLANTIC OCEAN	44.0 X	57.0 CM	JOHNSTON
BASLE	25.5 X	35.0 CM	MUNSTER
BASSE-LOUISIANE ET FLORIDE OCCIDENTALE...	19.1 X	40.6 CM	BLONDEAU
BAYE DE L'ACUL/BAYE DAME-MARIE/PORT FRANCOIS/MOLE ST. NICOLAS/BAYE DES	58.4 X	45.1 CM	DEPOT DE LA MARINE
BEATAM MEDICENT OMNES GENERATIONES	23.0 X	35.0 CM	SCHERER
BEDFORD SHIRE...	38.7 X	47.6 CM	SPEED
BEDFORD...	27.3 X	33.7 CM	KIP
BEDFORDSHIRE	17.8 X	26.7 CM	ELLIS
BEDFORDSHIRE	19.1 X	30.5 CM	MOLL
BEDFORDSHIRE	17.8 X	11.4 CM	OWEN & BOWEN
BEDFORDSHIRE AND THE SITUATION OF BEDFORD DESCRIBED WITH THE ARMES OF	38.1 X	50.8 CM	SPEED
BEDFORDSHRIRE	11.4 X	14.0 CM	SELLER
BEEMSTRA. AGRI BIEMSTRANI, 1617...	36.5 X	47.0 CM	VAN DEN KEERE
BELEGERINGHE VAN HET SLOT GENNEP DOOR...DEN PRINCE VAN ORAIGNIEN. GHED	31.0 X	39.0 CM	HONDIUS
BELGICARUM PROVINCIARUM NOVA DESCRIPTIO	25.0 X	33.5 CM	VAN DEN KEERE
BELGII NOVI, ANGLIAE NOVAE ET PARTIS VIRGINIAE	44.5 X	55.9 CM	JANSSON
BELGII REGII TABULA, IN QUA OMNES PROVINCIAE AB HISPANIS AD ANNUM 1684	47.0 X	54.0 CM	VISSCHER
BELGII SIVE GERMANIAE INFERIORIS ACCURATISSIMA TABULA. AUCTORE HENRICO	48.0 X	61.0 CM	HONDIUS
BELGII SIVE GERMANIAE INFERIORIS...TABULA. 1631	39.0 X	50.0 CM	HONDIUS
BELGII VETERIS TYPUS. PATRUS KAERIUS CAELAVIT	38.0 X	48.0 CM	HONDIUS
BELGII VETERIS TYPUS. PETRUS KAERIUS CELAVIT ET EXCUD. AMSTELODA	37.5 X	49.0 CM	VAN DEN KEERE
BELGIUM	20.0 X	25.0 CM	TALLIS
BELGIUM FOEDERATUM	47.0 X	57.0 CM	VISSCHER
BELGIUM FOEDERATUM...	31.8 X	45.7 CM	DE WIT
BELGIUM REGIUM...CARTE DES PAYS BAS CATHOLIQUES, AMSTERDAM, CHEZ JEAN	51.0 X	60.0 CM	COVENS & MORTIER

Title	Size	Publisher
BELGIUM, SIVE INFERIOR GERMANIA POST OMNES IN HAC FORMA, EXACTISSIME D	43.0 X 55.5 CM	GOOS
BELGIUM, SUE GERMANIA INFERIOR	13.5 X 17.5 CM	PTOLEMY (1596-1621 ...
BELIZE VIEW TAKEN FROM THE HARBOUR	14.0 X 19.1 CM	BARCLAY
BELLEVUE, THE COUNTY SEAT OF SARPY COUNTY, ON THE WEST SIDE OF THE MIS	14.0 X 22.9 CM	FRANK LESLIE'S ILLU...
BERGARUM AD ZONAM	40.0 X 50.0 CM	BLAEU
BERKSHIRE	23.5 X 19.1 CM	WILKES
BERMUDAS	22.0 X 29.0 CM	MOUNT & PAGE
BERNE (VIEW)	21.0 X 30.0 CM	MUNSTER
BERWICKSHIRE	11.4 X 14.0 CM	SELLER
BESCHREIBUNG ENGELLANTS UND SCHOTTLANDTS	25.4 X 16.5 CM	MUNSTER
BESCHRIJVINGHE DER ZEE CUSTEN VANT LANDT VAN ARGARBE...	32.4 X 50.8 CM	WAGHENAER
BIRD'S EYE VIEW OF HOLYOKE, MASS. 1816	61.0 X 86.4 CM	BAILEY & HAZEN
BIRD'S-EYE VIEW OF ANDERSONVILLE PRISON FROM THE SOUTH-EAST	35.6 X 48.3 CM	KEYSTONE PUBLISHING...
BIRD'S-EYE VIEW OF NEW ORLEANS	13.3 X 18.8 CM	ANON
BIRD'S-EYE VIEW OF PHILADELPHIA	49.8 X 74.9 CM	HARPER'S WEEKLY
BIRDS EYE VIEW OF FORT LYON-COL.	16.9 X 22.1 CM	U.S.
BIRDS-EYE VIEW OF AUBURN. PLACER COUNTY, CAL.	48.9 X 80.3 CM	ELLIOTT PUBLISHING CO.
BISHORPICK OF DURHAM	11.4 X 14.0 CM	SELLER
BOHEMIA REGNUM JUXTA XII. CIRCULOS DIVISUM, CUM COMITATU GLACENSI ET D	48.9 X 57.2 CM	SEUTTER
BOHEMIA...	38.7 X 47.6 CM	SPEED
BOLEDUCH. LE PLANT ET POURTRAICT DE BOLDUC UN DES VILLES CAPITALES DE	29.5 X 34.0 CM	DE BELLE FOREST
BORNEO INSULA	14.0 X 21.7 CM	DE BRY
BOSTON	20.0 X 14.7 CM	BAEDEKER
BOSTON	10.2 X 17.8 CM	BLUNT
BOSTON	24.1 X 17.8 CM	GERSTMAYR
BOSTON & BUNKER HILL VON DER OSTSEITE (VIEW)	18.7 X 28.6 CM	RENNER
BOSTON AND ADJACENT COUNTRY	16.6 X 10.0 CM	MELISH
BOSTON WITH CHARLESTOWN AND ROXBURY. UNDER THE SUPERINTENDENCE OF THE	29.5 X 37.1 CM	SDUK
BOSTON WITH ITS ENVIRONS	22.6 X 32.4 CM	GORDON
BOSTON. THE ILLUSTRATIONS DRAWN, & ENGRAVED BY J. WATKINS. THE PLAN, D	32.4 X 26.0 CM	TALLIS
BOWLES'S NEW ONE-SHEET MAP OF THE INDEPENDENT STATES OF VIRGINIA, MARY	48.3 X 63.5 CM	BOWLES
BOWLES'S NEW POCKET DRAUGHT OF FALKLAND ISLANDS...PUBLISH'D AS THE ACT	46.4 X 70.5 CM	BOWLES
BOWLES'S NEW POCKET MAP OF THE DISCOVERIES MADE BY THE RUSSIANS ON THE	45.1 X 61.3 CM	BOWLES
BOWLES'S NEW POCKET MAP OF THE DISCOVERIES MADE BY THE RUSSIANS ON THE	46.4 X 62.2 CM	BOWLES
BOWLES'S NEW POCKET MAP OF THE DISCOVERIES MADE BY THE RUSSIANS ON THE	45.1 X 61.3 CM	BOWLES
BOWLES'S NEW POCKET MAP OF THE EAST PART OF THE RUSSIAN EMPIRE IN ASIA	49.5 X 55.9 CM	BOWLES
BOWLES'S NEW POCKET MAP OF THE FOLLOWING INDEPENDENT STATES OF NORTH A	49.5 X 64.8 CM	BOWLES
BOWLES'S NEW POCKET MAP OF THE UNITED STATES OF AMERICA; THE BRITISH P	47.0 X 50.8 CM	BOWLES
BOWLES'S NEW...MAP OF THE LAND OF CANAAN...	47.0 X 57.8 CM	BOWLES
BRABANTIA	24.0 X 32.0 CM	DE BRUYN
BRABANTIA	24.0 X 32.0 CM	DE BRUYN
BRABANTIA DUCATUS	40.0 X 50.0 CM	BLAEU
BRABANTIA DUCATUS, MACHLINIAE URBIS DOMINIUM. PETRUS KAERIUS CAELAVIT	35.0 X 50.0 CM	VAN DEN KEERE
BRABANTIA...FRANCISCUS HOGENBERGIUS IN UBIORUM METROPOLI...MDLXXXI	36.0 X 41.5 CM	HOGENBERG
BRABANTIAE DESCRIPTIO	23.5 X 31.5 CM	VAN DEN KEERE
BRABANTIAE DUCATUS CUM ADJACENTIBUS PROVINCIIS	60.0 X 51.0 CM	VISSCHER
BRABANTIAE...DESCRIPTIO. JACOBO A DAVENTRIA AUCT	36.5 X 50.0 CM	ORTELIUS
BRABANTIAE...DESCRIPTIO. JACOBO A DAVENTRIA AUCT	36.5 X 50.0 CM	ORTELIUS
BRASILIA ET PERUVIA	36.8 X 41.9 CM	DE JODE
BRASILIA GENERIS NOBILITATE ARMORUM ET LITTERARUM SCIENTIA...	38.1 X 49.5 CM	BLAEU
BRAZIL	16.5 X 18.4 CM	MOLL
BRAZIL	34.3 X 26.7 CM	TALLIS
BRAZIL	20.0 X 25.0 CM	TALLIS
BRAZIL	38.1 X 31.8 CM	THOMAS, COWPERTHWAI...
BRAZIL. DRAWN & ENGRAVED BY J. DOWER...LONDON PUBLISHED BY HENRY TEESD	41.3 X 33.7 CM	TEESDALE
BRECKNOC COMITATUS PARS OLIM SILURUM	26.7 X 31.8 CM	KIP
BRECKNOCKSHIRE	11.4 X 14.0 CM	SELLER
BREDA OBESSSA... (sic)	41.0 X 52.0 CM	ANON
BREKNOKE...	38.7 X 47.6 CM	SPEED
BRITAIN AS IT WAS DIVIDED...HEPTARCHY	38.7 X 47.6 CM	SPEED
BRITAIN...	38.1 X 50.8 CM	SPEED
BRITANNIA...ANGLO-SAXONIUM...HEPTARCHIA	42.0 X 53.0 CM	BLAEU
BRITANNIA...HEPTARCHIA	41.9 X 52.7 CM	JANSSON

BRITANNICARUM INSULARUM TYPUS	36.8 X 52.1 CM	ORTELIUS
BRITISCHES, NORD-AMERICA GEZEICHNET NACH AUFNAHME DER HUDSONS-BAY	21.6 X 26.0 CM	RADEFELD
BRITISH AMERICA	19.7 X 24.8 CM	BRADFORD
BRITISH AMERICA	20.0 X 25.0 CM	TALLIS
BRITISH AMERICA	25.8 X 32.8 CM	TALLIS
BRITISH AMERICA	34.3 X 26.7 CM	TALLIS
BRITISH AMERICA	26.0 X 32.0 CM	TALLIS
BRITISH AMERICA	34.3 X 26.7 CM	TALLIS
BRITISH AMERICA	25.4 X 33.0 CM	TALLIS
BRITISH AND RUSSIAN AMERICA	22.0 X 27.0 CM	ARCHER
BRITISH COLONIES IN NORTH AMERICA	19.0 X 24.0 CM	KELLY
BRITISH COLONIES IN NORTH AMERICA	22.3 X 30.8 CM	WILLIAMS
BRITISH COLONIES IN NORTH AMERICA FROM THE BEST AUTHORITIES	19.1 X 22.9 CM	RUSSELL
BRITISH COLONIES OF NORTH AMERICA	19.7 X 24.8 CM	KELLY
BRITISH COLUMBIA, VANCOUVER ISLAND &C.	33.5 X 38.5 CM	STANFORD
BRITISH COLUMBIA, VANCOUVER ISLAND, AND THE VALLEY OF THE SASKATCHEWAN	22.9 X 30.6 CM	VIRTUE
BRITISH COLUMBIA/VANCOUVER ISLAND	43.0 X 30.5 CM	WELLER
BRITISH DOMINIONS IN AMERICA. DRAWN FROM THE LATEST AND BEST AUTHORITI	34.5 X 38.0 CM	KITCHIN
BRITISH GUAYANA	20.0 X 25.0 CM	TALLIS
BRITISH GUIANA ACCORDING TO SIR ROBERT SCHOMBURGK	22.9 X 14.0 CM	FULLARTON
BRITISH GUYANA	34.3 X 26.7 CM	TALLIS
BRITISH GUYANA	34.3 X 26.7 CM	TALLIS
BRITISH INDIA	20.0 X 25.0 CM	TALLIS
BRITISH ISLES	20.0 X 25.0 CM	TALLIS
BRITISH NORTH AMERICA	19.5 X 25.0 CM	FULLARTON
BRITISH NORTH AMERICA	20.3 X 25.4 CM	FULLARTON
BRITISH NORTH AMERICA	19.7 X 25.4 CM	FULLARTON
BRITISH NORTH AMERICA	49.0 X 51.0 CM	HALL
BRITISH NORTH AMERICA SHEET II WEST. CANADA WITH PART OF UNITED STATES	41.0 X 52.5 CM	FULLARTON
BRITISH NORTH AMERICA SHEET II, WEST. CANADA WITH PART OF UNITED STATE	40.6 X 52.7 CM	STANFORD
BRITISH NORTH AMERICA SHEET II. WEST. CANADA WITH PART OF UNITED STATE	40.6 X 52.1 CM	FULLARTON
BRITISH NORTH AMERICAN PROVINCES	39.4 X 67.3 CM	MOFFAT
BRITISH POSSESSIONS (NORTH AMERICA)	20.0 X 24.0 CM	DOWER
BRITISH POSSESSIONS IN AMERICA	20.0 X 25.0 CM	ARROWSMITH
BRITISH POSSESSIONS IN NORTH AMERICA	50.8 X 68.6 CM	PINKERTON
BRITISH POSSESSIONS IN NORTH AMERICA. FROM MR. ARROWSMITH'S MAP OF NOR	50.0 X 69.5 CM	PINKERTON
BRITISH POSSESSIONS IN THE MEDITERRANEAN	34.9 X 25.4 CM	TALLIS
BRITISH POSSESSIONS ON THE N.E. COAST OF SOUTH AMERICA	47.0 X 31.1 CM	FULLARTON
BRITISH POSSISSIONS IN NORTH AMERICA	31.1 X 43.2 CM	WALKER
BRITISH WEST INDIAN POSSESSIONS, NORTHERN	44.0 X 31.5 CM	FULLARTON
BRUXELLA	46.0 X 57.0 CM	BLAEU
BUCKINGHAM BOTH SHYRE, AND SHIRE...	38.7 X 47.6 CM	SPEED
BUCKINGHAMSHIRE	41.9 X 34.9 CM	MORDEN
BUCKINGHAMSHIRE	11.4 X 14.0 CM	SELLER
BUCKINGHAMSHIRE	10.8 X 6.4 CM	WALLIS & REID
BURGUNDIA...	43.2 X 57.2 CM	BLAEU
CABOOL, THE PUNJAB...	20.0 X 25.0 CM	TALLIS
CAERMARDEN...	38.7 X 47.6 CM	SPEED
CAERNARVO COMITATUS PARS OLIM ORDOVICUM	25.4 X 30.5 CM	HOLE
CAERNARVON BOTH SHYRE AND SHYRETOWNE WITH THE ANCIENT CITIE BANGOR DES	38.1 X 50.8 CM	SPEED
CAERNARVON...	38.7 X 47.6 CM	SPEED
CAERTE VANDE NIEUWE PASSAGIE BEZUYDEN DE STRATE MAGELLANI...	15.5 X 22.6 CM	SCHOUTEN
CALCUTTA	40.5 X 31.0 CM	SDUK
CALETENSIUM ET BONONI ENSIUM DITIONIS ACCURATA DELINATIO/VEROMANDUORUM	33.7 X 48.3 CM	ORTELIUS
CALIFORNIA ALSO UTAH, NEVADA, COLORADO, NEW MEXICO & ARIZONA	43.2 X 59.7 CM	JOHNSON
CALIFORNIA TERRITORIES OF NEW MEXICO & UTAH	43.2 X 62.2 CM	JOHNSON & BROWNING
CALIFORNIA, UTAH, LR. CALIFORNIA AND NEW MEXICO	43.0 X 30.5 CM	WELLER
CALIFORNIA...	42.5 X 29.8 CM	ETTLING
CAMBRIAE TYPUS	38.1 X 49.5 CM	ORTELIUS
CAMBRIAE TYPUS AUCTORE HUMFREDO LHUYDO, DENBIGIENSE CAMBROBRITANNO, PE	36.8 X 49.5 CM	MERCATOR
CAMBRIAE TYPUS. AUCTORE HUMFREDO LHUYDO	36.8 X 49.5 CM	MERCATOR
CAMBRIDGE	10.2 X 17.8 CM	CAPPER
CAMBRIDGE SHIRE	41.9 X 35.6 CM	MORDEN

CAMBRIDGESHIRE	24.1 X 19.1 CM	BELL
CAMBRIDGESHIRE	14.0 X 8.9 CM	CARY
CAMBRIDGESHIRE	17.8 X 26.7 CM	ELLIS
CAMBRIDGESHIRE	7.6 X 12.1 CM	LEIGH
CAMBRIDGESHIRE	17.8 X 11.4 CM	OWEN & BOWEN
CAMBRIDGESHIRE	11.4 X 14.0 CM	SELLER
CAMBRIDGESHIRE	11.4 X 15.2 CM	SELLER
CAMBRIDGESHIRE	10.8 X 6.4 CM	WALLIS & REID
CAMBRIDGESHIRE	23.5 X 19.1 CM	WILKES
CAMBRIDGSHIRE DESCRIBED...	38.7 X 47.6 CM	SPEED
CANAAN	38.1 X 52.1 CM	SPEED
CANAAN	38.7 X 47.6 CM	SPEED
CANAAN, PALESTINE	22.2 X 17.8 CM	MOLL
CANADA	20.5 X 25.0 CM	ARROWSMITH
CANADA	19.0 X 24.0 CM	ARROWSMITH
CANADA	10.5 X 23.5 CM	DURY
CANADA	20.0 X 25.0 CM	KELLY
CANADA	20.5 X 25.0 CM	MORSE
CANADA	20.0 X 24.8 CM	MORSE
CANADA	18.0 X 23.5 CM	THOMSON
CANADA	18.5 X 24.5 CM	VIRTUE
CANADA AND NOVA SCOTIA	48.0 X 60.0 CM	THOMSON
CANADA AND NOVA SCOTIA. DRAWN AND ENGRAVED FOR THOMSON'S NEW GENERAL A	48.9 X 59.7 CM	THOMSON
CANADA BY A.K. JOHNSTON F.R.G.S.	50.0 X 60.5 CM	JOHNSTON
CANADA EAST FORMERLY LOWER CANADA	31.1 X 39.4 CM THOMAS, COWPERTHWAI...	
CANADA IIE FEUILLE	29.2 X 43.2 CM	BONNE
CANADA LOUISIANE ET TERRES ANGLOISES	48.0 X 56.0 CM	D'ANVILLE
CANADA LOUISIANE ET TERRES ANGLOISES PER LE SR. D'ANVILLE...	39.4 X 64.8 CM	D'ANVILLE
CANADA ORIENTALE NELL'AMERICA SETTENTRIONAL DESCRITTA DAL P. MIO CORON	45.7 X 61.0 CM	CORONELLI
CANADA ORIENTALE...	44.5 X 59.7 CM	CORONELLI
CANADA WEST	30.5 X 40.6 CM	MITCHELL
CANADA WEST FORMERLY UPPER CANADA	32.0 X 40.0 CM	DESILVER
CANADA WEST FORMERLY UPPER CANADA	31.8 X 39.4 CM THOMAS, COWPERTHWAI...	
CANADA WEST OR UPPER CANADA	32.0 X 39.0 CM	COLTON
CANADA WEST, AND PART OF CANADA EAST	35.0 X 50.0 CM	BLACKIE & SON
CANADA, LOUISIANE, ETATS-UNIS	24.0 X 28.9 CM	DELAMARCHE
CANADA, NEW BRUNSWICK AND NOVA SCOTIA	40.0 X 32.0 CM	TEESDALE
CANADA, NEW BRUNSWICK ETC.	26.0 X 37.0 CM	BLACK
CANADA, NEW BRUNSWICK, ETC.	25.2 X 37.5 CM	BLACK
CANADA, NEW BRUNSWICK, NOVA SCOTIA, CAPE BRETON ISLAND, PRINCE EDWARD	62.2 X 53.3 CM	BARTHOLOMEW
CANADA, NEW BRUNSWICK, NOVA SCOTIA, ETC.	22.0 X 27.0 CM	ARCHER
CANADA, NOVA SCOTIA & NEW BRUNSWICK &C.	50.0 X 60.5 CM	PHILIP
CANADA-WEST SHEET	62.2 X 53.3 CM	BARTHOLOMEW
CANDIA	7.6 X 10.8 CM	ORTELIUS
CANDIA CUM INSULIA ALIQUOT CIRCA GRAECIAM	33.7 X 47.6 CM	MERCATOR
CANDIA INSULA, OLIM CRETA	13.5 X 17.5 CM PTOLEMY (1596-1621 ...	
CANIBALES INSULAE	41.5 X 53.1 CM	BLAEU
CANTIUM VERNACULE KENT	38.5 X 50.0 CM	JANSSON
CANTIUM VERNACULE KENT	38.1 X 49.5 CM	VALK & SCHENK
CAPE BRETON	21.0 X 26.7 CM	BELLIN
CAPE FEAR RIVER, WITH THE COUNTIES ADJACENT, AND THE TOWNS OF BRUNSWIC	23.9 X 17.8 CM	POLITICAL MAGAZINE
CAPE LOOKOUT SHOALS	57.0 X 44.0 CM	U.S. COAST SURVEY
CAPE POGE	10.2 X 17.8 CM	BLUNT
CAPE VIRGIN MARY AT THE NORTH ENTRANCE OF MAGELLAN'S STREIGHTS (VIEW)	20.3 X 38.1 CM	ANSON
CARACAS AND GUIANA	49.5 X 59.1 CM	THOMSON
CARACCAS AND GUIANA. ENGD. BY J. MOFFAT...	50.2 X 59.7 CM	THOMSON
CARACCAS AND GUYANAS	19.1 X 24.1 CM	NEELE
CARCHI, ET LIMONIA	12.0 X 16.5 CM	CORONELLI
CARDIGAN SHYRE...	38.7 X 47.6 CM	SPEED
CARMARTHENSHIRE	11.4 X 14.0 CM	SELLER
CARMARTHENSHIRE	10.8 X 6.4 CM	WALLIS & REID
CAROLINA	8.9 X 12.4 CM	SPEED
CAROLINA BY H. MOLL	19.1 X 27.9 CM	MOLL

CAROLINAE FLORIDAE NEC NON INSULARUM BAHAMENSIUM...	42.5 X 57.8 CM	CATESBY
CARTA DEL GOLFO DI S. LORENZO	22.2 X 35.6 CM	BELLIN
CARTA ESFERICA DE LA COSTA DE AFRICA DESDE CO BOJADOR HASTA CO VERDE E	64.8 X 54.6 CM	VARELA Y ULLOA
CARTA ESFERICA DE LAS ISLAS ANTILLAS CON PARTE DE LA COSTA DEL CONTINE	90.2 X 59.7 CM DIRECCION HIDROGRAFICA	
CARTA GEOGRAFICA DELLA AMERICA MERIDIONALE	35.6 X 45.1 CM	ALBRIZZI
CARTA MARINA NUOVA TAVOLA	17.8 X 24.1 CM PTOLEMY (1561-99 VE...	
CARTA MARITTIMA DEL LEVANTE	40.6 X 50.8 CM	LEVANTO
CARTA MARITTIMA DELLA COSTA LIGUSTICA...	40.0 X 50.8 CM	CORONELLI
CARTA NUOVA DELL' ARABIA	28.5 X 35.0 CM	ALBRIZZI
CARTA PARTICOLARE DELLA MERA INCONITA CON LA GRONLANDIA OCCIDENTALE E	47.0 X 74.9 CM	DUDLEY
CARTA RAPPRESENTANTE IL PORT DI BOSTON	21.6 X 17.8 CM GAZZETTIERE AMERICANO	
CARTA RAPPRESENTE L'ISOLA DELLA GIAMMACA	20.3 X 31.8 CM GAZZETTIERE AMERICANO	
CARTAGENA HARBOUR SURVEYED BY H.M.S. SCORPION	63.5 X 95.3 CM	ADMIRALTY
CARTE CHOROGRAPHIQUE DU ROYAUME DES PAYS BAS. COMPRENANT LA DIVISION T	195.0 X 130.0 CM	DE BOUGE
CARTE CONTENANT LE ROYAUME DU MEXIQUE ET LA FLORIDA	40.3 X 51.8 CM	CHATELAIN
CARTE CONTENANT LE ROYAUME DU MEXIQUE ET LA FLORIDE...	40.6 X 52.1 CM	CHATELAIN
CARTE D'AMERIQUE	48.3 X 61.0 CM	DE L'ISLE
CARTE D'AMERIQUE DRESSEE POUR L'USAGE DU ROY...PAR GUILLAUME DE L'ISLE	48.3 X 59.7 CM	BUACHE
CARTE D'AMERIQUE, DIVISEE EN SES PRINCIPAUX PAYS, DRESSEE SUR LES MEMO	94.0 X 124.5 CM	CLOUET
CARTE D'UN TRES GRAND PAIS NOUVELLEMENT DECOUVERT DANS L'AMERIQUE SEPT	38.1 X 44.5 CM	HENNEPIN
CARTE D'UNE PARTIE DE L'AMERIQUE POUR LA NAVIGATIONS	49.5 X 92.7 CM	BUACHE
CARTE D'UNE PARTIE DE L'AMERIQUE SEPTENTRIONALE	34.6 X 45.4 CM	BELLIN
CARTE D'UNE PARTIE DE LA MER DE CHINE. 1798	69.1 X 49.2 CM	DEPOT DE LA MARINE
CARTE D'UNE PARTIE DU GRAND OCEAN A L'E ET S.E. DE NOUVELLE GUINEE	24.0 X 37.0 CM	LA PEROUSE
CARTE DE COURS DE RIVIERE DE SAGUENAY	19.7 X 28.6 CM	BELLIN
CARTE DE L'ACADIE ISLE ROYALE	21.6 X 33.0 CM	BELLIN
CARTE DE L'AMERIQUE DU NORD	49.5 X 38.1 CM	ANDRIVEAU-GOUJON
CARTE DE L'AMERIQUE ET DES MERS VOISINES 1763	45.7 X 30.5 CM	BELLIN
CARTE DE L'AMERIQUE SEPTENTRIONALE ET DES ANTILLES	43.2 X 29.2 CM	DELAMARCHE
CARTE DE L'AMERIQUE SEPTENTRIONALE...	27.9 X 35.6 CM	BELLIN
CARTE DE L'ARABIE DU GOLFE PERSIQUE, ET DE LA MER ROUGH AVEC L'EGYPTE,	21.6 X 31.8 CM	BONNE
CARTE DE L'EMPIRE D'ALLEMAGNE	48.0 X 53.0 CM	DE VAUGONDY
CARTE DE L'EMPIRE D'ALLEMANGE; LES ROUTES DES POSTES	48.0 X 53.0 CM	DE VAUGONDY
CARTE DE L'EMPIRE DE LA CHINE, DE LA TARTARIE...AVEC LES ISLES DU JAPO	31.8 X 21.0 CM	BONNE
CARTE DE L'EMPIRE DE PERSE...	31.8 X 42.5 CM	BONNE
CARTE DE L'ENTREE DE LA RIVIERE DE CANTON	22.5 X 21.0 CM	BELLIN
CARTE DE L'ENTREE DE LA RIVIERE DE KOUROU	21.6 X 16.5 CM	BELLIN
CARTE DE L'ENTREE DE LA TAMISE AVEC LES BANCS	45.1 X 88.9 CM	MORTIER
CARTE DE L'ENTREE DU GOLPHE DU CHILOS ET DU PORT DE CACHAO AU CHILI	21.6 X 16.5 CM	BELLIN
CARTE DE L'INDE DRESSEE POUR LA COMPAGNIE DES INDES PAR LE SR. D'ANVIL	48.3 X 104.1 CM	D'ANVILLE
CARTE DE L'ISLE DE JAMAIQUE...1758	21.0 X 31.5 CM	BELLIN
CARTE DE L'ISLE DE LA BARBADE	55.0 X 40.0 CM	BELLIN
CARTE DE L'ISLE DE LA BARBADE	20.3 X 15.2 CM	BELLIN
CARTE DE L'ISLE DE LA BARBADE POUR SERVIR A L'HISTOIRE GENERAL DES VOY	20.3 X 15.2 CM	BELLIN
CARTE DE L'ISLE DE LA JAMAIQUE	21.6 X 31.8 CM	BONNE
CARTE DE L'ISLE DE LA JAMAIQUE AUX ANGLOIS AVEC LES PASSAGES ENTRE CET	24.1 X 31.8 CM	BUACHE
CARTE DE L'ISLE DE LA MARTINIQUE COLONIE FRANCOISE DE L'UNE DES ISLES	45.7 X 58.4 CM	COVENS & MORTIER
CARTE DE L'ISLE DE SAINT CHRISTOPHLE SITUEE A 17 DEGREZ 30 MINUTES DE	13.3 X 24.1 CM	LABAT
CARTE DE L'ISLE DE SAINTE CROIX AU SUD DES ISLES VIERGES/CARTE DE L'IS	22.2 X 17.1 CM	BELLIN
CARTE DE L'ISLE DE SAINTE LUCIE. DRESSEE AU DEPOST DES CARTES ET PLANS	87.6 X 55.9 CM	BELLIN
CARTE DE L'ISLE DE ST. DOMINGUE	21.6 X 30.5 CM	BONNE
CARTE DE L'ISLE DE ST. DOMINGUE UNE DES GRANDES ANTILLES, COLONIE FRAN	32.1 X 21.0 CM	BONNE
CARTE DE L'ISLE DE TERRE-NEUVE	28.6 X 36.2 CM	BELLIN
CARTE DE L'ISLE ST. PIERRE	21.6 X 15.9 CM	BELLIN
CARTE DE L'ISLE ST. THOMAS E UNE DES VIERGES	22.9 X 35.6 CM	BELLIN
CARTE DE L'ISTHME DE PANAMA ET DES PROVINCES DE VERAGUA, TERRE FERME E	20.3 X 29.2 CM	BELLIN
CARTE DE L'OCEAN ATLANTIQUE	49.5 X 63.0 CM	LATTRE
CARTE DE L'OCEAN PACIFIQUE AU NORD DE L'EQUATEUR, ET DES COTES QUI LE	48.9 X 56.5 CM	LOTTER
CARTE DE LA BAYE DE HUDSON	22.5 X 30.5 CM	BELLIN
CARTE DE LA BAYE DE HUDSON PAR N. BELLIN...	21.6 X 29.2 CM	BELLIN
CARTE DE LA BAYE DE PANAMA DANS L'AMERIQUE MERIDIONALE	21.6 X 17.1 CM	BELLIN
CARTE DE LA CALIFORNIA SUIVANT 1. CARTE MANUSCRIT 1604...	29.0 X 38.5 CM	DE VAUGONDY
CARTE DE LA CALIFORNIE	29.2 X 38.1 CM	DE VAUGONDY

Titre	Dimensions	Auteur
CARTE DE LA CALIFORNIE ET DES PAYS NORD-OUEST SEPARES DE L'ASIE PAR LE	29.2 X 36.8 CM	DE VAUGONDY
CARTE DE LA CAROLINE ET GEORGIE	18.7 X 28.6 CM	BELLIN
CARTE DE LA FLORIDE DE LA LOUISIANE	22.2 X 30.5 CM	BELLIN
CARTE DE LA FLORIDE, DE LA LOUISIANE ET PAYS VOISINS. POUR SERVIR A L'	22.2 X 30.5 CM	BELLIN
CARTE DE LA FLORIDE, DE LA LOUISIANE, ET PAYS VOISINS POUR SERVIR A L'	22.9 X 30.5 CM	BELLIN
CARTE DE LA FLORIDE, DE LA LOUISIANE...	21.6 X 30.5 CM	BELLIN
CARTE DE LA GONAVE, DRESSEE SUR LES OPERATIONS GEOMETRIQUES FAITES EN	58.4 X 88.9 CM	DEPOT DE LA MARINE
CARTE DE LA GUYANE FRANCOISE ET L'ISLE DE CAYENNE FRANCOISE ET L'ISLE	58.1 X 40.6 CM	BELLIN
CARTE DE LA HOLLANDE ET D'UNE PARTIE DES ETATS VOISINS, POUR SERVIR A	74.0 X 66.0 CM	DE BEAURAIN
CARTE DE LA LOUISIANE	52.1 X 92.7 CM	D'ANVILLE
CARTE DE LA LOUISIANE ET DE LA FLORIDE PAR M. BONNE INGENIEUR	33.0 X 21.6 CM	BONNE
CARTE DE LA LOUISIANE ET DU COURS DU MISSISSIPI	43.8 X 59.7 CM	COVENS & MORTIER
CARTE DE LA LOUISIANE ET DU COURS DU MISSISSIPI...	43.2 X 59.1 CM	COVENS & MORTIER
CARTE DE LA LOUISIANE ET DU COURS DU MISSISSIPPI	48.5 X 65.0 CM	DE L'ISLE
CARTE DE LA LOUISIANE ET DU COURS DU MISSISSIPPI	48.3 X 66.0 CM	DE L'ISLE
CARTE DE LA LOUISIANE PAR LE SR. D'ANVILLE. DRESSEE EN MAI 1732, PUBLI	52.1 X 92.1 CM	D'ANVILLE
CARTE DE LA LOUISIANE, ET DE LA FLORIDE	31.8 X 20.3 CM	BONNE
CARTE DE LA LOUISIANE, ET DE LA FLORIDE	32.0 X 21.1 CM	BONNE
CARTE DE LA LOUSIANE	48.3 X 64.8 CM	BUACHE
CARTE DE LA MANCHE	57.2 X 86.4 CM	MORTIER
CARTE DE LA NOUVELLE ZEELANDE	48.0 X 38.0 CM	BONNE
CARTE DE LA NOUVELLE ZEELANDE PAR M. BONNE...	34.5 X 23.0 CM	BONNE
CARTE DE LA PARTIE DE L'OCEAN VERS L'EQUATEUR ENTRE LES COTES D'AFRIQU	48.3 X 64.8 CM	BUACHE
CARTE DE LA PARTIE DE LA COTE NORD-OUEST DE L'AMERIQUE	75.0 X 58.8 CM	DEPOT DE LA MARINE
CARTE DE LA PARTIE DE SAINT-DOMINGUE HABITEE PAR LES FRANCOIS	23.5 X 30.5 CM	D'ANVILLE
CARTE DE LA PARTIE FRANCOIS DE ST. DOMINGUE FAITE PAR BELLIN INGR. DE	37.5 X 48.3 CM	VARLE
CARTE DE LA PARTIE MERIDIONALE DE LA PRESQU'ISLE DE L'INDE QUI COMPREN	48.6 X 69.8 CM	DEPOT DE LA MARINE
CARTE DE LA PARTIE MERIDIONALE DU BRESIL...	21.6 X 31.8 CM	BONNE
CARTE DE LA PARTIE NORD, DES ETATS-UNIS DE L'AMERIQUE SEPTENTRIONALE	21.6 X 31.1 CM	BONNE
CARTE DE LA PARTIE ORIENTALE DE LA NOUVELLE FRANCE OU DU CANADA DEDIEE	40.0 X 55.9 CM	BELLIN
CARTE DE LA PARTIE SEPTENTRIONALE DE LA MER DU SUD	26.0 X 37.0 CM	DUPUIS
CARTE DE LA PARTIE SEPTENTRIONALE DU NOUVEAU MONDE QU'SONT COMPRISES L	26.7 X 45.7 CM	VIVIEN
CARTE DE LA PARTIE SUD DES ETATS UNIS DE L'AMERIQUE SEPTENTRIONALE	21.6 X 31.8 CM	BONNE
CARTE DE LA PARTIE SUD DES ETATS UNIS...	21.6 X 31.8 CM	BONNE
CARTE DE LA RIVIERE DE RICHELIEU ET DU LAC CHAMPLAIN	30.5 X 13.7 CM	BELLIN
CARTE DE LA SUISSE	49.0 X 73.5 CM	COXE
CARTE DE LA TERRE VAN-DIEMAN	23.5 X 34.5 CM	BONNE
CARTE DE LA VALLEE DE MEXICO ET DES MONTAGNES VOISINES...	39.4 X 45.7 CM	HUMBOLDT
CARTE DE LA VIRGINIE ET DU MARYLAND	48.3 X 64.1 CM	DE VAUGONDY
CARTE DE LA VIRGINIE, DE LA BAYE CHESAPEACK, ET PAYS VOISINS	19.1 X 29.2 CM	BELLIN
CARTE DES ANTILLES FRANCOISES ET DES ISLES VOISINES	64.2 X 37.1 CM	DE L'ISLE
CARTE DES ARCHIPELS DES ILES SALOMON, DE LA LOUISIADE ET DE LA NOUV. L	49.3 X 75.5 CM	DEPOT DE LA MARINE
CARTE DES BAYES RADES ET PORTE DE PLAISANCE	19.7 X 28.6 CM	BELLIN
CARTE DES CERCLES DU HAUTE ED DU BAS RHIN	48.0 X 53.0 CM	DE VAUGONDY
CARTE DES COMTEZ DE HAINAUT, DE NAMUR ET DE CAMBRESIS. PAR GUILLAUME D	47.0 X 67.0 CM	DE L'ISLE
CARTE DES COSTES DE LA FLORIDE FRANCOISE	20.6 X 14.4 CM	BELLIN
CARTE DES COSTES DE LA FLORIDE FRANCOISE	20.3 X 14.0 CM	BELLIN
CARTE DES COTES DE GUZERAT, DE CONCAN ET DE CANARA. 1798	69.0 X 48.2 CM	DEPOT DE LA MARINE
CARTE DES COTES DE L'AMERIQUE ET DE L'ASIE	38.5 X 50.0 CM	ROBINSON
CARTE DES COTES DE L'AMERIQUE ET DE L'ASIE DEPUIS LA CALIFORNIE JUSQU'	50.2 X 68.6 CM	LA PEROUSE
CARTE DES COTES DE L'AMERIQUE MERIDIONALE DEPUIS LE PARALLELE 36 30' L	90.7 X 61.8 CM	DEPOT DE LA MARINE
CARTE DES COTES DE L'ASIE SUR L'OCEAN CONTENANT LES BANC ISLES ET COST	56.0 X 87.0 CM	MORTIER
CARTE DES DEUX FLORIDES ET DE LA LOUISIANE INFERIEURE...	40.4 X 67.0 CM	POIRSON
CARTE DES DEUX FLORIDES ET DE LA LOUISIANE INFERIEURE...	40.6 X 66.0 CM	POIRSON
CARTE DES ENVIRONS DE LA MER-NOIRE OU SE TROUVENT L'UKRAYNE LA PETITE	49.5 X 64.1 CM	SANTINI
CARTE DES ENVIRONS DE LA VILLE DE MEXIQUE POUR L'HISTOIRE GENERALE DES	20.3 X 15.9 CM	BELLIN
CARTE DES ETATS-UNIS D'AMERICA	22.9 X 24.0 CM	MALTE-BRUN
CARTE DES ETATS-UNIS DE L'AMERIQUE DU NORD ET MEXIQUE...	22.9 X 27.9 CM	HACHETTE
CARTE DES ETATS-UNIS DE L'AMERIQUE SEPTENTRIONALE COPIEE ET GRAVEE SUR	122.0 X 142.0 CM	TARDIEU
CARTE DES ILES SANDWICH	54.8 X 76.7 CM	DEPOT DE LA MARINE
CARTE DES INDES ET DE LA CHINE	57.2 X 86.4 CM	MORTIER
CARTE DES ISLES ANTILLES OU DU VENT AVEC LA PARTIE ORIENTALES DES ISLE	31.8 X 20.3 CM	BONNE
CARTE DES ISLES BERMUDES OU DE SOMMER TIRE DE L'ANGLOIS	20.3 X 33.0 CM	BELLIN

CARTE DES ISLES CANARIES	21.0 X 27.9 CM	BELLIN
CARTE DES ISLES D'ACORES...	50.2 X 54.0 CM	MORTIER
CARTE DES ISLES DE JAVA, SUMATRA, BORNEO &C	25.5 X 29.0 CM	BELLIN
CARTE DES ISLES DE LA SOCIETE...	29.0 X 43.5 CM	COOK
CARTE DES ISLES DE SAINT PIERRE ET MIQUELON LEVEE PAR ORDRE DE M. LE D	58.4 X 88.9 CM	BELLIN
CARTE DES ISLES DU JAPON	21.5 X 29.0 CM	BELLIN
CARTE DES ISLES KOURILES D'APRES LA CARTE RUSSE DRESSEE ET GRAVEE PAR	24.1 X 26.7 CM	LAURENT
CARTE DES LACS DU CANADA	19.7 X 29.2 CM	BELLIN
CARTE DES NOUVELLES DECOUVERTES AU NORD DE LA MER DU SUD, TANT A L'EST	47.0 X 66.7 CM	BUACHE
CARTE DES NOUVELLES DECOUVERTES AU NORD DE LA MER DU SUD, TANT A L'EST	47.0 X 66.7 CM	DEZAUCHE
CARTE DES NOUVELLES DECOUVERTES AU NORD DE LA MER DU SUD...	44.5 X 62.2 CM	SANTINI
CARTE DES PAYS-BAS CATHOLIQUES...PARIS, CHEZ L'AUTEUR, SUR LE QUAY DE	49.0 X 63.0 CM	DE L'ISLE
CARTE DES POSSESIONS ANGLOISES DANS L'AMERIQUE SEPTENTRIONALE POUR SER	62.2 X 72.4 CM	IMBERT
CARTE DES POSSESIONS ANGLOISES & FRANCOISES DU CONTINENT DE L'AMERIQU	45.7 X 57.2 CM	OTTENS
CARTE DES PROVINCES DE TABASCO, CHIAPA, VERAPAZ, GUATIMALA...ET YUCATA	21.0 X 34.3 CM	BELLIN
CARTE DES PROVINCES UNIES DES PAYS-BAS...PAR G. DE L'ISLE, GEOGRAPHE,	48.0 X 63.0 CM	DE L'ISLE
CARTE DES VOYAGES DU CAPE. CARVER...	26.7 X 34.3 CM	CARVER
CARTE DES XVII PROVINCES DES PAYS BAS TIREE DE PLUSIEURS CARTES FAITES	66.0 X 82.0 CM	JAILLOT
CARTE DU BRABANT	64.0 X 64.0 CM	DE L'ISLE
CARTE DU CANADA OU DE LA NOUVELLE FRANCE	49.5 X 58.0 CM	COVENS & MORTIER
CARTE DU CANADA OU DE LA NOUVELLE FRANCE ET DES DECOUVERTES QUI Y ONT	49.5 X 64.8 CM	DE L'ISLE
CARTE DU CANADA OU DE LA NOUVELLE FRANCE ET DES DECOUVERTES...PAR GUIL	50.8 X 66.0 CM	BUACHE
CARTE DU CANADA OU DE LA NOUVELLE FRANCE ET DES DECOUVERTES...PAR GUIL	50.2 X 57.2 CM	COVENS & MORTIER
CARTE DU CANADA OU DE LA NOUVELLE FRANCE ET DES DECOUVERTES...PAR GUIL	50.2 X 65.4 CM	DE L'ISLE
CARTE DU CANADA OU DE LA NOUVELLE FRANCE, & DES DECOUVERTES QUI Y ONT	40.5 X 52.0 CM	CHATELAIN
CARTE DU CANADA OU DE LA NOUVELLE FRANCE, & DES DECOUVERTES QUI Y ONT	40.6 X 52.1 CM	CHATELAIN
CARTE DU CANADA, QUI COMPREND LA PARTIE SEPTENTRIONALE DES ETATS-UNIS	50.8 X 66.0 CM	DEZAUCHE
CARTE DU CHILI DEPUIS LE SUD PEROU JUSQU'AU CAP HORN, AVEC PARTIE DES	34.3 X 21.0 CM	BONNE
CARTE DU COMTE DE FLANDRE. PARIS, CHEZ L'AUTEUR, SUR LE QUAI DE L'HORL	60.0 X 65.0 CM	BUACHE
CARTE DU COMTE DE KENT ET DU PAS DE CALAIS...	57.2 X 85.1 CM	BELLIN
CARTE DU COURS DU FLEUVE DE SAINT LAURENT DEPUIS LA MER JUSQU'A QUEBEC	60.3 X 86.4 CM	BELLIN
CARTE DU COURS DU FLEUVE DE SAINT LAURENT DEPUIS QUEBEC JUSQU A LA MER	60.3 X 89.5 CM	BELLIN
CARTE DU COURS DU FLEUVE ST. LAURENT	19.1 X 29.8 CM	BELLIN
CARTE DU DUCHE DE LUXEMBOURG	48.0 X 53.0 CM	DE VAUGONDY
CARTE DU DUCHE DE LUXEMBOURG ET SOUVERAINETE DE SEDAN. PAR DU VAL GEOG	37.5 X 48.3 CM	DU VAL
CARTE DU FONDS DE LA BAYE DE HUDSON QUE LES ANGLOIS APPELLENT BAYE JAM	20.3 X 14.0 CM	BELLIN
CARTE DU GOLPHE DE ST LAURENT	14.0 X 22.0 CM	BELLIN
CARTE DU GOLPHE DU MEXIQUE ET DES ISLES DE L'AMERIQUE	27.9 X 37.5 CM	BELLIN
CARTE DU GRAND OCEAN, OU MER DU SUD	36.0 X 49.0 CM	ROBINSON
CARTE DU GROENLAND DRESSEE ET GRAVEE PAR LAURENT	19.7 X 25.4 CM	PREVOST D'EXILES
CARTE DU JAPAN ET DE LA COREE...	21.5 X 27.5 CM	LE ROUGE
CARTE DU KAMTSCHATKA DRESSEE ET GRAVEE PAR LAURENT	52.1 X 29.8 CM	PREVOST D'EXILES
CARTE DU KATAY OU EMPIRE DE KIN, POUR SERVIR A L'HISTOIRE DE JENGHIZ K	20.3 X 31.8 CM	BELLIN
CARTE DU MEXIQUE DE LA NLLE. ESPAGNE	29.2 X 40.6 CM	BONNE
CARTE DU MEXIQUE ET DES ETATS UNIS PARTIE MERIDIONALE	47.0 X 64.8 CM	DEZAUCHE
CARTE DU MEXIQUE ET DU NOUVELLE ESPAGNE	45.0 X 58.5 CM	SANTINI
CARTE DU PEROU AVEC UNE PARTIE DES PAYS QUI EN SONT A L'EST...	31.8 X 21.0 CM	BONNE
CARTE DU PEROU OU SE TROUVENT LES AUDIENCES DE QUITO, LIMA ET LA PLATA	43.2 X 31.1 CM	BONNE
CARTE DU THEATRE DE LA GUERRE, COMPRENANT LES PAYS-BAS ET PARTIE DES P	47.0 X 61.0 CM	DESNOS
CARTE DU WAEIGATZ OU DETROIT DE NASSAU	15.2 X 29.2 CM	ANON
CARTE ENCYPROTYPE DE L'AMERIQUE SEPTENTRIONALE...	52.7 X 69.9 CM	BRUE
CARTE GENERAL D'UNE PARTIE DE LA COTE DU NORD OUEST DE L'AMERIQUE	49.5 X 38.0 CM	ROBINSON
CARTE GENERAL DE LA CAROLINE...	56.2 X 46.4 CM	MORTIER
CARTE GENERAL DES DECOUVERTS DE L'ADMIRAL FONTE	30.5 X 38.1 CM	DE VAUGONDY
CARTE GENERALE DE CANADA A PETIT POINT	8.9 X 14.0 CM	LA HONTAN
CARTE GENERALE DE L'AMERIQUE DU NORD. DRESSEE PAR A.H. DUFOUR	32.4 X 50.2 CM	DUFOUR
CARTE GENERALE DE L'AMERIQUE DU NORD...	32.4 X 50.2 CM	DUFOUR
CARTE GENERALE DE L'OCEAN ATLANTIQUE OU OCCIDENTAL...	60.5 X 89.5 CM	DEPOT DE LA MARINE
CARTE GENERALE DE LA CAROLINE	57.2 X 47.0 CM	MORTIER
CARTE GENERALE DE LA HOLLANDE AVEC LES ROUTES DE POSTES. 1810	76.0 X 92.0 CM	KRAYENHOFF
CARTE GENERALE DE LA MER ROUGE. 1798	59.5 X 86.5 CM	DEPOT DE LA MARINE
CARTE GENERALE DE LA NOUVELLE HOLLANDE ET DES ARCHIPELS DE GRAND OCEAN	49.5 X 75.5 CM	BEAUTEMPS-BEAUPRE
CARTE GENERALE DE LA TARTARIE CHINOISE	52.0 X 81.0 CM	D'ANVILLE

233

CARTE GENERALE DES DECOUERTES DE L'AMIRAL DE FONTE ET AUTRES NAVIGATE	27.0 X 37.0 CM	DE VAUGONDY
CARTE GENERALE DES DECOUVERTES DE L'AMIRAL DE FONTE, ET AUTRES NAVIGAT	29.2 X 38.1 CM	DE VAUGONDY
CARTE GENERALE DES DECOUVERTES DE L'AMIRAL DE FONTE...PAR THOMAS JEFFE	30.5 X 38.1 CM	DE VAUGONDY
CARTE GENERALE DES DIX ET SEPT PROVINCES DES PAYS-BAS	37.0 X 52.0 CM	TASSIN
CARTE GENERALE DES DIX SEPT PROVINCES DES PAIS BAS. PARIS, PAR M. TAVE	30.0 X 37.0 CM	TAVERNIER
CARTE GENERALE DES DIXSEPT PROVINCES DES PAIS-BAS...PAR M. TAVERNIER,	53.0 X 41.5 CM	TAVERNIER
CARTE GENERALE DES ETATS-UNIS DES HAUT ET BAS-CANADA...	36.8 X 50.8 CM	BRUE
CARTE GENERALE DES ETATS-UNIS, DU CANADA ET D'UNE PARTIE DES PAYS ADJA	37.5 X 51.4 CM	BRUE
CARTE GENERALE DES ROYAUME D'ANGLETERRE, ESCOSSE ET IRLANDE	39.4 X 51.4 CM	SANSON
CARTE GENERALE DU CANADA, DE LA LOUISIANE, DE LA FLORIDE, DE LA CAROLI	48.9 X 66.0 CM	SANTINI
CARTE GENERALE DU CANADA, DE LA LOUISIANE...FLORIDE, CAROLINE...VIRGIN	47.6 X 64.8 CM	SANTINI
CARTE GENERALE DU MONDE, OU DESCRIPTION DU MONDE TERRESTRE & AQUATIQUE	39.7 X 46.7 CM	MORTIER
CARTE GENERALE DU PEROU DE LA BOLIVIE, DU CHILI ET LA PLATA...	50.8 X 36.8 CM	BRUE
CARTE GENERALS DES TREIZE ETATS UNIS...	41.3 X 56.8 CM	COVENS & MORTIER
CARTE GEOGRAPHIQUE DE L'AMERIQUE MERIDIONALE	59.2 X 42.3 CM	BONNE
CARTE GEOGRAPHIQUE STATISTIQUE ET HISTORIQUE DE L'AMERIQUE	48.3 X 64.1 CM	BUCHON
CARTE GEOGRAPHIQUE STATISTIQUE ET HISTORIQUE DE LA CAROLINA DU NORD	44.5 X 60.3 CM	BUCHON
CARTE GEOGRAPHIQUE, STATISTIQUE ET HISTORIQUE DE GEORGIE	45.7 X 61.0 CM	BUCHON
CARTE GEOGRAPHIQUE, STATISTIQUE, ET HISTORIQUE DU TERRITOIRE D'ARKANSA	35.6 X 35.6 CM	BUCHON
CARTE HYDROGRAPHIQUE DE LA BAYE DE LA HAVANE AVEC LE PLAN DE LA VILLE	56.5 X 40.0 CM	BELLIN
CARTE MARINE DE LA MER CASPIENE LEVEE SUIVANT LES ORDRES DE S.M. CZARI	88.9 X 60.3 CM	OTTENS
CARTE MARINE DES ENVIRONS DE L'ISLE D'OLERON A L'USAGE DES ARMEES DU R	58.4 X 47.0 CM	MORTIER
CARTE MARITIME DEPUIS LA RIVIERE DE BORDEAUX JUSQUES A ST. SEBASTIEN A	57.8 X 47.0 CM	MORTIER
CARTE MARITIME DES ENVIRONS DE DIEPPE DEPUIS PONT ASSELANE JUSQUES AU	58.4 X 47.0 CM	MORTIER
CARTE NOUVELLE CONTENANT LA PARTIE D'AMERIQUE LA PLUS SEPTENTRIONALE,	59.7 X 48.3 CM	VISSCHER
CARTE NOUVELLE DE L'AMERIQUE ANGLOISE CONTENANT LA VIRGINIE, MARY-LAND	60.3 X 91.4 CM	MORTIER
CARTE NOUVELLE DE L'AMERIQUE ANGLOISE CONTENANT TOUT CE QUE LES ANGLOI	59.7 X 48.9 CM	LOTTER
CARTE NOUVELLE DE L'AMERIQUE ANGLOISE CONTENANT TOUT CE QUE LES ANGLOI	49.5 X 62.2 CM	LOTTER
CARTE NOUVELLE DE LA COMTE DE HOLLANDE ET DE LA SEIGNEURIE D'UTRECHT.	40.5 X 62.0 CM	COVENS & MORTIER
CARTE NOUVELLE DE LA MER DU SUD	59.7 X 96.5 CM	DE LETH
CARTE NOUVELLE DE TOUT L'EMPIRE DE LA GRANDE RUSSIE DANS L'ESTAT OU IL	47.6 X 65.4 CM	OTTENS
CARTE NOUVELLE DU CREMASCO	47.0 X 39.4 CM	MORTIER
CARTE NOUVELLE DU PADOUAN	57.2 X 86.4 CM	MORTIER
CARTE PARTICULIERE DE ISTHMUS OU DARIEN...CARTAGENE	57.2 X 86.4 CM	MORTIER
CARTE PARTICULIERE DE L'AMERIQUE SEPTENTRIONALE OU SONT COMPRES LE DET	57.2 X 87.6 CM	MORTIER
CARTE PARTICULIERE DE LA CAROLINE	48.3 X 61.0 CM	MORTIER
CARTE PARTICULIERE DE LA COTE OCCIDENTALE D'ECOSSEE...PAR ORDRE DU CON	87.6 X 58.4 CM	DEPOT DE LA MARINE
CARTE PARTICULIERE DE VIRGINIE, MARYLAND, PENNSILVANIE, LA NOUVELLE IA	51.4 X 80.0 CM	MORTIER
CARTE PARTICULIERE DE VIRGINIE, MARYLAND, PENNSILVANIE, LA NOUVELLE JA	57.2 X 87.6 CM	MORTIER
CARTE PARTICULIERE DES POSTES DE FRANCE	57.2 X 86.4 CM	MORTIER
CARTE PARTICULIERE DU FLEUVE SAINT LOUIS DRESSEE SUR LES LIEUX AVEC LE	36.8 X 45.7 CM	CHATELAIN
CARTE PARTICULIERE DU HAVRE DE BOSTON...	58.4 X 87.6 CM	DEPOT DE LA MARINE
CARTE POUR SERVIR AU JOURNAL DE MR. LE MARQUIS DE CHASTELLUX	17.8 X 26.7 CM	DEZOTEUX
CARTE QUI REPRESENTE LES DIFFERENTES CONNAISSANCES QUE L'ON VUE DES TE	30.5 X 34.3 CM	DE VAUGONDY
CARTE REDUITE DE GRAND BANC ET D'UNE PARTIE DE L'ISLE DE TERRE NEUVE D	56.5 X 81.9 CM	BELLIN
CARTE REDUITE DE L'EXTREMITE DE L'AMERIQUE MERIDIONALE DANS LA PARTIE	19.1 X 29.2 CM	FREZIER
CARTE REDUITE DE L'ISLE DE SAINT DOMINGUE...	55.7 X 89.0 CM	BELLIN
CARTE REDUITE DE L'OCEAN ORIENTAL DEPUIS LE CAP DE BONNE ESPERANCE, JU	56.0 X 84.0 CM	D'APRES DE MANNEVIL...
CARTE REDUITE DE L'OCEAN SEPTENTRIONALE COMPRIS ENTRE L'ASIE ET L'AMER	55.9 X 85.7 CM	BELLIN
CARTE REDUITE DE LA COTE OCCIDENTALE DE L'AMERIQUE DEPUIS 9 DE LATITUD	84.7 X 56.1 CM	DEPOT DE LA MARINE
CARTE REDUITE DE LA PARTIE DE LA COTE DU CHILI COMPRISE ENTRE LE 22E E	84.5 X 56.4 CM	DEPOT DE LA MARINE
CARTE REDUITE DE LA PARTIE DE LA COTE DU PEROU COMPRISE ENTRE LE 7E ET	84.8 X 55.1 CM	DEPOT DE LA MARINE
CARTE REDUITE DE LA PARTIE LA PLUS MERIDIONALE D'AMERIQUE	21.6 X 16.5 CM	BELLIN
CARTE REDUITE DE LA PARTIE MERIDIONALE DE L'ILE D'HAINAN PARCOUROE EN	42.6 X 57.4 CM	DEPOT DE LA MARINE
CARTE REDUITE DE LA PARTIE ORIENTALE DE LA NOUVELLE ESPAGNE DEPUIS LE	21.6 X 62.2 CM	HUMBOLDT
CARTE REDUITE DE LA PARTIE SEPTENTRIONAL DE L'ISLE DE TERRE NEUVE DRES	61.6 X 80.0 CM	BELLIN
CARTE REDUITE DE LA ROUTE D'ACAPULCO A MEXICO	39.4 X 19.1 CM	HUMBOLDT
CARTE REDUITE DES COSTES DE L'ACADIE DE L'ISLE ROYALE ET DE LA PARTIE	23.5 X 57.2 CM	CHABERT
CARTE REDUITE DES COSTES DE LA LOUISIANE, ET DE LA FLORIDE	56.5 X 85.1 CM	BELLIN
CARTE REDUITE DES COSTES ORIENTALES DE L'AMERIQUE SEPTENTRIONALE	54.5 X 87.5 CM	BELLIN
CARTE REDUITE DES COTES DE L'ACADIE	55.9 X 85.7 CM	CHABERT
CARTE REDUITE DES COTES ORIENTALES DE L'AMERIQUE SEPTENTRIONALE	59.1 X 87.6 CM	DEPOT DE LA MARINE
CARTE REDUITE DES DEBOUQUEMENTS DE ST. DOMINGUE LEVEE, DRESSEE ET PUBL	61.0 X 91.4 CM	CHASTENET-PUISEGUR

CARTE REDUITE DES DESTROITS DE MALACCA, SINCAPOUR...	55.0 X 90.0 CM	BELLIN
CARTE REDUITE DES ILES DE FRANCE ET DE BOURBON. 1798, NOUVELLE EDITION	58.1 X 87.2 CM	DEPOT DE LA MARINE
CARTE REDUITE DES ISLES ANTILLES...POUR SERVICE DES VAISSEAUX DU ROI	87.6 X 56.5 CM	BELLIN
CARTE REDUITE DES ISLES BRITANNIQUES EN CINQ FEUILLES...PREMIERE FEUI	55.9 X 61.6 CM	BELLIN
CARTE REDUITE DES MERS DU NORD...	55.9 X 86.4 CM	DEPOT DE LA MARINE
CARTE REDUITE DU GLOBE TERRESTRE	22.2 X 34.3 CM	BELLIN
CARTE REDUITE DU GOLPHE DE ST. LAURENT CONTENANT L'ISLE DE TERRE-NEUVE	56.5 X 89.5 CM	DEPOT DE LA MARINE
CARTE REDUITE DU GOLPHE DU MEXIQUE ET DES ISLES DE L'AMERIQUE	52.1 X 78.7 CM	BELLIN
CARTE REDUITE, DES COTES DE L'ACADIE, DE L'ISLE ROYALE, ET DE LA PARTI	58.4 X 87.6 CM	DEPOT DE LA MARINE
CARTE TOPOGRAPHIQUE DES ENVIRONS DE CHARLEROY JUSQU'A PHILIPPEVILLE. P	63.0 X 48.0 CM	LE ROUGE
CARTE TOPOGRAPHIQUE DES FORTS, VILLE, CITADELLE D'ANVERS ET DE SES ENV	50.0 X 69.0 CM	JAILLOT
CARTE TRES CURIEUSE DE LA MER DU SUD	81.3 X 139.7 CM	CHATELAIN
CARTE UNIVERSELLE DU MONDE...AMERIQUE SEPTENTRIONALE	41.7 X 57.9 CM	DU VAL
CARTE VAN T'VRYE...EEN GEDEELTE VAN VLAENDEREN...DOOR C.I. VISSCHER. H	38.0 X 42.0 CM	VISSCHER
CARTES DES ISLES PHILIPPINES CELEBRES ET MOLUQUES	15.0 X 23.0 CM	BELLIN
CARTES DES NOUVELLES DECOUVERTES AU NORD DE LA MER DU SUD...A PARIS, Q	45.4 X 63.5 CM	DE L'ISLE
CARTES DES ROYAUMES D'ESPAGNE ET DE PORTUGAL	48.0 X 53.0 CM	DE VAUGONDY
CARTES DES ROYAUMES D'ESPAGNE ET DE PORTUGAL. LES ROUTES DES POSTES	48.0 X 53.0 CM	DE VAUGONDY
CARTES TYPO-GEOGRAPHIQUES, INVENTEES ET IMPRIMEES PAR FIRMIN DIDOT. FR	35.6 X 38.7 CM	DIDOT
CARTHAGENA INDE SPAANSCHE WEST INDIEN	18.4 X 26.0 CM	TIRION
CARTHAGENE (VIEW)	20.3 X 10.2 CM	MALLET
CASTELLI AT SANTFLITAM	40.0 X 50.0 CM	BLAEU
CAVENDISH PLUNDERS & BURNS PAITA	10.2 X 15.2 CM	NEWBERY
CEILAN	6.5 X 7.5 CM	MULLER
CELEBERRIMI FLANDRIAE COMITATUS TYPUS	33.0 X 48.0 CM	VAN DEN KEERE
CENTRAL AMERICA	22.2 X 26.7 CM	CHAMBERS
CENTRAL AMERICA	34.3 X 26.7 CM	TALLIS
CENTRAL AMERICA (GUATEMALA)	20.0 X 25.0 CM	TALLIS
CENTRAL AMERICA I	30.5 X 39.4 CM	SDUK
CENTRAL AMERICA II	31.1 X 39.4 CM	SDUK
CENTRAL AMERICA II	31.1 X 39.4 CM	SDUK
CENTRAL AMERICA II, INCLUDING TEXAS, CALIFORNIA...	31.8 X 39.4 CM	SDUK
CERCLE DE BASSE SAXE	48.0 X 53.0 CM	DE VAUGONDY
CERCLE DE FRANCONIE	48.0 X 53.0 CM	DE VAUGONDY
CERCLE DE SOUABE	48.0 X 53.0 CM	DE VAUGONDY
CERCLE DE WESTPHALIE	48.0 X 53.0 CM	DE VAUGONDY
CETTE CARTE DE CALIFORNE ET DU NOUVEAUX MEXIQUE...	23.0 X 34.0 CM	DE FER
CEYLON	20.0 X 25.0 CM	TALLIS
CEYLON ET LES MALDIVES	19.0 X 16.0 CM	SANSON
CHAMPAGNE LATINE CAMPANIA, COMITATUS	38.1 X 50.2 CM	BLAEU
CHAMPAIGNE ET BRIE, ETC.	40.0 X 49.5 CM	SANSON
CHANNEL ISLANDS	20.0 X 25.0 CM	TALLIS
CHARLES TOWN SOUTH CAROLINA, WITH A CHART OF THE BARS & HARBOUR	19.1 X 19.7 CM	COWLEY
CHARLESTON	24.1 X 17.8 CM	GERSTMAYR
CHARLESTON HARBOR AND ITS APPROACHES	79.5 X 81.0 CM	U.S. COAST SURVEY
CHARLESTON HARBOUR	18.4 X 10.2 CM	BLUNT
CHARLESTON, AND ADJACENT COUNTRY	16.7 X 10.3 CM	MELISH
CHARLESTON, SOUTH CAROLINA (VIEW)	12.7 X 15.2 CM	JACKSON
CHARLOTTE BAY. PUBLISHED ACCORDING TO ACT OF PARLIAMENT BY J.F.W. DES	71.1 X 101.6 CM	DES BARRES
CHART AND PLAN OF THE HARBOUR OF NEW YORK & THE COUNY. ADJACENT FROM S	41.9 X 24.3 CM	POLITICAL MAGAZINE
CHART CONTAINING PART OF THE ICY SEA WITH THE ADJACENT COAST OF ASIA &	45.7 X 53.3 CM	JEFFERYS
CHART EXHIBITION THE BRITISH POSSESSIONS IN NORTH AMERICA; THE ATLANTI	16.7 X 38.8 CM	MCGREGOR
CHART EXHIBITION THE DISCOVERIES OF THE SECOND AMERICAN GRINNELL EXPED	28.5 X 45.5 CM	KANE
CHART FOR THE JOURNAL OF MR. LE MARQUIS DE CHASTELLUX BY MR. DEZOTEUX.	17.8 X 26.0 CM	ROBINSON
CHART FOR THE JOURNAL OF MR. LE MQUIS. DE CHASTELLUX. BY MR. DEZOTEUX	18.1 X 23.5 CM	DEZOTEUX
CHART ILLUSTRATIVE OF THE VOYAGES AND TRAVELS OF CAPTAINS ROSS, PARRY	26.0 X 35.0 CM	SMITH
CHART OF BEHRING'S STRAIT, UPON MERCATOR'S PROJECTION	19.7 X 19.7 CM	PHILLIPS
CHART OF HUDSON'S STRAIT & SIR THOS. ROWE'S WELCOME, SHEWING THE TRACK	18.4 X 36.8 CM	PARRY
CHART OF LONG ISLAND SOUND	17.8 X 43.2 CM	BLUNT
CHART OF NORTH ATLANTIC OCEAN WITH TRACKS OF THE SHIPPING TO WEST INDI	53.3 X 62.9 CM	MOFFAT
CHART OF PART OF THE COAST OF LABRADORE, FROM CAPE CHARLES TO SANDWICH	43.2 X 61.0 CM	FADEN
CHART OF SOUTH AMERICA, COMPREHENDING THE WEST INDIES...	53.5 X 60.5 CM	JEFFERYS
CHART OF THE ATLANTIC OCEAN	48.9 X 41.3 CM	LIZARS

CHART OF THE BAHAMA ISLANDS/THE BERMUDAS OR SUMMER ISLANDS/ISLAND OF C	50.0 X 58.6 CM	THOMSON
CHART OF THE COAST OF AMERICA & ASIA FROM CALIFORNIA TO MACAO ACCORDIN	38.7 X 48.9 CM	ROBINSON
CHART OF THE DISCOVERIES & ROUTE OF HIS MAJESTY'S SHIPS HECLA & GRIPER	34.9 X 94.6 CM	MURRAY
CHART OF THE DISCOVERIES TO THE NORTH OF JAPAN INCLUDING JESO, STATEN	38.1 X 48.3 CM	LA PEROUSE
CHART OF THE HIGHLANDS & LOWLANDS OF THE WORLD/PRINCIPAL VOLCALOES & I	21.6 X 27.9 CM	BARNES & BURR
CHART OF THE ISLAND OF CORSICA FROM THE TOPOGRAPHIC SURVEY MADE BY ORD	31.8 X 22.2 CM	FADEN
CHART OF THE ISLAND OF NEWFOUNDLAND	38.7 X 31.8 CM	GOLD
CHART OF THE N.W. COAST OF AMERICA AND THE N.E. COAST OF ASIA, EXPLORE	43.2 X 69.9 CM	FADEN
CHART OF THE NEW ARCHIPELAGO, DISCOVER'D BY THE RUSSIANS, IN THE SEAS	15.2 X 20.3 CM	CONDER
CHART OF THE NORTH WEST COAST OF AMERICA EXPLORED BY THE BOUSSOLE & AS	38.7 X 49.5 CM	ROBINSON
CHART OF THE NORTHERN PASSAGE BETWEEN ASIA & AMERICA	50.0 X 59.0 CM	THOMSON
CHART OF THE NORTHERN PASSAGE BETWEEN ASIA & AMERICA. DRAWN & ENGRAVED	49.5 X 58.4 CM	THOMSON
CHART OF THE NORTHWEST COAST OF AMERICA AND THE NORTHEAST COAST OF ASI	39.7 X 67.9 CM	FADEN
CHART OF THE NORTHWEST COAST OF AMERICA. EXPLORED BY THE BOUSSOLE, AND	35.9 X 48.6 CM	ROBINSON
CHART OF THE SANDWICH ISLANDS	27.3 X 45.1 CM	COOK
CHART OF THE SUPPOSED COURSE OF THE FLORIDA STREAM. LONDON PUBLISH'D M	39.4 X 15.9 CM	GOLD
CHART OF THE WORLD ON MERCATOR'S PROJECTION	53.3 X 80.0 CM	LIZARS
CHART OF THE WORLD ON MERCATOR'S PROJECTION	30.5 X 45.1 CM	WYLD
CHART OF THE WORLD ON MERCATORS PROJECTION SHOWING THE DIRECTION OF TH	44.0 X 57.1 CM	JOHNSTON
CHART SHEWING THE TRACK OF THE FRENCH SHIPS THROUGH THE MOLUCCAS TO BA	22.9 X 26.7 CM	FORSTER
CHART VAN DEN INSELN TRINIDAD, TABAGO AND MARGARETHA...	21.9 X 40.3 CM	WEIMAR GEOGRAPHISCH...
CHART, CONTAINING THE COASTS OF CALIFORNIA, NEW ALBION, AND RUSSIAN DI	45.7 X 111.1 CM	SAYER & BENNETT
CHARTA COSMOGRAPHICA CUM VENTORUM PROPRIA NATURA ET OPERATIONE	21.6 X 29.2 CM	APIANUS
CHARTE MARITIMA CHE CONTENE LA COSTA SETENTRIONALE DE NEGROPONTE E LE	41.0 X 51.0 CM	CORONELLI
CHARTE UBER DIE XIII VEREINIGTE STAATEN VON NORD-AMERICA	44.5 X 57.2 CM	GUSSEFELD
CHARTE VON AMERIKA AUS DER ALTESTEN NOCH UNEDIRTEN WELTCHARTE DES DIEG	66.0 X 49.5 CM	GUSSEFELD
CHARTE VON DEN VEREINIGTEN STAATEN VON NORD-AMERICA MIT LOUISIANA	30.2 X 41.6 CM	ANON
CHARTE VON DEN VEREINIGTEN STAATEN VON NORD-AMERICA NEBST LOUISIANA	47.0 X 68.6 CM	GUSSEFELD
CHARTE VON NORD-AMERICA	41.3 X 29.8 CM	ANON
CHARTE VON NORD-AMERICA PRAG...1818	41.9 X 29.8 CM	WEIMAR GEOGRAPHISCH...
CHARTE VON WEST INDIEN NACH DER GROSSEN CHARTE DES B. EDWARDS...	43.5 X 61.6 CM	GUSSEFELD
CHEKIAN, E KIANGSI, PROVINCIE DELLA CHINA...	45.7 X 61.0 CM	CORONELLI
CHESHIRE	11.4 X 14.0 CM	SELLER
CHICAGO IN 1812	10.8 X 18.4 CM	BLANCHARD
CHILE AND PART OF THE VICEROYALTY OF LA PLATA	41.3 X 25.4 CM	CAREY
CHILI	27.9 X 35.6 CM	DE LAET
CHILI AND LA PLATA	20.0 X 25.0 CM	TALLIS
CHILI AND LA PLATA	34.3 X 26.7 CM	TALLIS
CHILI, LA PLATA & URUGUAY	38.1 X 31.8 CM	THOMAS, COWPERTHWAI...
CHILI, MAGELLANS-LAND	16.5 X 18.4 CM	MOLL
CHILI, PARAGUAY, THE ARGENTINE CONFEDERATION AND URUGUAY	25.4 X 20.3 CM	MITCHELL
CHINA	43.2 X 53.3 CM	FULLARTON
CHINA	49.5 X 61.0 CM	JOHNSTON
CHINA	50.2 X 61.0 CM	JOHNSTON
CHINA	39.4 X 44.5 CM	LIZARS
CHINA	17.1 X 19.1 CM	MOLL
CHINA	20.0 X 25.0 CM	TALLIS
CHINA A NEW DESCRIPTION...	14.0 X 13.3 CM	MORDEN
CHINA AND JAPAN	33.0 X 43.2 CM	TEESDALE
CHINA DIVIDED INTO ITS GREAT PROVINCES ACCORDING TO THE BEST AUTHORITI	35.2 X 35.9 CM	CAREY
CHINA REGIO ASIE	7.6 X 10.2 CM	ORTELIUS
CHINA VETERIBUS SINARUM REGIO NUNC INCOLIS TAME DICTA	40.6 X 49.5 CM	BLAEU
CHINA VETERIBUS SINARUM REGIO NUNC INCOLIS TAME DICTA	40.5 X 49.5 CM	JANSSON
CHORO-TOPOGRAPHISCHE KAART DER NOORDELYKE PROVINCIEN VAN HET KONIGRYK	87.0 X 96.0 CM	KRAYENHOFF
CHRISTINAE SKANTZ OCH STATEN CHRISTINAE HAMNS BELAGRING AF HOLLANDERNE	12.8 X 13.0 CM	CAMPANIUS HOLM
CHURFURSTENTHUM, UND MARCH BRANDEBURG	30.5 X 48.9 CM	SANSON
CINCINNATI	8.7 X 15.7 CM	ANON
CIRCUMJACENT THE POLE	25.0 X 25.0 CM	SDUK
CITY OF BALTIMORE	30.5 X 36.8 CM	COLTON
CITY OF BURLINGTON, CHITTENDEN CO.	30.5 X 38.1 CM	GRAY
CITY OF DES MOINES FROM SOUTH PARK HILL	32.1 X 40.6 CM	ANDREAS
CITY OF LOUISVILLE (VIEW)	15.2 X 22.9 CM	APPLETON
CITY OF LOUISVILLE. A.C. WARREN. E.P. BRANDARD. ENTERED ACCORDING TO A	13.3 X 22.9 CM	APPLETON

CITY OF MONTREAL 1830	20.3 X	23.5 CM	WALKER
CITY OF NEW YORK 1842	38.1 X	30.5 CM	MORSE
CITY OF PANAMA FROM THE SEA (VIEW)	12.1 X	17.8 CM	COLBURN
CITY OF PROVIDENCE. FROM PROSPECT HILL. A.C. WARREN, R. HINSHELWOOD...	22.9 X	13.3 CM	APPLETON
CITY OF WASHINGTON	40.6 X	33.0 CM	DESILVER
CITY OF WASHINGTON	29.2 X	36.8 CM	TANNER
CITY OF WASHINGTON	31.8 X	39.7 CM THOMAS, COWPERTHWAI...	
COAST OF NEW GRANADA CABO LA VELA TO CAYOS RATONES CHIEFLY FROM SPANIS	47.6 X	61.0 CM	ADMIRALTY
COELI STELLATI CHRISTIANI HAEMISPHAERIUM PRIUS	43.2 X	50.8 CM	CELLARIUS
COELISTALLATI CHRISTIANI HAEMISPHAERUM POSTERIUS	44.5 X	52.1 CM	CELLARIUS
COLOMBIA	41.7 X	51.6 CM	HALL
COLOMBIA	37.5 X	26.7 CM	SMITH
COLPHE ON L'ITALIA	8.5 X	12.0 CM	COTOVICUS
COLTON'S CONNECTICUT WITH PORTIONS OF NEW YORK & RHODE ISLAND	32.5 X	40.0 CM	COLTON
COLTON'S JAPAN NIPPON, KIUSIU, SIKOK...	33.0 X	40.6 CM	COLTON
COLTON'S MAP OF THE OIL DISTRICT OF PENNSYLVANIA, COMPRISING PART OF T	80.0 X	72.7 CM	COLTON
COLTON'S MEXICO	33.0 X	39.4 CM	COLTON
COLTON'S NEW MAP OF THE STATE OF TEXAS	40.6 X	62.2 CM	COLTON
COLTON'S TERRITORIES OF NEW MEXICO AND UTAH	31.8 X	39.4 CM	COLTON
COLTON'S TERRITORY OF ALASKA (RUSSIAN AMERICA) CEDED BY RUSSIA TO THE	33.0 X	43.2 CM	COLTON
COLTON'S TEXAS COMPILED FROM J. DE CORDOVA'S LARGE MAP	40.6 X	61.6 CM	COLTON
COLTON'S WASHINGTON AND OREGON	33.0 X	40.6 CM	COLTON
COLUMBIA	33.7 X	41.3 CM	DOWER
COMITATIS CANTABRIGIENSIS VERNACULE CAMBRIDGE SHIRE	41.3 X	51.4 CM	JANSSON
COMITATUM HANNONIAE ET NAMURCI DESCRIPTIO	38.0 X	50.0 CM	BLAEU
COMITATUS BERCHERIAE VULGO BARKSHYRE...	22.9 X	32.4 CM	HOLE
COMITATUS DORCESTRIA, SIVE DORSETTIA; VULGO ANGLICE DORSET SHIRE	38.1 X	50.2 CM	BLAEU
COMITATUS DORCESTRIA. VULGO ANGLICE DORSET SHIRE	37.5 X	49.5 CM	JANSSON
COMITATUS FLANDRIA. T'AMSTERDAM GEDRUCKT BIJ CLAES JANSS VISSCHER INDE	46.0 X	56.5 CM	VISSCHER
COMITATUS FLANDRIAE NOVA TABULA. PARIS, PIERRE MARIETTE, RUE ST-JACQUE	39.0 X	50.5 CM	MARIETTE
COMITATUS FLANDRIAE TABULA	47.0 X	56.0 CM	DE WIT
COMITATUS HANNONIAE	47.0 X	58.0 CM	VISSCHER
COMITATUS HANNONIAE TABULA...	46.4 X	58.4 CM	VISSCHER
COMITATUS MANSFELDIA	38.1 X	50.2 CM	HONDIUS
COMITATUS NAMURCI...	47.0 X	57.0 CM	VISSCHER
COMITATUS NAMURCI...GEDRUCKT T'AMSTERDAM BY FREDERICK DE WIT	47.0 X	54.0 CM	DE WIT
COMITATUS ZELANDIAE NOVA DESCRIPTIO ANNO 1645. N. VISSCHER EXCUDEBAT	47.0 X	56.0 CM	VISSCHER
COMITATUS ZELANDIAE...	47.0 X	57.0 CM	VISSCHER
COMITATUS ZUTPHANIA. 1617	37.0 X	48.0 CM	VAN DEN KEERE
COMITATUS ZUTPHANIA. AUTH. NICOLAO GEILKERCKIO.	40.0 X	52.5 CM	HONDIUS
COMMISSION EUROPEENE DE DELIMITATION DE LA BULGARIE. CROQUIS GENERALE	69.0 X	400.0 CM	GREAT BRITAIN
COMTE DE FLANDRES	48.0 X	53.0 CM	DE VAUGONDY
COMTE DE HAINAULT ET DE CAMBRESIS	48.0 X	53.0 CM	DE VAUGONDY
COMTE DE NAMUR	43.0 X	57.0 CM	JAILLOT
COMTE DE NAMUR	57.2 X	86.4 CM	MORTIER
CONGO, REGNUM CHRISTIAN IN AFRICA	10.2 X	12.7 CM	BERTIUS
CONNECTICUT	35.6 X	29.2 CM	BRADFORD
CONNECTICUT	22.9 X	29.2 CM	LUCAS
CONNECTICUT	15.2 X	18.4 CM	SCOTT
CONNECTICUT	29.2 X	35.6 CM	TANNER
CONNECTICUT/RHODE ISLAND	19.7 X	25.4 CM	BRADFORD
CONTINENT ARCTIQUE	14.5 X	11.0 CM	MALLET
COOCHETOPA PASS TO THE WASATCH MOUNTAINS	78.7 X	57.8 CM	U.S.
CORCYRA	18.5 X	12.0 CM	COTOVICUS
COREA AND JAPAN	49.5 X	63.5 CM	THOMSON
CORFU	10.5 X	14.5 CM	PORCACCHI
CORNWALL	19.1 X	24.1 CM	FULLARTON
CORNWALL	11.4 X	14.0 CM	SELLER
CORNWALL	38.7 X	47.6 CM	SPEED
CORNWALL	10.8 X	6.4 CM	WALLIS & REID
CORPORUM COELESTIUM MAGNITUDINES	41.9 X	50.8 CM	CELLARIUS
CORSICAE	8.5 X	12.5 CM	ORTELIUS
CORSICAE ANTIQUA DESCRIPTIO/SARDINAE ANTIQUA DESCRIPTIO	26.0 X	10.5 CM	MOLL

CORSICAE ISOLA, OLIM CYRNUS	34.0 X 45.0 CM	PTOLEMY (1596-1621 ...
CORSO DEL FIUME DELL AMAZONI, DESCRITTO DAL P. COSMOGRAFO CORONELLI, D	27.9 X 45.7 CM	CORONELLI
COSTES ET RIVIERES DE VIRGINIE, DE MARILAND ET DE NOUVELLE ANGLETERE	19.1 X 24.1 CM	MICHAULT
COTE DU NORD-OUEST DE L'AMERIQUE RECONNUE PAR LES FREGATES FRANCAISES	36.0 X 49.5 CM	ROBINSON
COTE NORD-OUEST DE L'AMERIQUE...1E PARTIE	76.4 X 61.5 CM	DEPOT DE LA MARINE
COTE NORD-OUEST DE L'AMERIQUE...2E PARTIE	75.5 X 61.0 CM	DEPOT DE LA MARINE
COTE NORD-OUEST DE L'AMERIQUE...3E PARTIE	76.8 X 61.3 CM	DEPOT DE LA MARINE
COTE NORD-OUEST DE L'AMERIQUE...IVE PARTIE	74.5 X 61.4 CM	DEPOT DE LA MARINE
COTE NORD-OUEST DE L'AMERIQUE...VE PARTIE	72.5 X 61.5 CM	DEPOT DE LA MARINE
COUNTY AND TOWNSHIP MAP OF OREGON AND WASHINGTON	50.8 X 36.8 CM	MITCHELL
COUNTY MAP OF ARKANSAS, MISSISSIPPI AND LOUISIANA	53.0 X 34.9 CM	MITCHELL
COUNTY MAP OF COLORADO, WYOMING, DAKOTA, MONTANA	49.5 X 36.8 CM	MITCHELL
COUNTY MAP OF FLORIDA	26.7 X 34.0 CM	MITCHELL
COUNTY MAP OF ILLINOIS	34.3 X 27.3 CM	MITCHELL
COUNTY MAP OF TEXAS	35.6 X 54.0 CM	MITCHELL
COUNTY MAP OF TEXAS	27.9 X 34.3 CM	MITCHELL
COUNTY MAP OF TEXAS	26.7 X 34.3 CM	MITCHELL
COUNTY MAP OF TEXAS	22.9 X 30.5 CM	MITCHELL
COUNTY MAP OF TEXAS	27.3 X 34.0 CM	MITCHELL
COUNTY MAP OF TEXAS	26.7 X 34.3 CM	MITCHELL
COUNTY MAP OF TEXAS	27.3 X 34.0 CM	MITCHELL
COUNTY MAP OF THE STATE OF TEXAS	35.6 X 53.3 CM	MITCHELL
COUNTY MAP OF THE STATE OF TEXAS	35.6 X 53.3 CM	MITCHELL
COUNTY MAP OF THE STATE OF TEXAS	35.6 X 53.3 CM	MITCHELL
COUNTY MAP OF THE STATE OF TEXAS	35.6 X 53.3 CM	MITCHELL
COUNTY MAP OF THE STATE OF TEXAS, SHOWING ALSO PORTIONS OF THE ADJOINI	35.6 X 54.6 CM	MITCHELL
COUNTY MAP OF THE STATE OF TEXAS, SHOWING ALSO PORTIONS OF THE ADJOINI	35.6 X 54.6 CM	MITCHELL
COUNTY MAP OF UTAH AND NEVADA	29.2 X 35.6 CM	MITCHELL
COURS DU FLEUVE SAINT LOUIS DEPUIS SES EMBOUCHURES JUSQUA LA RIVIERE D	21.6 X 35.6 CM	BELLIN
COURS DU MISSISSIPI ET LA LOUISIANE...	21.6 X 16.5 CM	DE VAUGONDY
COURSE OF THE RIVER MISSISSIPPI FROM THE BALISE TO FORT CHARTRES; TAKE	112.0 X 34.5 CM	SAYER
COURTRAY EN FLANDRE. N. COCHIN FECIT (VIEW)	13.5 X 50.0 CM	COCHIN
CRETA...	33.7 X 48.3 CM	ORTELIUS
CRUCHLEY'S NEW MAP OF THE WORLD ON MERCATOR'S PROJECTION SHOWING THE D	92.0 X 165.0 CM	CRUCHLEY
CUBA	29.2 X 43.8 CM	LUCAS
CUBA INSULA/HISPANIOLA INSULA/INS. JAMAICA/INS. S. JOANNIS/I.S. MARGAR	14.5 X 18.0 CM	JANSSON
CULIACANAE AMERICAE REGIONIS DESCRIPTIO/HISPANIOLA, CUBAE ALIARUMQUE	36.0 X 50.0 CM	ORTELIUS
CULIACANAE AMERICAE.../HISPANIOLAE, CUBAE ALIARUM QUE INSULARUM...	45.0 X 50.0 CM	ORTELIUS
CUM SUO APPARATU VOLUCRUM ET QUADRUPEDUM A MDCC	22.0 X 33.0 CM	SCHERER
CUMBERLAND	10.2 X 17.8 CM	CAPPER
CUMBERLAND	7.6 X 12.1 CM	LEIGH
CUMBERLAND	11.4 X 14.0 CM	SELLER
CUMBERLAND...	38.7 X 47.6 CM	SPEED
CUMBRIA SIVE CUMBERLANDIA...	28.6 X 31.8 CM	KIP
CURACAO	22.9 X 29.2 CM	LUCAS
CUSCO	17.8 X 10.2 CM	MALLET
CUSCO	26.7 X 35.6 CM	OGILBY
CUSCO (BIRD'S EYE PLAN)	8.9 X 14.0 CM	LASOR A VAREA
CUST VAN HOLLANT TUSZCHEN DE MAES ENDE TEXEL	43.0 X 53.0 CM	GOOS
CYPRI INSULAE DESCRIPTIO	17.0 X 13.0 CM	COTOVICUS
CYPRI INSULAE NOVA DESCRIPT	36.0 X 50.0 CM	ORTELIUS
CYPRUS	9.5 X 11.0 CM	MUNSTER
CYPRUS INS.	35.5 X 49.5 CM	MERCATOR
CYPRUS INS.	35.5 X 49.5 CM	MERCATOR
DALMACIA NOVA TABULA	12.7 X 17.1 CM	PTOLEMY (1548 VENICE)
DANIA POMERANIA DVC MECHLE BURGICUS 1699	23.0 X 33.0 CM	SCHERER
DANISH ISLANDS IN THE NORTH ATLANTIC OCEAN	46.4 X 30.5 CM	FULLARTON
DARBIESHIRE DESCRIBED 1666	38.7 X 47.6 CM	SPEED
DARIEN	22.9 X 30.5 CM	ARROWSMITH
DAS HEILIG JUDISCH LANDT...	26.7 X 33.0 CM	MUNSTER
DAS REICH MEXICO	19.1 X 26.0 CM	WERNER
DAUPHINE	57.2 X 86.4 CM	MORTIER
DAVENPORT, IOWA, AS SEEN FROM SOUTH WEST (VIEW)	33.3 X 41.3 CM	ANDREAS

238

DAWSON'S MAP OF THE DOMINION OF CANADA	55.8 X	82.5 CM	DAWSON BROS.
DE CUSTEN VAN NOORWEGEN EN FINMARCKEN VAN WTWEERCLIPPEN TO AEN DE NOOR	43.0 X	55.0 CM	JACOBSZ
DE FERO DE SCHELAND, ORKNAY ET HEBRIDES	20.0 X	14.5 CM	MALLET
DE GOLF VAN MEXICO, DE EILANDEN EN HET OMLEGGENDE LAND	48.0 X	58.0 CM	ELWE
DE HEERLICHEYT VAN OVER. YSSEL.	39.0 X	59.5 CM	GOOS
DE INSULIS BRITANNICIS, ALBIONE QUAE EST...	8.0 X	13.0 CM	MUNSTER
DE ISLANDIA INSULA...	26.5 X	19.0 CM	CAMOCIO
DE JERSEY ET DE GARNESEY	20.0 X	14.5 CM	MALLET
DE L'AMERIQUE EN GENERAL	31.8 X	55.2 CM	CLOUET
DE NOVIS INSULIS	10.2 X	14.6 CM	MUNSTER
DE SINU BAYE LA BAYE...	14.0 X	17.0 CM	DE BRY
DE STADT EN HAVEN VAN PORTO BELLO	17.8 X	25.4 CM	TIRION
DE STOEL DES OORLOGS IN ITALIEN...	59.1 X	73.7 CM	VISSCHER
DECIMA ASIAE TABULA	36.8 X	55.9 CM	PTOLEMY (1513-20 ST...
DECIMA EUROPE TABULA	38.7 X	54.0 CM	PTOLEMY (1482-86 ULM)
DEFINITIONS GEOGRAPHIE SIGNIFIE DESCRIPTION DE LA TERRE COROGRAPHIE	31.8 X	25.4 CM	CLOUET
DELAWARE	35.6 X	29.2 CM	BRADFORD
DELAWARE	25.4 X	20.3 CM	LEWIS & ARROWSMITH
DELAWARE	27.3 X	21.6 CM	LUCAS
DELAWARE	22.9 X	29.2 CM	LUCAS
DELAWARE	18.4 X	15.2 CM	SCOTT
DELAWARE AND MARY-LAND	27.9 X	31.8 CM	BURR
DELAWARE, FROM THE BEST AUTHORITIES	40.8 X	22.8 CM	CAREY
DELFLANDIA-SCHIELANDIA	40.0 X	50.0 CM	BLAEU
DELINEATIO NOVA ET VERA PARTIS AUSTRALIS NOVI MEXICI CUM AUSTRALI PART	23.5 X	35.0 CM	SCHERER
DELL' ISOLE DELLA BRETTAGNE, DELL' ALBIO	7.5 X	13.5 CM	MUNSTER
DENBIGH COMITATUS PARS OLIM ORDOVICUM	26.7 X	31.8 CM	KIP
DENBIGH COMITATUS PARS OLIM ORDOVICUM	26.7 X	31.8 CM	KIP
DENBIGH SHIRE	38.7 X	47.6 CM	SPEED
DENBIGHSHIRE	38.1 X	50.8 CM	SPEED
DENMARK	17.1 X	19.1 CM	MOLL
DENMARK	20.0 X	25.0 CM	TALLIS
DEPARTEMENT DE LA MEUSE INFERIEURE	55.0 X	62.0 CM	CHANLAIRE
DER GRUNDRISS VON DER STAT DESS HEYL DOMINICUS...LA VILLE DE SAN DOMIN	17.8 X	11.4 CM	MALLET
DER NOERDLICHE THEIL DES GROSSEN WELT MEERES NACH DEN NEUESTEN BESTIMM	50.2 X	66.7 CM	REICHARD
DER NOERDLICHE THEIL DES GROSSEN WELT MEERES...WEIMAR IM VERLAGE DES	50.2 X	66.7 CM	REICHARD
DERBYSHIRE	24.1 X	19.1 CM	BELL
DERBYSHIRE	11.4 X	14.0 CM	SELLER
DERBYSHIRE	11.4 X	15.2 CM	SELLER
DES POSTES DE L'ITALIE	57.2 X	86.4 CM	MORTIER
DESCRIPCION DE LAS INDIAS DEL NORTE	15.8 X	22.6 CM	DE BRY
DESCRIPCION DE LAS INDIAS DEL NORTE	16.5 X	22.5 CM	HERRERA
DESCRIPCION DEL AUDIENCIA DE LOS CHARCAS	15.2 X	16.5 CM	HERRERA
DESCRIPTIO DEL DESTRICTO DEL AUDIENCIA DEL ESPAGNOLA	19.5 X	21.6 CM	DE BRY
DESCRIPTIO GERMANIAE INFERIORIS	24.0 X	32.0 CM	DE BRUYN
DESCRIPTIO GERMANAIAE INFERIORIS	38.0 X	51.0 CM	ORTELIUS
DESCRIPTIO TOTIUS GALLIAE BELGICAE. PYRRHO LIGORIO NEAPOLIT. AUCTORE.	37.5 X	49.0 CM	TRAMEZINI
DESCRIPTION DE BERGEN-SUR-ZOOM...APUD JOANNEM JANSSONIUM	22.5 X	53.5 CM	HONDIUS
DESCRIPTION DE LA CITE, VALETTE	20.0 X	14.0 CM	RAIGNAULD
DESCRIPTION DU BRABANT. BRABANTIAE DUCATUS TABULA. ANNO 1629	39.0 X	50.0 CM	HONDIUS
DESCRIPTION DU PAYS DE HAINAULT. COMITATUM HANNONIAE ET NAMURCI DESCRI	39.0 X	50.0 CM	HONDIUS
DESCRITTIONE DELL L'ISOLA ET TERRA DI SANTA CROCE, OVERO MONDO NUOVO	10.2 X	14.0 CM	PORCACCHI
DESCRITTIONE DEL MAPPAMONDO	10.2 X	14.6 CM	PORCACCHI
DESIGNATIO ORBIS CHRISTIANI	15.2 X	19.1 CM	HONDIUS
DESTROIT DE MAGELLAN, TERRE ET ISLES MAGELLANICQUES	19.1 X	24.1 CM	SANSON
DEVONSHIRE	11.4 X	14.0 CM	SELLER
DEVONSHIRE	10.2 X	10.2 CM	SIMONS
DEVONSHIRE	10.8 X	6.4 CM	WALLIS & REID
DEVONSHIRE...	38.7 X	47.6 CM	SPEED
DIAGRAM OF ST. AUGUSTINE LAND DISTRICT SHEWING THE TOWNSHIPS IN WHICH	21.6 X	17.8 CM	U.S.
DIAGRAM OF THE STATE OF MISSOURI. OFFICE OF THE SURVEYOR GENERAL FOR T	45.1 X	55.2 CM	U.S.
DIAGRAM OF THE STATE OF MISSOURI; SAINT LOUIS	45.1 X	56.5 CM	CLARK
DIE ERST GENERAL TAFEL	31.0 X	36.0 CM	MUNSTER

DIE ERST GENERAL TAFEL DIE BESCHREIBUNG UND DEN CIRKEL DES GANTZEN ERD	31.1 X 36.2 CM	MUNSTER
DIE INSEL HISPANIOLA, ODER SAN DOMINGO	21.6 X 29.2 CM	BAUMGARTEN
DIE INSEL HISPANIOLA, VON DEN INDIANERN GENANT HAYTI	19.7 X 29.2 CM	BAUMGARTEN
DIE ZEE CUSTEN VAN BISCAIJEN...	33.0 X 50.8 CM	WAGHENAER
DINANT VILLE CELEBRE DE L'EVECHE DE LIEGE...	44.0 X 38.0 CM	LE CLERC
DIR NATUR IST SPARSAM CUSCO IN WEST INDIEN (VIEW)	10.2 X 14.0 CM	MEISNER
DISCORSE INTORNO ALLA CARTA DA NIVIGARE	11.4 X 14.6 CM	PORCACCHI
DISCORSO INTORNO ALLA CARTA DA NAVIGARE	10.2 X 14.0 CM	PORCACCHI
DISCORSO INTORNO ALLA CARTA DA NAVIGARE	10.2 X 14.0 CM	PORCACCHI
DISCOVERIES IN WESTERN AUSTRALIA FROM DOCUMENTS FURNISHED TO THE COLON	49.0 X 60.0 CM	ARROWSMITH
DISCOVERIES OF ADMIRAL DE FONTE & OTHERS, BY M. DE L'ISLE	19.7 X 25.4 CM	GENTLEMAN'S MAGAZINE
DISCOVERIES OF THE EXPEDITION UNDER THE COMMAND OF CAPTAIN FRANKLIN R.	69.0 X 128.0 CM	FRANKLIN
DISCRETIONE VERA DE L'ANTICA CITA DI GIERUSALEM (VIEW)	22.9 X 27.9 CM	CALLOT
DISIGNO DELL'ISOLA...	30.5 X 44.5 CM	LAFRERI SCHOOL
DISTRICT OF COLUMBIA	25.4 X 19.1 CM	BRADFORD
DITIO TRANSISULANA...	37.0 X 48.5 CM	VAN DEN KEERE
DIVERSA ORBIS TERRAE...IN PLANUM ORTHOGRAPHICA PROJECTIO	51.0 X 59.0 CM	SCHENK
DIVERSI GLOBI TERR-AQUEI	50.0 X 58.0 CM	SEUTTER
DIVERSI GLOBI TERR-AQUEI...	49.5 X 57.2 CM	SEUTTER
DIVERSI GLOBI TERR-AQUI STATIONE VARIANTE ET VISU INTERCEDENTE...	50.0 X 58.2 CM	SEUTTER
DIXMUNDE EN FLANDRE (VIEW)	14.5 X 50.0 CM	COCHIN
DOESBURG. VILLE TRES FORTE DU COMTE DE ZUTPHEN...	44.0 X 38.0 CM	LE CLERC
DOMINIA ANGLORUM IN AMERICA SEPTENTRIONALI	50.0 X 54.5 CM	HOMANN
DOMINIA ANGLORUM IN AMERICA SEPTENTRIONALI SPECIALIBUS MAPPIS LONDINI	55.2 X 49.5 CM	HOMANN
DOMINIA ANGLORUM IN AMERICA SEPTENTRIONALI...	50.8 X 55.9 CM	HOMANN
DOMINIA ANGLORUM IN AMERICA SEPTENTRIONALI...	50.0 X 55.0 CM	HOMANN
DOMINIA ANGLORUM IN PRAECIPUS INSULIS AMERICAE	48.9 X 55.2 CM	HOMANN
DOMINICA	22.9 X 29.2 CM	LUCAS
DOMINII FRISIAE TABULA...	48.0 X 57.0 CM	VISSCHER
DOMINION OF CANADA	23.0 X 30.0 CM	BARTHOLOMEW
DOMINION OF CANADA	22.0 X 27.0 CM	MACKENZIE
DOMINION OF CANADA (EAST CENTRAL SHEET) BY KEITH JOHNSTON F.R.S.E.	32.5 X 42.5 CM	JOHNSTON
DOMINION OF CANADA (EASTERN SHEET) NEW BRUNSWICK, NOVA SCOTIA, PRINCE	32.5 X 42.5 CM	JOHNSTON
DOMINION OF CANADA (EASTERN SHEET) SHOWING NEW BRUNSWICK, NOVA SCOTIA,	42.5 X 55.5 CM	JOHNSTON
DOMINION OF CANADA (WEST CENTRAL SHEET) BY T.B. JOHNSTON	32.5 X 42.5 CM	JOHNSTON
DOMINION OF CANADA (WESTERN SHEET)	43.8 X 57.2 CM	JOHNSTON
DOMINION OF CANADA (WESTERN SHEET)	44.0 X 57.2 CM	JOHNSTON
DOMINION OF CANADA (WESTERN SHEET) BY KEITH JOHNSTON. F.R.S.E.	42.5 X 55.5 CM	JOHNSTON
DOMINION OF CANADA SHOWING NEW BRUNSWICK & NOVA SCOTIA, WITH PRINCE ED	44.1 X 57.0 CM	JOHNSTON
DOMINION OF CANADA. DISTRICTS OF ALGOMA, PARRY SOUND, ALSO PART NIPISS	40.6 X 61.0 CM	BELDIN
DOMINION OF CANADA//DOMINION OF CANADA (EASTERN PROVINCES) & NEWFOUNDL	20.0 X 28.0 CM	BARTHOLOMEW
DORSETSHIRE	14.0 X 8.9 CM	CARY
DORSETSHIRE	11.4 X 14.0 CM	SELLER
DORSETSHYRE...	38.7 X 47.6 CM	SPEED
DRENTIA	40.0 X 50.0 CM	BLAEU
DT DE MAGELLAN	10.2 X 15.2 CM	MALLET
DU LAC DE LEMAN (VIEW)	15.0 X 16.0 CM	MUNSTER
DUCATUM LIVONIA ET CURLANDIA...	48.5 X 58.0 CM	OTTENS
DUCATUS EBORACENSIS PARS ORIENTALIS; THE EASTRIDING OF YORKESHIRE	38.1 X 48.3 CM	BLAEU
DUCATUS EBORACENSIS. ANGLICE YORKSHIRE	38.1 X 49.5 CM	VALK & SCHENK
DUCATUS GELDRIAE ET COMITATUS ZUTPHANIAE TABULA	46.5 X 55.5 CM	DE WIT
DUCATUS GELDRIAE ET ZUTPHANIAE	47.0 X 57.0 CM	VISSCHER
DUCATUS LUTZENBURGENSIS NOVA ACCURATA DESCRIPTIO	39.5 X 50.0 CM	JANSSON
DUCATUS LUTZENBURGI NOVISSIMA ET ACCURATISSIMA DELINEATIO	46.0 X 56.0 CM	VISSCHER
DUCATUS LUTZENBURGICI TABULA NUPERRIME IN LUCEM EDITA	46.5 X 55.5 CM	DE WIT
DUCATUS LUTZENBURGICUS. CUM PRIVILEG.	12.0 X 17.4 CM	GOOS
DUCATUS UPLANDIA	37.5 X 49.5 CM	BLAEU
DUCHE ET LEGATION DE FERRARE	57.2 X 86.4 CM	MORTIER
DUODECIMA ASIE TABULA	29.2 X 39.4 CM	PTOLEMY (1482-86 ULM)
DURHAM	10.2 X 17.8 CM	CAPPER
DURHAM	7.6 X 12.1 CM	LEIGH
EAST CANADA	20.0 X 25.0 CM	TALLIS
EAST CANADA & NEW BRUNSWICK	25.4 X 33.0 CM	TALLIS

EAST CANADA AND NEW BRUNSWICK	34.3 X	26.7 CM	TALLIS
EAST CANADA AND NEW BRUNSWICK	26.7 X	34.3 CM	TALLIS
EAST CANADA AND NEW BRUNSWICK	25.6 X	33.5 CM	TALLIS
EAST CANADA AND NEW BRUNSWICK	34.3 X	26.7 CM	TALLIS
EAST CANADA OR LOWER CANADA AND NEW BRUNSWICK	32.0 X	39.0 CM	COLTON
EAST CANADA, AND NEW BRUNSWICK	26.0 X	32.0 CM	TALLIS
EAST INDIES	17.1 X	19.1 CM	MOLL
EASTERN END OF DEER ISLAND...	42.9 X	44.6 CM	U.S. COAST SURVEY
EASTERN HEMISPHERE	35.6 X	29.2 CM	BRADFORD
EASTERN HEMISPHERE	20.0 X	25.0 CM	TALLIS
EASTERN HEMISPHERE/WESTERN HEMISPHERE	26.0 X	32.0 CM	TALLIS
EASTERN STATES WITH PART OF CANADA	19.4 X	24.1 CM	CAREY & WARNER
EASTERN UNITED STATES	26.0 X	37.0 CM	BLACK
ECLIPSE HARBOUR LABRADOR	38.1 X	31.8 CM	U.S. COAST SURVEY
ECONOMIC MAP OF COLORADO	64.8 X	89.5 CM	HAYDEN
EDENBURGUM SCOTIAE METROPOLIS (VIEW)	34.3 X	45.7 CM	BRAUN & HOGENBERG
EGENTLICKE BESCHRYVINGE DES ISELSTROOMS, SAMPT ITTELICKE OMLIGGENDE ST	13.5 X	35.5 CM	KREFFELDT
EGYPT	20.0 X	25.0 CM	TALLIS
EIGENTLICHE UND WOLFORMIERTE CARTE DARINNEN ZUFINDEN EIN THEIL DES GEL	20.0 X	45.0 CM	ANON
EMISFERO TERRESTRE SETTENTRIONALE TAGLIATO SU L'EQUATORE	32.0 X	41.0 CM	ZATTA
EMPIRE OF JAPAN	22.9 X	40.6 CM	ARROWSMITH
EMPIRE OF JAPAN	39.4 X	31.8 CM	BALDWIN & CRADOCK
ENGELLANDT, MIT DEM ANSTOSSENDEN REICH SCHOTTLANDT, SO VORZEITEN ALBIO	30.5 X	35.6 CM	MUNSTER
ENGLAND & WALES	14.0 X	8.9 CM	CARY
ENGLAND AND WALES	20.0 X	25.0 CM	TALLIS
ENGLAND AND WALES...	34.3 X	26.0 CM	TALLIS
ENSDA. DE CARUPANO	17.8 X	23.5 CM	FIDALGO
ENSENA. DE UNARE	17.9 X	23.8 CM	FIDALGO
ENTRANCE TO CAPE FEAR RIVER-NORTH CAROLINA	78.0 X	65.5 CM	U.S. COAST SURVEY
ENVIRONS DE PARIS	48.0 X	53.0 CM	DE VAUGONDY
ENVIRONS OF ST. LOUIS/LEAD REGION/ENVIRONS OF LEXINGTON/ENVIRONS OF NA	15.2 X	13.4 CM	ANON
EPISCOPATUS DUNELMENSIS VULGO THE BISHOPRIC OF DURHAM BY ROBT. MORDEN	36.8 X	41.9 CM	MORDEN
EPISCOPATUS LEODIENSIS PROVINCIA, AUCTORE IOHANNE A SCHILDE	34.0 X	24.0 CM	DE JODE
EQUISSE DES OPERATIONS DU SIEGE DE CHARLESTON CAPITALE DE LA CAROLINA	36.8 X	29.2 CM	RAMSAY
EREFALL-DIGHEETZ FORTE	12.8 X	12.5 CM	CAMPANIUS HOLM
EROBERUNG DER VESTUNG PROVANCON ZU PORTO CALVO IN BRASILIA...	27.0 X	35.0 CM	MERIAN
ERYN, HIBERNIAE BRITANNICAE INSULAE, NOVA DESCRIPTIO. IRLANDT	35.6 X	48.3 CM	ORTELIUS
ESQUISSE DU MUSKINGHUM/ESQUISSE DES RIVIERES MUSKINGHUM ET GRAND CASTO	24.1 X	52.1 CM	CREVECOEUR
ESSEX	24.1 X	19.1 CM	BELL
ESSEX	17.8 X	26.7 CM	ELLIS
ESSEX	19.1 X	30.5 CM	MOLL
ESSEX	21.0 X	26.7 CM	MOULE
ESSEX	22.2 X	34.9 CM	PIGOT & CO.
ESSEX	11.4 X	14.0 CM	SELLER
ESSEX	10.8 X	6.4 CM	WALLIS & REID
ESSEX	23.5 X	19.1 CM	WILKES
ESSEX DEVIDED INTO HUNDREDS...	38.7 X	47.6 CM	SPEED
ESTANCIA DE SAN JORGE URUGUAY	21.6 X	24.8 CM	WELLER
ESTAT ET SEIGNEURIE DE L'EVESCHE DE LYEGE	44.0 X	57.0 CM	JAILLOT
ESTATS DE L'EGLISE ET DE TOSCANE	57.2 X	86.4 CM	MORTIER
ESTATS DE LA COURONNE DE SUEDE	16.5 X	22.0 CM	CHIQUET
ESTATS DE POLOGNE	57.2 X	86.4 CM	MORTIER
ETATS DE LA COURONNE D'ARAGON	48.0 X	53.0 CM	DE VAUGONDY
ETATS DU GRAND-SEIGNEUR EN ASIE...	48.0 X	55.5 CM	DE VAUGONDY
ETATS UNIS	19.1 X	24.1 CM	MONIN & FREMIN
ETATS UNIS ET GRANDES ANTILLES	29.8 X	22.2 CM	CHAMOUIN
ETATS-UNIS D'AMERIQUE	41.9 X	52.7 CM	BUCHON
ETATS-UNIS DE L'AMERIQUE SEPTENTRIONALE AVEC LES ISLES ROYALE, DE TERR	47.4 X	62.7 CM	DELAMARCHE
ETATS-UNIS ET N. BRETAGNE	21.6 X	28.6 CM	ANTOINE
ETHNOGRAPHISCHE KARTE VON NORDAMERIKA	37.1 X	39.7 CM	PERTHES
EUR. X TAB.	35.0 X	46.0 CM	PTOLEMY (1578-1730 ...
EUROP...	38.7 X	47.6 CM	SPEED
EUROPA EXACTISSIME DESCRITPA	38.0 X	51.0 CM	HONDIUS

EUROPA, AD MAGNAE EUROPAE GERARDI MERCATORIS IMITATIONEM, RUMOLDI MERC	38.5 X 47.0 CM	MERCATOR
EUROPAE	34.0 X 46.0 CM	ORTELIUS
EUROPAE	34.3 X 46.4 CM	ORTELIUS
EUROPE	40.6 X 48.3 CM	CAREY
EUROPE	16.5 X 18.4 CM	MOLL
EUROPE	13.5 X 17.5 CM PTOLEMY (1596-1621 ...
EUROPE	20.0 X 25.0 CM	TALLIS
EUROPE, FROM THE BEST AUTHORITIES	23.5 X 22.9 CM	TEGG
EXACTISSIMA FLANDRIAE DESCRIPTIO...AD CORDATUM LECTOREM N. STOPIUS. VE	49.8 X 41.6 CM	STOPIUS
EXQUISITA & MAGNO ALIQUOT MENSIUM PERICULO LUSTRATA ET IAM RETECTA FRE	35.6 X 46.4 CM	HONDIUS
EXQUISITA & MAGNO ALIQUOT MENSIUM PERICULO LUSTRATA ET IAM RETECTA FRE	34.9 X 45.7 CM	MERCATOR
EXTREMA AMERICAE VERSUS BOREAM, UBI TERRA NOVA NOVA FRANCIA, ADJACENTI	44.7 X 56.6 CM	BLAEU
F DELFINUM	14.2 X 20.9 CM	DE BRY
FACIES POLI ARCTICI ADIACENTIUMQUE EI REGIONUM EX RECENTISSIMIS ITINER	31.8 X 35.6 CM	WEIGEL
FALKLAND ISLANDS AND PATAGONIA	34.9 X 25.4 CM	TALLIS
FALKLAND ISLANDS AND PATAGONIA	34.3 X 26.7 CM	TALLIS
FALKLAND ISLANDS AND PATAGONIA	20.0 X 25.0 CM	TALLIS
FALKLAND ISLES	14.0 X 23.0 CM	HADFIELD
FAMAGUSTA	15.0 X 23.0 CM	BRAUN & HOGENBERG
FERNERE LAUF DES FLUSSES ST. LAURENTZ VON QUEBEC BIS AN SEE ONTRAIO	18.4 X 28.6 CM	BELLIN
FEZZAE ET MAROCCHI REGNA AFRICAE CELEBERRIMA, DESCRIBEBAT ABRAH. ORTEL	38.7 X 50.2 CM	BLAEU
FISHING VILLAGE CARTHAGENA (VIEW)	12.7 X 22.9 CM	GOLD
FLANDERS OF SPANISH NETHERLANDS	17.1 X 19.1 CM	MOLL
FLANDERS OR THE SPANISH NETHERLANDS WITH YE ARCHBISHOPRICK OF CAMBRESI	17.8 X 25.4 CM	MOLL
FLANDRE ESPAGNOLE ET FLANDRE HOLLANDOISE	43.5 X 56.5 CM	JAILLOT
FLANDRIA	24.0 X 32.0 CM	DE BRUYN
FLANDRIA BOREALIS...	23.0 X 33.5 CM	HOGENBERG
FLANDRIA ET ZEELANDIA COMITATUS	41.5 X 53.0 CM	BLAEU
FLANDRIA GERARDUS MERCATOR RUPELMANDANUS DESCRIBEBAT	38.0 X 50.0 CM	ORTELIUS
FLANDRIA GERARDUS MERCATOR RUPELMANDANUS DESCRIBEBAT	38.0 X 50.0 CM	ORTELIUS
FLANDRIA PETRUS KAERIUS CAELAVIT	23.0 X 31.0 CM	VAN DEN KEERE
FLANDRIA, BARBANTIA E HOLANDA NOVA	12.7 X 17.1 CM PTOLEMY (1548 VENICE)
FLANDRIA, BRABANTIA ET HOLANDA NUOVA	20.0 X 25.0 CM PTOLEMY (1561-99 VE...
FLANDRIAE COMITATUS...	47.0 X 56.0 CM	VISSCHER
FLANDRIAE PARTES DUAE	41.5 X 52.0 CM	BLAEU
FLANDRIAE TEUTONICAE PARS ORIENTALIOR	38.0 X 50.0 CM	BLAEU
FLINT...	38.7 X 47.6 CM	SPEED
FLINTSHIRE	11.4 X 14.0 CM	SELLER
FLINTSHIRE	11.4 X 15.2 CM	SELLER
FLORIDA	35.6 X 29.2 CM	BRADFORD
FLORIDA CALLED BY YE FRENCH LOUISIANA	20.3 X 27.9 CM	MOLL
FLORIDA, ET REGIONES VICINAE	27.9 X 35.6 CM	DE LAET
FLORIDAE AMERICAE PROVINCIAE	37.0 X 45.5 CM	DE BRY
FONDEADERO DE LA GUAYRA	17.0 X 23.4 CM	FIDALGO
FORT CHAMBLY	12.7 X 20.3 CM	FADEN
FORT D.A. RUSSELL, W.T. GENERAL PLAN	20.8 X 16.1 CM	U.S.
FORT GEORGE, ASTORIA (VIEW)	12.1 X 17.1 CM	COLBURN
FORT GIBSON, INDIAN TERRITORY, GENERAL PLAN OF POST 1874	18.2 X 20.4 CM	U.S.
FORT LARAMIE, WYOMING TERRITORY. GENERAL PLAN OF POST, 1874	16.5 X 21.7 CM	U.S.
FORT LEAVENWORTH, KANSAS	16.3 X 20.8 CM	U.S.
FORT MCKAVETT, TEXAS. GENERAL PLAN OF POST 1874	17.1 X 21.8 CM	U.S.
FORT RANDALL, DAKOTA TERRITORY 1873	21.4 X 17.2 CM	U.S.
FORT SILL, INDIAN TERRITORY-GENERAL PLAN OF THE POST 1874	18.0 X 21.4 CM	U.S.
FORT SMITH TO THE RIO GRANDE	55.2 X 128.3 CM	U.S.
FORT SMITH-ARKANSAS (VIEW)	14.8 X 21.9 CM	STEVENS
FORT UTAH, VALLEY OF THE GREAT SALT LAKE (VIEW)	12.7 X 19.1 CM	ACKERMANN
FORT VANCOUVER W.T. (VIEW)	15.2 X 22.8 CM	STEVENS
FORUM IULII, ET HISTRIA	13.5 X 17.5 CM PTOLEMY (1596-1621 ...
FRANCE	16.5 X 18.4 CM	MOLL
FRANCE	20.0 X 25.0 CM	TALLIS
FRANCE PICARDIE CHAMPAIGNE CUM REGIONIBUS ADIACENTIBUS	35.6 X 40.0 CM	MERCATOR
FRANCE, DIVIDED INTO CIRCLES AND DEPARTMENTS	33.3 X 37.5 CM	CAREY
FRANCE...	38.7 X 47.6 CM	SPEED

FRANCIAE COMITATUS	10.2 X 13.3 CM	BERTIUS
FRIBURG IM BRISGEW (VIEW)	19.5 X 36.0 CM	MUNSTER
FRISE OCCIDENTALE	43.2 X 58.4 CM	MORTIER
FRISE ORIENTALE	20.0 X 17.0 CM	MUNSTER
FRISIA OCCIDENTALIS AUCTORIBUS ADRIANO METIO ET GERARDO FREITAG	39.0 X 50.0 CM	HONDIUS
FRISIA OCCIDENTALIS, 1579...	36.0 X 49.0 CM	ORTELIUS
FRISIA OCCIENTALIS	40.0 X 50.0 CM	BLAEU
FRISIAE OCCIDENTALIS TYPUS	24.0 X 32.0 CM	DE BRUYN
FRISIAE OCCIDENTALIS TYPUS	23.0 X 31.0 CM	VAN DEN KEERE
FRISLANDA SCOPERTA DA NICOLE ZENO PATRITIO VENETO CREDUTA FAULOSA...	24.8 X 30.5 CM	CORONELLI
FROM THE NORTHERN BOUNDARY OF CALIFORNIA TO THE COLUMBIA RIVER FROM EX	69.9 X 58.4 CM	YOUNG
FUGURA NATURALIS AMERICAE AUSTRALIS...	22.4 X 34.9 CM	SCHERER
FURNES (VIEW)	15.0 X 50.0 CM	COCHIN
GALLAPAGOS ISLANDS, DESCRIBED BY AMBROSE COWLEY IN 1684/THE ISLAND SAN	13.6 X 12.2 CM	ANON
GALLIA NOVA TABULA	13.3 X 17.1 CM	PTOLEMY (1548 VENICE)
GALLIAE BELGICHAE ROMAE MDLXIIIII FERANDO BERTELI EXCUDEBAT	34.9 X 47.4 CM	BERTELLI
GALLIAE REGNI POTENTISS. NOVA DESCRIPTIO, IOANNE IOLIVETO AUCTORE	35.0 X 50.5 CM	ORTELIUS
GALLIAE REGNUM	13.5 X 17.5 CM	PTOLEMY (1596-1621 ...
GALLOFLANDRIA...AUCTORE MARTINO DOUE GALLO-FLANDRO	38.0 X 50.5 CM	BLAEU
GALVESTON ENTRANCE, TEXAS	34.3 X 43.2 CM	U.S. COAST SURVEY
GALVESTON IN TEXAS (VIEW)	10.2 X 15.2 CM	HILDBURG INSTITUT
GAND, CAPITALE DU COMTE DE FLANDRES & LA PLUS GRANDE VILLE DES PAIS BA	39.0 X 33.5 CM	LE CLERC
GAND. LE RESA ALLI ALLEATI DELLA CITTA DI GANDA, CAPITALE DELLA FLANDR	46.0 X 38.0 CM	WOLFF
GANDE (VIEW)	43.0 X 33.5 CM	LE CLERC
GEBEIT MISSOURI. GEBEIT OREGAN	19.7 X 26.7 CM	WERNER
GEGEND UM DIE MEXICANISCHE SEE/DIE PROVINZEN MEXICO, PANUCO, UND TLASC	24.1 X 36.2 CM	BAUMGARTEN
GELDRIA	36.5 X 48.5 CM	DE JODE
GELDRIA ET TRANSISULANA	37.0 X 49.0 CM	VAN DEN KEERE
GELDRIA ET ZUTPHANIA	40.0 X 50.0 CM	BLAEU
GELRIA ET ZUTFANIA	24.0 X 32.0 CM	DE BRUYN
GELRIA ET ZUTFANIA	23.0 X 31.0 CM	VAN DEN KEERE
GELRIAE, CLIVIAE...	37.0 X 50.0 CM	ORTELIUS
GENERAL CHART OF DELAWARE AND CHESAPEAKE BAYS AND THE SEA COAST FROM C	78.7 X 63.3 CM	U.S. COAST SURVEY
GENERAL CHART SHEWING THE TRACK OF H.M. SHIPS FURY AND HECLA, ON A VOY	25.4 X 59.7 CM	PARRY
GENERAL CHART SHEWING THE TRACK OF HMS HECLA & GRIPER, FROM THE ORKNEY	25.4 X 61.0 CM	PARRY
GENERAL CHART...TO SHEW THE TRACK...TO THE GULPH OF PEKIN IN CHINA 179	55.9 X 92.7 CM	BARROW
GENERAL MAP OF BRITISH NORTH AMERICA, SHOWING THE ROUTE OF LORD MILTON	18.9 X 27.3 CM	MILTON & CHEADLE
GENERAL MAP OF EXPLANATIONS AND SURVEYS IN CALIFORNIA	60.3 X 44.5 CM	U.S.
GENERAL MAP OF EXPLORATION & SURVEYS IN CALIFORNIA UNDER DIRECTION OF	184.2 X 61.0 CM	WILLIAMSON
GENERAL MAP SHOWING THE COUNTRIES EXPLORED & SURVEYED BY THE U.S. & ME	38.1 X 48.6 CM	COLTON
GENERAL PLAN OF FORT BUFORD, DAKOTA TERRITORY 1874	17.5 X 19.0 CM	U.S.
GENERAL VIEW OF INDEPENDENCE	12.7 X 20.3 CM	WEST SHORE
GENERAL VIEW OF THE CITY OF MONTREAL, CANADA	36.0 X 48.0 CM	HARPER'S WEEKLY
GENERALKARTE VON NORDAMERICA SAMT DEN WESTINDISCHEN INSELN	99.1 X 114.3 CM	SCHRAEMBL
GENEVE. GENSS (VIEW)	23.0 X 34.0 CM	MERIAN
GEOGNOSTISCHE KARTE DER VEREINIGTEN STAATEN, CANADA &C.	38.1 X 49.5 CM	LYELL
GEOGRAPHIAE SACRAE TABULA	19.7 X 27.9 CM	SANSON
GEOGRAPHICAL, HISTORICAL, AND STATISTICAL MAP OF CONNECTICUT	24.1 X 29.2 CM	CAREY & LEA
GEOGRAPHICAL, STATISTICAL & HISTORICAL MAP OF HISPANIOLA OR ST. DOMING	43.2 X 53.3 CM	CAREY & LEA
GEOGRAPHICAL, STATISTICAL, AND HISTORICAL MAP OF ALABAMA	30.5 X 22.9 CM	CAREY & LEA
GEOGRAPHICAL, STATISTICAL, AND HISTORICAL MAP OF ALABAMA	30.5 X 22.9 CM	CAREY & LEA
GEOGRAPHICAL, STATISTICAL, AND HISTORICAL MAP OF FLORIDA	30.5 X 24.1 CM	CAREY & LEA
GEOGRAPHICAL, STATISTICAL, AND HISTORICAL MAP OF FLORIDA	29.2 X 24.1 CM	CAREY & LEA
GEOGRAPHICAL, STATISTICAL, AND HISTORICAL MAP OF GEORGIA	29.2 X 22.9 CM	CAREY & LEA
GEOGRAPHICAL, STATISTICAL, AND HISTORICAL MAP OF ILLINOIS	30.5 X 21.6 CM	CAREY & LEA
GEOGRAPHICAL, STATISTICAL, AND HISTORICAL MAP OF INDIANA	27.9 X 21.6 CM	CAREY & LEA
GEOGRAPHICAL, STATISTICAL, AND HISTORICAL MAP OF KENTUCKY	28.6 X 45.7 CM	CAREY & LEA
GEOGRAPHICAL, STATISTICAL, AND HISTORICAL MAP OF LOUISIANA	29.2 X 33.0 CM	CAREY & LEA
GEOGRAPHICAL, STATISTICAL, AND HISTORICAL MAP OF LOUISIANA	29.2 X 33.7 CM	CAREY & LEA
GEOGRAPHICAL, STATISTICAL, AND HISTORICAL MAP OF MEXICO	38.1 X 36.8 CM	CAREY & LEA
GEOGRAPHICAL, STATISTICAL, AND HISTORICAL MAP OF MICHIGAN TERRITORY	36.8 X 26.7 CM	CAREY & LEA
GEOGRAPHICAL, STATISTICAL, AND HISTORICAL MAP OF NEW HAMPSHIRE	30.5 X 22.9 CM	CAREY & LEA
GEOGRAPHICAL, STATISTICAL, AND HISTORICAL MAP OF NEW HAMPSHIRE	30.5 X 22.9 CM	CAREY & LEA

GEOGRAPHICAL, STATISTICAL, AND HISTORICAL MAP OF NEW YORK	30.5 X	45.7 CM	CAREY & LEA
GEOGRAPHICAL, STATISTICAL, AND HISTORICAL MAP OF NORTH CAROLINA	27.9 X	48.3 CM	CAREY & LEA
GEOGRAPHICAL, STATISTICAL, AND HISTORICAL MAP OF NORTH CAROLINA	27.9 X	47.0 CM	CAREY & LEA
GEOGRAPHICAL, STATISTICAL, AND HISTORICAL MAP OF PENNSYLVANIA	29.2 X	44.5 CM	CAREY & LEA
GEOGRAPHICAL, STATISTICAL, AND HISTORICAL MAP OF TENNESSEE	29.2 X	47.0 CM	CAREY & LEA
GEOGRAPHICAL, STATISTICAL, AND HISTORICAL MAP OF VERMONT	30.5 X	24.1 CM	CAREY & LEA
GEOGRAPHICAL, STATISTICAL, AND HISTORICAL MAP OF VIRGINIA	41.9 X	52.1 CM	CAREY & LEA
GEOLOGICAL CHART OF PART OF IOWA, WISCONSIN, AND ILLINOIS	58.4 X	45.7 CM	OWEN
GEOLOGICAL MAP OF LONG & STATEN ISLANDS WITH THE ENVIRONS OF NEW YORK,	11.4 X	64.8 CM	MATHER
GEOLOGICAL MAP OF MISSISSIPPI	40.6 X	33.0 CM	COLTON
GEOLOGICAL MAP OF PARTS OF MINNESOTA AND WISCONSIN, DESIGNED TO SHOW P	25.4 X	19.1 CM	NORWOOD
GEOLOGICAL MAP OF THE PROVINCE OF NOVA SCOTIA AND PART OF NEW BRUNSWIC	32.4 X	45.7 CM	CANADA
GEOLOGICAL MAP OF THE U.S.	26.7 X	45.7 CM	COWPERTHWAIT
GEOLOGICAL MAP OF THE U.S. & TERRITORIES	40.6 X	58.4 CM	ASHER & ADAMS
GEOLOGICAL RECONNOISSANCES IN CALIFORNIA	29.2 X	38.1 CM	TYSON
GEORGETOWN AND THE CITY OF WASHINGTON	31.8 X	39.4 CM	JOHNSON & WARD
GEORGETOWN AND THE CITY OF WASHINGTON CAPITAL OF UNITED STATES	30.5 X	40.6 CM	COLTON
GEORGIA	35.6 X	29.2 CM	BRADFORD
GEORGIA	15.9 X	18.4 CM	SCOTT
GEORGIA AND ALABAMA	12.8 X	16.3 CM	ANON
GEORGIA AND ALABAMA	15.9 X	21.0 CM	BURGESS
GEORGIA, FLORIDA & ALABAMA	27.3 X	21.6 CM	BARNES & BURR
GERMANIA	36.2 X	50.2 CM	ORTELIUS
GERMANIA	13.5 X	17.5 CM PTOLEMY (1596-1621 ...	
GERMANIA ANTIQUA	48.0 X	53.0 CM	DE VAUGONDY
GERMANIA NOVA TABULA MDXXXXII	12.7 X	17.1 CM PTOLEMY (1548 VENICE)	
GERMANIA VULGO TEUTSCHLANDT	49.0 X	56.5 CM	BLAEU
GERMANIAE INFERIORIS, GALLIAE BELGICAE DICTAE CONTINENTIS...PER MATHIA	30.5 X	48.5 CM	DE JODE
GERMANY	19.1 X	19.1 CM	MOLL
GERMANY	20.0 X	25.0 CM	TALLIS
GEZIGT VAN'T SPAANSCHE VELK PENSACOLA...IN DE GOLF VAN MEXIKO...VAN DE	16.5 X	25.4 CM	TIRION
GIAPPONE	20.3 X	21.6 CM	BORDIGA
GIBRALTAR, MALTA AND IONIAN ISLES	20.0 X	25.0 CM	TALLIS
GLAMORGAN SHYRE	38.7 X	47.6 CM	SPEED
GLAMORGANSHIRE	7.6 X	12.1 CM	LEIGH
GLAMORGANSHIRE	11.4 X	15.2 CM	SELLER
GLAMORGANSHIRE	10.8 X	6.4 CM	WALLIS & REID
GLOCESTERSHIRE CONTRIVED INTO THRE SEVERALL HUNDREDS & THOSE AGAIN INT	38.1 X	49.5 CM	SPEED
GLOCHESTERSHIRE...	38.7 X	47.6 CM	SPEED
GLOUCESTERSHIRE	23.5 X	19.1 CM	WILKES
GLOUCESTERSHIRE CONTRIVED INTO THIRTY THRE SEVERALL HUNDREDS...THE CIT	38.1 X	51.4 CM	SPEED
GOLFE OF CANADA	25.0 X	34.5 CM	PURCHAS
GOUVERNEMENT GENERALE DE CHAMPAGNE	57.2 X	86.4 CM	MORTIER
GRAECIA	40.6 X	52.1 CM	BLAEU
GRAECIA	36.0 X	47.5 CM	MERCATOR
GRAECIA VETUS	48.0 X	53.0 CM	DE VAUGONDY
GRAECIAE UNIVERSAE SECUNDUM HODIERNUM SITUM NEOTERICA DESCRIPTIO	36.2 X	51.4 CM	ORTELIUS
GRAECIAE UNIVERSAE SECUNDUM HODIERNUM SITUM NEOTERICA DESCRIPTIO	36.2 X	50.8 CM	ORTELIUS
GRAEFSCHAPPE VAN HOLLANDT	26.0 X	36.5 CM	VAN DEN KEERE
GRAETIA NOVA TABULA	12.7 X	17.1 CM PTOLEMY (1548 VENICE)	
GRAETIA NUOVA TAVOLA	17.8 X	24.1 CM PTOLEMY (1561-99 VE...	
GRAND RIVER HARBOR, OHIO	25.4 X	43.8 CM	U.S.
GRAND TARTARIE	57.2 X	86.4 CM	MORTIER
GRANDE OCEANO OUVERO QUINTA PARTE DE MONDE	20.0 X	25.0 CM	BELLIN
GRAY'S ATLAS MAP OF TEXAS	41.9 X	63.5 CM	GRAY
GRAY'S GEOLOGICAL MAP OF THE U.S. BY CHARLES H. HITCHCOCK	38.1 X	64.8 CM	GRAY
GRAY'S MAP OF CALIFORNIA	68.6 X	40.6 CM	GRAY
GREAT FALLS OF MISSOURI	17.7 X	10.0 CM	ANON
GREAT SALT LAKE TO THE HUMBOLDT MOUNTAINS	52.1 X	45.1 CM	U.S.
GREAT TARTARY/THE ISLE OF JAPON	17.1 X	18.4 CM	MOLL
GREECE	38.7 X	47.6 CM	SPEED
GREECE	39.5 X	51.0 CM	SPEED
GREECE	8.0 X	12.5 CM	SPEED

GREECE	20.0 X 25.0 CM	TALLIS
GRENADA	22.9 X 29.2 CM	LUCAS
GRENADA DIVIDED INTO ITS PARISHES	46.5 X 61.5 CM	JEFFERYS
GROENINGHEN. PORTRAICT DE LA VILLE DE GROENINGHEN AVECQ LE CHASTEAU OU	20.0 X 27.5 CM	HUBERTI
GROENLAND	9.5 X 13.0 CM	BERTIUS
GROENLANDE	15.0 X 10.5 CM	MALLET
GROLLA OBSESSA ET EXPUGNATA...	38.0 X 50.0 CM	BLAEU
GRONDVLAKTE VAN NIEUW ORLEANS DE HOOFDSTAD VAN LOUISIANA/DE UITLOOP VA	34.0 X 45.5 CM	TIRION
GRONINGA DOMINIUM	40.0 X 50.0 CM	BLAEU
GRONINGA DOMINIUM AUCTORE BARTHOLDO WICHERINGE. EXCUDEBAT IOANNES IANS	38.0 X 50.0 CM	HONDIUS
GRONINGA DOMINIUM. ANNO 1621	37.0 X 48.0 CM	VISSCHER
GRONINGAE ET OMLANDIAE DOMINIUM...	47.0 X 57.0 CM	VISSCHER
GRUNDRISS VON DER STADT BOSTON	16.5 X 16.5 CM	BELLIN
GUADALOUPE	22.9 X 29.2 CM	LUCAS
GUAIANA	27.9 X 35.6 CM	DE LAET
GUELDRE ESPAGNOL	43.2 X 58.4 CM	MORTIER
GUELDRE ESPAGNOLE OU QUARTIER DE RUREMONDE...	43.0 X 56.0 CM	JAILLOT
GUIANA SIVE AMAZONUM REGIO	37.5 X 49.5 CM	BLAEU
GUIANA SIVE AMAZONUM REGIO	37.5 X 49.0 CM	HONDIUS
GUIDE THROUGH OHIO, MICHIGAN, INDIANA, ILLINOIS, MISSOURI, WISCONSIN,	50.8 X 68.6 CM	COLTON
GUIENNE ET GASCOIGNE	48.3 X 59.7 CM	MORTIER
GUILELMI ET JOANNIS BLAEU THEATRUM ORBIS TERRARUM SIVE ATLAS NOVUS PAR	38.1 X 24.1 CM	BLAEU
GUINEA	38.1 X 50.8 CM	BLAEU
GUINEE	14.0 X 10.2 CM	MALLET
GULF OF AMAPALLA ALIAS FONSECA	16.5 X 21.2 CM	MOLL
GUYANE PORTUGAISE ET PARTIE DU COURS DE LA RIVIERE DES AMAZONES	21.6 X 45.7 CM	BELLIN
HABES HIC NOVAM & ACCURATISSIMAM DESCRIPTIONEM TRACTUS ILLIUS FLANDRIA	37.0 X 52.0 CM	MERCATOR
HAEMISPHAERIUM STELLATUM BOREALE ANTIQUUM	43.2 X 50.8 CM	CELLARIUS
HAEMISPHAERIUM STELLATUM BOREALE CUM SUBIECTO HAEMISPHAERIO TERRESTRI	42.5 X 50.2 CM	CELLARIUS
HAERLEM. THANTWERPEN BY PHILLIPS GALLE, 1573	28.0 X 34.0 CM	GALLE
HALIFAX	20.1 X 14.7 CM	BAEDEKER
HAMPSHIRE	17.8 X 11.4 CM	OWEN & BOWEN
HAMPSHIRE	11.4 X 14.0 CM	SELLER
HANNONIA	23.5 X 31.0 CM	VAN DEN KEERE
HANNONIA NAMURCUM COMITATUS. PAR GERARDUM MERCATOREM	35.0 X 46.0 CM	MERCATOR
HANNONIAE COMITATUS	24.0 X 32.0 CM	DE BRUYN
HANTSHIRE...	38.7 X 47.6 CM	SPEED
HARBOR OF DUBUQUE	35.6 X 27.9 CM	U.S.
HARBOR OF MANITOWOC WISCONSIN	31.1 X 33.0 CM	U.S.
HARPERS FERRY FROM THE BLUE RIDGE (VIEW)	16.5 X 18.4 CM	BARTLETT
HAUTE ETHIOPE...ET LE ZANGUEBAR	40.0 X 50.5 CM	SANSON
HAVRE DE GRACE	17.8 X 23.5 CM	ANON
HAYTE OR ST. DOMINGO	30.2 X 47.6 CM	LUCAS
HEBRIDES INSULAE	8.0 X 12.5 CM	SPEED
HEIRSOLYMA CLARISSIMA TOTIUS ORIENTIS CIVITAS INDAEQUE METROPOLIS (VIE	34.0 X 49.0 CM	BRAUN & HOGENBERG
HELVETIA	7.6 X 10.2 CM	ORTELIUS
HELVETIAE DESCRIPTIO AEGIDIO TSCHUDI AUCT.	34.5 X 45.5 CM	ORTELIUS
HELVETIAE SEU SUICIAE...CHOROGRAPHIA VERA ET ELEGANS	39.0 X 52.0 CM	DE JODE
HEMISPHAERIUM ORBIS ANTIQUI, CUMZONIS, CIRCULIS, ET SITU POPULORUM DIV	41.9 X 50.8 CM	CELLARIUS
HEMISPHERE OCCIDENTAL DRESSEE EN 1720 POUR L'USAGE DU ROY SUR LES OBSE	50.8 X 50.8 CM	DE L'ISLE
HEMISPHERE SEPTENTRIONAL POUR VOIR PLUS DISTINCTEMENT LES TERRES ARCTI	46.0 X 46.5 CM	COVENS & MORTIER
HEMISPHERE SEPTENTRIONALE POUR VOIR PLUS DISTINETEMENT LES TERRES ARCT	45.7 X 45.7 CM	DE L'ISLE
HEMISPHERE SEPTENTRIONALE and HEMISPHERE MERIDIONALE	45.7 X 60.3 CM	OTTENS
HEMISPHERIU AB AEQUINOCTIALI LINEA AD CIRCULU POLI ARTICI/HEMISPHERIU	33.0 X 52.1 CM	DE JODE
HEREFORD SHIRE	8.3 X 12.1 CM	VAN DEN KEERE
HEREFORDSHIRE	11.4 X 14.0 CM	SELLER
HEREFORDSHIRE	10.8 X 6.4 CM	WALLIS & REID
HEREFORDSHIRE...	38.7 X 47.6 CM	SPEED
HERGEST'S ISLANDS DISCOVERED BY THE DAEDALUS STORE SHIP, LIEUT. HERGES	24.1 X 19.1 CM	EDWARDS
HERTFORDSHIRE	24.1 X 19.1 CM	BELL
HERTFORDSHIRE	10.2 X 17.8 CM	CAPPER
HERTFORDSHIRE	21.0 X 26.7 CM	MOULE
HERTFORDSHIRE	17.8 X 11.4 CM	OWEN & BOWEN

245

HERTFORDSHIRE	11.4 X 14.0 CM	SELLER
HERTFORDSHIRE BY ROBT. MORDEN	36.2 X 44.5 CM	MORDEN
HET NOORDER DEEL VAN T'GRAEFSCHAP VLEANDREN...T'ANTWERPEN, GEDRUCKT BI	40.0 X 48.0 CM	VERBIEST
HET WESTINDISCH EILAND MARTENIQUE...	30.5 X 36.8 CM	TIRION
HIBERNIA	7.6 X 10.2 CM	ORTELIUS
HIBERNIA REGNUM VULGO IRELAND	38.5 X 50.0 CM	BLAEU
HIBERNIA REGNUM VULGO IRELAND	38.1 X 50.2 CM	BLAEU
HIBERNIA...	33.7 X 47.0 CM	JANSSON
HIBERNIAE BRITANNICAE INSULAE, NOVA DESCRIPTIO...	49.0 X 34.5 CM	ORTELIUS
HIBERNIAE REGNUM	58.4 X 48.3 CM	HOMANN
HIBERNIAE...	35.6 X 48.3 CM	ORTELIUS
HIERSOLYMA URBS SANCTA (VIEW)	33.0 X 42.0 CM	BRAUN & HOGENBERG
HISPALENSIS CONVENTUS DELINEATIO...	34.3 X 45.7 CM	ORTELIUS
HISPANIA ANTIQUA	48.0 X 53.0 CM	DE VAUGONDY
HISPANIA NOVA	14.0 X 18.6 CM	HONDIUS
HISPANIA NOVA TABULA	13.3 X 17.1 CM	PTOLEMY (1548 VENICE)
HISPANIAE ET LUSITANIAE COMPLURA PIA LOCA IMMACULATAE VIRGINAE DICATA.	28.5 X 36.0 CM	SCHERER
HISPANIAE NOVA DESCRIPTIO, DE INTEGRO MULTIS INCOLIS, SECUNDUM HYDROGR	38.1 X 50.8 CM	HONDIUS
HISPANIAE NOVAE NOVA DESCRIPTIO	13.5 X 19.0 CM	JANSSON
HISPANIAE NOVAE SIVE MAGNAE RECENS ET VERA DESCRIPTIO	35.0 X 50.5 CM	ORTELIUS
HISPANIAE NOVAE SIVE MAGNAE...	33.7 X 44.5 CM	DE BRY
HISPANIOLA	10.2 X 13.3 CM	LANGENES
HOLLAND	20.0 X 25.0 CM	TALLIS
HOLLAND OR THE SEVEN UNITED PROVINCES, AND THE NETHERLANDS	44.5 X 37.5 CM	CAREY
HOLLANDIA COMITATUS	40.0 X 50.0 CM	BLAEU
HOLLANDIAE BATAVOR VETERIS INSULAE ET LOCORUM ADIACENTIUM EXACTA DESCR	37.5 X 52.0 CM	TRAMEZINI
HOLLANDIAE COMITATUS	75.0 X 56.0 CM	VISSCHER
HOLLANDIAE COMITATUS. HOLLANDIA...DELINEATIO. AMSTELODAMI PETRUS KAERI	37.5 X 51.5 CM	VAN DEN KEERE
HOLLANDIAE PART SEPTENTRIONALE	38.1 X 49.5 CM	BLAEU
HOLLANDIAE TYPUS	24.0 X 32.0 CM	DE BRUYN
HOLLANDIAE...NOVA DESCRIPTIO...	35.0 X 48.7 CM	ORTELIUS
HOLLANDIAE...NOVA DESCRIPTIO...	35.0 X 48.7 CM	ORTELIUS
HOLY ILAND/GARNSEY/FARNE/IARSEY	40.0 X 51.0 CM	VALK & SCHENK
HOLY ISLAND STAPLES AND BARWICK...DEDICATED TO CAPT. WILL DAVIES VICE	44.5 X 55.9 CM	COLLINS
HOLY ISLAND/GARNSEY/FARNE/JARSEY	38.7 X 47.6 CM	SPEED
HOLY ISLAND/GARNSEY/FARNE/JARSEY	8.0 X 12.5 CM	SPEED
HONDIUS HIS MAP OF CYPRUS	14.0 X 18.5 CM	MERCATOR
HONDIUS, HIS MAP OF ICELAND	13.0 X 18.5 CM	MERCATOR
HOOFSTAD EN HAVEN VAN'T EILAND PORTO RICO IN DE WESTINDIEN	17.8 X 26.0 CM	TIRION
HOTCHKISS' GEOLOGICAL MAP OF VIRGINIA AND WEST VIRGINIA. THE GEOLOGY B	33.0 X 50.8 CM	ROGERS
HULST (VIEW)	20.0 X 28.0 CM	HUBERTI
HUMBOLDT MOUNTAINS TO THE MUD LAKES	52.1 X 45.1 CM	U.S.
HUNGARIAE	50.8 X 57.2 CM	SCHENK
HUNGARIAE DESCRIPTIO. WOLFGANGO LAZIO AUCT...	34.9 X 49.5 CM	ORTELIUS
HUNGARY	17.8 X 19.1 CM	MOLL
HUNGARY	20.0 X 25.0 CM	TALLIS
HUNTINGDON SHIRE, DIVIDED INTO ITS HUNDREDS	34.3 X 24.1 CM	BOWEN
HUNTINGDONENSIS COMITATUS HUNTINGTON SHIRE	39.4 X 49.5 CM	JANSSON
HUNTINGDONSHIRE	39.4 X 31.8 CM	WALKER
HUNTINGTON BOTH SHIRE AND SHIRE TOWNE WITH THE ANCIENT CITIE ELY DESCR	38.1 X 49.5 CM	SPEED
HUNTINGTON...	38.7 X 47.6 CM	SPEED
HUUM. HOY. (VIEW)	19.0 X 36.0 CM	MERIAN
HUY AU PAYS DE LIEGE (VIEW)	20.0 X 27.5 CM	HUBERTI
HUY. VILLE DU DIOCESE DE LIEGE SUR LA MEUSE...	44.0 X 37.0 CM	LE CLERC
HYDROGRAPHICAL CHART OF THE WORLD ON WRIGHT OR MERCATOR'S PROJECTION W	44.5 X 50.8 CM	THOMSON
HYPOTHESIS PTOLEMAICA SIVE COMMUNIS PLANETARUM MOTUS PER ECCENTRICOS,	43.2 X 50.8 CM	CELLARIUS
I DE ST HELENE (VIEW OF PORT)	20.0 X 14.5 CM	MALLET
I. D HISPANIOLA ET P. RICO	20.0 X 14.5 CM	MALLET
I. DE GUAVANHI OU DE ST. SALVADOR	20.0 X 14.5 CM	MALLET
I. LADRONES	14.0 X 18.4 CM	DE BRY
I.O. WIGHT	19.1 X 30.5 CM	MOLL
IAMAICA	11.4 X 14.6 CM	LASOR A VAREA
IAPONIA INSULA.	7.6 X 10.2 CM	ORTELIUS

IE. D'HORN	20.0 X 14.5 CM	MALLET
IEHOVA	8.5 X 12.3 CM	LINSCHOTEN
IERUSALEM	20.3 X 33.0 CM	MERIAN
IERUSALEM ET SUBURBIA EIUS...	51.4 X 74.9 CM	VAN ADRICHEM
IL CANADA, LE COLONIE INGLESI, CON LA LOUIGIANA E FLORIDA	31.0 X 41.0 CM	ZATTA
IL CUSCHO CITTA PRINCIPALE DELLA PROVINCIA DEL PERU	26.7 X 36.8 CM	RAMUSIO
IL DUCATO DI MEKLENBURGO CHE E PARTE DELLA BASSO SASSONIA...IL TUTTO P	43.2 X 57.8 CM	ROSSI
IL MARYLAND IL JERSEY MERIDIONALE LA DELAWARE, E LA PARTE ORIENTALE DE	33.0 X 43.2 CM	ZATTA
IL PAESE DE SELVAGGI OUTAGAMIANI MASCOUTENSI ILLINESI...	33.0 X 42.5 CM	ZATTA
IL PAESE DE' SELVAGGI OUTAGAMIANI, MASCOUTENSI, ILLINESI, E PARTE DELL	31.8 X 41.9 CM	ZATTA
IL PAESE DE' SELVAGGI OUTAUACESI, E KILISTINESI INTORNO AL LAGO SUPERI	31.8 X 41.9 CM	ZATTA
IL PAESE DE' SELVAGGI OUTAUCE SI, E KILISTINE SI INTORNO AL LAGO SUPER	33.0 X 43.8 CM	ZATTA
IL REGNI DI SUEZIA, DANIMARCA E NORVEGA	30.5 X 40.6 CM	ZATTA
IL VERO DISEGNO DEL MIRABILE ASSEDIO DELLA FORTISSIMA CITA DE ANVERSA	37.5 X 50.0 CM	LAFRERI SCHOOL
ILLINOIS	35.6 X 29.2 CM	BRADFORD
ILLINOIS	36.2 X 28.9 CM	BRADFORD
ILLINOIS	40.6 X 33.0 CM	COLTON
ILLINOIS	22.9 X 29.2 CM	LUCAS
ILLINOIS	30.2 X 22.2 CM	LUCAS
ILLINOIS	35.6 X 27.9 CM	MORSE
ILLINOIS	45.7 X 27.9 CM	SWINSTON
ILLINOIS & MISSOURI	25.1 X 19.1 CM	MORSE
ILLINOIS AND MISSOURI	15.6 X 12.6 CM	ANON
IMAGO TOTIUS ORBIS TERRAQUEI CUM SUO APPARATU AB AUCTORE NATURAE IN SU	23.0 X 33.0 CM	SCHERER
IMPERII SINARUM NOVA DESCRIPTIO. AUCTORE JOH VAN LOON	47.0 X 52.7 CM	VAN LOON
INDEPENDENT TARTARY	25.4 X 33.0 CM	TALLIS
INDEPENDENT TARTARY	20.0 X 25.0 CM	TALLIS
INDIA EXTREMA	25.4 X 34.3 CM	MUNSTER
INDIA OR THE MOGUL'S EMPIRE	17.1 X 19.1 CM	MOLL
INDIA ORIENTALIS	14.5 X 18.5 CM	MERCATOR
INDIA ORIENTALIS	13.5 X 17.5 CM	PTOLEMY (1596-1621 ...
INDIA QUAE ORIENTALIS DICTUR, ET INSULAE ADIACENTES...	38.0 X 49.0 CM	HONDIUS
INDIA QUAE ORIENTALIS DICTUR...	39.0 X 46.0 CM	VALK & SCHENK
INDIA TERCERA NOVA TABULA	12.7 X 16.5 CM	PTOLEMY (1548 VENICE)
INDIAE ORIENTALIS	34.0 X 48.0 CM	ORTELIUS
INDIAE ORIENTALIS INSULARUMQUE ADIACENTIUM TYPUS	35.0 X 50.0 CM	ORTELIUS
INDIAN TERRITORY	61.0 X 81.3 CM	U.S.
INDIAN TERRITORY, DRAWN FROM MAPS & SURVEYS FURNISHED BY THE ENGINEER	31.8 X 39.4 CM	COLTON
INDIANA	35.6 X 29.2 CM	BRADFORD
INDIANA	35.6 X 28.6 CM	BRADFORD
INDIANA	40.0 X 33.0 CM	COLTON
INDIANA	27.9 X 21.6 CM	FINLEY
INDIANA	27.9 X 22.2 CM	LUCAS
INDIANA	22.9 X 29.2 CM	LUCAS
INDIARUM ORIENTALIUM OCCIDENTALIUMQUE DESCRIPTIO, DEDICATA PET. MAFFEI	25.4 X 49.5 CM	MAFFEIUS
INDIE OCCIDENTALI	18.0 X 30.5 CM	BELLIN
INFERIORIS GERMANIAE PROVINCIARUM NOVA DESCRIPTIO	41.0 X 53.5 CM	ANON
INGHILTERRA	36.8 X 34.3 CM	ALBRIZZI
INGILTERRA ET SCOTIA	21.6 X 17.8 CM	CAMOCIO
INS KLEINE GEBRACHTE KARTE VON DEM MITTNAEGTIGHEN MEERE	20.2 X 35.5 CM	BELLIN
INS. CEILAN QUAE INCOLIS TENARISIN DICITUR	34.3 X 49.5 CM	HONDIUS
INS. CEILAN QUAE INCOLIS TENARISIN DICITUR	34.5 X 49.5 CM	JANSSON
INSULA BORNEO ET OCCIDENTALIS PART CELIBIS CUM ADJACENTIBUS INSULIS	41.9 X 52.1 CM	JANSSON
INSULA CANDIA EJUSQUE FORTIFICATIO	46.0 X 55.5 CM	DE WIT
INSULA CANDIA...	44.5 X 55.2 CM	DE WIT
INSULA GADITANA...	38.1 X 50.2 CM	BLAEU
INSULA JAMAICAE	11.4 X 12.7 CM	MORDEN
INSULA MALTA...CUM URBIBUS ET FORTALITIIS	44.5 X 54.0 CM	DE WIT
INSULA PUNA	15.9 X 12.1 CM	HULSIUS
INSULAE ALBION ET HIBERNIA	38.0 X 45.0 CM	BLAEU
INSULAE AMERICANAE	38.0 X 52.5 CM	BLAEU
INSULAE AMERICANAE	46.5 X 56.0 CM	VISSCHER
INSULAE AMERICANAE	46.0 X 56.0 CM	VISSCHER

INSULAE AMERICANAE IN OCEANO SEPTENTRIONALI CUM TERRIS ADIACENTIBUS	37.5 X 51.4 CM	VALK & SCHENK
INSULAE AMERICANAE IN OCEANO SEPTENTRIONALI...	38.1 X 52.7 CM	BLAEU
INSULAE AMERICANAE...	45.7 X 55.2 CM	VISSCHER
INSULAE ANTILLAE FRANCICAE SUPERIORIS CUM VICINIS INSULIS...	33.0 X 35.6 CM	WEIGEL
INSULAE ANTILLES	6.5 X 8.0 CM	MULLER
INSULAE BALEARIDES ET PYTIUSAE	28.0 X 37.0 CM	MERIAN
INSULAE BALEARIDES...	38.1 X 49.5 CM	JANSSON
INSULAE BALY...	14.0 X 17.0 CM	DE BRY
INSULAE CANARIAE ALIAS FORTUNATAE DICTAE	38.5 X 50.0 CM	BLAEU
INSULAE INDAE ORIENTALIS PRAECIPUAE...	34.3 X 47.0 CM	MERCATOR
INSULAE INDIAE ORIENTALIS PRAECIPUA	34.0 X 48.0 CM	HONDIUS
INSULAE INDICAE CUM TERRIS CIRCUMVICINIS	23.0 X 35.0 CM	SCHERER
INSULAE JAMAICAE	49.5 X 59.0 CM	SEUTTER
INSULAE MALDIVES	6.5 X 7.5 CM	MULLER
INSULAE MELITAE VULGO MALTE NOVA ET ACCURATA DESCRIPTIO	41.0 X 50.5 CM	JANSSON
INSULAE MOLOCCAE	6.5 X 7.5 CM	MULLER
INSULAE SARDINIAE NOVA ET ACCURATA DESCRIPTIO	41.0 X 51.0 CM	JANSSON
INSULAE SONDAE	6.5 X 7.5 CM	MULLER
INSULARUM ALIQUOT MARIS MEDITERRANEI	33.7 X 48.9 CM	ORTELIUS
INSULARUM ARCHIPELAGI SEPTENTRIONALIS SEU MARIS AEGAEJ ACCURATA DELINE	47.6 X 57.2 CM	DE WIT
INSULARUM BRITANNICARUM ACURATA DELINEATIO	39.0 X 50.5 CM	JANSSON
IOWA	40.6 X 55.9 CM	BRADLEY
IOWA	32.4 X 40.6 CM	COLTON
IOWA AND WISCONSIN	35.6 X 28.6 CM	BRADFORD
IRELAND	18.4 X 17.8 CM	MOLL
IRELAND	44.5 X 53.3 CM	SELLER
IRELAND	20.0 X 25.0 CM	TALLIS
IRELAND, DIVIDED INTO THE PROVINCES AND COUNTIES	24.1 X 14.0 CM	BICKHAM
IRLANDA	38.1 X 32.4 CM	ALBRIZZI
IRLANDA	12.4 X 14.0 CM	PORCACCHI
IS. COCOS	20.0 X 14.5 CM	MALLET
IS. DE CUBA ET DE JAMAICA	20.0 X 14.5 CM	MALLET
IS. DE MAN D'ANGLESEY	20.0 X 14.5 CM	MALLET
IS. DI CAPRI	22.0 X 28.0 CM	CORONELLI
ISCHIA	8.5 X 12.5 CM	ORTELIUS
ISLAND OF BARBADOS/ISLAND OF ST. LUCIA/ISLAND OF ST. VINCENT/CHART OF	24.8 X 19.1 CM	LONDON MAGAZINE
ISLAND OF JAMAICA	14.0 X 22.9 CM	FULLARTON
ISLAND OF TRINIDAD/BRITISH GUYANA	46.0 X 31.0 CM	FULLARTON
ISLANDIA	9.0 X 13.0 CM	BERTIUS
ISLANDIA	33.7 X 48.9 CM	ORTELIUS
ISLANDIA	34.0 X 49.0 CM	ORTELIUS
ISLANDIA	10.5 X 14.5 CM	PORCACCHI
ISLANDS IN THE ATLANTIC	49.5 X 59.7 CM	PHILIP
ISLANDS IN THE ATLANTIC	20.0 X 25.0 CM	TALLIS
ISLANDS IN THE ATLANTIC. ENGRAVED BY J. & C. WALKER. PUBLISHED BY BALD	39.7 X 33.0 CM	SDUK
ISLANDS IN THE INDIAN OCEAN	20.0 X 25.0 CM	TALLIS
ISLANDS OF THE ATLANTIC	35.0 X 24.5 CM	TALLIS
ISLE D IRLANDE	20.0 X 14.5 CM	MALLET
ISLE DE CAYENNE	20.0 X 14.5 CM	MALLET
ISLE DE CAYENNE (VIEW)	15.2 X 10.2 CM	MALLET
ISLE DE CIPRE	19.0 X 26.5 CM	RAIGNAULD
ISLE DE MALTHE	37.5 X 52.5 CM	DE FER
ISLE DE ST. DOMINGUE	20.3 X 27.9 CM	LE ROUGE
ISLE DE STE. HELENE (VIEW OF WHOLE ISLAND)	20.0 X 14.5 CM	MALLET
ISLE DE TERRE NEUVE	20.0 X 14.5 CM	MALLET
ISLE DE WIGH	20.0 X 14.5 CM	MALLET
ISLE DE ZOCOTORA	20.0 X 14.5 CM	MALLET
ISLE ET ROYAUME DE CANDIE	16.5 X 22.0 CM	CHIQUET
ISLE OF GUERNSEY	11.4 X 14.0 CM	SELLER
ISLE OF JERSEY	11.4 X 14.0 CM	SELLER
ISLE OF MAN	11.4 X 14.0 CM	SELLER
ISLE OF SABLE	10.2 X 17.8 CM	BLUNT
ISLE OF ST. DOMINGO OR HISPANIOLA	45.7 X 74.3 CM	FADEN

ISLE OF WIGHT	7.6 X	12.1 CM	LEIGH
ISLE OF WIGHT	11.4 X	14.0 CM	SELLER
ISLES ACORES	20.0 X	14.5 CM	MALLET
ISLES BRITANNIQUE...	23.0 X	18.0 CM	SANSON
ISLES CANARIES	20.0 X	14.5 CM	MALLET
ISLES CARIBES	20.0 X	14.5 CM	MALLET
ISLES DE MADAGASCAR DITE DE ST. LAURENS	20.0 X	14.5 CM	MALLET
ISLES DE MADERA	20.0 X	14.5 CM	MALLET
ISLES DE SALOMON	20.0 X	14.5 CM	MALLE
ISLES DES CANARIES ET DU CAP VERD	20.0 X	14.5 CM	MALLE
ISLES DES LARRON	15.2 X	9.5 CM	MALLE
ISLES DU CAP-VERD	10.2 X	15.2 CM	MALLET
ISLES DU CAP-VERD	20.0 X	14.5 CM	MALLET
ISLES DU JAPON	15.2 X	10.2 CM	MALLET
ISLES LUCAYES	20.0 X	14.5 CM	MALLET
ISOLA CUBA NOVA	16.0 X	25.0 CM	PTOLEMY (1561-99 VE...
ISOLA CUBA NOVA	19.7 X	24.8 CM	PTOLEMY (1561-99 VE...
ISOLA D'ISLANDA	22.9 X	30.5 CM	CORONELLI
ISOLA D'ISLANDIA	30.0 X	38.0 CM	CORONELLI
ISOLA DE IAMES O'GIAMACA POSSEDUTTA DAL RE BRITANNICO DIVISA IN PARROC	22.2 X	29.2 CM	CORONELLI
ISOLA DE JAMES, O GIAMAICA, PESSEDUTTA DAL RE BRITANNICO DIUISA IN PAR	47.0 X	30.5 CM	CORONELLI
ISOLA DEL GIAPONE E PENISOLA DI COREA	46.0 X	61.0 CM	CORONELLI
ISOLA DEL GIAPONE E PENISOLA DI COREA	46.0 X	61.0 CM	CORONELLI
ISOLA DI CAPO BRETON DE CANADA	12.0 X	16.4 CM	CORONELLI
ISOLA DI CENGO CYTHERA	15.5 X	21.0 CM	LASOR A VAREA
ISOLA E CITTA DI CARTAGENA NELL. AMERICA	12.1 X	21.7 CM	CORONELLI
ISOLE ANTILI, LA CUBA, E LA SPAGNUOLA, DESCRITTE, E DEDICATE...	42.7 X	25.7 CM	CORONELLI
ISOLE ANTILLE, CUBA, ANTIGUA, BARBADOS...	33.0 X	42.0 CM	ZATTA
ISOLE ANTILLI LA CUBA, LA SPAGNUOLA, DESCRITTO E DEDICATE DAL PADRE MA	26.0 X	43.2 CM	CORONELLI
ISOLE DELL'INDIA...	45.0 X	60.0 CM	CANTELLI DA VIGNOLA
ISOLE FILIPPINE	40.5 X	31.0 CM	ZATTA
ISOLE NELLE PIAGGE DELLA NUOVA SPAGNA DE CARTAGENA	38.1 X	29.2 CM	CORONELLI
ISTHMUS OF PANAMA	20.0 X	25.0 CM	TALLIS
ISTHMUS OF PANAMA	26.0 X	33.0 CM	TALLIS
ITALIA	13.5 X	17.5 CM	PTOLEMY (1596-1621 ...
ITALIA NOVA TAVOLA	12.7 X	17.1 CM	PTOLEMY (1548 VENICE)
ITALIA SECUNDUM DOMINATUS DESCRIPTA PER IOANNEM BAPTISTAM NICOLOSIUM.	40.0 X	45.7 CM	NICOLOSI
ITALIA...	38.7 X	47.6 CM	SPEED
ITALY	18.4 X	18.4 CM	MOLL
ITALY AND SARDINIA FROM THE BEST AUTHORITIES	36.5 X	38.1 CM	CAREY
ITALY WITH THE ADDITION OF THE SOUTHERN PARTS OF GERMANY AS FAR AS PET	63.5 X	111.1 CM	FADEN
ITALY, WITH ITS POLITICAL DIVISIONS, TOWNS, RIVERS	45.7 X	96.5 CM	DAVIES
ITINERA VARIA AUCTORIS	25.4 X	20.3 CM	SELIGMANN
IUDEA SEU TERRA SANCTA	57.2 X	86.4 CM	MORTIER
IUDEA, SEU TERRA SANCTA QUAE HEBRAEORUM SIVE ISRAELITARUM...	48.3 X	58.4 CM	SCHENK
J.H. COLTON'S MAP SHOWING THE OIL REGION OF WEST VIRGINIA...1865	52.7 X	44.8 CM	COLTON
JAMAICA	26.0 X	34.9 CM	HALL
JAMAICA	22.9 X	29.2 CM	LUCAS
JAMAICA	8.9 X	12.7 CM	SPEED
JAMAICA	48.0 X	61.0 CM	STANFORD
JAMAICA	26.7 X	34.9 CM	TALLIS
JAMAICA	20.0 X	25.0 CM	TALLIS
JAMAICA	26.0 X	34.3 CM	TALLIS
JAMAICA	34.3 X	26.7 CM	TALLIS
JAMAICA	41.9 X	59.7 CM	THOMSON
JAMAICA FROM THE LATEST SURVEYS; IMPROVED AND ENGRAVED BY THOMS JEFFER	46.0 X	61.2 CM	LAURIE & WHITTLE
JAMAICA, AMERICA SEPTENTRIONALE AMPLA INSULA...	51.0 X	58.0 CM	VISSCHER
JAMAICA/BARBADOS	38.7 X	47.6 CM	SPEED
JAPAN	6.5 X	7.5 CM	MULLER
JAPAN & COREA	26.0 X	33.7 CM	TALLIS
JAPAN AND KOREA	20.0 X	25.0 CM	TALLIS
JAPAN I.	14.0 X	17.1 CM	MERCATOR
JAPAN MANDSHURIA (SHOWING THE COURSE OF THE AMUR RIVER). THE KURILE IS	45.1 X	30.5 CM	FULLARTON

IAPAN NIPPON, KIUSIU, SIKOK...	33.0 X 38.7 CM	JOHNSON & BROWNING
IAPONIA	34.3 X 44.5 CM	MERCATOR
IAPONIA REGNUM	41.9 X 57.2 CM	BLAEU
IAPONIA REGNUM	41.5 X 57.0 CM	COVENS & MORTIER
JAPONIAE INSULAE DESCRIPTIO	35.5 X 48.5 CM	ORTELIUS
JOHNSON'S CALIFORNIA, TERRITORIES OF NEW MEXICO AND UTAH	43.2 X 61.0 CM	JOHNSON & WARD
JOHNSON'S MEXICO	29.2 X 36.8 CM	JOHNSON
JOHNSON'S MEXICO	27.9 X 39.4 CM	JOHNSON
JOHNSON'S MEXICO	29.2 X 36.8 CM	JOHNSON & WARD
JOHNSON'S MEXICO	29.2 X 36.8 CM	JOHNSON & WARD
JOHNSON'S NEBRASKA DAKOTA, MONTANA AND KANSAS	31.8 X 39.4 CM	JOHNSON
JOHNSON'S NEBRASKA, DAKOTA, COLORADO & KANSAS	31.8 X 39.4 CM	JOHNSON
JOHNSON'S NEBRASKA, DAKOTA, COLORADO, IDAHO & KANSAS	31.8 X 39.4 CM	JOHNSON
JOHNSON'S NEBRASKA, DAKOTA, IDAHO AND MONTANA	43.2 X 58.4 CM	JOHNSON
JOHNSON'S NEW MAP OF TEXAS	39.4 X 59.7 CM	JOHNSON
JOHNSON'S NEW MAP OF THE STATE OF TEXAS	41.9 X 62.2 CM	JOHNSON
JOHNSON'S NEW MAP OF THE STATE OF TEXAS	41.9 X 62.2 CM	JOHNSON
JOHNSON'S NEW MAP OF THE STATE OF TEXAS	41.9 X 62.2 CM	JOHNSON
JOHNSON'S NEW MAP OF THE STATE OF TEXAS	41.9 X 62.2 CM	JOHNSON & WARD
JOHNSON'S NEW MAP OF THE STATE OF TEXAS	41.9 X 36.8 CM	JOHNSON & WARD
JOHNSON'S NEW MAP OF THE STATE OF TEXAS	41.9 X 62.2 CM	JOHNSON & WARD
JOHNSON'S NEW MEXICO	29.2 X 36.8 CM	JOHNSON & WARD
JOHNSON'S NEW MILITARY MAP OF THE U.S. SHOWING THE FORTS, MILITARY POS	41.3 X 56.5 CM	JOHNSON
JOHNSON'S NEW MILITARY MAP OF THE U.S. SHOWING THE FORTS, MILITARY POS	41.3 X 56.5 CM	JOHNSON & WARD
JOHNSON'S NEW MILITARY MAP OF THE U.S...	40.6 X 57.8 CM	JOHNSON & WARD
JOHNSON'S NORTH AMERICA	55.9 X 43.2 CM	JOHNSON & WARD
JOHNSON'S ONTARIO, OF THE DOMINION OF CANADA	42.5 X 58.5 CM	JOHNSON
JOHNSON'S TEXAS	39.4 X 55.2 CM	JOHNSON
JOHNSON'S TEXAS	42.5 X 58.4 CM	JOHNSON
JOHNSON'S TEXAS	43.2 X 59.7 CM	JOHNSON
JOHNSON'S TEXAS	43.2 X 58.4 CM	JOHNSON
JOHNSON'S TEXAS	43.2 X 59.7 CM	JOHNSON
JOHNSON'S TEXAS	43.2 X 58.4 CM	JOHNSON
JOHNSON'S TEXAS	43.2 X 59.7 CM	JOHNSON
JOHNSON'S UNITED STATES	42.5 X 57.8 Cm	JOHNSON
JOHNSON'S WASHINGTON AND OREGON	31.1 X 39.4 CM	JOHNSON & WARD
JOHNSON'S WASHINGTON AND OREGON	31.8 X 40.0 CM	JOHNSON & WARD
JUDAEA SEU TERRA SANCTA...	58.4 X 83.8 CM	JAILLOT
JUDAEAE SEU TERRAE ISRAELIS TABULA GEOGRAPHICA...	35.6 X 48.3 CM	JANSSON
JUDEE OU TERRE SAINTE SOUS LES TURCS	24.1 X 21.6 CM	DE VAUGONDY
KAART VAN DE GEHEEL WERELD	18.0 X 29.0 CM	GRAVIUS
KAART VAN DE TWEE PLATTE WARELDS BOLLEN	17.5 X 30.0 CM	GRAVIUS
KAART VAN HET WESTELYK GEDEELTE VAN NIEUW MEXICO EN VAN CALIFORNIA	32.4 X 34.9 CM	TIRION
KAART VAN PERU MET EEN GEDEELTE...	33.0 X 21.0 CM	BACHIENE
KAART VAN VAN DIEMENS LAND OPGIENOOMEN DOOR KAPITEIN FURNEAUX IN MAAR	21.0 X 14.0 CM	COOK
KAARTE VAN DE GOLF VAN MEXICO EN HET ZUYD-AMERICA WAAR IN PORTO-BELLO	18.4 X 30.5 CM	RATELBAND
KAARTJE VAN HET NOORDER DEEL VAN AMERICA	18.0 X 24.5 CM	GRAVIUS
KANSAS	48.3 X 66.0 CM	RAND MCNALLY
KANSAS AND THE TERRITORIES OF ARIZONA, COLORADO, NEW MEXICO, UTAH AND	41.9 X 64.8 CM	WALLING & GRAY
KARTE VON AUSTRALIEN ODER POLYNESIEN...BIS 1789 ENTWORDEN IM JAHR 1792	46.5 X 66.0 CM	WEIGEL
KARTE VON DEM LAUFE DES FLUSSES ST. LAURENS...	19.1 X 30.5 CM	BELLIN
KARTE VON DEN KUSTEN DES FRANZOSISCHEN FLORIDA	20.3 X 14.0 CM	BELLIN
KARTE VON DEN SEEN IN CANADA	19.1 X 28.6 CM	BELLIN
KARTE VON DER INSEL BARBADE ZUR ALLGEMEINEN GESCHICHTE DER REISEN	14.6 X 19.7 CM	BELLIN
KARTE VON DER INSEL MONTREAL UND DEN GEGENDEN UMBER...1760	22.9 X 27.9 CM	BELLIN
KARTE VON DER INSELWELT POLYNESIEN...1795	47.0 X 64.0 CM	VON REILLY
KARTE VON NEU ENGLAND	20.3 X 29.2 CM	BELLIN
KENNEBEC AND SHEEPCOT RIVERS, MAINE	97.5 X 59.0 CM	U.S. COAST SURVEY
KENT WITH HER CITIES AND HER EARLES...	38.7 X 47.6 CM	SPEED
KENTUCKY	35.6 X 29.2 CM	BRADFORD
KENTUCKY	27.9 X 48.3 CM	CAREY
KENTUCKY	26.0 X 47.0 CM	CAREY
KENTUCKY	29.2 X 48.3 CM	LUCAS

KENTUCKY	29.5 X 48.9 CM	LUCAS
KENTUCKY	15.2 X 18.4 CM	SCOTT
KENTUCKY	16.5 X 36.2 CM	WEIMAR GEOGRAPHISCH...
KENTUCKY & TENNESSEE	19.1 X 25.4 CM	MORSE
KENTUCKY AND TENNESSEE	12.6 X 16.1 CM	ANON
KENTUCKY AND TENNESSEE	25.4 X 39.4 CM	FENNER, SEARS & CO.
KENTUCKY AND TENNESSEE	30.5 X 41.9 CM	MORSE & BREESE
KOOS BAY-OREGON	49.5 X 65.0 CM	U.S. COAST SURVEY
KOPPENHAVEN (VIEW)	19.1 X 26.7 CM	ANON
KREMLENAGRAD...	37.5 X 48.9 CM	BLAEU
L'ACADIA, LE PROVINCIE DI SAGADAHOOK E MAIN, LA NUOVA HAMPSHIRE, LA RH	31.8 X 41.9 CM	ZATTA
L'AFRIQUE	17.0 X 23.0 CM	CHIQUET
L'AFRIQUE	46.5 X 58.5 CM	DE VAUGONDY
L'AFRIQUE	57.2 X 86.4 CM	MORTIER
L'AFRIQUE DIVISEE EN SES PRINCIPALES PARTIES, OU LES EMPIRES, LES MONA	50.8 X 73.0 CM	DE VAUGONDY
L'ALSACE	57.2 X 86.4 CM	MORTIER
L'AMERICA	32.0 X 40.5 CM	ZATTA
L'AMERICA DIVISA NE SUOI PRINCIPALI STATI	30.5 X 40.6 CM	ZATTA
L'AMERICA DIVISA NE SUOI PRINCIPALI STATI DI NUOVA PROJEZIONE. VENEZIA	30.5 X 40.6 CM	ZATTA
L'AMERICA SETTENTRIONALE	39.4 X 54.6 CM	ROSSI
L'AMERICA SETTENTRIONALE. NUOVAMENTE CORRETTA ET ACCRESCIUTA SECONDO L	41.0 X 56.0 CM	ROSSI
L'AMERIQUE	17.8 X 14.0 CM	FAURE
L'AMERIQUE	38.1 X 49.5 CM	VAN LOCHOM
L'AMERIQUE DIVISEE EN SES PRINCIPAUX ETATS ASSUJETTIE AUX OBSERVATIONS	48.3 X 66.0 CM	SANTINI
L'AMERIQUE DIVISEE PAR GRANDS ETATS	30.5 X 44.5 CM	JANVIER
L'AMERIQUE DIVISEE PAR GRANDS ETATS...CHEZ LATTRE...	31.1 X 45.1 CM	JANVIER
L'AMERIQUE DRESSEE POUR L'ETUDE DE LA GEOGRAPHIE...	28.0 X 31.3 CM	BRION DE LA TOUR
L'AMERIQUE MERIDIONALE	17.0 X 22.0 CM	CHIQUET
L'AMERIQUE MERIDIONALE	14.0 X 19.1 CM	LA FEUILLE
L'AMERIQUE MERIDIONALE	57.2 X 86.4 CM	MORTIER
L'AMERIQUE MERIDIONALE DRESSEE SUR LES OBSERVATIONS...	45.7 X 60.0 CM	DE L'ISLE
L'AMERIQUE SELON LES NOUVELLES OBSERVATIONS DE MSSRS DE L'ACADEMI DES	47.0 X 66.0 CM	VAN DER AA
L'AMERIQUE SEPTENTRIONALE DIVISEE EN SES PRINCIPAUX ETATS PAR LE SR. J	30.5 X 44.5 CM	JANVIER
L'AMERIQUE SEPTENTRIONALE DRESSEE SUR LES OBSERVATIONS DE MR. DE L'ACA	47.0 X 58.4 CM	COVENS & MORTIER
L'AMERIQUE SEPTENTRIONALE...	30.5 X 44.5 CM	JANVIER
L'AMERIQUE...	25.4 X 26.7 CM	BRION DE LA TOUR
L'AMERIQUE...	33.0 X 45.7 CM	CASSINI
L'AMERIQUE...	49.5 X 66.0 CM	VAN DER AA
L'ANCIEN ET LE NOUVEAU MEXIQUE	34.3 X 23.5 CM	BONNE
L'ANCIEN MONDE ET LE NOUVEAU	21.6 X 40.6 CM	BONNE
L'ANCIEN MONDE ET LE NOUVEAUX EN DEUX HEMISPHERES	21.0 X 40.6 CM	BONNE
L'ARCHIDUCHE D'AUSTRICHE	57.2 X 86.4 CM	MORTIER
L'ASIE	57.2 X 86.4 CM	MORTIER
L'ASIE	19.7 X 27.3 CM	SANSON
L'ASIE DIVERSEE EN SES PRINCAPALES REGIONS	49.0 X 58.0 CM	COVENS & MORTIER
L'ASIE SUIVANT LES NOUVELLES DECOUVERTES DONT LES POINT PRINCIPAUX SON	22.9 X 55.2 CM	DE FER
L'EMPIRE DE JAPON...	48.3 X 53.3 CM	DE VAUGONDY
L'EMPIRE DE LA CHINE AVEC LA TARTARIE CHINOISE	48.0 X 54.0 CM	SANTINI
L'EMPIRE DU GRAND SEIGNEUR DES TURCS	57.2 X 86.4 CM	MORTIER
L'EMPIRE DU JAPON EN SEPT PRINCIPALES PARTIES...	48.3 X 53.3 CM	DE VAUGONDY
L'ESPAGNE	57.2 X 86.4 CM	MORTIER
L'ETAT DE LA REPUBLIQUE DE VENISE	57.2 X 86.4 CM	MORTIER
L'EUROPE	48.0 X 53.0 CM	DE VAUGONDY
L'EUROPE	57.2 X 86.4 CM	MORTIER
L'EVERSCHE DE LIEGE	57.2 X 86.4 CM	MORTIER
L'EVESCHE DE LIEGE. DIOECESIS LEODIENSIS...	46.0 X 54.0 CM	HONDIUS
L'ILE DE TERRE NEUVE ET LE GOLFE DE SAINT LAURENT	20.3 X 30.5 CM	KEYSER
L'ILE DE TERRE NEUVE ET LE GOLFE DE SAINT LAURENT SELON LES MEILLEURS	21.0 X 31.8 CM	BERNARD
L'INDE...L'EMPIRE DU GRAND MOGOL...	34.3 X 54.0 CM	SANSON
L'INDE...L'EMPIRE DU GRAND MOGOL...	33.7 X 54.0 CM	SANSON
L'IRLANDE SUIVANT LES NOUVELLES OBSERVATIONS	25.4 X 38.1 CM	VAN DER AA
L'ISLE D'ISCHIA DANS LE VOISINAGE DE NAPLES	38.0 X 48.0 CM	MORTIER
L'ISLE DAUPHINE	57.2 X 86.4 CM	MORTIER

L'ISLE DE CYPRE	10.0 X 15.0 CM	MUNSTER
L'ISLE DE TERRE NEUVE L'ACADIE OU LA NOUVELLE ECOSSE	21.0 X 31.8 CM	BONNE
L'ISLE DE TERRE-NEUVE L'ACADIE, OU LA NOUVELLE ECOSSE, L'ISLE ST. JEAN	21.6 X 32.4 CM	BONNE
L'ISLE DE TERRE-NEUVE, L'ACADIE, OU LA NOUVELLE ECOSSE, L'ISLE ST JEAN	21.5 X 31.5 CM	BONNE
L'ISLE ET ROYAUME D'IRLAND...	40.6 X 50.8 CM	DU VAL
L'ISLE ET ROYAUME DE SARDAGNE	57.2 X 86.4 CM	MORTIER
L'ISLE ST. DOMINGUE OU ESPAGNOLE DECOUVERTE EN 1492 PAR LES ESPAGNOLS	22.9 X 33.0 CM	DE FER
L'ISLE ST. DOMINGUE OU ESPAGNOLE DECOUVERTE L'AN 1492...CHEZ DANIEL GE	43.2 X 57.8 CM	DE FER
L'ISOLE BRITANNICHE...	41.0 X 51.0 CM	ROSSI
L'ITALIE	57.2 X 86.4 CM	MORTIER
LA BAJA D'HUDSON TERRA DI LABRADOR E GROENLANDIA CON LE ISOLE ADIACENT	31.8 X 41.3 CM	ZATTA
LA BAJA D'HUDSON...	30.0 X 40.5 CM	ZATTA
LA BARBADE UNE DES ANTILLES AUX ANGLOIS DIVISEE PAR PAROISSES/ISLE ST.	27.9 X 21.0 CM	LE ROUGE
LA BATAILLE DE SENEFFE...	44.0 X 37.0 CM	LE CLERC
LA BERMUDE AUX ANGLOIS.../LA JAMAIQUE AUX ANGLOIS	27.3 X 20.3 CM	LE ROUGE
LA BRETAGNE DIVISEE EN SES NEUF EVESCHES	48.0 X 61.0 CM	JAILLOT
LA CALIFORNIE OU NOUVELLE CAROLINE	44.5 X 64.8 CM	DE FER
LA CHASTELLENIE D'IPRE. HENRICUS HONDIUS EXCUDEBAT (VIEW)	39.0 X 49.0 CM	HONDIUS
LA CHINE ROYAUME	41.3 X 53.3 CM	SANSON
LA CHINE ROYAUME. A PARIS: CHEZ PIERRE MARIETTE, RUE S. IACQUE A L'ESP	41.9 X 53.3 CM	SANSON
LA CHINE, SUIVANT LES NOUVELLES OBSERVATIONS	39.5 X 32.5 CM	VAN DER AA
LA DELFLANDE ET SCHIELANDE, AVEC LES ISLES...HENRICI HONDII, 1629	46.0 X 55.0 CM	HONDIUS
LA FLANDRE GALLICANE. FLANDRIA GALLICA CONTINENS CASTELLANIAS INSULENS	40.0 X 51.0 CM	HONDIUS
LA FLANDRE IMPERIALE ET PROPRIETAIRE	40.0 X 50.0 CM	HONDIUS
LA FLORIDA/GUASTECAN REG./PERUVIAE AURIFERAE REGIONIS TYPUS	33.0 X 46.4 CM	ORTELIUS
LA FLORIDA/PERUVIAE AURIFERAE REGIONIS TYPUS/GUASTECAN REG.	33.0 X 45.7 CM	ORTELIUS
LA FLORIDE	22.9 X 30.5 CM	VAN DER AA
LA FLORIDE...	33.3 X 40.3 CM	VAN DER AA
LA GRECE	16.5 X 22.0 CM	CHIQUET
LA GRENADE DIVISEE PAR QUARTIERS AVEC SES PORTS ET MOUILLAGES D'APRES	43.8 X 59.1 CM	LATTRE
LA GUYANE FRANCOISE, AVEC PARTIE DE LA GUYANE HOLLANDOISE; SUIVANT LES	21.3 X 31.4 CM	BONNE
LA HOLLANDE MERIDIONALE...ZUYT HOLLAND. HENRICI HONDII, 1629	45.0 X 55.0 CM	HONDIUS
LA HOLLANDE OU LES PROVINCES UNIES DES PAYS BAS...AVEC LEURS CONQUESTE	40.0 X 53.0 CM	DANET
LA HOLLANDE OU LES VII PROVINCES UNIES	49.0 X 58.0 CM	LE ROUGE
LA HOLLANDE. COMITATUS HOLLANDIAE. HENRICI HONDII, 1629	40.0 X 51.0 CM	HONDIUS
LA JAMAIQUE.../LA BERMUDE	27.0 X 20.0 CM	LE ROUGE
LA LORRAINE	57.2 X 86.4 CM	MORTIER
LA LOUISIANA, PARTE SETTENTRIONALLE...	25.4 X 41.9 CM	CORONELLI
LA LOUISIANA, PARTE SETTENTRIONALLE...	26.7 X 43.2 CM	CORONELLI
LA MAPPE MONDE OU LE GLOBE TERRESTRE REPRESENTE EN DEUX HEMISPHERES, L	55.2 X 80.0 CM	HERISSON
LA MARTINIQUE UNE DES ANTILLES FRANCOISES DE L'AMERIQUE DRESSEE SUR LE	48.3 X 63.5 CM	LE ROUGE
LA MER ROUGE	57.2 X 86.4 CM	MORTIER
LA MOCHA (ENGRAVED SCENE)	11.7 X 15.6 CM	HULSIUS
LA MOREE	57.2 X 86.4 CM	MORTIER
LA NUOVA FRANCIA	26.7 X 36.8 CM	RAMUSIO
LA NUOVA FRANCIA	26.7 X 36.8 CM	RAMUSIO
LA PARTIE MERIDIONALE DES PAYS-BAS, CONNUE SOUS LE NOM DE FLANDRE...PA	44.5 X 60.0 CM	NOLIN
LA PARTIE OCCIDENTALE DELLA NUOVA FRANCIA O CANADA	33.7 X 43.8 CM	ZATTA
LA PARTIE PLUS OCCIDENTALE DE LA FLANDRE TEUTONIQUE. FLANDRIAE PARS OC	40.0 X 50.0 CM	HONDIUS
LA PARTIE PLUS ORIENTALE DE LA FLANDRE TEUTONIQUE PARS FLANDRIAE ORIEN	40.0 X 49.0 CM	HONDIUS
LA PENNSYLVANIE EN TROIS FEUILLES...	66.0 X 132.1 CM	LE ROUGE
LA PENSILVANIA, LA NUOVA YORK, IL JERSEY SETTENTRIOLE: CON LA PARTIE O	33.7 X 43.8 CM	ZATTA
LA PRINCIPAUTE D'ORANGE ET COMTAT DE VENAISSIN, PAR IAQUES DE CHIEZE O	38.1 X 50.2 CM	BLAEU
LA PRINCIPAUTE DE LIEGE ET LE DUCHE DE LIMBOURG	48.0 X 53.0 CM	DE VAUGONDY
LA REPUBBLICA D'OLLANDA	41.0 X 31.0 CM	ZATTA
LA RHEINLANDE. RHINOLANDIAE, AMSTELANDIAE...HENRICI HONDII, 1629	45.0 X 55.0 CM	HONDIUS
LA RUSSIE BLANCHE OU MOSCOVIE	57.2 X 86.4 CM	MORTIER
LA SCANDINAVIE	57.2 X 86.4 CM	MORTIER
LA SEIGNEURIE D'OUEST-FRISE OU FRISE OCCIDENTALE...	43.0 X 57.0 CM	JAILLOT
LA SEIGNEURIE D'OVER-YSSEL...	56.0 X 43.0 CM	JAILLOT
LA SEIGNEURIE D'UTRECHT	43.0 X 56.0 CM	JAILLOT
LA SEIGNEURIE D'UTRECHT	43.2 X 58.4 CM	MORTIER
LA SEIGNEURIE DE GRONINGUE	44.0 X 58.0 CM	JAILLOT

LA SEIGNEURIE DE MALINES. MECHLINIA DOMINIUM ET AERSCHOT DUCATUS. AUCT	41.0 X	51.0 CM	HONDIUS
LA SICILE	57.2 X	86.4 CM	MORTIER
LA SPAGNUOLA, DESCRITTA...E DEDICATA ALL'ILLUSTRISS SIG. GIUSTIMIANO L	22.2 X	29.2 CM	CORONELLI
LA SUEZIA	41.9 X	31.8 CM	ZATTA
LA TABLES DES ISLES NEUVUES	25.4 X	34.3 CM	MUNSTER
LA TERRA DE HOCHELEGA NELLA NOVA FRANCIA	26.7 X	36.8 CM	RAMUSIO
LA TERRA DE HOCHELEGA NELLA NOVA FRANCIA	26.7 X	36.8 CM	RAMUSIO
LA TERRA DE HOCHELEGA NELLA NOVA FRANCIA	26.7 X	35.6 CM	RAMUSIO
LA VELUWE, LA BETUNE ET LE COMTE DE ZUTPHEN DANS LE DUCHE DU GUELDRE..	43.0 X	57.0 CM	JAILLOT
LA VELUWE, LA BETUNE...	57.2 X	86.4 CM	MORTIER
LA VERA CITA DI GIERUSALEM COME SI TROVA OGNI (VIEW)	22.9 X	27.9 CM	CALLOT
LA VERA CRUZ OR ST. JUAN DE ULUA	17.8 X	11.4 CM	KITCHIN
LA VERA DESCRITTIONE DELLA GALLIA BELGICA	39.0 X	30.0 CM	ANON
LA VERITABLE DESCRIPTION DU SIEGE DE PHILIPSBOURG PAR LES FRANCOIS	45.7 X	48.3 CM	DE LETH
LA WEST-FRISE AUTREMENT DITE LA HOLLANDE SEPTENTRIONALE	45.0 X	55.0 CM	HONDIUS
LACUS LEMANNI...	40.6 X	52.1 CM	BLAEU
LAKE ONTARIO	22.2 X	25.4 CM	KITCHIN
LANCASHIRE	10.2 X	17.8 CM	CAPPER
LANCASHIRE	11.4 X	14.0 CM	SELLER
LATIUM	13.5 X	17.5 CM	PTOLEMY (1596-1621 ...
LATIUM NUNC COMPAGNA DI ROMA	36.8 X	72.4 CM	MERCATOR
LE BRABANT	63.0 X	51.0 CM	LE ROUGE
LE BRABANT ESPAGNOL QUI COMPREND LES QUARTIERS DE BRUSSELLES, DE LOUVA	44.0 X	57.0 CM	JAILLOT
LE BRETAGNE	57.2 X	86.4 CM	MORTIER
LE CANADA OU PARTIE DE LA NOUVELLE FRANCE DANS L'AMERIQUE SEPTENTRIONA	47.0 X	59.7 CM	OTTENS
LE CANADA OU PARTIE DE LA NOUVELLE FRANCE...	57.2 X	87.6 CM	MORTIER
LE CANADA OU PARTIE DE LA NOUVELLE FRANCE...CONTENANT LA TERRE DE LABR	48.3 X	59.7 CM	JAILLOT
LE CERCLE DE BAVIERE	48.0 X	53.0 CM	DE VAUGONDY
LE COLONIE UNITE DELL' AMERICA SETTENTR. DI NUOVE PROJEZIONE...	31.8 X	41.9 CM	ZATTA
LE COLONIE UNITE DELL' AMERICA SETTENTRIONALE	32.0 X	42.5 CM	ZATTA
LE COMTE DE DRENTE & LA SEIGNEURIE DE WESTERWOLD...CORNELI PYNACKER, 1	38.0 X	49.0 CM	HONDIUS
LE COMTE DE FLANDRE	57.2 X	86.4 CM	MORTIER
LE COMTE DE HAYNAUT, DIVISE EN FRANCOIS ET ESPAGNOL. PAR SANSON. A PAR	43.5 X	57.0 CM	JAILLOT
LE COMTE DE HAYNAUT...LE COMTE DE CAMBRESIS...PAR I.B. NOLIN	46.0 X	57.0 CM	NOLIN
LE COMTE DE HOLLANDE	57.2 X	86.4 CM	MORTIER
LE COMTE DE NAMUR. NAMURCUM COMITATUS. 1632	39.0 X	50.0 CM	HONDIUS
LE COMTE DE NAMUR. PAR F. DU VIVIER INGENIEUR ET GEOGRAPHE...PARIS, CH	42.0 X	54.0 CM	DU VIVIER
LE COMTE DE ZEELANDE	57.2 X	86.4 CM	MORTIER
LE COMTE DE ZEELANDE...	43.0 X	57.0 CM	JAILLOT
LE COMTE DE ZUTPHEN. COMITATUS ZUTPHANIA EXCUDIT JOANNES JANSSONIS	38.0 X	49.0 CM	HONDIUS
LE DOMAINE D'UTRECHT. EPISCOP. ULTRAIECTINUS, 1628	37.0 X	49.0 CM	HONDIUS
LE DUCHE DE BRABANT. PARTIE MERIDIONALE	57.2 X	86.4 CM	MORTIER
LE DUCHE DE BRABANT. PARTIE SEPTENTRIONALE	57.2 X	86.4 CM	MORTIER
LE DUCHE DE BRABANT...	48.0 X	80.0 CM	JAILLOT
LE DUCHE DE GUELDRE. DUCATUS GELDRIAE...AUCTORE BALTHAZARO FLOR. A BER	39.0 X	50.0 CM	HONDIUS
LE DUCHE DE LUCXEMBOURG DIVISE EN QUARTIER WALON ET ALLEMAND	52.0 X	62.0 CM	JAILLOT
LE DUCHE DE LUXEMBOURG	57.2 X	86.4 CM	MORTIER
LE DUCHE DE LUXEMBOURG DIVISE EN FRANCOIS ET ESPAGNOL	43.8 X	57.0 CM	JAILLOT
LE DUCHE DE MILAN	57.2 X	86.4 CM	MORTIER
LE GOUVERNEMENT DE L'ISLE DE FRANCE	40.6 X	52.1 CM	BLAEU
LE GOUVERNEMENT GENERALE DE L'ISLE DE FRANCE	57.2 X	86.4 CM	MORTIER
LE GRAND PLANT ET VRAY PORTRAIT DE LA VILLE DE BRUSSELLES	32.0 X	40.0 CM	DE BELLE FOREST
LE ISOLE DELLA SONDA, MOLUCCHE, ET FILIPPINES...	47.5 X	34.5 CM	CASSINI
LE ISOLE DI TERRA NUOVA E CAPO BRETON	43.2 X	31.8 CM	ZATTA
LE ISOLE DI TERRA NUOVA E CAPO BRETON	42.0 X	32.0 CM	ZATTA
LE ISOLE DI TERRA NUOVA E CAPO BRETON DI NUOVA PROJEZIONE. VENEZIA 177	43.2 X	34.3 CM	ZATTA
LE LIMBOURG	43.2 X	55.9 CM	MORTIER
LE LIMBOURG...	43.5 X	57.0 CM	JAILLOT
LE NOUVEAU MEXIQUE	21.0 X	31.4 CM	BONNE
LE NOUVEAU MEXIQUE AVEC LA PARTIE SEPTENTRIONALE DE L'ANCIEN, OU DE LA	21.0 X	31.8 CM	BONNE
LE NOUVEAU MEXIQUE AVEC...NOUVELLE ESPAGNE	21.6 X	31.8 CM	BONNE
LE NOUVEAU MEXIQUE ET LA FLORIDE: TIREES DE DIVERSE CARTES ET RELATION	31.1 X	54.3 CM	SANSON
LE PAIS D'ENTRE SAMBRE ET MEUSE ET LES ENVIRONS DE NAMUR, DINANT, CHAR	39.0 X	50.0 CM	DE FER

LE PARAGUAY	21.0 X 27.3 CM	SANSON
LE PEROU DANS L'AMERIQUE MERIDIONALE DRESSE SUR LES DIVERS RELATIONS D	48.3 X 57.8 CM	DE FER
LE PLAN DE L'ISLE DE ST. JAN ET PTO RICO	20.0 X 14.5 CM	MALLET
LE PORT AU PRINCE DANS L'ISLE DE ST. DOMINGUE	22.2 X 17.1 CM	BELLIN
LE POURTRAICT DE LA TRES NOBLE VILLE D'ANVERS AINSI QU'ELLE SE COMPORT	30.0 X 41.0 CM	DE BELLE FOREST
LE ROYAUME D'ANGLETERRE...	47.6 X 51.4 CM	DE VAUGONDY
LE ROYAUME D'ECOSSE	86.4 X 57.2 CM	MORTIER
LE ROYAUME D'ESPAGNE AVEC SES CONFINS	14.6 X 21.6 CM	LA FEUILLE
LE ROYAUME D'IRLAND	86.4 X 57.2 CM	MORTIER
LE ROYAUME DE BOHEMIA	48.0 X 53.0 CM	DE VAUGONDY
LE ROYAUME DE DANEMARK	16.5 X 22.0 CM	CHIQUET
LE ROYAUME DE DANEMARK	57.2 X 86.4 CM	MORTIER
LE ROYAUME DE FRANCE	16.5 X 22.0 CM	CHIQUET
LE ROYAUME DE FRANCE	48.0 X 53.0 CM	DE VAUGONDY
LE ROYAUME DE FRANCE	57.2 X 86.4 CM	MORTIER
LE ROYAUME DE FRANCE ET LES CONQUETES DE LOUIS GRAND	45.7 X 57.2 CM	LOTTER
LE ROYAUME DE HONGRIE	57.2 X 86.4 CM	MORTIER
LE ROYAUME DE NORWEGE	22.0 X 16.5 CM	CHIQUET
LE ROYAUME DE POLOGNE	48.0 X 53.0 CM	DE VAUGONDY
LE ROYAUME DE SIAM	86.4 X 57.2 CM	MORTIER
LE TYROL	48.0 X 53.0 CM	DE VAUGONDY
LE VIEUX MEXIQUE OU NOUVELLE ESPAGNE AVEC LES COSTES DE LA FLORIDE	22.5 X 33.5 CM	DE FER
LE VIEUX MEXIQUE OU NOUVELLE ESPAGNE AVEC LES COSTES DE LA FLORIDE...	22.9 X 33.0 CM	DE FER
LE VRAY PORTRAICT DE LA VILLE D'OOSTENDE LAQUELLE FUT ASSIEGEE PAR LAR	20.0 X 27.5 CM	HUBERTI
LEICESTER BOTH COUNTYE AND CITIE DESCRIBED	38.1 X 50.8 CM	SPEED
LEICESTERSHIRE	24.1 X 19.1 CM	BELL
LEICESTERSHIRE	14.0 X 8.9 CM	CARY
LEICESTERSHIRE	11.4 X 14.0 CM	SELLER
LEICESTERSHIRE...	38.7 X 47.6 CM	SPEED
LEODIENSIS DIOCESIS TYPUS	38.0 X 49.0 CM	ORTELIUS
LEODIENSIS DIOCESIS TYPUS	38.0 X 49.0 CM	ORTELIUS
LEODIENSIS DIOECESIS	38.0 X 50.0 CM	BLAEU
LEODIENSIS DIOECESIS TYPUS	33.5 X 48.0 CM	MERCATOR
LEODIENSIS EPISCOPATUS	24.0 X 32.0 CM	DE BRUYN
LEODIENSIS EPISCOPATUS	23.5 X 31.0 CM	VAN DEN KEERE
LEODIENSIS EPISCOPATUS...PER NICOLAUM VISSCHER AMST. BAT.	46.5 X 56.5 CM	VISSCHER
LEODIUM. LEIGE. LUTICH (BIRD'S EYE VIEW)	28.5 X 37.5 CM	MERIAN
LEODIUM. LIEGE. LUTICH. (PANORAMIC VIEW)	22.0 X 33.0 CM	MERIAN
LES COSTES AUX ENVIRONS DE LA RIVIERE DE MISISIPI	22.5 X 33.5 CM	DE FER
LES COTES DE LA GRECE ET L'ARCHIPEL PAR LE SR. D'ANVILLE...OCTOBRE M.D	55.2 X 72.4 CM	D'ANVILLE
LES DESERTS D'EGYPTE	57.2 X 86.4 CM	MORTIER
LES DIX-SEPT PROVINCES DES PAYS-BAS	44.0 X 57.0 CM	DESNOS
LES DIX-SEPT PROVINCES DES PAYS-BAS	86.4 X 57.2 CM	MORTIER
LES DIX-SEPT PROVINCES DES PAYS-BAS...PARIS	44.0 X 57.0 CM	JAILLOT
LES DUCHES DE STIRIE, DE CARINTHIE, DE CARNIOLE	57.2 X 86.4 CM	MORTIER
LES ENVIRONS DE LONDRES	48.3 X 55.9 CM	COVENS & MORTIER
LES ETATE UNIS DE L'AMERIQUE SEPTENTRIONALE...	31.8 X 21.6 CM	BONNE
LES ETATS UNIS...	18.4 X 22.2 CM	HERISSON
LES ISLES ANTILLES &C. ENTRE LESQUELLES SONT LUCAYES ET LES CARIBES	38.7 X 55.2 CM	SANSON
LES ISLES ANTILLES...	21.0 X 30.5 CM	SANSON
LES ISLES BRITANNIQUES	57.2 X 86.4 CM	MORTIER
LES ISLES BRITANNIQUES SUIVANT LES NOUVELLES OBSERVATIONS	25.4 X 38.1 CM	VAN DER AA
LES ISLES DE L'AMERIQUE	22.5 X 33.5 CM	DE FER
LES ISLES ET COSTE DE LA DALMATIE	16.5 X 22.0 CM	CHIQUET
LES ISLES MOLUCQUES; CELEBES GILOLO, &C...	18.4 X 24.1 CM	SANSON
LES ISLES MOLUCQUES	19.0 X 16.0 CM	SANSON
LES ISLES PHILIPPINES/ISLAS DE LOS LADRONES...	19.0 X 16.0 CM	SANSON
LES ISLES PHILIPPINES/ISLAS DE LOS LANDRONES OU ISLE DE LARRONS. A DE	24.4 X 19.1 CM	SANSON
LES MONTAGNES DES ALPES	57.2 X 86.4 CM	MORTIER
LES MONTS PYRENEES	57.2 X 86.4 CM	MORTIER
LES PETITES ANTILLES OU LES ISLES DU VENT	23.5 X 16.5 CM	BELLIN
LES PROVINCES APPELEES PAIS BAS CONNUES SOUS LES NOMS DE FLANDRE ET DE	53.0 X 41.0 CM	DE FER
LES PROVINCES DES PAY-BAS CATHOLIQUES VULGAIREMENT CONNUES SOUS LE NOM	44.0 X 59.0 CM	SANSON

LES PROVINCES DES PAYS-BAS CATHOLIQUES	57.2 X 86.4 CM	MORTIER
LES PROVINCES DES PAYS-BAS CATHOLIQUES...	47.0 X 65.0 CM	JAILLOT
LES PROVINCES UNIES DES PAYS-BAS...	49.0 X 60.0 CM	DE VAUGONDY
LES PROVINCES UNIES OU LA PARTIE SEPTENTRIONALE DES PAYS-BAS CONNUE SO	46.0 X 60.0 CM	NOLIN
LES PROVINCES-UNIES DES PAYS-BAS	48.0 X 53.0 CM	DE VAUGONDY
LES ROYAUMES D'ANGLETERRE, D'ECOSSE ET D'IRLANDE	16.5 X 22.5 CM	CHIQUET
LES ROYAUMES DE SUEDE ET DE NORWEGE	48.0 X 53.0 CM	DE VAUGONDY
LES XVII PROVINCES DES PAYS-BAS	16.5 X 22.0 CM	CHIQUET
LES XVII PROVINCES DITES LES PAYS-BAS, PAR ET CHEZ LE SR. LE ROUGE	50.0 X 57.0 CM	LE ROUGE
LIEGE (VIEW)	23.0 X 31.0 CM	GUICHARDIN
LIEGE 1693 (PANORAMIC VIEW)	17.0 X 50.0 CM	PERELLE
LIEGE ET PARTIE DE L'EVESCHE DE LIEGE	21.0 X 46.5 CM	NOLIN
LIMBURGENSIS DUCATUS TABULA NOVA, EXUSA SUMPTIBUS IOAN. BAPTISTAE VRIN	40.0 X 48.5 CM	VRIENTS
LIMBURGENSIS DUCATUS, 1616	37.0 X 48.5 CM	VAN DEN KEERE
LIMBURGI...VALCKENBURGI NOVA DESCRIPTIO	47.0 X 57.0 CM	VISSCHER
LIMBURGUM	40.0 X 50.0 CM	BLAEU
LINCOLNIAE COMITATUS UBI OLIM INSEDERUNT CORITANI...	29.8 X 34.9 CM	KIP
LINCOLNSHIRE	7.6 X 12.1 CM	LEIGH
LINCOLNSHIRE	11.4 X 14.0 CM	SELLER
LINCOLNSHIRE	11.4 X 15.2 CM	SELLER
LINCOLNSHIRE	10.8 X 6.4 CM	WALLIS & REID
LIVONIAE ET CURLANDIAE DUCATUS CUM INSULIS ADJACENTIB.	48.9 X 57.2 CM	LOTTER
LOMBARDIA ET MARCHIA TARUISINA	13.5 X 17.5 CM PTOLEMY (1596-1621 ...
LONDINUM...	23.0 X 36.5 CM	MUNSTER
LOTHARINGIE DUCATUS	36.2 X 26.0 CM PTOLEMY (1513-20 ST...
LOUISIANA	35.6 X 29.2 CM	BRADFORD
LOUISIANA	27.3 X 33.0 CM	BURR
LOUISIANA	41.3 X 46.0 CM	CAREY
LOUISIANA	33.0 X 40.0 CM	COLTON
LOUISIANA	27.3 X 43.5 CM	LUCAS
LOUISIANA	26.7 X 34.3 CM	TANNER
LOUISIANA AND MISSISSIPPI	15.6 X 12.5 CM	ANON
LOUISIANA BY DE RIVIER MISSISSIPPI	19.1 X 15.2 CM	LAW
LOUISIANA, AS FORMERLY CLAIMED BY FRANCE, NOW CONTAINING PART OF BRITI	17.8 X 22.9 CM	KITCHIN
LOUISIANA, AS FORMERLY CLAIMED BY FRANCE, NOW CONTAINING PART OF BRITI	17.8 X 22.9 CM	LONDON MAGAZINE
LOUISIANA...& SPANISH AMERICA	17.8 X 22.9 CM	KITCHIN
LOUVAIN. LE POURTRAICT ET DESCRIPTION DE LA VILLE DE LOUVAIN	29.0 X 35.0 CM	DE BELLE FOREST
LOVELL'S GROVE. NO. WEYMOUTH, MASS. (VIEW)	45.4 X 63.8 CM	BUFFORD
LOW ARCHIPELAGO OR PAUMOTU GROUP	21.6 X 29.2 CM U.S. EXPLORING EXPE...
LOWER CANADA	35.6 X 29.2 CM	BRADFORD
LOWER CANADA, NEW BRUNSWICK, NOVA SCOTIA, PRINCE EDWARD IS...	61.0 X 48.3 CM	ARROWSMITH
LOWER CANADA, NEW BRUNSWICK, NOVA SCOTIA, PRINCE EDWARDS ID. NEWFOUNDL	62.9 X 53.3 CM	ARROWSMITH
LUCENBURGUM URBS... (VIEW)	36.0 X 47.0 CM	BRAUN & HOGENBERG
LUCQUES OU LUCA...PIERRE MORTIER	41.3 X 52.1 CM	MORTIER
LUIGIANA	43.8 X 28.6 CM	ANON
LUIGIANA INGLESE, COLLA PARTE OCCIDENTALE DELLA FLORIDA, DELLA GIORGIA	33.0 X 41.9 CM	ZATTA
LUTZEBURG	8.1 X 10.5 CM	ORTELIUS
LUTZENBOURG. LUTZENBURGUM...URBS...	23.3 X 31.5 CM	LIEFRINCK
LUTZENBURG	9.7 X 13.3 CM	HONDIUS
LUTZENBURG	8.7 X 12.2 CM	VAN DEN KEERE
LUTZENBURG (VIEW)	9.6 X 14.6 CM	MEISNER
LUTZENBURG DUCATUS	38.0 X 50.0 CM	BLAEU
LUTZENBURGENSIS DUCATUS VERISS DESCRIPT. IACOBO SURHONIO MONTANO AUCTO	36.7 X 49.5 CM	ORTELIUS
LUTZENBURGENSIS DUCATUS VERISS. DESCRIPT.	23.4 X 31.8 CM	DE BRUYN
LUTZENBURGENSIS DUCATUS VERISS. DESCRIPT. IACOBO SUHONIO MONTANO AUCTO	23.3 X 31.0 CM	VAN DEN KEERE
LUTZENBURGENSIS DUCATUS VERISS. DESCRIPT. IACOBO SURHONIO MONTANO AUCT	36.5 X 49.0 CM	ORTELIUS
LUTZENBURGENSIS DUCATUS. JACOBO SURHONIO MONTENSI AUCTORE. PETRUS KAER	18.5 X 25.5 CM	GOOS
LUTZENBURGUM	38.8 X 50.0 CM	BLAEU
LUXEMBOURG (VIEW)	11.0 X 15.0 CM	PERELLE
LUXEMBOURG LUTZENBURGUM	35.0 X 41.0 CM	BRAUN & HOGENBERG
LUXEMBOURG, UNE FORTERESSE TRES-CELEBRE DE LA DUCHE DE CETTE NOM...	49.5 X 57.0 CM	SEUTTER
MADISON, DANE COUNTY	40.6 X 29.2 CM WALLING, TACKABURY ...
MADRID	30.5 X 36.8 CM	SDUK

MAESTRICHT (VIEW)	27.0 X	40.0 CM	ANON
MAGNAE BRITANNIAE ET HIBERNIAE TABULA	38.7 X	50.2 CM	BLAEU
MAGNAE BRITANNIAE ET HIBERNIAE TABULA	38.0 X	50.0 CM	BLAEU
MAGNAE BRITANNIAE ET HIBERNIAE TABULA	38.1 X	49.5 CM	HONDIUS
MAGNI DUCATUS LITHUANIAE...EXACTA DESCRIPTIO	75.0 X	73.0 CM	BLAEU
MAGNI MOGOLIS IMPERIUM	36.2 X	48.9 CM	HONDIUS
MAINE	35.6 X	29.2 CM	BRADFORD
MAINE	35.6 X	29.2 CM	BRADFORD
MAINE	33.0 X	26.7 CM	BURR
MAINE	38.1 X	30.5 CM	MORSE & BREESE
MAINE, NEW HAMPSHIRE & VERMONT	20.0 X	25.1 CM	MORSE
MAINE, NEW HAMPSHIRE, MASSACHUSETTS, VERMONT, CONNECTICUT & RHODE I.	26.7 X	19.7 CM	MEYER
MAINE, NEW HAMPSHIRE, VERMONT	22.9 X	27.9 CM	BARNES & BURR
MAIORES MINORES QUE INSULAE HISPANIOLA, CUBA...	27.9 X	35.6 CM	DE LAET
MAIORICA	10.5 X	14.5 CM	PORCACCHI
MALAY ARCHIPELAGO	20.0 X	25.0 CM	TALLIS
MALINES. LE VRAY PLANT ET POURTRAICT DE LA VILLE DE MALINES	28.0 X	34.0 CM	DE BELLE FOREST
MALTA	10.5 X	14.5 CM	PORCACCHI
MANOA O DEL DORADO (VIEW)	10.5 X	14.1 CM	HULSIUS
MAP 5 TO ILLUSTRATE ROUTE FOLLOWED FROM PIRARA TO TORONG	31.5 X	22.9 CM	SCHOMBURGK
MAP 6 TO ILLUSTRATE ROUTE FOLLOWED BETWEEN "OUR VILLAGE" AND TORONG	22.9 X	25.3 CM	SCHOMBURGK
MAP AND ELEVATION OF THE SHUBENACADIE NAVIGATION FROM HALIFAX HARBOUR	11.4 X	31.0 CM	ANON
MAP AND ELEVATIONS OF THE SHUBENACADIE NAVIGATION FROM HALIFAX HARBOUR	12.7 X	32.4 CM	FADEN
MAP AND PROFILE OF THE CANADA DE LAC UVAS	55.2 X	75.6 CM	U.S.
MAP AND PROFILE OF THE CANADA DE LAS UVAS; FROM EXPLORATIONS...BY LT.	55.9 X	76.2 CM	WILLIAMSON
MAP AND PROFILE OF THE CHAMPLAIN CANAL	19.7 X	49.5 CM	GEDDES
MAP AND PROFILE OF THE TEJON PASS	55.9 X	83.8 CM	U.S.
MAP EXHIBITING THE HARBOUR OF HALIFAX AND THE SHUBENACADIE CANAL...	11.5 X	32.1 CM	MCGREGOR
MAP OF A PORTION OF CHILE WITH THE INTERMEDIATE MOUNTAIN RANGES AND PA	25.4 X	43.2 CM	BALDWIN & CRADOCK
MAP OF ASHLAND	50.8 X	66.0 CM	SCHRADER
MAP OF BALTIMORE PREPARED FOR THE STRANGER'S GUIDE IN BALTIMORE. MURPH	28.6 X	52.7 CM	MURPHY & CO.
MAP OF BRITISH COLUMBIA COMPILED FROM THE MAP OF THE PROVINCE RECENTLY	15.2 X	62.2 CM	TRUTCH
MAP OF BUFFALO HARBOR, N.Y.	27.3 X	36.2 CM	U.S.
MAP OF CAPE BRETON...	11.6 X	19.9 CM	MCGREGOR
MAP OF CLEAR CREEK TOWNSHIP	39.4 X	31.9 CM	KINGMAN BROS.
MAP OF COLOMBIA, AND BRITISH GUYANA, INCLUDING THE STATES OF NEW GRANA	22.2 X	27.9 CM	WYLD
MAP OF COLORADO TERRITORY, AND NORTHERN PORTION OF NEW MEXICO SHOWING	52.1 X	53.3 CM	GILPIN
MAP OF DALLAS TOWNSHIP-MAP OF HUNTINGTON TOWNSHIP	39.7 X	65.7 CM	KINGMAN BROS.
MAP OF EASTERN TEXAS	33.0 X	48.3 CM	HARDESTY
MAP OF GILLIAM'S TRAVELS IN MEXICO, INCLUDING TEXAS AND PART OF THE UN	48.3 X	47.0 CM	GILLIAM
MAP OF HUNTINGTON COUNTY	41.0 X	32.1 CM	KINGMAN BROS.
MAP OF INDIAN TERRITORY AND OKLAHOMA	55.9 X	74.9 CM	FULLARTON
MAP OF JACKSON TOWNSHIP	39.4 X	31.9 CM	KINGMAN BROS.
MAP OF JAMAICA PREPARED FROM THE BEST AUTHORITIES UNDER THE DIRECTION	63.0 X	159.0 CM	HARRISON
MAP OF KANSAS, NEBRASKA, AND COLORADO...DACOTAH	29.2 X	35.6 CM	MITCHELL
MAP OF KHORASAN AND NEIGHBOURING COUNTRIES	62.2 X	82.5 CM	WELLER
MAP OF LOUISIANA FROM D'ANVILLE'S ATLAS	30.5 X	49.5 CM	HARRISON
MAP OF LOUISIANA REPRESENTING THE SEVERAL LAND DRISTRICTS...	39.4 X	41.9 CM	U.S.
MAP OF LOUISIANA, TEXAS, ARKANSAS, AND INDIAN TERRITORY	20.6 X	26.7 CM	MITCHELL
MAP OF MASSACHUSETTS, CONNECTICUT & RHODE ISLAND	43.2 X	55.2 CM	FINLEY
MAP OF MEXICO, CENTRAL AMERICA, & WEST INDIES	30.5 X	50.2 CM	MITCHELL
MAP OF MEXICO...	29.2 X	50.2 CM	MITCHELL
MAP OF MINNESOTA TERRITORY	33.0 X	40.6 CM	DESILVER
MAP OF MINNESOTA TERRITORY	33.0 X	40.6 CM	DESILVER
MAP OF MINNESOTA TERRITORY	33.0 X	40.6 CM	DESILVER
MAP OF MINNESOTA TERRITORY	33.0 X	40.6 CM	DESILVER
MAP OF MINNESOTA TERRITORY	33.0 X	40.6 CM THOMAS, COWPERTHWAI...	
MAP OF NEW BRUNSWICK, P.E.I. AND NOVA SCOTIA	14.6 X	27.2 CM	BAEDEKER
MAP OF NEW HAMPSHIRE & VERMONT	32.0 X	40.0 CM	DESILVER
MAP OF NEW HAMPSHIRE & VERMONT	38.1 X	30.5 CM THOMAS, COWPERTHWAI...	
MAP OF NEW JERSEY COMPILED FROM THE LATEST AUTHORITIES	32.0 X	40.0 CM	DESILVER
MAP OF NEW YORK CITY SOUTH OF 135TH STREET SHOWING NEW ARRANGEMENT DOC	195.0 X	66.0 CM	DRIPPS
MAP OF NEWFOUNDLAND...	12.0 X	15.6 CM	MCGREGOR

256

Title	Dimensions	Publisher
MAP OF NORTH AMERICA	26.7 X 22.9 CM	BURGESS
MAP OF NORTH AMERICA	23.8 X 20.3 CM	ROBINSON
MAP OF NORTH AMERICA EXHIBITING THE RECENT DISCOVERIES GEOGRAPHICAL &	47.6 X 36.2 CM	WYLD
MAP OF NORTH AMERICA...	26.7 X 21.6 CM	ROBINSON
MAP OF NORTH AMERICA...	26.7 X 21.6 CM	ROBINSON
MAP OF NORTH AMERICA...& RECENT DISCOVERIES IN POLAR REGIONS	35.6 X 27.9 CM	MITCHELL
MAP OF NORTH AND SOUTH CAROLINA	19.1 X 23.5 CM	MORSE
MAP OF NORTHWEST TEXAS AND PAN HANDLE	30.5 X 24.1 CM	HARDESTY
MAP OF NOVA-SCOTIA FROM LATE SURVEYS...	19.3 X 24.1 CM	MCGREGOR
MAP OF OREGON TERRITORY	35.6 X 57.5 CM	PARKER
MAP OF OREGON TERRITORY	35.6 X 55.9 CM	PARKER
MAP OF OREGON TERRITORY WEST OF THE CASCADE MOUNTAINS	44.5 X 26.7 CM	U.S.
MAP OF OREGON, WASHINGTON, IDAHO AND PART OF MONTANA	26.7 X 34.3 CM	MITCHELL
MAP OF OREGON, WASHINGTON, IDAHO, AND PART OF MONTANA	27.9 X 34.3 CM	MITCHELL
MAP OF PART OF THE NORTH WEST TERRITORY INCLUDING THE PROVINCE OF MANI	40.6 X 63.5 CM	BELDIN
MAP OF PART OF THE PROVINCES OF RIO DE JANEIRO AND THE MINAS GERAES WI	36.5 X 48.2 CM	ANON
MAP OF PASSES IN THE SIERRA NEVADA	76.8 X 50.2 CM	U.S.
MAP OF POLAND WITH APPENDAGES	17.1 X 20.3 CM	GENTLEMAN'S MAGAZINE
MAP OF PORTION OF THE ARCTIC SHORES OF AMERICA TO ACCOMPANY CAPTN. MC.	34.0 X 50.2 CM	ARROWSMITH
MAP OF PRINCE EDWARD ISLAND IN THE GULF OF ST. LAWRENCE...	11.0 X 17.1 CM	MCGREGOR
MAP OF PUBLIC SURVEYS IN CALIFORNIA	89.5 X 76.2 CM	U.S.
MAP OF PUBLIC SURVEYS IN CALIFORNIA	91.4 X 78.7 CM	U.S.
MAP OF SCANDINAVIA	41.9 X 33.0 CM	ANON
MAP OF SIKKIM	21.6 X 22.9 CM	ROYAL GEOGRAPHICAL ...
MAP OF SOUTH AMERICA	44.5 X 32.5 CM	KITCHIN
MAP OF SOUTHERN TEXAS	33.0 X 48.3 CM	HARDESTY
MAP OF STANDARD TIME ADOPTED BY THE RAILWAYS OF UNITED STATES	22.2 X 27.9 CM	IVISON & BLAKEMAN
MAP OF TEXAS	32.4 X 50.2 CM	MAST, CROWELL & KIR...
MAP OF TEXAS	32.4 X 50.2 CM	MAST, CROWELL & KIR...
MAP OF TEXAS	26.7 X 21.6 CM	OLNEY
MAP OF TEXAS	26.7 X 21.6 CM	ROBINSON
MAP OF TEXAS AND THE COUNTRIES ADJACENT. WASHINGTON, FOR THE STATE DEP	53.3 X 81.9 CM	U.S.
MAP OF TEXAS FROM THE MOST RECENT AUTHORITIES	31.1 X 38.1 CM	MITCHELL
MAP OF TEXAS FROM THE MOST RECENT AUTHORITIES	30.5 X 37.5 CM	TANNER
MAP OF THE ARGENTINE REPUBLIC SHEWING THE LINE OF RAILWAY BETWEEN ROSA	38.1 X 45.7 CM	MACGREGOR
MAP OF THE ARKANSAS SURVEYING DISTRICT SHOWING THE EXTENT OF PUBLIC SU	38.7 X 42.5 CM	U.S.
MAP OF THE BASIN OF THE ST. LAWRENCE SHOWING ALSO THE NATURAL AND ARTI	88.0 X 190.0 CM	ANDREWS
MAP OF THE BLACK LEAD MINES &C. IN CUMBERLAND	19.7 X 24.1 CM	GENTLEMAN'S MAGAZINE
MAP OF THE BOUNDARY DIFFERENCES	18.4 X 26.0 CM	MACLURE & MACDONALD
MAP OF THE BRITISH NORTH AMERICAN PROVINCES AND ADJOINING STATES	39.4 X 67.4 CM	MCGREGOR
MAP OF THE BRITISH POSSESSIONS IN NORTH AMERICA	22.5 X 27.0 CM	WYLD
MAP OF THE CITY AND COUNTY OF NEW YORK, WITH ADJACENT COUNTRY	125.7 X 49.5 CM	BURR
MAP OF THE CITY AND TOWN OF MANCHESTER, N.H.	40.8 X 68.9 CM	HURD
MAP OF THE CITY OF HUNTINGTON	65.4 X 84.7 CM	KINGMAN BROS.
MAP OF THE CITY OF NEW YORK	38.7 X 30.5 CM	PEABODY & CO.
MAP OF THE CITY OF QUEBEC	20.0 X 20.5 CM	NEELE
MAP OF THE COUNTRIES ROUND THE NORTH POLE	30.5 X 27.9 CM	SMITH
MAP OF THE COUNTRY AROUND PHILADELPHIA	17.8 X 22.2 CM	GENTLEMAN'S MAGAZINE
MAP OF THE COUNTRY BETWEEN...ARKANSAS & NEW MEXICO...EXPLORED IN 1849,	68.6 X 149.9 CM	MARCY
MAP OF THE COUNTRY DRAINED BY THE MISSISSIPPI	37.2 X 50.6 CM	ANON
MAP OF THE COUNTRY UPON THE UPPER RED RIVER EXPLORED IN 1852	41.3 X 85.7 CM	MARCY
MAP OF THE COUNTY OF OXFORD FROM ACTUAL SURVEY BY A. BRYANT IN THE YEA	189.2 X 148.0 CM	BRYANT
MAP OF THE COUNTY OF SOMERSET, FROM ACTUAL SURVEY MADE IN THE YEARS 18	134.6 X 182.9 CM	GREENWOOD
MAP OF THE COUNTY OF SUFFOLK	45.7 X 83.8 CM	BURR
MAP OF THE COUNTY PALATINE OF CHESTER, FROM AN ACTUAL SURVEY...	57.2 X 67.9 CM	GREENWOOD
MAP OF THE DEPARTMENT OF THE COLUMBIA...	80.0 X 102.9 CM	U.S.
MAP OF THE DISTRICT OF MAINE, PART OF MASSACHUSETTS	30.5 X 19.7 CM	MORSE
MAP OF THE DOMINION OF CANADA BETWEEN THE BEAUFORT SEA AND THE SOUTHER	14.7 X 29.7 CM	BAEDEKER
MAP OF THE EASTERN PORTION OF BRITISH NORTH AMERICA INCLUDING GULF OF	66.0 X 117.0 CM	ANDREWS
MAP OF THE EASTERN TOWNSHIPS OF LOWER CANADA	24.8 X 40.6 CM	DEAN & MUNDAY
MAP OF THE ENVIRONS OF BOSTON DRAWN AT BOSTON IN JUNE 1775	20.3 X 25.4 CM	ALMON
MAP OF THE GENERAL GOVERNMENT ROADS IN THE TERITORY OF MINNESOTA	45.7 X 31.8 CM	U.S.
MAP OF THE GOLD REGION IN UPPER CALIFORNIA	12.1 X 22.9 CM	FOSTER

MAP OF THE GOLD REGIONS OF THE FRAZER RIVER AND THE WASHINGTON TERRITO	41.9 X 35.6 CM	WYLD
MAP OF THE GREAT SALT LAKE AND ADJACENT COUNTY IN THE TERRITORY OF UTA	43.8 X 30.5 CM	WELLER
MAP OF THE GULF OF MEXICO, THE ISLANDS AND COUNTRIES ADJACENT	31.5 X 48.9 CM	KITCHIN
MAP OF THE HARBOUR AND THREE RIVERS OF PICTOU, AND THE POSITION OF THE	19.5 X 15.5 CM	MCGREGOR
MAP OF THE HARBOUR CITY AND ENVIRONS OF MONTREAL...	18.3 X 22.5 CM	MCGREGOR
MAP OF THE HARBOUR CITY AND ENVIRONS OF QUEBEC...	18.5 X 22.3 CM	MCGREGOR
MAP OF THE HARBOUR OF SYDNEY AND BRIDPORT AND THE POSITION OF THE GENE	18.9 X 23.5 CM	MCGREGOR
MAP OF THE INDIAN TERRITORIES WEST OF MISSOURI AND ARKANSAS, COMPILED	20.3 X 28.6 CM	SCHOOLCRAFT
MAP OF THE ISLAND OF BARBADOES	23.5 X 19.1 CM	EDWARDS
MAP OF THE ISLANDS OF MARTINICO, DOMINICO, GUARDALUPE, ST. CHRISTOPHER	23.7 X 27.7 CM	POLITICAL MAGAZINE
MAP OF THE MEXICAN NATIONAL R.R. (LAREDO ROUTE)	61.0 X 59.7 CM	CRAWFORD
MAP OF THE NATIONAL ROAD BETWEEN CUMBERLAND AND WHEELING	15.2 X 28.6 CM	MELISH
MAP OF THE NEW YORK CENTRAL LINES	19.7 X 39.4 CM	MATTHEWS, NORTHRAP CO.
MAP OF THE PROGRESS OF HIS MAJESTY'S ARMIES IN NEW YORK, DURING THE LA	31.8 X 19.7 CM	GENTLEMAN'S MAGAZINE
MAP OF THE PROVIDENCE LINE & CONNECTION FOR BOSTON, PROVIDENCE...AND B	36.8 X 47.0 CM	CRAWFORD
MAP OF THE PROVINCES OF NEW BRUNSWICK AND PART OF LOWER CANADA...	19.8 X 23.5 CM	MCGREGOR
MAP OF THE RAILROADS IN THE UNITED STATES IN OPERATION AND PROGRESS...	100.0 X 106.0 CM	ANDREWS
MAP OF THE RIVER ST. LAURENCE AND TRIBUTARIES EXHIBITING THE SIGNEURIE	11.5 X 16.3 CM	MCGREGOR
MAP OF THE ROUTES IN NEW YORK, NEW ENGLAND & PENNSYLVANIA, DRAWN FOR T	14.1 X 15.4 CM	HARPER
MAP OF THE SEAT OF WAR IN NORTH AMERICA	40.0 X 55.2 CM	MELISH
MAP OF THE SEAT OF WAR TO ACCOMPANY THE AMERICAN CONFLICT	66.0 X 92.7 CM	CASE
MAP OF THE SOUTHERN & SOUTHWESTERN STATES	30.5 X 44.5 CM	WILLIAMS
MAP OF THE SOUTHERN COAST OF AUSTRALIA, FROM ENCOUNTER BAY TO KING GEO	32.0 X 77.0 CM	ARROWSMITH
MAP OF THE SOUTHERN PART OF THE UNITED STATES OF AMERICA	19.7 X 38.7 CM	RUSSELL
MAP OF THE SOUTHERN STATES OF AMERICA COMPREHENDING MARYLAND, VIRGINIA	36.8 X 49.5 CM	RUSSELL
MAP OF THE STATE OF ALABAMA	32.4 X 26.7 CM	BURR
MAP OF THE STATE OF CALIFORNIA, THE TERRITORIES OF OREGON & UTAH, & PA	40.0 X 33.0 CM	THOMAS, COWPERTHWAI...
MAP OF THE STATE OF KENTUCKY; WITH ADJOINING TERRITORIES	38.0 X 45.0 CM	RUSSELL
MAP OF THE STATE OF KENTUCKY; WITH THE ADJOINING TERRITORIES	37.5 X 45.1 CM	RUSSELL
MAP OF THE STATE OF MISSOURI	25.4 X 36.2 CM	HINTON, SIMPKIN & M...
MAP OF THE STATE OF NEW YORK	19.1 X 24.1 CM	MORSE
MAP OF THE STATE OF NEW YORK PUBLISHED IN 1826	43.2 X 55.2 CM	FINLEY
MAP OF THE STATE OF NEW YORK, WITH PART OF UPPER CANADA. ENGRAVED AND	40.0 X 24.8 CM	HINTON, SIMPKIN & M...
MAP OF THE STATE OF OHIO	39.4 X 33.0 CM	THOMAS, COWPERTHWAI...
MAP OF THE STATE OF OHIO DRAWN BY A. BOURNE...	48.3 X 41.3 CM	ATWATER
MAP OF THE STATE OF TEXAS	20.3 X 26.7 CM	MITCHELL
MAP OF THE STATE OF TEXAS	20.3 X 26.7 CM	MITCHELL
MAP OF THE STATE OF TEXAS	26.7 X 20.3 CM	MITCHELL
MAP OF THE STATE OF TEXAS	20.6 X 26.7 CM	MITCHELL
MAP OF THE STATE OF TEXAS	20.3 X 26.7 CM	MITCHELL
MAP OF THE STATE OF TEXAS	20.3 X 26.7 CM	MITCHELL
MAP OF THE STATE OF TEXAS	20.3 X 26.7 CM	MITCHELL
MAP OF THE STATE OF TEXAS	20.3 X 26.7 CM	MITCHELL
MAP OF THE STATE OF TEXAS	20.3 X 26.7 CM	MITCHELL
MAP OF THE STATE OF TEXAS	26.7 X 20.3 CM	MITCHELL
MAP OF THE STATE OF TEXAS	20.3 X 26.7 CM	MITCHELL
MAP OF THE STATE OF TEXAS...	32.4 X 39.4 CM	DESILVER
MAP OF THE STATES NORTH & SOUTH CAROLINA	25.4 X 39.4 CM	HINTON
MAP OF THE STATES OF ALABAMA AND GEORGIA	25.4 X 40.0 CM	HINTON, SIMPKIN & M...
MAP OF THE STATES OF CALIFORNIA THE TERRITORIES OF OREGON & UTAH...	39.4 X 33.0 CM	MITCHELL
MAP OF THE STATES OF INDIANA AND OHIO, WITH PART OF MICHIGAN TERRITORY	24.8 X 39.7 CM	FENNER, SEARS & CO.
MAP OF THE STATES OF MISSISSIPPI, LOUISIANA AND ARKANSAS TERRITORY	41.3 X 26.7 CM	FENNER, SEARS & CO
MAP OF THE STATES OF NORTH & SOUTH CAROLINA. ENGRAVED & PRINTED BY FEN	24.8 X 40.0 CM	HINTON, SIMPKIN & M...
MAP OF THE TERRITORY OF THE UNITED STATES FROM THE MISSISSIPPI TO THE	107.3 X 116.8 CM	U.S
MAP OF THE U.S. & TERRITORIES SHOWING THE EXTENT OF THE PUBLIC SURVEYS	71.8 X 142.2 CM	U.S
MAP OF THE U.S. AND THEIR TERRITORIES BETWEEN THE MISSISSIPPI AND THE	51.4 X 58.4 CM	U.S
MAP OF THE U.S. EXHIBITING THE PROGRESS MADE IN THE GEOLOGIC SURVEY...	43.8 X 71.8 CM	U.S
MAP OF THE U.S.A. SHOWING THE BOUNDARIES OF THE UNION & CONFEDERATE GE	42.5 X 70.5 CM	U.S
MAP OF THE U.S.A. SHOWING THE BOUNDARIES OF THE UNION AND CONFEDERATE	42.5 X 70.5 CM	U.S
MAP OF THE UNITED STATES	25.4 X 43.2 CM	ROBINSON
MAP OF THE UNITED STATES	25.4 X 42.5 CM	ROBINSON

258

MAP OF THE UNITED STATES & CANADA	26.7 X 44.5 CM	BURGESS
MAP OF THE UNITED STATES AND TERRITORIES, TOGETHER WITH CANADA &C.	33.7 X 53.3 CM	MITCHELL
MAP OF THE UNITED STATES AND TEXAS	26.7 X 44.5 CM	BURGESS
MAP OF THE UNITED STATES AND TEXAS	26.7 X 44.5 CM	BURGESS
MAP OF THE UNITED STATES ENGRAVED TO ILLUSTRATE MITCHELL'S SCHOOL AND	26.4 X 42.5 CM	MITCHELL
MAP OF THE UNITED STATES OF AMERICA	37.5 X 47.0 CM	CAREY
MAP OF THE UNITED STATES SHOWING THE FARM ANIMALS IN EACH STATE	44.5 X 61.0 CM	HILL & CO.
MAP OF THE UNITED STATES, AND TEXAS	44.5 X 58.4 CM	HARPER & BROS.
MAP OF THE UNITED STATES, CANADA	40.0 X 34.9 CM	FOOT
MAP OF THE UNITED STATES, CANADA, TEXAS & PART MEXICO	27.3 X 44.5 CM	OLNEY
MAP OF THE UNITED STATES, THE BRITISH PROVINCES, MEXICO...	86.4 X 109.2 CM	COLTON
MAP OF THE VALLEY OF THE ORINOCO RIVER	26.0 X 40.6 CM	NATIONAL GEOGRAPHIC...
MAP OF THE WEST INDIA & BAHAMA ISLANDS WITH THE ADJACENT COASTS OF YUC	52.7 X 76.8 CM	WYLD
MAP OF THE WESTERN MILITARY DEPARTMENTS, OF THE UNITED STATES, SHOWING	29.4 X 34.0 CM	U.S.
MAP OF THE WORLD FROM THE BEST AUTHORITIES	18.4 X 34.9 CM	MORSE
MAP OF THE WORLD ON MERCATOR'S PROJECTION...SHOWING THE CENTRAL POSITI	53.3 X 58.4 CM	BURR
MAP OF THE WORLD ON THE MERCATOR PROJECTION...	36.2 X 45.7 CM	MITCHELL
MAP OF UNITED STATES AND CANADA	32.4 X 27.9 CM	LIZARS
MAP OF UPPER CANADA EXHIBITING THE DISTRICTS & COUNTIES...	12.0 X 20.3 CM	MCGREGOR
MAP OF WESTERN TEXAS	47.0 X 30.5 CM	HARDESTY
MAP SHEWING DOMINION LANDS SURVEYED OR EXPLORED IN THE PROVINCE OF MAN	31.0 X 47.0 CM	CANADA
MAP SHEWING THE TOWNSHIPS SURVEYED IN THE PROVINCE OF MANITOBA AND NOR	65.5 X 96.5 CM	CANADA
MAP SHOWING THE LOCATION OF PUEBLOS IN NEW MEXICO	22.9 X 34.3 CM	U.S.
MAP: SHOWING INDIAN RESERVATIONS WITHIN THE LIMITS OF THE U.S.	53.3 X 83.8 CM	MORGAN
MAPA DE LAS PROVINCIAS DE VENEZUELA Y DEL REINO DE SANTA FE	24.5 X 32.0 CM	TORRENTE
MAPPA AESTIVARIUM INSULARUM, ALIAS BARMUDAS DICTARUM...ACCURATE DISCRI	40.6 X 53.3 CM	BLAEU
MAPPA AESTIVARUM INSULARUM ALIAS BARMUDAS	39.4 X 51.4 CM	HONDIUS
MAPPA AESTIVARUM INSULARUM ALIAS BARMUDAS DICTARUM	39.0 X 52.0 CM	HONDIUS
MAPPA AESTIVARUM INSULARUM ALIAS BARMUDAS...	40.0 X 53.0 CM	BLAEU
MAPPA AESTIVARUM INSULARUM...	39.4 X 51.4 CM	HONDIUS
MAPPA FLUXUS ET REFLUXUS...	34.3 X 41.1 CM	KIRCHER
MAPPA GEOGRAPHICA PROVINCIAE NOVAE EBORACI AB ANGLIS NEW YORK	71.0 X 57.0 CM	HOMANN
MAPPE MONDE PHYSIQUE SUR LA PROJECTION REDUITE DE MERCATOR...	36.8 X 50.8 CM	BRUE
MAPPE MONDE QUI COMPREND LES NOUVELLES DECOUVERTES FAITES JUSQUA CE JO	21.9 X 29.5 CM	LE ROUGE
MAPPE-MONDE GEO-HYDROGRAPHIQUE DESCRIPTION GENERALE DU GLOBE TERRESTRE	55.9 X 96.5 CM	MORTIER
MAPPE-MONDE GEO-HYDROGRAPHIQUE, OU DESCRIPTION GENERALE DU GLOBE TERRE	47.0 X 66.0 CM	JAILLOT
MAPPE-MONDE OU CARTE GENERALE DU GLOBE TERRESTRE, REPRESENTE EN DEUX P	14.6 X 16.5 CM	SANSON
MAPPE-MONDE, OU CARTE GENERALE DE LA TERRE, DIVISEE EN DEUX HEMISPHERE	44.5 X 70.5 CM	DE FER
MAPPE-MONDE...	33.5 X 45.5 CM	CHATELAIN
MAPPEMONDE	49.5 X 61.0 CM	JAILLOT
MAPPEMONDE PHILOSOPHIQUE ET POLITIQUE	52.1 X 76.2 CM	BRION DE LA TOUR
MAPPEMONDE POUR LA CONCORDE DE LA GEOGRAPHIE	14.0 X 27.0 CM	PLUCHE
MAPPEMONDE...	22.9 X 43.8 CM	CHATELAIN
MAR DEL NORT and MAR DI AETHIOPIA	43.2 X 55.9 CM	JANSSON
MARCA ANCONAE	13.5 X 17.5 CM	PTOLEMY (1596-1621 ...
MARCHIONATUS MORAVIAE AUCT I. COMENIO	38.1 X 53.3 CM	HONDIUS
MARCHIONATUS SACRI ROMANI IMPERII. CL. J. VISSCHER EXCUDEBAT. NICOLAUS	46.0 X 56.0 CM	VISSCHER
MARCHIONATUS SACRI ROMANI IMPERII. CL. J. VISSCHER EXCUDIT ANNO 1624	38.5 X 49.5 CM	VISSCHER
MARE DEL NORD...	45.0 X 60.0 CM	CORONELLI
MARE DEL SUD DETTO ALTRIMENTI MARE PACIFICO	45.7 X 58.4 CM	CORONELLI
MARE DEL SUD...	45.0 X 61.0 CM	CORONELLI
MARIONETHSHIRE DESCRIBED 1610	38.7 X 47.6 CM	SPEED
MARIS PACIFICI (QUOD VULGO MAR DEL ZUR) CUM REGIONIBUS CIRCUMIACENTIBU	37.5 X 50.8 CM	ORTELIUS
MARIS PACIFICI VULGO MAR DEL ZUR	20.3 X 27.9 CM	METELLUS
MARIS PACIFICI...	34.3 X 49.5 CM	ORTELIUS
MARITIMES	60.3 X 47.6 CM	ARROWSMITH
MARMARICA NUOVA TAVOLA	17.8 X 24.1 CM	PTOLEMY (1561-99 VE...
MARMARICA NUOVA TAVOLA	17.8 X 24.1 CM	PTOLEMY (1561-99 VE...
MARTINICO, ONE OF THE CARIBEE ISLANDS...ACCORDING TO THE OBSERVATIONS	34.5 X 36.7 CM	JEFFERYS
MARTINICO...	36.8 X 34.9 CM	UNIVERSAL MAGAZINE
MARTINIQUE	22.9 X 29.2 CM	LUCAS
MARYLAND	35.6 X 29.2 CM	BRADFORD
MARYLAND	28.9 X 36.2 CM	BRADFORD

MARYLAND	31.8 X 45.1 CM	CAREY
MARYLAND	28.6 X 49.5 CM	LUCAS
MARYLAND & DELAWARE	27.9 X 43.2 CM	SWINSTON
MARYLAND AND DELAWARE	26.7 X 34.3 CM	TANNER
MASSACHUSETTS	35.6 X 29.2 CM	BRADFORD
MASSACHUSETTS	29.8 X 45.7 CM	CAREY & LEA
MASSACHUSETTS	17.8 X 30.5 CM	DORR, HOWLAND & CO.
MASSACHUSETTS	15.2 X 18.4 CM	SCOTT
MASSACHUSETTS AND RHODE ISLAND	30.5 X 37.5 CM	MORSE
MASSACHUSETTS AND RHODE ISLAND	30.5 X 39.5 CM	TANNER
MASSACHUSETTS, CONNECTUCUT & RHODE ISLAND	21.6 X 27.9 CM	BARNES & BURR
MASSACHUSETTS, RHODE ISLAND & CONNECTICUT	21.6 X 27.9 CM	ATWOOD
MASSACHUSETTS, RHODE ISLAND & CONNECTICUT	20.0 X 24.8 CM	MORSE
MASTRICH (VIEW)	44.0 X 33.0 CM	LE CLERC
MECHLINIA DOMINIUM, ET AERSCHOT DUCATUS	41.0 X 52.0 CM	BLAEU
MEDITERANEO E GOLF DE SETALIA	8.5 X 12.0 CM	COTOVICUS
MER DE SUD OU PACIFIQUE CONTENANT L'ISLE DE CALIFORNIA	59.7 X 73.7 CM	MORTIER
MER DES ANTILLES ET GOLFE DU MEXIQUE. VENTS GENERAUX. DRESSE PAR CH. D	45.7 X 29.2 CM	DEPOT DE LA MARINE
MER MEDITERRANE	57.2 X 86.4 CM	MORTIER
MERIDA, SIERRA NEVADA (VIEW)	20.0 X 30.0 CM	GOERING
MERIONETH COMITATUS OLIM PARS ORDIWICUM	26.7 X 32.4 CM	KIP
MERIONETHSHIRE	11.4 X 14.0 CM	SELLER
MERS DU NORD	33.0 X 44.5 CM	BELLIN
MERVINIA; ET MONTGOMERIA COMITATUS	38.1 X 49.5 CM	JANSSON
MESSICO OU VERO NUOVA SPAGNA CHE CONTIENE EL NUOVO MESSICO-LA CALIFORN	31.1 X 40.6 CM	ZATTA
MESSICO...IL NUOVO MESSICO, LA CALIFORNIA...	31.0 X 41.0 CM	ZATTA
MEXICO	48.3 X 60.3 CM	ARROWSMITH
MEXICO	22.9 X 24.8 CM	ARROWSMITH
MEXICO	29.2 X 23.5 CM	CARY
MEXICO	26.0 X 36.8 CM	HALL
MEXICO	25.4 X 36.8 CM	HALL
MEXICO	25.4 X 37.1 CM	HALL
MEXICO	25.4 X 36.8 CM	HALL
MEXICO	22.9 X 29.2 CM	LUCAS
MEXICO	30.5 X 41.9 CM	MORSE & BREESE
MEXICO	25.4 X 33.0 CM	TALLIS
MEXICO & CENTRAL AMERICA	50.8 X 60.3 CM	HUGHES
MEXICO & GUATEMALA	30.5 X 38.1 CM	DESILVER
MEXICO & GUATEMALA	30.5 X 38.1 CM	MITCHELL
MEXICO & GUATEMALA	29.2 X 36.2 CM	TANNER
MEXICO & GUATIMALA	21.0 X 25.4 CM	DOWER
MEXICO & GUATIMALA	21.0 X 25.4 CM	DOWER
MEXICO & GUATIMALA	19.1 X 24.1 CM	FULLARTON
MEXICO & TEXAS	22.9 X 28.6 CM	ARCHER
MEXICO & TEXAS	28.6 X 22.9 CM	GRATTON & GILBERT
MEXICO AND CENTRAL STATES	40.6 X 50.8 CM	HALL
MEXICO AND CENTRAL STATES	41.0 X 51.0 CM	HALL
MEXICO AND GUATEMALA	30.5 X 38.1 CM	THOMAS, COWPERTHWAI...
MEXICO AND GUATIMALA	33.0 X 40.6 CM	TEESDALE
MEXICO AND GUATIMALA	33.7 X 40.6 CM	TEESDALE
MEXICO AND GUATIMALA CORRECTED FROM ORIGINAL INFORMATION COMMUNICATED	41.3 X 51.4 CM	HALL
MEXICO OR NEW SPAIN	9.5 X 6.4 CM	BOWEN
MEXICO OR NEW SPAIN	43.8 X 38.7 CM	CAREY
MEXICO OR NEW SPAIN	45.4 X 41.3 CM	CAREY
MEXICO OR NEW SPAIN	16.5 X 18.4 CM	MOLL
MEXICO OR NEW SPAIN IN WHICH THE MOTIONS OF CORTES MAY BE TRACED	29.2 X 38.1 CM	KITCHIN
MEXICO OR NEW SPAIN...	38.1 X 27.9 CM	KITCHIN
MEXICO, CALIFORNIA & TEXAS	25.4 X 36.8 CM	BLACK
MEXICO, CALIFORNIA & TEXAS	26.0 X 37.0 CM	BLACK
MEXICO, CALIFORNIA & TEXAS	26.0 X 36.8 CM	HALL
MEXICO, CALIFORNIA & TEXAS	26.0 X 36.8 CM	HALL
MEXICO, CALIFORNIA & TEXAS	26.7 X 33.0 CM	TALLIS
MEXICO, CALIFORNIA & TEXAS	24.8 X 32.4 CM	TALLIS

MEXICO, CALIFORNIA AND TEXAS	25.4 X 33.0 CM	TALLIS
MEXICO, CALIFORNIA AND TEXAS	20.0 X 25.0 CM	TALLIS
MEXICO, CALIFORNIA AND TEXAS	25.4 X 33.0 CM	TALLIS
MEXICO, GUATEMALA & WEST INDIES	20.3 X 25.4 CM	BRADFORD
MEXICO, GUATIMALA...	8.3 X 15.2 CM	BOYNTON
MEXICO, TEXAS, GUATIMALA...	11.4 X 15.2 CM	BOYNTON
MEXICO/CUSCO	26.7 X 47.6 CM	BRAUN & HOGENBERG
MEXIQUE	21.6 X 28.6 CM	ANTOINE
MEXIQUE	19.1 X 24.1 CM	MONIN & FREMIN
MEXIQUE-DE STADT MEXICO	15.2 X 10.2 CM	MALLET
MICHIGAN	13.5 X 16.9 CM	ANON
MICHIGAN	58.4 X 40.6 CM	ASHER & ADAMS
MICHIGAN	35.6 X 29.2 CM	BRADFORD
MICHIGAN	30.5 X 26.7 CM	BURR
MICHIGAN	32.4 X 38.1 CM	MORSE & BREESE
MICHIGAN	77.5 X 63.5 CM	U.S.
MICHIGAN TER.	22.9 X 30.5 CM	LUCAS
MIDDLE-SEX DESCRIBED	38.7 X 47.6 CM	SPEED
MIDDLE-SEXIA	39.0 X 41.0 CM	BLAEU
MIDDLESEX	11.4 X 14.0 CM	SELLER
MIDDLESEX	11.4 X 15.2 CM	SELLER
MIDDLESEX	23.5 X 19.1 CM	WILKES
MIDDLESEX OLIMA TRINOBANTIBUS HABITATA	27.3 X 26.0 CM	NORDEN
MIDLE-SEX, DESCRIBED WITH THE MOST FAMOUS CITIES OF LONDON AND WESTMIN	38.1 X 50.8 CM	SPEED
MILFORD HAVEN	44.5 X 56.5 CM	COLLINS
MISSION OF SAN CARLOS, AND BAY OF CARMEL, UPPER CALIFORNIA (VIEW)	11.1 X 19.6 CM	SMYTH
MISSISSIPPI	35.6 X 29.2 CM	BRADFORD
MISSISSIPPI	35.6 X 28.6 CM	BRADFORD
MISSISSIPPI	29.2 X 22.9 CM	LUCAS
MISSISSIPPI	22.9 X 29.2 CM	LUCAS
MISSISSIPPI CITY HARBOUR	40.6 X 43.2 CM	U.S. COAST SURVEY
MISSISSIPPI LOUISIANA & ARKANSAS	27.3 X 21.0 CM	BARNES & BURR
MISSISSIPPI RIVER AND ENVIRONS	21.6 X 42.5 CM	U.S.
MISSISSIPPI TERRITORY	31.1 X 35.6 CM	CAREY
MISSISSIPPI TERRITORY	25.4 X 20.3 CM	LEWIS & ARROWSMITH
MISSOURI	35.6 X 29.2 CM	BRADFORD
MISSOURI	29.2 X 35.6 CM	BRADFORD
MISSOURI	43.2 X 53.3 CM	BRADLEY
MISSOURI	29.5 X 32.7 CM	BURR
MISSOURI TERRITORY FORMERLY LOUISIANA	30.5 X 35.6 CM	CAREY
MISSOURI TO THE MOUTH OF TRAP CREEK	78.7 X 57.8 CM	U.S.
MITCHELL'S MAP OF ILLINOIS EXHIBITING ITS INTERNAL IMPROVEMENTS...PUBL	38.1 X 31.8 CM	MITCHELL
MITCHELL'S NATIONAL MAP OF THE AMERICAN REPUBLIC...	92.7 X 115.6 CM	MITCHELL
MODERN MAP OF NORTHAMPTON-SHIRE...	25.4 X 19.1 CM	ELLIS
MODERN PALESTINE	20.0 X 25.0 CM	TALLIS
MOMONIA, HIBERNICE MOUN ET WOUN; ANGLIC MOUNSTER	41.3 X 52.1 CM	BLAEU
MONA INSULA VULGO ANGLESEY/MONA INSULA: VULGO THE ISLE OF MAN/VECTIS I	50.2 X 55.9 CM	JANSSON
MONA INSULA VULGO ANGLESEY/MONA INSULA: VULGO THE ISLE OF MAN/VECTIS I	50.2 X 55.9 CM	JANSSON
MONDO NUOVO	10.5 X 14.5 CM	PORCACCHI
MONDO NUOVO	10.2 X 14.3 CM	PORCACCHI
MONMEDI EN LUXEMBOURG (VIEW)	14.5 X 50.0 CM	COCHIN
MONMOUTHSHIRE	23.5 X 19.1 CM	WILKES
MONMOUTHSHRIRE	19.1 X 30.5 CM	MOLL
MONTAGNE DE POTOSI	10.2 X 15.2 CM	MALLET
MONTANA	31.8 X 48.3 CM	RAND MCNALLY
MONTGOMERY COMITATUS QUI OLIM PARS ORDOVICUM	26.7 X 31.8 CM	KIP
MONTGOMERY SHIRE	38.7 X 47.6 CM	SPEED
MONTGOMERYSHIRE	11.4 X 14.0 CM	SELLER
MONTREAL	20.0 X 17.5 CM	BAEDEKER
MOREA	21.0 X 15.0 CM	CAMOCIO
MOSCAUW	34.9 X 49.5 CM	BRAUN & HOGENBERG
MOSCOVIA OR RUSSIA	16.5 X 17.8 CM	MOLL
MOSCOVIAE PARS AUSTRALIS AUCTORE ISACCO MASSA	38.7 X 50.8 CM	JANSSON

261

MOUNTAINS & RIVERS	26.0 X 37.0 CM	BLACK
MOUTH OF GALIEN RIVER MICHIGAN	49.5 X 77.5 CM	U.S.
MOUTH OF THE COLUMBIA RIVER...	43.2 X 67.9 CM	U.S. COAST SURVEY
MUD LAKES TO THE PACIFIC OCEAN	52.1 X 44.5 CM	U.S.
N. & S. CAROLINA, GEORGIA & FLORIDA	25.4 X 19.4 CM	MEYER
N.W. TERRITORY	15.2 X 17.8 CM	SCOTT
NAMURCUM COMITATUS	24.0 X 32.0 CM	DE BRUYN
NAMURCUM COMITATUS	24.0 X 32.0 CM	DE BRUYN
NAMURCUM COMITATUS	25.5 X 33.5 CM	MERIAN
NAMURCUM COMITATUS, AUCTORE IOHANN SURHONIO	41.0 X 51.0 CM	BLAEU
NAMURCUM COMITATUS. IOES. SURHON DESCR. AMSTERDAM, P. KAERIUS EXCUDIT,	38.0 X 50.0 CM	VAN DEN KEERE
NAMURCUM COMITATUS. PETRUS KAERIUS CAELAVIT	23.5 X 31.0 CM	VAN DEN KEERE
NAMURCUM, COMITATUS. IOES. SURHON DESCRIB. 1579	39.0 X 51.0 CM	ORTELIUS
NAMURCUM, COMITATUS. IOES. SURHON DESCRIB. 1579	39.0 X 51.0 CM	ORTELIUS
NAMURCUM...NAMEN. COLONIE EXC. IOHAN BUSSM	19.0 X 26.5 CM	QUAD
NANTUCKET HARBOR	35.9 X 43.7 CM	U.S. COAST SURVEY
NATAL	20.0 X 25.0 CM	TALLIS
NATOLIA NUOVA TAVOLA	17.8 X 24.8 CM PTOLEMY (1561-99 VE...
NATOLIA OLIM ASIA MINOR	13.5 X 17.5 CM PTOLEMY (1596-1621 ...
NATOLIAE, QUAE OLIM ASIA MINOR, NOVA DESCRIPTIO. AEGYPTI RE CENTOR DE	29.2 X 48.9 CM	ORTELIUS
NEBRASKA	39.4 X 58.4 CM	ASHER & ADAMS
NEBRASKA	41.9 X 55.9 CM	BRADLEY
NEBRASKA	41.9 X 55.9 CM	BRADLEY
NEBRASKA AND KANZAS	31.8 X 40.6 CM	COLTON
NEBRASKA AND KANZAS	32.4 X 40.0 CM	COLTON
NEBRASKA, DAKOTA, COLORADO, & KANSAS	31.8 X 39.4 CM	JOHNSON & WARD
NEOPOLITANUM REGNUM	13.5 X 17.5 CM PTOLEMY (1596-1621 ...
NEU BRAUNFELS IN TEXAS (VIEW)	10.2 X 15.2 CM	HILDBURG INSTITUT
NEUESTE KARTE VON OHIO	37.1 X 30.2 CM	MEYER
NEW AND ACCURATE CHART OF HUDSON'S BAY, IN NORTH AMERICA	17.5 X 22.6 CM	POLITICAL MAGAZINE
NEW BRUNSWICK & NOVA SCOTIA LAND COMPANY, MAP OF COMPANY'S TRACT OF LA	55.9 X 68.6 CM	CROSS
NEW BRUNSWICK, NOVA SCOTIA	123.0 X 158.0 CM	MACKINLAY
NEW BRUNSWICK, NOVA SCOTIA, NEWFOUNDLAND, AND PRINCE EDWARD ID.	32.0 X 39.0 CM	COLTON
NEW BRUNSWICK, NOVA SCOTIA, PRINCE EDWARD ISLAND, AND PART OF CANADA E	35.0 X 50.0 CM	BLACKIE & SON
NEW ENGLAND AND NEW YORK IN 1697	19.1 X 24.7 CM HINTON, SIMPKIN & M...
NEW ENGLAND AND NEW YORK IN 1697 FROM THE "MAGNALIA AMERICANA" ENGRAVE	19.1 X 24.8 CM HINTON, SIMPKIN & M...
NEW ENGLAND, NEW YORK, NEW JERSEY AND PENSILVANIA	20.0 X 27.5 CM	MOLL
NEW FOUND LAND. H. MOLL, FECIT.	16.2 X 10.8 CM	LA HONTAN
NEW GRANADA, SAVANILLA HARBOUR & RIO MAGDALENA TO BARRANQUILLA	45.7 X 61.0 CM	ADMIRALTY
NEW HAMPSHIRE	35.6 X 29.2 CM	BRADFORD
NEW HAMPSHIRE	40.0 X 32.4 CM	COLTON
NEW HAMPSHIRE	22.9 X 29.2 CM	LUCAS
NEW HAMPSHIRE BY SAM'L LEWIS. ENGRAVED FOR M. CAREY, SEXMEAR, SCUPT.	19.1 X 14.3 CM	CAREY & WARNER
NEW JERSEY	35.6 X 28.6 CM	BRADFORD
NEW JERSEY	35.6 X 29.2 CM	BRADFORD
NEW JERSEY	38.1 X 31.1 CM	COLTON
NEW JERSEY	35.6 X 27.9 CM	MORSE
NEW JERSEY	18.4 X 15.2 CM	SCOTT
NEW JERSEY	26.7 X 16.5 CM	SWINSTON
NEW JERSEY	35.6 X 29.2 CM	TANNER
NEW MAP OF KENT	41.5 X 53.5 CM	BOWLES
NEW MAP OF N. AMERICA...	152.4 X 152.4 CM	MONK
NEW MAP OF THE ENGLISH EMPIRE IN AMERICA VIZ VIRGINIA MARYLAND CAROLIN	50.2 X 59.1 CM	SENEX
NEW MAP OF THE ISLE OF MAN...	25.4 X 19.1 CM	KITCHIN
NEW MAP OF...NORTH AMERICA EXHIBITING THE UNITED STATES & TERRITORIES.	157.5 X 147.3 CM	MONK
NEW MEXICO	11.5 X 13.0 CM	MORDEN
NEW MEXICO AND ARIZONA	29.2 X 38.1 CM	GRAY
NEW NIEDERLAND (VIEW)	13.3 X 16.5 CM	DAPPER
NEW ORLEANS	18.3 X 20.2 CM	BAEDEKER
NEW POCKET MAP OF PORTUGAL	64.5 X 48.0 CM	BOWLES
NEW RAIL ROAD MAP OF THE UNITED STATES	39.8 X 66.8 CM	KINGMAN BROS.
NEW RAILROAD AND DISTANCE MAP OF KENTUCKY AND TENNESSEE	31.8 X 40.6 CM	WATSON
NEW SOUTH WALES	19.5 X 24.5 CM	KELLY

NEW SOUTH WALES	20.0 X 25.0 CM	TALLIS
NEW SOUTH WALES	43.0 X 30.5 CM	WELLER
NEW YORK	20.3 X 27.9 CM	BARNES & BURR
NEW YORK	10.2 X 17.8 CM	BLUNT
NEW YORK	35.6 X 29.2 CM	BRADFORD
NEW YORK	25.4 X 31.8 CM	BURR
NEW YORK	29.8 X 46.4 CM	LUCAS
NEW YORK	20.0 X 24.4 CM	MORSE
NEW YORK	30.5 X 38.1 CM	MORSE & BREESE
NEW YORK	15.2 X 18.4 CM	SCOTT
NEW YORK BAY AND HARBOR, NEW YORK	77.5 X 67.6 CM	U.S. COAST SURVEY
NEW YORK CITY	35.6 X 29.2 CM	BRADFORD
NEW YORK IN 1792 (VIEW)	29.8 X 46.4 CM	VALENTINE'S MANUAL
NEW YORK ISLAND & PARTS ADJACENT	26.5 X 17.0 CM	GORDON
NEW YORK, PENSYLVANIA, MARYLAND, NEW JERSEY, DELAWARE & VIRGINIA	26.7 X 19.7 CM	MEYER
NEW ZEALAND	42.5 X 32.4 CM	JOHNSTON
NEW ZEALAND	20.0 X 25.0 CM	TALLIS
NEW ZEALAND	35.6 X 26.0 CM	TALLIS
NEW-YORK AND ADJACENT COUNTRY	16.2 X 10.4 CM	MELISH
NEWBURG (VIEW)	35.6 X 53.7 CM	MEGAREY
NEWBURYPORT	10.2 X 17.8 CM	BLUNT
NEWFOUNDLAND AND NOVA SCOTIA	34.3 X 26.7 CM	TALLIS
NEWPORT	10.2 X 17.8 CM	BLUNT
NICARIA	12.0 X 16.5 CM	CORONELLI
NIEUPOORT...LAMBARTUS CORNELIJ DEDICABAT	35.0 X 45.0 CM	CORNELIS
NIEUWE AFTEEKENING VAN...DE STAD ENKHUISEN INDE ZUYDER ZEE...P.E. INV.	51.0 X 59.0 CM	VAN KEULEN
NIEUWE EN ALGEMEENE VAN AMERICA	34.3 X 41.9 CM	BACHIENE
NIEUWE KAART VAN HET WESTELYKSTE DEEL DE WEERELD	33.0 X 35.6 CM	TIRION
NIEUWE KAART VAN HET WESTELYKSTE DEEL DER WEERELD...	34.3 X 35.6 CM	TIRION
NIEUWE KAART, VAN T'LAND DONAWERT, EN HOCHSTETT &C ALWAAR DE ROEMWAARD	29.2 X 40.6 CM	ANON
NIEUWE PLATTE PASKAART VAN DE STRAAT DAVIDS, VAN 67 GRAADE TOT 73 GRAA	59.7 X 100.3 CM	VAN KEULEN
NLLE. GALLES MERIDLE. OU COTE ORIENTALE DE LA NOUVELLE HOLLANDE	34.5 X 23.5 CM	BONNE
NLLE. GALLES MERIDLE. OU COTE ORIENTALE DE LA NOUVELLE HOLLANDE	36.5 X 79.5 CM	BONNE
NOBILIS HANNONIAE COM. DESCRIPTIO. P. KAERIUS EXCUDIT 1616	37.0 X 48.0 CM	VAN DEN KEERE
NOBILIS HANNONIAE COMITATUS DESCRIP. AUCTORE IACOBO SURHONIO MONTANO	37.0 X 49.0 CM	ORTELIUS
NOBILIS HANNONIAE COMITATUS DESCRIP. AUCTORE IACOBO SURHONIO MONTANO.	37.0 X 49.0 CM	GALLE
NONA ASIAE TABULA	40.0 X 48.3 CM	PTOLEMY (1513-20 ST...
NOORD-POOL	17.8 X 23.5 CM	ANON
NOOTKA SOUND-PORT EFFINGHAM...	19.7 X 31.8 CM	MEARS
NORDLICHER THEIL DER VEREINIGTEN STAATEN	27.9 X 33.7 CM	REICHARD
NORFOLCIAE COMITATUS QUEM...	26.7 X 38.7 CM	KIP
NORFOLK	24.1 X 19.1 CM	BELL
NORFOLK	10.2 X 17.8 CM	CAPPER
NORFOLK	17.8 X 26.7 CM	ELLIS
NORFOLK	11.4 X 14.0 CM	SELLER
NORFOLK	10.8 X 6.4 CM	WALLIS & REID
NORFOLK A COUNTIE FLORISHING & POPULOUS DESCRIBED AND DEVIDED WITH THE	38.1 X 50.2 CM	SPEED
NORFOLK A COUNTIE FLORISHING & POPULOUS DESCRIBED AND DEVIDED WITH THE	39.4 X 50.8 CM	SPEED
NORFOLK A COUNTIE FLORISHING & POPULOUS...	38.7 X 47.6 CM	SPEED
NORFOLK BY ROBT. MORDEN	37.5 X 57.8 CM	MORDEN
NORTH & SOUTH CAROLINA	25.4 X 39.4 CM	FENNER, SEARS & CO.
NORTH & SOUTH WALES	58.4 X 41.9 CM	BARTHOLOMEW
NORTH AMERICA	28.6 X 24.8 CM	ARCHER
NORTH AMERICA	15.0 X 21.0 CM	ARCHER
NORTH AMERICA	25.5 X 20.5 CM	ARROWSMITH
NORTH AMERICA	26.0 X 43.5 CM	BANKES
NORTH AMERICA	35.6 X 29.8 CM	BRADFORD
NORTH AMERICA	25.4 X 19.7 CM	BRADFORD
NORTH AMERICA	35.6 X 29.2 CM	BRADFORD
NORTH AMERICA	38.1 X 30.5 CM	CHAPMAN & HALL
NORTH AMERICA	23.5 X 29.5 CM	CRUCHLEY
NORTH AMERICA	20.3 X 26.7 CM	CUMMINGS
NORTH AMERICA	10.0 X 12.0 CM	DURY

NORTH AMERICA	20.3 X 24.1 CM	FULLARTON
NORTH AMERICA	24.5 X 20.5 CM	FULLARTON
NORTH AMERICA	38.1 X 25.4 CM	HALL
NORTH AMERICA	38.1 X 27.9 CM	HALL
NORTH AMERICA	50.8 X 41.9 CM	HALL
NORTH AMERICA	57.5 X 44.0 CM	JOHNSTON
NORTH AMERICA	22.9 X 29.2 CM	LUCAS
NORTH AMERICA	39.4 X 32.4 CM	MITCHELL
NORTH AMERICA	24.5 X 19.5 CM	MORRISON & WEST
NORTH AMERICA	24.4 X 20.0 CM	MORSE
NORTH AMERICA	38.1 X 31.1 CM	MORSE & BREESE
NORTH AMERICA	43.8 X 53.3 CM	NEELE
NORTH AMERICA	50.8 X 71.1 CM	PINKERTON
NORTH AMERICA	23.5 X 20.3 CM	ROBINSON
NORTH AMERICA	38.1 X 30.5 CM	SDUK
NORTH AMERICA	38.1 X 30.5 CM	SDUK
NORTH AMERICA	38.1 X 30.5 CM	SDUK
NORTH AMERICA	22.0 X 35.0 CM	SMITH
NORTH AMERICA	26.7 X 35.6 CM	SMITH
NORTH AMERICA	35.6 X 24.1 CM	TALLIS
NORTH AMERICA	32.0 X 26.0 CM	TALLIS
NORTH AMERICA	35.6 X 24.1 CM	TALLIS
NORTH AMERICA	20.0 X 25.0 CM	TALLIS
NORTH AMERICA	34.3 X 26.7 CM	TALLIS
NORTH AMERICA	35.6 X 23.8 CM	TALLIS
NORTH AMERICA	35.6 X 24.1 CM	TALLIS
NORTH AMERICA	26.0 X 32.0 CM	TALLIS
NORTH AMERICA	38.4 X 32.1 CM	TANNER
NORTH AMERICA	37.1 X 30.2 CM	TANNER
NORTH AMERICA	50.2 X 60.3 CM	THOMSON
NORTH AMERICA	31.8 X 24.8 CM	WELLER
NORTH AMERICA & WEST INDIES	27.9 X 23.5 CM	HUNTINGTON
NORTH AMERICA ACCORDING TO THE LATEST OBSERVATIONS	14.5 X 16.5 CM	GRIERSON
NORTH AMERICA ACCORDING TO THE LATEST OBSERVATIONS...	15.2 X 17.8 CM	SENEX
NORTH AMERICA BRITISH POSSESSIONS	53.5 X 42.0 CM	LIZARS
NORTH AMERICA DIVIDED INTO ITS PRINCIPAL PARTS...	57.2 X 87.6 CM	BERRY
NORTH AMERICA DRAWN FROM THE LATEST & BEST AUTHORITIES BY THOS. KITCHI	34.0 X 37.0 CM	KITCHIN
NORTH AMERICA DRAWN FROM THE LATEST AND BEST AUTHORITIES	33.7 X 39.4 CM	HARRISON
NORTH AMERICA DRAWN FROM THE LATEST AND BEST AUTHORITIES	33.7 X 39.4 CM	KITCHIN
NORTH AMERICA FROM THE BEST AUTHORITIES	19.1 X 21.6 CM	BRIGHTLY
NORTH AMERICA FROM THE BEST AUTHORITIES	19.1 X 22.9 CM	RUSSELL
NORTH AMERICA FROM THE BEST AUTHORITIES	19.7 X 22.9 CM	TEGG
NORTH AMERICA FROM THE FRENCH OF MR D'ANVILLE IMPROVED WITH THE BACK S	47.6 X 55.2 CM	JEFFERYS
NORTH AMERICA SHEET IX PARTS OF MISSOURI, ILLINOIS, AND INDIANA	29.5 X 37.0 CM	SDUK
NORTH AMERICA SHEET VI NEW-YORK, VERMONT, MAINE, NEW-HAMPSHIRE, MASSAC	35.0 X 31.0 CM	SDUK
NORTH AMERICA SHEET VII PENNSYLVANIA, NEW JERSEY, MARYLAND, DELAWARE,	37.0 X 31.5 CM	SDUK
NORTH AMERICA SHEET VIII OHIO, WITH PARTS OF KENTUCKY AND VIRGINIA	35.5 X 31.5 CM	SDUK
NORTH AMERICA SHEET XV	32.0 X 39.0 CM	SDUK
NORTH AMERICA SHOWING ALL THE NEW DISCOVERIES 1797	19.1 X 21.6 CM	MORSE
NORTH AMERICA SHOWING ITS POLITICAL DIVISIONS AND RECENT DISCOVERIES I	34.6 X 27.0 CM	MITCHELL
NORTH AMERICA WITH WEST INDIES WHEREIN ARE DISTINGUISHED THE UNITED ST	30.5 X 44.5 CM	SAYER & BENNETT
NORTH AMERICA XIV FLORIDA	38.1 X 30.5 CM	WALKER
NORTH AMERICA, SHEET IV...	30.5 X 38.1 CM	SDUK
NORTH AMERICA, SHEET XV, UTAH, NEW MEXICO, TEXAS, CALIFORNIA &C. AND T	31.1 X 39.4 CM	SDUK
NORTH AMERICA, THE NORTHWEST AND MICHIGAN TERRITORIES	32.4 X 38.7 CM	BALDWIN & CRADOCK
NORTH AMERICA, WEST COAST: HARO AND ROSARIO STRAITS	95.4 X 63.2 CM	ADMIRALTY
NORTH AMERICA-SOUTH AMERICA	25.4 X 21.6 CM	BOWEN
NORTH AMERICA. N.R. HEWITT SC., 10 BROAD STR. BLOOMSBY. LONDON. DRAWN	59.1 X 49.5 CM	THOMSON
NORTH AMERICA. NEW YORK, VERMONT, MAINE...	35.6 X 30.5 CM	BALDWIN & CRADOCK
NORTH AMERICA...	14.6 X 19.4 CM	KITCHIN
NORTH AMERICA...	19.1 X 21.6 CM	MORSE
NORTH AMERICA...	26.7 X 21.6 CM	ROBINSON
NORTH AND SOUTH AMERICA	29.8 X 32.4 CM	GREENLEAF

264

NORTH AND SOUTH CAROLINA	32.4 X 26.7 CM	BURR
NORTH CAROLINA	29.2 X 36.8 CM	BRADFORD
NORTH CAROLINA	35.6 X 29.2 CM	BRADFORD
NORTH CAROLINA	20.3 X 25.4 CM	BRADFORD
NORTH CAROLINA	29.5 X 48.3 CM	CAREY
NORTH CAROLINA	30.2 X 36.8 CM	COLTON
NORTH CAROLINA	27.9 X 48.3 CM	LUCAS
NORTH CAROLINA	31.8 X 42.5 CM	MORSE
NORTH CAROLINA	15.2 X 18.4 CM	SCOTT
NORTH CAROLINA, SOUTH CAROLINA AND GEORGIA	19.7 X 24.8 CM	MORSE
NORTH CAROLINA, SOUTH CAROLINA AND GEORGIA	19.7 X 25.4 CM	MORSE
NORTH DAKOTA	34.3 X 57.2 CM	RAND MCNALLY
NORTH EAST GERMANY	34.3 X 41.9 CM	BOWEN
NORTH POLAR CHART	42.6 X 32.3 CM	JOHNSTON
NORTH POLAR CHART...HYDROGRAPHIC OFFICE, LONDON 1881	64.1 X 92.7 CM	ADMIRALTY
NORTH POLAR REGIONS WITH RESULTS OF LATEST EXPLORATIONS	29.5 X 23.0 CM	MACKENZIE
NORTH WALES	20.3 X 31.8 CM	MOLL
NORTH-WEST TERRITORY. MAP SHEWING DOMINION LAND SURVEYS BETWEEN WEST B	77.0 X 88.0 CM	CANADA
NORTHAMPTON DIVIDED INTO HUNDREDS...	32.4 X 22.9 CM	BOWEN
NORTHAMPTON SHIRE	38.7 X 47.6 CM	SPEED
NORTHAMPTONSHIRE	35.6 X 41.3 CM	MORDEN
NORTHERN AFRICA	20.0 X 25.0 CM	TALLIS
NORTHERN BOUNDARY OF CALIFORNIA TO THE COLUMBIA RIVER	68.6 X 58.4 CM	U.S.
NORTHERN HEMISPHERE	36.2 X 34.9 CM	FADEN
NORTHERN HEMISPHERE	58.4 X 58.4 CM	WYLD
NORTHERN INDIA	20.0 X 25.0 CM	TALLIS
NORTHERN ITALY	25.4 X 19.1 CM	GIBSON
NORTHERN ITALY	20.0 X 25.0 CM	TALLIS
NORTHERN PROVINCES OF THE UNITED STATES	49.5 X 58.4 CM	THOMSON
NORTHERN PROVINCES OF THE UNITED STATES	49.5 X 59.0 CM	THOMSON
NORTHERN PROVINCES OF THE UNITED STATES	49.5 X 59.1 CM	THOMSON
NORTHUMBERLAND	7.6 X 12.1 CM	LEIGH
NORTHUMBERLAND	11.4 X 14.0 CM	SELLER
NORTHUMBERLAND	38.7 X 47.6 CM	SPEED
NORTHWESTERN AMERICA SHOWING THE TERRITORY CEDED BY RUSSIA TO THE UNIT	29.2 X 36.8 CM	MITCHELL
NORVEGIA REGNUM VULGO NOR-RYKE	41.3 X 50.2 CM	BLAEU
NORWICH, CONN. (VIEW)	41.9 X 74.9 CM	RAU
NOTINGAMIAE COMITATUS OLIM PART CORITANIORUM	26.0 X 31.1 CM	KIP
NOTTINGHAM SHIRE	34.9 X 41.9 CM	MORDEN
NOTTINGHAMSHIRE	17.8 X 11.4 CM	OWEN & BOWEN
NOTTINGHAMSHIRE	11.4 X 14.0 CM	SELLER
NOTTINGHAMSHIRE	10.8 X 6.4 CM	WALLIS & REID
NOU GRECIA...	25.4 X 34.3 CM	MUNSTER
NOUVEAU MEXIQUE ET CALIFORNIE	11.0 X 14.0 CM	MALLET
NOUVELLE CALIFORNIE	47.0 X 57.2 CM	VANDERMAELEN
NOUVELLE CARTE DE L'AMERIQUE	43.2 X 53.3 CM	VAN DER AA
NOUVELLE CARTE DE L'AMERIQUE	43.2 X 53.3 CM	VAN DER AA
NOUVELLE CARTE DE L'AMERIQUE SEPTENTRIONALE DRESSEE SUR LES PLUS NOUVE	48.3 X 61.0 CM	CHATELAIN
NOUVELLE CARTE DES DECOUVERTES FAITES PAR DES VAISSEAUX RUSSIENS AUX C	50.2 X 66.7 CM	MULLER
NOUVELLE CARTE DES DECOUVERTES...RUSSIENS	45.7 X 63.5 CM	MULLER
NOUVELLE CARTE DES DIX-SEPT PROVINCES DES PAYS-BAS	46.0 X 56.0 CM	CHATELAIN
NOUVELLE CARTE DU GOUVERNEMENT DIVIL D'ANGETERRE A ET DE CELUY DE LA V	34.9 X 45.7 CM	CHATELAIN
NOUVELLE CARTE DU POLE ARTIQUE	17.8 X 20.3 CM	PICQUET
NOUVELLE CARTE POUR CONDUIRE A L'ASTRONOMIE ET LA GEOGRAPHIQUE ET POUR	50.8 X 62.2 CM	CHATELAIN
NOUVELLE ET EXACTE CARTE DU DUCHE DE BRABANT, L'ANNEE 1635. A AMSTERDA	38.5 X 48.0 CM	DANCKERTS
NOUVELLE REPRESENTATION DES COTES NORD ET EST DE L'ASIE POUR SERVIR DE	29.2 X 37.8 CM	DE VAUGONDY
NOVA ANGLIA	48.3 X 58.4 CM	HOMANN
NOVA ANGLIA	48.3 X 57.2 CM	HOMANN
NOVA ANGLIA	48.5 X 58.5 CM	HOMANN
NOVA ANGLIA NOVUM BELGIUM ET VIRGINIA	27.9 X 35.6 CM	DE LAET
NOVA ANGLIA NOVUM BELGIUM ET VIRGINIA	38.7 X 50.2 CM	JANSSON
NOVA ANGLIA NOVUM BELGIUM ET VIRGINIA. AMSTELODAMI JOHANNES JANSSONIUS	38.7 X 50.2 CM	JANSSON
NOVA ANGLIA, NOVUM BELGIUM ET VIRGINIA	38.1 X 50.8 CM	JANSSON

NOVA ANGLIA, NOVUM BELGIUM, ET VIRGINIA	38.7 X 50.8 CM	JANSSON
NOVA ANGLIA, NOVVUM BELGIUM ET VIRGINIA. AMSTELODAMI JOHANNES JANSSONI	38.7 X 50.8 CM	JANSSON
NOVA BARBARIAE DESCRIPTIO	35.6 X 51.4 CM	JANSSON
NOVA BELGICA ET ANGLIA NOVA	38.7 X 50.2 CM	BLAEU
NOVA BELGICA ET ANGLIA NOVA	38.1 X 50.8 CM	BLAEU
NOVA BELGICA ET ANGLIA NOVA	39.4 X 50.8 CM	BLAEU
NOVA BRABANTIAE DUCATUS TABULA. AUCTORE JUDOCO HONDIO. DIRCK GRYP SCUL	46.5 X 53.5 CM	HONDIUS
NOVA DELINEATIO TOTIUS ORBIS TERRARUM PER PETRUM VANDER AA	26.5 X 35.0 CM	VAN DER AA
NOVA DESCRIPTIO ORIENTALIS ET OCCIDENTALIS FRISIAE...ANNO 1617	37.0 X 49.0 CM	VAN DEN KEERE
NOVA ET ACCURATA NORMANDIAE DUCATUS TABULA...EDITA A PETRO PERSOY AMST	47.0 X 55.9 CM	DE WIT
NOVA ET ACCURATA POLI ARCTICI ET TERRARUM CIRCUM IACENTIUM DESCRIPTIO	40.6 X 52.1 CM	JANSSON
NOVA ET ACCURATA POLI ARCTICI ET TERRARUM CIRCUM IACENTIUM DESCRIPTIO	41.0 X 52.5 CM	JANSSON
NOVA ET ACCURATA POLI ARCTICI ET TERRARUM CIRCUM IACENTIUM DESCRIPTIO.	41.0 X 52.7 CM	JANSSON
NOVA ET ACCURATA POLI ARCTICI ET TERRARUM CIRCUMIACENTIUM DESCRIPTIO	40.6 X 53.3 CM	JANSSON
NOVA EUROPAE DESCRIPTIO AUCTORE IODOCO HONDIO	38.1 X 50.2 CM	HONDIUS
NOVA FRANCIA ET REGIONES ADIACENTES	27.9 X 35.6 CM	DE LAET
NOVA FRANCIA ET REGIONES ADIACENTES	27.9 X 35.6 CM	DE LAET
NOVA GROENLANDIAE TABULA	17.8 X 25.4 CM	CRANTZ
NOVA GROENLANDIAE TABULA A 59 GRADU USQUE AD 73	17.8 X 25.4 CM	CRANTZ
NOVA GUINEA ET INS SALOMONIS	9.0 X 13.0 CM	BERTIUS
NOVA GUINEA FORMA & SITUS	34.0 X 21.0 CM	DE JODE
NOVA HISPANIA, ET NOVA GALICIA. GUILJELMUS BLAEUW EXCUDIT	38.4 X 50.2 CM	BLAEU
NOVA HISPANIA, NOVA GALICA	27.9 X 35.6 CM	DE LAET
NOVA ORBIS TABULA IN LUCEM EDITA	47.0 X 86.4 CM	DE WIT
NOVA SCOTIA AND NEWFOUNDLAND	34.3 X 26.7 CM	TALLIS
NOVA SCOTIA AND NEWFOUNDLAND	34.3 X 26.7 CM	TALLIS
NOVA SCOTIA AND NEWFOUNDLAND	26.0 X 32.0 CM	TALLIS
NOVA SCOTIA DRAWN FROM SURVEYS BY T. KITCHIN	10.8 X 17.1 CM	LONDON MAGAZINE
NOVA SCOTIA...	20.0 X 25.0 CM	TALLIS
NOVA TABULA GEOGRAPHICA COMPLECTENS BOREALIOREM AMERICAE PARTEM: IN QU	59.7 X 48.3 CM	VISSCHER
NOVA TOTIUS AMERICAE DESCRIPTIO	43.2 X 54.6 CM	DE WIT
NOVA TOTIUS ORBIS TERRARUM DESCRIPTIO	31.4 X 44.1 CM	SPILBERGEN
NOVA TOTIUS TERRARUM ORBIS GEOGRAPHIA AC HYDROGRAPHICA TABULA	38.1 X 53.3 CM	HONDIUS
NOVA TOTIUS TERRARUM ORBIS GEOGRAPHICA AC HYDROGRAPHICA TABULA	40.6 X 54.6 CM	BLAEU
NOVA TOTIUS TERRARUM ORBIS GEOGRAPHICA AC HYDROGRAPHICA TABULA	37.5 X 54.0 CM	HONDIUS
NOVA TOTIUS TERRARUM ORBIS GEOGRAPHICA AC HYDROGRAPHICA TABULA	38.1 X 54.6 CM	HONDIUS
NOVA TOTIUS TERRARUM ORBIS GEOGRAPHICA AC HYDROGRAPHICA TABULA	38.0 X 54.5 CM	HONDIUS
NOVA TOTIUS TERRARUM ORBIS GEOGRAPHICA AC HYDROGRAPHICA TABULA	26.7 X 35.6 CM	MERIAN
NOVA TOTIUS TERRARUM ORBIS GEOGRAPHICA AC HYDROGRAPHICA TABULA	26.0 X 35.5 CM	MERIAN
NOVA TOTIUS TERRARUM ORBIS TABULA	47.0 X 55.9 CM	DANCKERTS
NOVA VIRGINIAE TABULA	37.5 X 48.3 CM	BLAEU
NOVA VIRGINIAE TABULA	37.5 X 47.9 CM	BLAEU
NOVA VIRGINIAE TABULA	38.1 X 50.2 CM	HONDIUS
NOVA VIRGINIAE TABULA	38.1 X 49.5 CM	HONDIUS
NOVA VIRGINIAE TABULA	13.0 X 19.0 CM	JANSSON
NOVA VIRGINIAE TABULA	18.4 X 25.4 CM	MERCATOR
NOVA VIRGINIAE TABULA	29.2 X 35.6 CM	OGILBY
NOVA VIRGINIAE TABULA PETRUS KAERIUS CAELAVIT	13.3 X 19.1 CM	MERCATOR
NOVA ZEMBLA EN'T WAYGAT	17.8 X 22.9 CM	ANON
NOVA-SCOTIA, NEW BRUNSWICK &C	38.1 X 30.5 CM	MORSE
NOVAE HISPANIAE, CHILI, PERUVIAE ET GUATIMALAE LITTORAE	49.0 X 56.0 CM	DE WIT
NOVI BELGII NOVAEQUE ANGLIAE NEC NON PENNSYLVANIAE ET PARTIS VIRGINIAE	45.7 X 54.0 CM	DANCKERTS
NOVI BELGII, NOVAE QUAE ANGLIAE NEC NON PENNSYLVANIAE ET PARTIS VIRGIN	45.7 X 54.6 CM	DANCKERTS
NOVI ORBIS SIVE TOTIUS AMERICAE...	27.5 X 34.3 CM	WEIGEL
NOVIS ET ACCURATA JAPANIAE TERRAE ESONIS	45.0 X 54.5 CM	VALK & SCHENK
NOVISSIMA ET ACCURATISSIMA SEPTENTRIONALIS AC MERIDINOALIS AMERICAE...	49.5 X 58.4 CM	DE WIT
NOVISSIMA ET ACCURATISSIMA SEPTENTRIONALIS ET MERIDIONALIS AMERICAE	48.3 X 58.4 CM	DE WIT
NOVISSIMA ET ACCURATISSIMA TOTIUS AMERICAE DESCRIPTIO	48.3 X 58.4 CM	DANCKERTS
NOVISSIMA ET ACCURATISSIMA TOTIUS AMERICAE DESCRIPTIO	43.2 X 59.1 CM	VISSCHER
NOVISSIMA ET ACCURATISSIMA TOTIUS AMERICAE DESCRIPTIO...	49.5 X 58.4 CM	DE WIT
NOVISSIMA ET ACCURATISSIMA TOTIUS HUNGARIAE TABULA PAR P. DU VAL GEOGR	39.4 X 47.6 CM	DANCKERTS
NOVISSIMA ISLANDIAE TABULA	37.5 X 48.3 CM	VALK & SCHENK
NOVISSIMAE PRAE CAETERIS ALIIS ACCURATISSIMA REGNORUM ANGLIAE, SCOTIAE	58.4 X 48.3 CM	DE WIT

NOVUM AMSTERDAMUM	12.7 X 16.5 CM	OGILBY
NOVUS ORBIS POTIUS ALTERA CONTINENS SIVE ATLANTIS INSULA...	39.7 X 55.9 CM	SANSON
NOVUS ORBIS SIVE AMERICA	50.0 X 57.5 CM	SEUTTER
NOVUS ORBIS SIVE AMERICA MERIDIONALIS ET SEPTENTRIONALIS, PER SUA REGN	49.5 X 58.4 CM	SEUTTER
NOVUS XVII INFERIORIS GERMANIAE PROVINCIARUM TYPUS	40.0 X 50.5 CM	BLAEU
NOVUS XVII INFERIORIS GERMANIAE PROVINCIARUM TYPUS. DE INTEGRO MULTIS	38.0 X 49.5 CM	VAN DEN KEERE
NUEVA HISPANIA TABULA NOVA	12.7 X 16.5 CM	PTOLEMY (1548 VENICE)
NUEVA HISPANIA TABULA NOVA	13.0 X 16.8 CM	PTOLEMY (1548 VENICE)
NUEVA HISPANIA TABULA NOVA	17.8 X 24.1 CM	PTOLEMY (1561-99 VE...
NUEVA HISPANIA TABULA NOVA	19.1 X 26.0 CM	PTOLEMY (1561-99 VE...
NUOVA CARTA DEL POLO ARTICO	27.9 X 33.0 CM	ALBRIZZI
NUOVA CARTA DEL POLO ARTICO SECONDO L'ULTIME OSSERVATIONI. A AMSTERDAM	29.8 X 35.6 CM	ALBRIZZI
NUOVA CARTA DELL'ISOLE BRITANNICHE DIVISE NEI TRE REGNI D'INGHILTERRA,	26.7 X 34.3 CM	ALBRIZZI
NUOVA ET ACCURATA CARTA DELL' ISOLE FILIPPINES, LADRONES, ET MOLUCCUS	28.0 X 35.0 CM	ALBRIZZI
NUOVA FRANCIA	26.7 X 37.5 CM	RAMUSIO
NUOVE SCOPERTE FATTA NEL 1765, E 69 NEL MARE DEL SUD	30.0 X 40.0 CM	ZATTA
NUOVE SCOPERTE...MARE DEL SUD	30.0 X 40.0 CM	ZATTA
OCCIDENTALIOR REGNI ANGLIAE DISTRICTUS COMPREHENDENS PRINCIPATUM WALLI	58.4 X 48.3 CM	MORTIER
OCCIDENTALIS AMERICAE PARTIS...	33.0 X 44.0 CM	DE BRY
OCEANIA, OR ISLANDS IN THE PACIFIC OCEAN, ON MERCATORS PROJECTION...	39.6 X 49.9 CM	FULLARTON
OCEANIE	34.0 X 25.0 CM	MONIN & FREMIN
OCEANIE...	28.5 X 38.0 CM	MIGEON
OCEANIQUE ORIENT	22.0 X 30.0 CM	TARDIEU
OCTAVA ASIE TABULA	35.6 X 38.1 CM	PTOLEMY (1513-20 ST...
OHIO	35.6 X 29.2 CM	BRADFORD
OHIO	35.6 X 28.6 CM	BRADFORD
OHIO	35.6 X 28.6 CM	BRADFORD
OHIO	26.7 X 30.5 CM	BURR
OHIO	33.0 X 40.6 CM	COLTON
OHIO	22.9 X 29.2 CM	LUCAS
OHIO	23.5 X 21.0 CM	WEIMAR GEOGRAPHISCH...
OHIO & INDIANA	19.1 X 25.1 CM	MORSE
OHIO AND INDIANA	12.5 X 15.5 CM	ANON
OLD PT. ROYAL	17.8 X 31.8 CM	GENTLEMAN'S MAGAZINE
ONTARIO	40.6 X 58.4 CM	ASHER & ADAMS
ONTARIO IN COUNTIES	27.0 X 34.3 CM	MITCHELL
OOST ENDE WEST VRIESLANDTS, 1568...	34.0 X 51.0 CM	ORTELIUS
OOST FRISE OU LE COMTE D'EMBDEN	43.2 X 58.4 CM	MORTIER
ORBIS DESCRIPTIO	18.4 X 26.7 CM	PTOLEMY (1561-99 VE...
ORBIS DESCRIPTIO	16.5 X 25.4 CM	PTOLEMY (1561-99 VE...
ORBIS DESCRIPTIO	19.0 X 26.0 CM	PTOLEMY (1561-99 VE...
ORBIS TERRAE COMPENDIOSA DESCRIPTIO	16.0 X 24.0 CM	PTOLEMY (1596-1621 ...
ORBIS TERRAE COMPENDIOSA DESCRIPTIO	16.5 X 24.5 CM	PTOLEMY (1596-1621 ...
ORBIS TERRAE...	15.9 X 24.1 CM	PTOLEMY (1596-1621 ...
ORBIS TERRARUM COGNITUS	8.5 X 16.0 CM	WELLS
ORBIS TERRARUM NOVA ET ACCURATA TABULA	48.5 X 57.0 CM	VALK
ORBIS TERRARUM NOVA ET ACCURATISSIMA TABULA	45.1 X 54.6 CM	GOOS
ORBIS TERRARUM NOVA ET ACCURATISSIMA TABULA	44.5 X 53.3 CM	VAN LOON
ORBIS TERRARUM NOVA ET ACCURATISSIMA TABULA, AUCTORE IOANNE A LOON	44.5 X 53.3 CM	VAN LOON
ORBIS TERRARUM TABULA RECENS EMENDATA ET IN LUCEM EDITA PER N. VISSCHE	30.5 X 47.0 CM	VISSCHER
ORBIS TERRARUM TABULA RECENS EMENDATA ET IN LUCEM EDITA PER N. VISSCHE	30.5 X 47.5 CM	VISSCHER
ORBIS TERRARUM TYPUS DE INTEGRO MULTIS IN LOCIS EMENDATUS	27.9 X 50.8 CM	PLANCIUS
ORBIS TERRARUM TYPUS...	40.6 X 56.5 CM	PLANCIUS
ORBIS TERRARUM VETERIBUS COGNITI TYPUS GEOGRAPHICUS	40.6 X 50.8 CM	JANSSON
ORBIS TYPUS UNIVERSALIS IUXTA HYDROGRAPHORUM TRADITIONEM EXACTISSIME D	31.8 X 47.0 CM	PTOLEMY (1522-41 ST...
ORBIS UNIVERSALIS DESCRIPTIO & HIBERNIA	12.7 X 16.5 CM	HONTER
ORBIS VETUS, ET ORBIS VETERIS ULTRAQUE CONTINENS, TERRARUM & TRACTUS A	40.0 X 54.6 CM	MORTIER
ORBIUM PLANETARUM TERRAM COMPLECTENTIUM SCENOGRAPHIA	43.2 X 50.8 CM	CELLARIUS
ORCADUM ET SCHETLANDIAE INSULARUM ACCURATISSIMA DESCRIPTIO	37.5 X 48.9 CM	JANSSON
OREGON	40.6 X 55.9 CM	ASHER & ADAMS
OREGON	27.3 X 35.6 CM	MORSE & BREESE
OREGON TERRITORY	26.7 X 31.8 CM	GREENLEAF
ORIENTALIOR DISTRICTUS REGNI ANGLIAE...CANTIUM...RUTLANDIAQ	58.4 X 48.3 CM	MORTIER

```
OTTAWA                                                            14.7 X  20.2 CM              BAEDEKER
OUTLET OF COLUMBIA RIVER                                          16.7 X   9.7 CM               MELISH
OUTLET OF THE SOUTH CHANNEL OF RIVER ST. CLAIR                    40.0 X  48.3 CM                 U.S.
OVER-ISSEL. DITIO TRANS-ISULANA. JOANNES JANSSONIUS EXCUD.        39.0 X  49.0 CM              HONDIUS
OVER-YSSEL                                                        40.0 X  50.0 CM                BLAEU
OVER-YSSEL...                                                     44.0 X  57.0 CM             VISSCHER
OVERLAND ROUTE TO INDIA                                           20.0 X  25.0 CM               TALLIS
OXFORD SHIRE                                                      41.9 X  35.6 CM               MORDEN
OXFORDSHIRE                                                       24.1 X  19.1 CM                 BELL
OXFORDSHIRE                                                       10.2 X  17.8 CM               CAPPER
OXFORDSHIRE                                                       14.0 X   8.9 CM                 CARY
OXFORDSHIRE                                                       17.8 X  26.7 CM                ELLIS
OXFORDSHIRE                                                        7.6 X  12.1 CM                LEIGH
OXFORDSHIRE                                                       19.1 X  30.5 CM                 MOLL
OXFORDSHIRE                                                       17.8 X  11.4 CM          OWEN & BOWEN
OXFORDSHIRE                                                       11.4 X  15.2 CM               SELLER
OXFORDSHIRE                                                       10.8 X   6.4 CM        WALLIS & REID
OXFORDSHIRE...                                                    38.7 X  47.6 CM                SPEED
OXONIUM COMITATUS VULGO OXFORD SHIRE                              38.1 X  49.5 CM       VALK & SCHENK
PACIFIC COAST FROM POINT PINOS TO BODEGA HEAD, CALIFORNIA         98.0 X  71.5 CM    U.S. COAST SURVEY
PACIFIC OCEAN                                                     19.7 X  24.4 CM                MORSE
PACIFIC STATES & THE TERRITORIES                                 27.9 X  20.3 CM             SWINSTON
PAGUS HISPANORUM IN FLORIDA (VIEW)                                26.7 X  35.6 CM               OGILBY
PAIS QUI SONT AUX ENVIRONS DE LA RIVIERE DE LA PLATA ET DU PAIS...16.5 X  10.2 CM               MALLET
PALAESTINA SIVE TOTIUS TERRAE PROMISSIONIS NOVA DESCRIPTIO        34.5 X  46.5 CM             ORTELIUS
PALAESTINA, VEL TERRA SANCTA                                      13.5 X  17.5 CM PTOLEMY (1596-1621 ...
PALATIUM BRUXELLENSE DUCIS BRABANTIAE                             36.0 X  46.0 CM             HARREWYN
PALATIUM MANSFELDICUM, PROPE LUTZENBURGUM                         42.0 X  52.0 CM                BLAEU
PALESTINAE VEL TERRAE SANCTAE TAB. II.                            33.0 X  52.1 CM              DE JODE
PALESTINAE VEL TERRAE SANCTAE, TAB. I.                            30.5 X  50.8 CM              DE JODE
PAMPATAR...MARGARITA                                              17.8 X  23.3 CM              FIDALGO
PARAGUAY, O PROV. DE LA PLATA                                     27.9 X  35.6 CM              DE LAET
PARAQUARIA VULGO PARAGUAY CUM ADJACENTIBUS.                       54.6 X  44.8 CM               BROWNE
PARIS.. PUBLISHED BY BALDWIN & CRADOCK...APRIL 1ST. 1834          38.7 X  52.1 CM                 SDUK
PARS FLANDRIAE TEUTONICAE OCCIDENTALIOR                           39.0 X  50.0 CM                BLAEU
PART OF SOUTH AUSTRALIA                                           33.5 X  24.5 CM               TALLIS
PARTE DE LA FRICA (WEST AFRICA)                                   26.7 X  36.8 CM              RAMUSIO
PARTE DELLA NUOVA SPAGNA, O DEL MEXICO DOVE SONO LE PROVINCIE DI GUADA 45.1 X  61.0 CM      CORONELLI
PARTE OCCIDENTALE D'UNE PARTIE D'ASIE OU SONT LES ISLES DE ZOCOTORA, D 59.1 X  86.4 CM       MORTIER
PARTE ORIENTALE DELLA FLORIDA DE LA GIORGIA E CAROLINA MERIDIONALE 33.0 X  42.5 CM             ZATTA
PARTE ORIENTALE DELLA FLORIDA, DELLA GEORGIA, E CAROLINA MERIDIONALE 31.8 X  41.9 CM           ZATTA
PARTICULAR DRAUGHTS AND PLANS OF SOME OF THE PRINCIPAL TOWNS AND HARBO 43.8 X  35.6 CM         BOWEN
PARTICULAR DRAUGHTS OF SOME OF THE CHIEF AFRICAN ISLANDS IN THE MEDITE 34.5 X  43.0 CM         BOWEN
PARTIE DE L'AMERIQUE SEPTENT QUI COMPREND LA NOUVELLE FRANCE OU LE CAN 49.5 X  60.3 CM    DE VAUGONDY
PARTIE DE L'AMERIQUE SEPTENT. QUI COMPREND LA NOUVELLE FRANCE OU LE CA 47.6 X  60.3 CM    DE VAUGONDY
PARTIE DE L'AMERIQUE SEPTENT. QUI COMPREND LA NOUVELLE FRANCE OU LE CA 48.0 X  60.0 CM    DE VAUGONDY
PARTIE DE L'AMERIQUE SEPTENTRIONALE                               57.5 X  43.5 CM                BONNE
PARTIE DE L'AMERIQUE SEPTENTRIONALE QUE COMPREND LE COURS DE L'HHIO, L 47.0 X  62.2 CM    DE VAUGONDY
PARTIE DE L'AMERIQUE SEPTENTRIONALE, QUI COMPREND LE CANADA, LA LOUISI 33.0 X  47.0 CM         BONNE
PARTIE DE L'AMERIQUE SEPTENTRIONALE, QUI COMPREND LE COURS DE L'OHIO,  61.6 X  47.6 CM    DE VAUGONDY
PARTIE DE L'AMERIQUE SEPTENTRIONALE, QUI COMPREND LE COURS DE L'OHIO,  49.5 X  62.2 CM    DE VAUGONDY
PARTIE DE L'AMERIQUE SEPTENTRIONALE, QUI COMPREND LE COURS DE L'OHIO.. 47.6 X  62.2 CM    DE VAUGONDY
PARTIE DE L'AMERIQUE SEPTENTRIONALE. QUI COMPREND LE CANADA, LE LABRAD 43.5 X  57.5 CM         BONNE
PARTIE DE L'ANGLETERRE                                            41.9 X  55.9 CM                FRICX
PARTIE DE L'ILE DE TERRE NEUVE NO. 37                             48.3 X  61.0 CM          VANDERMAELEN
PARTIE DE LA COTE NORD-OUEST DE L'AMERIQUE                        43.8 X  34.3 CM            VANCOUVER
PARTIE DE LA MER DU SUD COMPRISE ENTRE LES PHILLIPPINES ET LA CALIFORN 48.9 X  67.3 CM     LA PEROUSE
PARTIE DE LA NOUVELLE BRETAGNE                                    47.0 X  55.9 CM          VANDERMAELEN
PARTIE DE LA NOUVELLE GRANDE CARTE DES INDES ORIENTALES CONTENANT LES  53.0 X  60.5 CM          ELWE
PARTIE DE LA TERRE FERME DE L'INDIE OU L'EMPIRE DU MOGOL           10.2 X  14.0 CM              MALLET
PARTIE DE LITHUANIE OU SONT LES PALATINATS DE POLOCZK, WITEPSK, MSEISL 42.5 X  54.6 CM        SANSON
PARTIE DES ISLES ANTILLES, I PARTIE                               22.9 X  15.9 CM               BELLIN
PARTIE DU DUCHE DE MILAN                                          57.2 X  86.4 CM              MORTIER
```

PARTIE DU FLEUVE ST. LAURENT AVEC LE PASSAGE DE LA TRAVERSE ET LES ISL	24.1 X 30.5 CM	BELLIN
PARTIE DU MEXIQUE NO. 47	45.7 X 55.9 CM	VANDERMAELEN
PARTIE DU MEXIQUE NO. 65	45.7 X 53.3 CM	VANDERMAELEN
PARTIE MERIDION. DU DUCHE DE BRABANT	48.0 X 53.0 CM	DE VAUGONDY
PARTIE MERIDIONALE DE LA LOUISIANE, AVEC LA FLORIDE, LA CAROLINE ET LA	47.8 X 57.5 CM	SANTINI
PARTIE MERIDIONALE DE LA RIVIERE MISSISIPI	47.0 X 63.5 CM	DE FER
PARTIE MERIDIONALE DE MOSCOVIE DRESSEE PAR G. DE L'ISLE. A AMSTERDAM C	50.2 X 61.6 CM	COVENS & MORTIER
PARTIE MERIDIONALE DES ETATS DE CASTILLE	48.0 X 53.0 CM	DE VAUGONDY
PARTIE MERIDIONALE DU CERCLE D'AUTRICHE	48.0 X 53.0 CM	DE VAUGONDY
PARTIE MERIDIONALE DU COMTE DE HOLLANDE	44.0 X 57.0 CM	JAILLOT
PARTIE MERIDIONALE DU ROYAUME DE PORTUGAL	48.0 X 53.0 CM	DE VAUGONDY
PARTIE OCCIDENTALE D'AFRIQUE	22.5 X 32.5 CM	DE FER
PARTIE OCCIDENTALE DE CANADA, CONTENANT LES CINQ GRAND LACS...	21.1 X 31.8 CM	BONNE
PARTIE OCCIDENTALE DE LA NOUVELLE FRANCE	42.5 X 54.0 CM	BELLIN
PARTIE OCCIDENTALE DE LA NOUVELLE FRANCE OU CANADA	47.0 X 61.0 CM	BELLIN
PARTIE OCCIDENTALE DE LA NOUVELLE FRANCE OU CANADA	47.0 X 60.3 CM	BELLIN
PARTIE OCCIDENTALE DE LA NOUVELLE FRANCE OU DU CANADA	41.3 X 53.3 CM	HOMANN
PARTIE OCCIDENTALE DU CANADA ET SEPTENTRIONALE DE LA LOUISIANE AVEC UN	48.3 X 58.4 CM	SANTINI
PARTIE OCCIDENTALE DU CANADA, CONTENANT LES CINQ GRANDS LACS AVEC PAYS	21.0 X 31.1 CM	BONNE
PARTIE OCCIDENTALE DU CANADA...	48.3 X 56.5 CM	SANTINI
PARTIE ORIENTALE DE L'AMERIQUE ANGLOISE	57.2 X 87.6 CM	MORTIER
PARTIE ORIENTALE DE LA NOUVELLE FRANCE OU DU CANADA	47.0 X 62.2 CM	BELLIN
PARTIE ORIENTALE DE LA NOUVELLE FRANCE OU DU CANADA AVEC L'ISLE DE TER	57.2 X 49.5 CM	LOTTER
PARTIE ORIENTALE DE LA NOUVELLE FRANCE OU DU CANADA PAR MR. BELLIN ING	49.5 X 62.2 CM	HOMANN
PARTIE ORIENTALE DE LA NOUVELLE FRANCE OU DU CANADA, PAR MR. BELLIN IN	45.7 X 55.9 CM	HOMANN
PARTIE ORIENTALE DE LA NOUVELLE FRANCE OU DU CANADA. PAR. MR. BELLIN I	49.5 X 60.3 CM	BELLIN
PARTIE ORIENTALE DEL CANADA, NUOVA SCOZIA SETTENTRIONALE, E PARTE DI L	33.7 X 43.8 CM	ZATTA
PARTIE ORIENTALE DU CANADA AVEC LA NOUVELLE ANGLETERRE, L'ACADIE, ET L	48.3 X 58.4 CM	SANTINI
PARTIE SEPTENT. QUI COMPREND LA NOUVELLE FRANCE OU LE CANADA	47.5 X 60.5 CM	DE VAUGONDY
PARTIE SEPTENTRIONALE DE L'OCEAN PACIFIQUE OU L'ON A MARQUE LES DISCOU	38.7 X 49.5 CM	POIRSON
PARTIE SEPTENTRIONALE DE LA COURONNE DE CASTILLE	48.0 X 53.0 CM	DE VAUGONDY
PARTIE SEPTENTRIONALE DES PAYS BAS COMPRENANT LES ETATS GENERAUX DES P	48.0 X 66.0 CM	JANVIER
PARTIE SEPTENTRIONALE DU CERCLE D'AUTRICHE	48.0 X 53.0 CM	DE VAUGONDY
PARTIE SEPTENTRIONALE DU COMTE DE HOLLANDE...	43.5 X 58.0 CM	JAILLOT
PARTIE SEPTENTRIONALE DU DUCHE DE BRABANT	48.0 X 53.0 CM	DE VAUGONDY
PARTIE SEPTENTRIONALE DU ROYAUME DE PORTUGAL	48.0 X 53.0 CM	DE VAUGONDY
PARTS OF MISSOURI, ILLINOIS & INDIANA	32.4 X 36.8 CM	BALDWIN & CRADOCK
PARTS OF MISSOURI...TENNESSEE, ALABAMA, MISSISSIPPI & ARKANSAS	33.0 X 39.4 CM	BALDWIN & CRADOCK
PAS KAART VAN DE GOLFF VAN MEXICO DOOR VOOGT GEOMETRA...	50.8 X 58.4 CM	VAN KEULEN
PAS KAART VAN DE KUST VAN CAROLINA	50.8 X 58.4 CM	VAN KEULEN
PAS KAART VAN DE KUST VAN CAROLINA TUSSCHEN C. DE CANAVERAL EN C. H...	51.8 X 58.7 CM	VAN KEULEN
PAS KAART VAN DE KUST VAN CAROLINA...	51.8 X 52.7 CM	VAN KEULEN
PAS KAART VAN DE ZEE KUSTEN VAN VIRGINIA TUSSCHEN C HENRY EN T HOOGE L	51.1 X 57.8 CM	VAN KEULEN
PAS KAART VAN DE ZUYD-KUST VAN ESPANJOLA MET...NUEVO REYNE DE GRENADA.	52.1 X 58.4 CM	VAN KEULEN
PAS KAART VAN WEST INDIES...	50.8 X 58.4 CM	VAN KEULEN
PAS-KAART VANDE ZEE KUSTEN...NIEW ENGELAND...	51.4 X 58.4 CM	VAN KEULEN
PAS-KAART VANDE ZEE-KUSTEN, VAN, TERRA NOVA...FRANCIA NOVA CANADA EN A	50.8 X 58.4 CM	VAN KEULEN
PASCAART VANT CANAAL BEGRYPENDE IN SICH ENGELANDT, SCHOTLANDT EN IERLA	43.5 X 55.0 CM	JACOBSZ
PASCAART VANT CANAAL BEGRYPENDE IN SICH ENGLANDT, SCHOTLANDT EN JERLAN	43.0 X 53.0 CM	GOOS
PASCAARTE VAN 'T WESTELYCKSTE DEEL VAN DE MIDDELLANDSCHE ZEE/PASCAARTE	40.0 X 50.0 CM	JACOBSZ
PASCAARTE VANDE ZUYDER-ZEE, TEXEL ENDE VLIE-STROOM, ALS MEDE 'T AMELAND	43.0 X 53.0 CM	GOOS
PASCAERTE OM ACHTER YRLANDT OM TE ZEYLEN	43.5 X 54.5 CM	JACOBSZ
PASCAERTE VANDE VLAEMSCHE, SOUTE EN CARIBESCHE EYLANDEN ALS MEDE TERRA	44.5 X 54.0 CM	GOOS
PASCAERTE VANDE VLAEMSCHE, SOUTE, EN CARIBESCHE EYLANDEN, ALS MEDE TER	45.1 X 54.0 CM	GOOS
PASKAERT VAN DE NOORDELIJCKSTE KUSTE VAN AMERICA VAN GROELAND DOOR DE	43.2 X 54.0 CM	JACOBSZ
PASKAERTE VAN DE ZUYDT EN NOORDT REVIER IN NIEU NEDERLANT STRECKENDE V	50.5 X 60.0 CM	GOOS
PASKAERTE ZYNDE T'OOSTERDEEL VAN OOST INDIEN MET ALLES DE EYLANDEN DEE	44.0 X 53.5 CM	GOOS
PASKERT VAN DE ZEEUSCHE EN VLAEMSCHE KUSTEN, TONENDE ALLE DROOGHTEN, D	43.0 X 93.7 CM	GOOS
PAVILLONS ET COCARDES DES PRINCIPALES PUISSANCES DU GLOBE	45.7 X 57.8 CM	ANDRIVEAU-GOUJON
PAYS-BAS CATHOLIQUES	59.0 X 56.0 CM	DE VAUGONDY
PAYS-BAS CATHOLIQUES	48.0 X 53.0 CM	DE VAUGONDY
PEDEMONTIUM, MONSSERRATUS ET LIGURIA	13.5 X 17.5 CM	PTOLEMY (1596-1621 ...
PEMBROKESHIRE	11.4 X 14.0 CM	SELLER

```
PEMBROKESHIRE                                                    10.8 X   6.4 CM              WALLIS & REID
PEMBROKSHYRE...                                                  38.7 X  47.6 CM                     SPEED
PENBROK COMITATUS OLIM PARS DEMETARUM                            27.9 X  34.3 CM                       KIP
PENNSYLVANIA                                                     35.6 X  29.2 CM                  BRADFORD
PENNSYLVANIA                                                     33.0 X  48.3 CM                     CAREY
PENNSYLVANIA                                                     28.6 X  45.1 CM                     LUCAS
PENNSYLVANIA                                                     27.9 X  45.1 CM                     LUCAS
PENNSYLVANIA                                                     30.5 X  40.0 CM             MORSE & BREESE
PENNSYLVANIA                                                     15.2 X  18.4 CM                     SCOTT
PENNSYLVANIA                                                     26.7 X  34.3 CM                    TANNER
PENNSYLVANIA & NEW JERSEY                                        19.1 X  25.1 CM                     MORSE
PENNSYLVANIA AND NEW JERSEY                                      12.2 X  15.3 CM                      ANON
PENNSYLVANIA DRAWN FROM THE BEST AUTHORITIES                     19.1 X  33.7 CM                     MORSE
PENNSYLVANIA, NEW JERSEY, MARYLAND, DELAWARE...                  38.1 X  30.5 CM          BALDWIN & CRADOCK
PENNSYLVANIA, NOVA JARSEY ET NOVA YORK CUM REGIONIBUS            55.9 X  48.3 CM                    LOTTER
PENSYLVANIA NOVA JERSEY ET NOVA YORK CUM REGIONIBUS AD FLUVIUM DELEWAR 55.9 X 48.9 CM               SEUTTER
PEORIA, ILL. 1874. (VIEW)                                        66.7 X  94.0 CM           STROBRIDGE & CO.
PERSIA                                                           17.1 X  19.1 CM                      MOLL
PERSIA                                                           20.0 X  25.0 CM                    TALLIS
PERSIA NUOVA TAVOLA                                              45.7 X  62.2 CM PTOLEMY (1561-99 VE...
PERSIAE REGNUM                                                   13.5 X  17.5 CM PTOLEMY (1596-1621 ...
PERSPECTIVE MAP OF THE CITY OF HELENA, MONT. CAPITAL OF STATE, COUNTY 66.7 X 99.7 CM AMERICAN PUBLISHING...
PERU                                                              8.9 X  12.7 CM                   BERTIUS
PERU                                                             38.0 X  49.0 CM                     BLAEU
PERU                                                             41.9 X  30.5 CM                     CAREY
PERU                                                             27.9 X  35.6 CM                   DE LAET
PERU & BOLIVIA                                                   33.7 X  41.3 CM                     DOWER
PERU & BOLIVIA                                                   34.3 X  26.7 CM                    TALLIS
PERU & BOLIVIA                                                   35.6 X  25.4 CM                    TALLIS
PERU & BOLIVIA                                                   30.5 X  35.6 CM                    TANNER
PERU AND BOLIVIA                                                 48.5 X  60.0 CM                ARROWSMITH
PERU AND BOLIVIA                                                 20.0 X  25.0 CM                    TALLIS
PERU AND BOLIVIA                                                 41.3 X  33.7 CM                  TEESDALE
PERU AND THE AMAZONES COUNTRY                                    17.1 X  19.1 CM                      MOLL
PHILADELPHIA                                                     48.3 X  39.4 CM                  BRADFORD
PHILADELPHIA                                                     35.6 X  29.2 CM                  BRADFORD
PHILADELPHIA                                                     36.2 X  29.2 CM                  BRADFORD
PHILADELPHIA                                                     35.6 X  29.2 CM                    TANNER
PHILADELPHIA AND ADJACENT COUNTRY                               16.4 X  10.4 CM                    MELISH
PHYSICAL MAP OF THE UNITED STATES                               29.2 X  42.5 CM                WOODBRIDGE
PIAMONTE NOVA TAV.                                              13.3 X  17.1 CM PTOLEMY (1548 VENICE)
PICARDIAE BELGICAE REGIONIS DESCRIPTIO. JOANNE SURHONIO AUCTORE  33.0 X  50.8 CM                  ORTELIUS
PICARDIAE, BELGICAE REGIONIS DESCRIPTIO. IOANNE SURHONIO AUCTORE. CUM 33.0 X 50.8 CM               ORTELIUS
PICARDIE ET LES PAYS BAS CATHOLIQUES...                         37.0 X  52.0 CM                    SANSON
PINCO OU PORT DE LA CONCEPTION AU CHILI                         21.6 X  17.8 CM                    BELLIN
PLAN D'YORK EN VIRGINIE                                         29.8 X  38.1 CM                      ANON
PLAN DE BOSTON, AVEC LES SONDES ET LES DIRECTIONS POUR LA NAVIGATION. 50.8 X 85.1 CM            LE ROUGE
PLAN DE JEDO                                                    33.0 X  32.4 CM                CHARLEVOIX
PLAN DE L'ENTREE DU PORT DE BUCARELLI                           38.5 X  50.0 CM                  ROBINSON
PLAN DE L'ISLE VACHE A LA COSTE DU SUD DE S. DOMINGUE           21.6 X  16.5 CM                    BELLIN
PLAN DE LA BAIE D'YU-LIN-KAN ET DU MOUILLAGE DE SANGHIA         42.5 X  57.3 CM         DEPOT DE LA MARINE
PLAN DE LA BAIE DE GAALONG                                      42.7 X  57.4 CM         DEPOT DE LA MARINE
PLAN DE LA BAIE DE GABARUS SITUEE A LA COTE S.E. DE L'ISLE ROYALE... 58.4 X 39.4 CM               CHABERT
PLAN DE LA BAIE DE LYEOUNG-SOY                                  42.5 X  57.2 CM         DEPOT DE LA MARINE
PLAN DE LA BAIE DE MONTEREY                                     25.0 X  36.3 CM                  ROBINSON
PLAN DE LA BAIE DE NARRAGANSET DANS LA NOUVELLE ANGLETERRE      58.4 X  41.3 CM         DEPOT DE LA MARINE
PLAN DE LA BAIE DE TCHINKITANE (LA BAIA DE GUADALUPA DES ESPAGNOLS EN 21.7 X 16.7 CM             FLEURIEU
PLAN DE LA BAYE DE LA CONCEPTION SITUEE A LA COTE DU CHILY...   18.4 X  28.6 CM                   FREZIER
PLAN DE LA BAYE DE MANILLE                                      20.0 X  25.0 CM                      ANON
PLAN DE LA BAYE ET DU PORT DE RIO JANEIRO...VERISIE...PAR L'AUTEUR EN 49.5 X 31.8 CM D'APRES DE MANNEVIL...
PLAN DE LA RADE DE ARICA                                        17.8 X  29.2 CM                   FREZIER
PLAN DE LA RADE ET VILLE DU PETIT GOUAVE                        22.9 X  30.5 CM                    BELLIN
PLAN DE LA VILLE DE CAYENNE                                     22.2 X  15.9 CM                    BELLIN
```

270

PLAN DE LA VILLE DE PARAMARIBO SUIVANT LES PLANS HOLLANDOIS	22.2 X 15.2 CM	BELLIN
PLAN DE LA VILLE DE ROME	23.5 X 30.0 CM	DE FER
PLAN DE LA VILLE DE VIENNE	57.2 X 86.4 CM	MORTIER
PLAN DE LA VILLE ET DU PORT DE MACAO	22.5 X 18.0 CM	BELLIN
PLAN DE LA VILLE, CITE, UNIVERSITE ET FAUBOURGS DE PARIS	57.2 X 86.4 CM	MORTIER
PLAN DE PORT ET DE LA VILLE DE NANGASAKE	26.5 X 34.5 CM	CHARLEVOIX
PLAN DU CALLAO DE LIMA/PLAN DE L'ANSE ET PORT DE VALPARAISO	59.0 X 42.5 CM	DEPOT DE LA MARINE
PLAN DU PETIT GOAVE ET DE L'ACUL	16.5 X 20.3 CM	D'ANVILLE
PLAN DU PORT DAUPHIN	20.3 X 28.6 CM	BELLIN
PLAN DU PORT DE BALDIVIA/PLAN DE LA RADE DE SN JUAN BAUTISTA A LA POIN	56.8 X 41.2 CM	DEPOT DE LA MARINE
PLAN DU PORT DE LA HAIVE	20.3 X 28.6 CM	BELLIN
PLAN DU PORT DE SN CARLOS SITUE A LA PARTIE DU NORD DE L'ILE DE CHILOE	56.2 X 41.7 CM	DEPOT DE LA MARINE
PLAN DU PORT DE ST DIEGO/PLAN DU PORT ET DU DEPARTEMENT DE ST BLAS	36.5 X 24.5 CM	ROBINSON
PLAN DU PORT DE ST FRANCOIS	36.5 X 24.5 CM	ROBINSON
PLAN DU PORT DES FRANCAIS	37.0 X 50.0 CM	ROBINSON
PLAN DU PORT DES FRANCAIS 1786	49.7 X 69.0 CM	DEPOT DE LA MARINE
PLAN DU PORT ET VILLE DE LOUISBOURG	20.3 X 27.9 CM	BELLIN
PLAN DU PORT ET VILLE DE LOUISBOURG/PLAN DE LA VILLE DE LOUISBOURG/PLA	45.7 X 50.8 CM	HOMANN
PLAN DU PORT ROYAL	22.9 X 27.9 CM	BELLIN
PLAN DU PORT TOULOUSE/PLAN DE LA BAIE NERICHAC	59.7 X 40.6 CM	DEPOT DE LA MARINE
PLAN ET SIEGE DAMVILLERS, 1637	41.5 X 52.0 CM	BLAEU
PLAN FOR THE ALTERATION OF THE STREETS AROUND THE CAPITAL SUBMITTED BY	27.9 X 21.0 CM	U.S.
PLAN OF A SURVEY FOR A RAIL-ROAD...NO.2 FROM SPRINGFIELD TO ALBANY; 18	19.7 X 74.9 CM	BALDWIN
PLAN OF A SURVEY FOR THE PROPOSED BOSTON AND PROVIDENCE RAIL-WAY	18.4 X 106.0 CM	HAYWARD
PLAN OF AMELIA ISLAND IN EAST FLORIDA.../VIEW OF ENTRANCE INTO ST. MAR	50.8 X 61.0 CM	JEFFERYS
PLAN OF BALTIMORE	24.1 X 27.9 CM	MITCHELL
PLAN OF BOSTON	33.3 X 52.7 CM	MITCHELL
PLAN OF CINCINNATI AND VICINITY	26.7 X 28.6 CM	MITCHELL
PLAN OF FORT PITT OR PITTSBOURG	24.0 X 25.3 CM	KITCHIN
PLAN OF KENOSHA HARBOR WISCONSIN	33.0 X 50.8 CM	U.S.
PLAN OF MANHATTEN ISLAND (N.Y.)	14.7 X 49.4 CM	BAEDEKER
PLAN OF NORTH CUT AT MILWAUKEE	43.2 X 31.8 CM	U.S.
PLAN OF OSWEGO 1727	26.7 X 36.8 CM	HOWEN
PLAN OF OSWEGO HARBOUR	21.6 X 12.1 CM	BOUCHETTE
PLAN OF OSWEGO HARBOUR	21.6 X 12.7 CM	FADEN
PLAN OF OYSTER BAY AND PART OF MARIAS ISLANDS BY CAPT. J.H. COX 1789	29.8 X 22.9 CM	DALRYMPLE
PLAN OF PHILADELPHIA	27.9 X 33.0 CM	MITCHELL
PLAN OF PLACE D'ARMES AND ST. JAMES STREET AT MONTREAL FOR THE ELUCIDA	17.5 X 23.1 CM	MCGREGOR
PLAN OF PORT DES FRANCAIS ON THE NORTH WEST COAST OF AMERICA...BY THE	37.1 X 49.5 CM	ROBINSON
PLAN OF PORT ROYAL LAGUNA, COMMONLY CALLED THE LOGWOOD CREEKS	20.1 X 27.4 CM	JEFFERYS
PLAN OF PORT S. DIEGO IN CALIFORNIA...SURVEY 1782/PORT & DEPARTMENT OF	36.8 X 24.1 CM	ROBINSON
PLAN OF RACINE HARBOR	27.3 X 31.8 CM	U.S.
PLAN OF RINGOLD BARRACKS, TEXAS	21.7 X 17.3 CM	U.S.
PLAN OF STRASBURG	8.9 X 13.3 CM	MOLL
PLAN OF THE ANCHORING PLACE AT THE ISLAND QUIBO BY CAPT. JAMES COLNETT	37.5 X 52.1 CM	ARROWSMITH
PLAN OF THE BATTLE FOUGHT NEAR CAMDEN AUGUST 16TH 1780	21.2 X 18.9 CM	STEDMAN
PLAN OF THE BATTLE OF ECKEREN	38.1 X 48.3 CM	TINDAL
PLAN OF THE BATTLE OF MALPLAQUET	38.1 X 48.3 CM	TINDAL
PLAN OF THE BAY OF CONCEPTION IN CHILI...	25.4 X 36.8 CM	ROBINSON
PLAN OF THE BAY OF MONTEREY SITUATE IN NORTH CALIFORNIA	25.4 X 37.5 CM	ROBINSON
PLAN OF THE BAY, ROCK AND TOWN OF GIBRALTER, FROM AN ACTUAL SURVEY BY	50.8 X 72.4 CM	FADEN
PLAN OF THE CITY AND FORTIFICATIONS OF NAMUR	38.1 X 48.3 CM	TINDAL
PLAN OF THE CITY OF BARCELONA	38.1 X 48.3 CM	TINDAL
PLAN OF THE CITY OF BUENOS AYRES	18.9 X 10.9 CM	WILCOCKE
PLAN OF THE CITY OF DENDERMONDE	38.1 X 48.3 CM	TINDAL
PLAN OF THE CITY OF DOWAY	38.1 X 48.3 CM	TINDAL
PLAN OF THE CITY OF MONS	38.1 X 48.3 CM	TINDAL
PLAN OF THE CITY OF SAN DOMINGO	19.1 X 26.7 CM	JEFFERYS
PLAN OF THE CITY OF WASHINGTON, THE CAPITOL OF UNITED STATES OF AMERIC	27.6 X 34.0 CM	MITCHELL
PLAN OF THE CITY OF YPRES	38.1 X 48.3 CM	TINDAL
PLAN OF THE COUNTRY & CAMPS OF ALMANAR	38.1 X 48.3 CM	TINDAL
PLAN OF THE COUNTRY FROM FROGS PT. TO COTTON RIVER SHEWING...THE AMERI	43.2 X 21.6 CM	MARSHALL
PLAN OF THE DIFFERENT CHANNELS LEADING FROM KINGSTON TO LAKE ONTARIO;	22.2 X 24.8 CM	FADEN

PLAN OF THE FORTS ONTARIO AND OSWEGO, WITH PART OF THE RIVER & LAKE ON	19.1 X 10.2 CM	BALDWIN
PLAN OF THE GENERAL ATTACK UPON THE ISLAND OF GUADELOUPE	11.4 X 17.8 CM	LONDON MAGAZINE
PLAN OF THE HARBOUR AND FORTIFICATIONS OF LOUISBURG	9.7 X 17.0 CM	HALLIBURTON
PLAN OF THE HARBOUR OF LOUISBURG, AND THE TOWN & FORTIFICATIONS WHEN I	11.5 X 15.0 CM	MCGREGOR
PLAN OF THE HARBOUR OF NEW YORK AND PARTS ADJACENT	14.6 X 9.5 CM	CONDER
PLAN OF THE ISLE OF TRINIDAD, FROM ACTUAL SURVEYS MADE IN THE YEAR 179	49.0 X 64.1 CM	LAURIE & WHITTLE
PLAN OF THE LAND BETWEEN LAKE CHAMPLAIN AND FORT EDWARD ON THE HUDSON	26.5 X 16.5 CM	KITCHIN
PLAN OF THE OPERATIONS OF THE BRITISH & AMERICAN FORCES BELOW NEW ORLE	50.8 X 19.7 CM	JAMES
PLAN OF THE PORT AND DEPARTMENT OF S. BLAS...SURVEY IN NOV. 1777/PORT	36.8 X 24.1 CM	ROBINSON
PLAN OF THE PORT OF VERA CRUZ	20.0 X 25.2 CM	ANON
PLAN OF THE POSITION WHICH THE ARMY UNDER LT GEN. BURGOINE TOOK AT SAR	22.0 X 47.5 CM	STEDMAN
PLAN OF THE POST ROAD BETWEEN BUENOS AYRES AND SANTIAGO DE CHILE	14.8 X 37.4 CM	ANON
PLAN OF THE RIVER ST. LAWRENCE...SIEGE OF QUEBEC	17.1 X 23.5 CM	ENTICK
PLAN OF THE SEIGE OF CHARLESTOWN IN SOUTH CAROLINA	25.5 X 30.0 CM	STEDMAN
PLAN OF THE SEIGE OF YORK TOWN IN VIRGINIA	27.5 X 32.5 CM	STEDMAN
PLAN OF THE SIEGE OF CARDONA	38.1 X 48.3 CM	TINDAL
PLAN OF THE SIEGE OF CHARLESTOWN IN SOUTH CAROLINA	25.4 X 29.2 CM	CADELL
PLAN OF THE SIEGE OF CHARLESTOWN IN SOUTH CAROLINA	25.3 X 29.7 CM	STEDMAN
PLAN OF THE SIEGE OF CHARLESTOWN IN SOUTH CAROLINA	25.5 X 29.6 CM	TARLETON
PLAN OF THE SIEGE OF MENIN	38.1 X 48.3 CM	TINDAL
PLAN OF THE SIEGE OF YORK TOWN IN VIRGINIA	29.2 X 31.9 CM	STEDMAN
PLAN OF THE SIEGE OF YORK TOWN IN VIRGINIA	27.4 X 32.3 CM	STEDMAN
PLAN OF THE TOWN & FORT OF GRENADA. BY M. DE CAYLUS, ENGINEER GENERAL	22.2 X 17.8 CM	LONDON MAGAZINE
PLAN OF THE TOWN AND FORTIFICATIONS OF GIBRALTER, EXACTLY TAKEN ON THE	36.8 X 58.4 CM	BASIRE
PLAN OF THE TOWN AND FORTIFICATIONS OF MONTREAL OR VILLE MARIE IN CANA	17.8 X 24.8 CM	BALDWIN
PLAN OF THE TOWN AND HARBOUR OF SAN JUAN DE PUERTO RICO	21.0 X 29.8 CM	JEFFERYS
PLAN OF THE TOWN AND HARBOUR OF ST. AUGUSTIN IN EAST FLORIDA	16.7 X 24.0 CM	POLITICAL MAGAZINE
PLAN OF THE TOWN OF BASSETERRE THE CAPITAL OF GUADELOUPE FROM AN AUTHE	32.4 X 23.5 CM	JEFFERYS
PLAN OF THE TOWN, ROAD AND HARBOUR OF CHAGRE	26.7 X 20.3 CM	JEFFERYS
PLAN OF ZISAPATA BAY	22.2 X 29.2 CM	JEFFERYS
PLAN VAN DE HAVEN CARTHAGENA	17.8 X 30.5 CM	TIRION
PLAN...DE LA HAVRE DE MILFORT	20.3 X 27.9 CM	BELLIN
PLANIGLOBII TERRESTRIS MAPPA UNIVERSALIS, ULTRUMQ HEMISPHAERIUM ORIENT	47.0 X 56.5 CM	HOMANN
PLANISFERO DE MONDO NUOVO DESCRITTO DAL P. CORONELLI, COSMOGRAFO PUBLI	45.7 X 61.0 CM	CORONELLI
PLANISFERO DEL MONDO NUOVO, DESCRITTO DAL P. CORONELLI, COSMOGRAFO PUB	45.7 X 61.6 CM	CORONELLI
PLANISIPHERE GENERAL, POUR SERVIR A L'INTELLIGENCE DE LA NAVIGATION ET	20.3 X 31.8 CM	BONNE
PLANISPHAERIUM COPERNICANUM SIVE SYSTEMA UNIVERSE TOTIUS CREATI EX HYP	43.2 X 50.8 CM	CELLARIUS
PLANISPHAERIUM PTOLEMAICUM SIVE MACHINA ORBIUM MUNDI EX HYPOTHESI PTOL	41.9 X 49.5 CM	CELLARIUS
PLANISPHERE	26.7 X 47.0 CM	LEVASSEUR
PLANISPHERE SUIVANT LA PROJECTION DE MERCATOR	22.2 X 32.4 CM	BONNE
PLANO DEL PORTO E DEGLI STABILIMENTI DI PENSACOLA	18.4 X 26.0 CM	GAZZETTIERE AMERICANO
PLANO DEL PUERTO DE NAOS Y SUS ADYACENTES-ISTMO DE PANAMA	19.1 X 26.0 CM	FIDALGO
PLANO DELLA CITTA DI QUEBEC	24.8 X 23.5 CM	GAZZETTIERE AMERICANO
PLANO DI PORTO BELLO	20.3 X 25.4 CM	GAZZETTIERE AMERICANO
PLANS OF THE OLD & NEW CITY OF PEKING YE METROPOLIS OF CHINA	34.3 X 21.0 CM	HARRIS
PLANSIFERO DEL MONDO NUOVO...	45.7 X 61.0 CM	CORONELLI
PLANSIPHAERIUM COELESTE HYPOTHESIS PTOLEMAICA. EX FORMIS PETRI SCHENCK	50.8 X 57.2 CM	SCHENK
PLANISPHERE SUIVANT LA PROJECTION DE MECATOR	21.6 X 35.6 CM	BONNE
PLAT OF THE SEVEN RANGES OF TOWNSHIPS BEING PART OF THE TERRITORY OF T	61.6 X 34.9 CM	CAREY
PLAT OF THE SEVEN RANGES OF TOWNSHIPS...(OHIO)	60.6 X 33.3 CM	CAREY
PLATE LIV. MAP OF TEXAS & PART OF NEW MEXICO COMPILED...1857	41.3 X 68.6 CM	U.S.
PLYMOUTH SOUND, HAMOAZE AND CATWATER SURVEYED IN 1786	69.9 X 51.4 CM	SAYER
POICTOU. PICTONUM VICINARUM QUE REGIONUM FIDISS DESCRIPTIO. AUCTORE NO	36.2 X 50.2 CM	ORTELIUS
POLAND	17.8 X 19.7 CM	MOLL
POLAND AND OTHER COUNTRIES BELONGING TO THAT CROWNE ACCORDING TO THE N	47.0 X 28.6 CM	SENEX
POLAND BY ROBT. MORDEN	10.2 X 12.7 CM	MORDEN
POLAR REGIONS	20.0 X 20.0 CM	BLACK
POLAR REGIONS	18.0 X 24.0 CM	THOMSON
POLI ARCTICI, ET CIRCIMIACENTIUM TERRARUM DESCRIPTIO NOVISSIMA	42.9 X 48.9 CM	DE WIT
POLI ARCTICI, ET CIRCUMIACENTIUM TERRARUM DESCRIPTIO NOVISSIMA PER FRE	43.2 X 49.5 CM	DE WIT
POLI ARCTICI... and POLUS ANTARCTICUS...	43.2 X 49.5 CM	HONDIUS
POLIOMETRIA BRITANNICA DAT IS STEDENMEETING VAN GROOT BRITANNIEN	48.3 X 58.4 CM	COVENS & MORTIER
POLITICAL MAP OF NORTH AMERICA	21.6 X 26.7 CM	WOODBRIDGE

POLITICAL MAP OF NORTH AMERICA...	21.6 X	26.7 CM	WOODBRIDGE
POLITICAL MAP OF THE UNITED STATES, MEXICO...	27.3 X	45.7 CM	WOODBRIDGE
POLITICAL MAP OF THE UNITED STATES, MEXICO...	27.3 X	45.7 CM	WOODBRIDGE
POLONIA ET HUNGARIA NOVA TABULA	13.3 X	17.1 CM	PTOLEMY (1548 VENICE)
POLONIAE, LITUANIAEQ. DESCRIPTIO. AUCTORE WENCESLAV GODRECCIO; ET CORR	36.8 X	48.3 CM	ORTELIUS
POLUS ARCTICUS SIVE TRACT SEPTENTRIONALIS	21.6 X	27.9 CM	QUAD
POLUS ARCTICUS SIVE TRACT, SEPTENTRIONALIS. COLONIAE, EX OFFICINA TYPG	21.6 X	27.9 CM	QUAD
POLYNESIA	20.0 X	25.0 CM	TALLIS
POLYNESIA OR ISLANDS IN THE PACIFIC OCEAN	33.0 X	39.4 CM	COX
POLYNESIA OR ISLANDS IN THE PACIFIC OCEAN	26.0 X	35.6 CM	TALLIS
PORT AMHERST. PORT HALDIMAND. SURVEY'D AND PUBLISH'D ACCORDING TO ACT	74.9 X	55.9 CM	DES BARRES
PORT DICK, NEAR COOK'S INLET (VIEW)	18.4 X	23.5 CM	EDWARDS
PORT OF PROVIDENCE-RHODE ISLAND	48.9 X	39.2 CM	U.S. COAST SURVEY
PORT ROYAL IN JAMAICA	12.7 X	15.9 CM	GOLD
PORT TOWNSHEND WASHINGTON TERR...1858	36.2 X	29.2 CM	U.S. COAST SURVEY
PORTLAND	10.2 X	17.8 CM	BLUNT
PORTO RICO	22.9 X	29.2 CM	LUCAS
PORTO RICO & VIRGIN ISLANDS	23.5 X	61.0 CM	THOMSON
PORTO RICO AND VIRGIN ISLANDS	41.9 X	52.7 CM	CAREY & LEA
PORTO RICO AND VIRGIN ISLES/HAITI HISPANIOLA OR ST. DOMINGO...FEBY. 18	61.0 X	50.8 CM	THOMSON
PORTSMOUTH	10.2 X	17.8 CM	BLUNT
PORTUGALLIAE ET ALGARBIAE REGNA	46.0 X	56.5 CM	VISSCHER
PORTUGALLIAE QUE OLIM LUSITANIA...	33.7 X	50.2 CM	ORTELIUS
PORTUGALLIAE REGNUM	13.5 X	17.5 CM	PTOLEMY (1596-1621 ...
POSITION OF THE DETACHMENT UNDER LIEUTT. COLL. BAUM AT WALMSCOCK NEAR	27.4 X	34.6 CM	FADEN
POSITION OF THE ENGLISH & FRENCH FLEETS IMMEDIATELY PREVIOUS TO THE AC	21.6 X	25.4 CM	STEDMAN
POST AT BROWNSVILLE, TEXAS	21.1 X	16.1 CM	U.S.
POTOSI (VIEW)	28.6 X	35.6 CM	VAN DER AA
PRELIMINARY CHART OF GALVESTON BAY	49.5 X	42.2 CM	U.S. COAST SURVEY
PRELIMINARY CHART OF NORTH EDISTO RIVER	45.1 X	35.6 CM	U.S. COAST SURVEY
PRELIMINARY SURVEY OF OCRACOKE INLET NORTH CAROLINA...	45.1 X	36.8 CM	U.S. COAST SURVEY
PRELIMINARY SURVEY OF POINT REYES AND DRAKE'S BAY CALIFORNIA	21.6 X	24.8 CM	U.S. COAST SURVEY
PREMIER QUARTIER DE BRABANT, DONT LA CAPITALE EST LOUVAIN. PARS MERIDI	46.0 X	54.0 CM	HONDIUS
PREMIERE FEUILLE DES COTES DE LA COCHINCHINE. 1798	48.1 X	69.0 CM	DEPOT DE LA MARINE
PRESBITERI IOHANNIS SIVE ABISSINORUM IMPERIUM	7.6 X	10.2 CM	ORTELIUS
PRESBITERI IOHANNIS, SIVE ABISSINORUM IMPERII DESCRIPTIO	36.8 X	43.5 CM	ORTELIUS
PRESENT ASIA...	36.8 X	50.8 CM	WELLS
PRESQU'ISLE DE L'INDE...	19.1 X	24.1 CM	SANSON
PRIMA EUROPE TABULA//SECUNDA EUROPAE TABULA/(PTOLEMAIC WORLD)	40.6 X	53.3 CM	PTOLEMY (1511 VENICE)
PRIMA PARS BRABANTIAE CUIUS CAPUT LOVANIUM AUCTORE MICHAELE FLORENTIO	41.0 X	52.0 CM	BLAEU
PRINCE EDWARD ISLAND	18.4 X	34.9 CM	ASHBY
PRINCIPATUS GOTHA, COBURG ET ALTENBURG...	48.3 X	55.9 CM	HOMANN
PRINCIPATUS HENNENBERGENSIS	37.5 X	49.5 CM	HONDIUS
PRINCIPAUTE DE CATALOGNE	57.2 X	86.4 CM	MORTIER
PRINCIPAUTE DE TRANSILVANIE	57.2 X	86.4 CM	MORTIER
PROGRESS MAP OF THE UNITED STATES GEOGRAPHICAL SURVEYS WEST OF THE 100	40.6 X	55.9 CM	U.S.
PROPOSED CANAL FROM BAY VERT TO CUMBERLAND BASON	10.2 X	17.8 CM	TORBETT
PROPOSED CANAL FROM ST. PETER'S BAY TO BRAS D'OR LAKE	10.8 X	17.8 CM	TORBETT
PROSP. DER STATT NAMUR	14.0 X	36.0 CM	MERIAN
PROSPECT OF THE CAPE OF GOOD HOPE (VIEW)	21.0 X	15.0 CM	CHILD
PROVINCE OF CANADA (EASTERN SHEET) NEW BRUNSWICK, NOVA SCOTIA, PRINCE	44.0 X	57.5 CM	JOHNSTON
PROVINCE OF CANADA (EASTERN SHEET) NEW BRUNSWICK, NOVA SCOTIA, PRINCE	42.5 X	55.5 CM	JOHNSTON
PROVINCE OF CANADA (EASTERN SHEET), NEW BRUNSWICK, NOVA SCOTIA, PRINCE	44.5 X	57.2 CM	JOHNSTON
PROVINCE OF CANADA (WESTERN SHEET)	44.5 X	57.2 CM	JOHNSTON
PROVINCE OF CANADA (WESTERN SHEET)	44.0 X	57.5 CM	JOHNSTON
PROVINCE OF CANADA (WESTERN SHEET) BY KEITH JOHNSTON. F.R.S.E.	42.5 X	55.5 CM	JOHNSTON
PROVINCES DES PAIS BAS DIVISEES SUIVANT LES TRAITES...FAITS EN 1713, 1	47.0 X	62.0 CM	DE FER
PROVINCES UNIES DES PAIS-BAS CONNUES SOUS LE NOM DE HOLLANDE, PAR P. D	40.5 X	56.0 CM	DU VAL
PROVINCES UNIES DES PAYS BAS	41.0 X	44.0 CM	ANON
PROVINCES UNIES DES PAYS-BAS. PAR N. SANSON D'ABBEVILLE. GEOGR. DU ROY	41.0 X	51.0 CM	SANSON
PROVINCES UNIES DES PAYS-BAS. PARIS, JAILLOT D'APRES SANSON, 1700. COR	47.0 X	65.0 CM	JAILLOT
PROVINCIA DE BRAZIL	27.9 X	35.6 CM	DE LAET
PROVINCIAE SITAE AD FRETUM MAGELLANIS ITEMQUE FRETUM LE MAIRE	27.9 X	35.6 CM	DE LAET

PRUSSIA	20.0 X 25.0 CM	TALLIS
PTO. SANTO	17.8 X 23.4 CM	FIDALGO
PTOLEMAEI TYPUS	13.5 X 17.5 CM PTOLEMY (1596-1621 ...
PUERTO CABELLO	17.5 X 26.6 CM	FIDALGO
PUERTO CABELLO (VIEW)	20.1 X 30.6 CM	GOERING
PUGNAINTER COLUMBUM & FRANCISCUM PORESIUM (ENGRAVED SCENE)	19.7 X 15.9 CM	DE BRY
QUANTUNG, E FOKIEN	45.7 X 61.0 CM	CORONELLI
QUARTA ASIAE TABULA	38.7 X 53.3 CM PTOLEMY (1513-20 ST...
QUATRIEME QUARTIER DE BRABANT. BOISLEDUC. BRABANTIAE PARS ORIENTALIS..	46.0 X 54.0 CM	HONDIUS
QUEBEC	14.7 X 20.1 CM	BAEDEKER
QUEBEK, DE HOOFSTAD VAN KANADA; AAN DE RIVIER VAN ST. LAURENS: DOOR DE	33.0 X 43.2 CM	TIRION
QUESTA E LA VERA DESCRITTIONE DI TUTTA LA SPAGNA...	69.2 X 94.6 CM	GASTALDI
QUINTA ASIE TABULA	36.5 X 50.8 CM PTOLEMY (1513-20 ST...
RADNOR COMITATUS QUEM SILVRES OLIM INCOLUERUNT	27.3 X 32.4 CM	KIP
RADNORSHIRE	17.8 X 11.4 CM	OWEN & BOWEN
RADNORSHIRE	11.4 X 14.0 CM	SELLER
RAILROAD AND COUNTY MAP OF COLORADO	41.3 X 56.5 CM	CRAM
RAILROAD AND COUNTY MAP OF KANSAS	40.6 X 57.2 CM	CRAM
RAILROAD AND COUNTY MAP OF KENTUCKY AND TENNESSEE	24.1 X 30.5 CM	CRAM
RAILROAD MAP OF THE UNITED STATES TOGETHER WITH VARIOUS STEAMSHIP LINE	36.8 X 58.4 CM	BRADLEY
RECENS EDITA TOTIUS NOVI BELGII IN AMERICA SEPTENTRIONALI...	49.8 X 58.2 CM	LOTTER
RECENS EDITA TOTIUS NOVI BELGII, IN AMERICA SEPTENTRIONALI...	49.5 X 57.2 CM	SEUTTER
RECENTISSIMA NOVI ORBIS AMERICAE SEPTENTRIONALIS ET MERIDIONALIS TABUL	50.2 X 59.1 CM	ALLARD
RECENTISSIMA NOVI ORBIS SIVE AMERICAE	49.5 X 58.4 CM	DANCKERTS
RECONNAISANCE OF PORT GAMBLE WASH. TERR. 1856	30.5 X 22.2 CM	U.S. COAST SURVEY
RECONNAISSANCE OF THE S.E. END OF SAN CLEMENTE ISLAND CALIFORNIA	30.5 X 44.8 CM	U.S. COAST SURVEY
REGIO CANAAN...	48.9 X 56.5 CM	SEUTTER
REGIONES SUB POLO ARCTICO	41.0 X 53.0 CM	BLAEU
REGIONES SUB POLO ARCTICO AUCTORE GUILJELMO BLAEU	40.6 X 52.1 CM	BLAEU
REGIONIS, QUAE EST CIRCA LONDIUM SPECIALIS REPRAESENTATIO GEOGRAPHICA	48.3 X 55.9 CM	HOMANN
REGIONUM CIRCUMPOLARIUM LAPPONIAE ISLANDIAE ET GROENLANDIAE NOVA ET VE	29.0 X 36.0 CM	SCHERER
REGNI BOHEMIAE DESCRIPTIO	33.0 X 50.8 CM	ORTELIUS
REGNI D'ARACAN DEL PEGU DI SIAM DI CAMBOGE E DI LAOS	39.5 X 32.0 CM	ZATTA
REGNI HUNGARIAE, GRAECIAE, ET MOREAE...	50.2 X 57.8 CM	DANCKERTS
REGNI MEXICANI SEU NOVAE HISPANIAE...	48.3 X 57.2 CM	HOMANN
REGNI SINAE VEL SINAE PROPRIE MAPA ET DESCRIPTIO GEOGRAPHICA...	58.4 X 52.1 CM	HOMANN
REGNI SUECIAE IN OMNES SUAS SUBJACENTES PROVINCIAS ACCURATE DIVISI TAB	48.9 X 29.2 CM	HOMANN
REGNUM NEAPOLIS IN QUO SUNT APRUTIUM ULTERIUS ET CITERIUS...	58.4 X 49.5 CM	DE WIT
RELIGIONIS CATHOLICAE AUSTRALI AMERICAE IMPLANTATAE DESCRIPTIO GEOGRAP	21.7 X 34.2 CM	SCHERER
REPRAESENTATIO GEOGRAPHICA ITINERIS NAVIS VICTORIAE...1522	23.0 X 35.5 CM	SCHERER
RHENOLANDIAE ET AMSTELLANDIAE	40.0 X 50.0 CM	BLAEU
RHODE ISLAND	35.6 X 29.2 CM	BRADFORD
RHODE ISLAND	36.8 X 27.9 CM	BRADFORD
RHODE ISLAND	22.9 X 29.2 CM	LUCAS
RHODE ISLAND	27.9 X 22.2 CM	SWINSTON
RHODE ISLAND AND CONNECTICUT...	19.1 X 33.0 CM	MORSE
RHODUS	15.0 X 23.0 CM	BRAUN & HOGENBERG
RHODUS	12.0 X 18.0 CM	COTOVICUS
RIO COLORADO OF THE WEST, MAP NO. 1	37.5 X 88.9 CM	U.S.
RIO COLORADO OF THE WEST, MAP NO. 2	37.5 X 88.9 CM	U.S.
RIO DE JANEIRO (VIEW)	14.6 X 21.0 CM	DUNCAN
RIO DE LA PLATA	16.5 X 18.4 CM	MOLL
RIO GRANDE TO THE PACIFIC	55.9 X 127.0 CM	U.S.
RIO JANEIRO (VIEW)	10.9 X 16.6 CM	ANON
RIVER ODER GEGENT VON MIT DER EROBERUNG DER INSUL SCHEPENSAMBT WEG NEH	21.6 X 34.3 CM	ANON
RIVERS, MOUNTAINS	24.5 X 30.5 CM	MACKENZIE
RIVIERE DES LACS TO THE ROCKY MOUNTAINS	62.2 X 92.7 CM	U.S.
ROCK ISLAND CITY (VIEW)	10.2 X 15.2 CM	MEYER
ROCKY MOUNTAINS TO PUGET SOUND	62.2 X 91.4 CM	U.S.
ROMA	57.2 X 86.4 CM	MORTIER
ROMANI IMPERII	48.0 X 53.0 CM	DE VAUGONDY
ROMANIAE, (QUAE OLIM THRACIA DICTA) VICINORUMQ REGIONUM, UTI BULGARIAE	36.8 X 50.8 CM	ORTELIUS
ROUTE NEAR 32ND PARALLEL. MAP & PROFILE NO.1. FROM THE RED RIVER TO TH	54.0 X 144.8 CM	U.S.

274

ROUTE OF THE EXPEDITION A.D. 1825, FROM FORT WILLIAM TO THE SASKATCHAW	35.9 X	43.2 CM	FRANKLIN
ROUTE OF THE EXPEDITION FROM ISLE LA CROSSE TO FORT PROVIDENCE IN 1819	51.4 X	23.5 CM	FRANKLIN
ROUTE OF THE EXPEDITION FROM YORK FACTORY TO CUMBERLAND HOUSE AND...TR	25.4 X	56.5 CM	FRANKLIN
ROYAUME D'ANNAN COMPRENENT LES ROYAUMES DE TUMKIN ET DE LA COCHINCHINE	43.2 X	31.1 CM	SANSON
ROYAUME D'IRLANDE	48.3 X	54.0 CM	DE VAUGONDY
ROYAUME D'IRLANDE	47.6 X	53.3 CM	SANTINI
ROYAUME DE DANEMARK	48.0 X	53.0 CM	DE VAUGONDY
ROYAUME DE HONGRIE	48.0 X	53.0 CM	DE VAUGONDY
ROYAUMES D'ESPAGNE ET DE PORTUGAL	48.0 X	53.0 CM	DE VAUGONDY
ROYAUMES D'ESPAGNE ET DE PORTUGAL. LES ROUTES DE POSTES	48.0 X	53.0 CM	DE VAUGONDY
RUATAN OR RATTAN, SURVEYED BY LIEUT. HENRY BARNSLEY WITH IMPROVEMENTS	45.7 X	61.0 CM	JEFFERYS
RUSSIA CUM CONFINIJS	35.6 X	48.3 CM	MERCATOR
RUSSIA IN ASIA	20.0 X	25.0 CM	TALLIS
RUSSIA IN EUROPE	20.0 X	25.0 CM	TALLIS
RUSSIA VULGO MOSCOVIA DICTAE, PARTES SEPTENTRIONALIS ET ORIENTALIS. AU	41.9 X	53.3 CM	JANSSON
RUSSIAE, MOSCOVIAE ET TARTARIAE DESCRIPTIO AUCTORE ANTONIO IENKENSONO	34.9 X	44.5 CM	ORTELIUS
RUSSIAE...	35.6 X	44.5 CM	ORTELIUS
RUTLANDIAE...	28.6 X	21.6 CM	KIP
RUTLANDSHIRE	11.4 X	14.0 CM	SELLER
RUTLANDSHIRE	23.5 X	19.1 CM	WILKES
RUTLANDSHIRE...	38.7 X	47.6 CM	SPEED
S. GIOVANNI	11.4 X	15.2 CM	LASOR A VAREA
S. GIOVANNI	10.2 X	14.0 CM	PORCACCHI
S.M. ANNO AETATIS SUAE 60 (PORTRAIT)	16.2 X	13.3 CM	MUNSTER
SACRAMENTO GENERAL VIEW	12.7 X	22.9 CM	LONDON NEWS
SAINT PAUL M.T. (VIEW)	15.1 X	22.7 CM	STEVENS
SALT LAKE CITY (VIEW)	16.5 X	24.1 CM	DE BAR
SALT LAKE CITY UTAH (VIEW)	24.1 X	35.6 CM	LONDON NEWS
SAN FRANCISCO	19.5 X	24.5 CM	BAEDEKER
SAN FRANCISCO BAY TO NORTHERN BOUNDARY OF CALIFORNIA	68.6 X	58.4 CM	U.S.
SAN FRANCISCO BAY TO THE PLAINS OF LOS ANGELES FROM EXPLORATIONS & SUR	71.8 X	88.3 CM	PARKE
SAN FRANCISCO, CALIFORNIA, FROM THE BAY (VIEW)	18.4 X	34.9 CM	WHYMPER
SANTA BARBARA--UPPER CALIFORNIA (VIEW)	11.0 X	17.8 CM	SMYTH
SANTA FE CROSSING TO THE COOCHETOPA PASS	79.4 X	59.1 CM	U.S.
SANTVLIET: TABULA CASTELLI AD SANDFLIATUM...APUD IOAN. IANSSONIUM	37.0 X	49.0 CM	HONDIUS
SARDINIA	8.5 X	12.5 CM	ORTELIUS
SARDINIA/SCILIA	13.5 X	17.5 CM	PTOLEMY (1596-1621 ...
SAVOY & PIEDMONT	21.6 X	18.4 CM	MOLL
SAXONIAE SUPERIORIS LUSATIAE MISNIAEQUE DESCRIPTIO	34.9 X	48.9 CM	HONDIUS
SCANDINAVIA	14.0 X	19.1 CM	MOLL
SCHEMA CORPORIS SOLARIS PROUT AB AUTHORE ET P. SCHEINERO. ROMAE ANNO 1	37.0 X	42.0 CM	KIRCHER
SCHLAVONIAE, CROATIAE, CARNIAE, ISTRIAE, BOSNIAE...	33.0 X	45.7 CM	ORTELIUS
SCHONBERG'S MAP OF MEXICO	37.5 X	58.4 CM	SCHONBERG
SCOTIA REGNUM	34.9 X	40.6 CM	MERCATOR
SCOTIA...	41.9 X	54.6 CM	JANSSON
SCOTIAE TABULA	35.5 X	47.5 CM	ORTELIUS
SCOTIAE TABULA	36.8 X	48.3 CM	ORTELIUS
SCOTLAND	17.8 X	17.8 CM	MOLL
SCOTLAND	11.4 X	15.2 CM	SELLER
SCOTLAND	36.2 X	25.4 CM	TALLIS
SCOTLAND	20.0 X	25.0 CM	TALLIS
SCOTLAND WITH THE PRINCIPAL ROADS FROM THE BEST AUTHORITIES	33.0 X	36.8 CM	CAREY
SCOZIA	38.1 X	31.8 CM	ALBRIZZI
SEA COAST OF THE UNITED STATES FROM CAPE SMALL POINT MAINE TO CAPE COD	92.5 X	80.5 CM	U.S. COAST SURVEY
SECONDA ASIAE TABULA	36.8 X	40.6 CM	PTOLEMY (1513-20 ST...
SECONDE FEUILLE DES COTES DE LA COCHINCHINE. 1798	69.6 X	48.5 CM	DEPOT DE LA MARINE
SECONDE PARTIE DE LA CRIMEE LA MER NOIRE &C. RECTIFIES PAR DIVERSES OB	48.9 X	61.0 CM	COVENS & MORTIER
SECUNDA PARS BRABANTIAE CUIUS URBS PRIMARIA BRUXELLAE	41.5 X	52.5 CM	BLAEU
SEPTEMTRIONALES REG.	7.6 X	10.2 CM	ORTELIUS
SEPTENTRIONALIUM PARTIUM NOVA TABULA	17.8 X	24.1 CM	PTOLEMY (1561-99 VE...
SEPTENTRIONALIUM REGIONUM DESCRIP.	36.5 X	49.0 CM	ORTELIUS
SEPTENTRIONALIUM REGIONUM DESCRIP.	35.9 X	48.9 CM	ORTELIUS
SEPTENTRIONALIUM REGIONUM DESCRIP.	36.2 X	49.5 CM	ORTELIUS

SEPTENTRIONALIUM TERRARUM DESCRIPT.	14.5 X 20.0 CM		JANSSON
SEPTENTRIONALIUM TERRARUM DESCRIPTIO	37.0 X 39.5 CM		MERCATOR
SEPTENTRIONALIUM TERRARUM DESCRIPTIO. PER GERARDUM MERCATOREM CUM PRIV	36.8 X 39.4 CM		MERCATOR
SEPTIMA ASIE TABULA	33.7 X 53.3 CM	PTOLEMY (1513-20 ST...	
SEPTIME EUROPE TABULA	31.8 X 55.9 CM	PTOLEMY (1513-20 ST...	
SEVEN PROVINCES OF THE UNITED NETHERLANDS	17.1 X 19.1 CM		MOLL
SEVILLA/CADIZ/MALAGA (VIEWS)	34.0 X 47.5 CM		BRAUN & HOGENBERG
SEXTA ASIE TABULA	31.8 X 55.9 CM	PTOLEMY (1513-20 ST...	
SHROPSHIRE	36.2 X 41.9 CM		MORDEN
SHROPSHIRE	11.4 X 14.0 CM		SELLER
SHROPSHIRE	11.4 X 15.2 CM		SELLER
SHROPSHIRE	23.5 X 19.1 CM		WILKES
SHROPSHYRE...	38.7 X 47.6 CM		SPEED
SICILIA SARDINIA NOVA TABULA	13.3 X 17.1 CM	PTOLEMY (1548 VENICE)	
SICILIAE	8.5 X 12.5 CM		ORTELIUS
SICILIAE REGNUM	33.7 X 48.3 CM		MERCATOR
SIEGE D'OSTENDE EN 1601	31.0 X 44.0 CM		ANON
SIEGE ET PRISE DE THIONVILLE, 1643	44.0 X 54.0 CM		BLAEU
SIEGE OF BETHUNE	38.1 X 48.3 CM		TINDAL
SIEGE OF CITY OF AIRE, FORT ST. FRANCIS AND ST. VENANT	38.1 X 48.3 CM		TINDAL
SILESIAE DUCATUS...	38.1 X 48.9 CM		HONDIUS
SITKA OR NEW ARCHANGEL (VIEW)	16.5 X 24.1 CM		WHYMPER
SITKA, THE RUSSIAN POSSESSION ON THE NORTH WEST COAST OF AMERICA (VIEW	10.2 X 21.6 CM		LONDON NEWS
SITUS PARTIUM PRAECIPUARUM TOTIUS ORBIS TERRARUM	44.5 X 38.1 CM		TORNIELLO
SITUS TERRAE CANAAN	57.2 X 86.4 CM		MORTIER
SITUS TERRAE PROMISSIONIS, S.S. BIBLIORUM INTELLIGENTIUM EXACTE APERIE	36.8 X 48.3 CM		HONDIUS
SITUS TERRAE PROMISSIONIS. S.S. BIBLIORUM INTELLIGENTIAM EXACTE APERIE	36.8 X 49.5 CM		JANSSON
SITUS TERRAE PROMISSIONIS...PER CHR. ADRICHOM	37.0 X 50.0 CM		HONDIUS
SITUS TERRAE PROMISSIONIS...PER CHR. ADRICHOM	37.5 X 50.0 CM		JANSSON
SKETCH A SHOWING THE PROGRESS OF THE SURVEY...FROM 1832 TO 1865	44.4 X 69.1 CM		U.S. COAST SURVEY
SKETCH BY COMPASS OF NORFOLK SOUND	39.7 X 27.8 CM		DIXON
SKETCH BY COMPASS OF PORT BANKS...	38.1 X 27.9 CM		DIXON
SKETCH BY COMPASS OF PORT MULGRAVE...	40.6 X 27.9 CM		DIXON
SKETCH DISTINGUISHING THE PARTS OF NORTH EAST AMERICA BEST ADAPTED TO	18.7 X 11.1 CM		LONGMAN
SKETCH I SHOWING THE PROGRESS OF THE SURVEY IN SECTION NO. 9 FROM 1848	18.4 X 54.0 CM		U.S. COAST SURVEY
SKETCH I SHOWING THE PROGRESS OF THE SURVEY IN SECTION NO. 9, 1848 TO	19.1 X 28.6 CM		U.S. COAST SURVEY
SKETCH OF A PART OF THE MARCH & WAGON ROAD OF LT. COLONEL COOKE FROM S	29.2 X 56.5 CM		ABERT
SKETCH OF HURON HARBOUR SHOWING THE EXTENT OF REPAIRS MADE IN 1853	45.1 X 61.0 CM		U.S.
SKETCH OF MCLEOD'S HARBOUR ON THE WEST SIDE OF MONTAGU I...	30.0 X 29.5 CM		PORTLOCK
SKETCH OF MCLEOD'S HARBOUR, THE WEST SIDE OF MONTAGU IS.	31.8 X 30.5 CM		STOCKDALE
SKETCH OF MONROE HARBOR SHOWING THE EXTENT OF REPAIRS MADE IN 1854...	39.4 X 57.2 CM		U.S.
SKETCH OF NIAGARA RIVER BETWEEN QUEENSTON & CHIPPEWA	18.0 X 22.0 CM		ANON
SKETCH OF NOOTKA SOUND...	26.2 X 20.3 CM		ANON
SKETCH OF NORTH AMERICA SHEWING THE PROPOSED ROUTES OF CAPT. BACK	24.8 X 30.5 CM		MURRAY
SKETCH OF PART OF THE HUDSONS BAY COMPANY'S TERRITORY	28.6 X 32.4 CM		ARROWSMITH
SKETCH OF PORT ETCHES, SITUATED 5 LEAGUES NNE OF CAPE HINCHINGBROOK; T	20.3 X 29.5 CM		PORTLOCK
SKETCH OF PORTLOCK'S & GOULDING'S HARBOURS ON NORTH WEST COAST OF AMER	31.8 X 33.0 CM		STOCKDALE
SKETCH OF SOUTH FARALLON ISLAND	33.0 X 32.4 CM		U.S. COAST SURVEY
SKETCH OF THE ACTIONS FOUGHT AT SAN PASQUAL IN UPPER CALIFORNIA BETWEE	45.7 X 59.7 CM		EMORY
SKETCH OF THE COUNTRY ILLUSTRATING THE LATE ENGAGEMENT IN LONG ISLAND	31.1 X 19.7 CM		GENTLEMAN'S MAGAZINE
SKETCH OF THE GULF OF MEXICO SHOWING LINES OF DEEP SEA SOUNDINGS AND P	38.1 X 71.1 CM		U.S. COAST SURVEY
SKETCH OF THE HARBOUR OF SAMGANOODA, ON THE ISLAND OF OONALASKA...T. B	20.3 X 32.4 CM		HOGG
SKETCH OF THE LEAD MINE DISTRICT IN WASHINGTON COUNTY, MISSOURI TERRIT	47.0 X 39.4 CM		U.S.
SKETCH OF THE NORTH EASTERN BOUNDARY BETWEEN GREAT BRITAIN AND THE UNI	23.9 X 32.7 CM		WYLD
SKETCH OF THE NORTH EASTERN BOUNDARY BETWEEN GREAT BRITAIN AND THE UNI	24.1 X 32.4 CM		WYLD
SKETCH OF THE PUBLIC SURVEYS IN IOWA. DUBUQUE OCT. 24, 1851. GEORGE B.	44.5 X 56.5 CM		U.S.
SKETCH OF THE PUBLIC SURVEYS IN MICHIGAN	54.0 X 55.9 CM		U.S.
SKETCH OF THE PUBLIC SURVEYS IN MICHIGAN. DETROIT OCT. 21, 1851. CHARL	54.6 X 54.0 CM		U.S.
SKETCH OF THE PUBLIC SURVEYS IN WISCONSIN & TERRITORY OF MINNESOTA	44.5 X 53.3 CM		U.S.
SKETCH OF THE SURPRISE OF GERMANTOWN...	46.4 X 53.3 CM		FADEN
SKETCH OF VLAMINGO ROAD ON THE EAST SIDE OF AMSTERDAM ISLAND...	29.2 X 21.6 CM		DALRYMPLE
SKETCH SHOWING THE PROGRESS OF THE SURVEY ON THE ATLANTIC GULF OF MEXI	61.0 X 61.0 CM		U.S. COAST SURVEY
SNUG CORNER COVE IN PRINCE WILLIAM'S SOUND	14.0 X 19.7 CM		PELHAM

276

SOCIETAS IESU PER UNIVERSAM MUNDUM DIFFUSA	23.5 X 35.5 CM	SCHERER
SODUS BAY, WAYNE CO. N.Y.	39.4 X 31.8 CM	U.S.
SOMERSET SHIRE...	38.7 X 47.6 CM	SPEED
SOMERSETSHIRE	10.2 X 17.8 CM	CAPPER
SOMERSETSHIRE	14.0 X 8.9 CM	CARY
SOMERSETSHIRE	10.8 X 6.4 CM	WALLIS & REID
SOMERSETTENSIS COMITATUS: SOMERSET SHIRE	36.8 X 48.3 CM	VALK & SCHENK
SOUTH AMERICA	30.5 X 22.9 CM	ARROWSMITH
SOUTH AMERICA	27.9 X 21.0 CM	BARNES & BURR
SOUTH AMERICA	39.4 X 30.5 CM	CHAPMAN & HALL
SOUTH AMERICA	49.5 X 38.6 CM	FULLARTON
SOUTH AMERICA	43.2 X 54.0 CM	GALL & INGLIS
SOUTH AMERICA	37.5 X 74.3 CM	KITCHIN
SOUTH AMERICA	23.5 X 19.1 CM	NEELE
SOUTH AMERICA	68.6 X 49.5 CM	PINKERTON
SOUTH AMERICA	34.3 X 26.7 CM	TALLIS
SOUTH AMERICA	35.6 X 24.1 CM	TALLIS
SOUTH AMERICA	20.0 X 25.0 CM	TALLIS
SOUTH AMERICA	39.4 X 32.4 CM	THOMAS, COWPERTHWAI...
SOUTH AMERICA CORRECTED FROM OBSERVATIONS COMMUNICATED TO THE ROYAL SO	58.4 X 94.0 CM	SENEX
SOUTH AMERICA CORRECTED FROM THE OBSERVATIONS COMMUNICATED TO THE ROYA	64.5 X 89.5 CM	PRICE
SOUTH AMERICA FROM THE BEST AUTHORITIES	19.7 X 23.5 CM	TEGG
SOUTH AMERICA STATES. NEW GRANADA & VENEZUELA	41.2 X 53.0 CM	FULLARTON
SOUTH AMERICA, ACCORDING TO THE NEWEST AND MOST EXACT OBSERVATIONS...	58.0 X 97.0 CM	MOLL
SOUTH AMERICA. SHEET 1. ECUADOR, GRANADA, VENEZUELA, AND PARTS OF BRAZ	40.6 X 31.1 CM	SDUK
SOUTH AUSTRALIA	20.0 X 25.0 CM	TALLIS
SOUTH CAROLINA	35.6 X 29.2 CM	BRADFORD
SOUTH CAROLINA	22.9 X 29.2 CM	LUCAS
SOUTH CAROLINA	24.4 X 27.9 CM	LUCAS
SOUTH CAROLINA	15.2 X 18.4 CM	SCOTT
SOUTH DAKOTA	25.4 X 31.8 CM	TUNISON
SOUTH EASTERN ASIA BIRMAH-CHINA-JAPAN	31.8 X 40.6 CM	CHAPMAN & HALL
SOUTHERN & WESTERN STATES	8.3 X 15.2 CM	BOYNTON
SOUTHERN AFRICA (CAPE COLONY)	20.0 X 25.0 CM	TALLIS
SOUTHERN INDIA	20.0 X 25.0 CM	TALLIS
SOUTHERN ITALY	20.0 X 25.0 CM	TALLIS
SOUTHERN PORTS & HARBOURS IN THE UNITED STATES	41.2 X 29.6 CM	FULLARTON
SOUTHERN PROVINCES OF THE UNITED STATES	49.5 X 58.4 CM	THOMSON
SOUTHERN PROVINCES OF UNITED STATES	49.5 X 58.4 CM	THOMSON
SOUTHERN STATES	21.0 X 26.0 CM	APPLETON
SOUTHERN STATES WESTERN DIVISION	22.9 X 27.9 CM	SWINSTON
SOUTHERN STATES-WESTERN SECTION	21.6 X 27.9 CM	MATTHEWS, NORTHRAP CO.
SPAIN & PORTUGAL	15.9 X 18.4 CM	MOLL
SPAIN AND PORTUGAL	36.5 X 44.1 CM	CAREY
SPAIN AND PORTUGAL	20.0 X 25.0 CM	TALLIS
SPAINE...	38.7 X 47.6 CM	SPEED
SPANISH DOMINIONS IN N. AMERICA	18.4 X 24.1 CM	MACPHERSON
SPANISH DOMINIONS IN NORTH AMERICA	20.3 X 24.8 CM	LEWIS & ARROWSMITH
SPANISH DOMINIONS IN NORTH AMERICA MIDDLE PART	50.8 X 69.9 CM	PINKERTON
SPANISH DOMINIONS IN NORTH AMERICA, SOUTHERN PART	50.8 X 69.9 CM	PINKERTON
SPANISH DOMINIONS IN NORTH AMERICA. MIDDLE PART. PINKERTON'S MODERN AT	50.8 X 69.9 CM	PINKERTON
SPANISH NORTH AMERICA	24.8 X 39.4 CM	LONGMAN
SPANISH NORTH AMERICA	62.2 X 50.8 CM	THOMSON
SPECIMEN TRIGESINAE SEXTAE PARTIS EX GLOBO TERRESTRIUM...	82.5 X 16.5 CM	LOWIZIO
ST. AUGUS. DE FLORIDE (VIEW)	14.6 X 10.8 CM	MALLET
ST. CHRISTOPHERS	22.9 X 29.2 CM	LUCAS
ST. CHRISTOPHERS, OR ST. KITTS, SURVEYED BY ANTHONY RAVELL...ENGRAVED	46.7 X 61.7 CM	LAURIE & WHITTLE
ST. GEORGE'S RIVER AND MUSCLE RIDGE CHANNEL-MAINE	95.6 X 65.7 CM	U.S. COAST SURVEY
ST. JOHN	9.8 X 14.7 CM	BAEDEKER
ST. LOUIS AND ADJACENT COUNTRY	16.6 X 10.2 CM	MELISH
ST. LUCIA	22.9 X 29.2 CM	LUCAS
ST. PAUL TO RIVIERE DES LACS	62.2 X 92.7 CM	U.S.
ST. PAUL, MINNESOTA...(VIEW)	11.4 X 18.4 CM	RAWLINGS

ST. SALVADOR (VIEW)	11.1 X 16.7 CM	ANON
ST. THOMAS	20.0 X 14.5 CM	MALLET
ST. VINCENT	22.9 X 29.2 CM	LUCAS
STABILIMENTI DE FRANCESI INGLESI E SPAGNUOLI NELLE ISOLE ANTILLE...	31.8 X 41.9 CM	ZATTA
STAFFORD COUNTIE AND TOWNE WITH THE ANCIENT CITIE LICHFIELD DESCRIBED	38.1 X 50.8 CM	SPEED
STAFFORD COUNTIES AND TOWNE...	38.7 X 47.6 CM	SPEED
STAFFORDIAE COMITATUS PARS...	26.7 X 37.5 CM	KIP
STAFFORDSHIRE	11.4 X 14.0 CM	SELLER
STAFFORDSHIRE	11.4 X 15.2 CM	SELLER
STALIMENE	12.0 X 16.5 CM	CORONELLI
STATE OF NEVADA	80.0 X 61.0 CM	U.S.
STATE OF NEW YORK	20.3 X 24.1 CM	PICQUET
STATE OF OREGON	58.4 X 76.2 CM	U.S.
STATES OF AMERICA	19.1 X 22.9 CM	NUTTALL, FISHER & D...
STATES OF AMERICA FROM THE BEST AUTHORITIES	19.1 X 22.9 CM	RUSSELL
STATI UNITI D'AMERICA RIDOTTA DELLA CARTA PUBBLICATA A NUOVA YORK	33.0 X 27.9 CM	MAGGI
STATO DI MILANO PARTE OCCIDENTALE	61.0 X 45.5 CM	CORONELLI
STELLACOOM HARBOR WASHINGTON TERRITORY-BY W. FAIRFAX	30.5 X 39.4 CM	U.S. COAST SURVEY
SUCCESSION DES EMPEREURS DU JAPON AVEC UNE DESCRIPTION DU MEUTRE DE L'	38.1 X 50.8 CM	CHATELAIN
SUECIA NORUEGIA RUSSIA MOSCOVE TICA 1699	23.0 X 33.0 CM	SCHERER
SUFFOLK	24.1 X 19.1 CM	BELL
SUFFOLK	35.6 X 41.3 CM	MORDEN
SUFFOLK	11.4 X 14.0 CM	SELLER
SUFFOLKE DESCRIBED AND DIVIDED INTO HUNDREDS	38.7 X 47.6 CM	SPEED
SUFFOLKE DESCRIBED AND DIVIDED INTO HUNDREDS, THE SITUATION OF THE FAY	38.1 X 50.8 CM	SPEED
SUITE DE LA CARTE REDUITE DU GOLPHE DE ST. LAURENT CONTENANT LES COSTE	90.8 X 56.5 CM	DEPOT DE LA MARINE
SUITE DES ISLES ANTILLAS 2 PARTIE	22.2 X 17.1 CM	BELLIN
SUITE DU COURS DU FLEUVE DE ST. LAURENT	19.0 X 28.5 CM	BELLIN
SUITE DU COURS DU FLEUVE DE ST. LAURENT	19.1 X 27.9 CM	BELLIN
SUITE DU COURS DU FLEUVE ST. LOUIS DEPUIS LA RIVIERE D'IBERVILLE...	21.6 X 34.3 CM	BELLIN
SUMATRA	26.7 X 36.8 CM	RAMUSIO
SUMATRA, JAVA, BORNEO, &C.	19.5 X 25.0 CM	SANSON
SUPLEMENT POUR LES ISLES ANTILLES	31.8 X 21.0 CM	BONNE
SURREY	17.8 X 26.7 CM	ELLIS
SURREY	32.4 X 39.4 CM	WALKER
SURREY	10.8 X 6.4 CM	WALLIS & REID
SURREY DESCRIBED AND DIVIDED INTO HUNDREDS	38.1 X 51.4 CM	SPEED
SURREY...	38.7 X 47.6 CM	SPEED
SURRY	11.4 X 14.0 CM	SELLER
SURVEY OF HARBOR OF CLEVELAND, OHIO	26.0 X 45.1 CM	U.S.
SURVEY OF THE MOUTH OF CLINTON RIVER, MICHIGAN MADE IN 1853	29.2 X 37.5 CM	WAGNER & MCGUIGAN
SURVEY OF WINTER HARBOUR MELVILLE ISLAND JUNE 1820. J. WALKER, SCULPT.	24.1 X 17.1 CM	MURRAY
SUSSEX	24.1 X 19.1 CM	BELL
SUSSEX	10.2 X 17.8 CM	CAPPER
SUSSEX	7.6 X 12.1 CM	LEIGH
SUSSEX	11.4 X 14.0 CM	SELLER
SUSSEX...	38.7 X 47.6 CM	SPEED
SUSSEXIA SIVE SOUTHSEX, OLIM PARS REGNORUM	22.2 X 40.3 CM	KIP
SUSSEXIA...	22.2 X 38.7 CM	KIP
SUTHSEXIA VERNACULE SUSSEX	38.1 X 47.6 CM	JANSSON
SUTHSEXIA: VERNACULE SUSSEX	38.5 X 51.0 CM	JANSSON
SUYDT HOLLANDIAE	45.5 X 54.5 CM	DE WIT
SWEDEN & NORWAY	17.1 X 18.4 CM	MOLL
SWEDEN AND NORWAY	20.0 X 25.0 CM	TALLIS
SWEDEN, DENMARK, AND NORWAY FROM THE BEST AUTHORITIES	33.0 X 36.8 CM	CAREY
SWITZERLAND	17.8 X 19.1 CM	MOLL
SWITZERLAND	20.0 X 25.0 CM	TALLIS
SWITZERLAND ACCORDING TO THE BEST AUTHORITIES	22.2 X 29.2 CM	CAREY
SYLVADUCUS	40.0 X 50.0 CM	BLAEU
SYRIA	20.0 X 25.0 CM	TALLIS
SYSTEMA IDEAL QUO EXPRIMITUR, AQUARUM PER CANALES HYDRAGOGOS SUBTERRAN	36.5 X 41.5 CM	KIRCHER
SYSTEMA IDEALE PYROPHYLACIORUM SUBTERRANEORUM QUORUM MONTES VULCANI...	37.0 X 42.0 CM	KIRCHER
SYSTEME DE L'UNIVERS SELON TICHO	10.2 X 14.0 CM	MALLET

Title	Dimensions	Source
T'HOOGE HEEMRADSCHAP VAN DELFLAND MET ALLE DE STEDEN, DORPEN, AMBACHTE	50.0 X 59.0 CM	KRUIKIUS
T'HOOGE HEEMRAED-SCHAP VAN RHYNLAND	42.0 X 56.0 CM	DOU
TAB. XII ASIAE, TAPROBANUM...	34.3 X 35.6 CM PTOLEMY (1578-1730 ...
TABULA APHRICAE II	16.0 X 25.0 CM PTOLEMY (1561-99 VE...
TABULA ASIA XII	19.0 X 24.0 CM PTOLEMY (1561-99 VE...
TABULA ASIAE VI	12.7 X 17.1 CM PTOLEMY (1548 VENICE)
TABULA ASIAE XII	13.5 X 17.5 CM PTOLEMY (1596-1621)
TABULA COMITATUS FRISIAE...	46.5 X 55.0 CM	DE WIT
TABULA EUROPAE I	12.0 X 17.0 CM PTOLEMY (1548 VENICE)
TABULA EUROPAE II	13.3 X 17.1 CM PTOLEMY (1548 VENICE)
TABULA EUROPAE III	13.3 X 16.5 CM PTOLEMY (1548 VENICE)
TABULA EUROPAE IX	13.3 X 17.1 CM PTOLEMY (1548 VENICE)
TABULA EUROPAE IX	12.7 X 17.1 CM PTOLEMY (1548 VENICE)
TABULA EUROPAE V	13.3 X 17.1 CM PTOLEMY (1548 VENICE)
TABULA EUROPAE VI	13.3 X 17.1 CM PTOLEMY (1548 VENICE)
TABULA EUROPAE VII	13.3 X 17.1 CM PTOLEMY (1548 VENICE)
TABULA EUROPAE VIII	13.3 X 17.1 CM PTOLEMY (1548 VENICE)
TABULA EUROPAE X	18.4 X 25.4 CM PTOLEMY (1561-99 VE...
TABULA FLUXUS REFLUXUX, RATIONES IN MARI ANGLICO...	19.5 X 19.7 CM	KIRCHER
TABULA GEOGRAPHICA NOVA OMNIUM...REGNI GUIANA...GUALTHERO RALEGH...	34.0 X 45.5 CM	DE BRY
TABULA GEOGRAPHICO-HYDROGRAPHICA MOTUS OCEANI, CURRENTES, ABYSSOS, MON	33.7 X 55.2 CM	KIRCHER
TABULA INDIAE ORIENTALIS	45.5 X 56.0 CM	DE WIT
TABULA MAGELLANICA QUA TIERRA DEL FUEGO	41.3 X 53.3 CM	BLAEU
TABULA MAGELLANICA QUA TIERRAE DEL FUEGO CUM CELEBERRIMIS FREITIS A F.	40.6 X 53.3 CM	JANSSON
TABULA MODERNA BOSSINE SERVICE GRETIAE ET SCLAVONIE (GREECE)	41.6 X 54.3 CM PTOLEMY (1513-20 ST...
TABULA MODERNA ET NOVA HISPANIE	41.3 X 55.9 CM PTOLEMY (1513-20 ST...
TABULA MODERNA FRANCIE	38.7 X 54.6 CM PTOLEMY (1482-86 ULM)
TABULA MODERNA INDIA ORIENTALIS ET MERIDIONALIS	27.9 X 40.6 CM PTOLEMY (1522-41 ST...
TABULA MODERNA INDIAE	40.6 X 50.8 CM PTOLEMY (1513-20 ST...
TABULA MODERNA PRIME PARTIS APHRICAE	43.8 X 57.2 CM PTOLEMY (1513-20 ST...
TABULA MODERNA TERRA SANCTE	33.0 X 55.9 CM PTOLEMY (1513-20 ST...
TABULA NEOTERICA CRETE SIVE CENDIE INSULE	38.7 X 53.0 CM PTOLEMY (1513-20 ST...
TABULA NOVA ANGLIAE & HIBERNIAE	28.6 X 41.3 CM PTOLEMY (1522-41 ST...
TABULA NOVA PARTIS AFRICAE (SOUTH AFRICA)	30.5 X 42.5 CM PTOLEMY (1522-41 ST...
TABULA NOVA PARTIS AFRICAE (WEST AFRICA)	27.9 X 40.0 CM PTOLEMY (1522-41 ST...
TABULA NOVA TERRA SANCTAE	24.1 X 40.6 CM PTOLEMY (1522-41 ST...
TABULA NOVA TOTIUS ORBIS	27.9 X 45.7 CM PTOLEMY (1522-41 ST...
TABULA NOVARUM INSULARUM	27.9 X 34.3 CM	MUNSTER
TABULA NOVARUM INSULARUM...	25.5 X 34.0 CM	MUNSTER
TABULA OCTAVA ASIAE CONTINET SCYTHIAM EXTRA IMAUM MONTEM, & SERICAM	30.5 X 34.9 CM PTOLEMY (1522-41 ST...
TABULA PEUTINGERIANA	39.4 X 50.8 CM	HORNIUS
TABULA QUA HYDROPHYLACIUM...	20.4 X 34.2 CM	KIRCHER
TABULA QUARTA ASIA	30.5 X 45.7 CM PTOLEMY (1522-41 ST...
TABULA SECONDA AFRICAE (LIBYA)	34.3 X 54.6 CM PTOLEMY (1513-20 ST...
TABULA SUPERIORIS INDIAE ET TARTARIAE MAJORIS	27.9 X 33.0 CM PTOLEMY (1522-41 ST...
TABULAE EUROPAE I	18.0 X 25.0 CM PTOLEMY (1561-99 VE...
TARTARIAE	34.3 X 47.0 CM	ORTELIUS
TARTARIAE IMPERIUM	14.0 X 17.8 CM PTOLEMY (1596-1621 ...
TARTARIAE IMPERIUM	12.5 X 17.0 CM PTOLEMY (1596-1621 ...
TARTARIAE SIVE MAGNI CHAMI REGNI	33.7 X 47.0 CM	ORTELIUS
TARTARIAE SIVE MAGNI CHAMI REGNI TYPUS	35.0 X 47.5 CM	ORTELIUS
TARTARIAE SIVE MAGNI CHAMI REGNI TYPUS	35.5 X 47.0 CM	ORTELIUS
TARTARIAE SIVE MAGNI CHAMI REGNI TYPUS	7.6 X 10.8 CM	ORTELIUS
TARTARIAE SIVE MAGNI CHAMI REGNI TYPUS	34.9 X 47.0 CM	ORTELIUS
TARTARIAE SIVE MAGNI CHAMI REGNI TYPUS CONTINET HEC TABULA OEM TARTARI	34.9 X 47.0 CM	ORTELIUS
TAVARICA CHERSONESUS, HODIE PRZCOPSCA, ET GAZARA DICTUR. EXCUDEBANT JA	38.1 X 49.5 CM	PITT
TAVOLA DELLA GRAN GERMANIA, QUARTA DELL'EUROPA. TABULA EUROPAE IIII	12.7 X 16.5 CM PTOLEMY (1596-1621 ...
TAVOLA NUOVA D'ITALIA	18.4 X 24.1 CM PTOLEMY (1561-99 VE...
TAVOLA NUOVA DI SARDIGNA ET DI SICILIA	17.8 X 24.8 CM PTOLEMY (1561-99 VE...
TAVOLA NUOVA DI SCHIAVONIA	17.8 X 24.1 CM PTOLEMY (1561-99 VE...
TEGENWOORDIGE STAAT VAN DE WESTINDISCHE EILANDEN EN NOOD AMERICA	16.5 X 10.2 CM	TIRION
TEMISTITAN	10.5 X 14.5 CM	PORCACCHI
TENNASSEE	15.2 X 19.1 CM	SCOTT

279

Title	Dimensions	Source
TENNESSEE	35.6 X 29.2 CM	BRADFORD
TERCIA AFFRICE TABULA	30.5 X 55.9 CM	PTOLEMY (1482-86 ULM)
TERRA FIRMA AND THE CARIBBE ISLANDS	15.9 X 19.1 CM	MOLL
TERRA FIRMA. GUIANA AND THE ANTILLES ISLANDS	17.8 X 25.4 CM	MOLL
TERRA NOVA	29.2 X 38.1 CM	PTOLEMY (1522-41 ST...
TERRA NOVA	17.9 X 24.6 CM	PTOLEMY (1561-99 VE...
TERRA NOVA...	48.3 X 55.9 CM	DE WIT
TERRA SANCTA A PETRO LAICSTAIN PERLUSTRATA...ET A CHR. SCHROT IN TABUL	36.5 X 50.5 CM	ORTELIUS
TERRA SANCTA QUAE IN SACRIS TERRA PROMISSIONIS OL: PALESTINA	35.6 X 49.5 CM	MERCATOR
TERRA SANCTA SIVE PROMISSIONIS, OLIM PALAESTINA	46.5 X 56.0 CM	VISSCHER
TERRA SANCTA SIVE PROMISSIONIS, OLIM PALESTINA	46.0 X 55.0 CM	DE WIT
TERRA SANCTA, A PETRO LAICSTAIN PERLUSTRATA, ET AB EIUS ORE ET SCHEDIA	36.8 X 50.8 CM	ORTELIUS
TERRA SANCTA, SIVE PROMISSIONIS, OLIM PALESTINA	45.7 X 55.2 CM	DE WIT
TERRA SANCTA...	36.8 X 49.5 CM	ORTELIUS
TERRAE ARCTICA	6.5 X 7.5 CM	MULLER
TERRE ARTICHE DESCRITTE DAL P.M. CORONELLI M.C. COSMOGRAFO DELLA SEREN	45.7 X 61.0 CM	CORONELLI
TERRE FERME OU SONT LES GOVERNATIONS OU GOUVERNEMENS DE TERRE FERME, C	39.8 X 53.8 CM	SANSON
TERRE-FERME, PEROU, BRESIL PAYS DE L'AMAZON...	24.1 X 27.9 CM	DE VAUGONDY
TERRITOIRE DE VERONE	57.2 X 86.4 CM	MORTIER
TERRITORIES OF NEW MEXICO & UTAH	32.4 X 40.0 CM	COLTON
TERRITORIES OF NEW MEXICO AND UTAH	30.5 X 40.6 CM	COLTON
TERRITORY OF ARIZONA	52.1 X 43.2 CM	U.S.
TERRITORY OF ARIZONA	52.1 X 43.2 CM	U.S.
TERRITORY OF MONTANA	36.2 X 26.7 CM	MITCHELL
TERRITORY OF NEW MEXICO	74.3 X 61.6 CM	BIEN
TERTI AFRICAE TABULA	34.3 X 53.3 CM	PTOLEMY (1513-20 ST...
TERTIA PARS BRABANTIAE...MARCHIONATUS S.R.I. ANTVERPIA	42.0 X 52.5 CM	BLAEU
TEXAS	40.6 X 55.9 CM	ANON
TEXAS	57.2 X 40.0 CM	ASHER & ADAMS
TEXAS	35.9 X 28.6 CM	BRADFORD
TEXAS	19.7 X 26.4 CM	BRADFORD
TEXAS	20.3 X 26.7 CM	BRADFORD
TEXAS	35.6 X 29.2 CM	BRADFORD
TEXAS	19.7 X 26.4 CM	BRADFORD
TEXAS	41.9 X 57.2 CM	BRADLEY
TEXAS	26.0 X 22.2 CM	BURGESS
TEXAS	29.8 X 43.2 CM	CRAM
TEXAS	30.5 X 43.2 CM	CRAM
TEXAS	30.5 X 43.2 CM	GASKELL
TEXAS	20.3 X 27.0 CM	MITCHELL
TEXAS	20.3 X 27.0 CM	MITCHELL
TEXAS	20.6 X 27.0 CM	MITCHELL
TEXAS	20.3 X 26.7 CM	MITCHELL
TEXAS	21.0 X 27.0 CM	MITCHELL
TEXAS	23.5 X 31.8 CM	RAND MCNALLY
TEXAS	23.5 X 31.8 CM	RAND MCNALLY
TEXAS & INDIAN TERRITORY	31.8 X 24.1 CM	RAND MCNALLY
TEXAS, EASTERN PART; TEXAS WESTERN PART	104.1 X 67.3 CM	CRAM
TEXAS, NEW MEXICO & INDIAN TY.	21.6 X 27.3 CM	STUART
TEXAS, PART OF NEW MEXICO &C.	27.9 X 36.8 CM	BLACK
TEXAS, PART OF NEW MEXICO &C.	27.9 X 36.8 CM	BLACK
TEXAS, PART OF NEW MEXICO &C.	27.9 X 36.8 CM	BLACK
THAL VON CARACAS (VIEW)	20.3 X 29.8 CM	GOERING
THAT PART OF DISTURNELL'S TREATY MAP IN THE VICINITY OF THE RIO GRANDE	21.6 X 26.7 CM	U.S.
THE "FATHER OF WATERS"	96.5 X 8.9 CM	GLAZIER
THE ANTILLES OR WEST-INDIA ISLANDS...LONDON EDWARD STANFORD...	38.7 X 30.8 CM	SDUK
THE ARCTIC REGIONS SHOWING THE NORTH-WEST PASSAGE AS DETERMINED BY CAP	45.7 X 30.5 CM	FULLARTON
THE ARCTIC REGIONS, SHOWING THE NORTH-WEST PASSAGE AS DETERMINED BY CA	25.0 X 25.0 CM	FULLARTON
THE ATTACK OF QUEBEC	10.5 X 16.5 CM	LA HONTAN
THE AUSTRALIAN COLONIES	39.0 X 69.0 CM	SDUK
THE BAHAMAS	50.2 X 65.4 CM	STANFORD
THE BAY AND RIVER OF DELAWARE	18.4 X 21.6 CM	BLUNT
THE BAY OF CHESAPEAKE, FROM ITS ENTRANCE TO BALTIMORE	17.8 X 17.8 CM	BLUNT

THE BAY OF PANAMA AND GULF OF BALLONA	13.2 X 12.6 CM	ESQUEMELING
THE BISHOPRICK AND CITIE OF DURHAM	38.7 X 47.6 CM	SPEED
THE BISHOPRICK AND CITIE OF DURHAM. ARE TO BE SOLD BY HENRY OVERTON AT	38.1 X 48.3 CM	SPEED
THE BRITISH COLONIES IN NORTH AMERICA	25.0 X 35.0 CM	VIRTUE
THE BRITISH COLONIES IN NORTH AMERICA, FROM THE BEST AUTHORITIES	33.7 X 33.7 CM	GUTHRIE
THE BRITISH COLONIES IN NORTH AMERICA, FROM THE BEST AUTHORITIES	33.7 X 34.3 CM	GUTHRIE
THE BRITISH COLONIES IN NORTH AMERICA...	22.3 X 30.5 CM	VIRTUE
THE BRITISH GOVERNMENTS IN NTH. AMERICA LAID DOWN AGREEABLE TO THE PRO	20.3 X 23.5 CM	GENTLEMAN'S MAGAZINE
THE BRITISH ISLANDS AND PRIVILEGES IN THE WEST INDIES	17.8 X 29.8 CM	KITCHIN
THE BRITISH POSSESSIONS IN NORTH AMERICA	38.7 X 43.8 CM	LEWIS
THE CALIFORNIA GOLD DISTRICT-KANAHA BAR WHERE GOLD WAS FIRST FOUND (VI	24.1 X 35.6 CM	BORTHWICK
THE CANARY ISLANDS & A DRAUGHT OF THE FOUNTAIN TREE IN THE ISLAND OF F	18.5 X 22.5 CM	UNIVERSAL MAGAZINE
THE CITY OF BABYLON (VIEW)	33.0 X 47.0 CM	ANON
THE CITY OF LOUISVILLE, KENTUCKY/THE CITY OF NEW ORLEANS, LOUISIANA. P	40.0 X 33.0 CM	COLTON
THE COASTS OF ENGLAND & FRANCE FROM THE START, TO THE ISLES OF SILLY,	50.8 X 38.1 CM	SELLER
THE COASTS OF GUATEMALA AND MEXICO FROM PANAMA TO CAPE MENDOCINO, WITH	36.8 X 50.8 CM	ARROWSMITH
THE CONFEDERATE STATES...	50.8 X 61.0 CM	BARTHOLOMEW
THE COUNTIE AND CITIE OF LYNCOLNE...	38.7 X 47.6 CM	SPEED
THE COUNTIE OF LEINSTER...	38.7 X 47.6 CM	SPEED
THE COUNTIE OF NOTTINGHAM...	38.7 X 47.6 CM	SPEED
THE COUNTIE OF RADNOR...	38.7 X 47.6 CM	SPEED
THE COUNTIE OF WESTMORELAND...	38.7 X 47.6 CM	SPEED
THE COUNTY OF WARWICK...	38.7 X 47.6 CM	SPEED
THE COUNTY PALATINE OF CHESTER...	34.3 X 41.3 CM	MORDEN
THE COUNTY PALATINE OF LANCASTER...	41.9 X 36.2 CM	MORDEN
THE COUNTYE OF MONMOUTH...	38.7 X 47.6 CM	SPEED
THE COUNTYE PALATINE OF CHESTER...	38.7 X 47.6 CM	SPEED
THE COUNTYE PALATINE OF LANCASTER...	38.7 X 47.6 CM	SPEED
THE COURSE OF THE RIVER ST. LAURENCE, FROM LAKE ONTARIO, TO MANICOUAGA	43.8 X 62.9 CM	THOMSON
THE DISTRICT OF MAINE	40.6 X 31.8 CM	CAREY
THE DUTCH ISLANDS OF ST. EUSTATIA, SABA, AND ST. MARTINS; THE FRENCH I	26.5 X 20.9 CM	POLITICAL MAGAZINE
THE EMPIRE OF CHINA WITH ITS PRINCIPAL DIVISIONS DRAWN FROM THE SURVEY	48.3 X 62.9 CM	ROBERTS
THE EMPIRE OF JAPAN WITH PART OF THE CONTINENT OF ASIA SHOWING...NEW B	43.2 X 30.5 CM	WELLER
THE ENGLISH EMPIRE IN AMERICA	21.6 X 17.8 CM	MOLL
THE FIRST PRINCIPLES OF GEOGRAPHY AND ASTRONOMY MADE EASY BY INSPECTIO	30.5 X 59.7 CM	MARTIN
THE GALLAPAGOS ISLANDS DISCOVERED BY CAPT. JOHN EATON	13.8 X 13.0 CM	MOLL
THE GREAT AND SMALL BAY OF LE GRANDE, PART OF BRAZILE	14.6 X 21.0 CM	DAMPIER
THE GREAT BAY OF PLACENTIA	16.2 X 10.2 CM	LA HONTAN
THE GREAT RIVER MARANON OR THE AMASONS GEOGRAPHICALLY DESCRIBED BY SAM	15.9 X 36.2 CM	MOLL
THE GULF OF NICOYA, BY SOME CALL'D TH GULF OF SALINAS	16.5 X 21.0 CM	DAMPIER
THE HARBOR OF HOLMES' HOLE...	26.0 X 35.9 CM	U.S. COAST SURVEY
THE HARBOUR OF CASCO BAY AND ISLANDS ADJACENT BY CAPT. CYPRIAN SOUTHIC	42.5 X 52.1 CM	GRIERSON
THE HARBOUR OF CASCO BAY AND ISLANDS ADJACENT. BY CAPT. CYPRIAN SOUTHI	43.2 X 53.3 CM	MOUNT & PAGE
THE HARBOUR OF CHARLES TOWN IN SOUTH-CAROLINA FROM THE SURVEYS OF SR.	83.8 X 61.6 CM	DES BARRES
THE INVASIONS OF ENGLAND AND IRELAND...	38.7 X 47.6 CM	SPEED
THE ISLAND OF JAMAICA	20.3 X 27.9 CM	MOLL
THE ISLAND OF SABLE LIES IN LAT...	28.6 X 36.8 CM	JEFFERYS
THE ISLAND OF ST. CHRISTOPHERS	17.8 X 25.4 CM	MOLL
THE ISLAND OF ST. DOMINGO, CALLED BY THE SPANIARDS, HISPANIOLA, SUBJEC	33.0 X 47.2 CM	POLITICAL MAGAZINE
THE ISLANDS OF NEW ZEALAND	38.1 X 31.8 CM	SDUK
THE ISLANDS OF SCILLY	45.1 X 55.9 CM	COLLINS
THE ISLANDS OF THE EAST INDIES WITH THE CHANNELS BETWEEN INDIA, CHINA	22.9 X 29.8 CM	CAREY
THE ISLE OF CALIFORNIA, NEW MEXICO, LOUISIANE, RIVER MISISIPI AND THE	16.5 X 18.4 CM	MOLL
THE ISLE OF CALIFORNIA. NEW MEXICO. LOUISIANE. THE RIVER MISISIPI AND	16.2 X 18.4 CM	MOLL
THE ISLE OF MAN	38.7 X 47.6 CM	SPEED
THE ISLE OF WIGHT	8.0 X 12.5 CM	SPEED
THE ISLE OF WIGHT/SCILLY ISLANDS/HOLY ISLAND/FAIRN ISLANDS AND STAIPLE	20.3 X 31.8 CM	MOLL
THE ISLES OF MONTREAL AS THEY HAVE BEEN SURVEY'D BY THE FRENCH ENGINEE	25.4 X 33.0 CM	ANON
THE JERSEYS, &C. &C.	26.5 X 17.0 CM	GORDON
THE KINGDOM OF BOHEMIA	22.9 X 27.9 CM	ROLLOS
THE KINGDOM OF ENGLAND	18.4 X 18.4 CM	MOLL
THE KINGDOME OF CHINA	38.7 X 47.6 CM	SPEED
THE KINGDOME OF DENMARKE	39.4 X 50.8 CM	SPEED

THE KINGDOME OF DENMARKE...	38.7 X 47.6 CM	SPEED
THE KINGDOME OF ENGLAND	38.1 X 51.4 CM	SPEED
THE KINGDOME OF ENGLAND	38.7 X 47.6 CM	SPEED
THE KINGDOME OF ENGLAND	8.0 X 12.5 CM	SPEED
THE KINGDOME OF IRELAND	8.0 X 12.5 CM	SPEED
THE KINGDOME OF IRELAND...	38.7 X 47.6 CM	SPEED
THE KINGDOME OF PERSIA...	38.7 X 47.6 CM	SPEED
THE MAPE OF HUNGARI...	38.7 X 47.6 CM	SPEED
THE MISSION OF SAN FRANCISCO, UPPER CALIFORNIA (VIEW)	11.0 X 17.5 CM	SMYTH
THE MOST SURPRISING CATARACT OF NIAGARA IN CANADA (VIEW)	19.1 X 28.6 CM	MILLAR
THE NEW EL DORADO IN BRITISH AMERICA	35.6 X 24.1 CM	HARPER'S WEEKLY
THE NORTH AND EAST RIDINGE OF YORKSHIRE	38.7 X 47.6 CM	SPEED
THE NORTH AND EAST RIDINS OF YORKSHIRE	38.7 X 51.4 CM	SPEED
THE NORTH SIDE OF LARGEST OF QUEEN CHARLOTTE'S ISLANDS	20.3 X 33.0 CM	HOGG
THE NORTHERN HEMISPHERE	25.5 X 25.0 CM	CONDER
THE PACIFIC STATES, THE TERRITORIES...	50.8 X 61.0 CM	BARTHOLOMEW
THE PROVINCE OF CONNAUGH...	38.7 X 47.6 CM	SPEED
THE PROVINCE OF MOUNSTER	38.7 X 47.6 CM	SPEED
THE PROVINCE OF ULSTER	38.7 X 47.6 CM	SPEED
THE PROVINCES OF LA PLATA, THE BANDA ORIENTAL DEL URUGUAY & CHILE...	63.5 X 52.1 CM	ARROWSMITH
THE RIVER ST. LAWRENCE, ACCURATELY DRAWN FROM D'ANVILLE'S MAP PUBLISH'	35.6 X 41.9 CM	HARRISON
THE RIVER ST. LAWRENCE, ACCURATELY DRAWN FROM D'ANVILLE'S MAP. PUBLISH	33.5 X 42.0 CM	HARRISON
THE SEA COAST OF ITALY FROM CAPE DELLE MELLE TO MOUNT ARGENTATO WITH T	40.0 X 52.1 CM	MOUNT & PAGE
THE SEA COAST OF LANGUEDOC PROVENCE AND PART OF ITALY, FROM CAPE DRAGO	40.6 X 52.1 CM	MOUNT & PAGE
THE SEVERAL STATES & TERRITORIES OF THE UNITED STATES IN SQUARE MILES	35.6 X 85.1 CM	GILMAN
THE SOUTH EAST POINT OF YE ISLANDS OF RESOLUTION/A VIEW OF CAPE WALSIN	15.0 X 22.6 CM	ELLIS
THE SOUTH EASTERN STATES...ACCORDING TO CALVIN SMITH & TANNER	40.6 X 51.4 CM	FULLARTON
THE SOUTHERN PART OF THE PROVINCE OF NEW YORK: WITH PART OF THE ADJOIN	24.8 X 18.4 CM	LONDON MAGAZINE
THE STATE OF CAROLINA FROM THE BEST AUTHORITIES 1799	18.7 X 21.3 CM	PAYNE
THE STATE OF MARYLAND, FROM THE BEST AUTHORITIES	28.5 X 41.9 CM	LEWIS
THE STATE OF MASSACHUSETTS	34.3 X 48.3 CM	CAREY
THE STATE OF NEW YORK	43.2 X 53.3 CM	CAREY
THE STATE OF NORTH CAROLINA FROM THE BEST AUTHORITIES...	27.8 X 46.8 CM	LEWIS
THE STATE OF OHIO WITH PART OF OHIO UPPER CANADA ETC.	40.0 X 36.8 CM	CAREY
THE STATE OF PENNSYLVANIA FROM THE LATEST SURVEYS 1800	18.4 X 26.0 CM	PAYNE
THE STATE OF PENNSYLVANIA...	29.2 X 45.7 CM	CAREY
THE STATE OF SOUTH CAROLINA FROM THE BEST AUTHORITIES BY SAMUEL LEWIS	40.0 X 45.7 CM	CAREY
THE STATE OF SOUTH CAROLINA: FROM THE BEST AUTHORITIES...	38.9 X 44.3 CM	LEWIS
THE STATE OF TENNESSEE	26.7 X 54.6 CM	CAREY
THE STATE OF VIRGINIA FROM THE BEST AUTHORITIES	34.9 X 49.8 CM	LEWIS
THE THOUSAND ISLANDS OF ST. LAWRENCE RIVER REACHED BY THE RICHELIEU &	22.2 X 39.4 CM	MATTHEWS, NORTHRAP ...
THE TOWN & HARBOUR OF ST. JOHN, NEW BRUNSWICK	24.1 X 34.3 CM	ILLUSTRATED LONDON ...
THE TOWN OF BASSETERRE, GUADELOUPE (VIEW)	17.8 X 23.5 CM	LONDON NEWS
THE TOWN OF VALPARAISO ON THE COAST OF CHILI	17.8 X 22.9 CM	VANCOUVER
THE TOWNE OF PUERTO DEL PRINCIPE TAKEN & SACKT (VIEW)	15.9 X 11.4 CM	ESQUEMELING
THE TURKISH EMPIRE	38.7 X 47.6 CM	SPEED
THE TURKISH EMPIRE	39.4 X 50.8 CM	SPEED
THE UNITED STATES	27.9 X 43.8 CM	IVISON & BLAKEMAN
THE UNITED STATES OF AMERICA	38.1 X 65.4 CM	COLTON
THE UNITED STATES OF AMERICA AS SETTLED BY THE PEACE OF 1783	21.0 X 25.4 CM	ANON
THE UNITED STATES OF NORTH AMERICA	34.3 X 50.2 CM	BLACKIE & SON
THE UNITED STATES OF NORTH AMERICA WITH BRITISH TERRITORIES AND THOSE	53.3 X 62.9 CM	FADEN
THE UNITED STATES OF NORTH AMERICA WITH THE BRITISH TERRITORIES	53.3 X 64.8 CM	WYLD
THE UNITED STATES OF NORTH AMERICA WITH THE BRITISH TERRITORIES	54.0 X 64.0 CM	WYLD
THE UNITED STATES OF NORTH AMERICA WITH THE BRITISH TERRITORIES AND TH	54.6 X 64.8 CM	FADEN
THE UNITED STATES OF NORTH AMERICA: WITH THE BRITISH TERRITORIES AND T	53.0 X 63.2 CM	FADEN
THE UPPER TERRITORIES OF THE UNITED STATES	43.8 X 33.3 CM	CAREY
THE VIRGIN ISLANDS FROM ENGLISH AND DANISH SURVEYS	45.7 X 61.0 CM	JEFFERYS
THE VIRGIN ISLANDS SHEWING THE SET OF THE TIDE	19.1 X 41.9 CM	MURRAY
THE WEST INDIA ISLANDS	24.8 X 29.2 CM	DARTON
THE WEST INDIES ACCORDING TO THE BEST AUTHORITIES. ENGRAVED FOR GUTHRI	53.3 X 28.6 CM	GUTHRIE
THE WEST INDIES, AND GULF OF MEXICO. ENGRAV'D BY J. CARY. PUBLISH'D BY	34.6 X 22.9 CM	CARY
THE WEST INDIES...	19.1 X 27.9 CM	BANKES

THE WEST RIDINGE OF YORKESHYRE...	38.7 X 47.6 CM	SPEED
THE WESTERN COAST OF GREENLAND FROM BALL'S RIVER TO ICE GLANCE	17.1 X 22.9 CM	CRANTZ
THE WESTERN COAST OF GREENLAND, FROM BALL'S RIVER TO THE ICE GLANCE	16.5 X 22.9 CM	CRANTZ
THE WESTERN HEMISPHERE	34.0 X 34.0 CM	CRUCHLEY
THE WESTERN HEMISPHERE and THE EASTERN HEMISPHERE	51.4 X 88.3 CM	CARY
THE WORLD	47.0 X 64.8 CM	ANON
THE WORLD	20.0 X 25.0 CM	TALLIS
THE WORLD DRAWN BY A. ARROWSMITH HYDROGRAPHER TO PRINCE REGENT...	20.3 X 25.4 CM	ARROWSMITH
THE WORLD FROM THE BEST AUTHORITIES	20.0 X 31.5 CM	MCINTYRE
THE WORLD FROM THE DISCOVERIES & OBSERVATIONS MADE IN THE LATEST VOYAG	30.0 X 45.0 CM	ARROWSMITH
THE WORLD IN 3 SECTIONS	28.5 X 46.5 CM	DALRYMPLE
THE WORLD IN HEMISPHERES	29.5 X 57.0 CM	JOHNSTON
THE WORLD IN HEMISPHERES WITH COMPARATIVE VIEWS OF THE HEIGHTS OF THE	41.0 X 53.0 CM	FULLARTON
THE WORLD IN HEMISPHERES WITH COMPARATIVE VIEWS OF THE HEIGHTS OF THE	52.0 X 60.0 CM	JOHNSTON
THE WORLD IN PLANISPHERE	16.5 X 19.1 CM	MOLL
THE WORLD ON MERCATOR'S PROJECTION	49.5 X 59.7 CM	ARROWSMITH
THE WORLD ON MERCATOR'S PROJECTION	22.2 X 28.6 CM	FINLEY
THE WORLD ON MERCATOR'S PROJECTION	50.8 X 61.0 CM	PHILIP
THE WORLD ON MERCATOR'S PROJECTION	69.9 X 50.8 CM	PINKERTON
THE WORLD ON MERCATOR'S PROJECTION	36.8 X 57.2 CM	SMITH
THE WORLD ON MERCATOR'S PROJECTION	26.7 X 35.6 CM	TALLIS
THE WORLD ON MERCATOR'S PROJECTION	26.0 X 32.0 CM	TALLIS
THE WORLD ON MERCATOR'S PROJECTION	46.4 X 53.3 CM	TANNER
THE WORLD ON MERCATOR'S PROJECTION	34.3 X 41.3 CM	TEESDALE
THE WORLD ON MERCATOR'S PROJECTION, SHEWING THE VOYAGES OF CAPTAIN COO	22.2 X 31.8 CM	TALLIS
THE WORLD ON MERCATOR'S PROJECTION. DRAWN AND ENGRAVED BY J. DOWER...L	33.7 X 41.3 CM	TEESDALE
THE WORLD WITH THE LATEST DISCOVERIES	25.4 X 49.5 CM	SUDLOW
THE WORLD...	50.8 X 61.0 CM	JOHNSTON
THEATRE DE LA GUERRE DES COURONNES DU NORD	47.0 X 58.4 CM	MORTIER
THEATRE DES OPERATIONS DE L'ARMEE DU NORD, ET DESERT QUE LE GENERAL AR	25.4 X 21.6 CM	MARSHALL
THEORIA SOLIS PER ECCENTRICUM SINE EPICYCLO	43.2 X 50.8 CM	CELLARIUS
THIBET, MONGOLIA AND MANDCHOURIA	25.4 X 33.0 CM	TALLIS
THIBET, MONGOLIA...	20.0 X 25.0 CM	TALLIS
THIONVILLE EN LUXEMBOURG. N COCHIN SCULP. (PANORAMIC VIEW)	16.0 X 50.0 CM	COCHIN
THIONVILLE. POURTRAICT & DESCRIPTION DE THIONVILLE	12.5 X 15.5 CM	DE BELLE FOREST
THIRTY-MILES ROUND BOSTON	25.4 X 26.0 CM	SCOT'S MAGAZINE
THIS CHART OF KINGSLAE HARBOUR...BY CAPT. GREENVILE COLLINS	44.5 X 57.2 CM	COLLINS
THIS PLAN OF THE HARBOURS, TOWNS AND FORTS OF PORTO BELLO TAKEN BY EDW	43.2 X 58.4 CM	TOMS
THOFF VAN NASSOUME. EXCUDEBAT ROMBOUTIUS HOEYUS (VIEW)	39.0 X 52.0 CM	VAN DEN HOEYE
TIERRA FIRMA ITEM NUEVO REYNO DE GRANADA ATQUE POPAYAN	27.9 X 35.6 CM	DE LAET
TIERRA NOVA (SOUTH AMERICA)	13.3 X 17.1 CM	PTOLEMY (1548 VENICE)
TIERRA NUEVA	12.7 X 16.5 CM	PTOLEMY (1548 VENICE)
TIERRA NUEVA	19.1 X 26.0 CM	PTOLEMY (1561-99 VE...
TIERRA NUEVA	17.8 X 24.8 CM	PTOLEMY (1561-99 VE...
TIERRA NUEVA	19.0 X 26.0 CM	PTOLEMY (1561-99 VE...
TO CAPT. JOHN WOOD THIS MAP OF THE WORLD...IS HUMBLY DEDICATED	49.0 X 101.0 CM	MORDEN & BERRY
TO THE RIGHT HONORABLE JOHN LORD SOMMERS THIS MAP OF NORTH AMERICA ACC	57.8 X 96.5 CM	MOLL
TO THE RIGHT HONORABLE THE LORDS COMMISSIONERS...THIS CHART OF THE NOR	59.1 X 87.6 CM	DIXON
TOBAGO	22.9 X 29.2 CM	LUCAS
TOPOGRAPHICA REPRAESANTO BARBARICI PORTUS ET URBIS MUNITAE ORAN...DELI	50.8 X 58.4 CM	HOMANN
TOPOGRAPHIE DE LA ZELANDE EN 9 FEUILLES. PARIS, RUE DES GRANDS AUGUSTI	46.0 X 56.0 CM	LE ROUGE
TORNACI NERVORUM EPISCOPATUS PERANTIQUUS TOTAQ. TORNACESII DITIO...IOA	37.0 X 48.5 CM	VRIENTS
TORONTO	14.7 X 20.2 CM	BAEDEKER
TOTIUS AFRICAE NOVA REPRAESENTATIO	44.0 X 47.0 CM	HOMANN
TOTIUS ASIAE CONTINENS CUM PRAECIPUS INSULIS EIDEM ANNEXIS	22.0 X 33.0 CM	SCHERER
TOTIUS GRAECIA DESCRIPTIO	18.0 X 51.0 CM	BERTELLI
TOTIUS ORBIS COGNITI UNIVERSALIS DESCRIPTIO	35.6 X 49.5 CM	DE JODE
TOTIUS ORBIS COGNITI UNIVERSALIS DESCRIPTIO	30.0 X 50.5 CM	VAN DOETECHUM
TRACTUS REGNI ANGLIAE SEPTENTRION. IN QUO DUCATUS EBORACENSIS...ET LAN	48.3 X 58.4 CM	MORTIER
TRACTUS RHENI ET MOSAE	40.0 X 50.0 CM	BLAEU
TRAIECTUR. UTRECHT (BIRD'S EYE VIEW)	21.0 X 31.0 CM	MERIAN
TRANSSILVANIA	8.9 X 13.3 CM	BERTIUS
TRAP CREEK TO THE SANTA FE CROSSING	78.7 X 59.7 CM	U.S.

TREMAINE'S MAP OF THE COUNTY OF PRINCE EDWARD, UPPER CANADA, TORONTO,	154.9 X 125.1 CM	TREMAINE
TRIER ET LUTZEBORG	13.7 X 18.2 CM	MERCATOR
TRINIDAD	22.9 X 29.2 CM	LUCAS
TROISIEME FEUILLE DES COTES DE LA COCHINCHINE. 1798	69.7 X 48.5 CM	DEPOT DE LA MARINE
TROISIEME PARTIE DE LA CARTE D'ASIE, CONTENANT LA SIBERIE, ET QUELQUES	52.1 X 54.6 CM	D'ANVILLE
TROISIEME QUARTIER DE BRABANT, DONT LA CAPITALE EST ANVERS ET LE MARQU	47.0 X 54.0 CM	HONDIUS
TRUXILLO (VIEW)	28.6 X 34.3 CM	OGILBY
TRUXILLO (VIEW)	27.2 X 33.8 CM	OGILBY
TURCICI IMPERII	13.5 X 17.5 CM	PTOLEMY (1596-1621 ...
TURCICI IMPERII IMAGO	36.0 X 48.0 CM	HONDIUS
TURCICI IMPERII IMAGO	35.6 X 48.3 CM	HONDIUS
TURCICUM IMPERIUM	45.5 X 55.5 CM	DE WIT
TURCOMANIE GEORGIE COMMANIE	19.1 X 23.5 CM	SANSON
TURKEY IN ASIA	20.0 X 25.0 CM	TALLIS
TURKEY IN EUROPE	20.0 X 25.0 CM	TALLIS
TURKEY, IN EUROPE AND HUNGARY; FROM THE BEST AUTHORITIES	34.3 X 37.5 CM	CAREY
TURKY IN ASIA	17.1 X 19.1 CM	MOLL
TURKY IN EUROPE	17.1 X 19.1 CM	MOLL
TURQUIE EUROPEENE	48.0 X 53.0 CM	DE VAUGONDY
TUSCIA	13.5 X 17.5 CM	PTOLEMY (1596-1621 ...
TYCHONIS BRAHE CALCULUS, PLANETARUM CURSUS ET ALTITUDINES OBOCULOS PON	41.9 X 50.8 CM	CELLARIUS
TYPUS ASPECTUUM, OPPOSITIONUM ET CON IUNCTIONUM ETZ IN PLANETIS	43.2 X 50.8 CM	CELLARIUS
TYPUS ASPECTUUM, OPPOSITIONUM ET CON IUNCTIONUM ETZIN PLANETIS	43.2 X 52.1 CM	CELLARIUS
TYPUS FRISIAE ORIENTALIS...AUTHORE UBBONE. P. KEER. EXC.	39.5 X 50.0 CM	VAN DEN KEERE
TYPUS FRISIAE VETERIS...ITEMQE INSULAE BATAVORUM...DISPONENTE BERNHARD	48.0 X 40.0 CM	HALMA
TYPUS ORBIS DESCRIPTIONE PTOLEMAI	31.8 X 45.7 CM	PTOLEMY (1522-41 ST...
TYPUS ORBIS TERRARUM	9.5 X 13.3 CM	BERTIUS
TYPUS ORBIS TERRARUM	16.0 X 30.5 CM	CLUVER
TYPUS ORBIS TERRARUM	14.0 X 20.3 CM	HONDIUS
TYPUS ORBIS TERRARUM	34.3 X 49.5 CM	ORTELIUS
TYPUS ORBIS TERRARUM	36.0 X 49.0 CM	ORTELIUS
TYPUS ORBIS TERRARUM	35.6 X 49.5 CM	ORTELIUS
TYPUS ORBIS TERRARUM	33.0 X 48.9 CM	ORTELIUS
TYPUS ORBIS TERRARUM, AD IMITATIONEM UNIVERSALIS GERHARDI MERCATORIS	21.6 X 31.1 CM	QUAD
TYPUS ORBIS UNIVERSALIS	27.9 X 36.8 CM	MUNSTER
TYPUS ORBIS UNIVERSALIS	26.7 X 36.8 CM	MUNSTER
TYPUS TOTIUS ORBIS TERRAQUEI GEOGRAPHICE DELINEATUS ET AD USUM GLOBO M	22.0 X 35.0 CM	SCHERER
U. STATES' INDIAN FRONTIER IN 1840 SHEWING THE POSITIONS OF THE TRIBES	21.7 X 13.2 CM	CATLIN
U.S. OF N. AMERICA, SOUTH WEST SHEET	42.5 X 30.5 CM	ETTLING
U.S. PACIFIC RAIL ROAD EXP. & SURVEY WAR DEPARTMENT: GEOLOGICAL MAP OF	19.9 X 93.2 CM	U.S.
ULTRAIECTINI DOMINI...	47.0 X 57.0 CM	VISSCHER
ULTRAIECTUM DOMIN.	40.0 X 50.0 CM	BLAEU
ULTRAIECTUM DOMINIUM, 1616...	36.5 X 47.0 CM	VAN DEN KEERE
ULTRAIECTUM DOMINIUM, 1616...	36.5 X 47.0 CM	VAN DEN KEERE
ULTRAJECTUM DOMINIUM	36.5 X 47.0 CM	VISSCHER
UNDECIMA ASIAE TABULA	36.8 X 42.5 CM	PTOLEMY (1513-20 ST...
UNION MILITARY CHART	57.5 X 68.3 CM	MAGNUS
UNITED STATES	24.1 X 30.5 CM	ARROWSMITH
UNITED STATES	21.6 X 36.8 CM	BOYNTON
UNITED STATES	35.6 X 57.8 CM	BRADFORD
UNITED STATES	35.9 X 57.8 CM	BRADFORD
UNITED STATES	26.7 X 21.0 CM	DOWER
UNITED STATES	33.7 X 38.1 CM	DOWER
UNITED STATES	43.2 X 52.1 CM	GALL & INGLIS
UNITED STATES	41.9 X 50.8 CM	HALL
UNITED STATES	40.6 X 52.1 CM	HALL
UNITED STATES	40.6 X 50.8 CM	LIZARS
UNITED STATES	25.4 X 41.9 CM	MORSE
UNITED STATES	35.6 X 57.2 CM	SMITH
UNITED STATES	27.9 X 36.8 CM	SMITH
UNITED STATES	26.0 X 32.0 CM	TALLIS
UNITED STATES	24.1 X 33.7 CM	TALLIS
UNITED STATES	22.2 X 30.5 CM	TALLIS

UNITED STATES	20.0 X 25.0 CM	TALLIS
UNITED STATES	34.3 X 26.7 CM	TALLIS
UNITED STATES	22.2 X 30.5 CM	TALLIS
UNITED STATES	24.1 X 31.8 CM	TALLIS
UNITED STATES	34.3 X 40.6 CM	TEESDALE
UNITED STATES	33.7 X 40.6 CM	TEESDALE
UNITED STATES (WEST SHEET)	43.2 X 31.8 CM	ETTLING
UNITED STATES AND TERRITORIES	34.3 X 54.0 CM	MITCHELL
UNITED STATES AND TEXAS	49.5 X 61.0 CM	JOHNSTON
UNITED STATES AND TEXAS	49.5 X 61.0 CM	JOHNSTON
UNITED STATES AND TEXAS	49.5 X 62.0 CM	JOHNSTON
UNITED STATES GENERAL MAP	34.3 X 42.5 CM	CHAPMAN & HALL
UNITED STATES INCLUDING CALIFORNIA, TEXAS &C.	52.1 X 61.0 CM	PHILIP
UNITED STATES OF AMERICA	23.5 X 18.4 CM	BELL
UNITED STATES OF AMERICA	43.2 X 53.3 CM	CAREY & LEA
UNITED STATES OF AMERICA	41.9 X 73.7 CM	COLTON
UNITED STATES OF AMERICA	39.4 X 66.0 CM	COLTON
UNITED STATES OF AMERICA	42.5 X 54.0 CM	MELISH
UNITED STATES OF AMERICA	19.7 X 24.1 CM	NEELE
UNITED STATES OF AMERICA AND THE COURSE OF THE RIVER ST. LAURENCE FROM	41.5 X 23.0 CM	THOMSON
UNITED STATES OF AMERICA NORTHERN PART	51.4 X 69.9 CM	PINKERTON
UNITED STATES OF AMERICA SOUTHERN PART	52.1 X 69.9 CM	PINKERTON
UNITED STATES OF AMERICA...	43.2 X 54.0 CM	MELISH
UNITED STATES OF AMERICA...	41.3 X 49.5 CM	MELISH
UNITED STATES OF NORTH AMERICA	43.2 X 31.8 CM	ETTLING
UNITED STATES OF NORTH AMERICA	41.3 X 52.7 CM	FULLARTON
UNITED STATES OF NORTH AMERICA (EASTERN STATES)	57.5 X 44.0 CM	JOHNSTON
UNITED STATES OF NORTH AMERICA (EASTERN STATES)	57.2 X 44.2 CM	JOHNSTON
UNITED STATES, NORTH CENTRAL...COMPRISING MICHIGAN, ILLINOIS, WISCONSI	40.6 X 50.8 CM	FULLARTON
UNITED STATES, SOUTHERN PART.	26.0 X 37.0 CM	BLACK
UNITED STATES, TEXAS & ...THE CANADAS	29.2 X 47.6 CM	HUNTINGTON
UNITED STATES...	29.2 X 45.7 CM	CHAMBERS
UNITED STATES...	27.9 X 43.2 CM	COUNT & HAMMOND
UNITED STATES...COMPRISING MICHIGAN, ILLINOIS, WISCONSIN, IOWA, MINNES	40.6 X 50.8 CM	FULLARTON
UNITED STATES...SOUTH CENTRAL SECTION	51.4 X 40.0 CM	FULLARTON
UNIVERSALE DELLE PARTE DEL MONDO NUOVAMENTE RITROVATA	26.7 X 26.7 CM	RAMUSIO
UNIVERSALE NOVA	12.7 X 16.5 CM	PTOLEMY (1548 VENICE)
UNIVERSALIS COSMOGRAPHIA	12.7 X 16.5 CM	HONTER
UNIVERSALIS TABULA IUXTA PTOLEMAEUM	27.3 X 43.8 CM	SUDLOW
UNIVERSI ORBIS DESCRIPTIO	13.5 X 17.5 CM	PTOLEMY (1596-1621 ...
UNIVERSI ORBIS...	13.0 X 17.8 CM	PTOLEMY (1596-1621 ...
UNIVERSI...NAVIGANTIUM	13.0 X 17.1 CM	PTOLEMY (1596-1621 ...
UPPER AND LOWER CANADA	19.1 X 24.1 CM	BRADFORD
UPPER AND LOWER CANADA	26.0 X 35.0 CM	SMITH
UPPER CANADA	35.6 X 29.2 CM	BRADFORD
UPPER CANADA &C	61.0 X 50.8 CM	ARROWSMITH
UPPER CANADA &C. LONDON, PUBD 15 FEBY 1842, BY J. ARROWSMITH, 10 SOHO	63.5 X 53.3 CM	ARROWSMITH
UPPER CANADA &C., LOWER CANADA, NEW BRUNSWICK, NOVA SCOTIA, PRINCE EDW	61.0 X 95.0 CM	ARROWSMITH
URBIS DOMINGO IN HISPANIOLA	28.6 X 35.1 CM	OGILBY
UTAH	49.5 X 33.0 CM	RAND MCNALLY
UTAH, NEW MEXICO, TEXAS, CALIFORNIA ETC...	31.8 X 39.4 CM	COX
UTRECHT. CAPITALE DE LA PROVINCE D'UTRECHT, C'EST APRES AMSTERDAM LA P	44.0 X 37.0 CM	LE CLERC
UTRIUSQ TARTARIAE EUROPAE ET ASIATICAE DELINEATIO/INSULARUM INDICARU &	23.5 X 18.0 CM	SCHERER
UTRIUSQUE FRISIORUM REGIONIS NOVISS: DESCRIPTIO 1686	34.3 X 50.8 CM	ORTELIUS
UTRIUSQUE HEMISPHEREIO DELINEATIO	22.9 X 28.6 CM	WYTFLIET
VAL PARYSA (VIEW)	11.8 X 15.9 CM	HULSIUS
VALENTIAE REGNI...	34.3 X 49.5 CM	ORTELIUS
VALLETTA CITTA NOVA DI MALTA (VIEW)	27.5 X 35.0 CM	MERIAN
VALLEY OF GREEN RIVER TO THE GREAT SALT LAKE	52.1 X 45.1 CM	U.S.
VAN DIEMAN'S LAND OR TASMANIA	50.0 X 60.0 CM	JOHNSTON
VAN DIEMEN'S LAND	20.0 X 25.0 CM	TALLIS
VARE ALBEELDINGE VAN HET LEGER...MAURITIUS VAN NASSAU...TOT WATERVLIET	29.0 X 38.0 CM	CLAESZ
VARIOUS PLANS AND DRAUGHTS OF CITIES, TOWNS, HARBOURS &C.	30.5 X 21.5 CM	CONDER

VENEZUALA...	28.0 X 35.0 CM	DE LAET
VENEZUELA ATQUE OCCIDENTALIS PARS NOVAE ANDALUSIAE	27.9 X 35.6 CM	DE LAET
VENEZUELA CUM PARTE AUSTRALI NOVAE ANDALUSIAE	48.3 X 37.5 CM	BLAEU
VENEZUELA CUM PARTE AUSTRALI NOVAE ANDALUSIAE	37.5 X 48.3 CM	BLAEU
VENEZUELA CUM PARTE AUSTRALI NOVAE ANDALUSIAE	35.6 X 48.9 CM	HONDIUS
VENEZUELA CUM PARTE AUSTRALI NOVAE ANDALUSIAE	28.5 X 35.5 CM	OGILBY
VENEZUELA, NEW GRANADA, EQUADOR, AND THE GUYANAS	34.3 X 26.7 CM	TALLIS
VENEZUELS, NEW GRANADA...	20.0 X 25.0 CM	TALLIS
VENICE	48.0 X 35.0 CM	CAMOCIO
VERA EFFIGIES ET DELINEATIO INSULAE HELENAE...	61.0 X 48.3 CM	LINSCHOTEN
VERA ET EXACTA DEXCRIPTIO SPA VICI ARDUENNE CUM VICINIS MONTIBUS SYLVI	29.0 X 39.0 CM	VALDOR
VEREIN-STAATEN VON NORD-AMERICA MIT AUSNAHME FLORIDAS UND DER WESTLICH	34.9 X 39.4 CM	PERTHES
VEREINIGTE STAATEN VON NORD-AMERIKA	22.9 X 29.8 CM	WEIMAR GEOGRAPHISCH...
VERMONT	35.6 X 29.2 CM	BRADFORD
VERMONT	38.1 X 29.8 CM	CAREY
VERMONT	22.9 X 29.2 CM	LUCAS
VERMONT	27.3 X 22.2 CM	LUCAS
VERMONT & NEW HAMPSHIRE	35.6 X 27.9 CM	SWINSTON
VETERIS ET NOVAE BRITANNIAE	21.5 X 26.0 CM	CLUVER
VEUE ET PERSPECTIVE DE MOMMEDY. ISRAEL SULVESTRE DELIN. ET SCULPSIT 16	37.0 X 98.0 CM	SILVESTRE
VICTORIA	30.5 X 43.0 CM	WELLER
VICTORIA OR PORT PHILLIP	20.0 X 25.0 CM	TALLIS
VIEW OF ARSENAL & LIGHT HOUSE SITKA, NEW ARCKANGEL	12.1 X 19.1 CM	COLBURN
VIEW OF BALTIMORE, FROM FEDERAL HILL	46.7 X 70.5 CM	CONANT
VIEW OF BETHLEHEM-A MORAVIAN SETTLEMENT	16.5 X 22.9 CM	STOCKDALE
VIEW OF HONOLULU, OAHU, SANDWICH ISLANDS	12.1 X 19.1 CM	COLBURN
VIEW OF JAMES' ISLAND ONE OF THE GALAPAGOS/CHATHAM ISLAND AT STEPHENS	16.5 X 26.7 CM	COLNETT
VIEW OF NASSAU IN THE BAHAMAS	12.7 X 22.9 CM	GOLD
VIEW OF PART OF THE SOUTH SIDE OF THE ISLAND SAPAN, ONE OF THE LADRONE	17.1 X 21.6 CM	STOCKDALE
VIEW OF PORTLAND IN 1832, TAKEN FROM FORT PREBLE, ON PURPOODUCK POINT	15.2 X 34.3 CM	PENDLETON
VIEW OF ROSEAU, IN THE ISLAND OF DOMINICA. ENGRAVED BY GEORGE COOKE. L	19.1 X 12.7 CM	LONGMAN
VIEW OF ST. THOMAS, WEST INDIES, LATELY PURCHASED BY THE UNITED STATES	17.8 X 52.1 CM	HARPER'S WEEKLY
VIEW OF SULPHUR ISLAND	34.3 X 21.6 CM	HOGG
VIEW OF THE ANCHORAGES OF THE VESSELS AT THE ISLAND OF MOWEE	22.2 X 32.4 CM	ROBINSON
VIEW OF THE COUNTRY ROUND THE FALLS OF NIAGARA	16.7 X 10.3 CM	MELISH
VIEW OF THE ENGAGEMENT BETWEEN THE CAPES LA HOGUE & BARFLEUR	17.1 X 31.8 CM	ANON
VIEW OF THE ENGAGEMENT OFF THE ISLE OF MAN	18.4 X 27.3 CM	ANON
VIEW OF THE ISLAND OF ST. THOMAS, TAKEN FROM HAVENSICHT. ENGRAVED FROM	20.3 X 15.2 CM	LONGMAN
VIEW OF THE ISLE OF ST. THOMAS	12.1 X 16.5 CM	PHILLIPS
VIEW OF THE WEST BANK OF THE HUDSON RIVER 3 MILES ABOVE STILL WATER, U	19.7 X 40.4 CM	ANBUREY
VIEWS OF NORTH WEST COAST OF AMERICA EXPLORED BY THE BOUSSOLE IN 1786.	22.9 X 29.2 CM	ROBINSON
VIEWS OF THE NORTHWEST COAST OF AMERICA EXPLORED BY THE ASTROLABE IN 1	22.9 X 29.2 CM	ROBINSON
VILLAGE OF ALMANDRAL IN THE BAY OF VALPARAISO...	19.1 X 23.5 CM	VANCOUVER
VILLE DE BUENOS AYRES	20.3 X 16.5 CM	BELLIN
VIRGIN ISLANDS &C.	22.9 X 30.8 CM	LUCAS
VIRGINIA	35.6 X 29.2 CM	BRADFORD
VIRGINIA	31.1 X 47.6 CM	LUCAS
VIRGINIA	31.1 X 47.6 CM	LUCAS
VIRGINIA	30.5 X 39.4 CM	MORSE
VIRGINIA	15.2 X 18.4 CM	SCOTT
VIRGINIA (VIEW)	13.3 X 16.5 CM	DAPPER
VIRGINIA AND MARYLAND	27.0 X 20.0 CM	MOLL
VIRGINIA AND MARYLAND BY H. MOLL GEOGRAPHER	26.7 X 20.3 CM	MOLL
VIRGINIA ET FLORIDA	15.2 X 19.1 CM	MERCATOR
VIRGINIA ET FLORIDA	15.2 X 17.8 CM	PURCHAS
VIRGINIA ET FLORIDA	14.6 X 18.4 CM	PURCHAS
VIRGINIA ITEM ET FLORIDAE AMERICAE PROVINCIARUM NOVA DESCRIPTIO	18.7 X 25.7 CM	JANSSON
VIRGINIA PARTIS AUSTRALIS, ET FLORIDAE PARTIS ORIENTALIS...NOVA DESCRI	38.7 X 50.2 CM	BLAEU
VIRGINIA, MARYLAND AND DELAWARE	12.4 X 15.5 CM	ANON
VIRGINIA, MARYLAND EN DEUX FEUILLES PAR FRY ET JEFFERSON	67.3 X 101.6 CM	LE ROUGE
VIRGINIA, MARYLAND ET CAROLINA IN AMERICA SEPTENTRIONALI	48.3 X 58.4 CM	HOMANN
VIRGINIA, MARYLAND, PENNSILVANIA, EAST AND WEST NEW JERSEY	50.8 X 78.7 CM	MOUNT & PAGE
VIRGINIA, MARYLANDIA ET CAROLINA...	48.3 X 57.2 CM	HOMANN

286

VIRGINIA. S. LEWIS DEL.	20.0 X 25.1 CM	LEWIS & ARROWSMITH
VIRGINIAE ITEM ET FLORIDAE	34.3 X 48.3 CM	HONDIUS
VIRGINIAE ITEM ET FLORIDAE	34.3 X 48.3 CM	MERCATOR
VIRGINIAE ITEM ET FLORIDAE	19.1 X 25.4 CM	MERCATOR
VIRGINIAE ITEM ET FLORIDAE AMERICAE PROVINCIARUM, NOVA DESCRIPTIO	34.5 X 49.0 CM	MERCATOR
VIRGINIAE ITEM ET FLORIDAE AMERICAE...	34.2 X 48.3 CM	MERCATOR
VIRGINIAE PARS AUSTRALIS, ET FLORIDAE PARTIS ORIENTALIS...	38.1 X 50.8 CM	BLAEU
VIRGINIAE PARTIS AUSTRALIS, ET FLORIDAE PARTIS ORIENTALIS...	38.1 X 50.8 CM	BLAEU
VIRGINIAE PARTIS AUSTRALIS, ET FLORIDAE PARTIS ORIENTALIS...	28.9 X 35.4 CM	OGILBY
VIRGINIAE PARTIS AUSTRALIS, ET FLORIDAE...	40.0 X 38.4 CM	BLAEU
VIRGINIE, GRANDE REGION DE L'AMERIQUE SEPTENTRIONALE	28.9 X 35.6 CM	VAN DER AA
VIRGINIE, MARYLAND EN 2 FEUILLES PAR FRY ET JEFFERSON	67.0 X 98.7 CM	LE ROUGE
VIRGINIE, MARYLAND...	67.9 X 98.4 CM	LE ROUGE
VRAIJE DESCRIPTION DE L'ASSIEGEMENT D'ANVERS PAR LE...PRINCE DE PARME	37.5 X 44.0 CM	VRIENTS
VUE DE BOSTON	25.3 X 40.1 CM	HABERMANN
VUE DE LA BASSE VILLE A QUEBECK	25.2 X 39.6 CM	HABERMANN
VUE DE LA PLACE CAPITALE A QUEBECK	25.2 X 39.5 CM	HABERMANN
VUE DU COTE DU MOUGILAGE/PROFIL DU FORT DE VALPARAYSSO	19.1 X 29.2 CM	FREZIER
W. INDIES	24.1 X 30.5 CM	ARROWSMITH
WALES	38.7 X 47.6 CM	SPEED
WALES, NORTH COAST SHEET VII, POINT LYNUS TO ABERGELE...	47.0 X 62.9 CM	ADMIRALTY
WALLIA PRINCIPATUS VULGO WALES	38.1 X 49.5 CM	BLAEU
WARWICKSHIRE	24.1 X 19.1 CM	FULLARTON
WARWICKSHIRE	19.1 X 30.5 CM	MOLL
WARWICKSHIRE	11.4 X 14.0 CM	SELLER
WARWICUM NORTHAMTONIA HUNTINGDONIA CANTABRIGIA SUFFOLCIA OXONIUM BUCKI	36.8 X 47.0 CM	HONDIUS
WASHINGTON	23.5 X 27.4 CM	BAEDEKER
WASHINGTON	31.8 X 40.6 CM	COLTON
WASHINGTON, NEW ORLEANS, LOUISVILLE AND CINCINNATI	35.6 X 29.2 CM	BRADFORD
WEST AFRICA 1753	38.1 X 47.0 CM	SEALE
WEST CANADA	34.3 X 26.7 CM	TALLIS
WEST CANADA	24.8 X 32.8 CM	TALLIS
WEST CANADA	34.3 X 26.7 CM	TALLIS
WEST CANADA	20.0 X 25.0 CM	TALLIS
WEST CANADA	25.0 X 33.0 CM	TALLIS
WEST CANADA	25.4 X 33.0 CM	TALLIS
WEST CANADA	26.0 X 32.0 CM	TALLIS
WEST INDIA ISLANDS	30.5 X 35.6 CM	MORSE & BREESE
WEST INDIA ISLANDS	20.0 X 25.0 CM	TALLIS
WEST INDIA ISLANDS AND CENTRAL AMERICA	44.2 X 57.2 CM	JOHNSTON
WEST INDIES	17.8 X 29.2 CM	ANON
WEST INDIES	26.0 X 37.0 CM	BLACK
WEST INDIES	36.8 X 44.5 CM	BOWEN
WEST INDIES	35.6 X 29.2 CM	BRADFORD
WEST INDIES	24.8 X 40.0 CM	BRADFORD
WEST INDIES	35.5 X 44.5 CM	CRUCHLEY
WEST INDIES	22.9 X 29.2 CM	LUCAS
WEST INDIES	19.7 X 24.8 CM	MORSE
WEST INDIES	34.3 X 26.7 CM	TALLIS
WEST INDIES FROM THE BEST AUTHORITIES	19.1 X 23.5 CM	TEGG
WEST INDIES, WITH THE HARBOUR & FORT OF OMOA...	29.2 X 64.2 CM	POLITICAL MAGAZINE
WEST INDIES. ENGRAVED BY S. HALL, BURY STRT. BLOOMSBURY. EDINBURGH PUB	38.1 X 26.0 CM	BLACK
WEST MOUNTAIN MINING DISTRICT, BRIGHAM CANON...	29.2 X 30.5 CM	DONALDSON
WESTERN AFRICA	25.4 X 35.6 CM	TALLIS
WESTERN AFRICA	20.0 X 25.0 CM	TALLIS
WESTERN AUSTRALIA	20.0 X 25.0 CM	TALLIS
WESTERN AUSTRALIA	34.0 X 24.0 CM	TALLIS
WESTERN AUSTRALIA, FROM THE GOVERNMENT SURVEYS	24.0 X 32.0 CM	ARROWSMITH
WESTERN AUSTRALIA/SOUTH AUSTRALIA	31.0 X 43.0 CM	WELLER
WESTERN HEMISPHERE	35.6 X 29.2 CM	BRADFORD
WESTERN HEMISPHERE	33.0 X 33.0 CM	SDUK
WESTERN HEMISPHERE	20.0 X 25.0 CM	TALLIS
WESTERN HEMISPHERE	34.3 X 26.7 CM	TALLIS

WESTERN HEMISPHERE	24.1 X 34.9 CM	TALLIS
WESTERN HEMISPHERE	52.1 X 50.8 CM	THOMSON
WESTERN HEMISPHERE	78.7 X 78.7 CM	WYLD
WESTERN HEMISPHERE/EASTERN HEMISPHERE	27.9 X 45.1 CM	BARNES & BURR
WESTERN TERRITORY	49.5 X 88.9 CM	KINGSBURY
WESTERN TERRITORY	50.2 X 88.9 CM	U.S.
WESTMORELAND	20.3 X 26.7 CM	MOULE
WESTMORELAND	11.4 X 14.0 CM	SELLER
WESTMORLAND	19.7 X 32.4 CM	MOLL
WESTMORLAND	35.6 X 41.9 CM	MORDEN
WESTMORLAND	10.8 X 6.4 CM	WALLIS & REID
WESTMORLANDIA, LANCASTRIA, CESTRIA...CUM INSULIS MANIA ET ANGLESEY	36.8 X 41.9 CM	MERCATOR
WESTVRIESLAND	40.0 X 50.0 CM	BLAEU
WHEELING IN VIRGINIA (VIEW)	11.4 X 15.2 CM	MEYER
WIGHT ISLAND	38.7 X 47.6 CM	SPEED
WILKESBARRE, VALE OF WYOMING (VIEW)	16.5 X 17.8 CM	BARTLETT
WILLIAM CAMDEN CLARENCEUX OBIJT AO.D. 1623. AETATIS SUCE LXXIII. R. WH	29.2 X 19.1 CM	MORDEN
WILSHIRE	38.7 X 47.6 CM	SPEED
WILTONIAE...	27.9 X 35.6 CM	KIP
WILTSHIRE	11.4 X 14.0 CM	SELLER
WILTSHIRE	38.1 X 50.8 CM	SPEED
WILTSHIRE...	31.1 X 19.1 CM	MOLL
WISCONSIN	40.6 X 33.0 CM	COLTON
WISCONSIN AND IOWA	35.6 X 29.2 CM	BRADFORD
WISCONSIN SOUTHERN PART	31.8 X 39.4 CM	MORSE & BREESE
WORCESTER SHIRE DIVIDED INTO HUNDREDS...	22.9 X 32.4 CM	BOWEN
WORCESTERSHIRE	24.1 X 19.1 CM	BELL
WORCESTERSHIRE	10.2 X 17.8 CM	CAPPER
WORCESTERSHIRE	11.4 X 14.0 CM	SELLER
WORCESTERSHIRE DESCRIBED	38.7 X 47.6 CM	SPEED
WORLD ON MERCATOR'S PROJECTION	41.9 X 50.2 CM	HALL
XVII PROVINCIARUM GERMANIAE INFERIORIS DELINEATIO	47.0 X 57.0 CM	VISSCHER
YAM BAY ONEEHEOW...1786	19.7 X 27.9 CM	DIXON
YORK SHIRE	38.7 X 47.6 CM	SPEED
YORKSHIRE	38.5 X 51.0 CM	SPEED
YORKSHIRE E.R.	17.8 X 11.4 CM	OWEN & BOWEN
YORKSHIRE W.R.	17.8 X 11.4 CM	OWEN & BOWEN
YORKSHIRE WEST RIDING	19.7 X 26.7 CM	MOULE
YORKSHIRE, WEST RIDING	20.3 X 26.7 CM	MOULE
YPRES EN FLANDRE (VIEW)	17.0 X 51.0 CM	COCHIN
YPRES. GRAND VILLE RICHE & MARCHANDE... (VIEW)	42.0 X 36.0 CM	LE CLERC
YUCATAN CONVENTUS JURIDICI HISPANIAE NOVAE PARS OCCIDENTALIS, ET GUATI	28.3 X 35.6 CM	OGILBY
YUCATAN...	41.9 X 52.7 CM	BLAEU
ZE ZYPE. DE PURMER. DE WORMER. WATERLAND	35.0 X 47.0 CM	HONDIUS
ZEE CARTE VAN PORTUGAL...	33.0 X 50.8 CM	WAGHENAER
ZEELANDIA	40.0 X 50.0 CM	BLAEU
ZELANDE. ZEELANDIA COMITATUS. JOANNES JANSSONIUS	39.0 X 50.0 CM	HONDIUS
ZELANDIAE COMITATUS...	35.0 X 47.0 CM	VAN DEN KEERE
ZELANDIAE COMITATUS...	35.0 X 47.0 CM	VAN DEN KEERE
ZELANDIAE TYPUS	24.0 X 32.0 CM	DE BRUYN
ZELANDIAE TYPUS	23.5 X 31.5 CM	VAN DEN KEERE
ZELANDICARUM INSULARUM EXACTISSIMA ET NOVA DESCRIPTIO, AUCTORE D. IACO	33.5 X 46.7 CM	ORTELIUS
ZELANDICARUM INSULARUM EXACTISSIMA ET NOVA DESCRIPTIO, AUCTORE D. IACO	33.5 X 46.7 CM	ORTELIUS
ZIPA. AGRI ZUPANI NOVA DESCRIPTIO. 1617	37.5 X 48.0 CM	VAN DEN KEERE
ZUYDHOLLANDIA	40.0 X 50.0 CM	BLAEU

ERRATA FOR THE 1983 EDITION

The mapmaker "Holm" should have appeared as "Campanius Holm," and "Reilly" as "von Reilly." Starting with this edition all maps issued by permanent divisions of the United States government will be lumped under the heading "U.S." except for those issued by the U.S. Coast Survey, which will continue to be listed separately. The cumulative statistics have been corrected to reflect these changes. An effort is being made to keep such changes to a minimum.